THE CHEMICAL WARFARE SERVICE
ORGANIZING FOR WAR

MAJ. GEN. WILLIAM N. PORTER, *Chief of Chemical Warfare Service World War II.*

THE CHEMICAL WARFARE SERVICE: ORGANIZING FOR WAR

by

Leo P. Brophy

and

George J. B. Fisher

University Press of the Pacific
Honolulu, Hawaii

The Chemical Warfare Service: Organizing for War

by
Leo P. Brophy
George J. B. Fisher

ISBN: 1-4102-0487-1

Reprinted from the 1970 edition

University Press of the Pacific
Honolulu, Hawaii
http://www.universitypressofthepacific.com

UNITED STATES ARMY IN WORLD WAR II

Kent Roberts Greenfield, General Editor

Advisory Committee

(As of 1 January 1958)

Elmer Ellis
University of Missouri

Samuel Flagg Bemis
Yale University

Gordon A. Craig
Princeton University

Oron J. Hale
University of Virginia

W. Stull Holt
University of Washington

Maj. Gen. Oliver P. Newman
U.S. Continental Army Command

Brig. Gen. Edgar C. Doleman
Army War College

Brig. Gen. Frederick R. Zierath
Command and General Staff College

Brig. Gen. Kenneth F. Zitzman
Industrial College of the Armed Forces

Col. Vincent J. Esposito
United States Military Academy

T. Harry Williams
Louisiana State University

Office of the Chief of Military History

Maj. Gen. Richard W. Stephens, Chief

Chief Historian

Chief, Histories Division

Chief, Editorial and Publication Division

Editor in Chief

Chief, Cartographic Branch

Chief, Photographic Branch

Kent Roberts Greenfield

Col. Seneca W. Foote

Lt. Col. E. E. Steck

Joseph R. Friedman

Elliot Dunay

Margaret E. Tackley

v

History of

THE CHEMICAL WARFARE SERVICE

Organizing for War

... to Those Who Served

Foreword

General employment of toxic munitions in World War I made it necessary for the United States as a belligerent to protect its soldiers against gas attack, and to furnish means for conducting gas warfare. The postwar revulsion against the use of gas in no way guaranteed that it would not be used in another war; and to maintain readiness for gas warfare, Congress therefore authorized the retention of the Chemical Warfare Service as a small but important part of the Army organization.

Between world wars, officers of the Chemical Warfare Service anticipated that in another conflict the Service would again be principally concerned with gas warfare, and they concentrated on defense and retaliation against it. The almost equal preparedness of the United States and other nations for gas warfare acted during World War II as the principal deterrent to the uses of gas. That it was not used has obscured the very large and vital effort that preparations for gas warfare required at home and overseas. This effort involved large numbers of American scientists and the American chemical industry as well as the Chemical Warfare Service, and served not only the Army but also the other armed forces of the United States and those of Allied nations. And in World War II the Chemical Warfare Service and its civilian collaborators came up with some new major weapons, notably the 4.2-inch mortar, generators for large-area smoke screening, flame throwers, and incendiary and flame bombs. The Service acquired in addition an entirely new mission, that of preparing the nation against the hazards of biological attack. In fulfilling its responsibilities the Chemical Warfare Service during the war compiled a record of achievement that readers of this subseries both in and out of the Army, will find instructive.

Washington, D. C.
7 March 1958

R. W. STEPHENS
Maj. Gen., U. S. A.
Chief of Military History

The Authors

Dr. Leo P. Brophy holds an A.B. degree from Franklin and Marshall College and M.A. and Ph.D. degrees in history from Fordham University. After teaching history and sociology at Fordham and Seton Hall Universities, he joined the staff of the Chemical Corps Historical Office in 1945. He has specialized in administrative and logistic history. Since 1953 Dr. Brophy has served as Chief of the Chemical Corps Historical Office.

Col. George B. Fisher, a graduate of the Industrial College of the Armed Forces, was commissioned in the National Army during World War I and received a Regular Army commission in 1920. As a Chemical Warfare Service officer from 1929 until his retirement in 1947, he held a number of important training and administrative posts, including tours as Chief of the Training Division, Office of the Chief, CWS; Assistant Commandant of the Chemical Warfare School; director of Army civil defense schools in World War II; and Chemical Officer, Third United States Army in Europe. From 1951 until his death in 1956 he served as a consultant in the Chemical Corps Historical Office.

Preface

This is the first of three volumes devoted to the activities of the Chemical Warfare Service in World War II. Part One of the present volume traces the organization and administration of the Chemical Warfare Service from its origins in World War I up through World War II. Part Two deals with training of military personnel for offensive and defensive chemical warfare in the same period.

Even more than other elements of the Army, the Chemical Warfare Service (designated Chemical Corps after World War II) felt the effects of the government's restrictions on personnel and funds in the years between the two world wars. This was partly the aftermath of international efforts to outlaw gas warfare and partly the result of antipathy to that type of warfare on the part of various high government officials. Certain members of the War Department General Staff, including at times the Chief of Staff himself, were opposed to gas warfare. Consequently the Chemical Warfare Service was considered as more or less a necessary nuisance.

The movement toward general national preparedness that got under way in the late 1930's led to an increase in the stock levels of certain chemical warfare items. Included in 1938 Educational Order legislation providing for a build-up of a limited number of Army items was the gas mask. Later legislation and War Department directives enabled the Chemical Warfare Service to make still further preparations for gas warfare, offensive and defensive. These activities, continued throughout the war years, helped to deter the enemy from initiating gas warfare. During World War II, in addition to discharging its responsibility for gas warfare, the Chemical Warfare Service carried out a number of other chemical warfare missions for which it had little or no preparation in the prewar years. The service was also assigned a biological warfare mission.

Although any of the three volumes on the Chemical Warfare Service can be read as an entity, the first seven chapters of the present work will serve to illuminate the remainder of the CWS story. Against the background provided by Part One, the account of specific functions such as military training (covered in Part Two of this volume), research, procurement, and supply (covered in the second volume), and chemical warfare activities in the oversea theaters of operations (covered in the third volume) will emerge in clearer perspective.

A further word of explanation with regard to Part One may be of assistance to the reader. The aim here is to discuss developments in organization and administration primarily as they affected the Chief, Chemical Warfare Service, and his immediate staff and secondarily as they affected the commanders of Chemical Warfare Service field installations. Since these developments in almost all instances had their origin at a level higher than that of the Chief of the Chemical Warfare Service, pertinent background information on policy at the higher level is included.

Dr. Leo P. Brophy is responsible for Part One. He has been assisted in the research and writing on Chapters IV and V by Mr. Herbert G. Wing, formerly of the Historical Staff, Chemical Corps. The late Col. George J. B. Fisher, USA, was primarily responsible for Part Two. Colonel Fisher was taken ill before he was able to complete the research and writing of this portion of the volume. His work was taken up and completed by the staff of the Historical Office. Dr. Brophy wrote the section in Chapter XIII on the training of chemical mortar battalions, and the section in Chapter XVI on the training of the Army in the use of flame, smoke, and incendiaries. Dr. Brooks E. Kleber and Mr. Dale Birdsell assisted in the research of these and other chapters in Part Two.

The authors of this volume were greatly aided in their research by the competent staff of the Departmental Records Branch, Office of The Adjutant General, particularly Mrs. Caroline Moore; by Mr. R. W. Krauskopf of the staff of the National Archives; by Mr. Roger W. Squier, Office of the Comptroller of the Army; and by Mr. Michael D. Wertheimer, Office of the Deputy Chief of Staff for Personnel, Department of the Army. Mrs. Alice E. Moss supervised the typing of the manuscript.

The authors are indebted to the many veterans of the Chemical Warfare Service who through interviews and otherwise aided them in writing the volume. Among these were several whose assistance was most helpful: Maj. Gen. William N. Porter, Maj. Gen. Alden H. Waitt, Maj. Gen. Charles E. Loucks, Brig. Gen. Henry M. Black, Col. Harry A. Kuhn, Lt. Col. Selig J. Levitan, and Col. Raymond L. Abel.

In the Office of the Chief of Military History, Lt. Col. Leo J. Meyer, Deputy Chief Historian, and his successor, Dr. Stetson Conn, rendered valuable assistance. Final editing was accomplished by Mr. David Jaffé, senior editor, assisted by Mrs. Helen Whittington, copy editor. Mrs. Norma Sherris selected the photographs.

Washington, D. C.   LEO P. BROPHY
2 April 1958

Contents

PART ONE

Administrative Development

PART TWO

Military Training

     1. Chemical Mortar Battalions

     2. Chemical Mortar Companies

     3. Chemical Smoke Generator Battalions

     4. Chemical Smoke Generator Companies

     5. Chemical Companies, Air Operations

     6. Chemical Depot Companies (Aviation)

     7. Chemical Maintenance Companies (Aviation)

     8. Chemical Depot Companies and Chemical Base Depot Companies

     9. Chemical Maintenance Companies

Tables

Charts

Map

Illustrations

Illustrations are from Department of Defense files.

PART ONE

ADMINISTRATIVE DEVELOPMENT

CHAPTER I

Origins of the Chemical Warfare Service

The Chemical Warfare Service (CWS) came into being during an era of unprecedented change in the technology of war.[1] The introduction of gas warfare by Germany in April 1915 presented new problems of military techniques with which none of the Allied Powers was then prepared to cope. In the United States the War Department by the fall of 1915 began to show an interest in providing troops with protection against gas and assigned responsibility for the design and development of respirators to the Medical Department. In carrying out his responsibilities, The Surgeon General detailed certain Medical officers to the British and French Armies as observers, and these officers sent back periodic reports which included information on gas defense.[2] The Army took no steps to supply the troops with masks or to prepare for offensive gas warfare until the first part of 1917.

It was not the War Department but a civilian branch of the government that took the first step in preparation for the employment of toxic agents. Early in 1917 the Secretary of the Interior surveyed his department to determine how it might contribute to the national defense and decided that the Bureau of Mines, which, since its establishment in 1910, had been investigating poisonous gases in mines, might be utilized in assisting the Army and Navy in developing a gas war program. On 8 February, Van H. Manning, the director of the Bureau of Mines wrote to the chairman of the Military Committee of the National Research Council (NRC) offering the bureau's

---

[1] The Chemical Warfare Service was designated the Chemical Corps by Public Law 607, 79th Congress, on 2 August 1946. See the Bibliographical Note at the end of this volume for the location of sources cited in footnotes.

[2] *The Medical Department of the United States Army in the World War:* XIV, *Medical Aspects of Gas Warfare* (Washington: Government Printing Office, 1926), 27, hereafter cited as *Medical Aspects of Gas Warfare.*

services.[3] Formal action on the recommendation was taken on 3 April 1917, when the Military Committee of NRC appointed a subcommittee on noxious gases, to "carry on investigations into noxious gases, generation, and antidote for same, for war purposes."[4] Under the chairmanship of the director of the Bureau of Mines, the subcommittee included Ordnance and Medical officers from both Army and Navy as well as two members of the Chemical Committee of the National Research Council. The work of this group provided the genesis of the chemical warfare research effort of the United States in World War I.

The War Department's early lack of serious concern about the new type of warfare might be attributed to the fact that the effectiveness of a gas attack with the agents then in use was waning by 1917 because of the efficiency of antigas protection. It was not until the German Army in July 1917 began the use of dichloroethyl sulfide, the so-called mustard gas, as a liquid toxic filler for projectiles that the War Department began to give serious consideration to preparations for gas warfare. Mustard gas was persistent, it proved to be a high casualty producer, and it considerably widened the scope of chemical warfare.[5]

As the gas warfare needs of U.S. troops in France became known in Washington they were referred to the War Department bureau to which each seemed to relate. The basic requirement was a gas mask; this item, because of its prophylactic nature, was assigned to the Medical Department for procurement and distribution. Training of individuals in use of the mask then became a Medical responsibility.[6] The War Department assigned the responsibility for the manufacture and filling of gas shells to the Ordnance Department, which erected a new arsenal for this purpose at Edgewood, Maryland.[7] Engineer troops were selected for the projection of chemical

---

[3] (1) Van H. Manning, *War Gas Investigations,* Dept. of Interior Bull. 178–A (Washington: Government Printing Office, 1919). (2) Memo by G. S. Rice, Bureau of Mines, regarding early history of mask and gas investigations for the Army, 9 Jan 18. RG 7, NA.

[4] Rcd of Mtg. Mil Com NRC, 3 Apr 17. RG 70, NA.

[5] (1) John J. Pershing, *My Experiences in the World War* (New York: Frederick A. Stokes, 1931), I, 166–67. (2) Amos A. Fries and Clarence J. West, *Chemical Warfare* (New York: McGraw-Hill, 1921), p. 151.

[6] In September 1917, a Gas Defense Service, Sanitary Corps, Medical Department, was activated. This service, in which a group of forty-five chemists was commissioned, was placed in charge of training. In April 1918 the officers of the Gas Defense Service were transferred to the Corps of Engineers. See Report of the Director of Chemical Warfare Service, 1919, pp. 43–49. Hereafter cited as Rpt of CWS, with appropriate year.

[7] For detailed account of the building of Edgewood Arsenal, see Benedict Crowell, *America's Munitions, 1917–1918* (Washington: Government Printing Office, 1919), pp. 395–409.

agents, and a regiment of gas and flame troops, to be known as the 30th Engineers, was authorized.[8] Supplying gas alarms became a function of Signal Corps.[9] An agency for solving technical problems was at hand in the subcommittee on noxious gases mentioned above. In September 1917 this committee established a research and experiment station, financed by the War and Navy Departments and operated by the Bureau of Mines, at American University on the outskirts of Washington, D.C.[10] The Bureau of Mines also supervised research activities on war gases at many universities and industrial laboratories throughout the country as well as at laboratories of other government agencies.

Gas Warfare Organization, American Expeditionary Forces

The problems of gas warfare administration were in the meantime receiving serious consideration in the theater of operations under the urgency of an active gas warfare situation. A board of officers was appointed to plan a gas warfare organization for the American Expeditionary Forces (AEF) on 18 June 1917, a few days after General John J. Pershing's arrival in France.[11] The board analyzed the gas warfare establishments of the British, French, and German Armies and considered the recommendations of Dr. George A. Hulett of Princeton University, who had spent some time in England and France studying the use of gas in war. Following the board's recommendation, General Pershing decided to centralize the handling of all gas warfare matters under an independent agency. He reported his scheme of organization to Washington on 4 August 1917, recommending that a similar consolidation be adopted by the War Department.[12]

Two weeks later General Pershing assigned Lt. Col. Amos A. Fries, an Engineer officer who had served under him in the Philippines in 1905, as

---

[8] (1) WD GO 108, 15 Aug 17. (2) History of 1st Gas Regiment, Pt. I, p. 1. MS, n.d.

[9] Rpt of CWS, 1919, p. 3.

[10] *Medical Aspects of Gas Warfare*, pp. 35–36.

[11] Memo, Lt Col John McA. Palmer, C Opns Sec, Hq AEF, for CofS AEF, 30 July 17, sub: Gas and Flame Serv, Offensive and Defensive. Copy of this memo appears as Appendix II in History of Chemical Warfare Service, American Expeditionary Forces, a seventy-one-page detailed account of organization and administration, together with sixty-five supporting appendixes, which is apparently the official history written shortly after World War I. H–12 and H–13. This is hereafter cited as History of CWS, AEF.

[12] (1) Ltr, CinC AEF to TAG, 4 Aug 17, sub: Cml or Gas Serv. (2) James G. Harbord, *The American Army in France* (Boston: Little, Brown and Company, 1936), p. 128. Maj. Gen. James G. Harbord states that details of proposed organization were sent to War Department on 28 July.

Engineer in Charge of Gas.[13] As such Fries became the chief of the Gas Service, AEF, when it was officially established on 3 September 1917.[14] The following day Fries was raised to the rank of colonel and placed in command of the 30th Engineers, the gas and flame regiment.[15] He at once set up headquarters at Chaumont, where he would be in close touch with the General Headquarters (GHQ) of the American Expeditionary Forces.

The AEF order which established the Gas Service specified that the chief of the service would be "charged with the organization of the personnel, the supply of material and the conduct of the entire Gas Service, both Offensive and Defensive, including instruction." The first task confronting Fries was that of securing suitable officer personnel. Even before the Gas Service was officially established he had obtained the services of two Medical Department officers, Col. James R. Church, who had been observing the effects of gas on French troops, and Capt. Walter M. Boothby, who had been given a similar assignment with the British. Colonel Church headed the Medical Section of the Gas Service until December 1917 when he was succeeded by Col. Harry L. Gilchrist.[16] The Medical Section was responsible for training and instructing Medical officers and other personnel in the treatment of gas casualties, as well as for the inspection of methods and facilities for the care of gassed cases.[17]

From the other branches of the Army, including Engineers, Ordnance, Cavalry, and Infantry, Fries obtained some two hundred officers who, although they were assigned to the Gas Service, continued to hold commissions in their respective branches. These officers, as well as the enlisted men who were transferred to the Gas Service, were given a course of instruction in gas defense at the I Corps Gas School, which was activated on 15 October 1917.[18] The same month an Army Gas School, with courses in both defensive

[13] Cablegram (Pershing) 111–S, Paris, France, 18 Aug 17, Par. 19. WD Cables, P series, A.E.F. files, NA.

[14] (1) Interv, CmlHO with Maj Gen Amos A. Fries, USA (Ret.), 4 Aug 55. (2) Copy of AEF GO 31, 3 Sep 17. All AEF general orders cited in this chapter appear in Historical Division, Department of the Army, UNITED STATES ARMY IN THE WORLD WAR: 1917–1919, XVI, General Orders, G.H.Q., A.E.F. (Washington: Government Printing Office, 1948).

[15] Historical Division, Department of the Army, UNITED STATES ARMY IN THE WORLD WAR: 1917–1919, XV, Reports of Commander-in-Chief, A.E.F., Staff Sections and Services (Washington: Government Printing Office, 1948), 291, hereafter cited as Reports of Commander-in-Chief, A.E.F., Staff Sections and Services.

[16] (1) History of CWS, AEF, pp. 7–8. (2) Medical Aspects of Gas Warfare, pp. 39–50. (3) Fries and West, Chemical Warfare, p. 114.

[17] Medical Aspects of Gas Warfare, pp. 67–73.

[18] (1) AEF GO 45, 8 Oct 17. (2) Schedule, I Corps Gas School AEF. History of CWS, AEF, App. 13.

STOKES TRENCH MORTAR, *used by special gas troops of AEF, World War I. Picture taken in CWS training area, Chaumont, France, 1918.*

and offensive gas warfare, was started at Langres.[19] Later three other training schools were established.

The most serious problem which faced Fries when he became chief of the Gas Service, aside from the task of obtaining personnel, was that of providing for a supply of gas masks and other protective equipment for American troops. Just prior to Fries's appointment the British, upon request of Captain Boothby, had tested twenty thousand gas masks received from the United States and had found them entirely unsuitable for use on the battlefield.[20] Fries knew that he would have to look for other sources of supply and took immediate steps to purchase British masks, or box respirators, as they were called, and French M2 masks.[21] Second in importance to supplying the Army with masks was the task of equipping special gas troops with such weapons as cylinders, mortars, and projectors for the dispersion

[19] (1) AEF GO 46, 10 Oct 17. (2) Schedule of Instruction, AEF Army Gas School. History of CWS, AEF, App. 15.

[20] Amos A. Fries, History of Chemical Warfare Service in France, p. 4. MS.

[21] AEF General Order 53, 3 November 1917, made the Gas Service responsible for supplying all division, corps, and army gas officers with antigas supplies.

of agents. Fries also made arrangements to purchase these items from the British, and it was well that he did, for none were received from the United States until just before the close of the war.[22]

Colonel Fries was fortunate in securing the services of a very competent officer, Maj. Robert W. Crawford, whom he put in charge of procurement and supply activities in the Gas Service early in September 1917. The Procurement and Supply Division, as Crawford's unit came to be known, not only handled the purchase of matériel but also drew up plans for and supervised the construction of three separate gas depots in the First Army Area and four in the Second Army Area. These depots were placed in operation in October 1918 under depot officers who were on the staffs of the respective army gas officers.[23] Crawford also drew up plans for construction of phosgene-manufacturing plants, shell-filling plants, and a gas-mask repair plant. The proposed construction of phosgene and shell-filling plants in France was given up after Colonel Fries had studied the matter in detail and made a recommendation to that effect to General Pershing. The chief reason for abandoning those projects was the inability to obtain sufficient chlorine in France.[24] But the plan for building the mask repair plant was carried to completion, and in November 1917 four officers and 110 enlisted men of the Medical Department arrived from the United States to operate this plant.[25]

In addition to personnel, training, and procurement and supply responsibilities, the Gas Service, AEF, had definite technical responsibilities. In carrying out the latter responsibilities, General Fries' headquarters worked closely with the War Department.

Centralizing Chemical Warfare Activities

The start of centralizing chemical warfare activities within the War Department dates from October 1917, when an Office of Gas Service was set up, with Col. Charles L. Potter, an Engineer officer, as director. This move was an attempt to satisfy the need for an agency in Washington which would know everything that was going on with regard to chemical warfare both at home and abroad. The Gas Service was to be the "co-

[22] Fries and West, *Chemical Warfare*, p. 78.
[23] History of CWS, AEF, p. 48.
[24] Fries and West, *Chemical Warfare*, p. 104.
[25] *Medical Aspects of Gas Warfare*, p. 30.

ordinating agent" between the various bureaus and laboratories engaged in gas warfare activities, and all communications from abroad dealing with gas warfare were to be routed to that office. Provision was made for three assistants to the director of the new service, one from the Ordnance Department, another from the Medical Department, and a third from a newly created Chemical Service Section of the National Army, established under the same directive that established the Gas Service.[26] The Chemical Service Section was to consist of forty-seven commissioned and ninety-five enlisted personnel.

The Chemical Service Section, National Army, was created to fill a request of General Pershing, repeated five times between 26 September and 9 December 1917, for a chemical laboratory, complete with equipment and personnel, to investigate gases and powders.[27] Professor William H. Walker of the Massachusetts Institute of Technology (MIT) was commissioned a lieutenant colonel and made chief of the Chemical Service Section. Walker set out to recruit qualified personnel for a laboratory unit for overseas duty. In January 1918 the first members of this unit, consisting of about twenty-five officers and ten men, under the command of Col. Raymond F. Bacon, arrived in Puteaux, near Paris, where Colonel Fries had set up a laboratory. Here the scientists in uniform conducted experiments on gases until the close of the war. To satisfy the need for testing gas shells and fuzes and conducting other gas warfare experimentation, a test field was set up near Chaumont. This field was named Hanlon Field in September 1918 in honor of 2d Lt. Joseph T. Hanlon, the first Chemical Warfare officer to be killed in action.[28]

A development in connection with gas research in the theater was the inter-Allied gas conferences for the exchange of scientific information. Three such conferences were held during the war—in September 1917, March 1918, and October 1918. From the point of view of the American scientists the last was the most satisfactory, because by that time the Americans felt they had come to know as much about gas as their European co-workers. At this conference for the first time sat representatives from the

[26] Memo, CofS for TAG, 16 Oct 17, sub: Gas Serv of Army. CWS 322.095/101–140. The section of this directive dealing with the establishment of the Chemical Service Section, National Army, also appears in War Department General Order 139, 1 November 1917.

[27] Pershing's five cables are repeated verbatim in Memo, Col Potter, Dir Gas Serv, for CofS USA, 28 Dec 17. CWS 322.095/141–200.

[28] (1) History of CWS, AEF, pp. 18–19, 56–57. (2) Fries and West, *Chemical Warfare*, Ch. IV. (3) *Reports of Commander-in-Chief, A.E.F., Staff Sections and Services*, pp. 300–302.

laboratories in the United States, including Professors Elmer P. Kohler and Warren K. Lewis.[29]

Inter-Allied co-operation in the theater was not confined to research but extended to supply as well. At the suggestion of Winston S. Churchill, the Inter-Allied Commission for Chemical Warfare Supply was set up in May 1918.[30] Between May and November this commission, on which sat representatives of Great Britain, France, Italy, and the United States, held six meetings. By the time of the armistice the commission was said to be "gradually assuming the position of a board of directors, regulating production and distribution in accordance with existing needs." [31]

While the Chemical Service Section, National Army, was assisting the theater on the research program, Colonel Walker's headquarters was also taking steps to co-ordinate gas research activities in the United States. By January 1918 the number of troops doing research under the guidance of the Bureau of Mines at the American University Experiment Station and various other laboratories had risen to over two hundred officers and more than five hundred enlisted men. These were under the jurisdiction of various elements of the Army—Ordnance, Engineers, Signal, Sanitary Corps of the Medical Department, and the Chemical Service Section, National Army. Efficient administration demanded that these troops be placed under one Army agency. On 10 January Colonel Potter, chief of the Gas Service, recommended to the Chief of Staff that they be included in the Chemical Service Section. This request was favorably considered and on 15 February the authorized strength of the Chemical Service Section was raised to 227 officers and 525 enlisted men.[32]

In addition to its research activities, the Chemical Service Section, from early 1918 until the end of the war, was called on more and more by the Ordnance Department for recommendations on the manufacture of gases at Edgewood Arsenal. Thus, while the purpose behind the Chemical Service Section was to co-ordinate without integrating and without disturbing functions of the statutory bureaus of the War Department, it was becoming evident that the system was developing serious defects. What was needed was

---

[29] History of CWS, AEF, p. 52.

[30] (1) Pershing, *My Experience in the World War*, I, 357. (2) History of CWS, AEF, p. 27.

[31] History of CWS, AEF, p. 28.

[32] Marston T. Bogert and William H. Walker, History of the Chemical Service Section, Apps. C and D. This seven-page manuscript account, exclusive of appendixes, was written in 1919. H–131.

a greater degree of administrative centralization. Two additional factors were working toward this end. The large and growing number of scientists engaged in research in gas warfare was insisting on recognition. And there was increasing pressure by various officials for a responsible gas warfare organization within the zone of interior to parallel the one in the theater of operations.

The Chemical Warfare Service, National Army

In the spring of 1918 separate proposals were made both in the United States and in France to establish a gas corps. On 17 April Lt. Col. Marston T. Bogert, who had succeeded Colonel Walker as chief of the Chemical Service Section, recommended to the Chief of Staff that the section be replaced by a "chemical corps" which would be on a "basis more nearly like that occupied by the Engineering and Medical branches of the Army." [33] In this way, Bogert contended, chemists in the Army would be under the guidance and control of chemists. This suggestion was not favorably considered. [34] On 1 May Colonel Fries recommended to General Pershing that a gas corps be established in the AEF. Fries gave as his chief reason the very compelling fact that for the past year the enemy had been using gas as an essential part of every offensive and that the Gas Service, AEF, simply did not have the necessary administrative power to prosecute an effective gas program. [35] Pershing was favorably impressed by Fries's argument and on 3 June he cabled to the Chief of Staff in the United States requesting that a gas corps be activated. [36] This request, like Bogert's was not favorably considered. While it took no action on setting up a separate chemical or gas corps, the War Department did take definite steps in the spring of 1918 to establish a more strongly centralized organization for gas warfare. What was especially needed at that time was a "name" officer of rank and personality who could overcome obstacles and break log jams. This proved to be Maj. Gen. William L. Sibert, one of the builders of the Panama Canal

---

[33] Memo, Bogert, Cml Serv Sec NA, for CofS USA, 17 Apr 18, sub: Cml Serv Sec Pers. Bogert and Walker, History of the Chemical Service Section, App. C 1.

[34] 1st Ind, 6 May 18, to memo cited Note 33 above. Bogert and Walker, Hist of the Chemical Service Section, App. C 3.

[35] Ltr, C Gas Serv AEF to CinC AEF (Through: CG SOS), 1 May 18, sub: Reorganization of Gas Serv. History of CWS, AEF, App. 37.

[36] Cable 1240–S, CG AEF to CofS USA, 3 Jun 18. History of CWS, AEF, App. 38.

MAJ. GEN. WILLIAM L. SIBERT, *first Chief of the Chemical Warfare Service, June 1918–February 1920.*

and lately commander of the 1st Division in France. Appointment of Sibert as director of the Gas Service on 11 May 1918 was quickly followed by a number of administrative changes in line with the trend toward integration of chemical warfare functions which had been evident for some time.[37] On 25 June 1918 the President transferred the control experimental station at American University from the Bureau of Mines to the War Department.[38] Three days later the War Department formally established the Chemical Warfare Service, National Army, and sweepingly specified the transfer to the new organization of all facilities and functions applying to toxic chemicals.[39]

In World War I the United States had to rely on its allies, particularly the British, for chemical munitions. This situation was rapidly being corrected late in 1918. Manufacturing facilities in the Astoria section of New York City were by then capable of meeting all the requirements for protective equipment, and the production of toxic agents at the Edgewood Arsenal plants was totaling 675 tons per week.[40] Responsibility for the production of defensive items was put in the Gas Defense Production Division, CWS, headed by Col. Bradley Dewey, while supervision of toxics was placed in the Gas Offense Production Division, of which Col. William H. Walker was chief. Technical activities were divided between two divisions, a Research Division, headed by Col. George A. Burrell, and a Development Division,

[37] Colonel Potter was succeeded as Chief, Gas Service, on 30 January 1918 by Mr. Arthur Hudson Marks who served only a few days. Colonel Walker was Acting Chief, Gas Service, from that time until Sibert's appointment on 11 May. See Rpt of CWS, 1918, p. 5.
[38] Executive Order 2894, 25 Jun 18.
[39] WD GO 62, 28 Jun 18.
[40] Crowell, *America's Munitions,* pp. 407–09, 426–27.

CHEMICAL PLANTS, EDGEWOOD ARSENAL. *By 1918, toxic agents totaling 675 tons per week were being manufactured here.*

headed by Col. Frank M. Dorsey. To test gas munitions the War Department established a proving ground at Lakehurst, New Jersey, and adjoining this proving ground activated a training camp for gas troops, Camp Kendrick, under the Training Division. All activities connected with the medical aspects of gas warfare were placed in a Medical Division, headed by Col. William J. L. Lyster.[41]

The very day that the CWS was formally established, the War Department cabled Pershing informing him of the creation of the CWS and requesting him to cable back the names of the officers to be transferred to the new service as well as the numbers and grades of officers and men required in France.[42] The transfer of troops to the new service in the theater was made official on 16 July when an authorized strength of 916 officers and 7,264 enlisted men was approved for the Overseas Divsion, CWS, which was to be headed by a brigadier general.[43] Colonel Fries was thereupon raised to that rank. Later, the War Department, anticipating an in-

[41] Rpts of CWS, 1918 and 1919.
[42] Cable 1622–R, McCain to Pershing, 28 Jun 18. History of CWS, AEF, App. 39.
[43] Cable 1724–R, McCain to Pershing, 16 Jul 18. History of CWS, AEF, App. 41.

crease in the use of gas, authorized two additional gas regiments. This action raised the authorized strength of the Overseas Division to 1,315 officers and 17,205 enlisted men.[44] Because of the sudden collapse of the enemy nothing approximating that strength was ever attained, and as of 11 November 1918 the actual number of officers and men in the Overseas Division totaled 630 and 2,800 respectively. This compared with actual strength of the entire CWS on that date of 1,680 officers and 18,838 enlisted men.[45]

General Fries's headquarters, like the office of General Sibert, was organized along functional lines. Since the theater naturally placed greater emphasis on actual employment of gas on the battlefield, two divisions were set up for that purpose, an Offense Division and a Defense Division. Other divisions of the CWS, AEF, were: Procurement and Supply, Technical, Medical, and Intelligence.

With the establishment of the CWS the gas and flame regiment (the 30th Engineers) became the 1st Gas Regiment. The regiment had been activated in August 1917 under Maj. Earl J. Atkisson at Camp American University, Washington. In January 1918 the first two companies, A and B, arrived in France, where, through an arrangement between Fries and Maj. Gen. C. H. Foulkes of the British Army, they were given intensive training by the British Special Brigade, a gas brigade. Following this training they accompanied the British on actual gas operations on the field of battle. When two other companies arrived in France in March the officers and men of Companies A and B assisted in training the new arrivals. The facilities of the five gas schools in France were also utilized in training these and subsequent gas troops arriving from the United States.[46]

Troops of the 1st Gas Regiment were employed in operations on the Western Front during the summer and fall of 1918. Their biggest engagement was in the Meuse-Argonne offensive in which six companies of the regiment saw action. In this campaign gas troops expended some 489 Stokes mortar gas shells, 130 Livens projector gas drums, 206 Livens projector drums filled with high explosives, and over 2,800 smoke and thermite bombs.[47]

After the close of hostilities the War Department made a rapid start in demobilizing CWS troops and facilities. By June 1919 the troop strength of

---

[44] Cable 2027–R, Harris to Pershing, 7 Oct 18. History of CWS, AEF, App. 60.

[45] Rpt of CWS, 1919, pp. 14–15.

[46] (1) James Thayer Addison, *The Story of the First Gas Regiment* (Boston and New York: Houghton Mifflin, 1919), Ch. III. (2) Maj. Gen. C. H. Foulkes, *Gas, The Story of the Gas Brigade* (Edinburgh and London: William Blackwood and Sons, 1934), p. 298.

[47] History of CWS, AEF, p. 67.

the CWS had been reduced to 328 officers and 261 enlisted men, the government gas-mask factory in New York had been demobilized, 670 contracts had been adjusted, over a million dollars worth of surplus property had been disposed of, and the plants at Edgewood and Lakehurst were being put on a peacetime basis.[48] The majority of government-owned chemical plants throughout the country were yet to be sold or transferred to other government bureaus; that was a task which would run well into the following year.[49]

The War Department general order establishing the Chemical Warfare Service had provided that it would continue until six months after the termination of hostilities or until the general order itself was amended, modified, or rescinded. An act of Congress of 11 July 1919 extended the life of the CWS until 30 June 1920.[50] On 28 November 1919 the War Department defined the CWS peacetime mission as follows:

(a) The maintenance of a competent body of chemical warfare specialists with facilities for continuous research and experimentation.

(b) The maintenance of records.

(c) Provision for keeping in touch with civilian agencies for chemical research and chemical industries capable of being converted for the production of wartime material.

(d) The maintenance of such existing Government plants as may be decided necessary.

(e) The continuous training of the Army in chemical warfare.

(f) The maintenance of a supply of chemical warfare material sufficient to meet the initial requirements of the Army in time of war.[51]

Congress meanwhile began to study changes needed in military organization in the light of recent war experiences. Since the establishment of the Signal Corps in 1860 there had been no additions to the War Department technical services.[52] One of the questions now to be decided was, what should be done about Chemical Warfare? This matter was examined carefully by the military affairs committees of the Senate and the House of Representatives.

The recommendations of the officials of the War Department varied. Some suggested that the wartime CWS be abolished and its work appor-

---

[48] Rpt of CWS, 1919, pp. 15, 51.
[49] Rpt of CWS, 1920, p. 15.
[50] (1) General Order No. 62, 28 June 1918. (2) 41 *Stat.* 104.
[51] Rpt of CWS, 1920, p. 5.
[52] 12 *Stat.* 50.

tioned among the older established services. Others felt that the CWS should be retained. Newton D. Baker, the Secretary of War, believed that peacetime activities in this field would be principally in research and development, duties which the Corps of Engineers could handle.[53] The Chief of Staff, General Peyton C. March, who abhorred gas warfare, also felt that the Corps of Engineers should be given responsibility for preparations for gas warfare, which in peacetime should be restricted to its defensive aspects.[54] General Pershing, like most older line officers, disliked the idea of using toxic gas but he was not adamant on the subject; in fact, he was rather inclined toward retaining the Chemical Warfare Service as a separate department.[55]

The first powerful voice raised in support of an independent chemical service in the Army was that of Benedict Crowell, the Assistant Secretary of War and the man principally responsible for the success of the munitions program of 1917–18. Crowell, who had been educated as a chemist and believed that future warfare would depend largely on the work of men of science, strongly urged that the wartime CWS organization be made permanent.[56] This view of course was echoed by the two officers most closely identified with gas warfare in World War I, Sibert and Fries. Fries was particularly active. Less than two weeks after the close of hostilities he had obtained General Pershing's approval for his return to the United States in order to work for a permanent CWS.[57] He was a personal friend of both the chairman of the Senate Committee on Military Affairs, Senator George E. Chamberlain of Oregon, and the chairman of the House Committee on Military Affairs, Representative Julius Kahn of California. Fries lost no opportunity in conveying to those gentlemen his strong conviction of the need for a permanent chemical bureau in the Army.[58]

[53] S. Com. on Military Affairs, 66th Cong., 1st Sess., Hearings on S. 2715, *A Bill To Reorganize and Increase the Efficiency of the United States Army, and for Other Purposes,* 19 Aug. 19.

[54] (1) H. Com. on Military Affairs, 66th Cong., 1st Sess., Hearings on H. Res. 8287, *A Bill To Reorganize and Increase the Efficiency of the United States Army, and for Other Purposes,* 5 Sep 19, I, 53–54. (2) Peyton C. Marsh, *The Nation at War* (Garden City, N.Y.: Doubleday-Doran, 1932), pp. 333–36.

[55] H. Com. on Military Affairs, 66th Cong., 1st Sess., Hearings on H. Res. 8287, *A Bill To Reorganize and Increase the Efficiency of the United States Army, and for Other Purposes,* 1 Nov 19, I, 1507–08.

[56] H. Com. on Military Affairs, 66th Cong., 1st and 2d Sess., Hearings on H. Res. 8287, *A Bill To Reorganize and Increase the Efficiency of the United States Army, and for Other Purposes,* 9 Jan 20, II, 1804–05.

[57] Fries, History of CWS in France.

[58] Fries interv, 4 Aug 55.

Establishment of a chemical service as a permanent bureau of the War Department was also strongly advocated by leading chemical scientists and industrialists, who had come to regard the existence of such a service as a recognition of the growing importance of chemistry in the national economy.[59] The desire to assist these groups doubtless helped influence the decision of Congress in 1920 to write into its revision of the National Defense Act of 1916 a new section starting with the words: "There is hereby created a Chemical Warfare Service." [60]

The purpose of the wartime Chemical Warfare Service had been to handle all matters relating to toxic agents and ammunition together with gas defense material. Incendiaries and smokes had not been mentioned in the wartime charter of the Chemical Warfare Service although before the end of the war it had actually done considerable work on both these items. This fact is reflected in the wording of the revised National Defense Act, which accordingly enlarged the CWS field. Thus was completed the shift in emphasis from the "gas" service of 1917 to the "chemical" service of 1920.

The function of the new branch included the development, procurement, and supply of "all smoke and incendiary materials, all toxic gases, and all gas defense appliances." These duties were further extended to include "the supervision of the training of the Army in chemical warfare, both offensive and defensive . . . ; the organization, equipment, training, and operation of special gas troops, and such other duties as the President may from time to time prescribe." [61] The Chemical Warfare Service therefore took on service-wide training functions, together with responsibility for combatant troops, in addition to technical supply duties. For this work the National Defense Act authorized a chief of the service with the rank of brigadier general, one hundred officers, and twelve hundred enlisted men.

The Chemical Warfare Service was a product of the changing technology of war. Only reluctantly did the War Department provide for its activation. Many years would elapse before the new organization would be fully accepted in the military family. In fact, it would require the experience of a second world war to convince the War Department of the real need for a separate chemical service.

[59] See statement of Charles H. Herty, editor of the *Journal of Industrial and Engineering Chemistry*, in S. Com. on Military Affairs, 66th Cong., 1st Sess., Hearings on S. 2715, *A Bill To Reorganize and Increase the Efficiency of the United States Army, and for Other Purposes*, p. 408.

[60] Public Law 242, 66th Cong., Sec. 12a. War Department Bulletin 25, 9 June 1920, reproduces Section 12a *in toto*.

[61] *Ibid.*

CHAPTER II

The Years Between the Wars

The Issue of Gas Warfare

Announcement of the creation of the Chemical Warfare Service in 1920 as a branch of the permanent Military Establishment presumably settled an issue that had been discussed heatedly and at length. Actually, debate over functions of the CWS was to continue for many years. This perennial controversy had its roots in two spheres. One was the policy of the United States on gas warfare. The other was the reaction within the War Department itself to gas warfare.

For centuries the use of poisons for military purposes has been generally disavowed by civilized nations.[1] But not until the end of the nineteenth century, when the science of chemistry had advanced to a point where the use of toxics in warfare was being seriously considered, was the question raised as to whether toxics loaded into ammunition should be considered poisonous. Discussion of this point was listed on the agenda of an international conference, which, upon the initiative of the Russians, met at The Hague during the summer of 1899.

The proposal offered for consideration at the meeting would have bound the contracting powers to agree "to abstain from the use of projectiles, the sole object of which is the diffusion of asphyxiating or deleterious gases."[2] In instructions to the American delegates before they left to attend this conference, Secretary of State John Hay had stated, "The expediency of restraining the inventive genius of our people in the direction of devising means of defense is by no means clear . . . the delegates are therefore enjoined not to give the weight of their influence to the promotion of projects the

---

[1] Hugo Grotius, *De Jure Belli ac Pacis,* 1625, trans. Francis W. Kelsey (Oxford: Clarendon Press, 1925), III, 651–52.

[2] Carnegie Endowment for International Peace, Division of International Law, Pamphlet 8, *The Hague Declaration (IV, 2) of 1899 Concerning Asphyxiating Gases* (Washington: The Endowment, 1915).

realization of which is so uncertain." [3] The United States therefore did not subscribe to the antigas agreement, although a number of nations did.[4]

The refusal of the United States to participate in formal measures to outlaw the employment of toxic chemicals was not based on lack of sympathy with the purposes of the proposal. It was the result, rather, of unwillingness to act in the uncertain light of what was then only a nebulous possibility. Moreover, since The Hague antigas declaration specifically outlawed only projectiles, its phrasing could be interpreted as a stimulus to the devising of other means of dissemination. Because of this loophole the German attack at Ypres in April 1915, when chlorine gas was released from charged cylinders, did not violate the letter of The Hague declaration.[5]

The Hague antigas declaration was a casualty of the Ypres attack even though it did not specifically apply. Both the Central and Allied Powers developed and used toxics which were disseminated by a number of means, including projectiles, throughout the war. The spirit of The Hague declaration lived, however, to become a part of the effective Allied antigas propaganda weapon which in the period between the wars was to stimulate widespread public indignation against the "barbaric" and "inhuman" employment of toxics by the enemy.[6]

After the war there was wide reaction against use of gas in future military conflicts. The peace treaties signed by the Central Powers all contained the clause, "the use of asphyxiating, poisonous or other gases and all analogous liquids, materials or devices being prohibited, their manufacture and importation are strictly forbidden." [7] This wording presumably applied only to the defeated states. Subsequent agreements between the Allies and other powers were needed to insure universal prohibition of gas warfare.

The policy of the United States in the matter of toxic chemicals was clearly expressed at the Conference on the Limitation of Armament which met in Washington in 1921. This question was one considered earlier by a subcommittee on land warfare of which General Pershing was chairman.

---

[3] Ltr, Secy State to Hon. Andrew D. White *et al.,* 18 Apr 1899, in Special Missions, Department of State, Vol. IV, October 15, 1886–June 20, 1906. NA.

[4] The Hague antigas agreement was signed and ratified by twenty-five powers

[5] Cyrus Bernstein, "The Law of Chemical Warfare," *The George Washington Law Review,* X (June 1942), 889–915. Portions of this article were reproduced in *Chemical Warfare Bulletin,* XXVIII (October 1942), 174–86.

[6] For details on antigas propaganda, see: James M. Read, *Atrocity Propaganda: 1914–1919* (New Haven: Yale University Press, 1941), pp. 6, 95–99; and Horace C. Peterson, *Propaganda for War* (Norman, Okla.: University of Oklahoma Press, 1939), p. 63.

[7] Green H. Hackworth, *Digest of International Law* (Washington: Dept. of State, 1943), p. 269.

Pershing's group recommended that "chemical warfare should be abolished among nations as abhorrent to civilization." [8] Another report submitted at this time by the General Board of the Navy stated that it was believed "to be sound policy to prohibit gas warfare in every form and against every objective." [9] Both of these reports were considered by, and no doubt strongly influenced, the U.S. delegation at the Washington arms conference in formulating its proposal to prohibit the use of poison gas in war.

The U.S. proposal, incorporated as Article 5 in the Washington arms conference treaty covering the Use of Submarines and Noxious Gases in War, first pointed out that the employment of toxic war gases had been condemned by world opinion and prohibited in numerous existing treaties. It then announced that the contracting parties, "to the end that this prohibition shall be universally accepted as a part of international law binding alike the conscience and practice of nations, declare their assent to such prohibition, agree to be bound thereby as between themselves and invite all other civilized nations to adhere thereto." [10] The treaty was never ratified by France, one of the principal signatories, and therefore never came into effect.[11] It remains the only antigas convention the ratification of which the U.S. Senate has ever approved.

The proposition of outlawing gas warfare was revived at a conference held in 1925 at Geneva to consider regulating the international traffic in arms. Here the U.S. delegation introduced and obtained general agreement to what has been called the Geneva Gas Protocol. This instrument, after reiterating a general condemnation of the use of toxic agents in war, declared that the contracting parties had agreed to prohibit the use of such materials in the future and had further agreed "to extend this prohibition to the use of bacteriological methods of warfare and . . . to be bound as between themselves according to the terms of this declaration." [12] Although the U.S. delegation signed this protocol, the Senate refused to ratify it.

A cross section of opinion in the United States on the military usefulness of gas warfare and the prospects of preventing its employment by inter-

[8] Quoted by Sen. William E. Borah (R., Idaho) in *Congressional Record,* Vol. 68, Pt. I, p. 140.

[9] *Ibid.,* p. 143.

[10] U.S. Department of State, *Papers Relating to the Foreign Relations of the United States, 1922* (Washington: Dept. of State, 1938), I, 276, hereafter cited as Dept. of State, *Foreign Relations of the United States.*

[11] The other signatories were Great Britain, the United States, Italy, and Japan. France failed to sign this treaty because of the fact that it also greatly restricted submarine warfare.

[12] Dept. of State, *Foreign Relations of the United States, 1925* (Washington: Dept. of State, 1940), I, 89–90.

national agreement was brought out in Senate debates on the ratification of the Geneva Gas Protocol.[13] Some leading military figures were quoted as expressing agreement with eliminating gas as a weapon of war. Considerable opposition to ratification came from civilian groups, especially veterans' organizations. Despite the fact that the Senate did not approve it, the protocol was supported in principle by the executive departments of the U.S. Government. By the time World War II began, the Geneva Gas Protocol was adhered to by forty-two nations and was the most generally accepted expression of international opinion relating to the use of toxic agents in war.

The influence of national policy and of international agreements in limiting employment of toxic agents in war was of obvious concern to the War Department. This matter was clarified by Secretary of State Frank B. Kellogg on 7 December 1926 in a letter supporting continued military preparations in this field:

> All governments recognize that it is incumbent upon them to be fully prepared as regards chemical warfare, and especially as regards defense against it, irrespective of any partial or general international agreements looking to the prohibition of the actual use of such warfare. I have never seen any proposal seriously advanced by any government to provide that national preparation for the use of and for defense against chemical warfare, if such warfare should be used by an enemy contrary to treaty agreements, should be abolished or curtailed in the slightest.[14]

In agreement with this statement was the joint Army-Navy policy on chemical warfare which in 1934 was framed in these words:

> The United States will make all necessary preparations for the use of chemical warfare from the outbreak of war. The use of chemical warfare, including the use of toxic agents, from the inception of hostilities, is authorized, subject to such restrictions or prohibitions as may be contained in any duly ratified international convention or conventions, which at that time may be binding upon the United States and the enemy's state or states.[15]

All Presidents whose administrations spanned the interwar years sought to eliminate gas as a military weapon. Herbert Hoover and Franklin D. Roosevelt, who saw eye to eye on this issue, were particularly outspoken. President Hoover steadily urged elimination before the disarmament deliberations that took place while he was in office. By the time of President Roosevelt's inauguration the prospect of effective agreement among nations on the curtailment of armaments appeared to have vanished. In line, possibly,

---

[13] *Congressional Record*, Vol. 68, Pt. I, pp. 141–54, 226–29, 363–68.
[14] *Ibid.*, p. 366.
[15] Ltr, Jt Plng Com to JB, 17 Oct 34, sub: Use of Cml Agents. JB 325, Ser 542.

with this trend, Congress in 1937 passed a bill (S. 1284) to change the designation of the Chemical Warfare Service to Chemical Corps.[16] This the President promptly vetoed. The reasons given in the Roosevelt veto message clearly expressed the White House attitude and, *ipso facto,* that of the U.S. Government:

It has been and is the policy of this Government to do everything in its power to outlaw the use of chemicals in warfare. Such use is inhuman and contrary to what modern civilization should stand for.

I am doing everything in my power to discourage the use of gases and other chemicals in any war between nations. While, unfortunately, the defensive necessities of the United States call for study of the use of chemicals in warfare, I do not want the Government of the United States to do anything to aggrandize or make permanent any special bureau of the Army or the Navy engaged in these studies. I hope the time will come when the Chemical Warfare Service can be entirely abolished.

To dignify this Service by calling it the "Chemical Corps" is, in my judgment, contrary to a sound public policy.[17]

The War Department and Gas Warfare

Beginning in 1921 and continuing until 1941, the mission of the Chemical Warfare Service was the subject of almost continuous debate by the War Department General Staff (WDGS). During these years there was scarcely a time when the CWS felt that it enjoyed undisputed membership on the War Department team. Hence a great deal of energy was continually expended by the CWS in defending its statutory position. This fact had considerable bearing on the development of the new service.

The questions most frequently raised by the War Department were: Could the Chemical Warfare Service be eliminated and its duties distributed among other services? Could the Chemical Warfare Service be relieved of combat functions and its activities limited to technical and supply duties and to defensive training?

In 1924 the WDGS phrased a sentence which, constantly repeated in later years, came to be generally accepted as a statement of policy and a guide to the activities of the CWS: "Our peacetime preparations in chemical warfare will be based on opposing effectively any enemy employing chemical weapons." [18]

---

[16] This change, as already indicated, was eventually effected by Public Law 607, 79th Congress, 2 August 1946.

[17] Copy in CWS 011/1–20.

[18] Ltr, TAG to C CWS, 7 Jan 24, sub: CWS's Functions. AG 321.94 (1–2–24) (Misc.) M–C.

This statement was based on a War Department policy announcement which had attempted to clarify preceding general orders and other instructions relating to the establishment of the Chemical Warfare Service, particularly in the light of current developments toward international limitation of armaments. It had the merit of clearly stating an obviously desirable objective, yet the means to be followed to this end proved to be subject to widely varying interpretations. Some of the difficulties being encountered were brought to the attention of the War Department by the Chief, CWS (Maj. Gen. Amos A. Fries), in 1926, when some liberalizing of existing policy as to offensive means was proposed.[19] The staff study of CWS functions which followed carefully reviewed all the preceding actions and pointed to still further investigations that needed to be made but did not lead to immediate change in standing instructions.[20]

The War Department by this time had definitely veered away from planning the type of positional warfare characteristic of the campaigns in France in 1917 and 1918 and with which large-scale gas operations staged by chemical troops seemed intimately associated. Consequently, the existence of special gas troops was increasingly challenged, and the employment of gas by branches other than the CWS was increasingly favored by the staff. The CWS view was that gas had important uses in a war of movement as well as in static operations and that technical considerations necessitated the employment of special gas troops in either situation. These differing attitudes were never wholly reconciled, although at times the General Staff view appears to have been maintained somewhat less resolutely than that of the Chemical Warfare Service.

The mission of the Chemical Warfare Service with respect to its principal preoccupation, gas warfare, was therefore somewhat complex. Primarily the CWS was expected to provide insurance for American military forces against the shock of sudden gas attack. Hand in hand with this mission went responsibility for maintaining a state of readiness for quick retaliation. These two constituted explicit responsibilities. In a broader sense, an implicit function of the CWS was to provide military support for a national policy, that of dissuading others from resorting to the gas weapon. This was accomplished, as matters turned out, more by the strength of U.S. preparedness for toxic warfare than by the cogency of political agreements.

[19] (1) Ltr, C CWS to TAG, 9 Jun 26, sub: Functions of CWS. AG 321.94. (2) Public Law 457, signed 24 February 1925, raised the rank of the Chief, CWS, from brigadier general to major general.
[20] Memo, ACofS G–3 for CofS, 5 Nov 26, sub: CWS Functions. AG 321.94, Sec. 1, Functions of CWS.

Carrying Out the Peacetime Mission: 1920–39

To supplement the National Defense Act statement of CWS functions the War Department spelled them out in more detailed fashion via a series of general orders issued in 1920 and 1921. On 28 August 1920, for example, it defined the specific duties of the Chemical Warfare Service and the Ordnance Department with regard to the investigation, development, procurement, and supply of munitions: Ordnance retained the responsibility for the design, procurement, and supply of chemical shells, grenades, and bombs; the CWS was to fill them with gas, smoke, or incendiary agents. Later it defined the relationship of the CWS to the corps areas and, still later, outlined the storage and issue responsibilities and specified that the chemical warfare training of the Army be along both offensive and defensive lines.[21]

The signing by the U.S. delegation at the Washington arms confe nce of the proposal to outlaw gas warfare led the War Department in mid-1922 to modify its policy on the functions of the CWS.[22] The General Staff rescinded provisions of several general orders and promulgated two new general orders which suspended all work on toxic agents and restricted CWS activities in gas warfare to purely defensive measures.[23] Although the War Department eventually modified these directives, the change in policy which they represented was to exert a retarding influence on the CWS for many years.

For a decade and a half after the close of World War I appropriations for national defense were decidedly limited.[24] This was the era when the government and a good many citizens held high hopes for the early elimination of armed conflicts. It was the U.S. Government that initiated the call for the Washington conference of 1921–22, and it was an American Secretary of State who was coauthor of the Pact of Paris of 27 August 1928, aimed at outlawing war as an instrument of national policy (the so-called Kellogg-Briand agreement). During the 1920's the President and the Congress were insisting on economy in all branches of the national govern-

---

[21] WD GO 75, 23 Dec 20; WD GO 76, 28 Dec 20; WD GO 2, 14 Jan 21; WD GO 21, 21 May 21; WD GO 42, 17 Aug 21; WD GO 54, 28 Aug 1920.

[22] As indicated above, although the U.S. delegation signed this treaty and the U.S. Senate approved its ratification, the treaty never became operative.

[23] WD GO 24, 10 Jun 22, and WD GO 26, 17 Jun 22.

[24] Mark Skinner Watson, *Chief of Staff: Prewar Plans and Preparations,* UNITED STATES ARMY IN WORLD WAR II (Washington: 1950) (hereafter cited as *Prewar Plans*), Ch II.

TABLE 1—CONGRESSIONAL APPROPRIATIONS FOR CWS, 1922–46

Fiscal year	Appropriations	Fiscal year	Appropriations
1922[a]	$1,350,000	1935	1,257,369
1923	600,000	1936	1,388,330
1924	700,000	1937	1,483,608
1925	700,000	1938	1,525,180
1926	907,980	1939	2,867,300
1927	1,232,980	1940	2,091,237
1928	1,304,780	1941	60,092,532
1929	1,304,780	1942	1,067,461,059
1930	1,246,776	1943	620,546,241
1931	1,295,215	1944	340,025,000
1932	1,252,099	1945	[b]100
1933	1,222,000	1946[c]	[d]624,525,000
1934	1,255,563		

[a] 1922 was the first year for which funds were appropriated directly for the CWS. From 1918 to 1922 funds for the CWS were transferred from, or included in, other appropriations.

[b] This low figure is due to the fact that sufficient funds were appropriated in the previous fiscal year to take care of CWS needs in 1945.

[c] Surplus Appropriation Rescission Acts (P.L. 301, 8 Feb 46 and P.L. 391, 27 May 46) rescinded $1,024,351,000 of unexpended CWS appropriations for the years 1942–1946.

[d] This appropriation was made only two and one-half months before V-J Day (2 Sep 1945) and none of these funds were ever expended.

Source Budget of the United States, transmitted to Congress by the President.

ment. Following the stock-market crash of 1929 and the resultant depression, economy in the use of government funds became more of a watchword than ever.

If the Military Establishment as a whole felt the effects of the trend toward economy, the Chemical Warfare Service felt it in even greater degree. Since the necessity for a separate organization to supervise chemical warfare functions was seriously questioned by some of the highest ranking officers in the General Staff, the War Department was not prone to be oversolicitous for the welfare of the new service. The meager resources of the CWS until mid-1940 in terms of appropriations and personnel strength are indicated in Tables 1, 2, and 3. A glance at Table 2 will disclose that the quota of 101 officers and 1,200 enlisted men provided for in the National Defense Act of 1920 was not filled until after the close of fiscal year 1940.

Peacetime Organization

Within the confines of limited appropriations and personnel, the Chemical Warfare Service carried out its restricted peacetime mission. Ad-

TABLE 2—MILITARY STRENGTH OF THE CWS, 1918-46[a]

30 June	Actual strength CWS officers[b]	Actual strength enlisted men[c]	30 June	Actual strength CWS officers[b]	Actual strength enlisted men[c]
1918[d]	1,680	20,518	1933	77	413
1919[e]	328	261	1934	82	420
1920	108	1,544	1935	83	450
1921	79	442	1936	82	670
1922	84	518	1937	82	782
1923	64	363	1938	83	753
1924	70	424	1939	91	803
1925	89	424	1940	93	1,035
1926	79	417	1941	833	5,059
1927	80	418	1942	2,287	17,938
1928	81	450	1943	8,103	61,688
1929	76	425	1944	7,679	59,244
1930	78	413	1945	7,686	53,228
1931	77	451	1946	1,998	6,815
1932	73	425			

[a] For detailed figures on CWS military personnel strength in World War II see Appendixes A and B.

[b] Figures represent total strength reported as CWS by all commands and theaters. Officers of other branches or without branch assignments may have been serving with the CWS, but the number is judged not to be of significant size. Includes Regular Army, Reserve, Army of the U.S., and National Guard officers on active duty (except trainees) under the jurisdiction of the Chief, CWS.

[c] Includes enlisted men reported as CWS.

[d] Figures as of 11 November 1918.

[e] Figures as of 30 June from 1919 to 1946.

Source: Figures from 1918 to 1921 were taken from the annual report of the Chief, CWS, to the Secretary of War. Figures 1922–1941 from Tables, Actual Strength of the Military Personnel of the Army, Annual Reports of the Secretary of War to the President, 1922–41. Figures 1942–46 from draft table, Total Male Strength of the Army by Arm or Service, prepared by Statistics Br, Program Review and Analysis Div, Off, Comptroller of the Army.

ministratively, the CWS was a supply service of the Army, responsible to the War Department General Staff and to the Office of the Assistant Secretary of War for procurement and procurement planning activities. The Chief, CWS, was of course responsible for the organization and administration of his own service. In 1920 he set up an organization consisting of five divisions: Procurement and Supply, Technical, Medical, Industrial Relations (later called Procurement Planning), and Plans, Training, and Operations.[25] Except for the elimination of the Medical Division in 1932, this organization remained substantially unchanged throughout the peacetime period. From

[25] Rpt of CWS, 1921.

Table 3—Chemical Warfare Service Civilian Personnel Strength,
November 1918–December 1945

End of month	Total	OCCWS	Field	End of month	Total	OCCWS	Field
1918 11 November	784	180	604	1942 June	13,950	652	13,298
1923 June	820	20	800	July	16,045	655	15,390
1928 June	736	20	716	August	17,433	632	16,801
1931 June	742	27	715	September	19,708	657	19,051
1939 September	1,102	26	1,076	October	20,979	667	20,312
December	1,355	28	1,327	November	23,381	675	22,706
1940 March	1,464	28	1,436	December	25,611	655	24,956
June	2,221	30	2,191	1943 January	27,281	640	26,641
September	3,352	63	3,289	February	27,608	662	26,946
December	4,207	89	4,118	March	29,058	637	28,421
1941 March	6,048	116	5,932	June	28,038	596	27,442
June	5,477	139	5,338	September	25,639	521	25,118
July	5,227	184	5,043	December	24,810	502	24,308
August	5,276	194	5,082	1944 March	25,703	489	25,214
September	5,357	196	5,161	June	25,411	513	24,898
October	5,603	238	5,365	September	23,860	501	23,359
November	5,854	258	5,596	December	23,003[a]	474	22,529
December	7,268	335	6,933	1945 March	23,001	489	22,512
1942 January	10,060	369	9,691	June	22,824	457	22,367
March	12,646	596	12,050	September	11,303	399	10,904
April	12,667	604	12,063	December	7,671	353	7,318
May	13,354	626	12,728				

[a] For breakdown in this period see Table 6 where totals vary slightly, probably reflecting a later adjustment.
Source Figures 1918–1931 compiled from reports, "Civ Pers Strength," prepared by the Office of the Assistant and Chief Clerk to the SW. Figures 1939–1945 compiled from Office of the Comptroller, Dept of the Army, Statistics Br (Squier/Pentagon 2B673) from· (1) "Monthly Rpt of Pers Activities," WDAGO, (2) "Monthly Rpt of Authorizations and Strength for Pers Operating the Z of I Establishment," WDGS Contl Symbol SM-P2-39, (3) "Monthly Rpt of Pers Authorizations and Strengths for Establishments in Area of District of Columbia and Arlington County, Va.," WDMB Form 114, WDGS SM-P2-40, (4) draft reports of War Dept Monthly Strength in Statistics Br, Program Review and Analysis Div, Office of the Comptroller of the Army.

1920 until 1938 a dozen officers and a score of civilians constituted the entire personnel of the Chief's office.[26]

Each of the Chiefs made his own special contribution to the development of the Chemical Warfare Service. General Sibert devoted his mature judgment to the task of organizing the new service in World War I, and he had much to do with marshaling the sentiment which finally prevailed in 1920, when the decision was taken to make the emergency CWS organization a permanent element of the Army. General Fries, during his long

[26] The Chief's office was located in the Munitions Building in Washington, D.C.

tenure as Chief (1920–29), continuously displayed the aggressive capability that had made him conspicuously successful as head of the AEF Gas Service. He withstood all opposition from without while he molded the CWS into its ultimate peacetime form. During the next four years Maj. Gen. Harry L. Gilchrist brought to the Office of the Chief (OC) the prestige of an internationally known authority on gas casualties. A medical officer, he continued to emphasize, as had his predecessors, the scientific aspects of chemical warfare. Gilchrist's successor, Maj. Gen. Claude E. Brigham, an artilleryman, had executive and command experience which gave him a thorough insight into the strength and weakness of the Chemical Warfare Service as it existed in the middle 1930's. It was during Brigham's tour that the prospect of another major war began to take shape, and it became his responsibility to initiate a more vigorous preparedness program. To Maj. Gen. Walter C. Baker, who served from May 1937 to April 1941, fell the task of carrying out and extending this preparedness program into the emergency period.

Assisting the Chief, CWS, were an Advisory Committee of fifteen civilian authorities in chemistry and chemical engineering, a CWS Technical Committee, and a Chemical Warfare Board. The Advisory Committee, which was unofficial in capacity, was set up in the American Chemical Society in 1920. The members of the committee met periodically with CWS scientists and administrators to discuss policies and problems of research and development. The CWS Technical Committee, also set up in 1920, came into existence as the result of a need for co-ordination among interested branches of the armed forces in the development and standardization of chemical warfare items.[27] On the Technical Committee sat representatives of CWS and of the following: Field Artillery, Coast Artillery, Infantry, Air Corps, Cavalry, General Staff, National Guard Bureau, and the Assistant Secretaries of the War and Navy Departments. The Chemical Warfare Board was established at Edgewood Arsenal in 1923 to study and co-ordinate technical developments with tactical doctrine and methods.[28]

Research, development, training, manufacturing, and storage functions were centered at Edgewood Arsenal, Maryland. There in 1920 a functional type of organization was set up consisting of the following units: the

---

[27] OC CWS SO 74, 31 Mar 20.

[28] OC CWS SO 19, 21 May 23. For details on the Chemical Warfare Board, see Leo P. Brophy, Wyndham D. Miles, and Rexmond C. Cochrane, The Chemical Warfare Service: From Laboratory to Field, a volume in preparation for the series UNITED STATES ARMY IN WORLD WAR II.

CHEMICAL WARFARE SERVICE CHIEFS, *February 1920–April 1941. Top left, Maj. Gen. Amos A. Fries, 1920–29; right, Maj. Gen. Walter C. Baker, 1937–41; bottom left, Maj. Gen. Harry L. Gilchrist, 1929–33; right, Maj. Gen. Claude E. Brigham, 1933–37.*

Chemical Division and the Mechanical Division, each of which was engaged in research and development activities; the Plants Division, which was responsible for manufacturing; the Property Division, to which supply responsibilities were delegated; the Chemical Warfare School; and CWS troops.[29] Later a Safety and Inspection Division and a Medical Research Division were activated.

From a managerial standpoint the 1920's were a period of trial and error at Edgewood, when certain administrative procedures were inaugurated which later had to be modified. For example, before 1924 it was the practice to allocate funds to each division chief, who would disburse such funds and keep the necessary records pertaining to them. Each division, moreover, maintained its own storehouses, and it was not uncommon for one division to be short of certain items while another division had a surplus of these items. To rectify the condition a Planning Division (later called Administration Division) was set up in 1924. Another outstanding instance of how Edgewood profited through experience was in the field of research and development. Here each of three divisions (Chemical, Mechanical, and Medical Research) did all its own research and all its own engineering, which resulted in duplication of effort. A reorganization in 1928 largely remedied the situation by eliminating the Chemical and Mechanical Divisions and activating the following divisions: Research, Munitions Development, Information, Protective Development, and Engineering. After this reorganization, research was confined to the Research and Medical Research Divisions, and all engineering activities were concentrated in the Engineering Division. This was substantially the organization of Edgewood Arsenal at the start of the emergency period. At that time approximately nine hundred civilians were employed at Edgewood.[30]

Research and Development

Research and development was affected less than other functions by the action of the General Staff in 1922 which restricted CWS activities to the defensive. This was natural, and indeed inevitable, for it was not possible in doing research on a chemical agent or munition to make a nice distinction as to whether the item would be used by an enemy or by the

---

[29] Rpt of CWS, 1921.

[30] (1) Memo, TIG for C CWS, 1 Jun 27, sub: Survey WD Branches, Bureaus, and 1st Ind. CWS 333/2. (2) Edgewood Arsenal Organization Charts, 1921, 1922, 1929. (3) Memo, C Mfg and Supply Div for C CWS, 10 Jun 37. CWS 300.4/4.

U.S. Army. In February 1923 the War Department modified its former ruling to permit investigation of "various types of offensive gases and appliances against which defensive measures might be necessary." [31] During the peacetime period, therefore, the CWS conducted research and development on chemical agents, on the dispersion of those agents from airplanes, on smoke-producing materials, on the Livens projector, and on the 4.2-inch chemical mortar. Results of this research included the decrease in weight and increase in range of the 4.2-inch mortar, the development and standardization of sulphur trioxide in chlorosulfonic acid (FS), a smoke-producing material, and the design and installation of a filling plant for loading chemical munitions in Hawaii.

Some notable accomplishments in the defensive field were development of impregnite for gasproofing of clothing, improvement of the gas-mask canister to provide against irritant smoke, and development of a fully molded facepiece for the gas mask.[32]

The Chemical Warfare Service, in addition to conducting research and development on various aspects of chemical warfare, co-operated with other branches of the Army, with the U.S. Public Health Service, and with the Navy on projects of a quasi-public-health nature. In 1920 the service was directed to co-operate with the Medical Department and the Quartermaster Corps on the extermination of rodents and vermin.[33] Later the CWS worked on methods of exterminating the boll weevil and on improved methods for fumigating ships.[34]

Procurement and Supply

The peacetime restrictive policy of the War Department had a marked effect on CWS procurement and supply activities. Manufacture of all toxics was completely discontinued and the plants at Edgewood Arsenal fell into a state of disrepair. The only toxics in existence in the U.S. Army from 1922 to 1937 were some leftovers from World War I that were held in

---

[31] Memo, TAG for CGs All Corps Areas *et al.,* 5 Feb 23, sub: Confidential Instructions as to the Interpretation of GO 24 and GO 26. AG 353 (2–2–23) Misc.–M–C.

[32] (1) Rpts of CWS, 1921–27. (2) Lists of CWS R&D Proj Programs by fiscal years 1921–29. (3) Ltr, C CWS to CofS, 16 May 37, sub: Final Rpt on Status of Cml Warfare Readiness by Retiring C CWS. G–4/29895–1. (4) For a detailed discussion of research and development, see Brophy, Miles, and Cochrane, From Laboratory to Field.

[33] WD GO 67, 11 Nov 20.

[34] Rpts of CWS, 1926–27.

storage in the lone CWS storage depot at Edgewood and a small quantity that had been shipped from the Edgewood depot to Hawaii in 1921. Manufacture at Edgewood Arsenal was restricted to defensive items, chiefly gas masks.

While procurement was kept at a minimum there were no restrictions on procurement planning. The Procurement Planning Division of the Chief's office was responsible for drawing up and submitting its portion of industrial mobilization plans to the Office of the Assistant Secretary of War. Early in 1924 procurement district offices were activated in New York, Boston, Pittsburgh, Chicago, and San Francisco.[35]

The War Department general order No. 26, 1922, which restricted CWS research, procurement, and supply of poison gases to the defensive aspects of chemical warfare was not rescinded during the peacetime years or, as a matter of fact, at any later date. As mentioned above, it was modified in February 1923 but only with regard to research. Certain developments from the mid-thirties on, however, had the effect of nullifying the general order. This fact was brought out very well in a written discussion within the General Staff in the spring of 1936. Certain members of the staff were then contending that under General Orders No. 26 the Chemical Warfare Service had no authority to manufacture and supply toxic chemicals. In rebuttal, the chief of the War Plans Division (WPD), Brig. Gen. Stanley D. Embick, marshaled the following list of developments to prove that General Orders No. 26 was null and void:

a. Approval by the Secretary of War, 7 November 1934, of the Joint Board recommendation, to make all necessary preparations for the use of chemical warfare from the outbreak of war.

b. Approval by the Secretary of War, 21 August 1935, of the Joint Board recommendation, in regard to chemical warfare, that "adequate facilities must be available to meet the peace and wartime needs of both services [Army and Navy]."

c. Recommendations of the Secretary of War during the past two years for funds for the partial rehabilitation of the mustard gas plant at Edgewood Arsenal, for the manufacture of fifty tons of mustard gas, and for the three-year rearmament program for 4.2-inch chemical mortars.

d. Appropriations by the Congress of funds to cover c, above.

---

[35] War Department Bulletin 14, 1923, authorized the activation of these procurement district offices.

e. Army Appropriation Acts 1935 and 1936, containing the following language: "For . . . manufacture of chemical warfare gases or other toxic substances—or other offensive and defensive materials or appliances required for gas warfare purposes." [36]

The presentation of this list seems to have clinched the argument.

Training of Troops

The CWS training mission included staff supervision of the training of the Army in chemical warfare and the training of CWS military personnel, both Regular and Reserve. Training of the Army was conducted under the direction of "chemical" officers, who were CWS technical specialists assigned by the War Department to the staffs of division and Air Corps commanders as well as to corps area and department headquarters. "Gas" officers assisted in the training at lower echelons. The center of training of CWS personnel, as well as selected officers of the Navy and Marine Corps, was the Chemical Warfare School at Edgewood Arsenal. Reserve officers were trained through Army extension courses and through fourteen-day-on-duty training periods with the Army. Reserve Officers' Training Corps courses for prospective CWS officers were conducted at the Massachusetts Institute of Technology and at the Texas Agricultural and Mechanical College.

In 1923 the War Department modified the CWS training mission. Training of the noncombatant branches of the Army "other than the Chemical Warfare Service" was ordered confined to defensive aspects.[37] Training of the combatant arms was to include the "use of smoke, incendiary materials and nontoxic gases." Training of CWS personnel was to be conducted in accordance with the provisions of the National Defense Act, that is, it was to cover both the offensive and defensive aspects.[38]

---

[36](1) The Joint Army and Navy Board, usually called the Joint Board, was established in 1903 by agreement between the Secretaries of War and the Navy. It was composed of three Army members (Chief of Staff, Deputy Chief of Staff, and Chief, War Plans Division) and three Navy members (Chief of Naval Operations, his deputy, and director of Navy's War Plans Division). See Watson, *Prewar Plans,* pp. 79–81, for more details. (2) Also see Vernon E. Davis, History of Joint Chiefs of Staff in World War II, Vol. I, Ch. II. MS, OCMH. (3) Memo, WPD (Embick) for G–4, 31 Mar 36, sub: Manufacture and Supply of Essential Cml Agents. G–4, 29895.

[37](1)Memo, TAG for CGs All Corps Areas *et al.,* 5 Feb 23, sub: Confidential Instructions as to the Interpretation of GO 24 and GO 26. AG 353 (2–2–23) Misc.–M–C. (2) The question of whether the CWS had combatant or noncombatant duties remained unsettled in the War Department until the fall of 1941. See below, Chapter IX.

[38] See Note 37(1), above.

Relations With Other Elements of Armed Forces

To carry out its assigned mission, the Chemical Warfare Service had to maintain contact with other elements of the Army, such as the Quartermaster, Ordnance, Air Corps, and Medical Department, and with the Navy and the Marine Corps. Several media of liaison have already been mentioned, such as the CWS Technical Committee and the chemical and gas officers who served at headquarters and with troop units. In the Army, the CWS had particularly close relations in the peacetime years with the Medical Department which, as already indicated, had an interest in gas warfare dating back to World War I.[39] After the war, medical research on chemical warfare lapsed, but in 1922 a new Medical Research Division was set up at Edgewood Arsenal. This division was headed by Lt. Col. Edward B. Vedder, Medical Corps, a noted toxicologist. Vedder was directly responsible to the chief of the Medical Division, OC CWS, Colonel Gilchrist, who in 1929 was to be named Chief, CWS. It was largely through Gilchrist's influence that close relations between the CWS and the Medical Department were established. At the medical research laboratory at Edgewood trained research workers (about a dozen in number) of both organizations worked side by side.

CWS relations with the Navy dated back to World War I, when there was considerable apprehension that ships might be attacked with poison gas. At that time, the Chemical Warfare Service undertook research projects for the Navy, and naval personnel were furnished gas masks and trained in offensive and defensive gas warfare. After the war, as the result of the recommendations of a board of Navy officers headed by Rear Adm. William S. Sims, provision was made in the Navy for assigning various chemical warfare functions to specific bureaus. From 1921 on, these Navy bureaus maintained close liaison with the CWS.[40]

In February 1922 the Navy set up at Edgewood Arsenal a unit whose

---

[39] See above, Chapter I.

[40] (1) *Service Chemicals United States Navy,* 1939 (Washington: Government Printing Office, 1939), pp. 14–16. (2) Ltr, SecNav to the President, 7 Jul 17, 28801, Mat–1–ML 7/6, NA. (3) Memo, CNO for Div of Material, *et al.,* 30 Dec 20 sub: Board to Consider Possibilities of Gas Warfare and Methods of Defense Against Gas Attack. OP–22 in SecNav File 28801–16 to 80, NA. (4) Ltr, SecNav to Rear Adm William S. Sims, 8 Jan 21, sub: Board to Study Methods of Defense of Naval Vessels Against Gas Attack and Possibilities of the Offensive Use of Noxious Gases in Naval Warfare. OP–22, (431–2) in Sec Nav File 28801–16 to 80, NA. (5) Ltr, SecNav to SecWar, 29 Apr 21, sub: Gas Warfare. SecNav File 28801–33. (6) Ltr, SecWar to SecNav, 14 May 20, sub: Correspondence Relative to Gas Warfare. OCS 17230 in SecNav 28801–16 to 80, NA.

duties included maintaining liaison between the Army and the Navy on all matters pertaining to chemical warfare, co-ordinating research work in progress at Edgewood for various bureaus of the Navy, inspecting chemical warfare matériel manufactured at Edgewood Arsenal for the Navy, and planning certain courses of instruction for naval officers at the Chemical Warfare School. In May 1922 the Secretaries of the War and Navy Departments reached an agreement stipulating that the Navy would provide definite financial assistance to the Army for research in the means of defense against war gases. The following year the two Secretaries agreed that the CWS would be responsible for development and procurement activities relating to chemical warfare matériel for both the Army and the Navy.[41]

This arrangement had been in force a dozen years when the Navy began to develop doubts as to the ability of the CWS to make chemical warfare preparations for both services. In March 1935 the Chief of Naval Operations, in a letter to the Joint Board, stated that the chief of the Navy's Bureau of Construction and Repair felt that the CWS did not have the capacity to meet the requirements of the Army, the Navy, and the Marine Corps and that consequently he had recommended a reconsideration of the existing agreement between the Army and the Navy.[42]

The letter prompted the Joint Board to consult the other services and bureaus of the War and Navy Departments, and, on the basis of the replies received, the board decided on 21 August 1935 to renew the agreement of 1923.[43] Although the Navy as well as the Army approved this decision, less than two years later the Secretary of the Navy again raised the question of the Navy's dissatisfaction with the arrangement. Thereupon the Joint Board again took the matter under consideration and on 12 May 1937 reversed the decision of 21 August 1935.[44] The 1937 ruling of the Joint Board, which remained in effect throughout World War II, stated that while the Navy's

[41] (1) Memo, Capt Allen B. Reed, USN, Chmn Ex Com ANMB, for JB, 1 Apr 37, sub: Change in Agreement Between the Army and Navy Relative to Development and Proc of Cml Warfare Material. JB 325, Ser 605. (2) Ltr, SecNav to SecWar, 1 May 22, sub: Allotment of Funds to War Dept by Bur of Navy Dept for Gas Warfare Defense and Research Work OP-22 (431-25) in SecNav File 28801-61, NA. (3) Ltr, SecWar to SecNav, 19 May 22 G-4/6031 in SecNav File 28801-16 to 80, NA. (4) Ltr, Actg SecNav to SecWar 23 May 22, sub: Allotment of Funds to War Dept by Bur of Navy Dept for Gas Warfare Defense and Research Work. OP-22 (431-25) in SecNav File 28801-61, NA.

[42] Ltr, CNO (William H. Standley) to JB, 11 Mar 35, sub: Cml Warfare. AGO 29901-1.

[43] Ltr, Douglas MacArthur, USA, Senior Member Present JB, to SW, 21 Aug 35, sub: Cml Warfare. AGO 29901-1.

[44] Ltr, Malin Craig, USA, Senior Member Present JB, to SW, 12 May 37, sub: Change in Agreement between the Army and Navy Relative to Development and Proc of Cml Warfare Material. JB 325, Ser 605 This action was approved by the Secretary of War on 14 May 1937.

requirements in chemical warfare matériel in peace and war would generally be filled through the facilities of the CWS, the Navy might, if it deemed advisable, assign development or production of its chemical warfare requirements to sources other than the CWS. The ruling also listed certain procedures which both departments would have to observe. These included the mutual disclosure of their chemical warfare requirements and the mutual exchange of technical information obtained from outside sources.[45]

Industrial Mobilization Gets Under Way

On 8 September 1939, one week after the outbreak of war in Europe, President Roosevelt issued a proclamation of "limited national emergency."[46] This led to a greater emphasis on preparedness throughout the armed forces.[47] While all CWS activities felt the impact of this declaration, procurement was affected more than other functions. The main current of CWS developments in the emergency period was the industrial mobilization program.

The CWS took steps, under the guidance of the Office of the Assistant Secretary of War, to implement the educational order legislation enacted by Congress in June 1938.[48] This legislation had as its objective the training of selected industrial concerns in the manufacture of a half-dozen Army items, one of which was the gas mask. The first educational order contract was written by the Chemical Warfare Service in late 1939 and several more were awarded in 1940 and 1941.[49] The educational order program was the first real step, as far as the CWS was concerned, in the direction of industrial mobilization in the emergency period.

Other strides toward industrial mobilization were taken under the Munitions Program of 30 June 1940. The formulation of this program by the President, the National Defense Advisory Commission, and the War Department was the first important move to supply an expanding army with the implements of war.[50] In June 1940 Congress passed the first of five

---

[45] *Ibid.*

[46] Proclamation 2352.

[47] See R. Elberton Smith, *The Army and Economic Mobilization,* UNITED STATES ARMY IN WORLD WAR II (Washington: 1958).

[48] Public Law 18, 76th Cong., 1st Sess., 52 *Stat.* 707, 16 Jun 38.

[49] For more details on the educational order program in the CWS, see Brophy, Miles, and Cochrane, From Laboratory to Field.

[50] (1) See Watson, *Prewar Plans,* pp. 161–82, 318–21, for details on Munitions Program. (2) For details on this program in the CWS, see Brophy, Miles, and Cochrane, From Laboratory to Field.

supplemental appropriation acts for the fiscal year 1941 to finance this program. Included in those appropriations was over $57,000,00 for the Chemical Warfare Service, of which over $53,000,000 was for procurement and supply.[51]

The appropriation of funds in such unprecedented sums enabled the CWS to undertake a number of programs, some of which had been in the planning stages for a number of years. Among the important programs were the following: rehabilitation of old and construction of new facilities at Edgewood Arsenal, construction of new CWS arsenals at Huntsville, Alabama, and Pine Bluff, Arkansas, erection of new government-owned chemical plants in various parts of the country, acceleration of production activities at Edgewood Arsenal, and awarding of contracts through the procurement districts for such items as the gas mask and 4.2-inch mortar shells. Construction of the new arsenal at Huntsville began in July 1941 and at Pine Bluff in December 1941.

Passage of the Lend-Lease Act of 11 March 1941 gave further impetus to the CWS procurement and supply program.[52] Lend-lease appropriations enabled the CWS to undertake procurement activities on a larger scale. Between April and December 1941, the Chemical Warfare Service procured raw chemicals, gas masks, and other items for supply to Great Britain. Many of the items were manufactured at Edgewood, but a number were also secured through special contracts in the procurement districts.

Research and Development: A Change in Outlook

In late 1936 the General Staff had decided to cut research and development funds throughout the Army. The reason was a desire to get the Army equipped as soon as possible with the best matériel then available and to concentrate on that objective rather than on research and development of new matériel.[53] Consequently, the Army began to place more emphasis on work pertaining to plant design, specifications for items, and manufacturing directives than on pure research and development projects. From 1937 to 1939 much effort and money (for that period) went into the design, construction, and operation of a pilot mustard-gas shell-filling plant at Edgewood Arsenal. In November 1939 research and development was even more sharply subordinated to procurement under a policy of the Assistant Secretary of War

---

[51] CWS 314 7 Appropriations File.
[52] Public Law 11, 77th Cong.
[53] Watson, *Prewar Plans*, p. 42.

to abandon all basic research projects and all long-range development and to concentrate on completing development of the most promising items for which there was a definite military requirement.[54]

Research and development was not to be long hidden under a bushel. In June 1940 the National Defense Research Committee (NDRC) was set up by Presidential approval.[55] Division B (later expanded to Divisions 8, 9, 10, and 11) of NDRC, headed by Dr. James Bryant Conant, was set up to handle studies on bombs, fuels, gases, and chemical problems. Present at the first meeting of this division on 11 July 1940 were General Baker, Chief, CWS, and Lt. Col. Maurice E. Barker, chief of the Technical Division, OC CWS. Shortly thereafter the CWS proposed six projects for study by Division B, and by July 1941 this number had increased to sixteen. On 28 June 1941 NDRC and the Committee on Medical Research were included, by Executive order, under the jurisdiction of a newly created Office of Scientific Research and Development. Three months later the CWS recommended its initial medical project to the Committee on Medical Research, the first of seventeen such projects that would be undertaken before the close of World War II.

Included in the construction program which got under way at Edgewood Arsenal in the fall of 1940 was a new research center. Prior to that time research had been carried on in old, scattered buildings of World War I vintage, ill suited for the purpose and costly to maintain. The new research center was completed by the time war was declared. It consisted of a modern, two-story, laboratory building, animal and storage buildings, machine shops, powder and smoke laboratories, pilot plants, a power plant, and other necessary structures.[56] By that time also the CWS had acquired a new laboratory on the campus of the Massachusetts Institute of Technology.[57]

Limited Emphasis on Chemical Warfare Service Training

Of all the principal functions of the Chemical Warfare Service, training received least emphasis in the emergency period.[58] There were several reasons. First of all, war plans did not call for the use of gas offensively in the period of mobilization and therefore the War Department did not put a high priority on the training of chemical troops. More important was the

---

[54] Ltr, C CWS (Gen Baker) to CofS, 30 Apr 41 sub: Final Rpt. CWS 319.1/2183–2249.

[55] (1) James Phinney Baxter, 3rd, *Scientists Against Time* (Boston: Little, Brown and Company, 1947), pp. 17–19 and Chs XVIII and XIX. (2) Brophy, Miles, and Cochrane, From Laboratory to Field.

[56] Rexmond C. Cochrane, CWS Research and Development, pp. 50–51. MS.

[57] For more details on this laboratory, see below, Chapter VI.

[58] For more details on training in the emergency period, see below, Chapter IX.

uncertainty over the function of chemical combat troops in theaters of operation. Should CWS troops be employed to disperse toxic chemicals or should this be done by artillery or infantry using conventional-type weapons? Answers to this and several other basic questions on the CWS mission were not forthcoming until the fall of 1941. Until these answers were given CWS training activities continued to be limited.

During the emergency period the CWS continued to supervise the training of the Army in defensive gas warfare. In 1940 and 1941 the service faced the task of training fillers for existing CWS units which were being built up to full strength and training cadres and fillers for units being activated in the ground forces and air forces.[59] During this period also the Training Division of the Chief's office drew up Tables of Organization and Equipment for field units to carry out tasks resulting from recent technical developments, such as impregnating clothing to protect the wearer against gas vapors.[60] A Service Units Board, set up by the Chief, CWS, in May 1940, reviewed the mission and organization of CWS laboratory, depot, and maintenance units in the light of the operations in the European war and redefined their functions.[61] In the spring of 1941 the CWS organized a Replacement Center (later called Replacement Training Center) at Edgewood Arsenal. Between the date of its activation and the end of 1941 the center trained over seventeen hundred men, but this was less than one half of the number of troops coming into chemical units in that period.

Organizational Developments: 1940–41

The increase of CWS activities and the consequent expansion of personnel rolls made it necessary to set up more elaborate administrative machinery in the Chief's office and in the field. *(Charts 1 and 2. See also Tables 2 and 3.)* In July 1940 General Baker provided for an expanded organization in his office. Fiscal, Supply, Procurement, and Information Branches were raised to division status and thus placed on an administrative par with the Technical, Personnel, and Training Divisions. Since the Army was placing greater emphasis on procurement than on any of its other functions, the new Procurement Division was most imposing in its make-up. It included two subdivisions, designated Arsenal Procurement and Industrial Procurement. Each subdivision contained several sections and some of the sections had several

---

[59] For names and locations of CWS units, see below, Chapter IX.

[60] In July 1940 the Operations, War Plans, and Training Division became the Training Division. See Chart 1.

[61] OC CWS SO 25, 6 May 40.

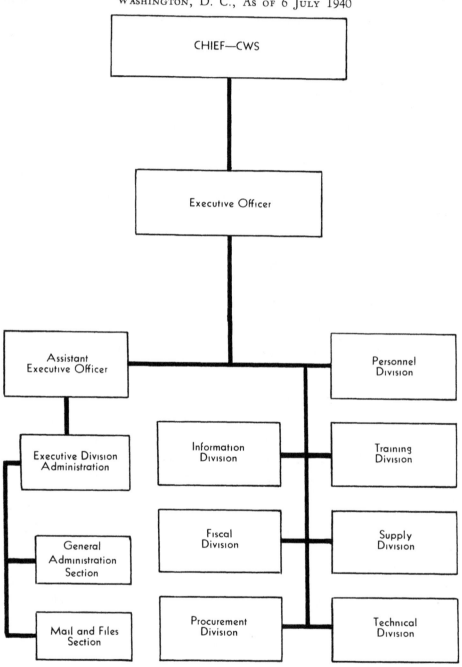

CHART 1—ORGANIZATION, OFFICE, CHIEF OF CHEMICAL WARFARE SERVICE,
WASHINGTON, D. C., AS OF 6 JULY 1940

CHIEF—CWS

Executive Officer

Assistant
Executive Officer

Personnel
Division

Executive Division
Administration

Information
Division

Training
Division

General
Administration
Section

Fiscal
Division

Supply
Division

Mail and Files
Section

Procurement
Division

Technical
Division

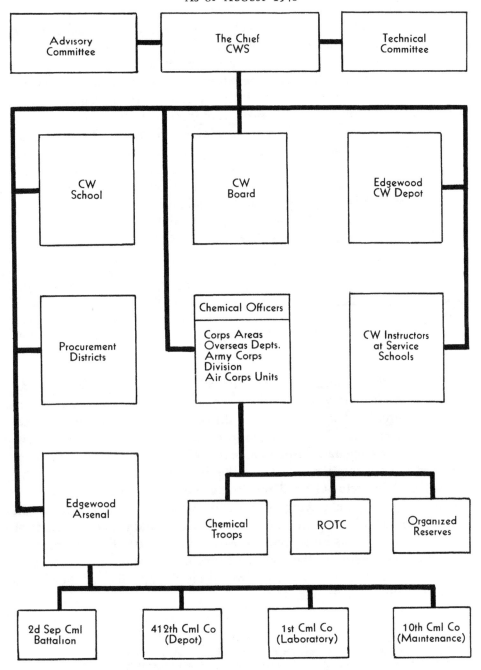

CHART 2—ORGANIZATION OF THE CHEMICAL WARFARE SERVICE,
As of August 1940

Advisory Committee

The Chief CWS

Technical Committee

CW School

CW Board

Edgewood CW Depot

Procurement Districts

Chemical Officers

Corps Areas
Overseas Depts.
Army Corps
Division
Air Corps Units

CW Instructors at Service Schools

Edgewood Arsenal

Chemical Troops

ROTC

Organized Reserves

2d Sep Cml Battalion

412th Cml Co (Depot)

1st Cml Co (Laboratory)

10th Cml Co (Maintenance)

branches.[62] Later this nomenclature was reversed, and sections became standard subdivisions of branches in all Army organizations.[63]

The initiation of procurement activities in the districts in mid-1940 led to an increase in the number of employees and to the development of district organizations to supervise expanding activities. Before 1939 each procurement district office was staffed by one officer and a stenographer or two, but in fiscal year 1940 several of the districts added a civilian engineer and a draftsman to the rolls. The increased appropriations in fiscal year 1941 enabled the districts to hire many more employees, so that by December 1940 the Boston district had 108 civilian employees, New York 82, Pittsburgh 373, and San Francisco 73. The vast majority of these were inspectors. By the end of 1940 the number of officers in the various districts ranged from five and twenty.[64] During 1941 the roster continued to grow. The following tabulation shows the comparative number of military and civilians in the five districts at dates indicated in 1941: [65]

District	Military	Civilians (Includes Inspectors)	Date
Boston	17	269	18 January
Chicago	22	265	27 March
New York	23	150	20 February
Pittsburgh	24	380	14 March
San Francisco	6	34	15 April

Although the organizational structures which were set up in the procurement districts in 1940 were essentially similar, there were enough variations to cause confusion. For example, each district but one had a separate fiscal unit; the one exception had a fiscal, property, and transportation unit. Almost all districts had separate inspection units. While the Office of the Chief reviewed the organizational charts of the districts, it did not insist on uniformity, and Inspector General reports on the procurement districts noted without comment the varying organizational patterns of the districts. In addition to lack of complete uniformity of organization there was lack of uniformity in administrative procedures in the districts. For instance, the district offices differed in the types of forms and records which they kept. This absence of standardization was to engage the attention of the Chief's office after the war got under way.

[62] OC CWS Off O 6, 6 Jul 40.
[63] For key personnel, OC CWS, 1940–45, see below, Appendix E.
[64] Figures based on various manuscript histories of chemical warfare procurement districts.
[65] IGD rpts of CWS proc districts for fiscal year 1941. CWS 335/10–15.

Between the summer of 1940 and the declaration of war, two changes were effected at CWS installations. In August 1940 Fort Hoyle, a Field Artillery installation adjacent to Edgewood Arsenal, was vacated and the land and buildings turned over to the CWS. This space was sorely needed in the period of expansion. In December 1940 an arsenal operations department was set up at Edgewood to supervise strictly arsenal functions such as production, service, and inspection.

General Baker retired as Chief, CWS, on 30 April 1941 and was succeeded on 31 May by Maj. Gen. William N. Porter.[66] The activities of the service continued to expand, and General Porter immediately began to take steps to crystallize the CWS mission, steps which would shortly result in still greater expansion of activities. Porter, like many other military men of the time, was convinced that American entry into the war was all but inevitable and that the CWS had to be prepared for nothing short of full-scale operations. Therefore in the summer of 1941 he reorganized his office.[67]

One feature of this organization of the Office of the Chief, CWS, was use of terminology then in general use throughout other technical services of the Army. Thus, the term "services" was used to designate the echelons having jurisdiction over the principal operating functions of CWS, namely, industrial, technical, and field (troops and training). General Porter selected Col. Paul X. English to head the Industrial Service, Col. Edward Montgomery, the Field Service, and Lt. Col. Maurice E. Barker, the Technical Service.

Development of the Chemical Warfare Service Mission in the Emergency Period

General Porter inherited several problems for which his predecessors in office had been unable, for a variety of reasons, to find satisfactory solutions. One was the impasse, already referred to, on the role of chemical troops in combat. Another was the division of responsibility for incendiary bombs between CWS and Ordnance, which was impeding production of these important munitions. A potential problem was the absence of specific official responsibility in the Chemical Warfare Service for an activity in which the CWS had an interest, namely, biological warfare (BW).

[66] For a biographical sketch of Porter, see below, Chapter V.
[67] (1) Interv, CmlHO with Maj Gen William N. Porter, USA (Ret.), 16 July 49. (2) OC CWS, Off O 12, 14 Jul 41, outlined the basic features of the new organization, leaving the details to be worked out later. The new organization was officially approved on 2 September 1941, as indicated in Chart 3.

CHART 3—ORGANIZATION, OFFICE, CHIEF OF CHEMICAL WARFARE SERVICE,
AS OF 2 SEPTEMBER 1941

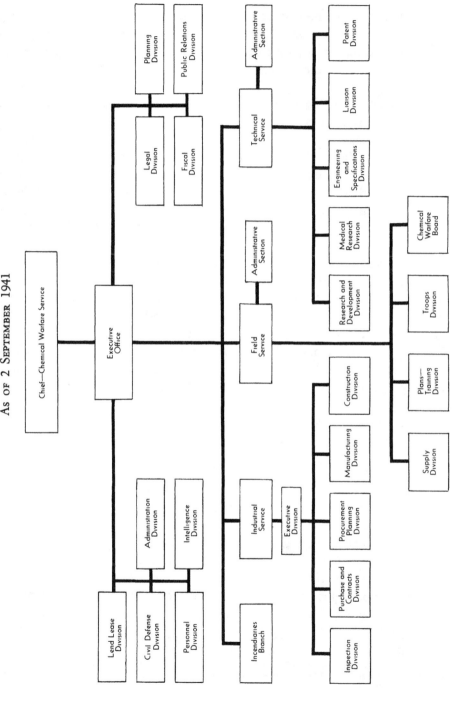

After Porter became Chief he made solution of these problems the first order of business. There were two concomitant circumstances in his favor: (1) the sense of urgency which marked U.S. military preparations in mid-1941; and (2) the receptive attitude of the Chief of Staff to proposals that promised to strengthen the nation's defenses. Porter was quick to take advantage of both.

In July 1941 the Chief, CWS, took action to get the question of weapons for chemical units settled. This he did by formally recommending to the Chief of Staff that the two active chemical weapons companies in the zone of interior be expanded to battalions and equipped with the 4.2-inch mortar.[68] The Chief, CWS, encountered some difficulty with this suggestion in the General Staff, but General George C. Marshall decided the issue by directing that General Porter's proposal be carried out.[69]

The division of responsibility for the incendiary bomb between Ordnance and Chemical Warfare Service dated back to 1920, when the War Department charged the CWS with the development of incendiary agents and the filling of incendiary munitions and Ordnance with responsibility for the procurement, storage, and issue of those munitions.[70] Neither Ordnance nor the CWS showed any marked enthusiasm for incendiaries in the peacetime years, although certain individuals, at least in the CWS, did. The CWS officer who perhaps more than anyone else was responsible for "selling" the Air Corps on the incendiary bomb was General Porter, who had been liaison officer at the Air Corps Tactical School at Maxwell Field (1933–37) and later (1937–41) liaison officer at GHQ Air Force headquarters at Langley Field. From Langley Field Porter went to Washington as Chief, CWS, thoroughly convinced that incendiaries were an absolutely indispensable munition for the winning of any future war.[71]

Two months after he assumed office, General Porter arranged for the recall to active duty of a colonel in the Reserves who had been intensely interested in incendiaries since World War I, Professor J. Enrique Zanetti of Columbia University. Porter sent Zanetti to London to obtain firsthand information on the bomb situation and upon his return put him in charge of the incendiary bomb program in the CWS.[72]

[68] Memo, C CWS for CofS, 26 Jul 41, sub: Cml Troops. CWS 320.2/266.

[69] See memo for rcd placed on returned copy of Memo, G–3 for TAG, 5 Sep 41, sub: Cml Troops. G–3/46556.

[70] WD GO 54, 28 Aug 20.

[71] (1) Memo, C CWS for G–3, 29 Nov 26, sub: Functions of the CWS. In OC CWS "black book on policy." (2) Memo, C Incendiaries Br OC CWS for C CWS, 2 Dec 41, sub: Development of Incendiary Bomb Program. CWS 471.6/1122. (3) Porter interv, 16 Jul 49.

[72] Porter interv, 16 Jul 49.

The issue of divided responsibility for the incendiary bomb program came up for consideration at a midnight conference on 15 July 1941 called by the Deputy Chief of Staff, Maj. Gen. Richard C. Moore. Represented at this conference were the Ordnance Department, Army Air Forces, and the Chemical Warfare Service. General Porter, representing the CWS, was emphatic in asserting that divided responsibility for the bomb program would not work, and to this proposition Brig. Gen. Carl A. Spaatz, Chief of Staff, Army Air Forces, lent his emphatic indorsement. The War Department announced its official decision on the matter on 3 September 1941 when it turned over responsibility for all phases of the incendiary bomb program to CWS.[73]

4.2-INCH CHEMICAL MORTAR, *used by Chemical units, World War II. Soldier is adjusting elevation of his weapon.*

The subject of biological warfare attracted but passing interest in the Chemical Warfare Service in the years between the two wars.[74] The chief of Medical Division, OC CWS, Maj. Leon A. Fox, lectured on the topic in the early 1930's at the Chemical Warfare School. His lectures reflected the general attitude of both the scientists and military men of the period, which was to minimize the potentialities of biological warfare.[75]

The later 1930's witnessed a marked change in thinking on biological warfare, a result of the simultaneous development of the science of bacteriology and airpower. By the 'forties the threat of this type of warfare

---

[73] (1) Notes of Conf in off of Gen Moore by Lt Col John T. Lewis, ASGS, 15 July 41, sub: Incendiary Bombs. CWS 471.6/241–280. (2) Ltr, TAG to CWS, 3 Sep 41, sub: Incendiary Bombs. CWS 471.6/29. (3) WD GO 10, 10 Sep 41. (4) Proceedings of the Proc Assignment Bd, OUSW, 17 Nov 41, with approval by Robert P. Patterson, USW, 18 Nov 41. CWS File 471.6/241–248. (5) WD GO 13, 24 Nov 41. (6) Porter interv, 16 Jul 49.

[74] See Brophy, Miles, and Cochrane, From Laboratory to Field, for a fuller treatment of biological warfare.

[75] Major Fox summarized his ideas in an article, "Use of Biologic Agents in Warfare," *The Military Surgeon*, LXXII (1933), 189–207.

was causing concern not only to the armed forces, but also to certain nonmilitary governmental agencies and to scientific associations. The reason for this is quite obvious: if a biological warfare attack were made on the civilian population, the attack would possibly be conducted on such a scale that every known resource would have to be employed to combat it. In the fall of 1940 Dr. Vannevar Bush, chairman of the National Defense Research Committee, suggested to Dr. Lewis H. Weed of the Health and Medical Committee of the Council of National Defense that consideration be given to the offensive and defensive aspects of biological warfare.[76] A few months later the National Institute of Health took the threat of biological warfare under advisement. The attitude of these scientific groups was not one of alarm. They believed that the relatively advanced state of public health in the United States put the population in a favorable position in the event of a biological attack, but at the same time they felt that the situation should be carefully watched.[77]

The Surgeon General and the Chief of the Chemical Warfare Service welcomed the assistance of nonmilitary agencies and groups. In the summer of 1941 The Surgeon General suggested to the National Defense Research Committee that a committee of scientists be set up to survey all phases of biological warfare, and about the same time the Chief, CWS, suggested to Mr. Harvey H. Bundy, special assistant to the Secretary of War, that a letter be prepared for the president of the National Academy of Science recommending the activation of a similar committee.[78] Secretary Henry L. Stimson that fall addressed such a letter to Dr. Frank B. Jewett, president of the National Academy of Science.[79] As a result of this letter a committee known as the WBC was set up, headed by Dean Edwin Broun Fred of the University of Wisconsin.[80] This group, which counted among its members outstanding authorities on human, animal, and plant pathology and bacteriology, was making a survey of the potentialities of biological warfare when the United States became involved in the war.

The Army had meanwhile been giving serious consideration to preparations against biological attack. Shortly after General Porter became Chief,

[76] Ltr, Bush to Weed, 28 Sep 40. WPD 4204–1.
[77] Capt Frank M. Schertz, History of Biological Warfare in the Chemical Warfare Service (1943), p. 16 MS.
[78] These letters are summarized in Memo for Rcd on Biological and Bacteriological Warfare, 1 Oct 1941, by Lt Col Richard C. Jacobs, Jr. WPD 4205–5.
[79] Ltr, SW to Jewett, 1 Oct 41 WPD 4204 BW.
[80] "WBC" is a reversal of the initials for committee on biological warfare.

CWS, he advised General Marshall that more consideration should be given to biological warfare, and he suggested that the responsibility go to the Chemical Warfare Service.[81] In August 1941 Brig. Gen. Harry L. Twaddle, Assistant Chief of Staff, G–3, informed General Marshall that in his judgment the Chemical Warfare Service was best equipped to handle this assignment.[82] Two months later Twaddle called on the Chief, CWS, to convey an oral directive from the Chief of Staff for the CWS to carry on research on biological warfare.[83] To supervise the function a new Biological Division was activated in the Office of the Chief.[84]

The emergency period saw not only the beginnings of industrial mobilization in the CWS but also the expansion of the CWS mission. Faced with the threat of war, the General Staff was less prone to deliberate on what activities the Chemical Warfare Service could carry on under War Department regulations and more inclined to assign definite responsibilities to the service. When the members of the General Staff could not agree, General Marshall personally intervened to decide the issue. Yet despite the progress made, the exact role of the CWS was not definitely decided until the war was well under way.

[81] Porter interv, 16 Jul 49.
[82] Memo, Twaddle for Marshall, 27 Aug 41, sub: Invisible Mil Offensive Attack, summarized in Schertz, History of Biological Warfare, p. 53.
[83] (1) Porter interv, 16 Jul 49. (2) Schertz, History of Biological Warfare, p. 148.
[84] OC CWS Organization Chart, 1 May 42.

CHAPTER III

Crystallizing the Wartime Mission

When the Japanese struck at Pearl Harbor on 7 December 1941 the Chemical Warfare Service, in spite of signs of improvement in its position, was still suffering from uncertainty as to its wartime mission. The fact that the course of international policy and events after World War I had seriously hindered CWS preparations for the possibility of gas warfare, together with the Presidential pronouncements against using toxic agents, and even against the permanent retention of a chemical warfare service in the Army, tended to lessen the vigor with which a gas warfare preparedness program could be pushed. Once the nation actually became involved in a fighting war in which toxics might be used against U.S. troops, this attitude of the executive department and particularly the War Department became much more realistic. The first year of the war was to witness a marked change in interpretation of the mission of the CWS.

A natural reaction to the events of 7 December was a War Department decision to authorize a sizable increase in CWS personnel. How these men would be utilized, into what units they would be formed, for what purposes the units would be used: these questions were as yet unanswered.

The Study of January 1942

The Secretary of State was among the first to raise a question as to the U.S. attitude toward gas warfare in World War II. In January 1942, Secretary of State Cordell Hull queried Secretary of War Stimson on the advisability of a unilateral declaration by the United States of its intention to observe the terms of the 1925 Geneva Gas Protocol prohibiting the use in war of poisonous gases.[1]

[1] Ltr, Secy State to SW, 12 Jan 42. Referred to in Memo, ACofS WPD for CoS, 4 Feb 42, sub: Prohibition of Use in War of Asphyxiating, Poisonous or Other Gases, and of Bacteriological Methods of Warfare. WPD 165–21. The British had attempted in December 1941 to obtain a statement of this nature from the Japanese but without much success. See reference to this attempt in Ltr, Secy State to SW, 17 Dec 42, with proposed communiqué by British Government. OPD 385 CWP, sec IIA.

As the basis for a reply to the Secretary of State, Mr. Stimson had access to a January 1942 study on toxic gases prepared by the War Plans Division of the General Staff. WPD had undertaken this study to determine existing capabilities of the United States in the event of gas warfare. In the course of preparing Mr. Stimson's reply, WPD had also consulted the Chief, CWS, and his views were subsequently expressed by the War Department.[2]

Mr. Stimson advised the Department of State against making any public statement which might indicate willingness by the United States to observe on a reciprocal basis the terms of the Geneva protocol. The Secretary pointed out that such a statement might, through the introduction of domestic controversy over the political and moral issues involved, impede preparation, reduce potential combat effectiveness, and be considered by the enemy an indication of national weakness. Regardless of treaty obligations, the War Department considered the only effective deterrent to gas warfare to be enemy fear of American retaliation, the capability for which should be maintained through active preparation and constant readiness. On the original correspondence Mr. Stimson succinctly penned: "I strongly believe that our most effective weapon on this subject at the present time is to keep our mouths tight shut."[3]

The WPD analysis of the state of gas warfare preparations sought to determine whether actual capabilities were reasonably adequate. The study brought to light some serious shortcomings and thereby paved the way for important corrective action. Immediate questions raised by the study involved the mission, mobilization, training, and disposition of chemical troops —all matters which, in prewar planning, had unfortunately been left for future decision. The study recommended that a decision be made on whether the Chemical Warfare Service was an arm or a service. It pointed out that the Munitions Program called for 18 regiments of CWS troops whereas the troop basis permitted but 2 combat battalions for an army of 56 divisions. The WPD study therefore proposed that six full-strength chemical battalions be activated at once and one battalion each be provided for the important U.S. bastions of Hawaii and Panama. Since tactical considerations plus availability of equipment indicated that the Air Corps would be the

---

[2](1) See Memo, C CWS for ACofS WPD, 25 Jan 42, sub: Prohibition of Use in War of Asphyxiating, Poisonous or Other Gases, and of Bacteriological Methods of Warfare. (2) Memo, ACofS WPD for CofS, 4 Feb 42, sub: Prohibition of Use in War of Asphyxiating, Poisonous or Other Gases, and of Bacteriological Methods of Warfare. Both in WPD 165-21.

[3] Ltr, SW to Secy State, 18 Feb 42. WPD 165-21. Interestingly, in spite of the title, none of this correspondence made any direct reference to bacteriological warfare. All discussion was on gas warfare.

first arm to use gas, the study asserted that first priority on chemical troops should be accorded to the Army Air Forces, and that Air Force A of the Munitions Program, comprising 147 officers and 5,777 enlisted men, should be activated and trained immediately. Other proposals included the provision of defensive chemical units (impregnating and decontaminating) for key U.S. outposts and for Australia, Iceland, and Northern Ireland; stockage of chemical munitions in every overseas theater, possession, and base with priority to areas proximate to the Japanese; activation of six regiments of chemical troops as soon as equipment was available; and training for all branches in smoke and gas operations.[4]

On 13 February 1942 General Marshall personally directed WPD to insure the activation of 4 chemical combat battalions and directed the Budget and Legislative Planning Branch of the War Department to procure funds for the equipment of 18 chemical regiments (later reduced to 24 battalions).[5] General Marshall ordered Lt. Gen. Lesley J. McNair to activate the four battalions along with nineteen chemical service companies before 1 July 1942. Following the 9 March 1942 reorganization of the Army into the Headquarters, Army Air Forces (AAF), Army Ground Forces (AGF), and Army Service Forces (ASF),[6] the AGF, heir to many GHQ functions, informed the Operations Division (OPD), War Department General Staff, that a directive was in preparation which would set up a program for training troops to operate under conditions of gas and smoke. By 23 March 1942 the Commanding General, Army Air Forces, had activated nearly three fourths of the authorized air chemical troops. About this time The Quartermaster General was instructed to ship impregnated clothing and decontamination matériel to the Pacific bases and the Western Defense Command.[7]

These operational decisions provided answers that the CWS had anxiously sought and supplied objectives toward which administrative and logis-

<hr />

[4] Memo, Lt Col Charles C. Herrick, WPD, for C Opns GP WPD, 10 Feb 42, sub: Use of Toxic Gases. WPD 165–23.

[5] (1) Memo, Col William T. Sexton, OCofS, for CofS, 8 Feb 42. (2) DF, WPD to G–3 and G–4, 13 Feb 42, sub: Augmentation of Equipment for CWS. Both in WPD 166–5.

[6] (1) WD Cir 59, 9 Mar 42. (2) Army Service Forces was known as the Services of Supply from March 1942 until 12 March 1943. Since it is best known by the earlier designation the term Army Service Forces will be used in the narrative of events from 9 March 1942 onward. Administratively, the CWS was under Army Service Forces and reported through ASF to the General Staff. See below, Chapter V.

[7] (1) Memo, Col Herrick, OPD, for Col St. Clair Streett, C Opns Gp OPD, 23 Mar 42, sub: Use of Toxic Gases. (2) Memo, Col James R. Townsend, C Resources & Reqmts Sec WPD, for Brig Gen Dwight D. Eisenhower, Feb 42, sub: Use of Toxic Gases. Both in WPD 165–23.

CWS Equipment *Army Exhibit, San Antonio, Texas, March 1942. The masks, from left to right, are: diaphragm, service, optical diaphragm (for use with field glasses), and civilian.*

tical action could be directed. By March 1942 the Chemical Warfare Service was thus embarked on a definite if modest mobilization project that was intended to assure the U.S. Army of at least a limited degree of readiness for gas warfare. In sum, this was an earnest of the active preparations and constant readiness to which the War Department had alluded in its reply to the Department of State.

The Concern of Mr. McCloy

While the WPD study was still in progress, Assistant Secretary of War John J. McCloy brought up another aspect of chemical warfare preparedness which, up to that time, had not been especially considered except by the CWS. McCloy asked the Chief of Staff whether the United States was prepared to assist the United Nations in the employment of toxic gases.[8] General Marshall referred the McCloy memorandum to the Chief, Chemical

[8](1) Memo, ASW for CofS, 25 Jan 42. CWS 470.6/2711–2754. (2) Interv, CmlHO with Maj Gen William N. Porter, USA (Ret.), 15 Sep 51.

Warfare Service, for comment and recommendation. Porter's reply concurred in the views and apprehensions expressed by Mr. McCloy and summarized certain specific steps considered necessary by way of preparation for gas warfare by the United Nations. Some of these measures were already under study by WPD. Porter now advanced a proposal that the chemical warfare needs of all the United Nations be surveyed to determine what assistance the United States should and could provide. "In most of our military preparations," he said, "we shall, for some time to come, be forced to follow a pacemaker. With the vast chemical industry of the United States and the highly trained scientific and technical men connected with it, we should be able to be ready for all-out gas warfare, if required, in a relatively short time, and in this particular do the pacemaking ourselves." [9]

As a result of the McCloy memorandum and General Porter's recommendations, the Assistant Chief of Staff, G–4, and the Assistant Chief of Staff, WPD, were directed to determine the requirements in chemical weapons and ammunition adequate to meet the needs of the United Nations in the event of gas warfare. [10] In addition, the Under Secretary of War, Mr. Robert P. Patterson, was requested to investigate current British and American production plans to learn what increase should be provided to meet the possible needs of the United Nations. [11]

This militant attitude reflected the increasing concern on the part of the War Department over the gas warfare situation in the late winter and early spring of 1942. The General Staff was at last beginning to regard realistically the several dimensions of the gas warfare problem: the capability of the United States to produce and use toxic agents; the ability of the United States and the rest of the United Nations to defend themselves against gas attack; the preparation—offensive and defensive—for gas warfare as a means of dissuading the enemy from using gas; and, behind all these considerations, the question whether the United States could indefinitely afford to surrender the initiative to the Axis in this important area. Thus the early months of 1942, a time of utmost difficulty for military planners generally, was also a period of serious concern over gas warfare. Would the enemy beat the United States to the punch and introduce gas before its nascent preparations materialized? Could the United States fulfill

[9] Memo, C CWS for CofS, 2 Feb 42, sub: Use of Gas. CWS 470.6/2711–2754.
[10] Memo, DCofS for ACofS G–4, 11 Feb 42, sub: Gas Warfare. WPD 165–24.
[11] (1) Memo, DCofS for USW, 11 Feb 42, sub: Gas Warfare. (2) Memo, SGS for Mr. McCloy, 14 Feb 42. Both in WPD 165–24.

its role in a coalition war of global proportions that was further complicated by the employment of toxic agents? Such questions the General Staff was now obliged to face.

During the prewar years, particularly 1940 and 1941, the Chemical Warfare Service had not always concealed its impatience with what appeared to be a lack of realism in the War Department's approach to the subject of gas warfare. By 1942 wishful thinking had ceased. It became the official view that the enemy might sooner or later resort to gas and that, if he did, the United States should beat him at his own game.[12]

The Porter Proposals

In addition to news of the steady succession of defeats suffered by the United Nations in the winter of 1941 and early spring of 1942, intelligence reports and rumors reaching the War Department hinted ever more strongly at the possibility of gas warfare. With the fall of Bataan the whole situation seemed to demand still closer study. The Assistant Chief of Staff, Operations Division, Maj. Gen. Dwight D. Eisenhower, called for the views of the Chemical Warfare Service in a memorandum that began with the ominous statement: "Present intelligence reports indicate the possibility of the outbreak of chemical warfare in the near future." [13] General Eisenhower specifically requested an estimate of the capability and probability of the Axis' waging gas warfare, an estimate of the power of the United States to retaliate, a report (co-ordinated with The Quartermaster General) on the distribution of protective equipment, another report (co-ordinated with the Army Air Forces) of the means for retaliation presently available overseas, and finally—for the CWS the most important—a report of such recommendations as the Chief, CWS, deemed advisable.[14] It was a red-letter day for the Chemical Warfare Service.

General Porter and his staff warmly welcomed the opportunity to present their case, and the CWS reply furnished the blueprint for the wartime

---

[12] (1) Memo, Col Herrick for C Opns Gp WPD, 10 Feb 42, sub: Use of Toxic Gases. WPD 166–5. (2) Memo for Rcd, Col Jay W. MacKelvie, WPD, 11 Feb 42. Both in WPD 165–23. (3) Ltr, SW to Secy State, 18 Feb 42. WPD 165–21.

[13] (1) Memo, ACofS OPD for CG SOS (Attn: C CWS), 27 Apr 42, sub: Cml Warfare. OPD 441.5. (2) Two days earlier, General Marshall had cabled all theater commanders, warning them not to use gas without the prior approval of the War Department. See CM–OUT 5049, 25 Apr 42.

[14] Memo, ACofS OPD for CG SOS (Attn: C CWS), 27 Apr 42, sub: Cml Warfare. OPD 441.5.

mission and program of the Chemical Warfare Service. The CWS stated that the probability of gas warfare was stronger than at any time since the beginning of the war and that the Axis had greater capabilities for waging gas warfare than did the United Nations. Whereas Great Britain could retaliate immediately in Europe, the long-established policy by which the United States left the initiative in gas warfare to the enemy had so hampered American preparations that retaliation, at the best, would be on a limited scale. The offensive and defensive training of the Army in chemical warfare was deficient. In the few hours of training allotted to chemical warfare the American soldier had learned little more than how to adjust his gas mask. Nor did inspection reports reveal a much better condition of training on the part of company grade officers. The CWS regarded the distribution and supply of protective clothing and equipment as entirely inadequate. Only a limited amount of chemical warfare offensive matériel was overseas for the use of the Army Air Forces, although it would initially be in the best position to retaliate.

General Porter therefore made a number of important recommendations aimed at placing the United States in the proper posture for offensive and defensive gas warfare. The very first of these was that definite objectives should be set up for the entire chemical warfare supply program. These would include filling the requirements of the United States and other United Nations for full-scale chemical warfare. Since preparations on such a scale naturally called for additional arsenal facilities, the Chief, CWS, pointed out that the present and projected chemical warfare production capacity of the United States was based solely upon the current Army Supply Program, which did not visualize the extent to which chemical warfare might develop. He therefore recommended that American production capacity for toxic agents be increased well beyond probable enemy capacities. On the defensive side the Chief, CWS, proposed that full protection be provided for all military and naval personnel stationed outside the continental United States, and he earnestly suggested that adequate gas and smoke training be injected into normal training routine and maneuvers.

The Chief, CWS, felt that chemical mortar battalions would provide the most effective means for large-scale retaliation on the ground and that such battalions should be activated on the general basis of one per division. Although the Army Supply Program had provided for a total of 28 battalions by 1944, by May 1942 only 4 chemical battalions and 3 separate chemical mortar companies—one each in Panama, Hawaii, and the United

States—had been activated, a fourth company having been lost in the Philippines. The CWS considered the 4.2-inch chemical mortar to be an ideal weapon for delivering gas, smoke, or high explosive shell in high concentrations in support of ground operations.

General Porter proposed the following basis for troop units for service support in the field:

Type	Basis
Maintenance Company	One per army
Decontaminating Company	One per army corps
Impregnating Company	One per army corps
Depot Company	One per army
Field Laboratory Company	One per theater of operations

He also believed that priority should be given to the chemical warfare requirements of the Army Air Forces and accordingly proposed the activation of the following troop units:

Type	Basis
Maintenance Company	One per air force
Impregnating Company	One per air force
Field Laboratory Company	One per air force

These service elements would be assigned to each air force in addition to the CWS units already authorized.[15]

For the Air Forces, General Porter further proposed that an over-all distribution scheme be prepared covering incendiary bombs, airplane spray tanks, and chemical bombs, based on the present location and anticipated future allocation of planes capable of employing those weapons in various theaters of operations.

General Porter not only recommended that the GHQ Umpire Manual be revised to include chemical warfare training for all parts of the Army but he also made other proposals to increase the efficiency and capability of CWS training. He requested that the Chemical Warfare Service receive control of the entire area of Gunpowder Neck, on which Edgewood Arsenal was situated, instead of having to share it with the Ordnance Department. This need arose out of the ever-increasing demand for additional space

---

[15](1) These were the following: chemical company (air bomb), chemical company (air operations), chemical company (depot aviation), chemical platoon (airdrome), chemical platoon (air force supply base), chemical platoon (air force service center), and chemical company (service aviation). (2) See Table 4 for final recommendations on air chemical units.

and range facilities in connection with both research and training which were carried on simultaneously at Edgewood. From this same problem arose General Porter's recommendation that, in any case, the Chemical Warfare Replacement Training Center (RTC) be relocated from Edgewood to a 35,000-acre tract outside the town of Gadsden, Alabama. The Chief, CWS, proposed that the student capacity of the Chemical Warfare School be increased from 200 student officers and 50 student enlisted men to at least 400 student officers and 150 student enlisted men. General Porter also recommended that the capacity of the CWS Officer Candidate School (OCS) be increased from 160 to at least 700 officer candidates. Finally, he suggested that a school for senior officers be provided at Edgewood Arsenal with an initial attendance by general officers of the Army.[16]

A few months earlier such proposals would have received scant attention at the General Staff level; now they were seriously studied and action on them was begun immediately. Within a week OPD sought their approval by the General Staff, with the exception of the ratio proposed by General Porter of one mortar battalion per armored or infantry division.[17] OPD recommended instead that twenty-eight chemical battalions be activated by 1944 with a maximum of fourteen by the end of 1942 and the General Staff concurred in the recommendations.[18]

All through the summer of 1942 the War Department was engaged in the implementation of General Porter's proposals. The War Department issued directives to insure adequate chemical warfare training and to provide for the immediate supply of impregnated clothing and other essential equipment to overseas forces. A priority list for the distribution of chemical warfare matériel was established with first priority given to the Far East. G–3 and ASF took measures to establish OCS and RTC facilities of sufficient size and to provide equipment for the program. By August the General Staff was ready to recommend the following additional steps to General Marshall: (1) that G–3 establish ratios for the constitution and activation of chemical warfare service troops (*Table 4*) and constitute and activate chemical mortar battalions on the basis of approved special projects rather

---

[16] Memo, C CWS for CG SOS, 11 May 42, sub: Cml Warfare; with tabs A–G. CWS 470 6/2730.

[17] (1) Memo, ACofS OPD for ACofS G–3, 18 May 42, sub: Cml Warfare Program. OPD 320.2. (2) The proposals, as revised by OPD, evolved from a conference between General Eisenhower, Brig. Gen. Robert W. Crawford, and Brig. Gen. Lehman W. Miller.

[18] The Assistant Chief of Staff, G–3, did not concur in the strength to be allotted the battalions, desiring they be at reduced strength until assigned to overseas task forces. G–3 also indicated that action had begun on revised training standards and on enlargement of the Replacement Training Center and the Officer Candidate School. See Memo, G–3 for OPD, 11 Jun 42. WDGCT 320.2.

TABLE 4—1942 PROPOSED MODIFICATION IN CWS TROOP BASIS

Type[a]	As of 25 May	Increase	Proposed 13 August
Ground Force Type Units			
Chemical Co (Maintenance)	12	0	12
Chemical Co (Depot)	9	2	11
Chemical Co (Decontamination)	26	0	26
Chemical Co (Impregnation)	30	0	30
Chemical Co (Field Laboratory)	5	0	5
Chemical Co (Smoke Generator)	21	0	21
Chemical Co (Composite)	2	7	9
Chemical Co (Mortar)	3	0	3
Chemical Bn (Mortar)	6	0	6
Air Force Type Units			
Chemical Co (Air Operations) (N)[b]	37	0	37
(M)	17	0	17
(L)	3	0	3
(D)	8	0	8
(C)	1	0	1
Chemical Co (Maintenance)	12	0	12
Chemical Co (Depot)	12	0	12
Chemical Co (Storage)	4	0	4
Chemical Co (Service Aviation)	11	0	11

[a] In addition to chemical sections in headquarters of units as authorized by approved Tables of Organization.

[b] A decrease in Air Force personnel led to the reorganization of the chemical company (air bombardment) and chemical company (air operations) into the chemical company (air operations) which had the same organization for all bombardment groups.

Source Tab E to Memo, ACofS OPD for CofS USA, 13 Aug 42, sub Revision in the Cml Warfare Program. OPD 385 CWP Sec IIA.

than assign one per division, and (2) that the Chief of Staff sign a letter requesting the Combined Chiefs of Staffs (CCS) to give early consideration to an over-all directive which could be used as a basis for production and allocation of chemical warfare material and troops available to the United Nations.[19] The new troop basis increased the size of the CWS to 4,970 officers and 47,192 enlisted men. (*Table 5*)

Several problems yet remained, such as formal confirmation of combat functions for the CWS, clarification of training responsibilities for CWS units, the adjustment of the Army Supply Program to handle prospective United Nations' requirements, and clarification of Air Force requirements together with improvement in co-ordination of the manufacture of chemical

[19] (1) Memo, OPD for CofS, 13 Aug 42, sub: Revision of Cml Warfare Program. OPD 385 CWP, sec IIA. (2) See below, Chapter IV.

TABLE 5—CWS TROOP BASIS, AS OF 13 AUGUST 1942

Type	Officer	Enlisted Men
Total	4,970	47,192
Air Force Type Units	828	14,609
Ground and Service Force Type Units	964	29,743
War Department Overhead (Arsenals, Schools, Procurement)	3,178	2,840

Source· Tab E to Memo, ACofS OPD for CofS USA, 13 Aug 42, sub Revision in the Chemical Warfare Program. OPD 385 CWP Sec IIA.

warfare equipment and aircraft.[20] In September 1942 OPD informed the ASF that the Chief of Staff had approved most of General Porter's major recommendations on gas warfare and that action had been taken to implement them.[21]

When cables reached the War Department in the latter part of November 1942 strongly suggesting that the enemy might soon resort to gas warfare, the Chief of Staff ordered the CWS to report on the status of overseas shipments of CWS supplies and on the extent of implementation of the protective equipment policy established the preceding June.[22] General Marshall apparently did not wish a gas warfare Pearl Harbor.

The Gas Mission Defined

General Marshall conveyed his concern over the potentialities of the gas warfare situation to Secretary Stimson in mid-December 1942 when the Chief of Staff expressed his conviction that the Germans would soon launch gas attacks on the United Nations.[23] Apparently both the director of the Office of Scientific Research and Development, Dr. Vannevar Bush, and the chairman of the National Defense Research Committee, Dr. James Conant, were present in the office of the Secretary of War when General

[20] Memo, ACofS OPD (Maj Gen Thomas T. Handy) for CofS, 13 Aug 42, sub: Revision of the Cml Warfare Program. The memos for record made on the OPD file copy provide an excellent means for tracing the steps taken by the War Department to implement General Porter's proposals. OPD 385 CWP, sec IIA.

[21] Memo, ACofS OPD for CG SOS, 2 Sep 42, sub: Revision in the Cml Warfare Program. OPD 385 CWP, sec IIA.

[22] Memo, CofS for CG SOS, 4 Dec 42, sub: Status of Cml Warfare Preparation. OPD 385 CWP, sec IIA. In June 1942 the War Department had established the policy of immediately furnishing overseas personnel with some protective clothing and ointment and of ultimately supplying them with complete sets of protective clothing together with a sufficient number of plants to reimpregnate the clothing after laundering. See Ltr, TAG to CGs All Overseas Depts *et al.,* 10 Jun 42, sub: Cml Warfare Protective Clothing. AG 420.

[23] Memo, Harvey Bundy for SW, 21 Dec 42. OPD 385 CWP, sec IIA.

Marshall made his remarks, for a week later both these distinguished scientists posed several incisive questions to Secretary Stimson relative to the fears expressed by the Chief of Staff. Bush and Conant asked whether the War Department had taken adequate steps to prepare American soldiers for defense against new German toxic agents.[24] Second, they inquired whether the United States was fully prepared to retaliate and, if so, whether a public announcement to that effect should be made.[25]

These pointed questions, raised by the two civilians who were principally responsible for marshaling the scientific skills of the nation for World War II, deserved serious study. Probably the questions were asked without full knowledge of the numerous measures taken by the War Department during 1942 to improve the capacity of the Army for waging gas warfare. But they served as the occasion for a hasty War Department survey of what had been accomplished under the Porter proposals. Harvey Bundy, special assistant to Secretary Stimson, incorporated the inquiries in a memorandum to Mr. Stimson on 21 December. Three days later it was in General Porter's hands for comment and recommendation.[26]

The Chief, CWS, indicated in rather broad terms what had been done and what remained to be accomplished. He assured the General Staff that the service gas mask was the best in the world and that it provided adequate protection against the German toxic agents to which Bush and Conant had referred. On the less favorable side, he pointed out that maneuver reports and inspections at ports of embarkation indicated that U.S. troops had received inadequate defensive training in the use of protective items other than the gas mask.[27] As for the ability of the United States to retaliate, General Porter stated that preparations included large stocks of mustard gas on hand and a large and steadily increasing capacity for its production. The Chief, CWS, reiterated his feeling that an overt threat of retaliation would serve no useful purpose and might be taken by the enemy as a sign of weakness.[28]

---

[24] The Germans were then thought to be preparing to employ both nitrogen mustard and hydrocyanic acid. Although the latter was a well-known agent in World War I, a serious problem had been that of producing adequate concentrations in the field. It was believed that the Germans might have solved this problem.

[25] Memo, Bundy for SW, 21 Dec 42. OPD 385 CWP, sec IIA.

[26] Memo, C Log Gp OPD for C CWS, 24 Dec 42, sub: Cml Warfare Preparedness of U.S. Army. OPD 385 CWP, sec IIA.

[27] These items included protective clothing, protective ointment, and gas detection equipment.

[28] (1) Memo, C CWS for OPD, 24 Dec 42, sub: Cml Warfare Preparedness of U.S. Army. OPD 385 CWP, sec IIA. (2) In this instance, the United States feared that Germany might

1-TON CHEMICAL CONTAINERS *awaiting shipment at a CWS storage yard,*
1943.

OPD promptly assembled representatives of the CWS, ASF G–3, G–4, AGF, and AAF to study the deficiencies noted by Porter. Upon examination of the vital training problem, the conferees concluded that the Army was not fully prepared to defend itself against gas attack because certain items of individual protective equipment had only recently been standardized and made available for training. They were of the opinion that the current training policy was satisfactory but that until production of the new equipment caught up with requirements the training program would be incomplete. In the meantime, one proposed solution was to re-emphasize priority for the chemical warfare training program of the Army, especially in field maneuvers. More important, it was decided that the Chief, CWS, as technical adviser to the Chief of Staff, ought to conduct any troop inspections necessary to determine the technical status of chemical warfare training. On the question of retaliation, the consensus was that the Army Air Forces could do little with the small stocks of gas munitions then overseas. The

initiate gas warfare. In May 1942 President Roosevelt had warned Japan against the use of gas in China and had promised retaliation if such acts continued. For details, see below, Chapter IV.

AAF and the CWS agreed that the immediate answer was a higher shipping priority.[29]

On the basis of General Porter's letter and the meetings held by representatives of the War Department General Staff, General Marshall informed the Secretary of War: (1) that the Army would be provided with new protective equipment by June 1943 (barring manufacturing priority difficulties); (2) that steps had been taken to expedite the training of the Army in the use of protective equipment; and (3) that American forces overseas were currently unprepared to retaliate but, granted the necessary shipping priorities, available equipment and munitions could be distributed by May 1943. The Chief of Staff concurred with General Porter that no public threats of retaliation should be made.[30] A more complete report on CWS and War Department accomplishments since May 1942 was submitted at the end of December in answer to General Marshall's inquiry of 4 December. This report thoroughly reviewed the chemical warfare status of the United States and listed steps taken toward readiness. The CWS recommended that higher priorities be given for critical materials needed in the completion of impregnating plants, that additional impregnating (later known as processing) companies be authorized, and that special directives governing the issue of impregnated clothing be published for all theaters where gas warfare was likely.[31]

The gas mission of the Chemical Warfare Service had thus crystallized by the close of 1942 as the result of almost a year of staff studies, discussion, alarms, and War Department directives. A number of factors had combined to bring about a more realistic attitude toward gas warfare than had been present at any time since 1918. Of these, the most impelling was the fear that the enemy might initiate gas warfare. Under the leadership of Secretary Stimson, Assistant Secretary McCloy, General Marshall, and General Porter, the War Department began active preparations to meet such a contingency in a manner that would insure American supremacy in this field.

[29] Memos for Rcd, 26 and 29 Dec 42, on Memo, ACofS OPD for CofS, 31 Dec 42, sub: Summary of Cml Warfare Preparations. OPD 385 CWP, sec IIA.

[30] Memo, ACofS OPD for CofS, 31 Dec 42, sub: Summary of Cml Warfare Preparations, with Tab A, Proposed Memo for SW. OPD 385 CWP, sec IIA.

[31] Memo, C CWS for ACofS OPD, 30 Dec 42, sub: Status of Cml Warfare Preparation. OPD 385 CWP, sec IIA.

CHAPTER IV

The United States Chemical Warfare Committee

The War Department's emphasis in early 1942 on preparation for retaliation gas warfare made evident the need for an agency to furnish advice on chemical warfare policy, to develop a procurement and supply program, and to co-ordinate these matters with the United Nations, particularly Great Britain.[1] In the late spring of 1942 the policy on gas warfare of the United States and Great Britain was announced in unilateral statements by Prime Minister Churchill and President Roosevelt.[2] On 10 May Churchill declared: "I wish to make it plain that we shall treat the unprovoked use of poison gas against our Russian ally exactly as if it were used against ourselves, and if we are satisfied that this new outrage has been committed by Hitler we will use our great and growing air superiority in the west to carry gas warfare on the largest possible scale far and wide upon the towns and cities of Germany." A month later President Roosevelt stated: "I desire to make it unmistakably clear that if Japan persists in this inhuman form of warfare against China or against any other of the United Nations, such action will be regarded by this government as though taken against the United States and retaliation in kind and in full measure will be meted out."[3]

[1] (1) As early as February 1942 the Chief, CWS, had voiced the need for such an agency. See Memo, C CWS for ACofS G–4, 24 Feb 42, sub Co-ord of Cml Warfare Allied Activities. CWS 400 12/17. Maj Gen. Brehon B. Somervell approved the procedure. See Memo, ACofS G–4 for C CWS, 25 Feb 42 G–4/34199. (2) Before the United States entered World War II there had been an exchange of information on chemical warfare through the assistant military attaché in London and through the representatives of the British Purchasing Commission in Washington.

[2] On 1 April 1942 Churchill had informed Roosevelt of assurances which the British had given Marshal Joseph Stalin—that any German use of gas against the USSR would lead to unlimited British retaliation. See Winston S. Churchill, *The Hinge of Fate* (Boston: Houghton Mifflin, Company, 1950), pp. 203, 329–30.

[3] (1) Churchill's statement and that of Roosevelt are quoted in CCS 106/2, 14 Nov 42, Allied Cml Warfare Program. This paper was the basis for Anglo-American gas warfare policy and co-ordinated procurement and supply of chemical warfare matériel. (2) The Chinese had repeatedly accused the Japanese of using gas. This charge was never definitely established.

These statements established the general gas warfare policy of the respective nations, but no organization had been established to implement co-ordination between the parallel policies of the United States and the British Commonwealth of Nations, and procedures for co-ordination of effort in event of enemy gas attack were necessary as well as preparation for a combined procurement and supply program. The British in 1940 had established the Inter-Service Committee on Chemical Warfare (ISCCW), a group representative of all services reporting to the British Chiefs of Staff; and the United States had the Chemical Warfare Service which represented the interests of the Army, the component Army Air Forces, and, by informal arrangement, the Navy. In August 1942 General Marshall brought the question of co-ordination to the attention of the Combined Chiefs of Staff and offered the services of the Chief of the Chemical Warfare Service as adviser to the CCS.[4] The Combined Chiefs referred this suggestion to the Combined Staff Planners (CPS) who created an *ad hoc* chemical warfare subcommittee headed by the Chief, CWS, which was to define the United Nations chemical warfare policy and draw up a directive upon which a co-ordinated United Nations chemical warfare procurement and supply policy could be based.[5] During discussions of initial drafts of a report within the *ad hoc* subcommittee, the British representative proposed establishment of a permanent subcommittee of the Combined Staff Planners to carry out the combined program.[6] This proposal was dropped during the *ad hoc* subcommittee meeting of 22 October 1942 upon general agreement to use existing agencies.[7] A week later the *ad hoc* subcommittee reported the results of its study to the Combined Staff Planners.[8]

The chemical warfare subcommittee recommended that gas warfare be

[4](1) Memo, CofS for U.S. Secretariat CCS, 27 Aug 42, sub: Allied Cml Warfare Program. WDCSA 470.71 (8–13–42). Reproduced as CCS 106, 28 Aug 42. (2) For the background of this recommendation, see above, Chapter III. Both in CWS 470.6/2754.

[5](1) CPS 45/D, 5 Sep 42, Allied Cml Warfare Program. (2) Memo, Secy JPS for Gen Porter *et al.*, 9 Sep 42, sub: Allied Cml Warfare Program. Both in CWS 314.7 USCWC file. (3) The subcommittee was dissolved following approval of CCS 106/2 at the 48th meeting of the CCS on 14 November 1942.

[6] Memo, Wing Comdr W. Oulton, RAF, for Gen Porter *et al.*, 19 Oct 42. CWS 314.7 USCWC File.

[7] Min of Mtg, CPS Subcom on UN Cml Warfare Program, 22 Oct 42. CWS 470.6/2754.

[8](1) Memo, C CWS for Brig Gen Albert C. Wedemeyer and Capt R. L. Conolly, USN, 11 Sep 42, sub: Allied Cml Warfare Program (CPS 45/D). (2) Memo, Porter for Secy CPS, 30 Oct 42, sub: Allied Cml Warfare Program. Both in CWS 470.6/2754. (3) Drafts and notes of the *ad hoc* subcommittee are filed in CWS 470.6/2754. (4) Other subcommittee members were: Capts. A. R. Early and O. K. Olsen, USN; Maj. Lawrence J. Lincoln, USA; and Wing Commander Oulton, RAF.

undertaken by both U.S. and British Commonwealth forces on the order of the Combined Chiefs of Staff after approval by appropriate governmental authority, or independently by any such nation, if in retaliation, on the decision of a representative especially designated for that purpose by its highest governmental authority.[9] It also recommended that either U.S. or British Commonwealth forces should provide evidence of the enemy's use of gas in case combined action was requested. When the decision to retaliate was made independently, the acting nation should give immediate, confirmed information to the Combined Chiefs of Staff who would then notify cobelligerents. Lastly, the subcommittee recommended that the CCS issue a directive for a co-ordinated chemical warfare procurement and supply program and included a suggested directive as a separate annex to the report. This proposed directive placed responsibility for the chemical warfare procurement and supply program in the United States with the Commanding General, Army Services Forces, who was to designate the Chief, CWS, and such other officers as he might deem appropriate as a committee to execute this responsibility. This group, in co-ordination with the U.S. Navy representative, would then contact the appropriate British agency which would be selected by the British Chiefs of Staff. Both the American and British agencies were to be staff in nature; where command decisions were required these were to be obtained through normal command channels. The proposed directive concluded with a list of specific functions which the two committees were to perform. The Combined Chiefs of Staff approved the report with but minor changes, and on 14 November 1942 it became an official document known as CCS 106/2.

Mission and Functions of the Committee

This document, CCS 106/2, described in some detail the duties of both American and British agencies in co-ordinating the chemical warfare procurement and supply program. It listed seven separate functions for which these agencies were responsible, six of which dealt exclusively with the production and supply of gas warfare matériel.[10] The Combined Chiefs of Staff directed these agencies to establish potential production capacity capable of rapid expansion to meet the needs of gas warfare while keeping

[9] In December 1942 the highest governmental authority in the United States was officially defined as the President, who, it was understood, could act on the recommendation of the U.S. Joint Chiefs of Staff. See JCS 176/1, 31 Dec 42, Allied Cml Warfare Program (Rpt by the JPS).

[10] These functions were substantially the same as those listed in the report by the chemical warfare subcommittee of the CPS.

current production on the minimum level compatible with this goal. The agencies were to provide for initial stocks at levels which would permit gas warfare to be carried on pending expansion of production; they were to establish uniform initial stock levels of all types of equipment for combined theaters, and they were to determine and maintain minimum levels of individual and collective protective equipment and to set up logistical factors for antigas equipment, gas weapons, and munitions. A further and very important function was the initiation of a program for standardizing and interchanging all types of chemical warfare equipment used by the United States and Great Britain. The directive concluded with the admonition that, in the execution of these policies, "the extent of the measures adopted would be limited to those compatible with a balanced over-all munitions program." [11]

To carry out these provisions the Commanding General, ASF, promptly established a committee headed by General Porter and including representatives chosen by G–2 and OPD of the War Department General Staff, the Requirements and Operations Divisions of the ASF, and the U.S. Navy.[12]

General Porter asked the chiefs of the Industrial, Technical, Operations, and Training Divisions of his office to appoint qualified officers to represent their divisions in the work required by the CCS directive. As the Chief, CWS, correctly observed, this work involved no small amount of time and travel.[13] Members of the Office of the Chief, CWS, eventually performed a great deal of the work of the committee.

The new committee, as yet undesignated, held its first meeting on 1

---

[11] CCS 106/2, 14 Nov 42, App. A, Directive for a Co-ordinated UN Cml Warfare Proc and Supply Program.

[12] (1) Ltr, CG SOS for C CWS, 1 Dec 42, sub: Allied Cml Warfare Program. SOS 470.6/2754 (later CCWCI). (2) On 30 November 1942 Admiral Ernest J. King directed that a naval representative be appointed. See Ltr, COMINCH to VCNO, 30 Nov 42, sub: Allied Cml Warfare Program. COMINCH file, FFI/S77/A16.3, serial 001441. (3) A British representative also sat with this committee. By its third meeting on 17 February 1943, a representative from the AAF had been named, and late in the year an AGF officer was appointed. CCWC 19/1, 17 Feb 43, Min of Mtg 17 Feb 43. CCWC, USCWC, and CWC papers cited in this chapter are located in CWS 314.7 USCWS file. (4) USCWC 142, 30 Mar 45, Performance of Responsibility for Carrying Out a Co-ordinated Anglo-American Cml Warfare Proc and Supply Program (U.S. Agency). Appendix A lists the members of the committee and subcommittees during the war. This document is an account of the USCWC to that date, prepared by the secretary, Lt. Col. Jacob K. Javits, CWS, and submitted by the chairman.

[13] (1) Memo. C CWS for C Ind Div et al., 19 Dec 42, sub: Allied Cml Warfare Program. CWS 470.6/2754. (2) The workload of the secretary and the OC CWS became such by 1944 that the Chief, CWS, requested that two officers and three civilians be provided for USCWC administration. Memo, C CWS for CG ASF, 1 Feb 44, sub: Co-ordinated Anglo-American Proc and Supply Program (Secretariat). CWS 314.7 USCWC File.

December 1942 to consider the Allied chemical warfare program.[14] Conduct of this meeting and of the subsequent monthly meetings followed the general procedures of the Joint Chiefs of Staff (JCS) committees.[15] For instance, matters brought up for consideration were, whenever practicable, presented in the form of a paper which the secretary circulated among the members before placing the item on the agenda.

At its second meeting, in January 1943, the committee adopted the name Combined Chemical Warfare Committee (CCWC) because it apparently considered its mission as being advisory to the Combined Chiefs of Staff. In March the newly appointed British representative on the CCWC, Lt. Col. Humphrey Paget of the Royal Engineers, took formal issue with this interpretation of the committee's position.[16] The British viewpoint was that the committee was simply an advisory body to the U.S. Joint Chiefs of Staff just as the British Inter-Service Committee on Chemical Warfare advised the British Chiefs of Staff. Paget argued that his role on the CCWC was that of a British liaison officer.[17] Colonel Paget's objections initiated a period of controversy and concern over the designation and role of the committee.

General Porter was visiting London to discuss implementation of CCS 106/2 at the time Colonel Paget's formal objections were received. The Operations Division of the War Department General Staff became concerned over the possibility of British pressure on General Porter for the establishment of an over-all combined committee to sit in London. The British had taken a renewed interest in chemical warfare, OPD felt, and might try to establish a combined committee in London despite the published British view of combined machinery as consisting of parallel joint agencies. OPD sought and obtained concurrence of the ASF, AAF, and the Navy

[14] Ltr, Gen Porter to Brig Gen John R. Deane, Secy JCS, 15 Dec 42, sub: Allied Cml Warfare Programs. CWS 470.6/2754. Reproduced as CCWC 6.

[15] For details on the operations of the JCS committee system, see Vernon E. Davis, History of Joint Chiefs of Staff in World War II, Vol. II, Development of JCS Committee Structure. MS.

[16] (1) CCWC 29/1, 19 Mar 43, Min of Mtg CCWC 19 Mar 43. (2) Lt. Col. D. J. C. Wiseman, Gas Warfare, volume I of Special Weapons and Types of Warfare, The Second World War: 1939–1945, Army (British War Office, 1951), p. 122. (3) Colonel Paget's predecessor, Col. F. C. Nottingham, had previously registered verbal protest at this interpretation. (4) The ARCADIA Conference in December 1941 had given precision to the word "combined" by reserving it to describe the machinery and action of the British-American partnership. The British thought of combined machinery as parallel joint committees in both capitals. See Duncan Hall, North American Supply, History Of The Second World War (United Kingdom Civil Series) (London: Her Majesty's Stationery Office, 1955), pp. 343, 347.

[17] Paget's views are summarized in a memorandum for the subcommittee, Title and Functions of CCWC, 25 March 1943

Department in the view that a combined committee should be located in Washington because the Combined Chiefs of Staff and most of its subordinate and supporting committees were located there. OPD further argued that since most of the assignments of chemical warfare matériel would be made from U.S. production, it was not logical that the assigning body sit in London. The Chief of Staff expressed his agreement with these views, and a cable was sent to General Porter stating the U.S. position.[18]

The United States had reversed its view of the committee function since the report of the JSP *ad hoc* committee when the Americans had argued for the use of existing agencies. It is possible that they regretted that decision. The Combined Chemical Warfare Committee appointed a subcommittee to examine the question of functions and derivation of authority for its group. This subcommittee inconclusively reported that the CCWC was neither combined nor joint. It did note that its functions more nearly approached those of a joint committee. When General Porter returned from London, the subcommittee report was taken up at the 30 April 1943 meeting, but the discussion bogged down because of conflicting views.[19]

Meanwhile, on 28 April 1943, the CCWC was officially notified that the ISCCW was the agency designated by the British Chiefs of Staff to act on CCS 106/2.[20] It became apparent that the British concept of parallel joint committees was the most acceptable solution to the organizational problem. At Lt. Gen. Brehon B. Somervell's suggestion, the CCWC therefore adopted the title, United States Chemical Warfare Committee (USCWC) at its May meeting.[21] The question of organization and functions was settled, and the arrangement worked so well that a subsequent attempt to rewrite CCS 106/2 to provide for a combined committee was abortive.

The two committees achieved close co-operation in carrying out the mission given them by the Combined Chiefs of Staff. As in the case of the Combined Chiefs of Staff, which drew strength from the personal friendship of Sir John Dill and General Marshall, the strong bonds between members of the American and British committees made it possible for all

---

[18] (1) Memo, ACofS OPD for CofS, 13 Mar 43, sub: Instructions to C CWS. OPD 385 CWP, sec IIB. This memo has in ink at the bottom "OK GCM" [George C. Marshall]. (2) CM–OUT 6548, 18 Mar 43.

[19] CCWC 34 and CCWC 34/1, 30 Apr 43. Min of Mtg CCWC 30 Apr 43. The second paper is a revised version of the minutes.

[20] Memo, Col Paget for C CWS. Also reproduced as CCWC 33.

[21] (1) Memo, CG ASF for C CWS, 6 May 43, sub: Allied Cml Warfare Program. Adopted as CCWC 35, (2) Memo, CofEngrs British Army Staff for C CWS, 6 May 43, No sub. CWS 314.7. USCWC file. (3) USCWC 38, 20 May 43. Min of Mtg 20 May 43.

their undertakings to be conducted with strength, forbearance, and mutual understanding.[22] As one of the principal members of the USCWC expressed it: "The British constantly pointed to the combined C.W. effort as the best combined effort throughout the war. Many, many times I've heard my British friends remark that they wished they could enjoy the same effective, smooth, pleasant co-operation with other U.S. agencies. And this model of co-operative effort was accomplished in spite of wide basic difference of opinion as to effectiveness of gas and use of gas."[23] The U.S. representatives, and particularly those from the Chemical Warfare Service, held the view that gas was a decisive weapon if dispersed in sufficient quantities at the right places and at the right time. The British, on the other hand, regarded gas as a supplementary weapon to be used in conjunction with high explosives and incendiaries.[24]

The two committees were able to co-operate more effectively not only through a continual exchange of information but also through occasional visits by official representatives. In September 1943, about six months after General Porter's visit to Great Britain, two other members of the USCWC, Brig. Gen. Alden H. Waitt and Lt. Col. Jacob K. Javits, visited London to confer with members of the ISCCW. At these meetings, discussion centered on varied subjects such as the allocation of the chemical warfare effort of the two countries, the interchangeability of protective equipment, chemical weapons, and munitions, and the co-ordination of logistical policies.[25] In February 1944 a British delegation headed by the ISCCW chairman, Air Marshal N. H. Bottomly, and including Maj. Gen. G. Brunskill of the British Directorate of Special Weapons and Vehicles, attended a meeting of the USCWC in Washington where the progress of the Anglo-

---

[22] Hall, *North American Supply,* pp. 348–49.

[23] Comments by Maj Gen Alden H. Waitt, USA (Ret.), 1955, on draft copy of this chapter.

[24](1) Wiseman, *Gas Warfare,* p. 126. (2) Rpt of AC CWS (USCWC 53/1, 27 Oct 43), for Fld Opns (Waitt) to USCWC, 27 Oct 43. (3) Unlike the U S. Army, the British Army had no central organization dealing with chemical warfare. Different arms and branches handled chemical warfare duties. For instance, Ordnance was responsible for the supply and maintenance of chemical weapons and equipment in the field; the Royal Engineers performed laboratory analysis; the Pioneer Corps furnished smoke companies; while staff advice was provided by GSC officers trained in chemical warfare and assisted at higher headquarters by technical officers who were trained chemists. The limited amount of matériel and manpower in the British Army was a governing factor in determining the effort which could be devoted to gas weapons. See USCWC 96, 21 Feb 44, Min of Mtg, 12 Feb 44.

[25](1) *Ibid.* (2) CCW (43) 4th Mtg, 10 Sep 43, Min of Mtg 8 Sep 43. CCW was the publications symbol for the British Inter-Service Committee on Chemical Warfare. (3) CCW (43) 5th Mtg, 8 Oct 43, Min of Mtg 5 Oct 43.

American chemical warfare program was discussed.[26] These visits, and others like them, definitely resulted in closer co-operation between the British and American committees.[27]

In carrying out its duties the USCWC worked through a subcommittee system. At first these subcommittees were *ad hoc* in nature, but on 8 November 1943, pressure of an ever-increasing number of War Department requests led to establishment of four permanent subcommittees: Chemical Warfare Operations, Gas and Smoke, Chemical Warfare Protective Equipment, and Incendiaries. Appointment of some *ad hoc* committees, however, continued, including such groups as the Joint Chemical Spray Project Subcommittee.[28] Membership on the subcommittees was not limited to USCWC members but was drawn from U.S. and British experts as needed.

Activities and Accomplishments

The USCWC continued in existence until after the close of World War II. During the war the committee co-ordinated supply between the U.S. services and with the British, it exchanged information on research; it brought about a broad program of interchangeability and standardization of all types of chemical warfare matériel used by U.S. and British Commonwealth forces; it prepared periodic reports of readiness for chemical warfare; and in conjunction with various committees of the Joint Chiefs of Staff it established a logistical basis for gas warfare. Unlike the ISCCW, its British counterpart, the USCWC dealt with incendiary agents and munitions and co-ordinated this program with the British Ministry of Aircraft Production and the Air Ministry.[29]

Co-ordination of Supply

To achieve the most effective use of raw materials, production facilities, manpower, and shipping the United States and the British Commonwealth of Nations had to co-ordinate their procurement and supply programs in

---

[26] See reference cited in Note 24(3) above.

[27] See excerpt from Rpt of Chmn ISCCW on Visit to U.S.A., Feb–Mar 44 Quoted in USCWC 112, 25 Apr 44. Note by the Secretary [Rpts of British Visitors, Feb–Mar 44].

[28] (1) See below, pages 72–73. (2) At the 30 October 1943 meeting, Col. H. Spencer Struble, ASF, suggested the establishment of the permanent subcommittees on the ground that the General Staff and the ASF were regarding the USCWC as an agency for the disposition of high echelon chemical warfare policies. See USCWC 54, 30 Oct 43, Min of Mtg 30 Oct 43, and USCWC 55, 11 Nov 43, Min of Adjourned Mtg of U.S. Cml Warfare Comm 8 Nov 43.

[29] Memo, Chmn USCWC for DCofS, 21 Jan 44, sub: Co-ordinated Cml Warfare Program. CWS 314.7 USCWC File.

HC M1 Smoke Pots in Use, *Rapido River, Italy, January 1944.*

World War II. Of these factors shipping was usually the most critical. CCS 106/2 provided that British and American agencies should initiate a program for the standardization and interchangeability of all types of chemical warfare equipment used by the respective nations. By this means the planners hoped that the various fighting fronts could be supplied with many chemical warfare items from the United States or Great Britain, whichever was closer, and valuable shipping space could be saved. Such items as toxic agents, bombs, flame throwers, smoke pots, incendiaries, and protective equipment were among those exchanged for this purpose.[30]

One of the earliest questions studied by the USCWC was the co-ordination of Anglo-American requirements for smoke-producing materials. Even before the formation of the USCWC in 1942 the United States and Great Britain had begun talks on this subject. Later, the invasion of French North Africa brought with it a need for smoke pots to screen the ports against German air attack. In the summer of 1943 the U.S. Army did not

[30] The secretary of the committee felt that the co-ordination of supply was the most important work of the USCWC. See Ltr, Jacob K. Javits to OCMH, 18 May 55.

yet have a large smoke pot of the type needed for starting and maintaining a good smoke screen. The USCWC, therefore, arranged for the British to supply large numbers of their No. 24 smoke pots until the United States should finish developing what was to become the M5 smoke pot.[31] This agreement was expanded to the establishment of a basic policy that, insofar as practicable, all troops in the European Theater of Operations (ETO) would use British smoke pots and all forces in the North African theater would be supplied with smoke pots by the United States. The two committees agreed that since the United States could not yet fulfill its responsibility for supply to the Mediterranean, 75 percent of that theater's requirements would be filled by the British and 25 percent from the United States. The British agreed to provide 600,000 smoke pots for U.S. forces in the ETO.[32] Early in 1944 the USCWC reciprocated by consenting to furnish floating smoke pots to Anglo-American forces in the European theater.[33] These plans worked out substantially as scheduled. Large-size U.S. smoke pots came off production lines in the spring of 1944. The United States supplied these pots to United Nations troops in the Mediterranean; the British supplied the forces in the ETO with land smoke pots, while the United States provided them with floating smoke pots.

Other examples of items in which co-ordination of supply was effected were gas bombs and tropical bleach. Until May 1944 the British supplied the U.S. Eighth Air Force in England with ten thousand phosgene-filled 500-pound bombs.[34] In the fall of 1943 USCWC representatives arranged for the procurement of fifteen thousand tons of tropical bleach from Great Britain, a measure which saved much valuable shipping space.[35] In the summer of 1944 the committee representatives made plans for the supply

[31](1)CCW (43) 33, 3 Oct 43, Rpt by AC U.S. CWS (Waitt). (2) USCWS 55, 11 Nov 43, Min of Adjourned Mtg of U.S. Cml Warfare Comm 8 Nov 43. (3) Brophy, Miles, and Cochrane, From Laboratory to Field.

[32](1) See Note 31 (1) above. (2) See reference cited in Note 12 (4) above.

[33] Ibid.

[34](1) USCWC Periodic Rpt of Readiness for Cml Warfare as of 1 Jan 45, p. 104. (2) USCWC 44, 24 Jan 43, Min of Mtg 24 Jan 43. (3) CCW (43) 29, 25 Aug 43, First Interim Rpt by Air Ministry Tech Subcom. (4) CCW (43) 4th Mtg, Min of Mtg 8 Sep 43, p 5. (5) The United States was anxious to have Great Britain supply persistent and nonpersistent gas bombs for the AAF in England. Various obstacles, including the inability to interchange the British 65-pound mustard bomb for use on U.S. aircraft, compelled the War Department to ship thousands of American bombs to England. See Memo for Rcd on Memo, ACofS OPD for CG AAF, 24 Jun 43, sub: Eighth Air Force Preparedness for Offensive Cml Warfare. OPD 385 CWP, sec IV. U.S. production of phosgene bombs resulted in the shipment of thousands to Great Britain in 1944–45. (6) Bleach is used in decontamination.

[35](1) See page 8 of reference cited in Note 31 (1) above. See reference cited in Note 12 (4) above.

of U.S. gas munitions for American aircraft operated by the Royal Australian Air Force in the Pacific.[36]

A representative of the U.S. Navy served on the USCWC to achieve close interservice co-ordination. As early as January 1943 conferences were held under committee auspices in order to improve integration of Army and Navy chemical warfare programs.[37] These conferences were followed in March by the establishment of the basis for the Navy's chemical warfare program.[38] This integration of procurement and supply simplified procedures and often led to considerable savings of men, matériel, and all-important shipping space. Many of the savings came in the field of protective equipment and supplies. The USCWC combined Navy, Marine Corps, and Merchant Marine requirements for bleach with those of the Army and reduced the total needs. When the committee discovered that Marine Corps requirements for decontaminating agent, noncorrosive (DANC), a special decontaminant for use on equipment, were greater than was indicated in the light of Army experience, the Marines were persuaded to reduce their estimates.[39]

Efforts to integrate requirements for impregnite and field impregnation plants began while the USCWC was studying the protective-clothing policy in late 1943.[40] As a result of committee efforts the Army agreed to assume the task of initial impregnation of Marine Corps uniforms and thus save supplies of critical acetylene tetrachloride, the solvent used in the impregnation process.[41] The United States also saved supplies of other chemicals as well as manpower, plants, and shipping space. Personnel shortages prevented the War Department from agreeing to a Navy proposal for the Army to handle reimpregnation of Navy and Marine Corps protective clothing in the event of gas warfare.[42]

---

[36] USCWC 121/6, 26 Aug 44, Min of Mtg 22 Aug 44.

[37] Ltr, VCNO to C CWS, 1 Jan 43, sub: Navy Cml Warfare Program.

[38] Ltr, King to VCNO, 6 Mar 43, sub: Cml Warfare Munitions Program. FF 1/S/77/A16–3. Incl to Memo, CofS for CG ASF, 9 May 43, same sub. OPD 385 CWP, sec III, case 39.

[39] See reference cited in Note 12 (4) above

[40] Impregnation is the process of treating ordinary clothing with a chemical solution to make it resistant to the action of vapor and very small drops of blister or nerve gases.

[41] (1) USCWC 124/4, 19 Sep 44, Min of Mtg Subcom on Protective Equipment 15 Sep 44. (2) USCWC 128/2, 9 Jan 45, Min of Mtg 2 Jan 45.

[42] (1) Memo by Secy USCWC, ca. Mar 45. (2) USCWC 128/4, ca. Jan 45, U S. Army Impregnation of U.S. Navy and U.S. Marine Corps Protective Clothing. (3) Some idea of the immensity of the task which the Navy proposed in the event of gas warfare may be gleaned from the comparative strengths of the Army and Navy on 30 June 1945 which were 8,266,373 and 3,855,969 respectively. The addition of nearly four million men with requirements for impregnation of clothing would have swamped Army resources, particularly as most of the Navy and Marine forces were in the Pacific.

The further development of such agents as cyanogen chloride made desirable the inclusion, in 1944, of a special type of activated charcoal in gas-mask canisters. Although the Navy was procuring its own gas masks at the time, it applied to the Army for a supply of this charcoal. The Army felt unable to furnish more than 20 percent of the amount requested, since charcoal was in such short supply that any additional allocation to the Navy would have crippled the Army's own program.[43] The USCWC resolved the problem by arranging for a reduction in Navy requirements so that the Army could meet Navy schedules. The committee endeavored to co-ordinate Army-Navy gas-mask procurement and attained such success that the Navy began using Army masks on a substantial scale, particularly for shore-based personnel.[44]

The Navy generally used Army air munitions for its chemical munitions program. Special requirements, such as phosgene for filling Navy rockets, were co-ordinated by the USCWC.[45] A need developed for the collection of additional basic information on the effectiveness and proper tactical use of chemical spray as well as for tests to ascertain just how much agent would be required. This research was especially desirable because the Army and the Navy had differing theories on the use of aerial spray.[46] The USCWC set up a special subcommittee, the Joint Chemical Spray Project Subcommittee, to handle the co-ordination of this task.[47]

This subcommittee studied test reports from U.S. and British installations and visited staff chemical officers of the Third Air Force, the AAF Board, and AAF Proving Ground Command to discover what information was available. The members found that considerable data existed on single-plane spray attacks but little on the use of several planes simultaneously for such attacks. The chairman of the USCWC wrote to the AAF and the

---

[43] (1) USCWC 82, 19 Jan 44, Min of Mtg Subcom on Protective Equipment 11 Jan 44. (2) Ltr, Chmn USCWC to Col L A Dessez, USMC, 18 Dec 43, sub: Co-ordinated Anglo-American Cml Warfare Proc and Supply Program (PC1 Charcoal for Navy Masks). Reproduced as USCWC 78/3

[44] (1) USCWC Rpt of Readiness for Cml Warfare as of 1 Jul 44, p. 164. (2) The Army mask was unsuitable for shipboard use because of the nature of the work performed. The canister for the Navy mask was placed behind the neck of the individual instead of at his side. This permitted ease of movement at crowded battle stations. One third of the masks used by the Navy needed diaphragms or other means of voice transmission. USCWC 97, 1 Mar 44, Min of Mtg Subcom on Protective Equipment 16 Feb 44.

[45] USCWC 113, 4 May 44, Min of Mtg 28 Apr 44.

[46] (1) Ltr Rpt, Jt Cml Spray Proj Subcom to Chmn USCWC, 27 Jan 45, sub: Rpt. Incl 3, Summary of Activities and Procedures, Sec III, p. 1. Hereafter cited as Jt Spray Proj Rpt. (2) See Note 31 (2) above.

[47] Memo, Chmn USCWC for Gen Waitt et al., 28 Mar 44, incl to USCWC 111, 25 Apr 44.

Navy requesting that the AAF set up a high-priority project to study formation spray attacks and that the Navy furnish the planes.[48] The AAF referred the question to the AAF Board which set up a first-priority board project. The first Navy test began at Dugway Proving Ground, Utah, on 29 June 1944, and the AAF tests started 10 July. The Navy theory of spraying was that it should be done at medium altitude (650–3,000 feet), while the AAF held that spray attacks should be executed either at tree-top level or above 10,000 feet. After the tests at Dugway the subcommittee agreed with Army Air Forces views that low level attacks were both safer and more effective.[49]

Interchangeability and Standardization of Matériel

Interchangeability and standardization of matériel offered great opportunities for logistic savings. During World War II the USCWC members learned that these goals were difficult to achieve in wartime without long experience in peacetime. Nonetheless, in World War II the United States and British Commonwealth of Nations made some progress in these fields. As the major portion of the Anglo-American gas effort would be from the air, the USCWC sought to interchange or standardize bombs, clusters, and spray tanks for use on U.S. or British aircraft.[50] The USCWC and the ISCCW agreed that in developing new items and in revising existing matériel, interchangeability should be sought if at all practicable. On 12 January 1943 the USCWC began discussions with the British Air Commission in Washington during which existing aircraft and munitions were analyzed and the most practical areas for standardization or interchangeability considered.[51] Similar work started in March on smoke agents and munitions.

The triple suspension bomb shackle made air chemical bombs generally interchangeable between British and American aircraft. But efforts to inter-

[48] Ltr, Chmn USCWC to CG AAF and CNO, 4 May 44, cited in Jt Spray Proj Rpt, Sec III, p. 5.

[49] *Ibid.*, Sec I, p. 1.

[50] Over a year before Pearl Harbor a CWS officer was serving on a standardization committee of the Army-Navy-British Purchasing Commission Joint Committee. See 1st Ind, 30 Nov 40, on Ltr, Recorder, Army-Navy-British Purchasing Comm Jt Com to C CWS, 27 Nov 40, sub: CWS Representative on Standardization Com of Army-Navy-British Purchasing Comm Jt Com. CWS 334.8/136–145. See also Memo, Recorder, Working Subcom in Standardization for Recorder, Jt Aircraft Com, 31 Mar 42, sub: Special Subcom for Standardization of Aircraft Bombs. Jt Aircraft Com 334.8.

[51] Memo for File, Lt Col Jacob K. Javits, Secy USCWC, 12 Jan 43, sub: Mtg British Air Comm, 11 Jan 43, on Aircraft Phases of Program. In CmlHo SOS GSCW 400.112/23.

LAYING SMOKE SCREEN *to conceal paratrooper landings near Lae, New Guinea, September 1943. Planes barely visible, extreme right, are Douglas A–20's, equipped with M10 spray tanks.*

change the British 65-pound mustard-gas bomb for use with U.S. bombers unfortunately were not successful. Rather than seek development of special bomb cases, the CWS attempted to have standard Ordnance bomb cases filled with gas and achieved notable success in the development of 500-pound and 1,000-pound nonpersistent gas bombs using the general purpose (GP) bomb case. Thanks to USCWC efforts, the British made their 500-pound phosgene bomb and their spray tanks suitable for use on American aircraft, thus bringing about a greater degree of readiness in the AAF in Great Britain during the earlier part of the war.[52] Tests arranged by the USCWC demonstrated that the U.S. M10 spray tank was satisfactory for British Typhoon aircraft. The American 100-pound bomb case, which could be filled with white phosphorus as well as mustard gas, was also interchangeable.

As the use of colored smoke for different munitions expanded, stand-

[52] See Note 45 above.

ardization of colors became increasingly desirable. In January 1944 the USCWC studied the colors then in use for signaling smokes. The committee not only co-ordinated Army, Navy, and Marine Corps requirements with those of the British but also obtained acceptance of four standard colors— red, yellow, green, and violet—plus blue for the British. Stocks of other colored smokes such as orange were gradually used up.[53]

By the time the USCWC and the British ISCCW came to consider the question of standardization of protective equipment, most items had been issued to the troops in the field. The committees decided that it would be more feasible at that late date to obtain interchangeability by training American and British troops to use each other's protective equipment than to attempt to standardize such items.[54] The USCWC, therefore, made arrangements with the British for the supply of training matériel and equipment for demonstrations and inaugurated publications to acquaint U.S. and British chemical officers with each other's matériel.[55] Although both committees considered it desirable to obtain standardization of one assault gas mask for British and American troops, their efforts to achieve these objectives were unsuccessful.

Research and Development

For purposes of general co-ordination of research and development as well as for standardization and interchangeability the USCWC and ISCCW found it desirable to exchange military characteristics and requirements for new items and revisions of existing items. The two committees also deemed it important to exchange information on the lines of research and development that would be followed.[56]

Among the outstanding accomplishments of the committees was the co-ordination of research on the effectiveness of gas warfare in the tropics. When delegations from the ISCCW visited the United States in February 1944 they exchanged papers on this topic with General Porter. Preliminary

[53](1) USCWC 81, 19 Jan 44, Min of Mtg Subcom on Gas and Smoke 11 Jan 44 (2) See reference cited in Note 24(3) above. (3) See Note 41(2) above. (4) USCWC Periodic Rpt of Readiness for Cml Warfare as of 1 Jan 45, p. 62.

[54] See Note 24(2) above.

[55](1) WD Pamphlet 3–1, 15 Jun 44, Comparison of U.S. and British Cml Warfare Offensive Equipment; WD Pamphlet 3–2, 6 Jan 44, Comparison of U.S. and British Cml Warfare Protective Equipment. These publications contained sufficient descriptive matter to enable troops in the field to requisition each other's matériel. (2) See reference cited in Note 12(4) above.

[56] See Note 31(1) above.

studies and research had indicated that gas possessed certain special advantages when used in tropical regions. The two committees eventually agreed that definite answers should be obtained on the behavior and usefulness of gas under such circumstances.[57] Representatives of the two committees, as well as of American, British, and Canadian chemical warfare agencies, and of the NDRC, concluded arrangements on 4 March 1944 for co-ordinated tests at American and British test stations.[58] The Advisory Committee on Effectiveness of Gas Warfare in the Tropics was established to co-ordinate planning and evaluate test results and was provided with a full-time Project Co-ordination Staff to do the work. The United States not only made use of test facilities on San José Island in the Gulf of Panama, but also organized and sent the Far Eastern Technical Unit to Australia to assist the British-Australian test station there and to support the Southwest Pacific Area (SWPA) in its efforts to prepare for gas warfare.[59]

The United States and Great Britain learned a great deal from these tropical experiments with gas. For instance, in 1944 it was discovered that clothing impregnated with British antivapor (AV) impregnite was toxic to the wearer when used in tropical areas and that British protective ointment was similarly irritating.[60] Co-ordinated action by the USCWC and ISCCW resulted in a requirement by Great Britain for twelve million tubes of the newly developed U.S. M5 protective ointment, and both British and Australian forces submitted requests for thousands of tons of American impregnite.[61] Since the M5 ointment was just getting into production, the USCWC set up priorities governing its issue, including initial issue to British troops in active Asiatic-Pacific tropical regions.[62]

---

[57] See reference cited in Note 24(3) above.

[58] (1) USCWC 101, 4 Mar 44, Effectiveness of Gas in Tropics. (2) USCWC 98/1, 4 Mar 44, Outline of San José Proj.

[59] (1) See below, Chapter V, for data on lease of San José Island by the Republic of Panama to U.S. Government. (2) Memo, Dir Proj Co-ord Staff (Dr. W. A. Noyes, Jr.) for Dugway Proving Ground, San José Proj, et al., 8 Mar 44, sub: Organization and Functions of the Proj Co-ord Staff. CWS 334.8. (3) Ltr, CG USASOS through CG USAFFE (MacArthur) to C CWS, 11 Aug 44, sub: Jt U.S.-Australian Cml Warfare Operational Tests. (4) For details on the organization, operation, and results of these projects and test stations, see (a) Brophy, Miles, and Cochrane, From Laboratory to Field; (b) Lincoln R. Thiesmeyer and John E. Burchard, *Combat Scientists* (Boston: Little, Brown and Company, 1947).

[60] See reference cited in Note 12(4) above.

[61] (1) USCWC 87/5, 13 Jun 44, Rpt by Subcom on Protective Equipment. (2) USCWC 110, 17 Apr 44, Note by Secy. (3) USCWC 124/5, 16 Sep 44, Allocation of M5 Ointment. (4) Incl to Memo, Chmn USCWC for CG ASF, 22 Sep 44, sub: Co-ordinated Anglo-American Cml Warfare Proc and Supply Program.

[62] USCWC 124/2, 14 Sep 44, Allocation of Production of M5 Ointment.

Preparing the Readiness Reports

At various times after Pearl Harbor the War Department sought reports of the current status of the U.S. chemical warfare effort.[63] Several months before the USCWC came into existence the Chief, CWS, had requested that all theater commanders be directed to furnish their latest operational and logistical data on chemical warfare matériel and personnel, as well as such offensive and defensive plans for gas warfare as they might have prepared.[64] Although the War Department had approved the request, no action was taken to obtain the information until after the committee raised the issue in December 1942. At the first meeting General Porter submitted a draft letter to theater commanders which the committee approved.[65] The War Department dispatched the letter and directed co-ordination with the Navy.[66]

As the theaters reported their chemical warfare status and plans to the Chemical Warfare Service, it became more and more apparent that American forces overseas were unprepared for powerful retaliation should the enemy initiate gas warfare. The USCWC used these theater plans to prepare logistical studies of gas warfare readiness and included much of the information in the USCWC semiannual reports of readiness.

Beginning in January 1943 the committee obtained information on the state of readiness of the Navy and the British. The USCWC then worked on the computation of logistical requirements for gas warfare, including the necessary reserves as well as the production capacity for key items. A full analysis was received from the British in April and the committee's first estimate appeared on 14 July.[67] Not until March 1944, however, did the USCWC publish its first full-scale report that covered the gas warfare situation as of 1 January 1944.[68]

---

[63] (1) Memo, ACofS OPD for CG SOS, 27 Apr 42, sub: Cml Warfare. OPD 441.5. (2) Memo, CofS for CG SOS, 4 Dec 42, sub: Status of Cml Warfare Preparation. (3) Memo, C Log Gp OPD for C CWS, 24 Dec 42, sub: Cml Warfare Preparedness of U.S. Army. Last two in OPD 385 CWP, sec IIA.

[64] Ltr, C CWS to ACofS OPD, 7 Sep 42, sub: Operational and Logistical Data. CWS 470.6/2754.

[65] (1) Min of Mtg of CCWC, 11 Dec 42. (2) The committee also agreed that joint and combined plans for chemical warfare should be requested for its use.

[66] Ltr, TAG to CINCSWPA *et al.,* 19 Dec 42, sub: Theater Plans for Cml Warfare. AG 381 (12–8–42) OB–S–E–M.

[67] This report was sent to Great Britain and reproduced as CCW (43) 28, 25 Aug 43, U.S. Cml Warfare Preparedness.

[68] USCWC 91/2, 15 Mar 44, Rpt of Readiness for Gas Warfare as of 1 Jan 44.

This report dealt with every phase of protection, offense, training, and intelligence. It included an estimate of enemy capabilities, mentioned the degree of protection provided American troops, gave the location of CWS units, and enumerated stockages of offensive and defensive chemical warfare items. Plans and principles for the employment of gas were discussed, and information was furnished on special projects. Thereafter the report appeared semiannually and was distributed to the Combined Chiefs of Staff and to all headquarters represented on the USCWC. The report then served as a day-to-day handbook on chemical warfare.[69]

Establishing a Logistical Basis for Gas Warfare

The Combined Chiefs of Staff in CCS 106/2 charged the USCWC with the task of establishing and maintaining initial stocks at levels which would enable gas warfare to be sustained pending expansion of production.[70] The USCWC performed much of this work in close conjunction with the Chemical Warfare Service and the War Department. An example of the many questions referred to the committee by the War Department was the important one of protective equipment supply policy. An initial issue of individual protective equipment had been provided for all U.S. troops moving overseas.[71] In September 1943 the improvement in the strategic situation led the ASF to suggest that an immediate survey be made of overseas *reserve* requirements for protective equipment with a view to reducing the amounts needed.[72] General Marshall referred the question to the USCWC for study and recommendation.

Earlier War Department policy on reserve stocks of protective clothing had been to divide the various theaters into three classes. In the first class were placed theaters where gas warfare was most likely and where U.S. forces would probably be in ground contact with the enemy when it began. The second class embraced those theaters where gas warfare might develop but where there would probably be no ground contact with the enemy. The third class comprised those theaters where gas warfare was unlikely. The planners assumed that all troops moving overseas would have minimum

---

[69] Beginning with the 1 July 1944 report, these semiannual reports of readiness covered all phases of chemical warfare including flame, smoke, and incendiaries.

[70] CCS 106/2, 14 Nov 42, with App. A.

[71] Ltr, TAG to CGs All Overseas Depts *et al.*, 10 Jun 42, sub: Cml Warfare Protective Clothing. AG 420 (23 May 42) (2), sec I.

[72] Memo, Maj Gen LeRoy Lutes, ASF, for OPD, 29 Sep 43, sub: Theater Levels for Cml Warfare Matériel. OPD 385 CWP, sec IV.

individual protective equipment and that these classes would apply only to theater reserves.[73] As planned by the Army Service Forces in 1943, those regions remote from ground and air attack, such as the Caribbean and South Atlantic, would have reserve stocks of protective equipment equal to 5 percent of the command strength. The ASF used the figure of 40 percent to calculate reserve requirements for Hawaii and the ETO. Where American soldiers were engaged in ground warfare in 1943—in North Africa, the Southwest Pacific Area, and elsewhere—a protective clothing reserve of 100 percent was authorized.[74]

The Subcommittee on Operations of the USCWC took what it considered a more realistic and detailed approach to the problem. The subcommittee felt that any regrouping of the theaters for purposes of reserve supply levels should be based on the type of operations that were planned and upon the activities and locations of specific numbers of troops within the theaters.[75] Accordingly, the USCWC recommended that the planners divide the troop strength of each theater into one or more classes of supply instead of placing the entire theater in one class. The committee reasoned that in certain theaters, such as SWPA, there were troops far to the rear— as in Australia—where enemy gas attack was improbable, whereas other troops in forward areas such as New Guinea were daily exposed to the possibility of Japanese use of gas. The USCWC suggested reserve levels of 100 percent for troops in forward areas within a theater, 50 percent for men in second class areas further to the rear, and only 5 percent for troops in the most remote areas. These levels applied to all types of protective equipment and supplies which would be used only if gas warfare started.[76] This policy the War Department directed the ASF to implement.[77]

[73] USCWC 54, 30 Oct 43, Min of Mtg 30 Oct 43.

[74] Memo, Dir Reqmts Div ASF for ACofS OPD, 6 Mar 43, sub: Cml Warfare Impregnating Program. AG 420 (23 May 43) (2), sec I. In addition, one set of protective clothing, over and above the individual T/BA authorization, was issued to troops sailing for Europe and the Southwest Pacific. In July 1943 the ETO became a first-class area because of the build-up there for the invasion of Europe.

[75](1) USCWC 57, 29 Nov 43, Min of Mtg Subcom on Opns 17 Nov 43 (2) USCWC 58, 29 Nov 43, Min of Adjourned Mtg Subcom on Opns 22 Nov 43

[76] Ltr, Chmn USCWC to CG ASF, 1 Dec 43, sub: Theater Levels for Cml Warfare Materials. OPD 385 CWP, sec IV.

[77](1) DF, Actg ACofS OPD to ACofS G–4 and CG ASF, 11 Dec 43, sub: Theater Levels for Cml Warfare Materials. OPD 385 CWP, sec IV. (2) Ltr, TAG to CINCSWPA et al., 24 Apr 44, sub: Cml Warfare Protective Clothing, Accessories, and Equipment. AG 420 (28 Mar 44) OB–S–D–SPOPP–M. This established final protective equipment requirements. (3) The USCWC also adopted a program by which the varying percentages of troops in different theaters would get two-layer protective clothing and one-and-one-half-layer protective clothing. These distinctions enabled the United States to save much manpower and matériel.

Another question which the War Department referred to the committee dealt with requirements for nonpersistent gases. The CWS had proposed the expansion of production facilities to create stockpiles of nonpersistent gas munitions which the AAF desired in 1944.[78] The USCWC suggested instead that sufficient facilities be created to sustain operational gas warfare. The desired stockpiles could be manufactured by these plants and the plants then placed in standby condition pending the outbreak of gas warfare. Such a step would, in effect, provide a broad production base that would make possible a considerable expansion in the event of gas warfare.[79] Although the War Department adopted this idea in principle, it authorized only one half of the production increase proposed by the USCWC.[80]

An important function of the USCWC was the determination of the amount of preparation that should be made for offensive gas warfare. The knotty question confronting the USCWC was the rate of military effort upon which levels of munitions supply in the theaters should be based. The Combined Chiefs of Staff had been careful to specify that any measures adopted in preparation for gas warfare should be "limited to those compatible with a balanced over-all munitions program." [81]

The USCWC undertook to make statistical studies of theater stocks of chemical munitions beginning in December 1943. From these studies the committee evolved certain fundamental principles upon which future committee recommendations were based. One principle was that in the event the Axis Powers used gas U.S. retaliation should be immediate and intensive, with airplanes flying 150 percent of their normal number of missions during the first fifteen days of gas warfare. After this initial effort, in which bomb loads would consist of 75-percent gas munitions and 25-percent high explosives, the normal number of aircraft missions would be flown with 50 percent of the bomb load consisting of gas.[82] Additional principles were that the European and Mediterranean Theaters of Operations, where the United Nations were on the strategic offensive, should have

[78] Memo, CG ASF for Chmn USCWC, 19 Jan 44, sub: Reqmts of Agents, Cml, CG, AC, and CC. SPRMP 470.6 (13 Jan 44). See also USCWC 88, 24 Jan 44, Min of Mtg Subcom on Opns 22 Jan 44.

[79] USCWC 86/2, 5 Feb 44, Rpt of Com.

[80] USCWC 86/3, 24 Apr 44, Reqmts of Agents, CG, AC, and CC.

[81] CCS 106/2, 14 Nov 42, Annex A.

[82] The 50-percent figure was gradually reduced in planning during 1944 and 1945 to 25 percent

special consideration and that a reserve of gas bombs should be created in the continental United States.[83]

In November 1943 and again in July 1944 the Army Air Forces raised the question of the adequacy of current theater stocks of chemical munitions. AAF experience in the European theater in 1944 revealed that theater gas-bomb stocks amounted to about 17 percent of one month's expenditure of the high explosive and incendiary bombs. As such a stock of gas bombs was believed to be inadequate, the AAF requested that the theater levels be reconsidered.[84] The commanding general of the Army Air Forces, General Henry H. Arnold, took up the question of theater gas stocks with his fellow members of the U.S. Joint Chiefs of Staff. He suggested that a study be made of American ability to retaliate and called attention to deficiencies in theater stocks of air chemical munitions.[85]

Instead of assigning the study to the USCWC, the Joint Chiefs handed it over to the Joint Staff Planners (JPS), who worked in close collaboration with the Joint Logistics Committee (JLC). The JPS and JLC designated members of a joint *ad hoc* subcommittee on which several members of the USCWC were called upon to serve, and the USCWC was asked to co-ordinate with the Joint Logistics Plans Committee on the study.[86] As prepared by this subcommittee, the study called for the use of gas in overwhelming quantities as a decisive weapon against the Japanese. But the study also pointed out certain deficiencies in the nonpersistent gas program and noted the need for tripling production facilities if bombing were continued over a long period. The subcommittee reduced the amount

[83](1)USCWC 121/7, 28 Aug 44, Min of Mtg 24 Aug 44. (2) See USCWC 127, 9 Dec 44, Capabilities of Implementing a Decision To Initiate Retaliatory Cml Warfare Against the Japanese. (3) During this period the committee persuaded the War Department to authorize the filling of three hundred thousand additional persistent gas bombs for storage in the United States. See Memo, Chmn USCWC for ACofS OPD, 14 Jun 44, sub: Co-ordinated Anglo-American Cml Warfare Proc and Supply Program (Cml Gas Bomb Levels), reproduced as USCWC 69/3, 15 Jun 44; and Memo, CG ASF for Chmn USCWC, 2 Aug 44, same sub.

[84](1) Memo, CG AAF for ACofS OPD, 1 Nov 43, sub: Theater Plans for Cml Warfare (Cml Gas Bomb Levels) (2) Memo, CG AAF for CofS (Attn: OPD), 12 Jul 44, sub: Theater Plans for Cml Warfare. (3) DF, OPD to CG ASF, 13 Jul 44, same sub. All in OPD 385 CWP, sec IV. (4) Initially the United States and Great Britain had agreed on a gas-bomb program at 25 percent of the total bomb program. The British later changed their basis to so many missions per month. See Memo for File, Col John C. MacArthur, 3 Apr 43, sub: General Porter's Mtg With Air Staff, Air Ministry, 2 Apr 43. CWS 314.7 USCWC File.

[85] JCS 825/1, 30 June 44, Implications of Retaliatory Cml Warfare Against the Japanese.

[86] Memo, Chmn USCWC for JLPC, 6 Jul 44, sub: Co-ordinated Anglo-American Cml Warfare Proc and Supply. Reproduced as USCWC 118/4.

of gas to be used in normal bombing missions from 50 to 30 percent of the total bomb load.[87]

Notwithstanding the subcommittee's recommendations to triple production facilities, the JLC and JPS recommended that there be no expansion of currently authorized production facilities except for certain loading plants. For planning purposes the committees proposed 1 January 1945 as a target date for readiness for retaliatory gas warfare.[88] After one more revision the Joint Chiefs approved the final version as JCS 825/4 on 16 October 1944. This study assumed that gas would be used only against Japan proper, the Ryukyus, and the Bonins and set a normal gas mission rate at 25 percent of the total tonnage.[89] Because of the time factor, the readiness date was set for 1 April 1945. In the study the planners indicated that the proposed mission rate would require the use of only about half the existing persistent gas capacity and two thirds of the nonpersistent capacity of the United States.[90]

In December 1944 the USCWC made recommendations to the General Staff on implementing these proposals. Among others, the committee suggested that theater commanders in the Pacific be notified of the proposed rate of air effort with gas, the levels of supply, and the date of readiness. The USCWC also recommended that gas bombs amounting to sixty days' supply be moved into continental U.S. reserve.[91] Three main problems confronted planners in their efforts to achieve gas warfare readiness in the Pacific. These were: (1) the movement of existing stocks to the Pacific; (2) the provision of storage facilities; and (3) the resumption of production, especially of empty bomb cases, without undue interference with the high explosive and incendiary bomb programs which were proving so successful in defeating the Axis.[92]

[87] (1) Of the gas bombs used, two thirds would be persistent and one third would be nonpersistent gases. See also JLC 144/3, 21 Sep 44, Capabilities of Implementing a Decision To Initiate Retaliatory Cml Warfare Against the Japanese. (2) For some USCWC comments, see USCWC 119/1, 10 Jul 44, Min of Mtg 6 Jul 44.

[88] JCS 825/2, 18 Aug 44, Capabilities of Implementing a Decision To Initiate Retaliatory Cml Warfare Against the Japanese. For USCWC work in connection with this study, particularly the logistical factors, see Memo, Chmn USCWC for Secy JLC, 25 Aug 44, same sub, submitted as USCWC 121/5; and USCWC 121/6, 26 Aug 44.

[89] The area restriction was due to the fact that friendly populations occupied the rest of Japanese-held areas.

[90] (1) JCS 825/4, 7 Oct 44, Capabilities of Implementing a Decision To Initiate Retaliatory Cml Warfare Against the Japanese. (2) DF, OPD to CG ASF, 17 Oct 44, sub: Capabilities of Implementing a Decision . . . (JCS 825/4). OPD 385 TS (16 Oct 44).

[91] (1) See Note 83(2) above. (2) USCWC 127/2, 15 Dec 44, Capabilities of Implementing a Decision To Initiate Retaliatory Cml Warfare Against the Japanese.

[92] USCWC 145/3, 4 Aug 45, Implementation of JCS 825 Series.

In March 1945 General of the Army George C. Marshall noted that some theater commanders had misinterpreted the provisions of JCS 825/4 as a directive for their readiness for gas warfare as of the planning date, including the forward area stockage of chemical munitions. The Chief of Staff expressed concern and suggested that a study be made, for it seemed that forward area stockage might be impracticable in view of the tight shipping situation.[93] The Joint Staff Planners studied the question and came up with their recommendations shortly after the defeat of Germany. They estimated that full readiness for swift and continuing retaliation against Japan would require the shipment of 113,500 tons of gas munitions from Europe and the United States, a possible reduction in the manufacture of incendiary bomb cases, the conversion of certain CWS and Ordnance units to handle gas munitions, and the provision of port capacity, labor, and storage facilities in forward areas of the Pacific. Because the JPS (and the Joint Intelligence Committee) considered the possibility that Japan would resort to gas as remote, they recommended that the United States produce and stockpile sufficient munitions to furnish the minimum amount needed for retaliatory gas warfare as of 1 November 1945, and that theater commanders be allowed to move these minimum levels of supply as far forward as shipping and other priorities would permit.[94]

As finally revised, the JPS-JLC report to the Joint Chiefs noted shortages of gas munitions in the Pacific. Although President Roosevelt's promise of swift retaliation required the presence of gas munitions in forward areas, the two committees could not agree on the advisability of forward area shipments and separated the question from that of production. They specified a minimum forward area stockage level in the Pacific of seventy-five days' supply, with ninety days' required in the China and India-Burma theaters. The planners also assumed that to end the war successfully with gas would require no more than three months' strategic bombing and six months of tactical bombing. They gave no directions which would require shipments to build up theater stocks nor was anything said about resuming production of toxic agents and munitions.[95] The JCS gave informal approval to the recommendations on 19 June 1945 and did not issue any

---

[93] JCS 825/5, 5 Mar 45, Theater Plans for Cml Warfare.

[94] JPS 484/5, 28 May 45, Theater Plans for Cml Warfare. The JPS felt that in view of the extremely tight shipping situation likely to last until after Operation OLYMPIC (the invasion of the island of Kyushu) the forward shipment of gas munitions should be avoided unless there was a likelihood gas would be used.

[95] JCS 825/6, 13 Jun 45, Theater Plans for Cml Warfare.

directives either authorizing theater commanders to raise stocks in forward areas or approving additional production.[96]

The Question of Initiating Gas Warfare

After the defeat of Germany, Army authorities in Washington suggested a re-examination of the existing American policy that called for the use of gas in retaliation only.[97] Several factors favored the use of gas against the Japanese. Meteorological conditions in Japan favored gas. The United States had predominant responsibility for the war in this area and was more convinced of the decisive value of gas than were the British. Finally, and probably most important, the high casualty rate suffered on Iwo Jima and on Okinawa so alarmed the War Department that it gave great emphasis to the study of every means which would shorten the war and save American lives. General Joseph W. Stilwell, then the commanding general of Army Ground Forces, suggested to the Chief of Staff the use of mobile weapons such as 4.2-inch chemical mortars, pack artillery, recoilless rifles, rockets, and self-propelled artillery, and the increased use of mechanized flame throwers and tank dozers. He also recommended that consideration be given to the use of gas in the planned invasion of Japan.[98] The director of the New Developments Division of the War Department General Staff, Brig. Gen. William A. Borden, felt that the best means of meeting the existing and anticipated conditions in the war against Japan would be by increasing effective mobile fire power including flame throwers. He further stated: "Efficient and proper employment of gas would be of great assistance." [99]

---

[96] (1) Decision of Jt CsofS on JCS 825/6, Jun 45. In JCS 825/6. (2) Memo, Dir Reqmts & Stock Contl Div ASF for Dir Plan Div, 17 Jul 45, sub: Comments on JCS 825/6. CWS 314.7 USCWC File.

[97] (1) The principal source for this section is OPD 385 TS, sec I-1945. (2) For the earlier viewpoint, see DF, CofS to C CWS, 3 Jan 44, sub: U.S. Policy Regarding Initiation of Gas Warfare. OPD 385 (27 Dec 43). This communication noted that use of gas against the Japanese at that time (1944) would give Germany an excuse to use gas in retaliation and that such employment of gas would endanger the planned invasion of the Continent as well as the civil population of the United Kingdom. In an interview after his capture, Hermann Goering stated that if the United States had resorted to chemical warfare, the Germans would have launched gas attacks on England. Intel Div Rpt 3897, CWS ETOUSA, 12 Jun 45, sub: Interrogation of Goering on Cml Warfare. CWS 319.1 ETO.

[98] Memo, CG AGF for CofS. Copy in CmlHO is Tab A to Memo, Dir NDD for CofS, 12 May 45, sub: Equipment for Use Against Japan. CWS 314.7 Cave Warfare File.

[99] Memo, Dir NDD for CofS, 12 May 45, sub: Equipment for Use Against Japan. CWS 314.7 Cave Warfare File.

A week after V-E Day, General Borden called a meeting of representatives of G–2, G–4, OPD, ASF, Ordnance, Engineers, and the CWS. The representatives discussed General Stilwell's recommendations and the possible solutions to two major problems: (1) What equipment would be best for overcoming the Japanese in their caves, pillboxes, and bunkers? and (2) How should this equipment be best employed? [100] The CWS set up a project under the Assistant Chief, CWS, for Field Operations to supervise and co-ordinate CWS activities in connection with the over-all Army project known as SPHINX.[101] As part of this program, the USCWC and the Chemical Warfare Service made extensive studies of the logistical requirements for gas warfare.[102]

Before June 1945 gas warfare studies had referred only to the question of retaliatory gas warfare. An OPD study of 4 June took up the question of the United States initiating gas warfare. While the study concluded that gas would be helpful, it pointed out that the United States would have to consider the effect on world opinion of using gas, for President Roosevelt had publicly condemned gas warfare. Furthermore, the study did not rate gas as the decisive weapon envisaged by the USCWC and the CWS.[103]

Nonetheless, on 14 June General Marshall sent to Admiral Ernest J. King another OPD study which recommended that the JCS immediately order an increased production of gas and that the principle of initiating gas warfare be informally discussed with President Harry S. Truman. If Truman should agree to a reversal of Roosevelt's policy on the use of gas, OPD suggested that Truman take up the question of altering current agreements with other United Nations members at the forthcoming Potsdam Conference. General Marshall added, that if Admiral King agreed with

[100] Min of Mtg with Gen Borden 14 May 45, dtd 15 May 45, sub: Equipment for Use Against Japan CWS 314.7 Cave Warfare File.

[101] Memo, C CWS for Dir NDD, 19 May 45, sub: Existing and Proposed Cml Weapons for Reduction of Japanese Fortifications. CWS 314.7 Cave Warfare File.

[102] (1) USCWC 127 series. (2) The final CWS report on SPHINX reached the conclusion that gas was the most promising weapon for reducing cave defenses and that the flame thrower was the most effective nongas weapon. See Memo, C CWS for Dir NDD, 9 Jul 45, sub: Final Summary Rpt on SPHINX Proj. CWS 314.7 SPHINX File.

[103] (1) Memo, Col Max S. Johnson, S&P Gp OPD, for Brig Gen George A. Lincoln, 4 Jun 45. (2) Memo, Gen Lincoln for ACofS OPD (Lt Gen John E. Hull), 9 Jun 45. Both in ABC 475 92 (25 Feb 44), sec 1–C. (3) OPD did not consult the CWS or the AAF in the preparation of this study, although these were the principal operating agencies concerned with the question. The USCWC was not consulted although supposedly an advisory body on gas warfare policy under CCS 106/2.

the proposed action, "I believe we should discuss the subject informally with General Arnold and Admiral Leahy." [104]

A copy of the OPD study reached Admiral William D. Leahy, who promptly expressed his opposition to the initiation of gas warfare. In writing to General Marshall, Admiral Leahy stated his belief that President Roosevelt's categorical statement to the press of 8 June 43 that "we shall under no circumstances resort to the use of such weapons [poisonous or noxious gases] unless they are first used by our enemies" had settled the question.[105] Nevertheless, Leahy added that he had ". . . no objection to a discussion with the President, by anyone who believes in gas warfare, of the possibility of a reversal of President Roosevelt's announced policy (8 June 1943)." He went on to express his astonishment that no adequate provision had yet been made for retaliation with gas in the Pacific.[106]

In all probability Admiral Leahy's response helped to discourage JCS consideration of the Army's proposal for initiating gas warfare. When the service chiefs went off to the Potsdam Conference in July they presumably also had in mind the thought of using a newer and more devastating weapon, even then being readied for test in the hot desert of New Mexico. After the first atomic bomb fell on Hiroshima the Pacific war rapidly came to a dramatic close.

Summary

While the United States Chemical Warfare Committee did not reach as high a position in the co-ordination of the combined Anglo-American gas warfare effort as perhaps many of its members desired, it nonetheless achieved a great deal, and probably all that was expected of it. After the usual initial controversies over mission, powers, and organization the USCWC settled down and became almost a model of co-operative effort, both with the U.S. services and with the British Inter-Service Committee

---

[104] (1) Memo, Marshall for King, 14 Jun 45, no sub. (2) Memo for Rcd, Col James K. Woolnough, S&P Gp OPD, 14 Jun 45, sub: U.S. Cml Warfare Policy. Both in OPD 385 TS, sec I–1945.

[105] Press Release, June 8, 1943. Annex to JCS 825, 18 Apr 44, Retaliatory Measures of Warfare Against Japan.

[106] Memo, Leahy for Marshall, 20 Jun 45. OPD 385 TS, sec I–1945. Leahy repeated his opposition to chemical warfare in his autobiography *I Was There* (New York: Whittlesey House, 1950), p. 440. Marshall explained that the lack of logistical preparation was due to the approach of U.S. forces within bombing range of the Japanese islands, as well as to the increased bomb loads carried by the B–29's, before which most gas warfare would have been of a tactical rather than strategic nature. See Memo, Marshall for Leahy (probably 21 Jun 45). OPD 385 TS, sec I–1945.

on Chemical Warfare. Although the committee lacked executive powers, the presence of representatives of interested organizations paved the way for the smooth passage of many USCWC recommendations through command channels.

Of all the committee's undertakings the co-ordination of supply seems to have been the most important and most successful. During World War II the most critical factor affecting both the British and American military effort was ship tonnage. Both the United States and Great Britain were committed to campaigns at the end of supply lines stretching across thousands of miles of ocean. While the decisive battle was to be fought only a scant few miles from England, much of the raw materials for the British war effort and all the finished American materiel had to be brought across the sea and in spite of intense German submarine activity. Every ton saved and every instance of crosshauling eliminated brought the day of ultimate victory that much closer. In the case of gas warfare matériel, an "insurance" item, it was even more important that its supply did not interfere more than absolutely necessary with that of items in every day use.

Two factors restricted the co-ordination of supply: one was the fact that there was a limit to the amount of matériel that Great Britain could provide for American troops in Europe and the Mediterranean; the other was the lack of standardization and interchangeability of items of British and American matériel. The USCWC manfully undertook to effect such standardization and interchangeability, but the lesson learned was that once war has started it is too late for any significant success in these fields. A number of items, especially aircraft munitions, were made interchangeable. In the field of protective equipment and clothing, interchangeability was obtained by training because so many of the items had already been standardized by each nation and issued to the troops in the field. But only over a considerable number of peacetime years did it appear possible to achieve any notable degree of standardization of the military items of two or more countries.

One of the steps which the USCWC and the British ISCCW took toward interchangeability and standardization was the interchange of information on the research and development programs of both nations and with Canada. Not only did this eliminate some duplication of effort, but it enabled the scientists to design items so that they could be used equally well by troops of any of these nations. The process of research and development is such a slow one, however, that significant results are hardly obtainable in the space of three or four years.

On a broader scale the USCWC prepared information for the use of U.S. and British agencies in the form of reports of readiness for gas warfare. These reports provided periodic information on intelligence, production, training, research, supply, and many other items of interest.

The USCWC participated in the planning for a logistical basis for chemical warfare, but in this instance the higher planning bodies in the Joint Chiefs of Staff committee system took over so much of the work that the role of the USCWC was pretty much limited to that of providing statistical calculations and recommendations for preparedness.

When the question of initiating gas warfare came under discussion in mid-1945 it is not too surprising that the committee, primarily established for procurement and supply co-ordination rather than for advice on policy, was not consulted. It is surprising that neither the Army Air Forces, as the principal arm for using gas, nor the Chemical Warfare Service, with the technical know-how was consulted. The reason for this is not clear, but it was possibly due to a desire to keep the circle of people debating the issue as small as possible, so that the pressure of public opinion for or against the use of gas might not be stirred by some incautious hint that the United States was considering its employment.

The operation of the committee does not appear to have differed materially from that of the various JCS committees. Toward the end of the war the lack of a secretariat and the strain on the facilities of the Office of the Chief of Chemical Warfare Service impelled the USCWC to seek additional administrative assistance.

Bonds between the USCWC and the Chemical Warfare Service were very close. On almost all subcommittees there was a plurality of CWS officers. The chairman and his principal assistant were the Chief, CWS, and his Assistant Chief for Field Operations. The various secretaries were CWS officers, and the Office of the Chief, CWS, provided the clerical assistance and most of the statistical and technical information on chemical warfare. It would appear that, although other organizations and nations had representation on the USCWC, the Chemical Warfare Service exerted the greatest amount of influence on decisions arrived at by the committee.

CHAPTER V

The Chief's Office
During World War II

General Porter remained Chief of the Chemical Warfare Service throughout the war and into the period of demobilization, retiring from active duty on 13 November 1945. His personality had a profound influence on the development of the CWS mission, and in a very definite sense the success of that mission was the measure of General Porter's accomplishment.

Porter was graduated from the U.S. Naval Academy in 1909 and commissioned in the Coast Artillery Corps the following year. In 1921 he transferred as major to the Chemical Warfare Service, where he served until his retirement from the Army. Although he lacked experience as a chemical officer in World War I, his peacetime assignments gave him an excellent background for his duties as Chief. After his graduation with distinction from the Command and General Staff School in 1927, he attended both the Army Industrial College and the Army War College.

Porter was an affable and diplomatic officer who lived on easy terms with most of his subordinates. He had the capacity for quickly sizing up a complicated problem and reaching a satisfactory solution with apparently little effort. He found time to listen to persons who wanted to catch his ear and he encouraged subordinates who were at considerable distances from headquarters to write him informal letters. A kindly reception of an earnest presentation of an idea, however, did not necessarily mean that Porter was convinced of its worth, although the person offering it might have thought so at the time. One of Porter's chief assets was his ability to conciliate members of his staff whenever they clashed over matters of policy or for other reasons. If, as sometimes happened, the conciliatory approach failed, he did not hesitate to take more drastic action. Another asset was his unusual ability to encourage his subordinates to put forth their best efforts. By not setting up impossible standards of performance, and by offering criticism in a kindly and courteous manner, he spurred on

most of his staff to put forth their best efforts. Occasionally personal pre-
dilections led Porter to overlook the shortcomings of some of his associates,
a trait not unrelated to his congeniality and his desire to accommodate. But
instances of either harshness or favoritism were rare, and generally speaking, Porter's personality inspired genuine respect and loyalty throughout
the service.[1]

Porter was able to attract to the CWS a number of eminent civilians
who, as emergency officers, naturally contributed to the success of his
administration, both in Washington and in the field installations.[2] He
either knew or quickly came to know the senior Reserve and emergency
officers on whom he had to rely so largely during the war. His intimate
acquaintance with the small group of Regular Army CWS officers aided
him in making assignments to key positions.

During the prewar years and on into the first few months of the war
the Chief, CWS, was under the direct jurisdiction of the Chief of Staff.
There was constant consultation between the General Staff and the CWS
staff over matters of policy. In March 1942, under a major War Department
reorganization, another echelon of command was placed between the supply
arms and services and the General Staff.[3] That echelon, commanded by
General Somervell, was the Services of Supply, or as it was later called,
the Army Service Forces. (*Chart 4*) From that time until after the close
of the war, policy matters were usually formulated after consultation
between ASF staff officers and their opposite numbers in the CWS. At
times War Department General and Special Staff officers had direct contact
with CWS personnel, as in the case of the United States Chemical Warfare
Committee, but such contact was the exception rather than the rule.[4]

General Porter himself had direct and intimate contact on matters of
policy affecting chemical warfare with the Combined and Joint Chiefs

---

[1] This estimate is based on the author's own observations and on interviews with numerous
officers and key civilians in the CWS during and after World War II.

[2] When war was declared the Washington headquarters was at 23d and C Streets, N. W., with
additional space in the Munitions Building. In 1942 a move was made from 23d and C Streets to
building Tempo F across the street. In January 1943 more adequate quarters were secured in AAF
Annex 1 at Gravelly Point, Virginia, and the entire office was moved there.

[3] For details on this reorganization see: (1) Ray S. Cline, *Washington Command Post: The
Operations Division,* UNITED STATES ARMY IN WORLD WAR II (Washington: 1951),
pp. 70–74, 90–93. (2) Frederick S. Haydon, "War Department Reorganization, August 1941–
March 1942," *Military Affairs,* XVI (1952), 12–29, 97–114. (3) John D. Millett, *The Organiza-
tion and Role of the Army Service Forces,* UNITED STATES ARMY IN WORLD WAR II
(Washington: 1954), Ch. II.

[4] Among War Department elements with which CWS had direct and formal contact were the
Operations Division and the War Department Manpower Board.

CHART 4—ORGANIZATION OF THE ARMY SERVICE FORCES,
AS OF 30 JUNE 1943

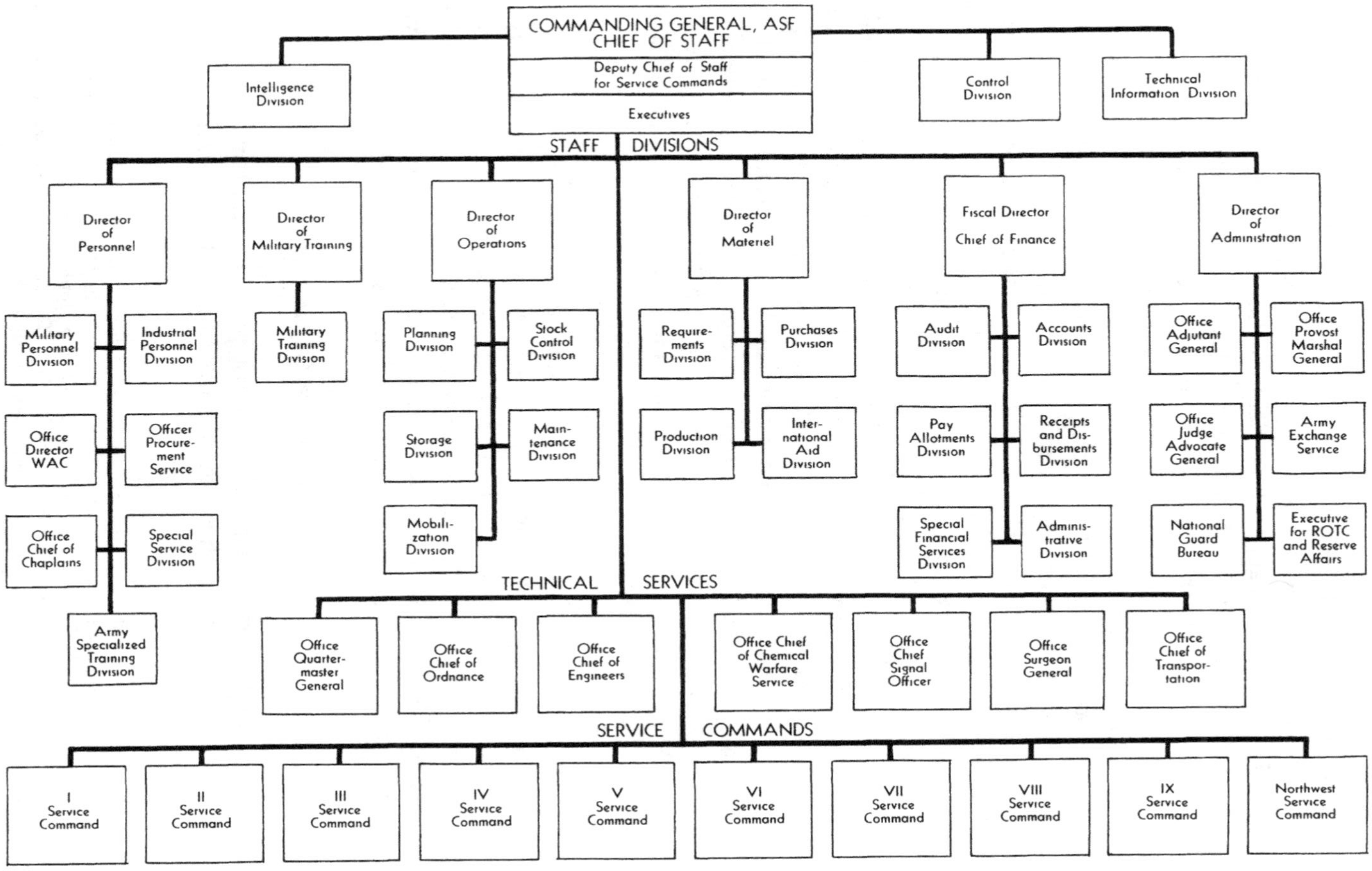

COMMANDING GENERAL, ASF
CHIEF OF STAFF
Deputy Chief of Staff for Service Commands
Executives

STAFF DIVISIONS

Intelligence Division

Control Division

Technical Information Division

Director of Personnel
- Industrial Personnel Division
  - Military Personnel Division
- Officer Procurement Service
  - Office Director WAC
- Special Service Division
  - Office Chief of Chaplains
- Army Specialized Training Division

Director of Military Training
- Military Training Division

Director of Operations
- Planning Division
- Stock Control Division
- Storage Division
- Maintenance Division
- Mobilization Division

Director of Materiel
- Requirements Division
- Purchases Division
- Production Division
- International Aid Division

Fiscal Director Chief of Finance
- Audit Division
- Accounts Division
- Pay Allotments Division
- Receipts and Disbursements Division
- Special Financial Services Division
- Administrative Division

Director of Administration
- Office Adjutant General
- Office Provost Marshal General
- Office Judge Advocate General
- Army Exchange Service
- National Guard Bureau
- Executive for ROTC and Reserve Affairs

TECHNICAL SERVICES

Office Quartermaster General

Office Chief of Ordnance

Office Chief of Engineers

Office Chief of Chemical Warfare Service

Office Chief Signal Officer

Office Surgeon General

Office Chief of Transportation

SERVICE COMMANDS

I Service Command
II Service Command
III Service Command
IV Service Command
V Service Command
VI Service Command
VII Service Command
VIII Service Command
IX Service Command
Northwest Service Command

381-812 O - 70 - 8

of Staff, with the General and Special Staffs, and with the commanding generals of the AAF and AGF. Officially he had to channel his communications through ASF headquarters. Seldom did this cause Porter any undue concern, for he had great respect for General Somervell's leadership in the supply field. Moreover, he realized the good work the ASF was doing on such matters as production controls, manpower utilization, and uniformity of administrative procedures. He felt that the ASF had a proper role in co-ordinating and directing the efforts of the chiefs of technical services, and he supported every move in that direction.[5] On the other hand, General Porter, like the chiefs of other technical services, opposed every effort by the Commanding General, ASF, or his staff to undercut the prerogatives of those statutory branches of the War Department.[6]

Porter did much of his business through personal contacts, characterized by absence of formality. He held frequent staff conferences with his principal assistants, a procedure which enabled him to keep informed of progress being made in his various fields of responsibility and to initiate action in line with ASF policies. These policies Porter became acquainted with at General Somervell's monthly staff conferences of technical services chiefs, as well as through communications from ASF headquarters. Unless absent from Washington, Porter always attended the ASF monthly staff conferences, accompanied by either Col. Harry A. Kuhn or Lt. Col. Philip J. Fitzgerald of his staff. After the OC CWS moved to Gravelly Point in January 1943, the Chief had a "situation room" set up, where charts and panels portraying CWS progress or lack of progress were displayed and discussed with members of his staff. In the situation room the shortcomings and deficiencies of the CWS were reviewed and analyzed. Through frequent visits to CWS field installations and overseas theaters, Porter was also enabled to gauge the strength and weaknesses of his service.

Early Wartime Organization

General Somervell felt that the most pressing problems facing the ASF before mid-1943 were those of organization and mobilization.[7] Two days

---

[5] Until April 1942 the term "supply arms and services" was used, when the ASF changed the designation to "supply services" (SOS GO 4, 9 Apr 42). In May 1943 the designation was again changed, this time to "technical services," and this term applied during and after the war.

[6] In 1943 Somervell presented a plan to the War Department which would have eliminated the technical services. Millett, *Army Service Forces.* Chapter XXIV.

[7] ASF Conf of CGs, Serv Comds, 22–24 Jul 43, p. 2.

after the ASF came into being Somervell issued an initial directive for the new organization which provided for the inclusion of a Control Division in his headquarters.[8] The mission of this division was to keep the commanding general, his staff, and his key assistants constantly advised on the status of the Army supply systems and other aspects of his work. The Control Division was to accomplish its mission through such measures as inspection aimed at determining the causes of delays and deficiencies, through analysis and evaluation of recurring reports and statistics, and through investigations of organizational procedures. On 27 March 1942, Somervell directed that units similar in character to the Control Division in his office be activated in all administrative elements under his command and that they be manned by competent personnel. He gave as the reason for establishing such units the fact that officers responsible for operations were usually so occupied with current assignments that they did not have the opportunity to survey the structure and procedures of their organizations as a whole. Thus, he went on to say, deficiencies were not detected and corrective action initiated at an early date.[9] The new control divisions in the technical services were to play a major role in all matters of an organizational and administrative nature.

In compliance with the directive of the Commanding General, ASF, a Control Division was established in the OC CWS on 11 April 1942.[10] Shortly thereafter the Chief, CWS, directed that the new division investigate and report on "the adequacy and correctness" of the organization of the CWS, with special reference to the Office of the Chief.[11] The CWS made every effort to carry out General Somervell's directive to secure competent individuals in staffing the Control Division. Col. Lowell A. Elliott became first chief of the division. Upon his departure for Europe in May 1942, Colonel Kuhn, commanding officer of the New York Chemical Warfare Procurement District, was made chief and served in this capacity for the duration of the war. Colonel Kuhn, who was to remain one of General Porter's closest advisers throughout the war, had been a CWS officer since World War I and had a broad background in the technical, training, and procurement activities of the service. To assist Kuhn, Porter brought in Reserve and emergency officers with outstanding experience in the business

---

[8] A copy of this directive is in Organizational Problems of the Army Service Forces, 1942–1945, I, 7–14, a five-volume manuscript compiled by the Historical Branch, ASF. In OCMH.

[9] Memo, Gen Somervell for All Staff Divs et al., 27 Mar 42, sub: Contl. oo 020/29.

[10] OC CWS Off O 17, 11 Apr 42.

[11] Leo P. Brophy, Organizational Development, Pt. 1 of Administration and Personnel Management, Vol II of History of the Chemical Warfare Service (1 Jul 40–15 Aug 45), p. 25.

world, as well as civilian employees with considerable training in business administration. It was particularly important that the Control Division engage only individuals of mature judgment, because of the nature of its functions. It was unfortunate that the name "Control" was applied to the division, for this designation did not stimulate ready acceptance by other elements of the Chemical Warfare Service on whose adequacy the Control Division had to report and with whom it had to work. In spite of its name, the Control Division was purely a staff and not a command unit, and its effectiveness depended chiefly on soundness of objectives and methods as well as on maintaining amicable relationships with the elements of the CWS and higher echelons. The division's effectiveness, as well as its methods of operation, developed gradually as the war went on.

The directive which provided for the organization of the OC CWS at the outbreak of the war had outlined an over-all organizational structure but left details to be worked out as time went on.[12] (See Chart 3.) Early in 1942 attempts were made to define more exactly the respective roles of the three services, Field, Technical, and Industrial, with regard to certain phases of the CWS mission.[13] After the activation of the Control Division in the Chief's office in April 1942, the OC CWS put forth more pronounced efforts to define the functions of each of its administrative elements and to fit each element into its proper niche in the over-all organization.[14] Sometimes the functions had been but recently delegated to the CWS, as in the case of the requirement for accumulating and correlating data on biological warfare, which was assigned orally in late 1941, and the price adjustment function, delegated in mid-1942. The administration of activities connected with biological warfare was placed in a Biological Division in the Technical Service, where it remained until mid-1943. Supervision of price adjustment activities was lodged with the Legal Division, because of the close association between price adjustment and legal functions such as drawing up and terminating contracts.

Some of the functions under consideration had been assigned originally to a separate administrative unit, but experience had indicated that such assignment was no longer practicable. This was the situation, for example, with the Incendiary Branch which had been set up when the incendiary program was turned over to the CWS in 1941. This branch co-ordinated all

---

[12] OC CWS Off O 12, 15 Jul 41.

[13] (1) OC CWS Off O 6, 14 Feb 42, and OC CWS Off O 11, 4 Mar 42. (2) See Chart 3 for organizational features of the Field, Technical, and Industrial Services.

[14] Memo, Ind Div OC CWS to Contl Br OC CWS, 30 Oct 42, sub: Overlapping and Duplication of Functions. CWS 310.

matters pertaining to incendiaries including their design and development, procurement, storage, and issue. It maintained contact with the Technical Service of the Chief's office on design and development, with the Industrial Service on the construction, procurement, and inspection facilities to manufacture the bomb, and with the Field Service on matters pertaining to the storage and issue of incendiaries to troops in the field. By June 1942 the incendiary program had been carried to the point where the functions associated with it could be assumed by the Technical, Industrial, and Field Services, and the branch was therefore eliminated.[15]

In still another instance, investigation revealed that closely allied or identical functions were being performed by various units of the OC CWS. The administration of legal activities was a case in point. Following the 15 July 1941 reorganization, three separate units of the Office of the Chief performed legal functions, namely, the Purchase and Contracts Division of the Industrial Service, the Patent Division of the Technical Service, and the Legal Division of the Executive Office. By early 1942, the OC CWS reached the conclusion that this setup was not making for the greatest efficiency. Furthermore, in May the ASF sent a directive urging the coordination of legal activities. The chief of the Control Division brought the matter to the attention of General Porter, pointing out that Control Division studies had demonstrated that the dispersion of legal functions among three administrative units was cumbersome and expensive. On 24 June 1942, therefore, all functions of a legal nature were placed under the jurisdiction of the Legal Division, OC CWS.[16]

Organizational developments, especially in the early period of the war, were affected to some extent by the military personnel situation. A number of Reserve officers in grades from first lieutenant to lieutenant colonel were being called to active duty, and in placing these officers the Army had to give consideration to rank as well as ability. The result was that it was often necessary to create organizational units to accommodate the rank of the officers. Organizational changes for this reason were continuously taking place in the early years of the war, particularly in the lower echelons.[17]

[15] OC CWS Off O 28, 2 Jun 42.

[16] (1) IOM, Contl Div OC CWS for C CWS, 30 May 42, sub: Co-ordination of Legal Work. CWS 101/12–13. (2) OC CWS Off O 32, 24 Jun 42.

[17] Reference will be made here to only the most significant over-all organizational developments in World War II. For details on minor organizational changes see Leo P. Brophy, History of the Chemical Warfare Service in World War II, Administration and Personnel Management. MS. OCMH.

Decentralization of Operations

A policy which had a marked effect on CWS organizational developments, both in the Chief's office and in the installations, was the ASF encouragement of decentralization of operations. The theory behind this policy was given expression by the chief of the Statistical Control Service in General Somervell's office; in discussing the functions of the recently activated control units, he said that one of the prime purposes of control was "to effect maximum decentralization of operation while maintaining centralization for co-ordination of broad policies and objectives." [18]

In conformity with this policy the Chemical Warfare Service gave considerable attention during the autumn of 1942 to the possibility of transferring elements of the Office of the Chief out of Washington. General Porter and his staff were reluctant to take this step for they realized it would make for administrative inefficiency. They had little choice in the matter, however. For a time they considered the possibility of moving all elements of the Chief's office to Edgewood but eventually gave up this idea as impractical.[19] General Porter and his assistants finally decided that certain units of the Industrial and Technical Divisions could be decentralized with the least loss of efficiency and in October 1942 made provision to move these to Edgewood. About the same time a newly activated Chemical Section of the Industrial Division, OC CWS, whose mission was to supervise the purchase of all chemicals for the CWS, was located in New York City. In 1943 a suboffice of the Chief was established at Baltimore, Maryland, with the following branches stationed there: Historical Branch of the Executive Office; Purchase Policies Branch of the Administrative Office of the Assistant Chief, CWS, for Matériel; Storage Branch of the Supply Division; and a branch of the Field Requirements Division.[20] This decentralization, which lasted throughout the remainder of the war, resulted in a need for additional personnel and in some loss in administrative efficiency.

Organizational Defects

The designation "service," applied to three major administrative units

---

[18] Brophy, Organizational Development, p. 28.

[19] (1) Interv, CmlHO with Maj Gen William N. Porter, USA (Ret.) 29 Apr 50. (2) Interv, CmlHO with Col Harry A. Kuhn, USA (Ret.) 16 Mar 50.

[20] (1) Memo, C Contl Br OC CWS for C CWS, 12 Oct 42, sub: Decentralization of OC CWS. (2) Memo, C Ind Div OC CWS for C CWS, 21 Oct 42, sub: Reorganization of Ind Div. (3) Memo, C Tech Div OC CWS for C CWS, 19 Oct 42, sub: Reorganization of Tech Div. All in CWS 310.1. (4) OC CWS Adm O 15, 11 Aug 43.

of OC CWS in July 1941, did not prove satisfactory. The term "service" implied command rather than staff functions; just as the Chief of the Chemical Warfare Service had command over the entire organization, so the chiefs of the smaller "services" under him assumed that they had command responsibility over their respective units. In certain matters the chiefs of the Industrial, the Technical, and the Field Services did have command responsibility. This was especially true with regard to installations, since each service was responsible for the conduct of activities at certain types of installations. The chief of the Industrial Service had jurisdiction over the arsenal and procurement districts, the chief of the Technical Service over the research laboratories and proving grounds, and the chief of the Field Service over the depots and training centers.[21] As a result of a suggestion from the Control Division, ASF, the three services of the OC CWS were renamed "divisions" on 28 July 1942.[22] The new divisions were intended to be "staff" organizations, although for some time they were allowed to retain a considerable degree of jurisdiction over installations. In order to standardize terms, the OC CWS also directed that organizations below division level be designated branches, sections, and subsections.[23] The desire of the Chief of the CWS to confine the activities of the new division chiefs mainly to staff activities was not entirely realized, and this was one of the factors which led to a major reorganization of the Chief's office in the spring of 1943.

Another and more important factor centered around serious personality differences among a few staff members in the Chief's office. Because procurement was an extremely important function in the early period of war, the chief of the procurement unit was called upon to take vigorous measures in order to get the job done. This pressure at times led to a tendency on the part of the unit to dominate other elements of OC CWS, with the result that personality clashes occurred among key officers. Perhaps because the Chemical Warfare Service was a relatively small organization where everybody in management knew almost everybody else, personal antagonisms were apt to be more pronounced than elsewhere. At any rate the situation as it existed in early 1943 was intolerable and needed correction. Something more than a shift of certain key officers was required, for there were also shortcomings in the over-all organizational pattern which de-

[21] (1) OC CWS Organizational Charts, 1 May 42. (2) IOM, C Contl Br OC CWS for C CWS, 30 Jul 42, sub: Installations CWS 31.
[22] Interv, CmlHO with Lt Col S J. Levitan, 17 Oct 55.
[23] OC CWS Off O 40, 29 Jul 42.

manded attention. These shortcomings in certain instances were not un-related to the strained personal relationships existing between key individuals.[24]

For example, there was a lack of co-operation on important operational matters between the Industrial and Technical Divisions. This difficulty dated back at least to 1941 when representatives of those units discussed some of the unsatisfactory conditions at a meeting. It was then disclosed that the Industrial Service had made contract awards in certain cases without first obtaining clearance on drawings and specifications, and that the Technical Service had not informed the Industrial Service when changes in drawings and specifications were contemplated but only after they were completed and approved.[25] The root of this whole problem was the unsatis-factory state of drawings and specifications at that time—unsatisfactory, that is, from the point of view of mass production of the item. Contractors working on items could not use the existing specifications and drawings and had to seek modifications through waivers and changes approved by the CWS. A large number of such waivers and changes were issued resulting in complete lack of uniformity in the same part produced by different manufacturers. Efforts were made during 1942 to co-ordinate the operations of the industrial and technical agencies by assigning to the deputy chief of the Industrial Division and the chief of the Technical Division the deter-mination of policy on such activities as continuance of research on a project, drawing up of preliminary and final drawings and specifications for equip-ment, and issuance of waivers for changes of such drawings and specifica-tions.[26] This innovation did not prove entirely successful, and as late as the spring of 1943 a number of unsatisfactory procedures had still not been corrected. The result was that items of inferior quality were being pro-cured.[27] Some action to insure that CWS items would measure up to specifications became vitally important.

General Porter found abundant proof that CWS matériel did not meet the standards required in the field, when he and Brig. Gen. Charles E. Loucks of his staff visited Europe in 1943. In England and North Africa

[24] This material is based on interviews with a number of key officers and civilians who were on duty in the Chief's office in World War II.

[25] IOM, C Proc Plng Div for C Ind Serv, 17 Nov 41, sub: Conf in Connection with Current Proc. CWS 337.

[26] Memo, C CWS for Chiefs Ind and Tech Divs, 25 Aug 42, sub: Co-ord of Ind and Tech Divs. CWS 334.2/282.

[27] (1) Interv, CmlHO with Col Charles E. Loucks (formerly CG RMA and C Ind Div OC CWS), 3 May 49. (2) Porter Interv, 16 Jul 49. (3) Interv, CmlHO with Col Harry A. Kuhn, USA (Ret.), 23 Jan 49.

the two generals saw some of the inferior items which had been sent out from the zone of interior, and the Chief returned to the United States determined to take drastic action with regard to uniformity of specifications and inspection of items. One of the first things he did was to direct the activation of an Inspection Division entirely independent of the Industrial Division. This change became part of a general reorganization of Porter's office which was made effective in May 1943.

Developments, May 1943–October 1945

Since its inception, the Control Division, OC CWS, had been conducting a survey aimed at improving organization.[28] On the basis of its findings the Control Division drew up an organizational chart and presented it to General Porter on his return from abroad in the spring of 1943. Among the objectives which the Control Division listed for the new organization were: reducing the number of persons reporting directly to the Chief; reducing the emphasis placed on the procurement function by striking a balance between that and other CWS functions; and improving the machinery for calculating CWS requirements. Porter studied the chart and submitted it to members of his staff for comment. It was the consensus that the proposed organization would be a definite improvement and General Porter then took the matter up with Maj. Gen. Wilhelm D. Styer, Chief of Staff, ASF, who gave his informal approval.[29] Porter thereupon issued a directive on 27 May 1943 which activated the new organization. (Chart 5) [30]

Under this setup there were to be two assistant chiefs, CWS, one for matériel and one for field operations. The Assistant Chief of CWS for Matériel was to "supervise and co-ordinate" the functions of development, procurement, inspection, and supply. These functions were to be administered by the following divisions: Technical, Industrial, Inspection, and Supply. The Assistant Chief of CWS for Field Operations was to "supervise and co-ordinate the preparation of plans for the utilization of chemical warfare matériel and troops." Under his jurisdiction were three divisions, Field Requirements, Training, and War Plans and Theaters. Other divisions, along with the executive branches, were directly under the supervision of

[28] Memo, C Contl Div OC CWS for C CWS, sub: Activities of Contl Div for the Period 15 Nov 42 to 31 Dec 43.
[29] (1) Porter interv, 16 Jul 49. (2) Memo, C CWS for CG ASF (Attn: Dir Mil Pers), 12 May 43, sub: Transfer of General Officer. CWS 210.3.
[30] OC CWS Off O 39, 27 May 43.

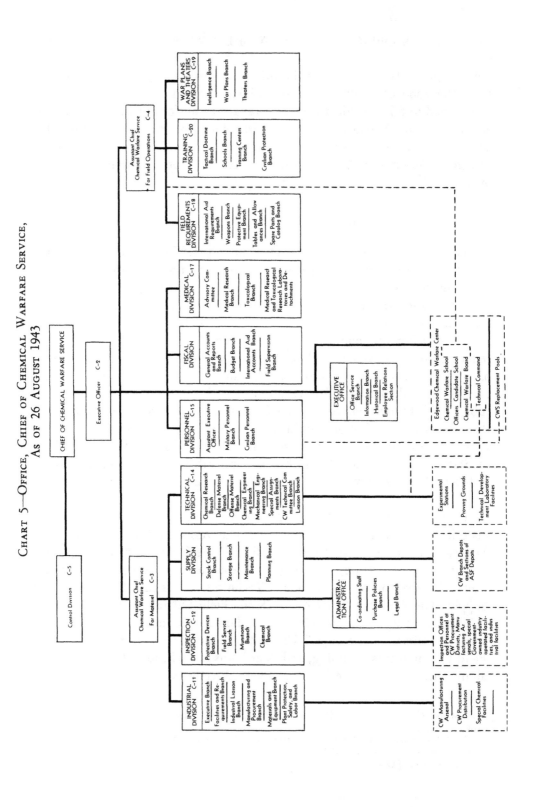

CHART 5—OFFICE, CHIEF OF CHEMICAL WARFARE SERVICE,
AS OF 26 AUGUST 1943

BRIG. GEN. ROLLO C. DITTO, CWS, *Assistant Chief of Matériel.*

BRIG. GEN. ALDEN H. WAITT, CWS, *Assistant Chief for Field Operations.*

the Chief, CWS. Brig. Gen. Rollo C. Ditto was appointed Assistant Chief of Matériel and General Waitt, Assistant Chief for Field Operations. Each continued in his respective post until the close of the war. In August 1943 General Ditto's tables of distribution called for 110 officers and 286 civilians and General Waitt's for 54 officers and 62 civilians. The total allotment of officers and civilians in OC CWS at that time was 215 and 585 respectively.[31] This large number is in great contrast to the small force that had manned the office in the peacetime years.

The 27 May 1943 reorganization of the Office of the Chief restricted command functions to the Chief himself and in a limited degree to the assistant chiefs. In their relations with General Porter the assistant chiefs were staff officers, but in regard to the divisions and installation under their jurisdictions they exercised command. For that reason their offices were generally referred to informally as "Matériel Command" and "Operations Command," instead of the Office of the Assistant Chief for Matériel and the Office of the Assistant Chief for Field Operations. Besides, the formal designations were much too long for day-to-day usage.

The new setup did a great deal to improve relationships among the

[31] OC CWS Off O 55, 5 Aug 43.

various elements of OC CWS. Better co-operation was attained between the Industrial and Technical Divisions. The Assistant Chief of CWS for Matériel now had jurisdiction over both divisions and he could act as arbiter in the event of differences over policy. The way was open, moreover, for making additional organizational changes aimed at better interdivision co-operation. The best example of this development was the activation of the Industrial Liaison Branch in the Industrial Division in August 1943.[32] This unit acted for the chief of the Industrial Division in all matters requiring concurrence by the chief of the Technical Division, such as the compilation of drawings and specifications and the clearing of requests for changes and waivers. Again, better co-ordination was attained between the industrial and the supply units in OC CWS because the Assistant Chief for Matériel could act as an arbiter whenever differences over policy or procedure arose between these divisions.

Better co-ordination of related activities was likewise attained under the Assistant Chief, CWS, for Field Operations. The close association of war plans and training had long been recognized, and for that reason General Waitt was given jurisdiction over both activities. A significant innovation was the incorporation of the intelligence function into Waitt's organization. Previously this unit had reported directly to the executive officer of OC CWS. The co-ordination of war plans, training, and intelligence under one jurisdiction in OC CWS was to prove very effective throughout the remainder of the war period.

Functions of the New Medical Division

For a decade and a half following World War I there had been a Medical Division in OC CWS. But in 1932 General Gilchrist had eliminated this division, and thereafter CWS and the Medical Department maintained co-ordination solely through the medical research group at Edgewood Arsenal. Just prior to World War II, increased emphasis began to be placed on the medical aspects of gas warfare, and a Committee on the Treatment of Gas Casualties was set up within the National Research Council. Later, when the Office of Scientific Research and Development (OSRD) was activated, the work was also carried on by its various committees and subcommittees.[33] The chemical warfare functions of the National Research

---

[32] OC CWS Adm O 14, 7 Aug 43.

[33] Data on the Medical Division was obtained from a six-page report prepared by Medical Division for Historical Branch, OC CWS, 13 June 1945.

Council and the Office of Scientific Research and Development overlapped, and by the spring of 1943 it was evident that there was need for a staff officer in the CWS who would co-ordinate all functions having to do with the medical aspects of chemical warfare. After consultation among the Secretary of War, The Surgeon General, and the Chief, CWS, Dr. Cornelius P. Rhoads of the Memorial Hospital, New York City, a renowned medical administrator, was selected for the post.[34] Dr. Rhoads was commissioned as a colonel in the Medical Corps and served as chief of the Medical Division until 18 April 1945 when he was succeeded by Col. John R. Wood, Medical Corps, who served until the close of the war.

The Surgeon General and the Chief, CWS, reached an agreement on 30 March 1943 on the responsibilities of the proposed Medical Division under Dr. Rhoads. They decided that the new division would be responsible for the conduct of research connected with the prevention and treatment of chemical warfare casualties; for carrying out toxicological studies required by the Chief, CWS; for investigating hazards to health of CWS employees engaged in producing chemical warfare agents; and for keeping The Surgeon General informed on the results of all investigations and studies.[35] The Medical Division was activated on 3 July 1943, and all medical and toxicological research being performed at Edgewood was placed under its supervision.[36] Before the close of 1943 new CWS medical laboratories had been set up at Camp Detrick, Maryland; Dugway Proving Ground, Utah; and Camp Sibert, Alabama; and a mobile laboratory unit had been activated at Bushnell, Florida. The Medical Division co-ordinated the research work performed in these laboratories as well as at various university laboratories and maintained liaison with The Surgeon General's Office, the NDRC, and the Canadian and British agencies carrying on chemical warfare research.[37]

Administrators later found that the research work and testing being carried on by the Medical Division overlapped that carried on by the Technical Division of the OC CWS. This overlapping was particularly pronounced in projects being conducted under tropical conditions. The

[34] (1) Porter interv, 29 Apr 50. (2) Interv, CmlHO with Dr. Cornelius P. Rhoads (C Medical Div OC CWS in World War II), 25 Sep 50.

[35] Memo, Lt Col George W. Perkins, OC CWS, for Brig Gen Charles C. Hillman, SGO, 30 Mar 43, sub. Proposed Medical Div for CWS. CWS 314.7 Policy File. The proposal was initialed by General Waitt and Brig. Gen. Paul X. English for CWS and General Hillman for SGO.

[36] OC CWS Off O 48, 3 Jul 43.

[37] For details on NDRC-CWS relationships, see Brophy, Miles, and Cochrane, From Laboratory to Field; and Baxter, *Scientists Against Time,* Chapter XVIII.

situation improved greatly as a result of the work of the Advisory Committee on Effectiveness of Gas Warfare in the Tropics and its operating agency, the Project Co-ordination Staff, which were set up in March 1944 after consultation among American, British, and Canadian representatives on chemical warfare.[38]

The committee, appointed by General Porter, was made up of two civilians, Dr. Conant and Dr. Roger Adams, and representatives from the U.S. Navy, Army Air Forces, and Army Ground Forces, British Army Staff, British Commonwealth Scientific Office, the Canadian Government, and the Australian Government. To the advisory committee the Project Co-ordination Staff submitted recommendations concerning such matters as allocation of problems to various field test agencies, co-ordination and standardization of testing methods, and the interpretation of data and results obtained from field tests. The Chief, CWS, appointed a prominent civilian scientist, Dr. W. A. Noyes, Jr., to head this staff and assigned two officers with the rank of lieutenant colonel as assistants. These three were on a full-time basis. The chairman of the committee, in addition, could receive assistance from representatives of the Medical Division, the Technical Division, and the Office of the Assistant Chief, CWS, for Field Operations. Representatives from the Navy and the British and Canadian chemical warfare agencies were on the staff, which had authority to communicate directly with stations and related projects in Australia, India, England, and the United States on questions of information.[39]

In order to carry out more effectively research on chemical warfare under tropical conditions, the United States and the Republic of Panama made arrangements early in 1944 to lease San José Island to the U.S. Army. This became a CWS installation, commanded during the war by a brigadier general. In September 1944, a San José Division was activated in the Chief's office, and the commanding general of the San José Project, Brig. Gen. Egbert F. Bullene, was made chief of this division in addition to his other duties.[40]

---

[38] For details, see above, Chapter IV.

[39] (1) OC CWS Adm [no number], 28 Mar 44. (2) Memo, C CWS for Secy USCWC, 3 Apr 44, sub: Advisory Com on Effectiveness of Gas in the Tropics. CWS 314.7 Gas Warfare File. (3) Memo, Noyes, Dir Proj Co-ord Staff, for Advisory Com on Effectiveness of Gas Warfare Matériel in the Tropics, 8 May 44, sub: Preliminary Copy of Memo to Fld Testing Agencies Outlining the Organization of the Proj Co-ord Staff. CWS 314.7 Gas Warfare File. (4) Memo, C CWS for CG ASF, 12 Mar 46, sub: Anglo-American Co-operation on Cml Warfare Development.

[40] (1) OC CWS Adm O 22, 27 Sep 44. (2) For details, see below, Chapter VI.

Special Projects Division

The WBC Committee on biological warfare turned in a report to the Secretary of War in June 1942 which served as the basis for Stimson's recommending to President Roosevelt that a civilian agency be delegated to supervise all aspects of this type warfare.[41] Upon Presidential approval, the War Research Service (WRS) headed by Mr. George W. Merck was set up in the Federal Security Agency in the summer of 1942. The WRS was a small co-ordinating organization which drew on the facilities, personnel, and experience of government and private institutions, including the medical services of the Army and Navy, the Chemical Warfare Service, the U.S. Public Health Service, the Department of Agriculture, G-2 of the Army, the Office of Naval Intelligence, the Office of Strategic Services, and the Federal Bureau of Investigation.[42] After the assignment of the biological warfare mission to the CWS in the fall of 1941, it will be recalled, a Biological Division was set up in the Chief's office.[43] Later this division was redesignated the Special Assignments Branch. Its first chief was Lt. Col. James H. Defandorf, who was succeeded in March 1943 by Col. Fraser Moffat. The Special Assignments Branch was subject to the technical supervision of the WRS.

The War Research Service secured the services of outstanding scientists and administrators for full-time duty with the armed forces. Among those whose talents were made available to the CWS was Dr. Ira L. Baldwin of the University of Wisconsin. Late in 1942 Dr. Baldwin was assigned to duty with the CWS with instructions to develop a research program, secure a location for a biological warfare installation, design laboratories, and recruit a staff.[44] By this time the WRS had decided that exhaustive investigation of biological warfare agents would require research and development on a scale not heretofore attempted and that the agency best equipped to carry out those activities was the Chemical Warfare Service.

Through co-operation with the WRS, Dr. Baldwin secured the services of a formidable group of scientists and technicians. A site outside Frederick, Maryland, was selected for a biological warfare installation and construction of the future Camp Detrick was begun in the spring of 1943. This

[41] Following the submission of this report the WBC Committee disbanded.

[42] "Biological Warfare, Report to the Secretary of War by Mr. George W. Merck, Special Consultant for Biological Warfare," *The Military Surgeon,* XCVIII (1946), 237–42. This is the so-called Merck Report, which appeared in various publications but with slight variations in the contents of certain paragraphs.

[43] See above, page 48

[44] Ltr, Baldwin to CmlHO, 5 Dec 52.

was the first of four biological warfare installations built during World War II. The others were the testing grounds at Horn Island, Pascagoula, Mississippi; the Granite Park installation at Tooele, Utah; and a production plant at Terre Haute, Indiana.

In December 1943 the Office of Strategic Services reported to the Joint Chiefs of Staff that there was evidence that the German Army was preparing to employ biological warfare.[45] This report led Secretary Stimson on 13 January 1944 to transfer responsibility for all biological warfare projects from the War Research Service to the Chemical Warfare Service. At the same time the Secretary directed that the Chief, CWS, co-operate with The Surgeon General on the defensive aspects, all under the direction of the Commanding General, Army Service Forces.[46] Later President Roosevelt confirmed this division of responsibility.[47] To co-ordinate biological warfare activities in his office, Stimson appointed Mr. George Merck as special consultant to the Secretary of War on biological warfare. Stimson also set up a United States Biological Warfare Committee (USBWC) to advise Merck on policy matters and to maintain liaison with British and Canadian representatives.[48]

This action by the Secretary of War led the Chief, CWS, in January 1944 to raise the Special Assignments Branch to the status of a division. The new division, known as the Special Projects Division, was headed successively by Cols. Martin B. Chittick, J. Enrique Zanetti, and H. N. Worthley.[49] In carrying out the main responsibility for biological warfare preparations the division supervised the activities of some 3,900 persons, of whom about 2,800 were Army personnel, about 1,000 Navy, and nearly 100 civilians. The majority of these were stationed at Camp Detrick, and the remainder were divided among the headquarters of the Special Projects Division in Washington and the other BW installations. The approved organization chart for 16 September 1944 listed 9 Army officers and 8 civilians and 6 Navy officers and 7 Navy enlisted men in the headquarters

[45] This report proved inaccurate. See Research and Development in the Special Projects Division (1 Jul 40–14 Aug 45), dated 20 Sep 45. CWS 314.7 R and D File.

[46] Memo, SW for CofS, 13 Jan 44, sub: BW. Cited in Rexmond C. Cochrane, Biological Warfare Research in the United States, History of the Chemical Warfare Service (1 Jul 40–15 Aug 45) p. 28.

[47] Merck Rpt.

[48] The USBWC was composed of representatives from the following headquarters: ASF, SGO, CWS, Navy Bureau of Medicine, Navy Bureau of Ordnance, AAF, New Developments Division of WD Special Staff, G–2, and Office of Strategic Services.

[49] OC CWS Off O [no number], 18 Jan 44.

office. Included in the activities of the Special Projects Division were administration and supervision of the work of scientists under contract in the universities, research institutes, and industries. Like the War Research Service before it, the Special Projects Division maintained liaison with various government and nongovernment technical groups.

Other Developments

From early 1944 till the close of the war very few important organizational changes took place in the Office of the Chief. The most significant development had something of a psychological aspect because it concerned the interpretation of the relationship of the Chief, CWS, to the installations. In the past, as has been mentioned, the chief of the Technical Division considered himself responsible for the administration of laboratories and proving grounds, the chief of the Industrial Division for arsenals and procurement districts, and the chief of the Supply Division for the depots. These relationships were portrayed graphically on the over-all organization chart of the OC CWS. (*See Chart 5.*) During 1944 the chief of the Control Division urged the Chief, CWS, to emphasize more strongly his direct command jurisdiction over the installations, and General Porter did this by signing a new organization chart dated 11 December 1944. For the first time during the war the installations were represented graphically as being directly under the command of the Chief, CWS. To understand fully this relationship, it is necessary to examine the administration of CWS field installations in World War II.

CHAPTER VI

Field Organization of the Chemical Warfare Service

The expansion of the Chemical Warfare Service field organization which began in the emergency period of course became much more rapid once war was declared. As part of the effort to meet the demands of a nation at war and at the same time supply the United Nations with the matériel to carry on war, activities at all existing CWS installations greatly increased, and the need for new installations arose.

The Procurement Districts

Most CWS procurement in World War II was effected through contracts awarded in the procurement districts.[1] The day after the United States declared war on Japan, General Porter recommended to the Under Secretary of War that the number of CWS procurement districts be increased from five to seven. He wanted to activate two new districts with headquarters at Atlanta and Dallas in order to tap the industrial capacity of the southeastern and southwestern sections of the United States. For some years War Department plans had called for the activation of a new district with headquarters at Birmingham, but General Porter argued for Atlanta rather than Birmingham on the ground that Atlanta was a more important center for industries useful to the Chemical Warfare Service. The Chief, CWS, further recommended that if the establishment of the two new districts was approved, the Atlanta district be placed immediately on a procurement basis and Dallas on a procurement planning basis for the first several months, pending a more accurate survey of the latter's capabilities. On 17 December 1941 the Office of the Under Secretary of War approved these recommendations.[2]

---

[1] For details, see Brophy, Miles, and Cochrane, From Laboratory to Field.
[2] Ltr, C CWS to USW, 9 Dec 41, and 1st Ind, sub: Additional Cml Warfare Proc Districts CWS 322 095/53.

Late in January 1942 the Office of the Chief, CWS, sent Maj. Herbert P. Heiss to Atlanta to establish a procurement district office.[3] A month later Col. Alfred L. Rockwood was transferred from the San Francisco Procurement District to assume command of the new Atlanta office, and Major Heiss then proceeded to Dallas to open the new office there. He arrived in Dallas on 2 March, and five days later the district was activated. With the creation of the Atlanta and Dallas districts, some of the territory formerly attached to the Pittsburgh and Chicago districts was put under jurisdiction of the new districts. The Atlanta district included the following states: Florida, Alabama, Georgia, North Carolina, South Carolina, Tennessee, and Mississippi; while the Dallas district included the states of Colorado, New Mexico, Texas, Oklahoma, Arkansas, and Louisiana. (*See Map, page 112.*) Early in 1943, Headquarters, ASF, and OC CWS decided that the continuation of the Atlanta office as a separate district office was not justified and, in April 1943, it was designated a suboffice of the Dallas district.

Of the twelve officers who were in charge of procurement districts during the war, seven were Regular Army officers and five were Reserve officers or were appointed from civilian life.[4] All the Regular Army officers had training and experience in procurement planning activities before the war and several of them had attended the Harvard University School of Business Administration for two-year periods. Every one of the Reserve officers had some experience in the industrial, financial, or commercial field. Lt. Col. Robert T. Norman, commanding officer of the Atlanta district and later executive officer of the Chicago district, had been associated for fourteen years with a Washington, D. C., securities and investment house. Col. Lester W. Hurd, commanding officer of the Boston district and later of the New York district, was a well-known architectural engineer in California. Colonel Heiss of the Atlanta and later of the Dallas districts had extensive banking and industrial experience. Heiss was the only commanding officer who had come into the Army from civilian life and who had not been a member of the Reserve. Col. Clarence W. Crowell, who

[3] Ltr, C CWS to CG Fourth Corps Area, 23 Jan 42, sub: Establishment of Atlanta Cml Warfare Proc District. CWS 322.095/36–65.

[4] Commanding officers of each of the procurement districts during the wartime period were: Atlanta, Major Heiss, Colonel Rockwood, Lt. Col. Robert T. Norman; Boston, Col. Sterling E. Whitesides, Jr., Col. Lester W. Hurd; Chicago, Col. Harry R. Lebkicher; Dallas, Col. H. P. Heiss, Col. Clarence W. Crowell; New York, Colonel Kuhn, Col. Patrick F. Powers, Colonel Whitesides, Colonel Hurd (in addition to his other duties as commanding officer of the Boston Procurement District); Pittsburgh, Col. Rollo Ditto, Col. Raymond L. Abel; San Francisco, Col. James W. Lyon.

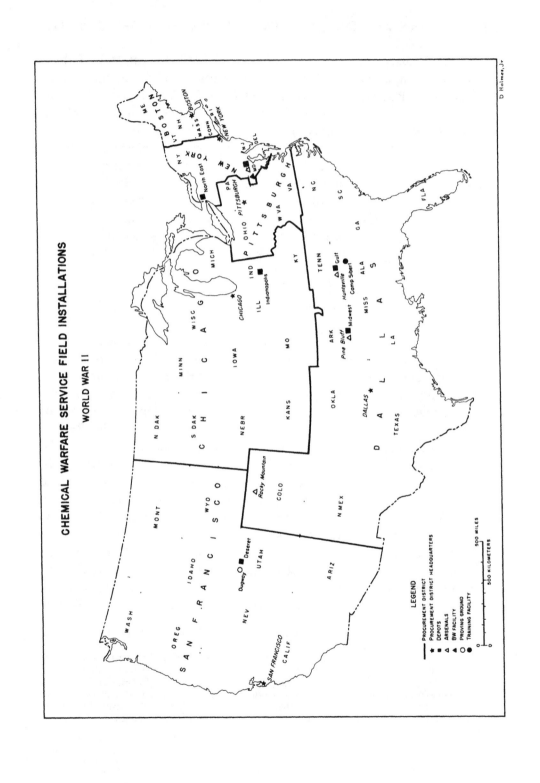

succeeded Colonel Heiss as commanding officer of the Dallas district, was vice president in charge of production at the Rochester Germicide Company, Rochester, New York. Col. Raymond L. Abel of the Pittsburgh district was a professor of chemical engineering at the University of Pittsburgh and had considerable practical experience in the field of petroleum engineering.

The United States entrance into the war brought such a vast increase in the number of contracts that the War Department decentralized authority for approval of many more contracts to the procurement districts.[5] On 13 December 1941 General Porter authorized the CWS districts to negotiate contracts up to and including $200,000.[6] On 3 January 1942 this authority was extended to contracts up to $1,000,000 and on 23 March this figure was raised to $5,000,000 at which level it remained throughout the war.[7]

The Chemical Warfare Service experienced certain difficulties in placing contracts on items other than the gas mask. Thanks to the educational order legislation, the CWS had access to the services of a number of large manufacturers experienced in gas-mask production. With other chemical warfare items the situation was somewhat different. Since the Industrial Mobilization Plan of 1939 was not put into effect, the CWS lost some well-established contractors allocated under that plan. It was necessary, therefore, to seek other potential contractors, who in many instances were small operators. While it would have been to the advantage of the government in certain cases to have had contractors with larger facilities, the small firms, generally speaking, did an outstanding job once they had converted their plants and had gained experience.[8]

Organizational Developments

The expansion of activities in the procurement districts necessitated a corresponding expansion of organization. Administrative units which formerly performed two or three functions were broken down into separate units. For example, in the Pittsburgh district there was a Fiscal, Property,

[5] For details on War Department contracts see Smith, *The Army and Economic Mobilization,* Chapter X

[6] See Memo, C CWS for USW, 23 Dec 41. CWS 160/658.

[7] (1) Ltr, C Ind Div OC CWS to COs Proc Districts and Arsenals, 3 Jan 42, sub: Authority to Contract. CWS 400 12/105. (2) Ltr, C CWS to COs Proc Districts and Arsenals, 23 Mar 42, sub· Approval of Awards and Formal Contracts. CWS 160/3011.

[8] Almost all CWS contractors had to convert their plants because 95 percent of CWS items were noncommercial. See CWS Presentation at SOS Staff Conference on Procurement and Production, 14 January 1943, page 2 in CWS 314.7 Procurement File.

and Transportation Section before December 1941, but in early 1942 separate sections were activated to deal with each of those functions. In the Boston district, inspection, plant protection, and production were all under an Engineering Division until 1942 when separate sections were established. The activation of these separate administrative units would not have been possible without the increased availability of officers.

Where the ever-growing workload did not account for the activation of new administrative units, the decentralization of operations in accordance with ASF policy did. In 1942 such functions as priorities and allocations and manpower utilization were decentralized to the installations. From 1943 to the close of the war, decentralization of operations took place on pricing analysis, public relations, property disposal, contract termination, and demobilization. Units to supervise these functions were set up in the district offices and other pertinent installations.

During the opening months of 1943 the Chief of the CWS directed all installations to activate control units in their organizations to assist the Control Division of his office to carry out its functions and to conduct control functions in the installations themselves.[9] He indicated the benefits which the commanding officers might expect from such units by describing the work of the Control Division of his office. This division, he stated, had recommended measures to integrate the organization and activities of the service and to reduce the number of persons engaged in administrative tasks and paper work.[10] Following receipt of General Porter's directive, all of the CWS installations set up control units.[11]

The outstanding accomplishment in the Chemical Warfare Service with regard to procurement district organization was the program of standardization of organization and procedures that was launched in the summer of 1943. In a letter to the commanding officer of each district the chief of the Control Division, OC CWS, stated that studies of record-keeping activities and work-simplification surveys made in the various districts indicated a marked disparity in the business practices of the districts. This resulted in certain districts utilizing more personnel than other districts to perform tasks of a similar extent and nature, an intolerable situation in the light of the manpower shortage. One step toward rectifying the

[9] See histories of CWS installations in World War II, MSS.

[10] Ltr, C CWS to CG EA, 23 Jan 43, sub: Contl Activities. CWS SPCWC 020.4 CWS (Control). Similar letters were sent to the various installations in January and February 1943.

[11] For the influence which ASF had on the internal developments of technical services such as CWS, see Millett, *Army Service Forces*, pages 304–08.

situation was the standardization of the district organizations. The chief of the Control Division of the Chief's office compiled a tentative draft of a manual outlining a uniform organization for procurement districts, on which he requested and received comments and suggestions by the commanding officers.[12]

On the basis of these recommendations, together with the principles of organization formulated by the ASF, a standard organization was set up in each district in September 1943. Local conditions dictated some variations, but in most respects all districts were organized in essentially the same manner from that time until the close of the war. The Chicago District, for example, shows the standard setup as of 15 August 1944. (*Chart 6*) [13] This organization was in conformity with ASF Manual M603 which was published in 1944. After publication of the manual, a study of the Chicago district as typical of all CWS procurement district organizations revealed that the district organization was in substantial agreement with the standards set up by the ASF.

The standardization of organization in the procurement districts and other CWS installations facilitated the standardization of administrative procedures. Before the Control Division survey of the districts, for example, each district office had its own forms and records system. This led to endless confusion in the Chief's office, where the data coming in from the installations had to be correlated. Until the forms and records were standardized it was extremely difficult to tell in what areas progress was being made.

Procurement District Headquarters and Field Inspection Offices

Following the activation of a separate Inspection Division in the OC CWS in May 1943,[14] the technical functions of the inspection offices at all CWS installations came under the jurisdiction of the new Inspection Division. The principle of divided jurisdiction was never entirely satisfactory to a number of installation commanders, who felt that since they

---

[12] Ltr, C Contl Div OC CWS to CO NYCWPD *et al.*, 31 Jul 43, sub: Standardization of Proc Districts. CWS 319 1.

[13] The representative of the Chemical Commodity Division reported to the chief of that division whose headquarters were in the New York procurement district. This division was set up in August 1944 to centralize the administration of procurement of chemicals. For details see Brophy, Miles, and Cochrane, *From Laboratory to Field.*

[14] See above, Chapter V.

CHART 6—CHICAGO PROCUREMENT DISTRICT, CHEMICAL WARFARE SERVICE,
AS OF 15 AUGUST 1944

GENERAL FUNCTIONS. The mission of this procurement district is to obtain material apportioned by the Chief, Chemical Warfare Service and assure its delivery to the proper destination at the desired time. The designated items are being procured from civilian firms, or if necessary, manufactured under the supervision of the Commanding General in commercially-operated, or government-operated plants.

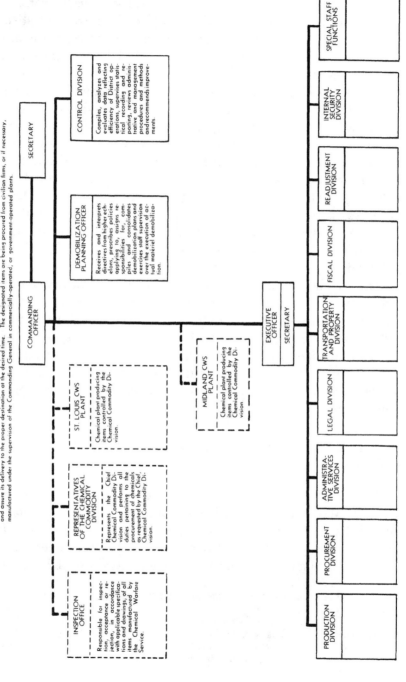

were generally responsible for the procurement of items they should be responsible for the quality of the items procured no less than for the quantity.[15] But the experience in the early part of the war of having the same officer responsible for both the production and inspection of items had not proved successful. The solution adopted was to take responsibility for inspection entirely out of the hands of the person accountable for production, the installation commander, and place it with an inspection officer responsible only to the chief of the Inspection Division, OC CWS.

From the point of view of operations, the system was effective because the quality of chemical warfare items improved greatly after the spring of 1943. The commanding officers of the procurement districts felt, however, that the same objectives could have been attained had the Chief, CWS, held them personally accountable for both quantity and quality of items. Such a procedure, they believed, would have avoided the administrative problems of divided authority that sprang up after separate inspection offices were activated in the districts.

Developments in 1945

Following V-E Day the Pittsburgh Procurement District was deactivated and the Boston and New York districts were consolidated under one commanding officer. This was the result of a requirement by ASF that for reasons of economy the number of CWS installations be reduced. In June 1945 Colonel Hurd, commanding officer of the Boston district, was named commanding officer of the New York district in addition to his other duties. During the preceding month, plans had been worked out to transfer part of the Pittsburgh district's business to the Chicago district and the remainder to the New York district and to set up a suboffice of the New York district in Pittsburgh. By V-J Day the transfers had been made, but owing to the sudden ending of the war the Pittsburgh suboffice was never activated.

The Chemical Warfare Center

The increased activities at Edgewood in research, training, manufacturing, and storage had, by the start of the war, made the designation

---

[15] Based on interviews and correspondence by the Chemical Corps Historical Office with installation commanders and key personnel of the Inspection Division, OC CWS.

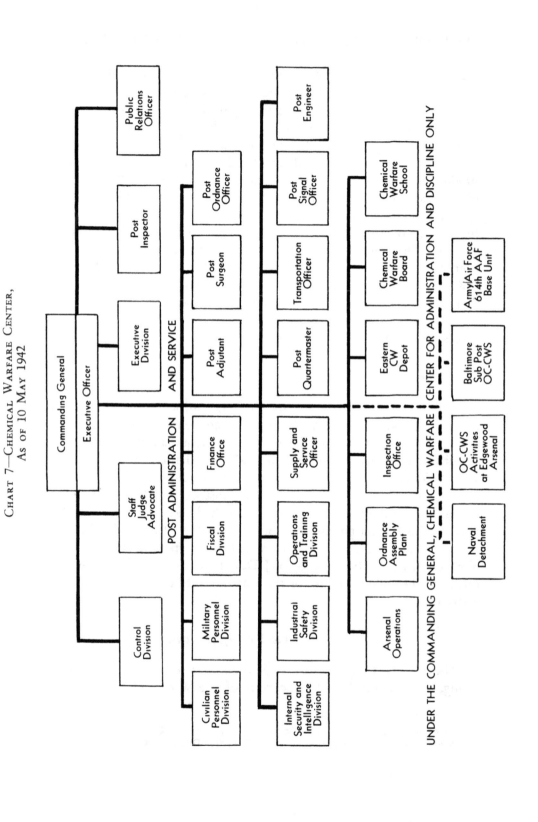

CHART 7—CHEMICAL WARFARE CENTER,
AS OF 10 MAY 1942

Commanding General

Executive Officer

Control Division

Staff Judge Advocate

Executive Division

Post Inspector

Public Relations Officer

POST ADMINISTRATION AND SERVICE

Civilian Personnel Division

Military Personnel Division

Fiscal Division

Finance Office

Post Adjutant

Post Surgeon

Post Ordnance Officer

Internal Security and Intelligence Division

Industrial Safety Division

Operations and Training Division

Supply and Service Officer

Post Quartermaster

Transportation Officer

Post Signal Officer

Post Engineer

Arsenal Operations

Ordnance Assembly Plant

Inspection Office

Eastern CW Depot

Chemical Warfare Board

Chemical Warfare School

Naval Detachment

OC-CWS Activities at Edgewood Arsenal

Baltimore Sub Post OC-CWS

Army Air Force 614th AAF Base Unit

UNDER THE COMMANDING GENERAL, CHEMICAL WARFARE CENTER FOR ADMINISTRATION AND DISCIPLINE ONLY

BRIG. GEN. RAY L. AVERY, *Commanding General, Chemical Warfare Center, Edgewood Arsenal, Md., 1942–46.*

Edgewood Arsenal a misnomer. Five days after Pearl Harbor, General Porter called this fact to the attention of the War Department in a letter recommending that a Chemical Warfare Center be activated at Edgewood. No action was taken on that recommendation, and on 23 February 1942 the Chief, CWS, again recommended that a center be set up under a commanding general, with several "intermediate" commanders to supervise the functions of research and development, training, and manufacturing. On 6 May 1942 the Secretary of War approved the recommendation, and four days later the Chemical Warfare Center was activated.[16]

Brig. Gen. Ray L. Avery, commanding general of Edgewood Arsenal, was put in charge of the new Chemical Warfare Center. (*Chart 7*) Avery remained in that post for the duration of the war, retiring from active service in April 1946. The organization of the center changed little throughout the war except for the activation of units to carry out newly assigned functions. For example, in February 1943 a Control Division was established, and in May the old Inspection Office was abolished and a new Inspection Office reporting directly to the chief of the Inspection Division, OC CWS, was activated.

The transfer of elements of the Chief's office to Edgewood in the fall of 1942 led to some administrative difficulties, particularly in personnel matters.[17] The Technical Division, OC CWS, for example, wanted to control its members located at Edgewood directly through the Washington office. The chief of the Technical Division felt that he could obtain more and better qualified employees in that way. The Chief, CWS, nevertheless, de-

---

[16](1) Ltr, C CWS to TAG, 12 Dec 41, and inds, sub: Cml Warfare Center. (2) Ltr, C CWS to TAG, 23 Feb 42, and inds, sub: Cml Warfare Center, EA, Md. Both in CWS 322.095/52. (3) EA GO 8, 20 Apr 42, and EA GO 18, 4 Dec 42.

[17] See above, Chapter V.

cided that all personnel activities at the Chemical Warfare Center should be processed through that headquarters and this procedure was adopted.

The duties of the commanding general of the Chemical Warfare Center corresponded closely to those of a post commander. They included personnel administration, internal security, public relations, post inspection, and post engineer functions for all elements of the center. The centralization of administration for those activities invariably made for a greater degree of efficiency. For example, it was far more effective to have one central office administer personnel functions than to have a half dozen independent offices scattered over the post, as was formerly the practice.[18]

The Arsenals

The Chemical Warfare Center included an Arsenal Operations Department which supervised strictly arsenal activities. As the new arsenals at Huntsville and Pine Bluff and later at Rocky Mountain [19] got into operation, the nature of arsenal activities at Edgewood changed. These new arsenals took over the bulk of the arsenal operations in the CWS, and the Edgewood plants eventually assumed the role of pilot plants, in addition to handling a number of "blitz" jobs.

On 6 May 1942 General Porter recommended to the Secretary of War that another CWS arsenal be erected near Denver, Colorado. Within a week Under Secretary of War Patterson issued a memorandum of approval for construction of the new arsenal.[20] This memorandum stated that the new installation would be used for producing certain gases and for loading operations and that the necessary funds, except for the purchase of land, would be made available to the CWS by the Army Air Forces.

Construction of the new arsenal, which was designated Rocky Mountain Arsenal, was begun in June 1942. As a result of the experience gained in building earlier CWS arsenals, the quality of its construction was superior to that of the others.

In the course of the war each of the CWS arsenals came to carry out much the same type of operation. Although the original plants at the new Pine Bluff and Rocky Mountain Arsenals were built to carry out certain specific operations, other types of plants were shortly erected at both arsenals. During the war, each of the CWS arsenals manufactured toxic

---

[18] Ltr, Asst Ex O to Comdt Cml Warfare School *et al.*, 20 Oct 42, sub: Centralization of Civ Pers Functions. CWS 314.7/7 Eastern Cml Dep.
[19] See below, pp. 167–68.
[20] WD Memo of Approval 438, 12 May 42.

agents, smoke and incendiary matériel, and with these filled shells, grenades, pots, and bombs supplied, as a rule, by the Ordnance Department.[21]

The physical layout of an arsenal was not without its effect upon the installation's organization and administration. Of all the CWS arsenals, Huntsville was by far the least compact. There, three separate plant areas had been erected, each separated by considerable distances, and each in turn separated from headquarters by several miles. Two of the plant areas were duplicates of each other, because Huntsville Arsenal was built on the theory that an enemy air attack was entirely feasible and that if one area were knocked out there was a chance that the other area might be saved. The third plant area at Huntsville was used for manufacturing and filling incendiaries. In setting up an organization for the post, General Ditto arranged for each area to have its own administrative units for engineering, personnel administration, property administration, storage, and transportation.[22] Although these units were responsible to higher echelon units at post headquarters, the supervision was more nominal than real. Because the system obviously made for duplication and added expense, it soon became necessary to set up a more centralized organization at Huntsville.

In contrast to Huntsville, Pine Bluff and Rocky Mountain Arsenals were compact, and therefore no basis existed for the duplication of administrative units. But those arsenals, like other CWS installations, were characterized by basic organizational and administrative defects in the early period of their existence. One of those defects was the fact that a great number of individuals reported directly to the commanding officer; in other words, there was not proper delegation of authority. Still more serious was the tendency on the part of commanding officers to organize and administer arsenals like other posts, camps, and stations. This tendency sprang from the limited experience of CWS officers in arsenal operations which were of course more technical than operations at other types of installations. Unlike the Ordnance Department, whose arsenal activities dated back many years and were carried on somewhat extensively even in peacetime, CWS operations came to a halt following World War I and

[21] (1) For details on construction and operations of CWS arsenals, see Brophy, Miles, and Cochrane, From Laboratory to Field. (2) See CWS Rpt of Production, 1 Jan 40 through 31 Dec 45, compiled by Production Br Proc Div, OC CWS in CWS 314.7 Production File.

[22] General Ditto served as commanding general of Huntsville Arsenal until he was appointed Assistant Chief, CWS, for Matériel in May 1943. He was succeeded by Col. Geoffrey Marshall. The commanding generals of the other arsenals were: Brig. Gen. Augustin M. Prentiss, Pine Bluff; General Loucks and, later, Brig. Gen. Alexander Wilson, Rocky Mountain.

were not resumed until the emergency period.[23] Consequently there were very few CWS officers, or civilians either, who were experts in arsenal activities. When war broke out, it was necessary for the Chief, CWS, to put his arsenals under the command of high ranking officers considered good administrators in the hope that they would utilize the services of Reserve officers who were experts in the technical operations.[24]

The defects in arsenal organization were largely overcome by the close of 1943. Under the ASF program for organizational improvement, both the Control and Industrial Divisions, OC CWS, reviewed closely the organization charts of the various arsenals. Where the charts did not conform to organizational standards, the commanding officers were contacted personally with a view to having them make the necessary changes.[25]

The Depots

At the time war was declared new depots at Huntsville and Pine Bluff were in the planning stages, and the site for another depot in northern Utah had not yet been selected.[26] The burden on the Edgewood Depot consequently was heavy, although the situation was somewhat eased by the procedure adopted by the Supply Division, OC CWS, during the emergency period of shipping equipment directly from points of manufacture to posts, camps, and stations throughout the country. The new depots at Huntsville and Pine Bluff were ready for partial operation in the fall of 1942. The site finally selected for the new depot in Utah was in Rush Valley, Tooele County, near the town of St. John. There by early 1942 the CWS erected an immense new installation comprising 370,000 square feet of closed storage space. In July 1942 this installation was designated the Deseret Chemical Warfare Depot.[27] Also in 1942, while the new depots were under construction, the Chemical Warfare Service acquired additional storage facilities in the following War Department general depots: San Antonio, Texas; Memphis, Tennessee; Atlanta, Georgia; Ogden, Utah; and New Cumberland, Pennsylvania. In March 1942 a large ware-

[23] (1) Constance McLaughlin Green, Harry C. Thomson, and Peter C. Roots, *The Ordnance Department. Planning Munitions for War*, UNITED STATES ARMY IN WORLD WAR II (Washington. 1955), Ch II. (2) Levin H. Campbell, *The Industry-Ordnance Team* (New York: McGraw-Hill, 1946), Ch. III.

[24] Porter interv, 29 Apr 50.

[25] Intervs, CmlHO with pers of Contl Div and Ind Div, OC CWS.

[26] History of the Deseret Chemical Warfare Depot to June 30, 1945, p. 3. MS.

[27] Ltr, TAG to C CWS, 14 Jul 42, sub: Designation of Deseret Cml Warfare Dep. AG 681.

house at Indianapolis, which the CWS had been occupying, was selected as a depot for spare parts.[28]

Originally the depots located at CWS arsenals had the same name as the arsenals, which led to confusion in the mails. In July 1943, therefore, the names of those depots were changed as follows: Edgewood Chemical Warfare Depot to Eastern Chemical Warfare Depot, Huntsville Chemical Warfare Depot to Gulf Chemical Warfare Depot, and Pine Bluff Chemical Warfare Depot to Midwest Chemical Warfare Depot.[29] The latter two depots were under the jurisdiction of the commanding officers of the arsenals to which they were attached. While not officially designated as a depot, a storage area at Rocky Mountain Arsenal was used to store items not shipped immediately to ports of embarkation.

In 1944 the CWS acquired the last of its wartime depots when 1,100 acres of the Lake Ontario Ordnance Works were transferred to the CWS and designated the Northeast Chemical Warfare Depot.[30] (*Chart 8*)

The administration of the Eastern, Gulf, and Midwest Depots had one characteristic in common:[31] in each case housekeeping functions were performed by an adjoining installation. In the case of the Eastern Depot the Chemical Warfare Center took care of those functions, while the Gulf and Midwest housekeeping functions were handled by Huntsville and Pine Bluff Arsenals respectively. In contrast to those three depots the other three —Deseret, Northeast, and Indianapolis—were responsible for their own housekeeping activities. In the CWS sections of general depots the Quartermaster Corps had responsibility.

Standardization of Depot Organizations

In no type of installation was such uniformity of organization achieved as in the depots. This was the result of the intense interest which the ASF showed in storage and distribution activities. Early in 1943 the ASF made a survey of operating and storage methods in typical depots under

---

[28] Interv, CmlHO with Col Oscar Gullans, 6 Dec 54. Gullans was commanding officer of the Indianapolis Depot during World War II.

[29] ASF Memo S50–4–43, 10 Aug 43, sub: Redesignation of CWS Br Deps.

[30] Ltr, TAG to C CWS, 27 Jun 44. AG 323.3.

[31] The commanding officers at the depots were: Col. Maurice S. Willett, Eastern; Col. Edward B. Blanchard and later, Col. William S. Bacon, Deseret; Lt. Col. Oscar Gullans, Indianapolis; and Maj. Homer J. Deschenes, Northeast. Officer in charge of depot operations at Gulf Depot was Maj. William C. Behrenberg and later, Maj. James H. Cochran. Officer in charge at Midwest Depot was Maj. Henry B. Merrill and later, Maj. Eldon B. Engle.

CHART 8—SCHEMATIC DIAGRAM, CHEMICAL WARFARE SUPPLY, AS OF 6 DECEMBER 1944

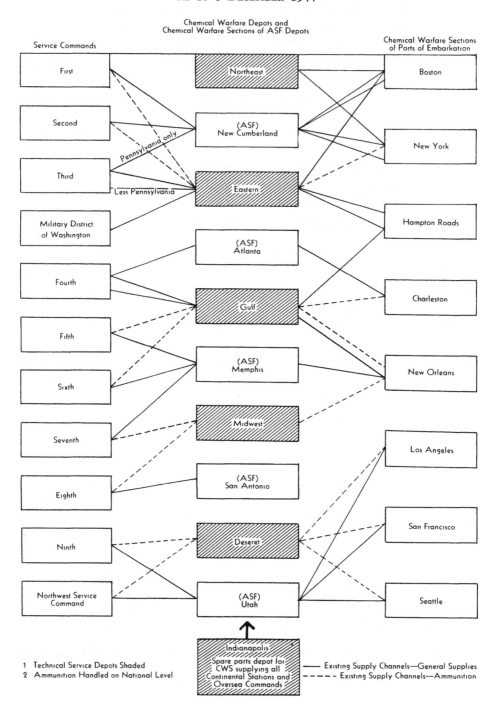

Chemical Warfare Depots and
Chemical Warfare Sections of ASF Depots

Service Commands

Chemical Warfare Sections
of Ports of Embarkation

First
Second
Third
Military District of Washington
Fourth
Fifth
Sixth
Seventh
Eighth
Ninth
Northwest Service Command

Northeast
(ASF) New Cumberland
Eastern
(ASF) Atlanta
Gulf
(ASF) Memphis
Midwest
(ASF) San Antonio
Deseret
(ASF) Utah

Pennsylvania only
Less Pennsylvania

Boston
New York
Hampton Roads
Charleston
New Orleans
Los Angeles
San Francisco
Seattle

Indianapolis
Spare parts depot for CWS supplying all Continental Stations and Oversea Commands

1 Technical Service Depots Shaded
2 Ammunition Handled on National Level

———— Existing Supply Channels—General Supplies
– – – – Existing Supply Channels—Ammunition

its jurisdiction. Its findings were published in Depot Operations Report No. 67, March 1943, which, after making a number of criticisms of current depot administration, went on to recommend basic organizational changes. Chief among the changes was the activation of storage, stock control, and maintenance units in all technical services headquarters and in all depots.

Pursuant to ASF directives the chief of the Supply Division, OC CWS, took immediate steps to reorganize his division to include Storage, Stock Control, and Maintenance Branches.[32] Col. Norman D. Gillet also directed the depots and the chemical sections of ASF depots to set up similar units. By the summer of 1943 this had been accomplished. By the fall, control units had also been activated in the depots, and the commanding officers could thereby better maintain organizational standards established by higher echelons. The publication of ASF Manual M417 in 1944 also served as a guide to depot commanders on organizational standards. Chart 9 shows a typical depot organization, that of the Eastern Depot, in April 1945.

Training Installations and Facilities [33]

Camp Sibert

The expanded training program of the Army had by late 1941 led to the need for additional CWS training facilities. In recognition of this fact, G-3 on 2 December 1941 advised the Chief, CWS, that a new chemical warfare replacement training center would be required in 1942.[34] With an adequate training area not available at Edgewood, it was necessary to consider locating the training center elsewhere. A survey of the Maryland countryside failed to disclose a large tract of reasonably priced land suitable for the purpose, and a decision was made to locate a site elsewhere. In the spring of 1942 an area near Gadsden, Alabama, in Etowah and Saint Clair Counties, was surveyed and selected. This site included 36,300 acres of sparsely inhabited rolling Alabama farmland, ample for a 5,000-man replacement training center and also able to accommodate, as stipulated by the CWS, eventual expansion to 30,000 to provide for unit training. Promise of good health conditions and suitability for year-round training led the

---

[32] See Leo P. Brophy, Organizational Development, pp. 247, 251–53.

[33] See below, Part Two, for details on CWS training activities during World War II.

[34] Memo, ACofS G-3 for C CWS, 2 Dec 41, sub: Expansion of CWS RTC Capacity. CWS 327 02/39.

CHART 9—EDGEWOOD ARSENAL, MARYLAND:

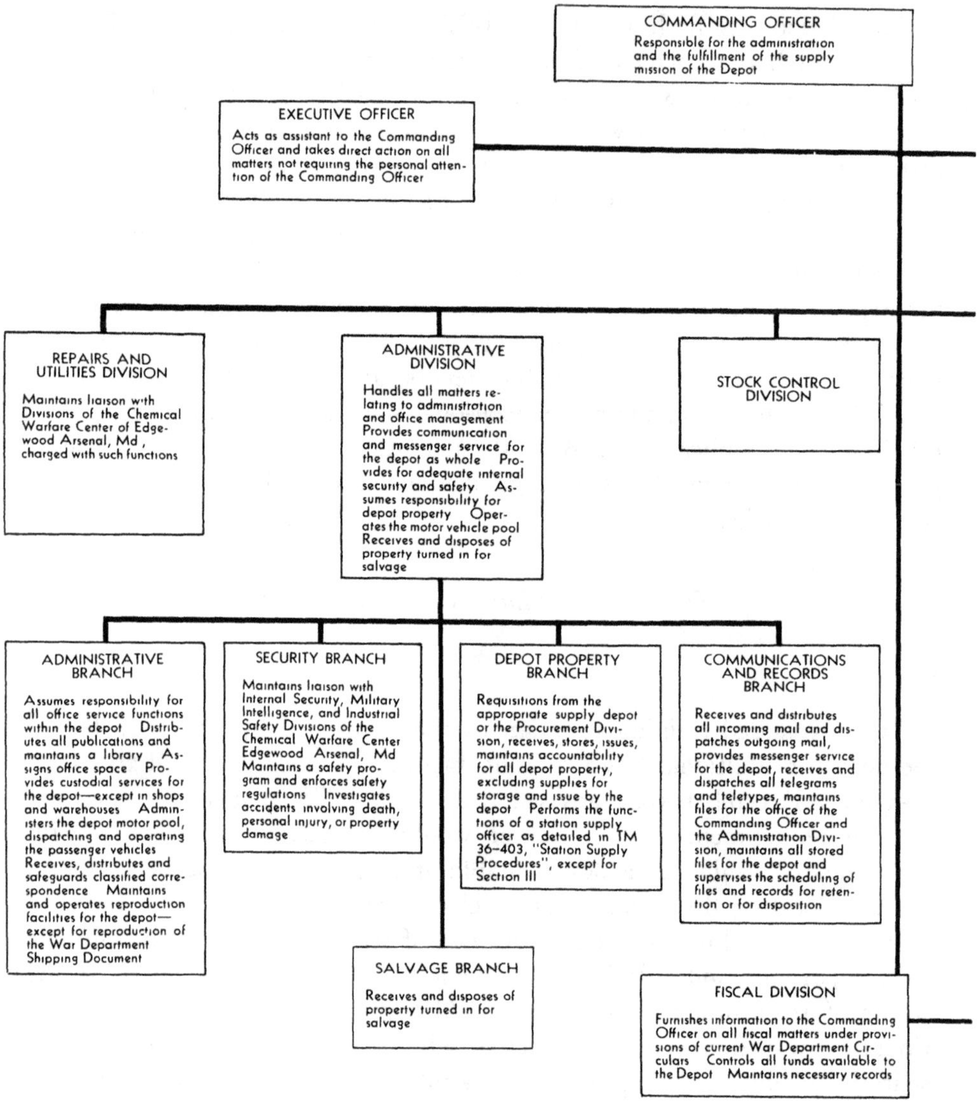

COMMANDING OFFICER

Responsible for the administration and the fulfillment of the supply mission of the Depot

EXECUTIVE OFFICER

Acts as assistant to the Commanding Officer and takes direct action on all matters not requiring the personal attention of the Commanding Officer

REPAIRS AND UTILITIES DIVISION

Maintains liaison with Divisions of the Chemical Warfare Center of Edgewood Arsenal, Md, charged with such functions

ADMINISTRATIVE DIVISION

Handles all matters relating to administration and office management Provides communication and messenger service for the depot as whole Provides for adequate internal security and safety Assumes responsibility for depot property Operates the motor vehicle pool Receives and disposes of property turned in for salvage

STOCK CONTROL DIVISION

ADMINISTRATIVE BRANCH

Assumes responsibility for all office service functions within the depot Distributes all publications and maintains a library Assigns office space Provides custodial services for the depot—except in shops and warehouses Administers the depot motor pool, dispatching and operating the passenger vehicles Receives, distributes and safeguards classified correspondence Maintains and operates reproduction facilities for the depot—except for reproduction of the War Department Shipping Document

SECURITY BRANCH

Maintains liaison with Internal Security, Military Intelligence, and Industrial Safety Divisions of the Chemical Warfare Center Edgewood Arsenal, Md Maintains a safety program and enforces safety regulations Investigates accidents involving death, personal injury, or property damage

DEPOT PROPERTY BRANCH

Requisitions from the appropriate supply depot or the Procurement Division, receives, stores, issues, maintains accountability for all depot property, excluding supplies for storage and issue by the depot Performs the functions of a station supply officer as detailed in TM 36–403, "Station Supply Procedures", except for Section III

COMMUNICATIONS AND RECORDS BRANCH

Receives and distributes all incoming mail and dispatches outgoing mail, provides messenger service for the depot, receives and dispatches all telegrams and teletypes, maintains files for the office of the Commanding Officer and the Administration Division, maintains all stored files for the depot and supervises the scheduling of files and records for retention or for disposition

SALVAGE BRANCH

Receives and disposes of property turned in for salvage

FISCAL DIVISION

Furnishes information to the Commanding Officer on all fiscal matters under provisions of current War Department Circulars Controls all funds available to the Depot Maintains necessary records

EASTERN CHEMICAL WARFARE DEPOT, AS OF 20 APRIL 1945

CONTROL DIVISION

Maintains liaison with Control Division of Chemical Warfare Center, Edgewood Arsenal, Maryland

STORAGE DIVISION

PERSONNEL DIVISION

Administer Military and Civilian Depot Personnel Co-ordinate personnel matters with Personnel Division, Edgewood Arsenal Perform personnel activities, such as placement training, evaluation, etc Administers efficiency rating program

MAINTENANCE DIVISION

Supervises and operates all maintenance and repair facilities for materials-handling equipment and other mechanical equipment used in the depot Develops preventive maintenance practices and supervises the application of regulations pertaining to proper use and preservation of depot equipment Performs first and second echelon maintenance on depot motor pool vehicles and maintains liaison with Motor Transportation Division of Chemical Warfare Center, Edgewood Arsenal, Md , with regard to maintenance and repair of motor pool vehicles

TRANSPORTATION DIVISION

Maintains liaison with Transportation Corps Division of Chemical Warfare Center of Edgewood Arsenal, Md

MILITARY PERSONNEL BRANCH

Maintains liaison with the Military Personnel Branch, Chemical Warfare Center, Edgewood Arsenal, Md Maintains records of the military personnel

CIVILIAN PERSONNEL BRANCH

Maintains liaison with the Civilian Personnel Branch, Chemical Warfare Center, Edgewood Arsenal, Md Maintains records of the civilian personnel

PLACEMENT SECTION

Develops good placement standards and practices in relation to assignments and reassignments, development, evaluation and promotion of employees, and in relation to plans for meeting increases or decreases of working force

TRAINING SECTION

Determines training needs and formulates training plans and procedures for the depot Administers certain training courses Evaluates the adequacy and effectiveness of the training program of the depot

TRANSACTIONS AND RECORDS SECTION

Processes all appointments, changes in status, separations and other types of personnel actions Maintains records of civilian personnel Prepares reports on personnel as required

PAYROLL SECTION

Maintains records relating to attendance, leave, and War Bonds Prepares all reports relating to leave, attendance, and War Bonds

FUND CONTROL BRANCH

Determine and certify as to the applicability and availability of funds prior to the incurrence of obligations Issue purchase authorization advice as requested Secures funds required by Depot and prepares any related budgetary estimates Processes all reimbursement transactions authorized at the Depot and processes all other collections made by the Depot

FISCAL ACCOUNTING BRANCH

Maintains fiscal accounting records pertaining to funds available to the depot Prepares required reports on the status of available funds Performs internal audit functions within the Depot as directed

COMMERCIAL VOUCHER BRANCH

Prepare and forward necessary forms to Finance Office for payment of purchases made through Procurement Division and Finance Office, Edgewood Arsenal, for Depot Receive necessary supporting papers including obligating documents, invoices and receiving reports Examine all such documents as to propriety, mathematical accuracy, and account classification Maintain liaison with Procurement Division and Finance Office, Edgewood Arsenal

GENERAL SHEKERJIAN, *Commanding General, Replacement Training Center, Camp Sibert, Alabama.*

CWS to determine on this location for its new training center.[35] The Chief of Engineers was accordingly directed in May 1942 to construct the housing facilities for a 5,000-man replacement training center with completion date set for 1 December 1942.[36] The new reservation was designated Camp Sibert in honor of the first Chief of the Chemical Warfare Service.[37] Col. Thomas J. Johnston was made commanding officer while construction was still under way. When the RTC was moved from Edgewood to Camp Sibert in the summer of 1942, Colonel Johnston became the camp commander and Brig. Gen. Haig Shekerjian, the RTC commander.

In the fall of 1942 the War Department authorized activation of a Unit Training Center (UTC) at Camp Sibert. Activation of the UTC, Chemical Warfare Service officials felt, would require another headquarters since the functions of replacement training and unit training were so different that it would be impracticable to include them under one command.[38] Therefore the UTC was activated as a separate CWS installation in September 1942. The War Department letter authorizing the installation was indorsed by the Fourth Service Command to the commanding general of the CWS Replacement Training Center instructing him to activate and assume command of the new Unit Training Center.[39] Accordingly General Shekerjian became responsible for replacement and unit training activities.

---

[35] Rpt of Investigation of Site for CWS RTC: Atlanta Engineering District, 28 May 42, reproduced as Appendix B in Training of Replacement, Fillers and Cadres (Through 30 June 1944), CWS History of Training, Pt. IV.

[36] Memo, CG SOS for CofEngrs, 19 May 42, sub: CWS RTC, Gadsden, Ala. Area. CWS 600.932/10.

[37] WD GO 47, 21 Sep 42.

[38] Interv, CmlHO with Brig Gen Egbert F. Bullene (formerly CO UTC), 27 Jan 50.

[39] Ltr, TAG to C CWS *et al.*, 27 Sep 42, sub: Establishment of CWS UTC, Gadsden, Ala. CWS 320.2.

This arrangement was not satisfactory to the Chief, CWS, who believed that efficient administration required separate commanding officers for the UTC and the RTC. By January 1943 the number of units in training at Sibert had reached fifty-four, as compared with thirteen two months before, and General Porter thereupon appointed Col. Egbert F. Bullene, chief of the Training Division in his office, as commanding officer of the Unit Training Center.[40] Bullene was promoted to brigadier general on 27 April 1943, so that both the RTC and the UTC were commanded by general officers each of whom enjoyed a status of relative independence. Meanwhile, Colonel

GENERAL BULLENE, *Commander, Unit Training Center, Camp Sibert, Alabama. (Photograph taken in 1952.)*

Johnston continued to command the post, providing services and utilities for both training centers. Between the two centers a rivalry developed, which was open and probably not unhealthy.

Within less than three months these administrative arrangements met with opposition from the commanding general of the Fourth Service Command, who objected to communicating with two general officers, each of whom commanded autonomous installations at the same military station. On 24 May 1943 he recommended to the ASF that existing instructions be amended to permit him to assign General Shekerjian as post commander and commanding general of the RTC, with Bullene, as Shekerjian's subordinate, to command the UTC.[41] General Porter opposed this recommendation but General Somervell sustained it, and appropriate orders were accordingly issued. The new arrangement continued in effect until the UTC operations were suspended in March 1944.

The commanding general of the service command had ample authority on which to base his recommendations of 24 May, for just twelve days before the ASF had designated Camp Sibert a Class I installation of the

[40] WD SO 41, Par 2, 27 Feb 43.
[41] Ltr. CG Fourth Serv Comd to CG ASF, 24 May 43, sub: Reassignment of Officers at Camp Sibert, Ala. AG 210.31 Camp Sibert.

Fourth Service Command.[42] This was in conformity with ASF policy in 1943 of emphasizing the role of the service commands in technical training.[43] The chiefs of the technical services resisted this policy because they naturally disliked surrendering direct control over their branch training. When General Porter heard that Camp Sibert had been made a Class I installation, he wrote a letter to General Somervell in which he questioned the wisdom of the move. "Great pains," he declared, "have been taken to insure the proper functioning of the training activities at Camp Sibert which are essential not only for their product but as a laboratory for the development of chemical warfare matériel of new and untried types . . . . the radical change proposed might well cancel a considerable part of the progress made." To this General Somervell replied that he was convinced the new system would work well, and he urged General Porter to give it "a fair and impartial trial." [44] Actual transfer was made in July 1943, and from that time until the close of the war the Chief, CWS, was responsible only for the promulgation of training doctrine, the establishment of student quotas, and the preparation of training programs.

West Coast Chemical School

In July 1943 the CWS asked the ASF for authority to establish a chemical warfare school toward the West Coast. The recommendation was advanced as a means of providing final instruction for military personnel moving into Pacific theaters of operations and of eliminating extensive travel for those selected at western stations for training in chemical warfare. The functions of the new school would be: (1) to provide for short technical refresher courses of one-week duration for CWS officers in the Far West who were scheduled for overseas duty; (2) to provide short courses for units gas officers who could not be economically sent to the Chemical Warfare School at Edgewood; (3) to conduct training for civilians, as directed by the Office of Civilian Defense; and (4) to meet requests of naval authorities for training naval personnel on the Pacific coast in gas defense.[45]

---

[42] AR 170–10, as amended 12 May 43. This regulation, originally issued 24 December 1942, defined a Class I installation as one coming under the jurisdiction of a service command and a Class IV installation as one subject to the chief of a technical service.

[43] Millett, *Army Service Forces,* pp. 326–29.

[44] Memo, C CWS for CG ASF, 3 Jun 43, and 1st Ind, 9 Jun 43. CWS 323.3 Sibert 43.

[45] Ltr, AC CWS for Fld Opns to CG ASF, 14 Jul 43, sub: Cml Warfare School. CWS 352.11.

The reaction of the ASF to the proposal for another chemical warfare school under the jurisdiction of the Chief, CWS, was not favorable. Instead, the chief of the Training Division, ASF, on 11 September 1943 directed that a chemical warfare school be set up at Camp Beale, California, as a Class I installation under the jurisdiction of the commanding general of the Ninth Service Command.[46] Such a school, known as the West Coast Chemical School, was activated in October 1943, and the first class assembled on 13 December.[47] As of 8 March 1944, 100 students were in attendance at the school, 56 of whom were officers and 44, enlisted men. These included personnel from the Army, Navy, Coast Guard, and Marine Corps.[48] Col. Maurice E. Jennings was named commandant of the school.

The school at Camp Beale was so located that it could operate with little interference from other activities at the post. Its physical layout consisted of six 2-story barracks buildings, two mess halls, a 1-story supply building, a 1-story headquarters building, and a 1-story building used for a library, a day room for enlisted men, a post office, and a publications supply room. The commanding general at Camp Beale was most cooperative in furnishing the school with any facilities it required.

Experience finally demonstrated, however, that it was not feasible to operate the school as an activity of a service command, and on 24 April 1944 General Porter requested the director of Military Personnel, ASF, to relocate the school at the Rocky Mountain Arsenal. The Chief, CWS, gave a number of reasons why he preferred to have the school at Rocky Mountain. There it would have the benefit of an environment meeting the special needs of the CWS, where the commanding general could furnish the school with chemical warfare matériel, and where the students would be impressed with all the activities of a CWS installation. More direct liaison would be afforded between the instructors at the school and the Chief's office, and thus the staff of the school could keep up to date on current developments in the CWS. The weather and terrain at Rocky Mountain Arsenal were more conducive to the use of smoke and chemical agents in training than at Camp Beale, and finally the housing and classroom facilities at the arsenal were more suitable for conducting classes.[49] General Porter's recom-

[46] TWX, C Tng Div ASF to CWS, c/o Dugway Proving Ground, 15 Oct 43. CWS 352.11.

[47] Ninth Serv Comd GO 135, 17 Oct 43.

[48] Memo, School Br, Mil Tng Div ASF for Dir of Mil Tng ASF, 8 Mar 44, sub: Tng Inspection of West Coast Cml Warfare School, Camp Beale, Marysville, Calif. CWS 333.

[49] Ltr, C CWS to CG ASF, 24 Apr 44, sub: Relocation of West Coast Cml Warfare School, Camp Beale, Calif. CWS 323.3.

mendation to move the school was approved by the ASF on 14 May 1944 and on 1 June by the Secretary of War.[50] From June 1944 until the close of the war the school, which was now renamed the Western Chemical Warfare School, was an activity of the Rocky Mountain Arsenal. Col. George J. B. Fisher succeeded Colonel Jennings as commandant when the school was moved to the Rocky Mountain Arsenal. In July 1945 Colonel Fisher was transferred to overseas duty and was succeeded by Col. Harold Walmsley, who remained commandant until the close of the war.

Research and Development Facilities

During the emergency period it became evident that the facilities for research, development, and testing at Edgewood were not adequate for the large-scale program being inaugurated. As mentioned above, a new technical research center had been constructed by December 1941, and by that time also a new CWS laboratory had been erected on the campus of the Massachusetts Institute of Technology.[51] Later the CWS acquired the use of a laboratory at Columbia University. Both laboratories became CWS installations.

Massachusetts Institute of Technology Laboratory.[52]

In the autumn of 1940 Bradley Dewey, president of the Dewey and Almy Chemical Company, who had headed the Gas Defense Production Division, CWS, in World War I and had kept up an active interest in the service in the peacetime years, suggested that a new CWS development laboratory be established at Massachusetts Institute of Technology.[53] The following February the proposition was discussed at a conference of high ranking CWS officers and outstanding scientists in Washington.[54] The

---

[50] Ltr, TAG to CG Ninth Serv Cmd and C CWS, 1 Jun 44, sub: Transfer and Redesignation of West Coast Cml Warfare School. AG 352 (29 May 44) OB–I–SPMOU–M.

[51] See above, Chapter II.

[52] Unless otherwise indicated this section is based on an unpublished installation history of MIT completed by CO CWS–MIT in World War II and Sylvester J. Hemleben, MIT CWS Development Laboratory, The History of Research and Development of the Chemical Warfare Service in World War II.

[51] (1) See above, Chapter I. (2) Ltr, Ex O OC CWS to Dr. Karl T. Compton, 15 Feb 41. CWS 400 112/114.

[54] The following representatives of CWS were at the conference: General Baker, C CWS; Colonel English, Executive Officer, OC CWS; and Colonel Barker, chief of the Technical Division, OC CWS. The following scientists were present: Dr. Lewis, Dr. H. E. Howe, Dr. Conant, and Bradley Dewey.

purpose of the conference was described in these words: "To consider the possibility of providing for additional development space and facilities for the Chemical Warfare Service in order that any new ideas, devices, or processes developed on the laboratory basis by the National Defense Research Committee might be tested out on a large scale to determine their probable application for military purposes." [55] Conference members decided to approach Dr. Karl T. Compton, president of MIT, on the possibility of the CWS obtaining additional facilities there.

By mid-March an agreement had been drawn up between the CWS and MIT which provided for a half-million dollar laboratory on grounds to be leased to the CWS upon approval of the War Department and the National Defense Research Committee.[56] Under this agreement the services of the MIT faculty, for advisory and consultant purposes, were made available to the Chemical Warfare Service. The new development laboratory when erected was made a Class IV installation of the CWS under Army Regulation 170–10 and was put under the command of Capt. Jacquard H. Rothschild. As of 28 May 1943 the organization chart of the installation called for 117 officers and 215 civilians. Because of the nature of its activities, the laboratory was organized along functional lines; the divisions were Protective Materials, Respiratory, Chemical Development, and Engineering and Test. The laboratory continued in operation until 21 August 1945.

Columbia University Laboratory.[57]

The transfer of the incendiary bomb program to the CWS in the fall of 1941 created the need for a laboratory devoted to the development of incendiary munitions. Col. J. Enrique Zanetti, whom General Porter had named as chief of the Incendiaries Branch in his headquarters, was a member of the Columbia University faculty in chemistry and was therefore intimately acquainted with the potentialities of the university's laboratories. Zanetti envisioned an arrangement between CWS and Columbia such as already existed between CWS and Massachusetts Institute of Technology: the university would lease laboratory and office space to the Chemical Warfare

[55] Ltr, Ex O OC CWS to CG EA, 17 Feb 41, sub: Additional CWS Development Facilities. CWS 334 8/146–48.

[56] 1st Ind, 20 Mar 41, on Ltr, C CWS to TAG, 28 Feb 41. CWS 111/16.

[57] This section is based on Bernard Baum, Columbia University CWS Laboratories, History of Research and Development of the Chemical Warfare Service in World War II, and Interv, CmlHO with Prof. J. Enrique Zanetti, 25 Sep 50.

Service and make available the services of its faculty members in engineering and chemistry, and CWS would establish an administrative unit at the university. Late in 1941 Colonel Zanetti approached Columbia's president, Nicholas Murray Butler, on the proposition, and in early 1942 President Butler agreed to the arrangement. On 31 January 1942 the War Department approved the proposition, and a formal contract, similar to the CWS-MIT contract was drawn up.[58]

In April 1942 Lt. Col. Ralph H. Talmadge was put in command of the Columbia laboratory, which was designated a Class IV activity. A peak personnel figure of 43 was reached at the laboratory in May 1943; of those, 23 were officers, and 20 were civilians. The civilian employees were not under federal civil service but were hired and trained by the university.

When the Incendiary Branch of the Chief's office was inactivated in June 1942, supervision of the Columbia CWS laboratory was turned over to the Technical Division, OC CWS. The scope of the laboratory's activities was broadened to include development work not only on the incendiary bomb but also on other items such as the 4.2-inch chemical mortar and the flame thrower. On 31 December 1943 the CWS-Columbia University contract was terminated and the laboratory's functions transferred to the Chemical Warfare Center.

Testing Facilities

The expansion of CWS research and development activities created a demand for new chemical warfare testing stations. At the start of the war all chemical warfare testing was done at Edgewood, where the Technical, Medical, and Inspection Divisions, the Chemical Warfare Board, the Chemical Warfare School, and the adjoining Aberdeen Proving Ground of the Ordnance Department all shared the same testing fields. By the time war was declared these facilities were already greatly overcrowded. To complicate matters still more, testing at the arsenal was becoming more hazardous because of the growth of populated areas adjacent to the arsenal. New testing grounds in a more sparsely populated locality were sorely needed. Experience had demonstrated that this new locality should be characterized by climatic and geographic features more favorable to the

[58] 1st Ind, 31 Jan 42, on Ltr, C CWS to TAG, 18 Jan 42, sub: Research Lab for Incendiaries at Columbia University, CWS 471.6/164 Incendiaries.

testing of various chemical warfare matériel than found in eastern Maryland.[59]

Dugway Proving Ground

On 3 January 1942 General Porter sent Maj. John R. Burns to Salt Lake City to investigate the possibilities of a testing ground in Utah. Major Burns, after conferring with the Army's district engineer and the representative of the Federal Grazing Service in Salt Lake City, recommended a tract some eighty-five miles southwest of the city, lying partly in the Salt Lake Desert and partly in the Dugway Valley. Burns' recommendation met with the approval of the OC CWS and the War Department, and a 265,000-acre stretch of land was acquired and developed into the CWS Proving Ground, Tooele, Utah.[60] On 1 March 1942 the installation was activated with Burns, then a lieutenant colonel, in command. From its inception to the close of the war Dugway conducted tests on both experimental and fully developed munitions.

Burns, raised to the rank of colonel in August 1942, was succeeded as commanding officer at Dugway on 28 November 1944 by Col. Graydon C. Essman who remained in command until the close of the war. The commanding officer at Dugway was responsible for both testing and housekeeping functions. To supervise the testing activities he appointed a director of operations.[61] Military strength at the post reached its peak in the summer of 1944, when there were over one hundred and fifty commissioned officers and over a thousand enlisted men on duty. These numbers included over one hundred members of the Women's Army Corps (WAC). There were few civilian employees at Dugway because of its inaccesibility.[62]

San José Project

The leasing of San José Island to the U.S. Government had been preceded by considerable reconnaissance of the Caribbean area for a suitable site to carry on chemical research under tropical conditions.[63] In the fall of 1943 Col. Robert D. McLeod, Jr., and Dr. Carey Croneis of the National Defense Research Committee made a thorough search of the territory adjoin-

[59] Ltr, C CWS to TAG, 14 Jan 42, sub: Test Area for CWS, included as Appendix B in Bernard Baum, Dugway Proving Ground, 1 Mar 47, Vol. 23 of History of Research and Development in the Chemical Warfare Service (1 Jul 40–31 Sep 45).

[60] (1) Executive Order 9053, 6 Feb 42. (2) WD GO 11, 5 Mar 42.

[61] Baum, Dugway Proving Ground, pp. 68–69.

[62] Ibid., pp. 52–58.

[63] See above, Chapter V.

ing the Panama Canal Zone for a peninsular site but found none suitable. Then by plane they searched the entire coast of Panama. They finally decided on San José, some sixty miles from the Pacific entrance to the canal, because the climate and topography were suitable and the foliage was of the desired character.[64] After consulting with the district engineer, Colonel McLeod forwarded his recommendations to the Chief, CWS, on 25 October 1943.[65]

General Porter wanted to make doubly sure of the suitability of the proposed site, so after reviewing McLeod's suggestions he sent General Bullene, whom he had selected to direct the project, to the Panama area. Bullene confirmed McLeod's findings, and thereupon the Chief, CWS, recommended to the General Staff that the island be acquired. The General Staff held up the recommendation pending assurance that the tests would not harm the rare animal, plant, or reptile life on the island. After Bullene secured a signed statement to that effect from the director of the National Museum in Washington, the General Staff gave its approval.[66]

On 9 December 1943, the Chief of Staff directed Lt. Gen. George H. Brett, Commanding General, Caribbean Defense Command, to lease San José Island for the period of the war and one year thereafter. General Brett was informed that General Bullene would arrive at the Caribbean Defense Command headquarters on 11 December and the command was to build "roads, trails and camp sites" for the San José Project. On 16 December, General Brett requested the government of Panama to lease the island to the government of the United States. To this request the Panamanian Government gave ready assent.[67]

Shortly after General Bullene's arrival in Panama, a crew of native workmen under the supervision of Mr. Russell Foster, engineer adviser to

[64] Dr. Ivan M. Johnston of the Arnold Arboretum of Harvard University described San José as follows: "The forests of San José most resemble in important details large areas of forest in Burma, Siam, Indo-China, Malaya, the Philippines and Formosa, and the woodland is similar to that of the Bonin and Luchu Islands." San José Proj Miscellaneous Rpt, Forest Types of San José Compared With Those of Southwestern Pacific and Southeastern Asia, 8 Dec 44, in Tech Lib, ACmlC, Md.

[65] (1) Interv, CmlHO with Col Robert D. McLeod, Jr., 28 Sep 44. (2) Ltr, Col McLeod to C CWS, 25 Oct 43, sub: Selection of Site for Tropical Tests. CWS files, Misc Series, Project Coordination, 601 (San José Project), NA. (3) Col. Robert D. McLeod, Jr., "Forty-five Days Under the Southern Cross," *Armed Forces Chemical Journal*, VIII (1954), No. 5–6.

[66] Bullene interv, 27 Jan 50.

[67] (1) Rad 5834, Marshall to CG CDC, 9 Dec 43. (2) Ltr, CofS CDC to Chargé d'Affaires, U.S. Embassy, Panama, 16 Dec 43. AG 470.6–1 (C). (3) Ltr, Minister of Foreign Relations, Govt of Panama, to Chargé d'Affaires, U.S. Embassy, Panama, 4 Jan 44. CWS 314.7 San José Project File.

the Corps of Engineers, landed on the beach at San José and began to cut a trail inland. Original plans called for the completion of the entire testing program within a period of about two months, and construction was undertaken with this time limit in mind. It was not long before drastic revisions of the time schedule had to be made. General Bullene insisted that every precaution be taken against the possible spread of malaria on the island, even though this precaution might slow up construction. His previous experience in the tropics had impressed upon him the need for such measures, and in addition it was well known that an important English project had failed because precautions against malaria had not been taken. After differences arose between the CWS and the Corps of Engineers on the building schedule, Bullene requested that the commanding general of the Caribbean Defense Command transfer responsibility for all construction to CWS jurisdiction.[68] This was done, and Russell Foster was transferred to CWS jurisdiction as an engineer adviser. Under Foster's supervision 300 buildings, some 3 miles of 20-foot roadway, 109 miles of 10-foot roadway, and 14 miles of foot trails were constructed by August 1944.[69]

From the project's inception until early in September 1944, military personnel rolls averaged about five hundred officers and enlisted men.[70] As the initial phases of the tests were concluded, the chemical companies were returned to the mainland.[71] By November 1944 there were 43 officers and 413 enlisted men attached to the San José Project, and a year later, with the war over, the number stood at 37 officers and 300 enlisted men.[72]

In addition to Army personnel, representatives from the following organizations were stationed at San José: U.S. Navy, British Army, Canadian Army, Royal Canadian Air Force, and the National Defense Research Committee. General Bullene described the project as a united effort of all these participants to secure certain technical data which would be useful in winning the war. Therefore he insisted that no distinction be made between nationals or organizations and directed that men be assigned to duties for which they were best qualified. Members of the NDRC, he

[68] Bullene Interv, 27 Jan 50.
[69] (1) Construction Status Rpt, San José Proj, Period Ending 15 Aug 44. CWS 314.7. (2) Interv, CmlHO with Russell Foster, 15 Sep 44.
[70] Ltr, CG San José Proj to TAG, 5 Sep 44, sub: Medical Pers Requirements, CWS 314.7 San José Project File.
[71] These were the 67th and 68th Chemical Smoke Generator Companies, the 27th Chemical Decontamination Company, and the 95th Chemical Composite Company.
[72] San José Proj Manning Tables, CWS 314.7 San José Project File.

ruled, were to occupy the position of commissioned officers and were to be accorded the same consideration as officers.[73]

By July 1944 the installation organization consisted of an administration director, a technical director, an intelligence officer, an advisory council, the adjutant, and the chief of the Army Pictorial Division, Signal Corps, which made films of the project. The administration director was responsible for the quartering, rationing, messing, supply, medical attention, discipline, and morale services for all persons on the project. The technical director, Colonel McLeod, was charged with the direction and supervision of all technical tests and the preparation of the reports of tests which would be forwarded to the commanding general through the Advisory Council. The Advisory Council was a very important element in carrying out the mission of the project. It was made up of the executive officer, technical director, chiefs of the principal technical divisions, and other designated key personnel. The duties of the Advisory Council were to analyze and interpret the technical data of the various tests as an aid to the commanding general in reaching sound conclusions in his reports to higher authority and to prepare such operational instructions for the using arms and services as were required.

In order to insure that the testing at San José would not be obstructed by administrative difficulties, the Chief, CWS, activated a San José Project Division in his office on 27 September 1944.[74] Under this arrangement the San José Project became a branch of the new division. General Bullene was made chief of the San José Project Division, at the same time retaining command at the project.

Biological Warfare Installations [75]

Mention has been made of the biological warfare installations established in World War II.[76] Camp Detrick, the first and most important of those installations, was activated on 17 April 1943 under the command of Lt. Col. William S. Bacon.[77] Bacon was succeeded by Cols. Martin B.

---

[73] San José Proj GO 8, 25 Apr 44.

[74] OC CWS Adm O 22, 27 Sep 44.

[75] Unless otherwise indicated, this section is based on Rexmond C. Cochrane, History of the Chemical Warfare Service in World War II (1 July 1940–15 August 1945), Biological Warfare Research in the United States (November 1947), 2 vols., MS, OCMH.

[76] See above, Chapter V.

[77] Ltr, TAG to C CWS, 17 Apr 43, sub: Designation of Camp Detrick, Md. AG 680.1 (4–7–43) OB–I–SPOPU–M.

Chittick and Joseph D. Sears. Actual construction of the camp, which came to occupy an area of more than five hundred acres, was not completed until June 1945. By then a small, self-contained city had been built containing more than 245 separate structures, including quarters for 5,000 workers. At the peak of operations in August 1945 there were at Camp Detrick 245 Army officers and 1,457 enlisted personnel, 87 Navy officers and 475 enlisted men, and 9 civilians, exclusive of civilian consultants.

By September 1944 the program at Camp Detrick, conducted jointly by civilian scientists and employees of the Chemical Warfare Service, the Medical Department, and the Navy, included research and development on mechanical, chemical, and biological methods of defense against biological warfare, production of agents and munitions for retaliatory employment, development of manufacturing processes through engineering and pilot plant studies, development of safety measures for protecting personnel on the post and its surrounding communities, and devising of suitable inspection procedures for production plants.[78] Within a year of its activation the technical staff had grown to such proportions, and the range of research operations was so wide, that it became difficult for key personnel in one unit to keep abreast of progress in other units. Consequently, a tendency toward duplication of effort developed in some of the laboratories, a problem not finally solved until almost the end of the war.

Horn Island, off the Mississippi coast, was selected as a field test site in early 1943, and construction got under way in June. No special structures, such as necessary at Camp Detrick, were required on the island aside from quarters for the test personnel and technical buildings adjacent to the grid area of the test site. The one unusual feature of the installation was an eight-mile narrow-gauge railroad which had to be constructed because building roads on the sandy island was not practicable. Track, locomotive, and wooden cars were shipped from Fort Benning, Georgia, and installed by a company of Seabees.

Administratively, Horn Island was a substation of Camp Detrick from its activation until June 1944 when it became a separate installation under the jurisdiction of the Special Projects Division, OC CWS.[79] Because of its

---

[78] Special Projects Div, CWS Organizational Chart, 11 Sep 44. In Cochrane, History of the CWS in WW II, Vol. II.

[79] Memo, AC of Opns, Special Projects Div for CO Camp Detrick and CO Horn Island, 17 June 44, sub: Administration of Horn Island, cited in Cochrane, History of CWS in WW II, Vol. II, 4A

proximity to the mainland, only the most restricted of field tests could be made on the island. As the biological warfare program expanded, it became obvious that a larger and more remote test area was necessary for the field program envisioned.

The biological warfare installation known as Granite Peak, a 250-square-mile area at Tooele, Utah, was activated in June 1944 as the principal large-scale test field. Administratively, Granite Peak was a subinstallation of Dugway Proving Ground, to which it was adjacent, and many of the administrative duties of the post were operated or supervised by the Dugway Proving Ground post commander. The biological warfare and chemical warfare field installations achieved a high degree of co-operation in their test activities. For example, the proving ground detachment flew all airplane missions required by Granite Peak operations, and existing Dugway facilities provided the meteorological forecasting service required at the Peak.[80] Nevertheless, Granite Peak retained full autonomy over all its technical operations. Its test operations reached their height in July 1945, when 10 Army officers and 97 enlisted men, and 5 Navy officers and 55 Navy enlisted men were engaged in conducting tests.

The Vigo Plant, near Terre Haute, Indiana, was an Ordnance Department plant which was turned over to the CWS in May 1944.[81] Its mission was the production of agents being developed at Camp Detrick. Vigo was considered to be a pilot plant rather than an arsenal, because of the experimental and highly technical nature of operations that were required before it could be proved for its intended purpose and accepted by the chief of the Special Projects Division and the Assistant Chief, CWS, for Matériel. Proof of the plant was considered to mean operation of all facilities at sufficiently high levels and for sufficient lengths of time to demonstrate the plant's capacity to perform its mission.[82] As plans for the operation of the Vigo Plant were made, it was proposed to limit the scale of operations to proving the plant, training personnel, providing end items for surveillance and proof testing, and accumulating material in anticipation of military requirements. The personnel involved in this operation in July 1945 con-

[80] Memo, O/C GPI for C Special Projects Div, 8 Sep 44, sub: Integration of Granite Peak and Dugway Activities, CWS SPCYF 141/1.

[81] Ltr, TAG to C CWS, CofEngrs, and CofOrd, 13 May 44, sub: Redesignation of Vigo Ord Plant, AG 322.

[82] Ltr, Special Projects Div to Tech Dir Camp Detrick and CO Vigo Plant, 5 Apr 45, sub: Assignment of Responsibility and Authority for Proving the Vigo Plant. CWS SPCYF 400.4.

sisted of 115 Army officers and 863 enlisted men, 32 Navy officers and 304 Navy enlisted men, and 65 civilians.

Organizational developments in the CWS during World War II included the expansion of existing organizational structures, particularly in the procurement districts, the activation of new administrative units in all installations to carry out functions delegated by the Army Service Forces, and the setting up of entirely new organizations such as the Chemical Warfare Center, the training center at Camp Sibert, and the new CWS laboratories, testing grounds, and biological warfare installations.

In its administrative no less than in its operational activities, the CWS felt the influence of the ASF. But only with regard to the depots was ASF influence direct and predominant. ASF headquarters specified that a standard organization be established in each depot. In the procurement districts and arsenals ASF initiative was never so pronounced. There the CWS generally inaugurated and carried to completion all actions of an administrative nature. These actions were, of course, subject to ASF approval.

In contrast to ASF activity at the depots, whose revised organizational structures were looked upon approvingly by key personnel in the CWS, the ASF decision to put Camp Sibert under the jurisdiction of the commanding general of the Fourth Service Command, was not viewed with favor by the Chief, CWS. General Somervell, nevertheless, stood by the ASF directive to make Sibert a Class I activity of the Fourth Service Command, as noted above. General Porter undoubtedly had that situation in mind when in September 1944 he set up the San José Project Division in his office to supervise all activities of the Panama installation. Porter was taking a precaution to insure that all responsibility for San José would remain under CWS control.

CHAPTER VII

Personnel Management

The proportion of civilians to military in the Chemical Warfare Service was far higher in World War II than in World War I.[1] In November 1918 there were only 784 civilians in the CWS as compared to 22,198 military, a ratio of 3.5 percent. During the peacetime period a marked change took place, the number of civilians usually exceeding the military. (*See Tables 2 and 3.*) The combined total of civilian and military personnel in the 1920's and 1930's was not large, so that personnel management functions presented no particular difficulty. As the Chief, CWS, himself phrased it in the spring of 1937, "The personnel duties devolving upon the Chief, Chemical Warfare Service, are not now onerous."[2] The Personnel Office, OC CWS, was staffed with one officer and one civilian clerk.

The situation began to change in the emergency period. From 1939 on there was a rise in both civilian and military personnel rolls, until a peak was reached in late 1942 for civilians, and in late 1943 for military. The greater increase, as might be expected, took place in the military rolls. However, as already mentioned, the proportion of civilians to military in World War II was far higher than in World War I. In December 1942 the number of civilians was 46 percent of the military, in December 1943, 36.5 percent, and in December 1944, 36 percent of the military.

Procurement and Assignment of Officers

In World War I the CWS obtained officers by transfer from other branches of the Army and by direct commissioning from civilian life. The

---

[1] In addition to the documentary sources cited throughout this chapter, information was obtained through interviews with key officers and civilians engaged in CWS personnel management activities in World War II. These included the following: General Porter, Brig. Gen. Henry M. Black, Brig. Gen. (later Maj. Gen.) Charles E. Loucks, Col. Herrold Brooks, Col. Charles H. McNary, Colonel Kuhn, Lt. Col. James B. Costello, Lt. Col. Evan H. Lewis, Lt. Col. Karl F. Erickson, Maj. Floyd Van Domelen, Capt. James Wills, Miss Norma G. Bussink, Mr. Forest C. Hall, Mr. Gerald M. Vest, and Dr. Victor G. Clare.

[2] 1st Ind, C CWS to TAG, 30 Apr 37, on Ltr, TAG to Chiefs WD Arms and Services, 21 Apr 37, sub: Pers Matters. CWS 200/1.

National Defense Act of 1920 set up a quota of one hundred officers, in addition to the Chief, for the CWS as the best possible estimate under the uncertain conditions which then prevailed. This quota, which in actual numbers was not obtained until 1940, was filled mainly by officers who had served successfully in the CWS in World War I. The background of these officers varied. Some had had scientific training and experience before entering the Army while others were military specialists. The CWS had a need for both.

As vacancies arose through attrition during the peacetime years, they were filled by details or transfers into the CWS from other arms and services, particularly the Coast Artillery Corps. In selecting such replacements it was the practice of the Chiefs of the CWS to select individuals having at least excellent military ratings [3] without special regard to technical qualifications. It was scarcely feasible to attempt to recruit scientific specialists from other branches of the peacetime Army. It became the policy, therefore, to rely on civilian scientists and engineers for developing the more technical aspects of the CWS program, under the general direction of officers who proved qualified to supervise research and development activities. In order to carry out the program more effectively, CWS detailed selected officers for two-year courses at the Massachusetts Institute of Technology and the University of Wisconsin.

All CWS officers, including in some instances those who supervised research and development work, received a variety of assignments in the course of their military careers. They were required to train and command troops, to serve as Special Staff officers in the field, to supervise procurement and supply activities, and on occasion to fill miscellaneous jobs listed as War Department overhead. The variety of assignments in the Chemical Warfare Service was wider than in most branches of the Army, and some otherwise good officers could not adapt themselves to the system. Undoubtedly there was greater need for specialization in officer assignments and from the mid-1930's on the CWS followed that policy. By the time of the emergency, CWS officers were generally classified as specialists in military field assignments, in research, or in procurement and supply. Of course the limited activities of the peacetime years restricted the degree of specialization. This was particularly true in the realm of procurement. The emergency brought to the CWS a desperate need for officers with industrial experience. Since Regular officers were not available in sufficient numbers, the CWS

---

[3] The highest military rating was "superior," which was followed by "excellent."

met the need by assignment of qualified Reserve officers and by direct commission of civilians with the necessary qualifications.

In addition to its relatively few Regular Army officers the CWS had a number of Reserve officers, who were generally assigned or attached to chemical regiments stationed throughout the country. In 1939 these Reserve officers totaled 2,100.[4] As the need became critical these officers were called to active duty. Unfortunately many could not pass the physical examination and were eliminated. From 1940 to 1942 the War Department effected transfer of Reserve officers from other branches under a procedure whereby The Adjutant General's Office circulated to the various arms and services the names and qualifications of especially able officers. In this way the CWS obtained some seventy officers, ranging in rank from second lieutenant to lieutenant colonel. But these sources did not come anywhere near filling the requirement for officers in the war period. The extent of the problem which the CWS faced in procuring officers may be gauged by a consideration of the number of officers who came into the service in the war years. In late 1943 this figure reached a peak of over eight thousand—in contrast to the less than one hundred Regulars of the peacetime years.

Civilians with proper qualifications provided an important source of officer procurement in 1941–42. The Personnel Division of the Chief's office and the procurement district offices carried out a program of contacting industries where qualified civilians might be available. Pamphlets listing the specifications of CWS officers were compiled and circulated. In this way numerous civilians were attracted to the Chemical Warfare Service and granted direct commissions.[5]

Another source of officer material was the Army Specialist Corps, fostered by the Army as a means of building up a quasi-military corps of scientific, technical, and administrative personnel.[6] This corps was activated in the spring of 1942. Its members, many of whom had minor physical

[4] For details on Reserves, see below, Chapter VIII.

[5] (1) Ltr, C SFCWPD to C CWS, 22 Apr 42, sub: Policy References Comms. (2) Ltr, C Pers Div OC CWS to Andrew P. Monroe, Vice President, N.J. Bell Telephone Co., 28 Apr 42. Both in CWS 210 1/421–499. (3) Ltr, C CWS to Hon. Wirt Courtney, House of Representatives, 21 Sep 42 CWS 210.1/500. (4) Summary of Staff Mtg, OC CWS, 27 Feb 42. CWS 337. (5) Memo, C Pers Div OC CWS for Col Edwin C. Maling, Cml Warfare School, 6 Apr 42. CWS 210.3/341–365.

[6] The Army Specialist Corps was activated under Executive Order 9078, 26 February 1942. See WD Bull 11, Sec. 11, 1942, and WD Army Specialist Corps Regulations (Tentative, 1942, G–1, 16545–46, Part III). For a general discussion of the Specialist Corps, see Millett, *Army Service Forces,* p. 101, and Henry P. Seidemann, "Army Specialist Corps," *Army Ordnance,* XXIII (1942), 502–04.

MAJ. GEN. DWIGHT F. DAVIS, *Director General of the Army Specialist Corps, with Lt. Col. William E. Jeffrey. Both are wearing the ASC uniform, distinguished by buttons and insignia of black plastic.*

defects, wore uniforms similar to those worn by the military, but the corps was civilian and not military. The program was discontinued in the fall of 1942 because it did not prove practical. During its existence some fifty Specialist Corps officers were assigned to the CWS, many of whom were integrated into the service as Army officers, upon the corps' deactivation.

After its establishment at Edgewood in early 1942, the Officer Candidate School became the chief source of officers so far as sheer numbers were concerned.[7] Graduates of the OCS were commissioned second lieutenants and were usually assigned to CWS units. Other assignments of CWS officers were to installations, to training centers, and to the Office of the Chief.

[7] For details on the OCS, see below, Chapter XIV.

A good many chemical warfare officers were assigned or attached in the zone of interior to the Army Ground Forces, the Army Air Forces, and the Army Service Forces. (*Chart 10*) [8]

The assignment of officers within the CWS was a function of the Office of the Chief. General Porter personally assigned the commanding officers of installations and members of his own staff, while commanding officers of installations were responsible for the selection of their subordinates through the Personnel Division, OC CWS. Although the commanding officers could not always obtain the officers they wanted, the situation was certainly not as bad as some commanders alleged. There developed a tendency in one or two installations to explain all administrative deficiencies on the ground that it was impossible to obtain the services of qualified officers. The evidence does not support this contention. [9] The trouble was not so much that qualified officers could not be obtained, although at times this problem did exist, but rather that there sometimes was a lack of appreciation of the potentialities of the officers on hand.

Promotion, Decorations, and Allotments

In order to assist the Personnel Division of his office in carrying out its functions, General Porter in the summer of 1942 appointed a Promotion and Decorations Board composed of the executive officer of his office and the chiefs of the Fielid, Industrial, and Technical Services. [10] Following the publication of the very important ASF Circular 39, 11 June 1943, the Chief, CWS, appointed a second board, known as an Allotment Board, to deal with the allotment of civilian and military employees to CWS units and installations. This Allotment Board consisted of the executive officer, the two assistant chiefs of CWS, the chiefs of the Control and Personnel Divisions, and a recorder from the Personnel Division who had no vote. [11] On 13 August 1943 the functions of the two boards were consolidated in an Allotment, Promotion, Separation, and Decoration Board. [12]

Before the creation of the Promotion and Decorations Board the administration of those activities in the CWS left much to be desired. Some

---

[8] For a detailed breakdown of the distribution of CWS military personnel from December 1941 to December 1945, see below, Appendixes A, B, and C.

[9] This conclusion is based on interviews with key personnel officers in CWS in World War II and on IOM, C Civ Pers Br OC CWS for C Pers Div OC CWS, 16 Feb 45. CWS 230.

[10] OC CWS Off O 36, 8 Jul 42.

[11] OC CWS Off O 46, 29 Jun 43.

[12] OC CWS Adm O 16, 13 Aug 43.

CHART 10—DISTRIBUTION OF CWS MILITARY PERSONNEL,
AS OF 30 JUNE 1944

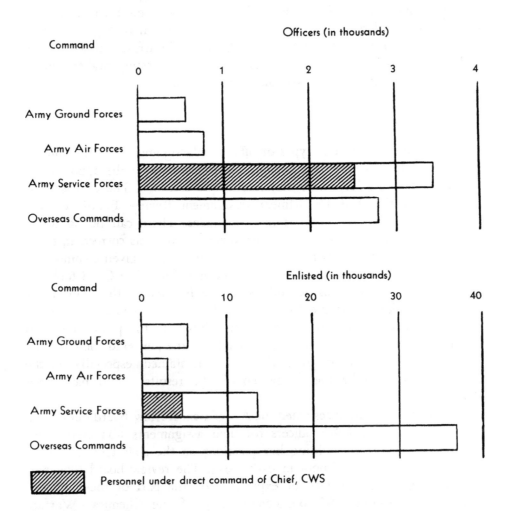

Personnel under direct command of Chief, CWS

Source. Appendix A

commanding officers were more prone than others to recommend promotions, and personal favoritism was all too often a determining factor. Once the board began to function effectively the situation greatly improved. The board's jurisdiction in all its functions—allotments, promotions, and decorations—was service-wide. Allotments of officers. as well as of enlisted men.

were on the basis of quotas furnished by The Adjutant General's Office, which the board would break down to the various elements of the CWS, such as installations, Office of the Chief, and training centers. After receiving notification of their quotas those elements would forward their military personnel requisitions to The Adjutant General through the Military Personnel Branch, OC CWS. The Chemical Warfare Service always had the prerogative, which it often exercised, of requesting higher quotas, but all such requests had to carry ample justification.

Malassignment of Officers

There were two general types of officer malassignment: the assignment of officers to duties that were not military functions; and the appointment of officers to posts for which they lacked qualifications. The criticisms of the CWS by the War Department Assignment Review Board centered chiefly around the first type of malassignment. There can be no doubt that this contention of the Assignment Review Board was correct. In many instances CWS civilians carrying out certain duties were given commissions and continued to do exactly the same work as before. The CWS took the position that circumstances beyond its control had led to the granting of these commissions, that the Civil Service Commission could not furnish qualified replacements, and that the only solution to the problem was to commission those civilians who were already on the job. Had these officers been removed from their posts, the CWS maintained, especially on the scale recommended by the review board, the results would have been disastrous.

One of the rare instances when the Assignment Review Board questioned the qualifications of CWS officers for their assignments was in the case of some dozen officers holding key positions on the staff and faculty of the Chemical Warfare School in early 1944. The review board took particular exception to the lack of experience on the part of these officers. Brig. Gen. Alexander Wilson, commandant of the Chemical Warfare School, generally agreed with this contention, although he held that the situation was not nearly so bad as one might gather from merely screening the Officer Qualification Records.[13] General Wilson outlined the history of how these officers came to occupy their posts. After the war broke out, he said, the number of Regular Army officers with experience in chemical

---

[13] WD AGO Form 0857.

warfare training was entirely inadequate and CWS Reserve officers, most of whom had had long experience in the field of chemistry, were placed in training posts. These officers, through experience, became expert in training and administrative duties. As understudies to these officers there were a number of other officers, recent college graduates, who had little or no practical civilian experience. In time, the older officers were assigned to overseas duty, and the only officers available to fill their places were the understudies, who, while they lacked civilian experience, had had several years of training in their present assignments.[14] The CWS did not find it possible to replace those officers.

Procurement and Utilization of Enlisted Personnel

Enlisted personnel rolls expanded in approximately the same proportion as officer rolls. From a total of 803 enlisted men in June 1939, the number rose to 5,591 in December 1941 and to a wartime peak of 61,688 in June 1943. The year and a half after Pearl Harbor was the period of greatest expansion. (*See Appendix B.*)

The majority of enlisted men assigned to the CWS went to the training center at Edgewood, which was later moved to Camp Sibert. Relatively few men were assigned to CWS installations. The Chief, CWS, was responsible for the assignment, promotion, and movement of those men in and out of the installations and for selecting those who were to attend special schools. Enlisted personnel were customarily not retained at the installations for long, since the service used them for overseas requisitions that it was continuously being called upon to fill.

Thanks to the Selective Service system, the CWS secured a number of unusually well-qualified enlisted men.[15] In June 1941, for example, there were thirty-two enlisted men with college degrees in the 1st Laboratory Company. Of these, seven had doctor's degrees and three had master's degrees. After activation of the Officer Candidate School, men of this caliber had opportunity to apply for admission. Many of the men assigned to the installations were very well qualified for minor administrative and clerical posts. The Chemical Warfare Center, particularly, utilized their

---

[14] 2d Ind, Comdt Cml Warfare School to CG Cml Warfare Center on Ltr, C Pers Div OC CWS to CG Cml Warfare Center, 11 Feb 44, sub: Correct Classification and Assignment of ASF Officers and Enlisted Men. CWS 200.3.

[15] Robert R Palmer, Bell I. Wiley, and William R. Keast. *The Procurement and Training of Ground Combat Troops*, UNITED STATES ARMY IN WORLD WAR II (Washington: 1948), pp. 17–18

services. When the great demand for men for overseas duty arose in 1943, all general service enlisted men were transferred from zone of interior installations to field service for eventual shipment overseas.[16] Men with varying degrees of physical disability replaced these enlisted men, but this move proved generally unsatisfactory. The situation was largely rectified when members of the Women's Army Auxiliary Corps (WAAC) were brought in as substitutes for the male personnel.

Negro Military Personnel

There were few Negro troops in the Army in the peacetime period, and prior to 1940 the number of Negro units provided for in the Protective Mobilization Plan (PMP) was decidedly limited.[17] No provision was made for any Negro chemical units. In the summer of 1940 the Assistant Chief of Staff, G–3, recommended modification of the PMP in order to provide more Negro units. The CWS initially felt the effects of the new policy when the 1st Chemical Decontamination Company, constituted as a white company in the PMP, was activated on 1 August 1940 at Fort Eustis, Virginia, as a Negro unit.[18]

In the summer of 1940 the War Department still had to work out many policy details on the employment of Negro troops. These included such items as the number of Negro troops to be called for active duty, the question of whether to use Negro or white officers with colored units, and the problem of what to do about the prevailing practice of segregating white and Negro troops. On 8 October 1940 the President approved the policy to be followed during the war.[19] Negro strength in the Army was to be maintained on the ratio of Negroes to the whites in the country as a whole, and Negro organizations were to be established in each major branch of the service, combatant as well as noncombatant. The existing War Department policy of not intermingling white and Negro enlisted personnel was to be continued. Negro Reserve officers eligible for active duty were to be assigned to Negro units and opportunity was to be given Negroes to attend officer candidate schools. The aviation training of Negroes as

[16] ASF Cir 39, 11 Jun 43.
[17] Ulysses G Lee, Employment of Negro Troops, a volume in preparation for the series UNITED STATES ARMY IN WORLD WAR II, is a detailed study of Negro troops throughout the Army.
[18] WD Ltr, AG 320 2 (7–10–40) M (Ret) M–C, 20 Jul 40.
[19] Memo, ASW for the President, 8 Oct 40. The President penciled his "OK" and initials on this memo. Cited in Lee, Employment of Negro Troops, Ch. IV.

pilots, mechanics, and technical specialists was to be accelerated, and at arsenals and Army posts Negro civilians were to have equal opportunity with whites for employment.

In conformity with the above policy the Replacement Center at Edgewood opened in 1941 with a capacity of 1,000 trainees—800 white and 200 Negro.[20] Negroes were trained in approximately this proportion at Edgewood and later at Camp Sibert. Since the percentage of Negro troops in Classes IV and V of the Army General Classification Test was much higher than that of white troops, the training of Negro troops as a whole presented greater difficulties than that of white troops.[21]

From the spring of 1942 until the summer of 1943 seventy-five CWS troop units composed of Negroes were activated at various installations throughout the country. The seventy-five units consisted of the following: 12 chemical maintenance companies (aviation), 7 chemical depot companies (aviation), 1 chemical company (air operations), 20 chemical decontamination companies, 3 chemical processing companies, 30 chemical smoke generator companies, and 2 chemical service companies. Forty-one of those companies were eventually assigned to duty overseas.[22]

As indicated by the large number of Negro chemical companies, the CWS had a relatively high percentage of Negro troops. As of 30 September 1943, over 17 percent of CWS enlisted men were Negro. The CWS percentage was exceeded only by those of the Quartermaster Corps, Transportation Corps, and Corps of Engineers.[23]

The chemical companies to which Negroes were assigned were, with one exception, service rather than combat in nature. The exception was the smoke generator company, and even this type of company in the early period of the war was considered more service than combat. Plans at that time called for the smoking of rear areas only, and the troops were trained for that mission. But as the war progressed these companies saw front-line action. Since the men were not trained for combat conditions, at first they made a poor showing. With experience these units improved tremendously and many of them had very good combat records.

The CWS trained about one hundred Negro officers at the Officer Candidate School. Upon graduation some of these officers were assigned to

---

[20] See, below, Part Two, for details on training of CWS troops.

[21] Classes IV and V were the two lowest levels of achievement.

[22] The 706th Chemical Maintenance Company (Aviation) was redesignated as 769th Chemical Depot Company (Aviation) as of 20 December 1943.

[23] Lee, Employment of Negro Troops, Ch. XIX.

chemical units, others were transferred to the Transportation Corps and the Air Forces, and those who were surplus were placed temporarily in the officers' pool at the Chemical Warfare Center.

There was one instance of marked unrest among Negro troops in the CWS. This outbreak, which occurred at Camp Sibert in July 1943, was occasioned by the improper advances of a white civilian clerk toward a Negro woman in the post exchange. Although the Negro soldiers showed no hostility toward their white officers, they were slow in obeying orders to disperse and return to their barracks. Perhaps the flare-up would have reached more serious proportions had the Negro troops not received assurance that the white clerk would be turned over to the civil authorities.[24]

Women's Army Corps Personnel in the Chemical Warfare Service

In the summer and early fall of 1942, shortly after President Roosevelt signed the bill establishing the Women's Army Auxiliary Corps, chemical officers, under ASF direction, made a study of possible employment of Waacs in the CWS.[25] It was decided that Waacs might be used as replacements for enlisted men doing housekeeping duties in arsenals, as fill-ins for certain types of civil service positions where it was impossible to obtain civilians, and perhaps in chemical impregnating companies in the zone of the interior. In the course of this study the Personnel Division, OC CWS, contacted the WAAC to ascertain what the chances were of securing the services of WAAC officers and auxiliaries. The Personnel Division was informed that all existing WAAC units had been earmarked for assignment outside the CWS but that, not withstanding this fact the CWS should submit a requisition, which would be filled if at all possible.[26]

On 7 January 1943 the Chief, CWS, sent his first requisition to the director of the WAAC for 160 auxiliaries to be made available at Pine Bluff Arsenal.[27] The quota requested was not filled at the time because there were then not enough Waacs to go around, but early in April the first installment was sent to Pine Bluff. Faced with a serious shortage of stenographers, typists, bus drivers, and dispatchers—positions for which

[24] Ltr, CG CWS UTC to C CWS, 20 Jul 43. CWS 000.7.

[25] Public Law 554, 15 May 42. For details on the WAAC and its successor, the WAC, see Mattie E. Treadwell, *The Women's Army Corps*, UNITED STATES ARMY IN WORLD WAR II (Washington: 1954). The Wacs in CWS are discussed on pages 321–26 of that volume.

[26] Memo, Maj Earl L. Shepherd, Pers Div OC CWS, for Col Herrold E. Brooks, C Pers Div OC CWS, 17 Nov 42, sub: WAAC. CWS 324.5 WAC.

[27] Ltr, C CWS to Dir WAAC (Through Mil Pers Div SOS), 7 Jan 43. CWS 324.5 WAC.

civilians could not be obtained—this installation used the Waacs to fill those vacancies.[28] A misunderstanding soon developed over the fact that the Waacs did not always replace enlisted men. The Waacs apparently had gone to Pine Bluff believing that such would be the case, although the correspondence between the Chief, CWS, and the director of WAAC discloses that the chief problem at Pine Bluff was the shortage of civilian personnel. Whatever the source of the misunderstanding, it became a serious morale factor at Pine Bluff Arsenal and led to a number of resignations in the summer of 1943 when the Women's Army Auxiliary Corps was integrated into the new Women's Army Corps, set up as an element of the Army by an act of Congress.[29]

Late in April 1943 Dugway Proving Ground became the second CWS installation to be assigned a WAAC unit, and in June Camp Detrick and the Chemical Warfare Center were assigned quotas of Waacs. Later WAC officers were assigned to the Office of the Chief, CWS, and to the Rocky Mountain and Huntsville Arsenals. The number of Wacs assigned to the CWS during the war totaled about seven hundred.[30]

WAC officers assigned to headquarters usually performed administrative duties such as those connected with time and payroll, with the motor pool, or with the public relations office. Enlisted Wacs assigned to the CWS, the vast majority of whom went to CWS installations, were employed in a variety of skilled and semiskilled occupations. General Porter summarized the situation well in a letter to Oveta Culp Hobby, director of the WAAC, on 5 July 1943, when he said:

> WAAC enrollees at Chemical Warfare Service installations are engaged in activities of wide scope and variety, embracing both skilled and semi-skilled occupations. The more specialized personnel are performing the work of chemists, toxicologists, lawyers, meteorologists, mechanical engineers, etc. Others with technical training are surgical and veterinarian assistants, motion picture projectionists, radio and teletype operators, glass blowers, draftsmen and photographers. In addition, of course, your Corps is supplying stenographers, typists, mail, code, file, stockroom personnel, and copy clerks; court reporters and librarians.[31]

One interesting feature of Waac assignment in the CWS which General

[28] Ltr, CG PBA to C CWS, 9 Jul 43. CWS 324.5 WAC.

[29] (1) Ltr, C Mil Pers Br OC CWS to CO 1st WAAC CWS Hq Det PBA (Through: CG PBA), 19 Aug 43. CWS 324.5 WAC. (2) Public Law 110, 1 Jul 45. This law provided for the changeover from the WAAC to the WAC within sixty days.

[30] Treadwell, *Women's Army Corps*, p. 321.

[31] (1) Public Law 110, 1 July 1943. (2) Ltr, C CWS to Dir WAAC, 5 Jul 43. CWS 324.5 WAC. The chief purpose behind General Porter's letter was to congratulate Director Hobby on the success of the WAAC project.

Porter did not mention in his letter to Director Hobby was the employment of Waacs in chemical impregnating companies in the zone of the interior. As mentioned above, this possibility had been considered in the fall of 1942. In April 1943 the CWS conducted an experiment with sixty Waacs at Edgewood Arsenal to determine whether they could be used on the work of impregnating protective clothes with chemicals. The experiment proved successful beyond all expectations, and henceforth Waacs were assigned to those units, which for semantic reasons were redesignated "processing companies." [32]

"Successful beyond all expectations" might be the phrase used to describe the reaction in CWS, from General Porter down, to the work of the Wacs. Those commanding officers and supervisors who were at first skeptical about employing Wacs on certain types of assignments, laboratory technicians for example, soon changed their minds once the young women got on the job. When in 1945 General Porter said of the Wacs, "We owe them a great debt," he was expressing the sentiment of every commanding officer and supervisor in the CWS.[33] The attitude of the WAC toward the CWS was likewise one of satisfaction. As the CWS WAC staff director, Capt. Helen H. Hart, expressed it, WAC personnel were accepted in all CWS installations "on an equal and respectful basis by the majority of CWS personnel," and this situation, Captain Hart went on to say, "resulted in WAC CWS Headquarter Detachments having some of the highest morale among all WAC Detachments in the field." [34]

The Expanding Civilian Rolls

The number of civilian employees in the Chemical Warfare Service jumped from about 7,000 at the outbreak of the war to a peak of over 28,000 in 1943.[35] The breakdown of CWS personnel by designated groups as of 31 December 1944 is shown in Table 6.

---

[32] See Ltr, AC CWS for Fld Opns to G–1 (Through: Dir Mil Pers Div ASF), 9 Jun 43, sub: Use of WAAC in Cml Impregnating Companies. CWS 324.5 WAC. This letter indicates that as of 31 May 1943 the Chief, CWS, requested the Commanding General, ASF, to change the designation from "Chemical Impregnating Company" to "Chemical Processing Company."

[33] Quoted in "Here Are the WACS," *Chemical Warfare Bulletin*, XXXI, No. 2 (1945), 4–11.

[34] Ltr, Capt Hart, CWS WAC Staff Dir, to CO HA, 3 May 44, sub: General George C. Marshall's Memorandum. AG 320.2 WAC. The CWS WAC staff director sent similar letters to the commanders of other installations. General Marshall in a memorandum of 6 April 1944 had urged all elements of the Army to realize the dignity and importance of the Wacs, and the CWS WAC staff director was commenting on this memorandum.

[35] See Table 3.

TABLE 6—ACTUAL STRENGTH OF CIVILIAN EMPLOYEES (FILLED POSITIONS),
31 DECEMBER 1944

Service and Grade or Other Groups	Employees
Total CWS	23,007
Departmental	475
Professional (P–1 through P–9)	19
Subprofessional (SP–1 through SP–8)	1
Clerical, Administrative and Fiscal (CAF–1 through 16)	438
Crafts, Protective and Custodial (CPC–1 through CPC–10)	15
Consultants without compensation, and $1 per annum or per month	2
Field	22,532
Professional (P–1 through P–6)	542
Subprofessional (SP–1 through SP–5)	396
Clerical, Administrative and Fiscal (CAF–2 through CAF–14)	5,318
Crafts, Protective and Custodial (CPC–3 and CPC–4)	1,646
Ungraded	14,601
Consultants and Experts	*29

* Includes 3 without compensations or at $1 per annum or $1 per month.
Source· CWS 230.

One of the earliest personnel requirements in the CWS in the emergency period was for trained inspectors. The need first arose out of the educational order program under which two hundred gas-mask inspectors were trained at Edgewood Arsenal before being sent out to perform their duties at the gas-mask plants in the procurement districts.[36] Later, in the summer and fall of 1940, the procurement district offices began hiring inspectors in connection with the procurement contracts they were awarding. These inspectors were sent to Edgewood Arsenal for training before assuming their responsibilities. After they had obtained experience on the job, these inspectors in turn retained newly hired apprentices.[37]

Another significant training project undertaken by the CWS in the fall of 1939 was the apprenticeship program. The project arose from efforts

[36] Ltr, CG EA to C CWS, 3 Dec 40, sub: Education Order Pers. CWS Files 230/681 (1939–42) Series, NA.
[37] For details on the training of inspectors in World War II, see Brophy, Miles, and Cochrane, From Laboratory to Field.

of the Assistant Secretary of War. In a letter of 13 September 1939 to the chiefs of all the arms and services the Assistant Secretary called attention to the problem of procuring an adequate supply of skilled labor for producing munitions. Even though there were great numbers of unemployed, he stated realistically, a full use of all the skilled men then idle would still leave a large deficit for meeting the war needs. As a solution he proposed the use of apprenticeship programs and urged the supply arms and services, in their field contacts with industry, to "foster and encourage apprenticeship training by relating such training to the needs of national defense." [38] The Office of the Chief, CWS, sent copies of this letter to all CWS procurement districts with instructions that they be guided by its contents.[39]

The CWS worked on plans for an apprenticeship training program at Edgewood Arsenal from late 1939 on, but it was not until January 1942 that such a program was actually launched.[40] At that time one hundred apprentices began courses in various crafts. Of that number only two eventually completed their training. The reason for this was not lack of ability or enterprise on the part of the young men, but rather the fact that almost to a man they were inducted into the armed services under the Selective Service Act. The one apprentice not inducted did finish his training. Another who returned to Edgewood as a regular employee after the war also finished his apprenticeship. On the basis of the record, the apprenticeship training program at Edgewood was anything but a success, especially in view of the fact that some of those apprentices had spent two years studying their crafts.[41]

As serious as the problem of obtaining suitable employees at Edgewood was the problem of retaining them once they had been hired. The chief source of difficulty was the wage rate system of the War Department. For a number of years the War Department had made efforts to keep the wage rates of its employees in line with localities where its installations were

[38] Ltr, Col Harry K. Rutherford, Ord Deputy Dir OASW, to Chiefs Supply Arms and Servs, 13 Sep 39, sub: Encouragement of Apprenticeship Tng. CWS 230/471–480.
[39] Ltr, Maj George F. Unmacht, Asst Ex O OC CWS, to All Cml Warfare Proc Districts, 20 Sep 39, sub: Encouragement of Apprenticeship Tng. CWS 230/471–480.
[40] (1) Ltr, ASW to C CWS, and 1st Ind, 26 Dec 39, sub: Apprentice Tng. CWS 230/471–480. (2) Memo, C CWS for CofS, 28 May 40, sub: Tng of Skilled and Semiskilled Workers. CWS 230/540.
[41] After the war a number of these men returned to Edgewood hoping to complete the training they had started, but unfortunately, except for the cases just cited, there was no opportunity for them to be taken back since the government no longer needed apprentices.

situated through the appointment of boards to survey wages. Such surveys had been made in Edgewood in April 1925, August 1929, and November 1939.[42] But the surveys could not keep up with rising wages in industry, and by the spring of 1940 the rates were again out of line. The CWS began to encounter the problem after its construction program got under way in the fall of 1940. Skilled and semiskilled workers began leaving government employ to work for private construction companies on the post, whose wage rates were about 50 percent higher than the government's. Later the same thing happened at Huntsville and Pine Bluff Arsenals.

Not only was the CWS losing employees to industry because of wage rates. It was also losing them to other nearby government installations. For, surprisingly, there was no uniform wage rate system throughout neighboring government installations, and employees were leaving Edgewood to accept higher rates of pay for the same type work at the naval installation at Bainbridge, Maryland, and at the Aberdeen Proving Ground.[43]

In the summer of 1941 the Personnel Division, OC CWS, requested the U.S. Employment Service (USES) to survey the situation at Edgewood. The USES readily complied and set up a wage scale of unclassified positions. This system did not prove satisfactory chiefly because the CWS did not have enough people trained to administer it. In the fall of 1941 the commanding officers at Edgewood and other CWS installations requested and received permission to raise the wages of their civilian employees. This they did by raising the grades of the laboring, craft, and mechanical positions (so-called upgraded), a procedure which led to trouble later on. What they should have done was to adjust the wage rates for all positions, white collar and ungraded, to conform to the percentage rise in general wage rates in the area. The grades of the jobs represented relative differences in skill levels, and by raising the grades for some jobs and not for others due recognition was not given to skill differentials. Since each installation was given authority to make its own grade adjustments, the entire wage structure soon became illogical and unworkable.

Late in December 1941 the Chief, CWS, in an effort to disentangle the wage rate situation, requested the director of personnel of the War

---

[42] Ltr, C Pers Div OC CWS to CG ASF (Attn: Ind Pers Div), 6 Jun 45, sub: Wage Fixing Procedures Prior to 28 Mar 34. CWS 248.

[43] (1) Ltr, CO EA to C CWS, 25 Apr 39, sub: Draftsmen at EA. CWS 230/431–470. (2) Interv, CmlHO with Col Henry M. Black, 8 Aug 50.

Department to appoint a specialist in wage administration to the CWS.[44] This request was given favorable consideration. A civilian wage specialist, Floyd Van Domelen, was commissioned in the CWS and assigned to the Personnel Division of the Chief's office in May 1942. He set to work immediately to draw up a wage rate plan, a task he completed by August 1942. The CWS was about to put the plan into operation when the ASF issued a directive to set up a wage administration system throughout its entire organization. In compliance, the CWS refrained from putting its own plan into operation and participated instead in the over-all ASF plan.

The ASF wage administration plan called for the activation of a Wage Administration Agency whose authority included setting wages for the laboring, craft, and mechanical employees in the field installations.[45] This agency was set up, and under its direction the CWS established alignments called ladder diagrams in each of its installations. These ladder diagrams set up the positions which were not subject to the Classification Act of 1923, as amended—laboring, craft, and mechanical positions—in accordance with the difficulty and responsibility of each job. The Wage Administration Agency then surveyed the wage rates in industrial establishments in the vicinity of each installation to determine the prevailing rate for each particular type of position and the resulting wage schedule was applied to the installation. The Wage Administration Agency collected its data on local wage rates through locality wage survey boards which it set up in the service commands. Representation on these boards was not confined to a single arm or service, but various appropriate elements of the ASF were represented. For example, the Locality Wage Survey Board which was activated at Aberdeen Proving Ground in the fall of 1942 under the commanding general of the Third Service Command had a CWS representative from Edgewood Arsenal.[46] In the opinion of perhaps the most competent authority on wage administration in CWS, the ASF methods of handling the wage problem were far superior to previous methods.[47] Once the new system began to function, other arms and services were no longer able to outbid the CWS for employees. The Navy still could, of course; over-all reform had to wait until a later day.

---

[44] Memo, C CWS for Dir Pers WD, 30 Dec 41. CWS 230/1436. The Chief, CWS, in this memorandum requested that Mr. Floyd Van Domelen be assigned to CWS. The request for Van Domelen was honored.

[45] Ltr, C Civ Pers Br APG to C CWS, 23 Nov 42, sub: Establishment of Wage Survey Bd. CWS 334.

[46] Ibid.

[47] Interv, Cml HO with Floyd Van Domelen, 24 Oct 50.

Administration From Washington

The activities of the emergency period led to an increase in the number of employees in the Chief's office. About a dozen civilians were added to the rolls as a result of the educational order program. Several of these were engineers and the remainder were clerk-stenographers.[48] During 1940 and 1941 the number of new employees continued to increase, so that by the time war was declared there were over 250 civilian employees in the overcrowded CWS headquarters offices in Washington. Included were employees with specialist, professional, and clerk-stenographer ratings. During the war this number was to be multiplied several times. In November 1942 the figure reached a wartime peak of 675 civilian employees. From then until the close of the war there was a progressive decline in numbers. (*See Table 3.*)

The advent of war brought about a revolutionary change in the functions and responsibility of the CWS in regard to personnel administration. Before Pearl Harbor the War Department procured, appointed, classified, and promoted all civilians. The only function left for the CWS was assignment. This procedure was too time-consuming and unwieldy for wartime. A week after the December attack, General Porter requested the Secretary of War to grant him authority to handle all civilian personnel functions in the CWS.[49] The Secretary of War answered this request, and perhaps others like it, with the issuance on 23 December 1941 of War Department orders authorizing decentralization of personnel administration to bureau, arm, and service levels. As a result of this and its other orders throughout 1942 and 1943, the War Department effected gradual decentralization to the field installation level.[50]

The decentralization of personnel administration from the War Department to the Chemical Warfare Service necessarily brought about a considerable increase in the responsibilities of the chief of the Personnel Division of General Porter's office. This post was occupied from 1938 until September 1942 by Col. Geoffrey Marshall. Colonel Marshall was succeeded by Col. Herrold E. Brooks who remained chief throughout the war. In

---

[48] (1) Memo, Ex O OC CWS for Adm Div OC CWS, 24 May 39. CWS 230/475. (2) Ltr, C CWS to ASW, 18 Oct 39, sub: Pers Whose Salaries Are Paid From Funds Allotted to the ASW. CWS 230/471–480.

[49] Memo, C CWS for SW, 15 Dec 41, sub: Delegation of Authority. CWS 230/436.

[50] WD Orders N, 23 Dec 41; WD Orders G, 1 Jun 42: WD Orders M, 13 Aug 42; WD Orders C, 29 Jan 43; WD Orders J, 3 Jun 43.

contrast to the situation in 1937, when the unit administering personnel activities in the Chief's office consisted of one officer, whose time was "considerably occupied on other than personnel work," and one clerk, there were in August 1944 nine officers and thirty-six civilians on duty with the Personnel Division of the Chief's office.[51] From 23 December 1941 until 1 September 1942 the Personnel Division of the Chief's office was responsible for administration of civilian activities in the OC CWS, as well as for prescribing regulations for the administration of civilians in the field installations. On 1 September 1942, under War Department orders, the commanding officers of the field installations assumed authority to make appointments and to carry out practically all other personnel functions.[52] From that time until the end of the war, the Personnel Division, OC CWS, acted merely as a staff agency with regard to the personnel administration and activities of the installations.

The administration of personnel functions in the Office of the Chief was handicapped in the early period of the war by a dearth of officers trained in personnel management. Since few officers with this training were available, it was necessary for officers on duty to learn through experience. Consequently it was difficult for the division to carry out all the recognized activities of a large industrial personnel organization. As the officers in the Personnel Division gained experience, the situation improved.

Recruitment of Civilian Personnel in the Office
of the Chief of Chemical Warfare Service

It is ironic that when the CWS was occupying inadequate headquarters in the city of Washington in the early period of the war it could have secured all the personnel it needed, but that when the headquarters was moved to more spacious quarters at Gravelly Point, Virginia, in January 1943, it was impossible to secure a sufficient number of employees. The Gravelly Point location was chiefly responsible for this predicament. Employees living in Washington had to pay two fares—one on the bus within the city and the other on the bus between Washington and Gravelly Point —and on the average it took an hour to get to work. The shortage of personnel in the Chief's office was not overcome until employees were able

---

[51](1) Ltr, TAG to Chiefs WD Arms and Services, 21 Apr 37, sub: Pers Matters. CWS 200/1. (2) Ltr, DC CWS to Dir Pers ASF, 17 Aug 44, sub: Justification for Pers Utilization. CWS 230.
[52](1) WD Orders N, 23 Dec 41; WD Orders M, 13 Aug 42. (2) OC CWS Organization Chart, 1 May 42.

to make car pool arrangements and until a number of civilians residing on the Virginia side of the Potomac were brought into the office.

After outbreak of war, the War Department received permission from the Civil Service Commission to recruit employees from a central pool in Washington. The Chief's office obtained its workers from this source until the pool was discontinued in January 1943. For several months thereafter OC CWS recruited employees on its own. Workers already on the job were urged to contact any of their acquaintances who might be likely prospects. Various CWS installations were combed for any surplus stenographers and typists. Later in 1943 the ASF set up another pool, or recruiting service, which it called the Pre-Assignment Development Unit. This agency remained active until the close of the war.

The CWS had considerable difficulty in obtaining qualified accountants, fiscal experts, and statisticians through the Civil Service Commission, both for the Chief's office and the installations. The need was met in part by dollar-a-year men and by experts from private industry who were loaned to the CWS.[53]

Training of Civilian Employees in the Office of the Chief of Chemical Warfare Service

As early as 10 July 1941 the Secretary of War called the attention of the chiefs of War Department bureaus, arms, and services to the importance of training civilian employees.[54] Soon after Pearl Harbor a training program got under way in the Chemical Warfare Service.[55] Training in the Chief's office consisted in the main of elementary and advanced instruction in stenography and typing, in the operation of machine records and automatic punch machines, and in interoffice correspondence routing and distribution.[56]

Employee Relations

Employee relations, which included counseling and personal services, had been traditionally carried on in the CWS in connection with other

---

[53] Interv, CmlHO with Col Harry A. Kuhn, USA (Ret.), 13 Oct 50.

[54] Memo, SW for Chiefs WD Bureaus, Arms, and Services, 10 Jul 41. CWS 314.7 Training File.

[55] See below, pages 173–76, for details of training in the CWS installations.

[56] Memo, C Pers Div OC CWS for C Pers Div ASF, 8 Sep 43, sub: Clerical and Stenographic Tng Course. CWS 353.

personnel activities, such as assignments, wage rates, and efficiency reports. Since the personnel offices supervised these functions, they felt that they should also deal with any problems arising in connection with the functions.

The theory that separate employee relations units were needed to carry on civilian personnel counseling originated in the ASF. In conformity with an ASF directive to appoint an employee counselor, General Porter brought Miss Dorothy A. Whipple, who had had experience counseling school teachers in the Detroit City school system, into his office in September 1942. Miss Whipple headed an Employee Relations Section in the Personnel Division until the reorganization of the Chief's office in 1943. As a result of that reorganization the Employee Relations Section was raised to the status of an executive branch, where it remained for the duration of the war.[57]

The separation of employee relations functions from other personnel functions did not make for improved administration. In many instances the Employee Relations Section had to consult with the Civilian Personnel Branch before any type of action could be taken or recommended. This was necessary because of the technical nature of the problems arising, such as job classification matters, and because the Civilian Personnel Branch had the complete personnel record of the employee in its files. It was a mistake to have attempted the separation of the functions.

Installation Management of Civilian Personnel

The Edgewood Arsenal employed more civilians than any other CWS installation. (*Table 7*) The difficulty which Edgewood experienced in the emergency period and in the first year of the war in obtaining and retaining civilian workers has already been mentioned. The differences in wage rates between the Chemical Warfare Center and other nearby installations, it will be recalled, was largely overcome as a result of the work of the Locality Wage Survey Board in the fall of 1942. These results did not come overnight, however, and in early 1943 the situation was still considered so critical that Brig. Gen. Paul X. English, chief of the Industrial Division, OC CWS, proposed that Edgewood Arsenal utilize military as well as civilian employees in its plant operations.[58] The chief of arsenal operations

---

[57] (1) Memo, Ex O OC CWS for file, 22 Sep 42, (2) Memo, C Pers Div OC CWS To All Concerned, 6 Oct 42. Both in CWS 230.6. (3) Employee Relations Monthly Rpt, 1 Jun–1 Jul 43. CWS 200 6.

[58] Ltr, C Civ Pers Div OC CWS to CG, Cml Warfare Center, 24 Jan 43, sub: Manpower at EA, Md. CWS 230.

TABLE 7—PEAK CIVILIAN PERSONNEL FIGURES AT PRINCIPAL CWS INSTALLA-
TIONS DURING WORLD WAR II

Installations	Peak figure	Date
Arsenals		
Huntsville	5,946	31 Mar 1944
Edgewood	8,886	31 Mar 1943
Pine Bluff	8,074	31 Mar 1944
Rocky Mountain	2,676	30 Jun 1945
Procurement Districts		
Atlanta	339	30 Sep 1942
Boston	1,042	31 Dec 1942
Chicago	1,721	31 Dec 1942
Dallas	373	30 Sep 1944
New York	1,200	31 Dec 1942
Pittsburgh	1,331	31 Dec 1942
San Francisco	453	31 Mar 1942
Depots		
Eastern	317	31 Dec 1942
Southwest–Gulf	633	31 Dec 1944
Midwest–Pine Bluff	411	30 Sep 1945
Deseret	532	30 Jun 1945
Indianapolis	319	30 Jun 1945
Northeast	91	30 Sep 1945
Biological Warfare Installations		
Camp Detrick	22	30 Jun 1945
Vigo Plant	180	30 Sep 1945
Granite Peak	0	-----------
Horn Island	0	-----------
Other CWS Installations		
Dugway Proving Ground	61	31 Dec 1944

Source Extracted from Station Files in custody of Mr. Michael D. Wertheimer, O Civ Pers, OACofS, G–1, DA.

at the Chemical Warfare Center, Col. Henry M. Black, contended that it would not be feasible to employ military and civilian workers in the same plant, chiefly because the military would become dissatisfied with working for what they would consider a lower rate of pay, and that the prospects of obtaining a sufficient number of the military to operate the plants seemed remote.[59]

[59] Black interv, 8 Aug 50.

The problem was referred to James P. Mitchell, chief of the Civilian Personnel Division, ASF, who decided against the utilization of military personnel at the manufacturing plants at Edgewood.[60] He believed that the civilian manpower situation at the Chemical Warfare Center could be improved by co-operative action between the ASF and the CWS. Toward that end Mr. Mitchell himself took the following specific steps: (1) he arranged with the Transportation Corps to make four additional buses available for service between Baltimore and Edgewood; (2) he detailed to the Baltimore area an ASF labor supply officer, who was to give every possible assistance to CWS; and (3) he directed the Civilian Personnel Division, ASF, to investigate the possibility of raising wage rates at the Arsenal Operations Department on the ground that it was a hazardous manufacturing unit. At the same time Mr. Mitchell requested the CWS to carry out the following procedures: (1) detail an officer or a civilian or both from the Chemical Warfare Center to the Baltimore office of the U.S. Employment Service with authority to interview the referrals who would be given priority, and hire those qualified; (2) keep a day-by-day record of the number of referrals, number interviewed, number employed, number rejected, and reasons for rejection; (3) maintain a daily list of new employees reporting for work and the number of separations with the reasons for separations; and (4) maintain a close check on the transportation system between Baltimore and Edgewood.[61]

Implementation of Mr. Mitchell's suggestions brought a definite improvement in the manpower situation at Edgewood. But the Chemical Warfare Center had to take an additional step before it solved its labor difficulties. Never able to obtain enough male employees the installation began hiring women in growing numbers. By January 1944, 40 percent of the employees of the arsenal operations were female. At that time approximately 45 percent of all employees were Negroes.[62] The same general pattern was characteristic of the other two CWS arsenals which were situated in the South, namely, Huntsville and Pine Bluff, both with a large percentage of Negro employees and female workers. Rocky Mountain Arsenal had a large

[60] (1) Mr. Mitchell later became Secretary of Labor. (2) For details on manpower problems at the War Department level, see Byron Fairchild and Jonathan P. Grossman, The Army and Industrial Manpower, a volume in preparation for the series UNITED STATES ARMY IN WORLD WAR II.

[61] See Note 58, above.

[62] Rpt of the CWS Pers Utilization Bd appointed by SO 20, OC CWS, 24 Jan 44. CWS 314.7 Pers File.

WOMEN AT PINE BLUFF ARSENAL *assembling M50 incendiary bombs.*

number of women employees but comparatively few of its workers were Negroes.

Arsenal employees were divided into the following broad categories: common labor, semiskilled mechanics, skilled mechanics, machine operators, maintenance and construction workers, chemical and mechanical engineers, production supervisors, and personnel for administrative duties such as accounting and plant protection. So far as sheer numbers went, recruitment of civilians at the Huntsville and Pine Bluff Arsenals was not nearly as difficult as at Edgewood. Both arsenals were located in predominately agricultural areas and had access to pools of seasonal labor. Workers were available in great numbers during the agricultural off-season periods but were more difficult to obtain at other periods. The Civil Service regional offices, the U.S. Employment Service, and the War Manpower Commission co-operated in recruiting civilian personnel for the arsenals.

At times when the manpower situation was stringent, those agencies assisted the arsenals in conducting recruiting campaigns. Advertisements were run in local papers, and employees were urged to hand out printed leaflets to their relatives and friends on the need for workers. A spectacular touch was added when airplanes dropped handbills about this need over the adjoining countryside. Recruitment of workers, in other respects, was not lacking in the elements of human interest. There was, for example, the incident at Huntsville Arsenal when, in the spring of 1943, the president of a college for Negro girls in Georgia stepped into the office of the commanding officer and offered the services of approximately one hundred young women in the graduating class. The offer was gratefully accepted. The young women from Atlanta University came to the arsenal fully aware of the rather distasteful nature of some of the work, but they did a job, which in the opinion of one qualified to judge, could hardly have been surpassed.[63]

Alabama and Arkansas agricultural workers, the most common type of employees readily available to the Huntsville and Pine Bluff Arsenals, were almost entirely unskilled laborers. Although their native intelligence was undoubtedly equal to that of any similar group in the United States, they were decidedly limited in educational background. A great many, particularly among the Negroes, could not read or write, and this made for difficulties in training them for semiskilled occupations. It was impossible, because of time restrictions, to attempt training for skilled occupations. Skilled workers, technicians, and typists had to be obtained from other areas, generally from localities considerably distant from the arsenals.

The differences in the wage scales between local industry and the government, such as existed at Edgewood, were not a problem at Pine Bluff and Huntsville Arsenals. The agricultural workers who went to work at Pine Bluff and Huntsville had never before done factory work and were completely unaccustomed to the comparatively high rates paid by the arsenals. A number of the Negro women who were hired had previously been engaged as domestics at a rate very far below that of the arsenals. Most of these workers had never experienced such prosperity, a fact which was not, as far as the war effort went, an unmixed blessing. In far too many instances, employees would not work any more days in a pay period than necessary for mere existence.

---

[63] (1) Interv, CmlHO with L. Wilson Greene, 27 Oct 49. Greene was in charge of manufacturing activities at Huntsville in World War II. (2) In the plants where these women were assigned to work there was usually a high concentration of tear gas, which made for physical discomfort.

Rocky Mountain Arsenal had access to a comparatively high number of skilled male workers, but to relatively few unskilled or semiskilled. For many years before the war, Denver was noted as a center for small-scale skilled industries. The advent of the emergency attracted a number of these skilled mechanics and technicians to the airplane and shipping industries on the west coast. Others remained at home, even though they were not able to carry on their trades because of shortages of raw material. Many of these skilled workers were willing to take employment only if it offered wages commensurate with the rates to which they had been accustomed. But they would not accept assignments as semiskilled workers, and consequently the arsenal had some difficulty in securing that type of labor.[64] Unskilled women workers, as already indicated, were plentiful and the arsenal experienced no difficulty in filling labor requirements in that group. From late 1943 on, prisoners of war (POW's) were used at Rocky Mountain, except in the plants area.[65]

In 1942, in an effort to secure semiskilled workers, the commanding general of Rocky Mountain Arsenal set up schools in Denver and the surrounding towns. Shortly after the arsenal was activated, a number of semiskilled workers were obtained from an unexpected source. The commanding general learned that sugar mill workers in the vicinity of Brighton, Colorado, had skills very similar to those required by chemical plant operators. General Loucks, commanding general of Rocky Mountain Arsenal, sent the chief of the Personnel Branch and his assistant to interview these workers. The two administrators found that they were usually occupied in their trade for a few months of the year and were very glad to go to work at Rocky Mountain Arsenal provided they were released for mill work from October to December. The arsenal readily agreed to this stipulation and the sugar mill workers were brought to the arsenal.

The centralization of personnel functions at the Chemical Warfare Center has already been referred to.[66] Huntsville Arsenal also experienced the need for a centralized personnel organization, for at that installation, where all activities were highly decentralized, personnel functions were no exception to the rule. Each operating division at the arsenal had its own personnel officers who were invariably officers of company grade subject to the command of the respective division chiefs. Although there was a personnel division at headquarters, it was lacking in effective authority.

[64] Van Domelen Interv, 24 Oct 50.
[65] History of Rocky Mountain Arsenal, II, 404–05, MS.
[66] See above, Chapter VI.

In the spring of 1944 an audit team from the Office of the Secretary of War visited Huntsville and found defects in the methods of wage administration employed at the arsenal. This discovery led to a survey by the Personnel Division, OC CWS, which resulted in a number of suggestions not only on wage administration but also on the centralization of civilian personnel functions, the substitution of civilians for military as personnel officers, and the training of operating officials in sound personnel practices. From July to December 1944 those measures were largely carried out at Huntsville and resulted in a marked improvement in personnel administration.[67]

At Pine Bluff and Rocky Mountain Arsenals the administration of civilian personnel functions was centralized almost from the start. At Pine Bluff the chief of the civilian personnel unit reported to the chief of the Administration Division of the Arsenal Operations Office, and at Rocky Mountain to the commanding general.

The Depots

Graded civilian employees at the depots, as at the arsenals and other CWS installations, were selected in accordance with civil service qualification standards and Classification Act salary schedules. Ungraded employees were hired on the basis of job descriptions, designations, and wage schedules approved by the Civilian Personnel Branch of the Chief's office.

Three of the CWS depots, Eastern, Midwest, and Gulf, were closely associated with Edgewood, Pine Bluff, and Huntsville Arsenals, respectively, and were faced with identical problems of personnel procurement. The outstanding need at depots, as at arsenals, was for skilled labor. Skilled workers were just not available, and it was necessary to train apprentices on the jobs. It took some time before a satisfactory staff of foremen was functioning at most of the depots. As at arsenals, many women were hired and trained to do jobs formerly handled by men, and many Negro workers were also brought in.

At the three remaining CWS depots, Indianapolis, Northeast, and Deseret, the procurement of workers, unskilled as well as skilled, was beset with difficulties. The Northeast Depot, in the Buffalo–Niagara Falls

---

[67] (1) Memo, C Civ Pers Br OC CWS for C Pers Div OC CWS, 25 May 44, sub: Rpt of Trip to HA, Ala. (2) Inspection of Civ Pers Administration, HA by Civ Pers Div, OSW, 23 Dec 44. Both in CWS 230.

vicinity, was in a labor area that was critical throughout the whole period of the war. At the time the depot was activated, the 190th Chemical Depot Company was brought from Edgewood for extended field training. This company remained for a little over a month, during which it rendered invaluable assistance in carrying out operations at the depot. The 190th Chemical Depot Company was replaced for a short time by troops of the 71st Chemical Company (Smoke Generator), but in September 1944 the 71st received change of station orders. Then, in the fall of 1944, the depot secured from the commanding general of the Second Service Command an allotment of fifty enlisted men who had returned from overseas. This experiment, unfortunately, did not prove satisfactory because of the caliber of men allotted, and very shortly the entire detachment was withdrawn.[68]

Although never able to obtain all the civilians it needed, the depot did secure the services of a corps of loyal and efficient workers from the following sources: (1) employees of the Lake Ontario Ordnance Works who stayed on the job after CWS took over the installation; (2) local residents; (3) seasonal employees such as school teachers and farmers; and (4) relatives of employees solicited through personal appeal.

The Indianapolis Depot was situated in an area dotted by defense plants which absorbed most of the available labor supply; in addition, two other armed forces depots in the vicinity competed with the CWS depot in procuring civilian employees. One of these was an Ordnance Department depot and the other an Army Air Forces depot. The CWS Indianapolis Depot managed, notwithstanding, to hire and train a number of civilians. In January 1945 prisoners of war provided a new source of labor.[69]

If the manpower situation at Buffalo, Niagara Falls, and Indianapolis was bad, it was much worse at the Deseret Depot in the remote reaches of Utah. There the labor supply was practically nonexistent, and an unusual recruitment program had to be initiated in the fall of 1943 by Lt. Col. William S. Bacon, the commanding officer. Bacon, who had had considerable experience with laborers of Mexican and Spanish ancestry, obtained permission to recruit outside the state of Utah and arranged for setting up recruiting offices in New Mexico. Experience had taught him that it was useless to attempt to employ these workers without making provisions for their families. He therefore provided for the transfer of as many married couples and children as the housing facilities at Deseret would permit. But

[68] History of the Northeast Chemical Warfare Depot, June 1944–August 1945, p. 32, MS.
[69] For a discussion on the use of POW's, see below, pages 181–82.

that was only the beginning of his project. He next had to make certain that they would remain on the job after they arrived at that isolated post. In other words, he had to provide the newcomers with the necessary shopping and recreational facilities. Under Colonel Bacon's direction, a grocery store, drug store, notion shop, restaurants, bars, and dance halls were erected. All profits accruing from these enterprises poured back into the general welfare fund. With so little in the vicinity to attract them, few of the workers had any desire to go outside the camp and thus their services were available day or night in the event of an emergency.[70] The entire project of recruiting and transporting these workers from New Mexico to Deseret was a unique and farsighted undertaking.

These workers, almost without exception unskilled, were the main source of labor at Deseret. A small number of other workers from Tooele and Salt Lake City came to work at the depot each day, after provision had been made with a public service company for their transportation.

There was no standard organization for administering personnel activities in the depots. Certain depots had no personnel units. The personnel activities of the Gulf Depot, for example, were administered by Huntsville Arsenal. The Eastern Depot had a personnel division until September 1942, when its functions were taken over by the personnel division of the Chemical Warfare Center. The other CWS depots each had personnel units.

The CWS sections of general depots were under the central administration of these depots, and therefore there were no separate personnel units at these sections. Their personnel allotments were based on the over-all allotments of the depots.

The Procurement Districts

The personnel requirements of the procurement districts included the following general categories: (1) chemists and engineers for chemical analyses and production methods; (2) clerical, administrative, and fiscal personnel; (3) inspectors; and (4) warehouse employees.

In recruiting employees, the procurement districts generally possessed certain advantages over the other types of CWS installations. All of the district offices, and even the suboffices, were located in large cities where a sizable pool of professional, skilled, and clerical labor was available. A great many of the district employees lived within easy commuting distance

[70](1) Ltr, Col Bacon to CmlHO, 21 Jul 50. (2) History of Deseret Chemical Warfare Depot, pp. 31–35.

of their work, and few problems of transportation arose. At the time war was declared and for about six months thereafter, there was an abundance of applicants for positions in all the procurement districts. The district office simply notified the local office of the U.S. Civil Service Commission or the U.S. Employment Service of its needs, and they were filled. A gradual deterioration set in thereafter, the result of a number of factors.

Among the most significant of these factors was the ability of private industry to pay higher wages than the government. It is ironic that in a number of instances those companies owed their prosperity to government contracts and yet they carried out recruiting campaigns which attracted employees away from government service. At times these recruiting campaigns became aggressive to the point of impropriety. Certain war contractors on the west coast for example, used the phrase "permanent jobs" in advertising vacancies; when the impropriety of this was called to their attention they obligingly changed the wording to "jobs with permanent companies." The only recourse open to the procurement district offices, under the circumstances, was to provide for more rapid promotions and this they did.

Another factor which complicated the personnel situation was the growth in the number of field inspection offices, the aftermath of the increased number of contracts. The CWS had to make provision with the Civil Service Commission to permit chief inspectors in certain field offices to hire all personnel under blanket authorities issued by the commission. As time went on the procurement districts, like other installations, hired more and more women to do jobs formerly done by men.

In all of the districts there were units administering personnel functions. These units became more and more standardized in the wake of the district reorganizations from July 1943 to the close of the war.[71]

There were no personnel units at the CWS sections of the ports of embarkation or at the CWS government-owned, privately operated plants. Requests for funds to cover authorization of civilian positions in the chemical sections of the ports were forwarded through the commanding officers of the ports to the Office of the Chief, CWS. It was incumbent upon port chemical officers to supply the Chief's office with pertinent data relating to the jobs, such as organization charts and job descriptions.[72] The OC CWS, particularly the Supply Division, kept close watch on all port activ-

[71] Ltr, C Contl Div OC CWS to CO NYCWPD *et al.,* 31 Jul 43, sub: Standardization of Proc Districts CWS 319.1.

[72] Memo, Ex O OC CWS for Port Cml Officers, 2 Nov 42, sub: Civ Pers Procedures. CWS 312.

ities. Personnel administration of CWS plants was a function of the procurement district in which the particular plant was located.

Employee Relations at Chemical Warfare Service Installations

The on-and-off-the-job problems of employees in the CWS were confined almost exclusively to the Chemical Warfare Center and the arsenals. Difficulties arose on such matters as housing, transportation, care of the children of working mothers, adequate eating accommodations, and recreation. The failure to solve these problems was a contributory factor to the comparatively high rates of absenteeism and turnover at certain CWS arsenals during the war.[73] To reduce the rates of absenteeism and turnover, employee relations officers were appointed at the various installations in 1943.

Although employee relations problems arose at all arsenals, they came up in varying forms and degrees. For example, the housing problem at Edgewood, Huntsville, and Pine Bluff grew out of an absolute shortage of housing units, and arrangements had to be made with the Federal Housing Authority to erect housing projects near those installations. At Rocky Mountain, the housing problem was confined to arrangements made by the installation for the rental of houses to new employees.

Transportation was another problem which varied in difficulty from place to place. All the arsenals were faced with this problem, which was aggravated by the rationing of gasoline and tires. Nevertheless, the situation was more serious at Huntsville and Pine Bluff than at Edgewood and Rocky Mountain, because most of the workers at the former installations had to travel long distances over poor secondary roads.

Employee problems at the arsenals differed in degree of difficulty also with respect to the provision of eating accommodations. All the arsenals felt the need for cafeterias, but the need was more pressing at Huntsville and Pine Bluff, where many of the workers brought lunches that were not conducive to the health and strength of efficient factory workers.

An employee relations problem of considerable importance, which was always present at Edgewood, Huntsville, and Pine Bluff, was the preservation of amicable relations between members of the white and Negro races. In matters of racial segregation the prevailing cultural patterns could not be entirely ignored, particularly in view of the urgent need for uninterrupted production. Therefore the procedure was followed of accepting a

[73] Huntsville Arsenal had a very high rate of absenteeism. See page 19 of report cited in Note 62, above.

certain amount of segregation, but of providing equal rights, facilities, and privileges to both races.

Training Civilian Workers

On-the-job training was widespread during the war at all CWS installations, particularly at the arsenals and depots. Under the circumstances, it could not have been otherwise. Hundreds of new employees were being hired, mostly in jobs of a semiskilled nature, and some provision had to be made immediately for training them at least in the fundamentals. Huntsville and Pine Bluff Arsenals had the services of a small cadre of experienced employees who had come from Edgewood Arsenal, but there were too few of these to train all new applicants. To supplement the number of instructors, the arsenals sent some of the most promising of the new employees to Edgewood for training and, upon their return, placed them as instructors to fresh recruits. Rocky Mountain Arsenal after activation was fortunate in having access to employees from all of the other CWS arsenals, employees who could act as instructors to new trainees.

Even before the new employee got to his job his training began. At the personnel office where he was hired he received instruction on his status and rights as a government worker. When he reported to the branch to which he was assigned he was instructed on the duties of his job and on matters of safety. Shortly after being hired he had the opportunity, if he was an employee of the Office of the Chief or of most CWS installations, of attending a course of about four hours' duration where CWS equipment and products were demonstrated to a small group of new, and even perhaps some old, employees. This introductory type of training was known as orientation training.

The matter of safety was brought to an employee's attention on many occasions, particularly if he was working in an arsenal. Practically every course and program conducted at CWS arsenals during the war included some instruction on safety.

The CWS received helpful guidance from a series of three training programs inaugurated by the ASF in August 1942, programs which had been developed co-operatively by the Army and the Industry Agency of the War Manpower Commission. These three programs, each of which covered ten hours of instruction, provided for the training of supervisors in the "basic skills of *how to instruct, how to lead, and how to manage the technical aspects of their jobs*" and were named respectively, Job Instructor

Training, Job Relations Training, and Job Methods Training.[74] Later a Job Safety Program was inaugurated and the four programs became known collectively as the "J" series.

The "J" series led to the inauguration of training programs on a large scale throughout the ASF. Those programs expanded far beyond the "J" series and were aimed at meeting the particular needs of zone of interior installations.

Arsenal Training Programs

Because of the nature of their operations, the arsenals needed more extensive training programs than other types of installations. Typical of all CWS arsenals was Rocky Mountain, which between the fall of 1942 and the end of 1945 conducted, in addition to the "J" series, some half dozen courses. These included the following courses offered on a continuing basis: a two-week to six-week course for inexperienced chemical engineers, a one-week course in analytical procedures for new chemists, and a four-week to eight-week course at factories for instrument makers and refrigerator plant operators. The following additional courses were given as indicated: a one-month course (four 2-hour sessions per week) in chemical plant operation and safety, conducted by the University of Colorado (course was given twice), a two-month course (two 2-hour sessions per week), conducted simultaneously by three Colorado universities (course given once), and a six-week course for laboratory technicians at the University of Denver (course given once).

The training program at Rocky Mountain Arsenal, elaborate as it was, did not provide any extensive training for clerks and stenographers. There was a good reason for this, namely, that Rocky Mountain was never faced with any serious shortage of workers in these categories. At Huntsville and Pine Bluff Arsenals, on the other hand, clerks and stenographers were at a premium all during the wartime period. Among the most important features of the training program at Huntsville and Pine Bluff was the training, on a continuous basis, of clerks and typists. The most promising candidates among the girls in the plants were transferred to the offices and trained as clerks and typists.

Since Huntsville and Pine Bluff were not situated near colleges or universities, these arsenals made no effort to carry out a co-operative training

---

[74] SOS Adm Memo 24, 18 Aug 42.

program with private educational institutions. The Chemical Warfare Center and Rocky Mountain Arsenal were more alike in this respect. The various colleges in Baltimore co-operated with the CWS in setting up courses for its employees. At times the U.S. Office of Education also co-operated. For example, in 1945 the CWS, in co-operation with the U.S. Office of Education and the University of Baltimore, organized a fifteen-week course, two and one-half hours per week, for supervisors. By July 1945, 178 supervisors had completed this course and the results, in the opinion of the commanding officer of the CWC, were excellent.[75]

In the administration of the training programs some arsenals did a better job than others. Those installations with the best civilian training records followed a few basic principles which made all the difference between good and bad administration. Among these principles the following three were outstanding: (1) all supervisors were required to take certain basic instruction, such as the "J" series; (2) the commanding officer personally encouraged the training programs; and (3) there was good co-ordination between the military and civilian key personnel on all training matters.

Depot Training

The most extensive training program at the depots, as at the arsenals, was on-the-job training. Within six months after the declaration of war, it was impossible to hire trained workers such as crane or fork lift truck operators, and consequently new employees had to be trained on the spot to perform these operations. The same situation prevailed at all of the depots throughout the wartime period.

The "J" series was introduced into the depots at the same time as at other installations. Courses at special training schools were also initiated. From 1943 until the close of the war, selected depot employees, both military and civilian, were dispatched to the Forest Products Laboratory, Madison, Wisconsin, to take a one-week course in packing and packaging.[76]

The training of depot employees was closely supervised by the Supply Division, OC CWS. Training units were set up at those depots where

---

[75] Ltr, CG Cml Warfare Center to C CWS, 23 Jul 45, sub: Information, Education, and Special Serv Activities. CWS 230.

[76] Ltr, C Storage Div OC CWS to CG Midwest Dep *et al.*, 23 Sep 44, sub: Packing and Packaging Course. CWS 352.

there were personnel organizations, such as the Indianapolis Depot and the Deseret Depot. At other depots such as Eastern, Midwest, and Gulf, the administration of training was the function of the training unit of the adjoining arsenal.

Training in the Procurement Districts

The most pressing manpower need of the procurement districts in the early part of the war was for inspectors. In the emergency period, as indicated above, newly hired inspectors were sent from the districts to Edgewood Arsenal for training. These employees upon their return to the districts helped train more recently hired inspectors. Once war got under way this method could not satisfy the greatly expanded need for inspectors.

To fill this need, the Chemical Warfare Service began an intensive drive to procure female as well as male employees. It scoured the colleges in the procurement districts for women who would qualify as inspector apprentices. Once trained, those college women did excellent work. For certain types of inspection, such as that of munitions, the training standards were lower, and a high school, vocational school, or even a grade school education was considered sufficient background. The minimum requirement for inspectors of chemicals always remained high: a college background in chemistry or chemical engineering.

The training of new inspectors was carried out in co-operation with the city and state departments of education and with various private schools. In the San Francisco district, for example, a course for inspectors was inaugurated in December 1941 in co-operation with the California State Department of Education. This course included instruction in measuring instruments and gauges, basic metallurgy as applied to inspection, and miscellaneous subjects such as principles of spring design and testing. The state of California furnished teachers for this course. In other districts, such as Boston, training was conducted almost entirely in private educational institutions such as the Durfee School at Fall River or Northeastern University in Boston. In still other districts, like Dallas, the district training unit itself conducted training courses for inspectors; a well-qualified civilian put in charge laid out the courses of instruction, obtained suitable texts, and arranged for the procurement of training films and other training aids.[77]

---

[77] Ltr, Ex O Inspection Off DCWPD to C CWS (Through C Inspection Div OC CWS), 14 Dec 43, sub: Recommendation for Award of Emblem for Meritorious Civ Serv. CWS 200.6.

Utilization of Employees

There was an extravagant waste of manpower in many war industries during World War II. This waste occurred not only in government plants but also in those operated by private industries. In some instances, cupidity or mismanagement or a combination of both was responsible. In a greater number of cases the cause was due to other factors, the most important being the extremely rapid expansion of the industrial facilities of the country as a result of the demand for matériel in the first year of the war. Contracts were let out to corporations or individuals who never had had experience in manufacturing the particular items called for in the contract. They had to learn by trial and error. Among other things, these manufacturers were totally unacquainted with the best methods of employing manpower in their plants, a technique they had to learn as time went on. Older government plants had a certain amount of experience, of course, in producing their particular products, but the tremendous increase in the demand for more and more of all types of items led them to place secondary emphasis on the conservation of manpower. The newer government plants, like the industries which converted to wartime manufacture, were in a more serious predicament.

The Chemical Warfare Service, like the other technical services, was faced with the problem of conserving manpower. As early as July 1942 the Commanding General, ASF, called attention to the need for better use of personnel. He informed the Chief, CWS, that many of the War Department offices were not using their employees to best advantage and urged a survey to ascertain the number and function of clerical workers by grade.[78] This was the beginning of a drive by General Somervell to conserve manpower, a drive which was to continue throughout the wartime period. Time and again he reiterated, either through personal statements or through official administrative action, the necessity for efficient utilization of personnel, both military and civilian.[79] In conformity with this policy great emphasis was placed on work simplification and work measurement programs throughout the ASF.[80]

[78] Memo, CG SOS for C CWS, 21 Jul 42.

[79] (1) ASF Adm Memo S–1, 10 Oct 42. (2) Ltr, CofS ASF to C CWS, 18 Jan 43. CWS 200. (3) Memo, CofS ASF for C CWS, 27 Jul 43, sub: Reduction in Operating Pers. CWS 223. (4) Address of CG ASF to Conf of Pers Contl Units of Tech Servs, Washington, D.C., 18 Jan 44. CWS 337.

[80] Work measurement consisted of comparing the amount of work performed by the same organization at different periods of time, or comparable organizations at the same period of time, by indicating a ratio of personnel to workload.

In June 1943, it was disclosed, General Somervell had promised General Marshall that he would reduce the number of ASF operating personnel by 105,000 and that Under Secretary of War Patterson and James Mitchell, director of ASF personnel, had assured Congress there would be a cut of at least 100,000 in civilian personnel in the ASF.[81] After the ASF apportioned this figure among its various elements, the Chemical Warfare Service was cut back 2,424 employees in July 1943.[82]

The CWS record for reducing the actual number of its personnel during the war was not outstanding. At times when many other branches and services were showing a decrease in their employment rolls, the CWS was showing an increase. But there was a very good reason behind the CWS increase: the expanded chemical warfare procurement program in the second half of the war. The CWS did not reach its peak of procurement before 1944.[83] Had the war continued, the Service would undoubtedly have reached peak procurement in 1945 or later, because at the time the war came to a close the demand for items like the flame thrower and the incendiary bomb was rising.[84] Although the CWS did not show a marked decline in the actual number of its employees, the CWS record in making the best use of its manpower was in the main impressive, as members of the ASF staff noted on various occasions.[85]

On 4 March 1943 General Porter appointed a Manpower Utilization Committee to supervise all projects aimed at conserving manpower in the CWS.[86] The Control Division, OC CWS, acted as the operating agency for this committee and, through the control units at the installations, administered work simplification and later work measurement programs on a continuing basis. On 24 January 1944 the Chief, CWS, appointed a Personnel Utilization Board of five military members, headed by General Loucks, to survey the employment needs of each CWS installation and make recommendations on better utilization of personnel.[87]

[81] Memo, Maj Robert G. Boyd for C Pers Div OC CWS, 23 Jun 43, sub: ASF Conf on Contl of Pers. CWS 200 3.

[82] Ltr, C CWS to CG ASF, 28 Jul 43, sub: Pers Allotment. CWS 200.3.

[83] This information was obtained from Statistical Branch, Office of Comptroller of the Army.

[84] See Special ASF Staff Conf Analysis, Period I Supply, 21 Mar 45. At that time the only two technical services with expanding procurement programs were the CWS and the Transportation Corps.

[85] (1) Memo, CofS ASF for C CWS, 8 Jun 44, sub: Work Simplification. CWS 310. (2) ASF Manpower Utilization Survey Team No. 6 Covering CWS Installations, Rpt on Spot Check of HA, Ala., 21 Feb 45. (3) ASF Manpower Utilization Survey Team No. 6 Covering CWS Installations, Rpt on Spot Check of PBA, Ark. Last two in CWS 230.

[86] OC CWS SO 55, 4 Mar 43.

[87] OC CWS SO 20, 24 Jan 44.

Utilization of Personnel at Arsenals

Of all CWS civilian personnel 85 percent was engaged in activities related to procurement.[88] This type of activity was the most amenable to work measurement, an operation on which the CWS put great emphasis, particularly at the arsenals. Both the Control and Industrial Divisions, OC CWS, scrutinized the personnel utilization reports of the arsenals very closely and called upon the commanding officers to explain any apparent failures to cut down the number of man-hours. In this way the arsenals became conscious of the importance of the work simplification and work measurement program and strove to make better records in their personnel utilization indexes.

Certain factors beyond the control of the Chemical Warfare Service mitigated against the optimum utilization of manpower at the arsenals. Among these were changing schedules of production, uncertain flow of components and raw materials, the relatively short period of actual operations, and empirical problems presented by the production of items never before manufactured. Under such conditions it was just not possible to make effective use of manpower at all times. That the Under Secretary of War appreciated the problems peculiar to manufacturing plants is indicated in Mr. Patterson's remark of May 1944 that it was often harder to re-staff a plant that had lost workers than it had been to staff the plant originally. Mr. Patterson therefore recommended that "each service should act with great caution in cutting down plant operation since it will be very difficult to get plants back into production." [89]

Another factor preventing effective use of personnel at the arsenals was the duplication of functions by the CWS and the service commands.[90] Army Regulation 170–10, as revised on 10 August 1942, provided that the service commands perform at technical services installations certain activities such as laundry, repair work, and maintenance. There were undoubtedly good reasons for this arrangement, but difficulties arose at CWS arsenals when service command workmen began to duplicate or supplement work done by CWS workmen.

The CWS did not eliminate its repair and maintenance crews at the

[88] Memo, Ex O OC CWS for Dir Pers ASF, 15 Jan 44, sub: Work Simplification Indices and Pers Requirements for Zone of Interior Establishments of Tech Servs. CWS 200.3.

[89] Memo, AC Contl Div for AC CWS for Matériel, 16 May 44, sub: ASF Staff Conf, 12 May 44 CWS 337.

[90] For details on service commands, see Millett, *Army Service Forces,* Chapter XXI.

arsenals with the revision of Army Regulation 170–10. The Chief, CWS, and the commanding officers of the arsenals felt that since the Chemical Warfare Service was responsible for the operation of the arsenals it was also responsible for their upkeep; it was just not possible to separate the two. At the Chemical Warfare Center a happy arrangement was worked out whereby the post engineer was made chief of the Service Division of the arsenal.[91] In this way the use of duplicate crews of workmen was avoided. At the other arsenals there was no such arrangement, and duplication and overlapping did occur. At times the situation bordered on the ridiculous. For example, at Rocky Mountain Arsenal, painters working under the post engineer would paint only the door frames and window casings of buildings. CWS painters would then have to paint the rest of the building. This procedure resulted in additional expense and loss in man-hours.[92]

The use of CWS repair and maintenance workers was, no doubt, contrary to Army Regulation 170–10 (revised). In July and August 1945 the ASF took steps to eliminate such practice by supplementing the Army Regulation with official circulars.[93] The circulars left the Chief, CWS, no alternative but to prepare for the transfer of some seven hundred service employees from the CWS to the service commands. This he was in process of carrying out when the war came to an end, but he did not take the action without a protest.[94]

Personnel Utilization at Other Chemical Warfare Service Installations

The work measurement program got under way in the depots as the result of an ASF directive of November 1944. Under that directive the Control and Supply Divisions of the Chief's office developed procedures for putting the plan in operation at CWS depots and chemical warfare sections of general depots.[95] The program was not in operation in the depots long enough for its efficiency to be properly judged.

CWS officials found that the work measurement program was not prac-

---

[91](1) Ltr, EX O Cml Warfare Center to C CWS, 28 Jul 45, sub: Post Engineer Activities at EA. CWS 231. (2) Interv, CmlHO and Mr. Gerald P. Schwarzkopf, C Serv Div, ACmlC, Md., 14 Oct 54.

[92] History of Rocky Mountain Arsenal, VII, 2234.

[93] ASF Cirs 265, 312 and 342 of 1945.

[94] Ltr, C CWS to CG ASF (Att: Dir of Pers) 28 Aug 45, sub: Pers Readjustments Under ASF Cirs 265 and 312. CWS 200.

[95] Activities of Contl Div OC CWS, 1 Jan 45–14 Aug 45, p. 9.

ticable in the procurement districts until uniformity of organization had been attained. As indicated above, standardization was achieved in the fall of 1943.[96] The CWS then submitted a list of the activities and operations of the procurement districts to the ASF for consideration in drawing up a uniform system of work measurement for all districts. Not until the spring of 1945 was the system formulated. Thus the war was practically over before the work measurement program got started in the procurement districts.

The utilization of personnel at CWS installations is somewhat difficult to assess. Perhaps if the work measurement program had been initiated earlier or if the war had continued it would be possible to pass judgment. Although, as indicated, ASF staff officers commented favorably upon personnel utilization at certain CWS arsenals, a War Department special board, the Gasser Board, which made a study in the summer and fall of 1945, was not always so favorably impressed.[97] Members of this board visited some of the CWS installations and on the basis of their observations made a number of recommendations on the more effective use of manpower.[98] The war ended before these recommendations could be thoroughly studied.

Use of Prisoners of War

One of the means by which the CWS attempted to overcome the shortage of manpower was through the use of prisoners of war. Late in December 1944 General Somervell urged General Porter to make greater use of POW's for certain types of work. Porter immediately directed his installation commanders to use the prisoners wherever possible and he put an officer in the Industrial Division, OC CWS, in charge of all POW activities.[99] In May 1945 more than 1,900 prisoners of war were at CWS installations, and over 1,900 more were at prisoner of war camps, working on CWS projects.[100]

[96] See above, Chapter VI.

[97] See Fairchild and Grossman, The Army and Industrial Manpower, Chapter III, for discussion of Gasser Board and other manpower boards and committees.

[98] Data on War Department Manpower Board surveys on certain installations are in WDMB file 333. Members of the survey teams discussed their findings with CWS officers, who were skeptical of surveys based on a few days' investigation. Van Domelen Interv, 24 Oct 50.

[99] (1) Ltr, CG ASF to C CWS, 21 Dec 44. (2) Ltr, C CWS to NYCWPD, 2 Jan 45, sub: Utilization of POW Labor on Essential Work. (3) Ltr, C CWS to CO HA, 3 Jan 45, sub: Utilization of POW Labor on Essential Work. Last two in CWS 230.

[100] Memo, C Plant Protection and Labor Br for Fiscal Div OC CWS, 28 May 45, sub: POW's at Cml Warfare Installations.

The efficiency of prisoner of war labor depended to no small extent on good supervision. Tests made in March 1945 indicated that the rate of production in well-supervised POW camps was four times greater than in poorly supervised camps.[101]

Guarding the Worker's Life and Health [102]

CWS responsibility for safety in its arsenals and plants became crystallized in July 1942. From then until the close of the war the service had responsibilities for plant protection, which included accident and fire prevention as well as measures designed to prevent sabotage and espionage, at the CWS arsenals and plants and at designated contractor plants.[103] To supervise these functions throughout the CWS a Plant Protection, Safety, and Labor Branch was activated in the Industrial Division, OC CWS, in mid-1942. This office was headed, for the duration of the war, by Col. James C. Sawders.

The Plant Protection, Safety, and Labor Branch, upon its inception, undertook a program aimed at educating arsenal and plant supervisory personnel on the importance of safety. The branch placed great emphasis on engineering improvements such as guarding and grounding machinery, and better ventilation. From early 1945 until the close of the war it stressed the safety training of all employees. The result of all this activity was remarkable: the CWS, which in 1942 and 1943 had one of the worst safety records of any element of the War Department, improved until by 1945 it had one of the best records.[104]

This record, commendable though it was, would have been even better had the safety training of all employees been initiated at an earlier date. Of course, the ideal situation would have been institution of a thorough-going safety program from the very start of the emergency period. Many accidents would have been avoided had that been done.

---

[101] Ltr, Lt Col James C. Sawders to C Contl Div OC CWS, 24 Mar 45, sub: Rpt of Official Travel. CWS 314.7 Pers File.

[102] The chief sources of information for this section were, in addition to the sources cited, interviews and correspondence with the following World War II officers who had had experience in intelligence and plant protection functions in CWS: Colonels MacArthur, Charles H. McNary, James C. Sawders, and Sidney L. Weedon.

[103] SOS Cir C-1, 22 Jul 42. Although this circular was superseded by SOS Circular 66, 22 September 1942, CWS responsibilities were not modified.

[104] Rpt, CWS Proc Conf Held at BCWPD, Boston, Mass., 24–25 Apr 45, pp. 40–43, remarks of Col James C. Sawders.

Sabotage and espionage were matters of immediate interest, not only to the Plant Protection, Safety, and Labor Branch but also to the Intelligence Branch of the Chief's office, which during World War II was headed by Lt. Col. Sidney L. Weedon. The Intelligence Branch had responsibility for security checks on officers, just as the Federal Bureau of Investigation did on civilians, as well as for counterintelligence activities.[105] When a fire or accident occurred which indicated the possibility of sabotage or espionage, the Intelligence Branch was concerned as to whether an officer was involved; in the same way the Plant Protection Branch was concerned about the possibility of civilians being involved. There were no known instances of sabotage or espionage in the CWS in World War II. It cannot be definitely stated that there were no cases of sabotage or espionage because of the difficulty of establishing such activities as the cause of fires and accidents. What can be stated definitely is that the Chemical Warfare Service was extremely vigilant in the security screening of prospective officers and employees.

CWS personnel rolls, military and civilian, expanded rapidly in the general mobilization of World War II. Reserve officers were brought into the service in great numbers, and civilians with special qualifications were given temporary commissions. These non-Regulars worked closely with the small cadre of CWS Regular officers to carry out the wartime mission. All during the war the CWS had access to a great number of qualified enlisted men, and from 1942 on, to competent WAC personnel.

The problem of filling civilian manpower needs was more difficult. Like all elements of the War Department the Chemical Warfare Service was faced with ever-tightening restrictions on the number of employees allotted. The CWS attempted to solve this problem by concentrating on retaining the people it had, by training them to be more efficient, and by conserving manpower generally through work simplification procedures.

---

[105] OC CWS Organization Charts, Aug 43 and Dec 44.

PART TWO

MILITARY TRAINING

CHAPTER VIII

Military Training
Responsibilities of the
Chemical Warfare Service

The military training responsibilities of the Chief of the Chemical Warfare Service were succinctly stated in the National Defense Act of 1920 as:

a. . . . supervision of the training of the Army in chemical warfare, both offensive and defensive, including the necessary schools of instruction. . . .
b. . . . training . . . of special troops. . . .[1]

Although amplified by subsequent administrative regulations, these provisions furnished the basic pattern followed in CWS training during World War II.

War Department directives provided that chemical warfare training should cover the fields of smoke, incendiary, and gas; yet the primary concern of the CWS prior to World War II was unquestionably with gas. Since the service had been created by Congress as an answer to the military threat of toxic chemicals, the status of the CWS as an independent technical service could scarcely have been justified if it were not prepared to cope with this major menace. Fear of gas was largely fear of the unknown, and its antidote was, in large measure, to acquaint troops with toxic agents and how to counteract them. To impart such understanding was the primary training responsibility of the Chemical Warfare Service and the point of departure for the whole CWS mission.

The training of troops in protection against war gases can be approached with two differing objectives in view. One is training to insure mere survival of an enemy attack. The other is a more aggressive type of training, in-

---

[1] WD Bull 25, 9 Jun 20.

tended to enable troops to advance through their own as well as the enemy's gas attacks. One is essentially negative; the other, an essentially positive approach. Circumstances combined with events to determine eventually a positive U.S. attitude toward training for gas warfare. Chemical officers were generally aggressive-minded, although before the war their enthusiasm was often curbed by opposition within as well as outside the Army.[2] Denied substantial funds for production and development of offensive matériel, CWS threw much energy into training channels, where such limitations were less hampering.

In addition to staff supervision of training of the entire Army in chemical warfare, the CWS was of course responsible for its own normal military and technical branch training. Since the number of CWS officers and troops was relatively small prior to 1940, this type of training presented no special problem. The National Defense Act appeared to give precedence to the more general training mission; and this was certainly the most challenging. By mutual agreement, chemical warfare training responsibilities in the early 1920's included training of the Navy and Marine Corps. The training activities of the CWS, therefore, came to reach, in some degrees, all elements of the armed forces.

Prewar Training of Chemical Warfare Service Personnel

The technical (branch) training of Regular and Reserve CWS officers and of CWS enlisted men conducted before the war, being necessarily limited, provided little procedural experience for solving complex training problems that were to confront the CWS after the beginning of hostilities. The duty strength of the officer corps of the Chemical Warfare Service had remained substantially unchanged for some years. In the month of the outbreak of war in Europe it included ninety Regular Army officers and approximately twenty-one hundred Reservists.[3]

Two factors tended to restrict the prewar training of Regular Army officers assigned to the CWS. One was the limited number of these officers; another, the diversified nature of their duties, some of which were highly technical. It was scarcely feasible to institute a sufficient number of courses to satisfy all the training requirements of CWS officers.

---

[2] See above, Chapter II.

[3] Annual *Report of the Secretary of War to the President, 1940* (Washington: Government Printing Office, 1940). Also, see above, Table 2.

Because of the slow turnover of officers during the decade preceding the European war, the problem of indoctrinating those transferring to the CWS from other branches was never pressing. Their military education was usually well advanced when they entered the Chemical Warfare Service. Attendance at a Chemical Warfare School course was required immediately after transfer, following which on-the-job training largely served to familiarize new officers with the specialized duties of the service.

Professional training of officers of the regular establishment was furthered by assigning them to courses of instruction at general and special service schools according to quotas established by the War Department. Some advanced training was accomplished at civilian schools, especially in the form of postgraduate work at the Massachusetts Institute of Technology and the Harvard School of Business Administration. Seven officers were normally detached each year for duty as students at military and civilian schools.

In all, more than one third of the officers assigned to the CWS before World War II were on training duty. Besides 7 students, these included: 9 officers assigned to faculties of general and special service schools; 2 instructors of ROTC units; 9 company officers with chemical troop units; 4 division chemical officers; and 2 officers on duty with the Training Division, Office of the Chief, CWS. The twelve chemical officers assigned to corps areas and overseas departments also had considerable training responsibilities. Training represented a major activity of Regular Army CWS officers.

Before World War II the Chemical Warfare Service had developed a relatively strong corps of Reserve officers, which included two distinct components, the branch assignment group and the corps area assignment group. The branch assignment group comprised officers whose mobilization assignment called for duty directly under the chief of branch. It consisted largely of men whose civilian backgrounds indicated a technical military occupational specialty appropriate to the CWS. In 1939 it included approximately 800 officers. Premobilization training of this group was a direct responsibility of the Chief, CWS, although in practice this training was generally decentralized to corps area chemical officers. The corps area assignment group also included many Reserve officers with technical experience in chemical fields. However, members of this group were slated for assignment to military units rather than to technical or procurement installations. There were approximately 1,300 corps area assignment Reserve officers in 1939. Responsibility for their training rested with corps area and department commanders, although the Chief, CWS, was vitally concerned with their readiness for war service.

The two principal means for training Reserve officers were army extension (correspondence) courses and associate training for 14-day periods with the Regular Army. These means were admittedly imperfect, yet nonetheless contributed measurably to the war preparation of the CWS Reserve. The extension course of the Chemical Warfare School offered in 1939 a total of eighteen subcourses prepared by the school for the instruction of CWS Reserve officers of all grades. One of these, Defense Against Chemical Warfare, was a required subcourse for study by Reserve officers of all arms and services. Associate training was, in theory, integrated with extension course training. A total of 453 Chemical Warfare Service Reserve officers were called to active duty for fourteen-day training periods during fiscal year 1939.[4]

For recruitment, the Reserves depended largely on the Reserve Officers' Training Corps. The unit maintained at Massachusetts Institute of Technology provided many highly trained technical officers. In 1935 a second CWS unit was authorized at Texas Agricultural and Mechanical College, from which source splendid troop leaders were obtained. Before the war the junior class of each unit, funds permitting, was brought to Edgewood Arsenal annually for summer training. Enrollment in these two units stood at 326 on 30 June 1939.[5]

The Regular Army enlisted strength of the Chemical Warfare Service in September 1939 totaled 759,[6] or less than two thirds of the number set by statute in 1920.[7] Eighty percent of these men were assigned to the handful of understrength CWS troop formations. The remainder were scattered in small detachments from Manila to Governors Island. Their training followed in general the conventional pattern of Army peacetime field operations. Promotion to grades of staff, technical, and master sergeant was based on written examinations conducted under direction of the Chief, CWS. Occasional courses of instruction at the Chemical Warfare School were provided for men seeking promotion under this system. The turnover among senior enlisted men was so slow in the prewar years that NCO courses were conducted infrequently. The eight-week course ending 26

---

[4] Annual *Rpt of SW to President, 1939,* p. 62.

[5] Annual *Rpt of SW to President, 1940,* p. 62.

[6] *Ibid.,* App. A, Table D.

[7] Section 12a of the National Defense Act specified that CWS would be allotted 1,200 enlisted men. See above, Chapter I.

May 1939 was the first NCO course that had been conducted since 1933. It was inevitable that, with so few Regular Army officers assigned to the CWS, considerable responsibility should devolve in peacetime upon the senior noncommissioned officers of this branch. Many of these men were commissioned during World War II and served with distinction in grades up to and including that of colonel.

Training of Other Branches

Although the Chief, CWS, had a statutory responsibility for supervising the training of the entire Army in chemical warfare, "both offensive and defensive," this fact was never taken by the War Department as a reason for relieving the unit commander of immediate responsibility for the readiness of his command for chemical combat.[8] Instead, the chemical training program was developed so as to strengthen rather than weaken that responsibility. Thus the War Department from time to time established standards of readiness and indicated the scope of assistance to be rendered by the Chemical Warfare Service to field commanders in meeting these standards.[9]

An underlying doctrine in training for gas defense was that slack defense invited attack while superior defense deterred attack. Good gas discipline could be expected to deny military advantage to an enemy employing poison gas—and thus to discourage him from such use. And gas discipline depended on sound training supplemented by dependable protective equipment.

Organization within the Army for defense against chemical attack was based on the proposition that unit commanders at each echelon have on their staff specialists capable of assisting them in gas defense training. According to basic training doctrine, these specialists fell into two categories.[10] The "chemical" officer was a CWS technical specialist assigned by superior authority to the staff of the commander of a division, corps, army, corps area, or department. At lower echelons the term "gas" officer (or noncommissioned officer) was used. Thus unit personnel were designated by unit commanders to serve as gas officers for regiments and bat-

---

[8] The unit commander was given this responsibility in the AEF gas manual, Defensive Measures Against Gas Attacks, 30 November 1917, p. 18.

[9] Ltr, TAG to All Corps Area and Dept Comdrs et al., 24 Jul 30, sub: Cml Warfare Tng and Tactical Assignment of Cml Warfare Troops to GHQ Reserve. AG 321.94 (5–17–30) (Misc.) M–C.

[10] Basic Field Manual, Vol. I, Field Service Pocketbook, Ch. 8, Defense Against Chemical Attack, 31 Dec 37, superseded in May 1940 by FM 21–40.

BASIC TRAINING, *Camp Roberts, California. Trainees receive instruction in decontamination procedures.*

talions and as gas noncommissioned officers for regiments, battalions, companies, or corresponding units of both ground and air troops.

After recruit instruction in use of the gas mask, training followed three well-defined phases: specialist training of unit gas officers and NCO's; basic training of units under direction of their gas officers and NCO's; and, finally, application of basic unit training in field problems involving gas situations.

The specialized training of unit gas officers and noncommissioned officers was therefore the starting point for the progressive training of combat forces in gas defense. This training was particularly the staff responsibility of chemical officers, who were charged with conducting special courses of instruction as frequently as necessary to insure that all units were provided with suitably trained gas officers and noncommissioned officers. The Basic Field Manual called for twenty-two hours of instruction for unit gas personnel. Opportunities were given for company grade line officers also to

GAS TRAINING FOR OFFICERS. *Wearing masks, officers enter gassed area. Specialist training, Camp Beale, California.*

receive this type of training, in more detail, at the Chemical Warfare School. Thus the training of unit gas officers and noncommissioned officers was a staff responsibility of the Chief, CWS, who was concerned with the training of instructors; the utilization of such unit personnel (and also of staff chemical officers) in the training of combat troops was a responsibility of unit command.

Unit training of combat commands in gas defense, as distinguished from individual training, stressed collective protection. The field phase of this training was intended to test the ability of the unit to meet gas situations according to the tactical employment of the arm. The overall standard set by the War Department contemplated "opposing effectively any enemy employing chemical weapons." [11] As head of a special staff section of the War Department, the Chief, CWS, was concerned with

[11] Ltr, TAG to C CWS, 7 Jan 24, sub: CWSs Functions. AG 321.94 (1-2-24) (Misc.) M-C. See above, pages 187-88.

how well gas discipline in the Army satisfied this standard and he accordingly advised the General Staff in matters pertaining to chemical warfare for inclusion in annual War Department training directives.[12]

Compared to the amount of organization and effort involved in defensive training, that devoted to offensive chemical warfare was relatively limited. Policy in this field was frequently reviewed by the War Department General Staff. Standard procedure was that chemical weapons developed for the U.S. Army should be produced "with a view to employment by one or more of the combatant branches"[13] (that is, by Infantry, Field Artillery, Air Corps, etc.). For such matériel, the CWS was in theory a producer and supplier only. But the Chemical Warfare Service was never content merely to purvey. It took the view that the stocks of smoke, incendiary, and gas munitions were specialties, the merits of which might be overlooked if not adequately utilized. Hence an important function of CWS officers detailed to the faculties of special service schools and the Command and General Staff School was to further the introduction of chemical warfare situations into instructional problems and at the same time assist in the development of doctrine covering the employment of chemical munitions by the several combat arms. The Chief, CWS, selected instructors for assignment to those schools with the utmost care.

Not all chemical weapons were suited to employment by one of the older arms. Such weapons constituted the armament of "special gas troops" and the technique of their employment was taught at the Chemical Warfare School.

Chemical Warfare School

The Chemical Warfare School at Edgewood Arsenal was, before the war, the most important single training agency of the CWS. It was in effect the fountainhead of chemical warfare training for the Army and its teachings were closely followed in the Navy and Marine Corps. It was also to some extent a laboratory for the development of chemical warfare tactics and techniques.

The school taught, almost exclusively, the offensive and defensive aspects of gas warfare. The military employment of smoke was treated

[12] Memo, sub: Policy on Cml Warfare Training, approved by C CWS on 7 Jun 29. CWS 352/940.

[13] Ltr, TAG to All Corps Area and Dept Comdrs et al., 4 Oct 27, sub: Cml Warfare Tng. AG 321.94 (9–27–27).

briefly, and some consideration was given to incendiary warfare. Impracticability of biological warfare was accented. The faculty emphasized that gas was an important development in military science; that wide use of the gas weapon in the next war was inevitable; that American gas warfare matériel, offensive and defensive, was superior, and, when employed together with the gas discipline so essential to troop protection, would ensure the ability of the U.S. Army to stage gas attacks more effectively than its enemies.

The great majority of students attending the school were from arms and services other than the CWS. Most of them were expected after graduation to become instructors in gas defense in their organizations or to supervise some phase of chemical warfare operations. Accommodations available at Edgewood Arsenal limited the capacity of the school to approximately fifty students. Normally, only five classes were conducted during the school year. Their duration varied from three to twelve weeks, and they ran without overlap. In an average year, resident students attended the school thirty weeks out of the fifty-two. The total number of graduates, as of 30 June 1939, was 2,809.[14] (*Table 8*)

TABLE 8—CHEMICAL WARFARE SCHOOL COURSES, SCHOOL YEAR
1937–38

Course	Length	Students
Total	—	ᵃ205
Field Officers	5 weeks	59
Navy Fall	3 weeks	41
Basic	6 weeks	34
Line and Staff	12 weeks	36
Navy Spring	4 weeks	35

ᵃ Regular Army–70 (includes 9 CWS officers); National Guard–19; Organized Reserves–15 (includes 11 CWS officers); Marine Corps–10, Navy–91.

Source Class records, Chemical Corps School.

The Chemical Warfare School had a tendency toward extroversion, naturally acquired through many years of teaching its military specialty to other elements of the armed forces. During prewar years the school was notably successful in bringing a working knowledge of gas warfare to

[14] Records. Cml C School.

a wide cross section of Army and Navy officers. It stood well among service schools on two counts: it had developed a liberal approach to military education, and it was held in high regard by its graduates.

Prior to 1939 three courses had been developed for the instruction of Army officers: the Basic, the Line and Staff, and the Field Officers' Courses. The Basic Course was essentially an elaborate unit gas officers' course which was attended in the late prewar years by an increasing number of National Guard and some Reserve officers. It was intended to strengthen the gas defense program by making available an increasing number of well qualified junior line officers to aid in unit training of ground and air forces. The Line and Staff Course (the longest prewar course conducted by the school) trained company grade officers, principally Regular Army, in both offensive and defensive chemical warfare. It presented a broad picture of gas warfare involving all combatant arms. The Field Officers' Course was designed to acquaint senior officers with the general features of chemical warfare from the viewpoint of battalion and regimental commanders. This midsummer course was timed for the convenience of officers graduating from or detailed to attend other Army schools, especially the general service schools.

In addition to these three standard courses for Army personnel, a Navy Course was conducted each spring and fall, integrated with the naval program of professional schooling. In order to assist in this instruction, naval personnel stationed at Edgewood Arsenal were attached to the faculty of the CW School.

Training Situation in 1939

In the two decades preceding World War II the CWS had developed a training organization that was well designed to serve the primary purpose of maintaining within the armed forces a healthy attitude toward gas warfare. If in these years the use of chemical weapons other than gas was not stressed, the omission must be attributed to the fact that other chemical weapons were still largely unperfected.

The training activities of the branch engaged a large and possibly disproportionate number of CWS officers. Training was in fact an engaging occupation. Trainers at times developed an evangelical approach toward gas warfare. The subject was novel and often welcomed by troops as a change from monotonous military exercises. Despite limited allotments of training time, the military concepts of the Chemical Warfare Service were well disseminated at the close of the interwar period.

Considerable training had been accomplished in connection with the projected mobilization of chemical combat troops. The composition of these troops and the tactics of their employment in conjunction with field armies were studied at service schools and in correspondence courses. The CWS expected that gas warfare would be resumed where it had left off in 1918; that the scale of gas casualties suffered by the American Army would be reduced because of improved defensive techniques; and that gathering momentum in the United States in the production of gas munitions during the final phases of World War I would quickly be regained in a new war so as to assure dominance in this field. In the view of the Chemical Warfare Service, at least, gas was a normal military weapon and, as a result of progressive training, the theory of its employment had become integrated into the main stream of Army tactical doctrine.

While no attempt was made to conceal training activities, every nation shrouded in secrecy its research and development in chemical warfare. The U.S. found it difficult to obtain precise information as to the size and scope of preparations for the offensive use of poison gas by other nations. Intelligence estimates were based to some extent on more readily obtainable information as to training activities in gas defense, which were generally accepted as an index to national intentions. The considerable attention given to chemical warfare defense in the United States Army was frequently noted by military attachés of the Washington embassies. As a result, both Germany and Japan came to a similar conclusion well before the outset of hostilities—the United States was making serious preparations for gas warfare.[15]

Actually the policy of President Roosevelt was to avert rather than to precipitate gas warfare. This policy was unmistakably announced in his veto message of 1937.[16] Despite Presidential intent some veering in attitude toward gas warfare is discernible in the years immediately preceding 1939. This trend coincided with the steady deterioration of international conciliation as a means of avoiding war which followed the rise of Mussolini and Hitler to power. It was reflected within the War Department as early as 1930, when a noticeable shift in emphasis from strictly defensive training in gas warfare took place.[17] The combatant status of the Chemical Warfare Service was reaffirmed in 1935 when Congress specified that the CWS,

[15] For a discussion of German estimate, see Herman Ochsner, History of German Chemical Warfare in World War II, Chemical Corps Historical Studies, No. 2, pp. 15 and 17.

[16] See above, Chapter II.

[17] See Note 9 above.

as well as the combatant arms, be included in the allotment of Reserve officers called to extended active duty.[18]

Having weathered much controversy in the two decades of its existence, the CWS by 1939 confidently felt that its seasoned training doctrine would contribute substantially to the success of any war into which the nation might be drawn.

[18] Public Law 408, approved 30 August 1935. This was the Thomason Act, which authorized the President to call one thousand Reserve officers to active duty every year for a period of active service not to exceed one year.

CHAPTER IX

Partial Mobilization:
1939-41

The beginning of large-scale war in Europe on 3 September 1939 was followed five days later by President Roosevelt's proclamation of a national emergency, accompanied by Executive Order 8244 which authorized an increase in the strength of the Army.[1] These developments marked the start of a new, more energetic stage of military activity—of preparations which for many months were animated by a hope of avoiding conflict, but which after the midsummer of 1940 were pointed increasingly toward the defeat of the Axis Powers.[2]

Chemical warfare training in the initial phase of partial mobilization showed slight advance beyond the normal procedures that already were in effect. But the nation's gradual girding for war during 1939 and 1940 pointed up certain basic deficiencies in the chemical preparedness program which became a matter of serious concern to the Chemical Warfare Service.

Chemical Troops in the Emergency Period

War Department planning at this time was based upon the quick marshaling of an Initial Protective Force (IPF) which was designed to resist invasion and to hold off an enemy pending mobilization under the Protective Mobilization Plan (PMP). The strengthening of the Regular Army and National Guard provided for by Executive Order No. 8244 was the first step in the development of this plan. The United States was not expected to use gas offensively during the IPF stage although it seemed likely that protection against gas attack would become important. The CWS regarded this prospect soberly and had developed its planning toward

---

[1] WD Bull 18, 12 Sep 39.
[2] The beginning of CWS industrial mobilization at this time is discussed in Brophy, Miles and Cochrane, From Laboratory to Field.

effective defense against any invader employing toxic agents. The offensive use of chemical warfare by U.S. troops was reserved, so far as Army planners could foresee, for later stages of war and for application if necessary on hostile soil. These factors tended to lower the priority under which the main body of chemical troops would be mobilized and accordingly to defer their training period.

The 90 officers and 759 enlisted men in the CWS in September 1939 were the hard core around which the tremendous expansion of the next four years was to develop. Within this allocation seven Regular Army chemical companies had been organized, all at reduced strength. These were:

Headquarters Company and Company A, 2d Separate Chemical Battalion, stationed at Edgewood Arsenal where they served as testing and demonstration units with the Chemical Warfare School (remainder of battalion inactive).

Company A, 1st Separate Chemical Battalion, assigned to Hawaiian Department and attached to the Hawaiian Division (remainder of battalion inactive).

Company C, 2d Chemical Regiment, stationed at Fort Benning, Ga., as a school troops unit with The Infantry School (remainder of regiment inactive).

412th Chemical Depot Company, on duty at Edgewood Chemical Warfare Depot.

1st Separate Chemical Company (pack), assigned to the Panama Canal Department.

4th Separate Chemical Company, assigned to the Philippine Department.

At the outset of the emergency period, the initial problem was to build up these active Regular Army companies to full strength, or as near full strength as possible under the emergency increase. Later the inactive Regular Army units could be mobilized to bring up to strength the 1st and 2d Chemical Regiments and the 1st and 2d Separate Chemical Battalions.[3] Once these measures had been accomplished, the main problems of CWS troop mobilization would revolve around activation of the additional combat and service units for which war planning then provided. These included ten chemical regiments and eighteen chemical service type companies.

Six of the regiments were officer-manned reserve organizations; four were designated as National Guard units and were allotted to corps areas (but not to individual states) for inclusion in mobilization planning. These,

---

[3] The 1st Chemical Regiment was at this time wholly inactive.

with the two regiments classed as Regular Army organizations, provided a total of twelve chemical regiments, the maximum combat chemical strength contemplated under full mobilization. These units were assigned to GHQ Reserve in the proportion of two regiments for each field army. The service companies on the other hand were intended for assignment organically to armies in the proportion of one field laboratory, one maintenance company, and one depot company to each army. This allocation of chemical troops upon mobilization had been provided for by the War Department in 1931, in a directive which with minor variations was the basis for 1939 planning.[4]

Originally, definite mobilization dates were set for these regiments and service companies.[5] This was later modified to leave open the date of activating chemical units under the Protective Mobilization Plan. The 1931 instructions already referred to thus provided for the selection of chemical units for activation "depending upon their relative state or organization and training." It was anticipated that at least two regiments together with appropriate service units would qualify for activation at about the time each field army mobilized.

There were two reasons for deferring a decision of the exact mobilization date for chemical troop units. First, there was general agreement that other types of combat units would be more urgently needed in the initial stages of an essentially defensive protective mobilization; second, there was continuing uncertainty within the War Department as to the exercise of combat functions by the CWS.

The Question of Combat Functions

Although prewar planning called for activating twelve chemical regiments under full mobilization, a situation had developed within the War Department which now effectively debarred activation of *any* chemical combat troops. Even though some increased War Department interest in the offensive employment of toxic gas had accompanied the rise of militarism in Europe, the combatants did not resort to gas warfare when the war began. By the spring of 1940 military campaigns of striking success had been fought in Europe without recourse to the gas weapon. This development, which was contrary to many expectations, was taken to justify

[4] Ltr, TAG to All Corps Area and Dept Cmdrs *et al.*, 4 Mar 31, sub: Allocation and Organization of Cml Troops. AG 320.2 CWS (2–9–31) (Misc.) M–C.
[5] Ltr, TAG to C CWS, 19 Dec 30, sub: Provisions for additional Chemical Units that may be required in a major emergency. AG 381 (11–28–30) (Misc.) C.

a detailed re-examination of gas warfare organization and planning within the American service.[6]

In a plan proposed by the War Department General Staff as a result of a study of this subject in 1940, it was observed that the "Chemical Warfare Service has been permitted since 1920 to organize and train chemical troops armed with weapons developed solely for the purpose of projecting chemicals."[7] The Chief, CWS, General Baker, objecting to such phraseology, replied: "This function was definitely assigned to it by law, which has *required* that they be so organized and trained under War Department orders."[8]

The mission of chemical troops was "to supplement the arms in the tactical employment of smoke, incendiary material and nontoxic agents."[9] From the CWS viewpoint, this was merely an interim function; the real reason for the existence of special gas troops was to insure means for waging large-scale gas warfare once use of the gas weapon had been initiated by an enemy. There was thus to be considered two missions for chemical combat troops; first, a necessarily limited pre-gas warfare mission of supporting military operations with nontoxic chemicals; and second, unrestricted employment of chemicals after the gas warfare phase of combat had begun.

Chemical troops were at this time (1940) armed with mortars, Livens projectors, chemical cylinders, irritant candles, and chemical land mines.[10] The projector and the cylinder were generally considered to be in need of improvement, and the 4.2-inch chemical mortar was in fact developed as the result of CWS effort to increase the capability of chemical troops to discharge nonpersistent gas. Yet production of this mortar—then regarded as the primary weapon of chemical troops—had been suspended since 1935, and after the lapse of some five years the 81-mm. mortar had been designated as the standard weapon for chemical troops. This arrange-

[6] Memo, Capt C. K. Gailey for ACofS WPD, 7 May 40, sub: CWS Program for National Defense. WPD 165–16.

[7] Ltr, TAG to C CWS, 2 Jul 40, sub: Combat Functions Now Exercised by the CWS. AG 320.2 (6–19–40) M–C.

[8] 1st Ind, 12 Jul 40, to Ltr, TAG to C CWS, 2 Jul 40, sub: Combat Functions Now Exercised by CWS. CWS 320.2/21.

[9] Ltr, TAG to All Corps Area and Dept Comdrs *et al.*, 4 Mar 31, sub: Allocation and Organization of Cml Troops. AG 320.0 CWS (2–9–31) (Misc.) M–C.

[10] (1) Chemical Warfare Service Field Manual, Vol. I, Tactics and Technique, 1 Aug 38. (2) Augustin M. Prentiss, *Chemicals in War* (New York: McGraw-Hill Book Company, 1937), pp. 346–83. (3) Alden H. Waitt, *Gas Warfare* (New York: Duell, Sloan and Pearce, 1943), pp. 88–99.

ment was unsatisfactory to the Chief, CWS, who maintained that the 81-mm. mortar was technically inadequate for major gas operations.

A settlement of this disagreement between the General Staff and the Chief, CWS, was aimed at in the 1940 proposal, which was "designated to relieve the Chemical Warfare Service of its combat functions" and distribute these among infantry, cavalry, and engineer troops. The branches would then determine military characteristics of weapons needed to undertake gas warfare missions within their appropriate spheres of tactical operation. The CWS pointed out that some of the conclusions advanced to support this proposal were tenuous.[11] Both the Infantry and the Cavalry expressed reluctance to undertake large-scale gas operations. Disagreement also developed within the War Department General Staff itself.[12] The net result was a decision which cleared the matter temporarily in the General Staff but which was far from satisfactory to the CWS.

Ensuing instructions were to the effect that the CWS would retain its combat functions, but that "combat units of Chemical Warfare Service will be limited to those now in being and future augmentations of the Army will make no provision for additional units of this character." The Chief, CWS, was at the same time directed to "determine and report upon his future needs for Reserve officers with the possibility of reducing the enrollment in the two Chemical Warfare Service ROTC units, or if need be, the elimination of one of the units.[13]

At a time when mobilization of the Army was moving forward at a rapid pace, this order confronted the Chemical Warfare Service with difficult questions about the future of a substantial number of Reserve officers who had been trained for active duty with chemical regiments. Another consideration which affected these units was the decision, arrived at earlier that the regiment was not the most satisfactory type of wartime organization for special gas troops. Instead of the regiment, the battalion was determined to be the largest tactical unit that could be utilized effectively for controlling chemical weapons operations.

The latter decision did not affect the status of the Reserve regiments. Actually the regimental organization provided an ideal peacetime arrangement, since it permitted an effective chain of command to supervise inactive duty training and facilitated the attachment of nontactical Reserve officers

[11] See Note 8, above.
[12] Papers relating to this staff study were filed in WPD 4286.
[13] Ltr, AGO to C CWS and CofOrd, 15 Jan 41, sub: Combat Functions Exercised by CWS. AG 320.2 (8–27–40) M–C–M.

to military units for instructional purposes. The Reserve regiments were widely distributed geographically and the officers assigned to them were relatively well trained. Although the regiments were destined never to be mobilized, as war grew imminent they became increasingly active not only in perfecting their own readiness for mobilization, but also in aiding in the chemical warfare training of other civilian components.

Although the 1940 staff proposals referred to above had to do with the exercise of combat functions by the Chemical Warfare Service, the crux of this matter was armament. The question of the official status of the 4.2-inch chemical mortar had been brought up so frequently by the CWS that it was almost continuously under study by the General Staff after 1935.[14]

When the Army was reorganized after World War I, it was assumed that war gases for the most part would be discharged by devices that differed essentially from conventional military weapons. But the later trend of munitions development was toward the conventional, rather than away from it. In 1940 the CWS was contending that no weapon was as useful in the tactical employment of gas as the 4.2-inch mortar. Yet there was nothing so technical about this mortar as to preclude its use by either infantrymen or artillerymen.

The G–4 position, repeatedly affirmed, was that standard and not special weapons should serve for chemical operations; and that since the combat arms used these standard weapons with explosive charges, there was no reason why they could not use the same weapons when loaded with gas and smoke charges. This view was summed up by Brig. Gen. George P. Tyner, ACofS, G–4: "I am against organizing 'chemical troops.' Why not use Infantry or Field Artillery to throw chemical ammunition? Another branch of the Army in the field is not necessary."[15] The Tyner view was in line with the military principle of simplicity: one less supply channel, one less organization in the chain of command, one less insignia in the combat zone, and, in the case of the chemical mortar, one less weapon to contend with. These all were worthy ends.

Yet the CWS was not convinced that the solution to the problem of gas warfare was as simple as G–4 maintained. Gas was a tricky weapon and its employment required special training not given by other branches. The 81-mm. mortar, which G–4 wished to substitute for the 4.2-inch chem-

---

[14] Representative staff action on such papers can be noted in G–4/29895–1.

[15] See penciled note in General Tyner's writing, initialed by him and dated September 1939. In G–4/29895–1.

ical mortar, was unsatisfactory as a means of projecting nonpersistent gas. On both these points the staff view differed from the CWS view. As far as the General Staff was concerned, they were closed issues in the spring of 1941, although the CWS never accepted their closure as final. As long as the General Staff maintained its position, the CWS could not activate the chemical combat units called for by prewar mobilization plans.

Action toward relieving the impasse between the General Staff and the CWS on the question of chemical combat troops was initiated by General Porter not long after his appointment as Chief, CWS. This took the shape of a formal recommendation of 26 July 1941 that each of the two active chemical weapons companies within the zone of interior (at Edgewood Arsenal and at Fort Benning) be expanded into battalions and equipped with 4.2-inch mortars.[16] This communication, with the concurrences of G–3, G–4, and the War Plans Division, was hand-carried to the Office of the Chief of Staff. In the course of subsequent staff discussion, however, the Porter proposal encountered objections, particularly from G–4 who now held out for armament of the battalions with the 81-mm. mortar. The matter was finally resolved by General Marshall, who approved activation of the two battalions and directed the Chief, CWS, to include in fiscal year 1943 estimates funds to equip these two battalions with 4.2-inch mortars.[17] Formal instructions to this effect were issued by the War Department on 10 September 1941.

This action clarified a question that had been of paramount concern to the Chemical Warfare Service for half a dozen years and which was seriously impeding training on the eve of the war. That the decision of the Chief of Staff was well taken is evident from the battle record established by this weapon in firing high explosive and smoke shells. The incident affords an interesting example of the willingness of General Marshall to hear the presentation of the chief of an Army service and on occasion to overrule staff action.

Chemical Service Units

Although the War Department General Staff repeatedly challenged the need for chemical combat troops, it did not object to "service" type chemical

[16] (1) See above, Chapter II. (2) Memo, C CWS for Cof S, 26 Jul 41, sub: Cml Troops. CWS 320.2/266.
[17] See memo for record on retained copy of Memo, G–3 for TAG, 5 Sep 41, sub: Cml Troops. In G–3/46556

TROOPS OF 3D CHEMICAL MORTAR BATTALION, *firing 4.2-inch mortars in le Tholy area, France, October 1944.*

units. Action to relieve the CWS of combat functions was in fact rationalized by a desire to enable the service to "devote full time to the organization and training of service troops required to perform essential service functions." [18]

Three types of chemical service units were authorized at the commencement of the emergency period: laboratory, maintenance, and depot companies. These companies were organized on paper for many years but only one, the 412th Chemical Depot Company, had ever been activated. In the spring of 1940, when it became apparent that augmentation of PMP would soon necessitate the mobilization of a number of these units, the CWS initiated a study to determine the adequacy of the existing organizational setup in meeting the wartime service and supply functions of the branch. Reasons for this action were partly military and partly technical.

The structure of chemical organizations in 1940 still bore the impress of 1918. Yet as the new war developed abroad it became apparent that many concepts of the earlier war were outmoded. Among the new realities,

[18] See Note 13 above.

WHITE PHOSPHORUS FROM 4.2-INCH MORTARS *falling on enemy-occupied town of le Tholy, France, October 1944.*

the most important with respect to chemical warfare was the growing dominance of air power. The range of gas was no longer held to the extreme range of artillery. Strategic bombardment implied that the entire communication zone as well as points in the zone of interior could be struck with gas. Nor was the mass of the attack to be limited by the quantitative restrictions imposed by ground methods. The prospects of gas warfare enlarged rapidly with expanding air power, and the defensive responsibilities of the Chemical Warfare Service increased in proportion.

CWS technical developments in the field of protection against gas meanwhile, had advanced so far as to suggest that the whole problem of technical field service for ground warfare be reviewed. Means were being perfected for impregnating and reimpregnating the uniform to afford protection against mustard gas vapor, yet no organizational provision had been made for accomplishing this in the field. As the scope of the problem of contamination (the quick destruction of persistent gas), increased with the rise of bombing capabilities, new techniques appeared for decontamination. Laboratory, maintenance, and depot units also required study in the light of recent operations in Europe. This entire task was assigned to a board of officers known as the Service Units Board.[19]

After two months of careful study the Service Units Board submitted a report which provided a working basis for the subsequent organization and training of all but one of the CWS service units employed by the ground and supply forces.[20] The board proposed the organization of two units hitherto unauthorized—the impregnating company and the decontaminating company. It redefined the functions of laboratory, maintenance, and depot companies. Tables of Organization and Equipment for all units were drawn up. It recommended that one of each of these five service companies be organized, equipped, and trained immediately as pilot units to test the adequacy of its proposals as a basis for later activations. These recommendations were approved with minor changes by the Chief, CWS, on 13 August 1940.[21]

In analyzing the training requirements for CWS service companies, the Service Units Board indicated that each type of unit would require certain specially trained individuals for jobs that had no exact counterpart in civilian industry. Individual training of such men prior to M Day was proposed. For unit training the board proposed a twenty-week, three-phase program involving military training, technical operations, and field training. The scope of strictly military training recommended is interesting in the light of standards later found necessary. It was limited to that "required in the initial development of a military organization and the insuring of a degree of discipline that will make certain compliance with instructions.[22]

Activation of Ground Service Units

Three new chemical service companies were activated in 1940 for duty with ground forces, in accordance with the recommendation of the Service Units Board. These were:

10th Company (Maintenance) activated at Edgewood Arsenal, 1 July 1940.

---

[19] The board was activated under OC CWS SO 25, 6 May 40.

[20] The exception was the smoke generator company, which was not proposed by the Service Units Board and which when finally organized functioned rather as a combat unit.

[21] Proceedings of a Board of Officers designated as the "Service Units Board," 2 July 1940. General Baker's approval of 13 August 1940 appears at end of document. CWS 381/313, Special, NA.

[22] *Ibid.*

1st Chemical Company (Laboratory) activated at Edgewood Arsenal,
1 August 1940.

1st Chemical Company (Decontamination) activated at Fort Eustis,
Va., 1 August 1940.[23]

An impregnating company was not provided at this time because mobile
impregnating apparatus was not yet standardized. With this exception, the
1940 activations provided opportunities to test out the organizational and
training requirements of the several types of chemical service units, inasmuch
as one depot company had previously been activated.

The experience thus gained was valuable in connection with the activation in the summer of 1941 of the next group of chemical units. This group
included one of each of the five types of units then authorized. Three of
them—the 3d Laboratory, 3d Maintenance, and 3d Depot Companies—
had been constituted in 1935 and assigned to the Eighth Corps Area for
mobilization. Actually only the 3d Maintenance and the 3d Depot Companies were activated in the Eighth Corps Area at Fort Sam Houston; the
laboratory unit was activated at Edgewood Arsenal. The 1st Chemical
Impregnating Company and the 2d Chemical Decontamination Company,
which had been constituted in 1940, were also activated at Edgewood
Arsenal.[24]

The procedure followed in organizing these 1940–41 units was to
supply the new organization with a cadre of trained personnel drawn from
one of the companies stationed at Edgewood Arsenal or Fort Benning.
Fillers were then supplied from the Edgewood replacement center or were
shipped from reception centers directly to the unit. Because of the leisurely
rate at which chemical units were then being mobilized, unit training presented no serious problem.

Plans for Air Service Units

The looming importance of aerial warfare necessitated consideration
of air as well as of ground organizations for chemical service functions.
This matter had already been studied by the GHQ Air Force and T/O's
had been prepared for organizations believed best suited for air needs.
The general scheme for chemical service units within the Air Corps was

---

[23] The decontamination company was comprised of Negro troops.

[24] All of the chemical units activated in 1940 and 1941 were redesignated after the service units
program was enlarged.

based on an analysis of requirements of the GHQ Air Force for CWS personnel, drawn up at Langley Field, Va., 28 January 1939.[25] Under this plan, a section from a chemical platoon, air base, was provided for each operating GHQ air base. These detachments were to be trained in chemical supply and maintenance functions. They were also to be prepared to conduct the chemical warfare training of tactical units. Their supply functions were to include the operation of chemical service points, where chemicals could be delivered directly to airplanes or poured into tanks before attachment. The plan also included the operation of air base distributing points, which were small chemical depots located near bases or advanced airdromes. It was not foreseen that units larger than platoons would be needed at operating air bases.

Rapid expansion of air power after 1940 necessitated activation of many additional chemical platoons for the Air Corps. Cadres and fillers for these units in most instances came from Edgewood Arsenal. In March 1941 a chemical service company, aviation, was set up for each numbered air force. Thereafter the separate chemical platoons serving bases within the air force area were drawn into the company organizations.

The organizational plan for air chemical units was at this time altogether tentative since the U.S. Army had no combat experience upon which such planning could be based. The CWS was interested in developing the project and was concerned with the technical training of the troops involved. But the determination of unit requirements devolved upon the GHQ Air Force and later upon the Army Air Forces.

Replacement Training at Edgewood Arsenal

Organization of a CWS Replacement Center at Edgewood Arsenal was directed by the War Department in 1940 in accordance with a scheme which provided for a general opening of replacement centers.[26] The replacement center system, which became operative in the spring of 1941, changed completely the peacetime arrangement for the introductory military training of enlisted personnel. Before the beginning of mobilization, recruit instruction had been handled by the units themselves and was an accepted feature of the general Army training program. The prewar replacement

[25] Rpt, Lt Col E. Montgomery, CmlO, GHQ Air Force, 28 Jan 39, sub: Analysis of the Requirements of the GHQ Air Force for Pers of the CWS. CWS 314.7 Personnel File.

[26] Ltr, TAG to Chiefs of Arms and Services *et al.*, 23 Oct 40, sub: Replacement Centers. AG 680.1 (10–15–40) M–C–M.

plans called for the establishment of replacement training centers to provide inductees with such basic military and elementary technical training as to enable them to be assimilated by Army units without difficulty. The units, freed from the necessity of giving basic training, could then concentrate on the job of preparing as teams for combat operations.[27] The supply of trained enlisted replacements was carefully planned under mobilization regulations to avoid a difficulty which had been serious in World War I— inability to maintain combat organizations at full strength by means of a steady supply of replacements provided through special installations organized for that purpose. While the planning, in principle, was sound, the replacement center system in practice left much to be desired because planning sights were set too low. The primary, long-range mission of the replacement centers was to furnish *loss* replacements; that is, to supply trained soldiers to fill vacancies as they developed in military units. As the number of centers and their expansion capacity were limited, the rapid expansion of the Army after Pearl Harbor compelled the War Department to send most inductees directly from reception centers to units in training. Although the training of *filler* replacements to bring newly mobilized units to authorized strength was also a replacement training center function, the centers were never able to meet both demands satisfactorily.[28]

Administrative control of the replacement centers was retained by the War Department which set up authorized capacities and regulated the movement of men into and out of the centers. In this way it was able to co-ordinate the utilization of manpower by military components with troop bases. Management of training within the centers was left to corps area commanders, except for the Signal, Ordnance, Armored, and CWS centers; control of the latter was retained by the War Department and exercised, in the case of the Edgewood Arsenal center, through the Chief, CWS.

The CWS Replacement Center with a capacity of 1,000 trainees, was the smallest of the twenty-one ground and service replacement centers opened in 1941.[29] Its mission was to receive, train, and forward to destination enlisted replacements for all CWS units.[30] The capacity authorized

[27] Palmer, Wiley, and Keast, *Procurement and Training of Ground Combat Troops*, pp. 170–71.
[28] (1) *Ibid.*, p. 172. (2) WD Mob Reg 3–1, par 33b(1), 23 Nov 40.
[29] (1) Ltr, AGO to Chiefs of Arms and Services, *et al.*, 25 Oct 40, sub: Replacement Centers. AG 680 1 (10–15–40) M–C–M. (2) Biennial *Report of the Chief of Staff of the United States Army to the Secretary of War, July 1, 1939, to June 30, 1941*, Chart 7.
[30] CWS PMP, 1940, par 12h. AG 381, Mob Plan.

was adequate for the training load foreseen under the then current CWS Protective Mobilization Plan, since a trainee capacity of 1,000 meant (at least in theory) that with the eight-week training schedule then in effect, some 6,000 replacements could be turned out annually. Organization of the center was to be completed by 15 February 1941, or one month prior to the opening date. Assignment of instructors to receive special advanced training for this duty was indicated. Accordingly a special Replacement Center Officers' Course, of nine weeks' duration, was conducted at the Chemical Warfare School from 15 December 1940 to 15 February 1941.

This course, in which fifty-two student officers were enrolled, broke with the past and enabled the school to prepare CWS personnel for specific branch operations. The course was designed to broaden the base of the individual's technical knowledge and at the same time prepare him to function as a replacement center trainer. However, subjects having to do strictly with training accounted for only 79 out of a total of 364 hours of instruction.[31] Applicable mobilization training regulations were not studied exhaustively, while the emphasis placed on gas defense training suggested that the school was still leaning heavily upon its peacetime curriculum. Yet the course was undoubtedly helpful in preparation for replacement center duty.

The Replacement Center Officers' Course raised an issue which certainly was not new in the Army but which was to plague the CWS continually during the war. A basic question in training was: Does the training fit the man for the job? The immediate corollary was: Is the man then assigned to duty for which he has been trained? The answer to the latter question would in many instances be no. Much training effort was wasted and standards of performance were at times unnecessarily low because students, after being trained for one type of duty, were assigned to another. An instance is seen in this early course at the Chemical Warfare School. Of the fifty-two officers attending the Replacement Center course, only seventeen were assigned to duty at the replacement center when it opened.[32]

Lt. Col. Henry Linsert, a Regular Army CWS officer, arrived at Edgewood Arsenal early in December 1940 to organize and take command of the replacement center. A site for the installation was selected in the troop area previously included in Fort Hoyle, where the necessary barracks, mess halls, and company administration buildings—seventy-nine structures in

---

[31] The complete curriculum of this course appears below, in Appendix F.

[32] Interv, CmlHO with Col Donald E. Yanka, 13 Jul 51. Colonel Yanka was a student in the Replacement Center Officers' Course.

all—were erected.[33] A pistol range was constructed and other facilities were staked out for later completion. The training organization provided for one battalion of four lettered companies (A, B, C, and D) plus a headquarters company, a band, and an enlisted specialists' school. In order to activate these units, seventy-four noncommissioned officers and thirty-two privates were furnished as cadres from CWS units then stationed at Edgewood Arsenal.

As of 29 April 1941 the actual trainee strength at the Replacement Training Center was 701 white and 226 Negro soldiers.[34] The training plan provided for assignment of up to 225 men to each lettered company, which carried also a permanent cadre of 3 (later 6) officers and 25 enlisted men. Training began on 15 March and continued until this entire group completed the prescribed course of instruction. At the end of the first training cycle, 648 soldiers had been processed at the replacement center and were shipped (June 1941) to various CWS units in the zone of interior. The second cycle produced in September 652 men, and the third cycle, completed in December, 447 more. Thus in 1941 the inductees receiving basic military training at Edgewood Arsenal before assignment to chemical units totaled 1,747. However the strength of CWS units shot up during the year from 1,506 to 5,591, so that the aggregate of 1941 replacement trainees was far short of the total number of soldiers required. As a result, many chemical units were obliged to accept as fillers substantial numbers of recruits who came directly from reception centers and who had to be absorbed without preliminary military training.

Replacement Training Programs

A perennial problem with every technical service is whether the accent in training should be placed upon the military or technical aspects of training. Both types were necessary. Yet the growing ferocity of modern warfare has tended to increase the emphasis that must be placed upon the purely military training if the technical soldier is to survive and function in the combat zone. In branches such as the CWS the strictly military side of the training program was necessarily subject to close staff supervision, while the more technical aspects of training were properly left to the branch

[33] Fort Hoyle was a field artillery station maintained within the Edgewood Arsenal military reservation until 1940.

[34] S. J. Hemleben and Louis Truncellito, CWS Summary of History of Training Through June 1945 (Revised) p. 79, MS.

concerned. Standing prewar instructions on this subject were embodied in War Department General Orders No. 7, 1927:

Military training is required for all recruits of noncombatant branches immediately upon their entrance into service. The responsibility for such training is placed upon the immediate commanding officer of each recruit. . . . This training will be regarded as purely military training, and as such should be conducted concurrently with special instruction and performance of technical duties pertaining to the branch to which the recruit is assigned.

In order to co-ordinate training among the arms and services under this general directive, a Board on Revision of Training Methods studied this matter and submitted a report to the War Department in 1934 which led to the publication a year later of the first series of mobilization training programs (MTP's). These early MTP's merely formalized the application of General Orders No. 7; they represented very largely the views of the several arms and services on allotment of time between basic military and branch technical training.

The training directive followed initially at the CWS Replacement Center was MTP 3–1, 18 September 1940, "For chemical regiments at unit training centers and for chemical troop replacements at enlisted replacement centers." This MTP, like all early ones, was admittedly tentative and subject to development in the light of experience. A revision of this program, undertaken while the first training cycle was in progress, was ready for use at the beginning of the second training cycle in June 1941. A second revision was completed in September and remained in force until after replacement center activities were transferred from Edgewood Arsenal.

The MTP used initially was unsatisfactory. It was designed to produce replacements for chemical weapons companies, although few such companies were then in existence and War Department policy did not then contemplate the formation of additional units of this type. Rather, the need was for fillers and loss replacements for chemical *service* companies and platoons, which required very different technical training from that provided for weapons units.

Another objection to the early program was the insufficient time allowed for the replacement training cycle. This cycle was initially set at eight weeks. All men were assigned to basic companies for the first two weeks during which period they received identical training. During this time schooling was emphasized and some technical training was introduced. At the beginning of the third week promising trainees were screened out for specialized training while the remainder continued in basic companies for the "technical" phase of the program.[35] Under current requirement rates for occupational specialists, 20 percent of CWS enlisted personnel were needed as truck drivers, clerks, and cooks.[36] Accordingly a fifth of the early trainees were selected to attend the replacement center specialists' school during the technical training phase, where they were instructed in one of these military occupational specialties.

It was found in practice that satisfactory development of the individual soldier could not be achieved within the time originally allotted. This was evident in connection with both military and technical training. More time was required for hardening and conditioning many inductees, while on the technical side more opportunity was needed for applicatory and group exercises. The same criticism of MTP's was made by other arms and services, so that in the fall of 1941 the replacement cycle was extended from eight to thirteen weeks.[37] Under the new setup, basic military training was emphasized at the start of the course and was continued to some extent during the first eight weeks; technical training was spread over the first nine weeks; while the last three to four weeks were employed in special technical exercises. This general allocation of time was found to be satisfactory. Later improvements in the training program were in the direction of more realistic military training and more specialized technical training. But it was now clear that, at this stage of mobilization, a well-indoctrinated replacement could be produced on a quarterly basis.

Conduct of Replacement Training

The group of young Reserve officers initially assigned to staff the replacement center proved to be satisfactory. The enlisted cadre on the other hand was less adequate. It was provided largely by Company A, 2d Separate Chemical Battalion, a unit that already had been stripped of cadre material to meet earlier calls. When the requirement arose for 106 men to provide overhead for the replacement center there simply were not that many men available of the type needed for this exacting duty. The men assigned were satisfactory although unseasoned soldiers, most of them without instruc-

---

[35] MTP 3–1, 23 Nov 40.

[36] Ltr, TAG to Chiefs of Arms and Servs et al., 25 May 41, sub: Changes in Incls. AG 324.71 (4–21–41) E–A.

[37] MTP 3–3, 26 Nov 41.

tional ability. A substantial number had to be replaced at the conclusion of the first training cycle.

The usefulness of the initial cadre no doubt would have been increased had these men been given specialist training at the Chemical Warfare School in a course paralleling the Replacement Center Officers' Course. This was not done. However, a two-week Replacement Center NCO Course was conducted at the school between the ending of the first and the beginning of the second RTC training cycle (26 May–7 June 1941). The course record of this class reveals that the seventy-one hours of instruction included little training that was directly helpful to the thirty students who attended.

Experience with the early training cycles clearly indicated that some inductees would be unable to undertake the standard course until after special development training. Defects most common were illiteracy, language difficulty, emotional instability, and physical defects. To accommodate such individuals, a Special Training Company was organized on 15 August 1941 in conformity with MTP 20–1. The unit consisted of two platoons, one for white and one for Negro troops. This RTC preparatory training had to be expanded with the growth of basic training activities; it was responsible for acclimating many men to military service who otherwise would have been rejected.

Early replacement training at Edgewood Arsenal was handicapped by the lack of training aids, training literature, and classroom facilities. Trainees were armed with the pistol, a poor substitute for the rifle in recruit training. Instructors were, at the outset, inexperienced in high-gear instructional procedure. Because training time was not efficiently allocated, graduates had to learn after joining chemical service units much that they should have been taught at the replacement center. Yet the 1941 trainees on the whole did compare favorably with those who later passed through the more highly developed CWS Training Center. Two reasons explain this fact. Most of the 1941 inductees proved to be of especially high caliber. And the instructors made up in enthusiasm what they lacked in experience.

The practice of officially referring to the installations as replacement *training* centers began in the spring of 1941. Previously, mobilization plans, mobilization training programs, and mobilization regulations had all omitted the word "training." The final adoption of the term served to emphasize the fact that training was the dominant function of the centers.

As training improved, it became increasingly apparent that the CWS center was inappropriately located. Edgewood Arsenal was selected in the first place because of the concentration of research and development as well as school and troop activities at this station. Some land was available, and a few barracks; yet neither area nor buildings were adequate to the needs of replacement training. Housing facilities could be supplemented by new construction, but there was no way to increase the land available for training purposes on narrow Gunpowder Neck. The limited number of ranges could not even meet requirements for CWS proving and experimental firing. Although a pistol range was developed, space was not available for a rifle range. The manufacturing activities of the arsenal were expanding rapidly during 1941 under priorities which impeded the development of needed replacement training facilities. Had requirements for CWS basic training remained at the projected levels of 1940, it might still have been possible to wedge this activity into the multiplicity of functions that were being undertaken on the constricted Edgewood reservation; but by the fall of 1941 it already was apparent that much more than the current capacity of the training center would be required.

The Chief, Chemical Warfare Service, was informed early in December 1941 that CWS replacement training capacity would have to be increased shortly to 2,430 trainees.[38] This step became necessary largely because of a recently approved increase in chemical service troops to meet expanding AAF requirements. The War Department wanted the additional replacement training load to be undertaken without construction of additional barracks. This could only be accomplished by the removal of an appropriate number of troops, including one Field Artillery battalion, from the Edgewood Arsenal reservation. In addition, it was necessary to project the construction of a number of new facilities, both administrative and instructional, in order properly to accommodate the greatly increased training activity. Planning was in progress when the Pearl Harbor attack occurred.

Gas Defense Training: 1939–41

During the period of limited emergency, the U.S. Army mobilized thirty-six divisions and activated seventy air force groups—together a phenomenal achievement. With these developments the Chief, CWS, was closely concerned as technical adviser to the War Department on gas defense training. It was his responsibility to counteract the inevitable tendency to neglect, in the rush of such rapid mobilization, a type of training for which need was not immediate. It was his job to see that a serious flaw—vulnerability to gas

[38] Memo, G–3 for C CWS, 2 Dec 41, sub: Expansion of CWS RTC Trainee Capacity. G–3/6457–364.

attack—did not develop in the course of preparations for battle. He had to push a military specialty, yet do it with tact and with a nice appreciation of larger objectives.

There was no lack, in 1939 of definite channels of responsibility for gas defense training. Under peacetime procedures the War Department set the objectives, the Chemical Warfare Service provided certain of the means, corps area commanders supervised training, and unit commanders were responsible for its execution. But this originally simple arrangement became more complicated as growing mobilization resulted in the appearance of an increasing number of ranking unit commanders with varying views as to how gas warfare directives should be interpreted.

The over-all War Department objective was stated as: "Our peacetime preparation in chemical warfare will be based on opposing effectively any enemy employing chemical agents and weapons.[39] This was amplified, as previously noted, by detailed instructions on gas defense training.[40]

A field interpretation and amplification of instructions on chemical warfare training appeared in a training memorandum issued by Headquarters, Sixth Corps Area, in December 1940.[41] This monumental directive presented a complete picture of chemical warfare training as presumably undertaken in the U.S. Army at that time. The memorandum meticulously considered every detail to insure observance of all instructions that bore in any way on the subject. Full compliance would have been gratifying in the CWS since troops so trained would unquestionably have been capable of meeting any enemy who chose to resort to gas warfare.

The Sixth Corps Area memorandum represents the high tide of training under the corps area system. The old Army had taken such directives in stride and had mastered the technique of according them a degree of compliance which satisfied higher authority. The new Army, on the other hand, was inclined to heed the full letter of formal instructions, a feat which in practice was seldom possible.

In peacetime training the CWS sought to cultivate respect for, while averting unreasoning fear of, war gases. This aim had been rather generally accomplished as long as training time was not at a great premium; but once the momentum of mobilization began to build up, unit commanders became

[39] Ltr, TAG to All Corps Area and Dept Comdrs *et al.*, 24 Jul 30, sub: Cml Warfare Tng and Tactical Assignment of Cml Warfare Troops to GHQ Reserve. AG 321.94 (5–17–30) (Misc.) M–C.

[40] Basic Field Manual, Vol. I, Ch. 8, 31 Dec 37.

[41] Tng Memo 13, Hq Sixth Corps Area, 4 Dec 40. See below, Appendix G.

increasingly reluctant to spare time for the degree of gas defense training which the CWS considered the minimum for realistic war preparation. In order to decide where emphasis should be placed, officers who never before had given the matter serious thought began to ask themselves what the prospects actually were of gas warfare.

The views of most military men on gas warfare as an offensive weapon were essentially pragmatic. *Was it really worth while?* There were two schools of thought on the matter. One group held that gas was a revolutionary weapon, that its possibilities should be exploited, and that it was folly for the nation to deny itself the fullest advantage of this or any other new development of military science. The other felt that experience of the war in Europe to date indicated that gas had only limited application in modern military operations, that it was always ineffective against good defense, and that it was an adjunct to positional warfare—a type of warfare never congenial to American military thinking. But while offensive gas warfare had both its advocates and opponents, no responsible officer questioned the need for gas *defense* training. The question was: How little training would meet essential needs?

Chemical Warfare Training of Ground Forces

As mobilization speeded up, a fundamental change began to appear in the old relationship between the CWS and the unit commanders directly responsible for gas defense training. Originally responsibility had been channeled from the War Department, through corps areas, to units. The first change in this pattern occurred in 1935, when air tactical units came under control of the GHQ Air Force. Training of ground force units was assumed by General Headquarters, U.S. Army, when that organization was activated in July 1940. Thereafter, unit commanders were reached, on matters relating to antigas defense, through one of these headquarters.

Only a skeleton GHQ staff moved into the Army War College in the summer of 1940. No chemical officer was included in General McNair's special staff until 1941, and GHQ continued without a formal chemical staff section until 10 January 1942.[42] This reflected General McNair's attitude on gas warfare and adversely influenced gas defense training of ground units throughout 1940 and 1941.

[42] (1) Greenfield, Palmer, and Wiley, *The Organization of Ground Combat Troops*, p. 26. (2) Interv, CmlHO with Col Thomas J. Ford, 11 Jan. 56. Colonel Ford was made Ground Chemical Officer in January 1942.

Although the GHQ Chief of Staff was sympathetic to limited training in defense against attack, he insisted that such training should not be extended to a point where it might interfere with his primary mission of training major elements of the field forces within the continental United States. General McNair believed that artillery was the most suitable ground arm for employing gas munitions; but he seriously questioned the advisability, from a military viewpoint, of resorting to gas warfare under any circumstances. He saw no merit in special gas troops and he declined to permit the introduction of gas situations into the large-scale maneuvers that were conducted in 1940 and 1941.[43]

Staff chemical officers, meanwhile as called for by existing tables of organization, were regularly provided for divisions and corps as these units were mobilized. To each of the four field armies then in existence and to each of the newly activated corps was assigned a senior CWS officer with considerable training experience. National Guard divisions took the field with their own chemical staff officers, many of whom were graduates of prewar courses at the Chemical Warfare School. The unit organizational setup for chemical warfare training of ground forces was adequate; yet training accomplishments during the period of partial mobilization were not satisfactory to the CWS. To a considerable degree this situation was the result of General McNair's attitude on gas warfare.

GHQ was primarily concerned with unit rather than replacement training, and it regarded gas defense training as essentially the latter type. During the early stage of mobilization, training of the individual soldier was exclusively the province of the War Department under the replacement training system. RTC training included a modicum of basic training in protection against gas attack, the amount of time devoted to this subject ranging from four to ten hours according to the applicable mobilization training program. For example, MTP 6–1, 1940, for field artillery replacements, prescribed five hours of training, which was expected to develop: "An ability to mask quickly and to wear the mask while performing military duties; an ability to identify the more common chemical agents and a knowledge of the means of defense against them."

The soldier processed through one of the twenty-one ground replacement centers thus presumably emerged with some idea of how to protect

---

[43](1) Ltr, Col Adrian St John, USA (Ret), to Hist Off OC CmlO, 21 Jun 51, no sub. (2) Ltr, OC CWS to CmlO Second Army, 19 Aug 41, no sub. CWS 354.2/101. (3) Addendum to Memo for Record on Memo, ACofS OPD for CofS USA, 13 Aug 42, sub: Revision in the Chemical Warfare Program. OPD 385 CWP Sec IIA (4–22). (4) Ford interv, 11 Jan 56.

RTC CLASSROOM TRAINING. *Soldiers in their second week of training learn how to identify different types of gases.*

himself under gas attack. As mobilization accelerated, however, increasing numbers of inductees had to be sent directly from reception centers to units without replacement center training. Instruction of these men in the rudiments of protection against war gases had therefore to be undertaken by unit commanders, usually with the assistance of unit gas personnel. Training of the latter, under standard operating procedure, was accomplished at special schools conducted by division and occasionally by corps chemical officers.

Anticipating that the training of regimental and battalion gas officers in such local schools would sometimes be difficult during the course of mobilization, the War Department announced a series of one-month classes at the Chemical Warfare School to provide this type of training.[44] In accordance with GHQ policy that the detail of students to service schools should be discretionary with unit commanders, no quotas were set. Thirteen of these

[44] Ltr, TAG to CGs of the Four Armies *et al.,* 7 Oct 40, sub: Tng of Regimental and Battalion Gas Officers AG 210.63 CW Sch (9–25–40) M–M.

classes conducted in 1941 graduated 686 unit gas officers, constituting a measurable contribution to the over-all gas defense program for the ground forces.

Individual training within units, as prescribed by War Department directives, was encouraged by GHQ. But, as indicated, when Army chemical officers proposed injection of gas situations into corps and army maneuvers, General McNair demurred. The formation of these large tactical units, the first in U.S. peacetime history, afforded opportunity to advance the final phase of chemical warfare training which previously had of necessity been neglected—that is, the culmination of individual and specialized gas defense instruction in field operations where large bodies of troops encountered simulated gas attacks under conditions requiring the use of gas masks. The Chemical Warfare Service felt that such a test was necessary in order to ascertain the real status of gas discipline within the field forces as well as for rounding out the entire chemical warfare training program. Yet, in the view of GHQ, this goal was considerably less important than the immediate task of developing command leadership and operating facility within corps and armies.

While the CWS supported as far as it could the position of chemical officers with field forces, the War Department General Staff was never inclined at this stage to question the training policies of GHQ. In retrospect, it is clear that on this issue General McNair assumed a calculated risk which was justified by subsequent events, although at the time the CWS felt that an important feature of chemical warfare training was being unduly neglected.

Army Air Forces Training

The approach to gas defense training in the Army Air Forces differed in several particulars from that developed in the ground forces. Beginning with the organization of the GHQ Air Force at Langley Field in 1935, able chemical officers were on duty with the highest air echelons.[45] Early appreciation of the importance of antigas protection of air bases led in 1936 to the conduct of a special Air Forces gas defense course at the Chemical Warfare School. The twenty air officers who graduated from this four-week course provided the nucleus for development of the GHQ Air Force gas protection scheme.

[45] After serving as instructor at the Air Tactical School, Maxwell Field, General Porter was on duty as air chemical officer at the time of his appointment as Chief, CWS, in 1941.

Compared to the problems confronting the ground forces, gas protection of air installations was in some respects simplified. Field units had to provide for defense against gas from both ground and air; air units were concerned only with the latter. Nevertheless, the AAF gave a great deal of thought to the protection of its bases against aerial gas attack.

Attempts to immobilize American air power by the immediate bombing of advanced U.S. air bases were clearly foreseen as the opening operations of air warfare. Before the commencement of hostilities in Europe, thinking among Air officers—undoubtedly influenced by the doctrines of Giulio Douhet—inclined to the belief that the earliest employment of gas warfare would be in the attack on airdromes.[46] That gas was not used for this purpose in the early stages of World War II resulted in somewhat lessened apprehension, although the Army Air Forces was never willing to dismiss entirely the threat of an enemy attempt to neutralize the growing air power of the United States through a gas attack. The AAF meant to be reasonably prepared and therefore gas defense measures were given serious and continued consideration, both under the GHQ Air Force and later, after air training became one of his functions, under the Chief of the AAF.

In individual training of Army Air Forces soldiers, the replacement training system worked out more satisfactorily than was the case with ground forces. Practically all AAF inductees passed through air replacement training centers, and therefore reached air units with some basic training in self-protection against war gases. MTP 1–1 (1940) prescribed six hours of instruction in defense against chemical attack for all AAF inductees. Inevitably there were times when this training was slighted, but this was the exception rather than the rule.

Because of the tremendous pressures under which AAF training was conducted, expecially in the early stages of mobilization, more advanced training in gas protection was necessarily limited. Schemes for the collective protection of airdomes were prepared and key personnel trained in operating procedures. A notable contribution to the advancement of individual and collective protection was the training of 385 air force officers in a series of seven Unit Gas Officers' classes conducted for the AAF by the Chemical Warfare School during 1941. The role of the Chemical Warfare Service in

[46](1) Giulio Douhet's *Air Warfare*, translated by Mrs. Dorothy Benedict, was reproduced by the Air Corps in December 1933. Copy in Army Library. This work was seriously studied at the Air Corps Tactical School. (2) Wesley F. Craven and James L. Cate, eds., *The Army Air Forces in World War II: Plans and Early Operations, January 1939 to August 1942* (Chicago: University of Chicago Press, 1948), p. 51.

gas defense training within the Army Air Forces was one of advancing the program as much as possible within the limitation imposed by more urgent air training requirements.

School Training

Involvement in war between 1939 and 1941 followed a gradient so gradual that it is difficult to reconcile events as they occurred with those that had been foreseen under the protective mobilization plan. Mobilization of the initial protective force, the springboard for PMP, was actually accomplished long before hostilities began. Yet operations of the Chemical Warfare School during the period of partial mobilization were not in accord with any section of the plan; and it is not possible to indicate a point at which implementation of the plan at the school did begin.

Removal of the school from Edgewood Arsenal to a location more advantageous from a training viewpoint had been scheduled under earlier war plans although this provision was eliminated from the plan which was current when mobilization began. The Chemical Warfare School had been housed for two decades in a two-story, hollow tile structure having two classrooms on the upper floor and administration and faculty offices on the ground floor. An adjoining building of identical size was occupied by the reproduction plant and the school detachment. Nearby temporary structures, build in 1918, were used for housing and messing students and for other school needs. With the facilities available it was difficult for the school to accommodate more than one class at a time.

The school commandant proposed, soon after the President's emergency proclamation in 1939, that steps be taken to increase the capacity of the school from fifty to one hundred students.[47] The War Department was reluctant to undertake the needed construction, since it was then seriously considering closing all service schools as a means of conserving officer strength.[48] Until this idea was dropped, no action was taken to relieve the school situation. However, in 1940, an enlargement program did get under way, which resulted in raising the school's capacity to two hundred students.

Additional academic facilities were provided by erecting a well-designed permanent structure between the two original tile buildings, thus merging

---

[47] Ltr, Comdt CW School to C CWS, 18 Sep 39, sub: Additional Facilities. CW Sch 352 11/148.

[48] Ltrs, TAG to C CWS, 7 Oct 38 and 18 Oct 39, sub: Schools. AG 352 (10-3-39) (10-9-39) M-C.

them into one spacious school edifice. The more than thirty new buildings added in this period included adequate barracks for student officers, mess halls, and supply facilities. Demonstration and outdoor training areas were also improved. Although this development was somewhat belated and despite the fact that it applied principally to officer students, it did enable the school, by 1941, to take a more active part in the accelerating chemical warfare training program.

The school staff and faculty at the beginning of the emergency period in 1939 included five CWS officers plus four officers attached from other components who served as part-time instructors. A year later the staff had increased to fourteen officers. There was no substantial change in this number during 1941.[49]

The suspension of courses at special service schools on 1 February 1940 did not affect the Chemical Warfare School.[50] This suspension enabled students who were attending courses longer than those given at Edgewood to participate in maneuvers in the spring of 1940. The Chemical Warfare School was permitted to begin its regular Line and Staff Course on 4 February with a class composed principally of Reserve officers. This step proved fortunate since most of the members of this class soon were called to extended active duty.

The 23d Line and Staff Officers class and the 13th Field Officers class conducted in 1940 were the last of these two series given at the Chemical Warfare School. Their termination by the War Department was in line with staff policy curtailing school attendance of Regular Army officers during the period of limited emergency. This marked the end of an era. Hereafter officer training at the Chemical Warfare School would concentrate on the preparation of emergency officers for war duty.

Instruction of Reserve Officers

On 27 August 1940 Congress authorized the calling of Reserve officers to active duty for periods of twelve consecutive months.[51] This in practice suspended the fourteen-day active duty arrangement which for years had been the mainspring of Reserve officer training. Had it been possible to foresee at the time that most of the Reservists who were called up under this authority would continue on duty through a major war, more adequate pro-

[49] Class records, Chemical Warfare School.
[50] Annual *Rpt of SW to President*, 1940, p. 63.
[51] Annual *Rpt of SW to President*, 1941, p. 73.

vision for their initial training could have been made. But the Army was then thinking in terms of limited mobilization and was concentrating on the immediate task of training the large numbers of enlisted men who were about to enter military service under the Selective Service System. The training of officers was not at this time given major consideration.

Among the first Reserve officers called for extended active duty were members of the corps area assignment group needed for special staff duty with the ground and air units to be mobilized during the limited emergency period. These men were products of the peacetime Reserve officers' training program and many of them had military experience extending back to World War I. Although they were comparatively well advanced in training when called up, the CWS would nevertheless have profited by their attendance at a school course according to the plan generally followed in the training of other special staff officers assigned to the divisions that were activated in 1940 and 1941.[52]

The mobilization of so many corps area assignment group officers to meet air and ground force T/O requirements for unit chemical officers had a retarding effect on the activation of branch assignment Reservists, for whom need soon developed under the rapidly expanding chemical warfare procurement program. The ceiling which the War Department set on the number of CWS Reserve officers that could be placed on extended active duty was taken to apply to both branches of the Reserve; the CWS felt bound to meet all requests for unit chemical troops, so that branch requirements were satisfied much more slowly than was desirable.[53] This situation directly affected the training of branch assignment personnel. By the time these officers were finally called to active duty, their services were so urgently needed that they could not be spared to attend basic or refresher courses prior to undertaking mobilization assignments.

Lack of an attempt at systematic school training of CWS nonregular officers in preparation for mobilization duty marked not only the period of partial mobilization, but in fact extended throughout the entire war period. There were on active duty with the CWS, on 31 December 1940, 270 nonregular officers. Not more than half of these officers had ever attended any school course. Except for OCS training, the ratio of nongraduates to all officers on duty increased instead of declined in succeeding years. This situation apparently resulted from want of a clear CWS policy on the school-

---

[52] Palmer, Wiley, and Keast, *Procurement and Training of Ground Combat Troops,* pp. 435–36.
[53] Interv, CmlHO with Col Geoffrey Marshall (former Comdt, Cml C Sch), 15 May 51.

ing of officers initiated and firmly maintained from the outset of the national emergency.

The CWS protective mobilization plan contemplated that training of other components at the Chemical Warfare School would be discontinued upon mobilization, when the school would reorganize for its primary mission of training CWS troops. Two types of courses were specified in the new setup: successive thirty-day refresher classes of seventy-five officers, and a series of classes for enlisted specialists (meteorologists).[54] This program would have proven inadequate, even had it been followed. Yet there was no evident inclination in 1940 to extend the school training of CWS officers. In recommending to the War Department the courses to be conducted at the school between 1 July 1940 and 30 June 1941, the CWS proposed only six courses, none of them specifically for preparation of Chemical Warfare Service officers for active duty.[55]

The negligible utilization of the Chemical Warfare School during the period of limited emergency in training CWS personnel for war duty is apparent from an analysis of courses conducted at the school during the calendar years 1940 and 1941. The only notable departure in 1940 from the normal prewar program of the school was the inclusion of a four-week refresher course for the training of eighteen newly commissioned Thomason Act Reserve officers. During 1941, aside from the schooling of replacement center troops already described, no training of officers in performance of CWS branch functions was undertaken; yet in this year more than 600 additional emergency officers were called to duty.

Since so few of the incoming officers were receiving formal training, the chemical warfare school in 1941 was not being utilized to full capacity. This was to some extent a result of the hiatus into which the chemical warfare program of the Army had drifted—a situation which was to be remedied soon after Pearl Harbor. The unused capacity of the school was employed meanwhile principally in furthering the training of the Army in gas protection by means of a series of Unit Gas Officers' classes. Although CWS officers were occasionally assigned to these classes, they were set up for and principally attended by line officers, ground and air.

Progress toward rearming in the period of 1939–41 has been described as "halting and confused."[56] These adjectives also describe chemical war-

[54] CWS PMP, 1940, par 12d and Annex 7, AG 381 Mob Plan.
[55] Memo, C CWS for ACofS, G–3, 7 Jun 40, sub: Courses at CW School. CWS 352.13.
[56] Watson, *Prewar Plans and Preparation*, p. 83.

fare training as it was carried forward during this period. A major factor was the passive attitude of the War Department General Staff toward this training, prior to the regeneration that followed the events of Pearl Harbor. At the same time the Chemical Warfare Service was nervously seeking more realistic antigas training. Often it was the unit commander who finally decided how far this training should be extended in his organization. In view of the conflicting attitudes on chemical warfare, it is remarkable that training in this field had advanced as well and as far as it had by 7 December 1941.

CHAPTER X

The Civilian Defense Mission

One of the first steps taken by Hon. Fiorello H. La Guardia as Director of the Office of Civilian Defense, after that office had been set up, was to request specifically that the War Department provide for the training of ten successive classes of civilians to be selected by his office.[1] The Secretary of War approved La Guardia's request to set up schools for the training of civilians, and on 21 May 1941 directed the activation of the first of these schools.[2]

CWS Prewar Interest in Civilian Defense

CWS interest in civilian defense had extended back for some years. As early as 1930, Col. Charles R. Alley, a CWS officer who had spent some time on military attaché duty and who was impressed by the importance being accorded gas defense in European programs for civilian protection, made a detailed study of measures for protection of American civilians against enemy attack. Colonel Alley's proposals were the first of a number of recommendations presented to the War Department General Staff during the 1930's covering aspects of civilian protection over which the CWS felt concern. During this period the developing threat of aerial warfare against civilian populations was closely observed, particularly any means being perfected overseas to counteract the effects of the two types of agents which the CWS was charged by law with developing and producing—war gases and incendiaries. It was the view of the Chemical Warfare Service that the Military Establishment had an inescapable responsibility to the civilian in

---

[1] (1) Executive Order No. 8757. (2) For discussion of civilian defense at War Department level, see Stetson Conn, Byron Fairchild, and Rose C. Engelman, Guarding the United States and Its Outposts, a volume in preparation in the series UNITED STATES ARMY IN WORLD WAR II.

[2] Memo, Dir Mil Pers Div SOS for C CWS, 5 Mar 43, and Inds, sub: Civilian Protection Schools. SOS SPG, AO/020 General (2–17–43)–13.

MAYOR FIORELLO H. LA GUARDIA, *New York City, first Director of Civilian Defense, left, and Maj. Gen. William N. Porter, Chief of Chemical Warfare Service, at graduation of first civilian defense class. Chemical Warfare School, Edgewood, Maryland, 12 July 1941.*

the matter of protection against air attack and that this responsibility should be defined.[3]

The reaction of the General Staff to the several proposals submitted by the CWS during this period was mixed. The dominant staff view was that nothing should be done that would unduly alarm the general public on the hazards attending strategic bombardment.[4] Americans were known to be sensitive to the implications of gas warfare; for this reason the War Department determined not to incur the charge of jingoism by emphasizing the danger of gas attacks. At the same time Colonel Sherman Miles of War Plans Division (WPD) felt that the matter should not be entirely neglected.[5] The Chief, CWS, was accordingly directed in 1936 to prepare a pamphlet containing information that would be useful to military authorities responsible for carrying out measures of passive protection against aerial attacks.[6] The Chemical Warfare Service was chosen for the task because its concern with both gas and incendiaries brought it more prominently into this field than other technical agencies of the War Department. In the preparation of this publication, the CWS was directed to confer with the Ordnance Department on the effects of explosive bombs, with the Corps of Engineers on the design of bombproof shelters, and with the Medical Department on related health measures. Co-ordination of views of all War Department bureaus that could contribute technical assistance to civilian defense was thus assured.

This document was duly prepared in the Office of the Chief, CWS, with the assistance of other branches. It was approved by the War Department and was reproduced by multilith process at the Chemical Warfare School in 1936 under the title, *Passive Defense Against Air Attack*.[7] Only 200 numbered copies, bound in red covers and classified "secret," were published. By War Department direction, copies of this 43-page pamphlet were transmitted to each corps area commander and to overseas departments where they were filed for use when needed.

---

[3](1) Ltr, C CWS to TAG, 28 Jul 36, sub: Legislation to Govern Government Production of Antigas Equipment. WPD 3942. (2) Memo, C CWS for CofS, 12 Sep 39, sub: Protection of the Civil Population against Air or other Attack. WPD 4078–12 to 24.

[4](1) Memo for Rcd, Brig Gen W. Krueger, Asst CofS, WPD, 8 Apr 37, sub: Anti-gas Protection of Civilians in War, WPD 3942. (2) Memo Brig Gen George V. Strong, Asst CofS WPD for G–4, 3 Oct 39, sub: Gas Masks for Civilian Population WPD 4078–14.

[5] Memo, Sherman Miles to Asst CofS WPD, 3 Sep 36, sub: Legislation to Govern the Production of Anti-gas Protective Equipment. WPD 3942.

[6] The 1936 directive is referred to and briefly quoted in draft memo, W. K. [Walter Krueger], Asst CofS WPD for CofS, Mar 37, sub: Provision for Anti-gas Protection of Civilians in War. WPD 3942.

[7] CW School Publication No. 135, 1930. CWS 314.7 CW School File.

With the publication of the passive defense pamphlet the General Staff dismissed, for the time being, further consideration of civilian defense. Yet during the next two years steady deterioration of the political situation in Europe led foreign governments to give increasing attention to problems of civilian protection. Full reports of these developments were obtained by the CWS through military attachés like Colonel Alley and from other sources. Early in 1939 Maj. Gen. Walter C. Baker again brought this matter officially to the attention of the War Department, proposing that military responsibility for the protection of U.S. citizens from aerial attack be more sharply determined. Among matters of concern to the CWS at this time were arrangements for production of gas masks for civilian use, agreement on channels for release of authoritative information that would allay undue alarm over war gases and incendiaries, and procedure for instruction of selected civilians in technical phases of air raid precautions. General Baker pointed out that "until a general plan has been adopted the chemical plan cannot be developed." [8] The recommendations he presented in this letter provided the basis for an outline plan for the Army's approach to civilian defense, a plan prepared by the War Plans Division after the German invasion of Poland.[9] This staff study represented the first frank recognition by the War Department of responsibility in the matter of civilian defense and provided the groundwork for a realistic approach to problems that were to loom large during the next four years.

In reviewing the WPD study after it had been referred to the Chemical Warfare Service for comment, General Baker recommended particularly that the development of civilian instructors and the specialized training of selected civilians be undertaken by the War Department.[10] This proved to be the precise direction in which extensive training activities of the CWS were to tend less than two years later.

Preparation of Instructional Material

In June 1940 the New York City Fire Commissioner, John J. McElligott, sent a representative to Washington to confer with the Chief, CWS on the problem of familiarizing fire fighters with methods of combating gas and

---

[8] Ltr, C CWS to TAG, 9 Jan 39, sub: Protection of Civilian Population Against Air or Other Attacks. CWS 470.6/732.

[9] Memo, WPD for CofS, 20 Feb 40, sub: Protection of Civilian Population from Air and Other Attack. WPD 4078-3.

[10] Memo, C CWS for WPD, 30 Sep 39, no sub. CWS 470.6/732.

incendiary attacks. This and similar requests from responsible municipal authorities for technical assistance on civilian defense problems were duly reported by the CWS to the War Department and were instrumental in getting the department to initiate the compilation of needed instructional and training literature.[11] The CWS was directed to prepare a pamphlet "to furnish the local Civil Defense organization with information as to the methods employed in Chemical Warfare and the means of combating them." [12] This manuscript, eventually published by the Office of Civilian Defense as *Protection Against Gas* (GPO, 1941), served as a wartime guide for this type of civilian training.

Behind the comprehensive group of textbooks, handbooks, and planning guides eventually published by the OCD is the story of the peacetime interest of a senior CWS officer in civilian defense matters. For several years preceding World War II, Col. Adelno Gibson had collected standard manuals and other writings on civilian defense from most of the countries of Europe. Colonel Gibson communicated his enthusiasm for the subject to others. In 1938, as Second Corps Area Chemical Officer, he presented to senior Reserve officers in the New York area a problem then being studied by the CWS. This involved the provision of authentic information for the general public on the effects of gas and incendiary bombing.[13]

One of these officers, Lt. Col. Walter P. Burn, an advertising executive, became interested in this problem and decided to make it the subject of a thesis which he was about to write in preparation for promotion. The thoroughness with which Burn developed this subject and his novel approach to the popularizing of instructional material impressed CWS officers who had the matter under study. Burn's thesis was available at the time the Office of Civilian Defense was created and it was accordingly supplied to that Office for study. As a result, the OCD requested the services of Colonel Burn and made him chief of the Training Division. It was largely due to Colonel Burn's ability and initiative that the impressive schedule of OCD training publications was launched so promptly. As chief of the Training Division, OCD, Burn was responsible for the preparation of training litera-

[11] (1) Copies of municipal communications were filed in CWS 470.6/732. (2) Ltr, TAG to Corps Area & Army Comdrs, 6 Jul 40, sub: Protection of the Civil Population from Air and Other Attack. AG 385 (6–27–40) M–C–M. (3) Ltr, TAG to C CWS, 23 Aug 40, sub: Instructional Matter. AG 383 (8–7–40) M–C.

[12] Ltr, TAG to C CWS, 12 Aug 40, sub: Preparation of Pamphlet entitled "Defense Against Chemical Warfare." AG 062.1 (8–3–40) P (C).

[13] Ltr Col Walter P. Burn, Ret, to Cml C Hist Off, 1 Jan 57.

GAS DEFENSE TRAINING FOR CIVILIANS *at the Chemical Warfare School, Edgewood, Maryland, 1941.*

ture, manuals and films; the design of insignia and special uniforms; the recruitment of skilled writers and artists who served on a voluntary basis; and the enlistment for special missions of national organizations such as the American Legion, the Boy Scouts, and the Red Cross.[14]

The incendiary bombing of British urban centers, which had become extremely ominous by the late summer of 1940, was viewed with special apprehension by the U.S. citizens on the Altantic seaboard. New York City sent technical observers to England to obtain first-hand information on combating incendiary fires. Increasingly urgent calls upon the War Department for technical data on which to base defensive planning finally forced it to direct that, pending completion of official instructional literature, the best information available should be issued to civilian authorities.[15] The War Department was moving cautiously but steadily toward full co-operation

[14] (1) Ltr, Col Adelno Gibson, CWS, Librarian Army War College, to Hist Br, CWS, 25 May 44. (2) Ltr, Maj Gen L. D. Gasser, C Protection Br OCD to Col W. P. Burn, 8 May 42. OCD Protection Br Control & Communications Sec Dispatched Corres File NA.

[15] Ltr, AGO to C CWS, 23 Aug 40, sub: Instructional Matter to be Furnished the Civil Population. AG 383 (8–7–40) M–C.

with civilian agencies charged with protection of U.S. citizens against aerial attack.

In line with this approach, the CWS, at the request of representatives of the National Board of Fire Underwriters, conducted a demonstration at Edgewood Arsenal on 9 October 1940, at which magnesium and oil incendiary bombs were ignited and extinguished.[16] This demonstration was the first of hundreds staged by the CWS during the war to inform civilians about the character of incendiary bombs and the methods of handling them.

As another important step in preparation for more active participation in the civilian protection program, the Chief, CWS, was directed in February 1941 to prepare a short course of instruction to be given on a volunteer basis to representatives of fire departments of large cities.[17] An outline for a three-day course was prepared by the Chemical Warfare School in which instructional time was evenly divided between the handling of incendiaries and protection against war gases.

The school staff then proceeded to develop a more extensive instructor-training course intended to qualify selected civilians for the task of teaching volunteer workers at local levels. In a sense, the Army had to provide such a course as a measure of self-defense. It was clear that civilian officials would look to the military for technical instructions upon which to base the more general training of civilians in connection with the national air raid precaution program that the United States would doubtless be obliged to adopt. It was equally clear that the Army, even at the beginning of 1941, was much too busily employed in military training to embark on an extended scheme for the training of civilians. A two-week course for a limited number of carefully selected top echelon civilians appeared to provide a solution which was within the ability of the War Department and which at the same time would enable it substantially to satisfy the need for disseminating authentic doctrine on the more technical aspect of civilian defense.

The Chemical Warfare School made a careful study of this subject and early in 1941 developed a course of instruction which promised to meet these requirements. As originally developed at the school this course included:

a. Incendiaries (22 hours): To afford technical instruction in characteristics of and in methods of coping with incendiary bombs.

b. Gas defense (26 hours): To acquaint students with war gases likely

[16] Ltr, OC CWS to CO EA, Md, 1 Oct 40, sub: Incendiary Bombs. CWS 470.6/732.
[17] Ltr, AGO to C CWS, 25 Feb 41, sub: Special Instruction at the CW School for Members of Fire Departments. AG 362.01 (1–22–41) M–C

to be used against noncombatants and with methods of protection against such agents.

c. High explosive bombs (17 hours): To afford familiarity with the action of HE bombs and with practical measures of protection from their effects.

d. Training methods (10 hours): To provide practical and theoretical instruction in training of local civilians in air raid precautions.

School Training at Edgewood Arsenal

The Office of Civilian Defense took such an interest in the course set up at Edgewood in June 1941 that it sent steno-typists to record the lectures. OCD had to co-ordinate these lectures with the texts and illustrations which it prepared. For that reason, and also because the OCD was getting numerous requests to visit Edgewood from governors, mayors, and other officials, as well as from writers interested in Civilian Defense, General Gasser on 21 July 1941 requested the Secretary of War to designate a liaison officer between Edgewood Arsenal and the Office of Civilian Defense.[18] After consultation between Maj. Gen. William Bryden, Deputy Chief of Staff and General Porter, Chief, CWS, 1st Lt. John N. Dick, a CWS Reserve officer called to active duty in 1940, was appointed to this post.[19] Dick had formerly been Mayor La Guardia's personal representative in Washington and was consequently no stranger to the Director of the Office of Civilian Defense.[20] At the same time Dick was named liaison officer he was made chief of a new activated Civilian Protection Division, OC CWS. In July 1942 this division was redesignated a branch.[21] That same month Lieutenant Dick was succeeded by Col. George J. B. Fisher as chief of the branch and in July 1943 Colonel Fisher was succeeded by Lt. Col. Willard A. Johnston. In the May 1943 reorganization of the Chief's Office the Civilian Protection Division became a branch of the Training Division.[22] Late in 1943 the branch

[18] Ltr, Brig Gen L. D. Gasser to SW, 21 Jul 41, sub: Request for Immediate Appointment of Liaison Officer at Edgewood Arsenal to Coordinate Relationships with the Office of Civilian Defense CWS 314.7 Civilian Defense File.

[19] (1) Memo, DCofS for WD Member of the Board for Civilian Defense (Brig Gen L. D. Gasser, Ret), 1 Aug 41, sub: Request for Appointment of Liaison Officer to Edgewood Arsenal to Co-ordinate Relationships with Office of Civilian Defense. (2) Ltr, TAG to 1st Lt John N. Dick, through the C CWS, 14 Aug 41, sub: Designation of Liaison Officer. Both in CWS 314.7 Civilian Defense File.

[20] (1) Interv, CmlHO with Col John N. Dick, 21 Mar 56. (2) The Washington Daily News, December 23, 1941.

[21] (1) OC CWS Off O 14, 30 Jul 41. (2) OC CWS SO 100, 5 Aug 41. (3) OC CWS Off O 40, 29 Jul 42.

[22] OC CWS Organization Chart, 12 Jun 43.

was deactivated, because by that time the CWS civilian protection mission had been accomplished.

The accommodation of civilian classes at the Chemical Warfare School during the summer and fall of 1941 did not impose an undue strain on school facilities. As has been indicated, the school at that particular period was not being fully utilized in the training of CWS personnel. However, the Chief, CWS, was convinced that all existing capacity of the school, and much more, would soon be needed for military training. While civilian defense training was accepted as a necessary contribution to an aspect of national defense in which the CWS had long been interested, it was clear that arrangement would have to be made for eventually carrying forward this work at other locations. General Porter in August 1941 accordingly sent two officers to survey sites where similar schools of instruction could be established. As a result of this survey, four additional locations for the future conduct of civilian defense training were tentatively selected in Texas, California, and Illinois.

In the eleven classes conducted at Edgewood Arsenal prior to 7 December 1941, 466 students from thirty-seven states were graduated. Out of this relatively small group came many leaders to head civilian defense bodies in every section of the country after war was declared. At the same time these prewar classes provided invaluable experience in working out solutions to problems that were without precedent in American experience.

Instead of merely instructing in a few essentially military techniques, the school faculty soon found itself confronted with the task of expounding a new thesis—how civilians might survive in modern war. It was fundamental that civilian protection was self-protection; that civilians themselves must organize and operate their own defense setup. This doctrine had to be rationalized and to some extent it had to be qualified. Overlapping of military and civilian authority needed clarification, and areas where one superseded the other had to be defined. For example, military control of the air raid warning system, of handling unexploded bombs, and of area smoke screening all was mandatory—for reasons which had to be made clear. On the other hand, development of the warden system, of rescue parties, and of fire-fighting services were all matters within civilian jurisdiction.

These and similar procedures that fell under OCD control obviously had to be elucidated before groups such as were attending the classes. The school undertook, whenever possible, to have nonmilitary subjects taught by civilians. For this purpose, members of the OCD staff and other qualified speakers came frequently to Edgewood to lay before succeeding classes

DEMONSTRATION IN DECONTAMINATION PROCEDURES *for civilians. Men in protective clothing and gas masks mark off gassed area. Chemical Warfare School, Edgewood Arsenal, Md.*

matters of important civilian defense procedure. Yet there was never any question, either of this stage or later, that here was a U.S. Army school following military instructional procedures but adapting itself to the training of civilians.

The fact that the students were on a military reservation attending an Army school gave prestige to the instruction at a time when this was most needed. It was frequently noted that a young officer wearing a second lieutenant's uniform would be listened to more respectfully than a speaker in civilian garb discussing a subject on which he was a nationally recognized authority. The confidence with which instruction was accepted was one of the rewarding features of this early training activity. Even though pedagogically the course may not have rated high at the beginning, this fact was incidental since the students who had volunteered for this training were at Edgewood Arsenal to learn; and that is what they proceeded to do. To some extent it was a case of student and instructor learning at the same time and of each recognizing the other as pioneering in a new field. There was at first a great deal of lecturing and not enough group discussion and applied work. The tendency of the school was to emphasize, it may be unduly, those subjects which for years had been its specialty. Yet there was much praise and little criticism from the students who derived a feeling of direct and personal participation in preparation for war which they could have gotten in no other way.

For these early classes at the Chemical Warfare School, sessions began on a Monday morning and ended at noon on the second succeeding Saturday. A charge of $23.00 per student was made for meals during the twelve-day period. This and other incidental costs were usually paid by the municipality or corporation by which the student was employed although often these expenses were borne by the patriotic volunteer. A prorated charge of $60.00 per student covered cost of ammunition and other outright expenses incurred in connection with this instruction. Army appropriations were reimbursed to this extent by emergency funds made available to OCD, thus satisfying a legal restriction that military appropriations should not be expended in the training of civilians.

During the fall of 1941, in response to insistent demands, the Chemical Warfare School extended its civilian defense instruction into nearby areas. This step was taken as an aid in the protection of industrial plants against aerial attack, a matter of utmost concern at the time. The work involved demonstrations and seminars at Boston, Princeton, Philadelphia, and Pittsburgh. The course at Princeton consisted of a two-day session conducted for the special benefit of CWS Reserve officers who were preparing for active participation in the New Jersey state civil defense program.

Reserve officers contributed materially to the development of civilian defense at this early stage, especially in the East. Notable in this connection was the work of Col. J. Enrique Zanetti, a CWS Reserve officer and Columbia University professor, who wrote and lectured extensively on this subject and demonstrated the burning of incendiaries before many interested groups.[23] Local officials charged with developing civilian defense organiza-

---

[23] In the fall of 1941 the Chief, CWS, put Colonel Zanetti in charge of the incendiary bomb program in the CWS See above, Chapter II.

tions very often pressed into service CWS officers who were acquainted with technical features of air raid protection.

The twelfth civilian defense class was enjoying its mid-course week end when the Japanese struck at Pearl Harbor. The final week of instruction for this class had to be conducted by a skeletonized staff because on 8 December the Chief, CWS (General Porter), directed the school to provide a group of experienced instructors for an urgent training mission on the Pacific Coast. As the details of the Pearl Harbor disaster became known, fear grew that other shattering blows might be imminent. The Office of Civilian Defense was especially concerned over reactions in west coast metropolitan centers. The Chemical Warfare Service had at that moment the only organized staff of instructors qualified to direct the type of training that would quickly develop competent leadership in civilian defense at local levels. Accordingly the War Department was asked by the OCD to dispatch a group of officers to California for the purpose of undertaking the instruction of local leaders in civilian defense operations.

This request was immediately granted. A group of nine CWS officers, headed by Lt. Col. George J. B. Fisher, reached San Francisco on 13 December and after hurried consultation with the Commanding General, Western Defense Command, and the regional director of civilian defense, was prepared to commence its training mission. Employing blitz tactics and a condensation of the course developed at Edgewood Arsenal, simultaneous three-day classes of instruction were conducted at San Francisco and Oakland. One instructional party moved quickly north to Portland, Seattle, and Spokane, while the other proceeded south to Los Angeles, Long Beach, and San Diego.

Public interest ran high; enrollment constantly exceeded the 250 students each class was intended to accommodate. Large groups witnessed the demonstrations and control center exercises. College auditoriums, public academies, and civic buildings were made available for instructional purposes. War had found the west coast with civilian protection programs still inadequate and incomplete—a situation which citizens of all ranks now undertook to correct. Hearty co-operation was afforded each training party. The doctrine stressed was that knowledge plus proper organization would enable American citizens to withstand anything the Japanese could bring to bear against them. This philosophy had a tonic effect. When the CWS contingent returned east in mid-January it was with the feeling that a measurable contribution had been made toward relieving the shock of the initial impact of war upon the Western states.

War Department Civilian Protection Schools

The early desire of General Porter to relocate civilian training was influenced by two considerations. First, he wished to free facilities at Edgewood Arsenal for strictly military usage. Secondly, the eastern location of the school was manifestly a handicap to students from the Far West. The latter circumstance was particularly disturbing to the Office of Civilian Defense. After the series of ten classes originally requested was completed on 28 November 1941 the OCD then asked that six more classes be conducted at Edgewood Arsenal, at the same time hoping that a number of additional schools would be established.

Already the Commission on Colleges and Civilian Defense had offered the co-operation of the nation's colleges in the civilian defense program. OCD decided that the use of college facilities for civilian defense schools was desirable and accordingly arranged for a meeting between Dr. Francis J. Brown, executive secretary of the Commission, and a group of Army officers, to study this possibility. This meeting, held in Washington on 5 December 1941, made a number of proposals which OCD adopted and laid before the War Department. Among these were recommendations; (1) that six branch schools, each with a capacity for fifty students, be established, (2) that these schools be located in colleges well distributed geographically, (3) that all schools be controlled and operated by the War Department, and (4) that necessary funds be made available by OCD and U.S. Office of Education.[24] The Chief, CWS, was in due time directed by the War Department to establish and operate these schools at locations selected by him.[25]

The two schools first established were opened on 15 February 1942 at Leland Stanford Jr. University (California) and at Texas Agricultural and Mechanical College—two of the four sites that had been selected tentatively by the CWS the preceding August. The next month a third school was ready to open at Amherst College in Massachusetts. Conduct of civilian instruction at the Chemical Warfare School terminated on 31 March 1942, by which time a fourth school was in operation at University of Maryland.[26] The opening in June of schools at the University of Florida, Purdue University (Indiana), and finally at the University of Washington (Seattle) completed the original program as proposed by the OCD.

---

[24] Ltr, OCD to TAG, 10 Dec 41, sub: CD Schools for 1942. AG 352 (12–10–41).

[25] Ltr, AGO to C CWS, 16 Jan 42, sub: CD Schools for 1942. AG 352 (12–10–41).

[26] The Maryland school was originally intended to serve instead of the Edgewood school as a mother institution for the six branch schools. Later this was found to be impracticable.

It was necessary to make a few changes in the locations initially selected. The school established at the University of Florida was not well attended so it was decided in August 1942 to transfer its staff and faculty to southern California where insistent demand for this training had developed. Thus a school at Occidental College, Los Angeles, opened on 1 September 1942 and continued in successful operation until the training program was terminated. Another adjustment made in November 1942 was the transfer of the Texas A. & M. school to Loyola University, New Orleans. The University of Maryland school was closed in September 1942, primarily in order to provide personnel for another training activity.

Each of these facilities, designated as War Department Civilian Protection Schools, was organized under a common pattern which followed experience gained at Edgewood Arsenal. A staff of six officer-instructors and an enlisted detachment of twenty-five men plus several clerical assistants were provided for each school, the senior officer in each instance being designated as school director. Cost of housing and meals, usually supplied by the university, was borne by the individual student. Outdoor instructional areas, including stage setting for a night incendiary demonstration, were set up by military personnel. Under their contract with the War Department, universities where schools were located were reimbursed only for actual expenses incurred. This sum scarcely compensated the institutions for extensive use made of their facilities, the value of which had to be written off as a contribution to the national defense.

With the opening of the first branch schools in February 1942 the original twelve-day course developed at the Chemical Warfare School was shortened to nine days (sixty-six hours) of scheduled instruction. This change was occasioned in part by the fact that certain instruction given at Edgewood Arsenal could not be duplicated elsewhere. By streamlining the course and eliminating interesting but nonessential periods it was found that a satisfactory program of basic training in civilian defense could be completed by the end of the second Wednesday.

As finally organized, the general Civilian Defense Course included nine subcourses as follows:

Aerial Attack (7 hours): To acquaint the student with the general features of aerial action, including hostile operations and military countermeasures thereto—thus leading to a clearer conception of the factors in modern war which necessitate development of civilian protection.

Civilian Defense Organization (3 hours): To insure familiarity with the general outlines of organization on national, regional, state, and local levels by which civilian defense is integrated to meet the problems presented by aerial attack.

Bomb Disposal (4½ hours): Presenting characteristics of explosive bombs and the general problem of disposing of unexploded bombs; definition of respective responsibilities of civilian agencies and military agencies in handling unexploded bomb situations.[27]

Incendiary Protection (9 hours): To impart understanding of the essential features of incendiary munitions, and of means and methods by which they can be controlled without recourse to organized fire-fighting units.

Gas Protection (11 hours): Consideration of the nature and characteristics of gases that may be employed against civilian targets; methods of protection against them; civilian organization of gas defense.

Plant Protection (5 hours): Problems of organization and technical preparation of industrial plants, hospitals, and other large facilities as distinct from community protection.

Citizens Defense Corps (17½ hours): To induce appreciation of the corps as an integrated team capable of coping with the various types of incidents, through review of functions of each unit and through exercises involving their combined employment under the control center.

Local Training (3½ hours): To prepare students to actively and effectively participate in local programs of civilian defense training.

General Subjects (5½ hours): Miscellaneous exercises and conferences not otherwise included.

By instructional directives, each of these subcourses was broken down into a suitable number of lectures, conferences, demonstrations, and exercises to insure the most effective approach to the designated objective. An instructor's period guide was provided by the Civilian Protection Branch, OC CWS, for each lesson phase. A standardized schedule indicated the sequence of instruction to be followed, text references, and academic procedure. Although each school director was authorized to make modifications to meet local conditions or to emphasize local problems, such variations were incidental. The school authorities realized that only within a firm overall pattern was it possible to reflect instructionally the frequent changes being made in the technique of protection against air attack.

Teaching procedure at the schools was based on FM 21–5, Military Training, and TM 21–250, Army Instruction. The texts employed were publications of the U.S. Office of Civilian Defense, supplemented oc-

---

[27] Instructions in handling of unexploded bombs and related subjects were generally given by Ordnance officers.

casionally by military manuals. Pertinent OCD publications were usually supplied in sufficient quantities to provide one for each student to be used at school and retained after graduation. Much of the resident instruction was explanation, demonstration, and application of matter contained in these texts. The atmosphere of the schools reflected the precision and thoroughness associated with the military service. Behind the immediate purpose of quickly imparting needed knowledge was the implicit responsibility of imbuing each graduate with a sense of confidence in the armed forces of the United States.[28]

The immediate and continued success of those schools was due in large measure to the experience and capability of the instructors who were assigned to these faculties. These Reserve officers were in many instances professional college and university teachers who fitted readily into this new type of semimilitary training conducted in an academic environment.

A reorganization of the teaching program of War Department Civilian Protection Schools was undertaken in December 1942. By this time civilian defense organization at local levels had been completed, the Citizens' Defense Corps was well established, and there was diminished need for the general course as originally developed at the Chemical Warfare School. However, definite requirement was now felt for more specialized instruction than was possible in the standardized course. A group of four shorter courses was accordingly worked out by the Civilian Protection Branch, OC CWS, including:

Basic Protection Course (6 days): Thorough grounding in technique applicable to community protection—handling of incendiaries, unexploded bombs, and gas situations; air raid wardens duties; blackouts; panic prevention; training the general public; and similar basic problems with which all were concerned.

Plant Protection Course (6 days): To specialize in training of selected plant personnel in problems of organization and technical preparation of industrial plants, hospitals, and other large institutions or facilities as distinct from community protection. This course was generally similar to the basic course except that the point of view was that of the plant or institution rather than the municipality.

Staff Course (5 days): Embraced command organization for control of combined units in air raid action; strategy of civilian protection; integration of military and civilian security agencies; planning and execution of local

---

[28] WD Civilian Protection Schools, Instruction Directive, 6 Feb 43.

programs; organization and direction of the Citizens' Defense Corps; control center exercises.

Gas Specialists Course (5 days): To qualify senior (local) gas officers and gas reconnaissance agents for performance of their duties; instruction of the general public, and equipment and training of Citizens' Defense Corps enrollees.

With the concurrence of the OCD, these shorter courses replaced the original basic course after 1942. During the first six months of 1943 approximately twenty of them were conducted at each WDCP school, scheduled in accordance with the training requirements of regional OCD authorities.

Miscellaneous Activities

Each WDCP school was called upon for considerable service over and above the resident instruction of civilian students. At colleges where these schools were located, the college laboratories served as practical substitutes for chemical field laboratories. The prospect of Japan delivering at least a token gas attack against the United States was by no means fantastic; should such attack be made, it was important to identify accurately the agents used.[29] For this reason, qualified instructors in analytical chemistry on the faculties of these colleges were given special instruction at Edgewood Arsenal in detection of war gases and arrangements were made with service commands to have samples of any enemy chemical agents dropped within the zone of the interior dispatched to the nearest school for analysis and positive identification.

The number of Negroes trained at WDCP schools was relatively small. This no doubt was due to the limited employment of Negroes as instructors and as executives in local civilian defense organizations. Three classes of all-Negro students were conducted in the fall of 1942 at the Prairie View (Texas) Normal and Industrial College by the faculty of the Texas A. & M. school. One hundred and fifty-one men and women from several southern states were trained in these classes. The instructional staff was altogether satisfied with the caliber of these students and would have welcomed the opportunity to train additional Negroes had they been needed.

---

[29] Japan did drop incendiaries from naval aircraft and released balloons which landed within continental United States. See Conn *et al.,* Guarding the U.S, Ch. III, and Wesley F. Craven and James L. Cate, eds, *The Army Air Forces in World War II: VI, Men and Planes* (Chicago: University of Chicago Press, 1955), pp. 113, 116–18. Hereafter cited as Craven and Cate, *Men and Planes.*

An important feature of extracurricula work of the schools was conducting plant protection seminars. These were held in every section of the country, an outgrowth of the work originally undertaken in this field by the Chemical Warfare School in the autumn of 1941. Word of such exercises held in the Southwest was carried home by Mexican graduates of the Texas school and led the Mexican Government formally to write the Americans to stage a plant protection exercise at Monterrey, Nuevo Léon. This exercise was successfully accomplished in September 1942 and occasioned a request from the Republic of Mexico for a more elaborate civilian defense program to be conducted in Mexico City.[30] The project was arranged through the Coordinator of Inter-American Affairs. With concurrence of the State Department, a party headed by the U.S. Director of Civilian Defense (James M. Landis) and including experienced CWS instructors flew to the Mexican capital in May 1943 for a three-day series of conferences to acquaint local and national authorities with U.S. civil defense procedures.

The most spectacular training activity of CWS in World War II was an outgrowth of the biweekly incendiary demonstration conducted by the University of Maryland WDCP school. This exercise constantly attracted large groups of spectators from Washington, military as well as civilian, a fact which influenced the school director, Col. Joseph D. Sears, to develop the demonstration into an outstanding spectacle. After observing the popular interest thus awakened and appreciating the desirability of carrying to a larger audience the lessons taught in the exercise, the OCD requested the War Department to make this a traveling unit. The War Department was unwilling to increase the personnel then allotted to civilian defense training but countered with the proposal that the Maryland school be closed and its staff utilized for this purpose. Under this arrangement a mobile unit named ACTION OVERHEAD was organized.

This undertaking put the CWS squarely into the show business. It required building up a staff with theatrical experience, including stage managers, lighting and sound effects men, and narrators. Personnel of the unit included nine officers and thirty-five enlisted men, more than the normal WDCP school complement, yet certainly small for the task at hand. The 15,000-word script followed in the show was developed principally by Colonel Sears and was finally approved by the Office of the Chief, CWS, and OCD on 31 August 1942, by which time ACTION OVERHEAD, in a caravan of fourteen trucks, was ready for the road.

[30] Ltr, US Direc OCD to Col G. J. B. Fisher, OC CWS, 17 Dec 42, no sub, and inclosures. General File Off Dir OCD, 093–Latin American Countries–Mexico, NA.

Throughout the performance the Army's instructional sequence of explanation, demonstration, and application was steadily followed. The hour and a half demonstration was divided into two sections. In the first section the various types of bombs used in air attack were displayed, explained, and detonated. Then followed demonstrations of correct methods of counteraction, usually undertaken by local units of the Citizens' Defense Corps. Stressed throughout this part of the exercises were practical knowledge, foresight, and calmness in the face of air attack. The second section opened with display of a typical control center, manned insofar as possible by local civilian defense volunteers. After explanation of the setup and operation of the control center, the demonstration field was blacked out for a simulated air attack. When possible, a flight of planes from a nearby Army Air Force base was employed, the dropping of live bombs being represented by static detonation of high explosives and incendiaries. In cities where the AAF was unable to co-operate in providing aircraft, sound strips were used to simulate their approach.

During 1942 and 1943 ACTION OVERHEAD was presented before 2¼ million people in more than one hundred American cities, giving a realistic interpretation of air attack and of civilian defense in action.

Supervision of War Department Civilian Protection Schools

Prior to the reorganization of the War Department in March 1942, civilian defense matters were handled by the Civil Defense Branch, Office of the Assistant Chief of Staff, G–3. After the creation of the Services of Supply, these functions were transferred to the Civil Defense Section of the Office of Chief of Administrative Services (SOS).[31] The latter organization thereafter co-ordinated all War Department activities in this field, including conduct of schools. Since the training was essentially technical in nature, its supervision was left with the CWS—the principal concern of the Services of Supply being that the schools met the requirements of OCD and that they were efficiently conducted.

Close liaison had to be maintained between the Office of the Chief, CWS, and the Office of Civilian Defense in training and related activities. The general operating procedure was for the OCD to indicate *what* teaching was desirable, the War Department then determining *how* the instructional aim would be attained. Army relations with the OCD were handled through the

[31] Ltr, C of Adm Servs SOS to CGs Air & Ground Forces, *et al.*, 31 Mar 42, sub: Civilian Defense. SPAAC 020 (3–29–42).

Board of Civilian Protection. The OCD Training Division was an important agency of the Board of Civilian Protection and its activities were directed by the Army member of that board. In addition to continuous development of the curriculum, which was a joint CWS-OCD project, the Training Division was solely responsible for the allotting to regional directors of quotas for civilian students.

At the end of a year of wartime operation, the OCD formally requested that the WDCP schools be continued. In approving this proposal, the U.S. Director of Civilian Defense was advised:

The War Department is agreeable to the continuation of these schools during the calendar year 1943, provided it is your judgment they are serving an essential purpose.

The Chief, Chemical Warfare Service, has been informed accordingly, and he is being directed to continue, as long as these schools are conducted by the War Department, to operate them in such a manner as will most effectively aid you in meeting the important responsibilities of your office.[32]

The question of how far these schools were "serving an essential purpose" began to present itself in the spring of 1943. For understandable reasons the active concern of the War Department with the civilian defense program gradually lessened as the war progressed. In the course of two years the Office of Civilian Defense, starting from scratch, had developed a nationwide scheme of civilian self-protection against air raids that was reasonably adequate, so that need for advanced training in this field was beginning to lack urgency. The doubt and unrest that arose after the shocking events of December 1941 had been supplanted by a sense of national confidence inspired by victories that began with the Battle of Midway. The gradual build-up of United Nations strength finally forced the Axis powers to assume the strategic defensive, which left them impotent to undertake serious action against the U.S. mainland. At the same time shortages of manpower at home obliged the Army by 1943 to curtail every activity that did not contribute directly to military victory overseas.

Early in 1943 the prospects of enemy attack were reviewed by the Combined Chemical Warfare Committee for study of the Policy for Gas Defense of the U.S. A study prepared by this group on 20 May 1943 reported the following conclusions:

(1) At present the enemy does not possess the means to deliver sustained gas attacks against the United States.

(2) The enemy probably does possess the means to deliver surprise and sporadic gas attacks against vital coastal installations in the United States.

[32] Ltr, C of Adm Serv to Dir OCD, 26 Dec 42, no sub. SPAAC 352.

(3) The enemy is not now capable of delivering any attacks against inland installations.

(4) Ample warning will be given before the enemy can get into a position which will enable him to deliver regular and sustained gas attacks against the United States.[33]

Although this report was made primarily with a view to determining policy as to protection of military installations in the zone of interior, its application to civilian defense was clear. The hazard of enemy gas attack against American cities had diminished to the point of negligibility.

Nor was this situation the result solely of the deterioration of enemy capabilities. U.S. defensive measures had progressively advanced until they promised to deny important advantage to the attacker. The American public had become acquainted with the characteristics of air raids and had developed more confidence in its ability to withstand their effects. The likelihood of creating panic in heavily populated areas by a show of air power had greatly diminished.

The gas protection phase of the civilian defense program, developed under CWS guidance, took into account certain psychological or morale-sustaining ends as well as the physical protection of the individual. It involved protective matériel plus organization, with the two blended into a functional entity. Civilian gas masks had been procured by the CWS and were stored by the OCD in quantities sufficient to permit issuance of one to every civilian whose duty required him to remain in a gassed area.[34] The civilian gas protection organization insured echelonment of responsibility and technical competence where this was needed. It provided for the execution of antigas measures by civilians themselves under procedures authenticated by military experience and training. Although fortunately the defensive scheme was never subjected to the test of combat, it did provide ground for assurance that the threat of poison gas could be countered successfully.

What had been accomplished in the field of gas defense was paralleled in other fields of air raid protection. Large industrial plants had developed operational procedures which promised to avert serious disruption of production in consequence of aerial attack. Fire-fighting organizations had become acquainted with the characteristics of incendiary bombing, against which defensive measures were introduced. State and municipal plans for evacuation,

[33] Agenda, Meeting OCWC, 20 May 43.
[34] CWS procured over 6½ million noncombatant masks for adults and over 1½ million for children. CWS Report of Production, 1 January 1940 through 31 December 1945, pp. 20–21.

rescue, medical assistance, and other aspects of passive defense were developed. The ability of U.S. citizens to withstand assault by air was increasing rapidly at the same time that enemy capability of initiating such assault was on the wane. This fact, recognized by Congress as well as by the general public, resulted in decision to terminate the WDCP school program. The schools accordingly were discontinued effective 21 July 1943.[35]

During their operation a total of 274 classes were conducted with an average attendance of 37.7 trainees. Graduates included men and women from every state in the Union as well as from Canada and Mexico. Over one fifth of the 10,328 enrolled students were Army and Navy officers, some of whom were trained for civilian protection duty in the zone of interior, others in the theaters of operation.

Although it now appears that the operation of WDCP schools after midsummer of 1943 was not justified, the War Department willingly agreed to continue aid to OCD in its training operations by providing CWS instructors as needed for technical training in state civilian defense schools.[36] It further agreed to maintain two educational facilities, one on each coast, where Army training of civilians could be undertaken again if occasion demanded. This commitment lead to the activation of the West Coast Chemical Warfare School at Camp Beale, California, in the fall of 1943, while plans were made for resuming civilian training at the CW School if necessary. However, OCD training activities virtually ceased with the closing of WDCP schools.

At the same time that it was diminishing within the zone of interior, the need for training in air raid precaution was being emphasized abroad as the extent of occupied territory increased. Civilian protection in occupied areas was a function of Military Government, although few officers designated for such duty had received any training in this specialty. The Chemical Warfare School was directed in September 1943 to prepare an air raid protection course to qualify CWS personnel to function as staff air raid protection officers in each theater of operations and for the training of officers of other branches for this type of duty within their units.[37] Well-qualified instructors released by the closing of WDCP schools were available for this purpose. A series of seven 1-week classes, each averaging 43 students, was completed at the Chemical Warfare School by the end of 1943. This brought to a close an interesting if somewhat unusual CWS training activity.

---

[35] Ltr, AGO to CGS of SCs, 29 Jul 43, sub: WDCP Schools. SPX 352 (8 Jul 43).
[36] WD Memo 4590-4-43, 24 Mar 43, sub: Training of civilians.
[37] Ltr, TAG to C CWS 16 May 43, sub: Civ Defense Instruction of Selected Officers for Expeditionary Forces. SPX 353 (3-12-43) OB-S-SPAAC-M.

CHAPTER XI

Official Publications

"Training literature" was the imposing description applied to the wartime products of the CWS publication agency. This term was only partially appropriate. It did serve, however, to underwrite the idea that all texts required for military training were to be found in the list of official publications.

Volume of Wartime Publications

The War Department publications that were available at the beginning of the war period are listed in a thin, pocket-size pamphlet of twenty-one pages. The corresponding list and index of 16 May 1945 was a 386-page quarto volume, FM-6, while two additional field manuals (21–7 and 21–8) were required to enumerate the various films and graphic training aids that were eventually provided. The contrast between the 1940 and 1945 listings affords an interesting sidelight on America's unpreparedness for war when the period of national emergency began. Not only did the Army lack the military publications needed in a major war effort, but, to a considerable extent, it lacked a realization of the necessity for such publications. And the means for producing them scarcely existed.

The situation of the Chemical Warfare Service as to training publications, while unfavorable, was probably neither better nor worse than that of the Army as a whole. Listed in the first issue of FM 21–6, 2 January 1940, were six CWS publications. Two were volumes of the field manual series, three were technical manuals describing chemical munitions, and one was a training regulation (Examination for Gunners). Besides, the Chemical Warfare Service had two training films—one produced in 1930 and one in 1933 —as well as a portfolio of graphic training charts. There was in addition some miscellaneous printed matter in the form of extension (correspondence) courses, technical bulletins, specifications covering supplies procured by the CWS, a nomenclature and price list of chemical munitions, and so forth. This modest group of prewar publications was a mere token compared to the flood of printed materials which the CWS was soon to sponsor.

The renaissance of the Chemical Warfare Service in the emergency period meant a marked stimulation of the development and production of CWS matériel, all of which required description or other treatment in official literature. The remarkable progress made during the war in producing fire and smoke weapons alone accounted for many new publications. A glance at the number and status of these publications as of 1 July 1945 indicates the task involved in the preparation of CWS training literature during World War II. At that time the following had been published or were being prepared for publications:[1]

	In Print	In Preparation
Field Manuals	10	6
FM Changes	13	2
Technical Manuals	34	10
TM Changes	40	3
Technical Bulletins	90	25
TB Changes	8	5
Training Circulars	8	3
Training Films	23	4
Film Bulletins	17	1
Film Strips	25	5
Graphic Training Aids	52	10

In addition to this series of publications, the CWS was particularly concerned with the preparation of FM 21–40, Defense Against Chemical Attack, and TM 8–285, Treatment of Casualties from Chemical Agents. The following logistical documents also were prepared for official publication:

62 Supply Bulletins
28 Supply Catalog Pamphlets
4 Modification Work Orders
2 Lubrication Orders
1 War Department Pamphlet

Setting Up the Publications Program

The prewar official Army manual was well written, but in a staid and unexciting style. It was directed toward the instructor rather than to the

---

[1] Memo, Tng Div OC CWS to Control Div, 21 Jul 45, sub: Quarterly Report of Publications Analysis. CWS 314.7 Publications File. This report also lists translations of CWS publications as follows: Into Chinese, 4; into French, 18; into Russian, 2.

trainee. Into the enlarged World War II publications program was introduced a new element, reader interest. Deliberate effort was made in writing to capture and hold attention. Illustrations, both photographic and "art," were lavishly employed. The Publications Division, AGO, in time established an editorial and art staff to assist preparing agencies in this work. The skills of the advertising expert and commercial illustrator were utilized in producing attractive formats. The new manuals were often striking departures from the publications of the past, yet such departures were necessary if the mass of new instructional material was to be quickly translated into usable knowledge. The preparation of publications to meet the standards of World War II required the development of a group of technical specialists—writers, editors, and illustrators—not previously available to the Chemical Warfare Service.

The CWS manuals published before the war were prepared under the general supervision of the Training Division of the Chief's Office. That division was responsible for obtaining War Department authorization for proposed publications, for arranging for the writing of manuals, and for obtaining concurrences, when necessary, of other arms and services to final drafts.

Three agencies at Edgewood Arsenal were engaged from time to time in writing manuals. The preparation and review of training regulations and manuals had been a function of the Chemical Warfare Board since 1925.[2] The Research Division kept two civilians employed in writing CWS technical reports and in preparing technical matter for inclusion in other publications. The Chemical Warfare School prepared tactical texts either for its own use or for official publication. Experienced officers serving with chemical troops were sometimes called on for assistance. The task of preparing a prewar manual was undertaken by whoever chanced to know most about a particular subject, and the task of reconciling divergent viewpoints of several writers was attempted with varying success by the Training Division in Washington. Occasionally the Training Division took a hand at writing. The system represented a defensive rather than a positive approach to the problem of providing the War Department texts needed to delineate the CWS mission. As soon as the pressure for new publications became urgent, a better scheme for producing them had to be devised.

Of the three offices concerned with the preparation of publications at

[2] Ltr, OC CWS to Pres CW Bd, 14 Dec 25, sub: Duties of Chemical Warfare Board. CWS 334/182

Edgewood Arsenal, the Chemical Warfare Board most nearly represented the over-all viewpoint of the CWS. The preparation of all field and technical manuals was centralized under the board in February 1941 as the first step toward development of a group specializing in the writing of manuals.[3] The writing of CWS technical bulletins by the technical agency was continued; with this exception the board was to co-ordinate and carry forward the entire publications program. The board's small staff of two officer-writers and one civilian artist was gradually built up to eight officers, four enlisted men, and seven civilians in the course of the next year and a half.[4]

In these months the CWS developed a capable nucleus of a manual writing agency. There was at the start a definite advantage in having this unit grow up within the framework of the Chemical Warfare Board. Once the child matured, difficulties arose. The work of the board's publications section was somewhat outside the main current of board activities, and its volume grew so fast as to make supervision by the board a continuing problem. The section had in fact become an almost separate entity when, in the fall of 1942, it was dissolved and its functions assumed by the newly established Training Aids Section, an independent agency of the Chemical Warfare Center.[5] This section operated under the Training Division, OC CWS,[6] and was responsible for preparing training literature, films and film strips, and tables of organization and allowances for chemical units. All personnel who had been working on the preparation of publications were transferred from the board to the Training Aids Section.[7]

This reorganization was advantageous to both the board and the Training Division. It freed the board from a considerable flow of administrative work that was interfering with its own important duties, and it enabled the Training Division to deal directly rather than indirectly with one of its essential operating agencies. By the time the Training Aids Section broke away, it no longer needed the administrative guidance that the board had initially provided although its success during the remainder of the war period was evidence of the sound development that marked its early growth.

The Training Aids Section remained an operating agency of the Office of the Chief located at the Chemical Warfare Center until June 1943 when, with its equipment and staff, it became a division of the Chemical Warfare

[3] Ltr, OC CWS to CG EA, 18 Feb 41, sub: Training Literature. CWS 300.7/212.
[4] CWS Hist of Tng, Pt. VI, Mil Tng Publications (1 Jul 39–30 Jun 44), p. 11.
[5] OC CWS, Off O 60, 20 Sep 42.
[6] See below, Chapter XVI, for details of activities of Training Division, OC CWS.
[7] OC CWS, SO 207, 20 Sep 42.

School.[8] The reasons for this action are not entirely clear. There is no indication that the work of the Training Aids Section had suffered because of the nature of its administrative status between September 1942 and June 1943. It is true that during this period the preparation of publications was somewhat hampered by lack of enough competent technicians, especially civilians, to enable the section to keep abreast of the demands made upon it. A great deal of highly specialized equipment, including cameras, enlargers, and automatic typewriters, had been procured, so that the section was becoming well equipped to meet all calls made upon it. But the problem of personnel was tougher, with greater difficulty in obtaining qualified civilians in 1943 than in 1941 and 1942. The Training Aids Section had placed too much reliance at the start on the services of officers and enlisted men who, after becoming experienced in the work of the Training Aids Section, were often reassigned to other duties. The CWS no doubt expected that by merging the training aids unit with the Chemical Warfare School the latter, with its larger reserve of personnel, would be able to facilitate the work of writing, illustrating, and editing. Actually the Training Aids Division suffered rather than benefited by this arrangement in that it was expected to contribute to the needs of the school for training aids while receiving little help from the school for its own manpower needs.

The preparation of official publications continued to be a responsibility of the Chemical Warfare School until July 1944. While under the school, the Training Aids Division had a somewhat autonomous status since the school authorities had neither the time nor experience to assume active control of the publications program. On 19 July a new administrative procedure, one that proved most satisfactory, was announced.[9] It abolished the Training Aids Division of the school, and placed the function of preparing official publications in the Tactical Doctrine Branch, Training Division, OC CWS. A field office of the Tactical Doctrine Branch was set up at the Chemical Warfare Center, and to it was assigned the publications personnel and facilities that during the preceding year had been accommodated within the organic structure of the school. Thereafter the Chief's Office, instead of *supervising* the preparation of official CWS publications, actually assumed full responsibility and accomplished this work during the remainder of the war period by means of its own field operating agency.

The trial-and-error organizational experience of the CWS publications

---

[8] OC CWS, Adm O 12, 14 Jun 43
[9] OC CWS, Adm O 15, 19 Jul 44.

agency followed in part from the failure at the beginning to measure properly the matériel and personnel requirements of this entirely new type of producing unit. Appropriate budgetary needs were only grudgingly met when they could no longer be avoided. At the time the agency was separated from the Chemical Warfare Board in September 1942, $25,000 was set aside to cover its operating expenses for the remainder of the fiscal year; this proved to be less than half the sum actually needed. The staff of the Tactical Doctrine Branch ultimately included 38 officers, 4 enlisted men, 4 enlisted women, and 49 civilians; of these, 4 officers and 3 civilians served in Washington. Funds allocated to the CWS publications program for fiscal year 1945 approached a half million dollars.[10]

The Pattern of Military Publications

The pattern of official War Department publications was firmly set at the beginning of hostilities, under the general provisions of the 310 series of Army Regulations. A general directive issued by the War Department in January 1941 may be taken as launching in earnest the World War II publications program. The system of military publications was supervised by the Operations and Training Division, War Department General Staff.[11] The principal standardized publications at this time were field manuals, technical manuals, training circulars, mobilization regulations and training programs, tables of organization and equipment, training films, and film strips. Although this system was somewhat expanded, the essential pattern was not altered during the war. The basic number "3" served to identify all CWS publications in each category.

The publications system was based on two types of documents—the field manual and the technical manual. The field manual group included a general series, covering the fundamental employment of combined arms and services, and a particular series, containing instructions on the employment of specific units of the several arms and services. The technical manual group, on the other hand, described matériel, its maintenance and operation, and contained other data more specialized in nature than was considered appropriate for inclusion in field manuals. These two groups furnished basic doctrine for the employment of CWS procedures and materials.

Although the field and technical manuals were conceived as being relatively permanent in form, the demand for increasing CWS support

[10] Interv, CmlHO with Lt Col Norman E. Niles, 20 Aug 52.
[11] Ltr, TAG to Chiefs of Arms, et al., 27 Jan 41, sub: Training Literature. AG 062.12.

throughout World War II called for constant amendment and change to accepted doctrine. Revision of these manuals could not keep pace with requirements, and two new series of publications, the training circular and the technical bulletin (War Department as contrasted with CWS), were therefore adopted to permit the ready dissemination of tentative data.

At first the training circular was employed to amend both field and technical manuals, as well as to announce new training policies. Toward the end of the war the importance of the training circular diminished, especially after the appearance of the technical bulletin. The somewhat belated addition of the latter to the list of official publications was necessitated by the striking technological advances of America's munitions program. Introduced as a means for quick publication of technical information, the technical bulletin was exempt from prior review by The Adjutant General. It represented the largest single item in the CWS publication program. Other publications standardized during the war and with which the CWS was particularly concerned were supply bulletins and spare parts catalogs.[12]

In the field of visual training aids, the film bulletin was introduced during the war to complement the training film in much the same way that the technical bulletin complemented the technical manual. It dealt with new military developments, not necessarily based on doctrine, but issued for the information of officers and enlisted men.

The graphic training aid (GTA), used to some extent before the war, was widely employed in training. Two types were standardized as official publications. War Department graphic training aids were those of Army-wide application. In this category were a number produced by CWS for training in defense against gas attack. A larger number were Chemical Warfare Service GTA's, intended only for use in the training of chemical personnel.

Through this wide range of publications—manuals, bulletins, films, film bulletins, graphic training aids—ran two divergent currents. One was the distinction between the tactical and the technical publications, as represented by the field manual and the technical manual. The other was the need for quick dissemination of data on new technical developments, without too great a disturbance of the old and well established. These views could be accommodated within the scheme of official publications. The Chemical Warfare Service emphasized the technical rather than the tactical and the new methods and materials rather than the old.

---

[12] Spare parts catalogs, published under ASF imprint, are discussed in Brophy, Miles, and Cochrane, From Laboratory to Field.

The Preparation of Manuals

Before March 1942, responsibility for the formulation of doctrine for employment of chemical munitions rested with the CWS. Under the 1942 reorganization of the War Department the AAF and the AGF were made responsible for development of tactical and training doctrine for the weapons which they used, and CWS responsibility was confined to the preparation of suitable instructions covering the technical care and use of the matériel it supplied. Within the Training Division, OC CWS, the Tactical Doctrine Branch was responsible for co-ordinating, supervising, and finally for actually authoring a manuscript. This name was adopted in deference to Pentagon practice, the Tactical Doctrine Branch of the Office of the Director of Military Training, ASF, being the office through which CWS publications were cleared.[13] Even tactical doctrine pertaining to CWS service troops was cleared with the combat forces before publication. In the case of incendiary bombs, matters of tactical employment were decided by the Army Air Force. With such munitions as smoke generators and mechanized flame throwers, the line between tactics and technique was not always clear; the CWS sometimes had to provide acceptable tactical answers. Yet where tactical doctrine appeared in CWS publications, this was formulated by or in agreement with the using arm and was not a principal contribution of the CWS.

At the outset of the war, field manuals covering tactical and logistical aspects of chemical warfare had already been published. The only wartime addition to this series was the publication of six manuals covering field operations of chemical service units.

Five CWS technical manuals had been published at the time of Pearl Harbor. These were:

> TM 3–205 The Gas Mask
> TM 3–215 Military Chemistry and Chemical Agents
> TM 3–240 Meteorology
> TM 3–250 Storage and Shipment of Dangerous Chemicals
> TM 3–305 Use of Smokes and Lacrimators in Training

Among the considerable number of CWS items then standardized, only the gas mask and chemical agents were discussed in War Department technical literature. It was therefore necessary, after war was under way, to publish technical descriptions of certain equipment already being supplied to troops,

[13] WD Cir 59, 2 Mar 42.

and at the same time to prepare for publication descriptions of new chemical items as they appeared for the first time in the Army supply program—mechanical smoke generators, field impregnating plants, incendiary bombs, mechanized flame throwers, napalm, and so on. For without detailed instructions on how munitions should be used and maintained, they quickly become a liability in a theater of operations.

The genesis of the technical description of a military item was to be found in data accumulated during the stage of research and development. Such data were used by the Technical Division at the Chemical Warfare Center to prepare CWS technical bulletins. Thirty-seven of these were published between 1940 and 1943. Although of limited circulation, they were important in providing a starting point for the development of the "3-series" of War Department technical bulletins, publication of which was first undertaken in 1943.[14] The function of the CWS publication agency was to take such essentially technical information as had been developed while the item was being designed and eventually produced, and translate it into a manuscript meeting the needs of a lay reader, providing suitable illustrations, and generally adapting the material to the standards set by The Adjutant General for official publication. A few of the CWS technical bulletins thus found their way into publication as War Department technical manuals although the more general procedure was for them to appear, in 1944 and 1945, as War Department technical bulletins. In practice, most of the "3–series" of technical bulletins appeared so late that no attempt was made to incorporate them in the more permanent medium of the technical manual.

While the CWS publication agency in time acquired a polished professional approach in the production of attractive and useful manuals, it necessarily had to seek from others much of the substance which it incorporated into them. The source most generally drawn on, other than the Technical Command, was the Chemical Warfare School. The school over a number of years had developed a series of locally reproduced texts covering features of tactics and technique not included in the scanty list of official publications. Some of these, as appropriations permitted, were accepted and printed by the War Department as official texts. Thus three of the five CWS technical manuals available at the beginning of the war were based on texts originally developed for use at the Chemical Warfare School.[15] This general type of procedure continued throughout the war; the unofficial school texts

[14] WD Cir 297, 13 Nov 43.
[15] TM 3–215, Military Chemistry and Chemical Agents; TM 3–240, Meteorology; TM 3–305, Use of Smokes and Lacrimators in Training

were steadily laid aside as additional War Department publications became available, while many of the latter that were processed by the Chemical Warfare Service were derived at least in part from school publications. As early as February 1941, unofficial texts had ceased to be used in teaching at the Chemical Warfare School.[16]

The debate over official and unofficial texts persisted in some measure throughout the war. There was continuing complaint, even when a War Department manual was available, that the coverage was incomplete and had to be supplemented to meet local training needs. Often this was true. Yet ASF policy was that the soldier should be trained with the same document that would be available to him in the field and that no local publication should take the place of this official text. Any compromise with this policy would have been unfortunate, since uniformity in training was essential whether the training was done in Louisiana, in northern Ireland, or in Burma.

One useful bridge between the official and unofficial publication was the "tentative" manual, numbered and approved by the War Department for use only at special service schools. Several Chemical Warfare School texts had this status until time and experience determined the desirability of official publication. An example is FM 3–5 which appeared in June 1942 as Tactics of Chemical Warfare, prepared under the direction of the Chief, CWS, for use at the Chemical Warfare School only; later this was superseded by two War Department field manuals: (1) Characteristics and Employment of Ground Chemical Munitions and (2) Characteristics and Employment of Air Chemical Munitions.

The Chemical Warfare Board, after it ceased to be responsible for the writing of publications, continued to review many of the manuscripts processed by the Tactical Doctrine Branch, a procedure which enabled the writing agency to take full advantage of the board's experience in all fields of chemical warfare.

Procedures to be followed in the preparation of official publications were set forth in great detail in ten mimeographed pages of ASF Circular 62, issued in March 1944. By this time the technical services were turning out a steady stream of well written and attractively illustrated publications; Circular 62 added little to what was then known, although it did authenticate existing practices and provided a permanent record of the manual writing

---

[16] Memo, Asst Comdt to C Tng Div, OC CWS, 25 Feb 41, sub: Use of School Texts. CWS 300.7/206–231.

procedures in vogue in the ASF during World War II. One object of this lengthy directive was to limit the multiplicity of War Department publications, although the success of the effort was questionable.

The steps ordinarily involved in the preparation of an official publication appear somewhat complicated, yet they were necessary to insure system and order in such a large publications program as that of the U.S. Army in World War II. When a new CWS publication was needed, or when a change in an existing publication was desirable, the CWS made a pertinent recommendation to the ASF. If approved, the CWS then prepared a full statement of the scope of the publication and an outline of the proposed manuscript. This, after review, was referred by the ASF to The Adjutant General who studied the project from the viewpoints of essentiality and appropriate medium of publication. If TAG concurred, the outline was returned to the CWS where it served as the blueprint for the preparation of the manuscript. Informal concurrences were obtained from air and ground forces headquarters as well as other interested agencies as the work progressed so that formal concurrences to the completed manuscript could be obtained quickly as a routine matter. The final manuscript with illustrations was sent to the ASF for approval and for securing necessary outside concurrences. Headquarters, ASF, then referred the manuscript to The Adjutant General, who reviewed for conformity with editorial standards and with media requirements; afterwards it was either returned to the Chemical Warfare Service for any essential changes or was transmitted to the printer for reproduction. After printing, distribution to troops also was handled by TAG. The same general procedure was followed in processing graphic training aids and film projects.[17]

Speeding Up the Program

As the publication program began to gain momentum, there appeared danger that it might bog down unless something was done to reduce the excessive time lapse between the initial approval and the final distribution of a printed pamphlet. In the case of some CWS manuals, the interval ran to as much as eight months.

This time was consumed in three ways: first, in writing and illustrating;

---

[17] The Signal Corps was responsible for the production of film materials of all sorts. See George Raynor Thompson, Dixie R. Harris, Pauline M. Oakes, and Dulany Terrett, *The Signal Corps: The Test,* a volume in UNITED STATES ARMY IN WORLD WAR II, Chapter XIII.

second, in obtaining concurrences of interested commands; third, in printing and binding. The ASF undertook to control the time spent on writing by assigning a deadline to each project as it was approved and by requiring submission of regular progress reports until the pamphlet was completed. But shortcuts had to be developed in the matter of concurrences and also in the printing of manuals.

The handling of concurrences to CWS publications by ground and air forces was greatly simplified by the ASF in November 1943 under a procedure which permitted the publication of new technical manuals without advice or consent of other agencies.[18] It also delegated to technical services full responsibility for approval of these publications, without reference to the ASF—a real departure from the initial procedure referred to above. This action was clearly dictated by the urgent necessity for speed in getting technical literature into the hands of troops. The line between the technical manual and the field manual was now more sharply drawn. Into the technical manual went instruction as to *what* was to be done about the maintenance and operation of new equipment, thus leaving for later publication in a field manual specific instructions for crew or individual equipment operation in the field. This meant the elimination of doctrine from technical manuals, and with it, much of the prepublication concern of the combat forces with these pamphlets. Upon distribution, copies of new technical manuals were circulated for comments which, wherever appropriate, were published later as technical bulletins or as changes to technical manuals.

The mushrooming of the Army publications program had the effect of clogging the Government Printing Office with work so that, by the summer of 1943, as much as three months were required merely for the printing of CWS manuals. In order to cut this time, use of the Chemical Warfare School reproduction plant was proposed. This plant was well equipped for offset printing which, under AGO policy, was acceptable for editions of less than 30,000 copies. Since most CWS publications fell within this limit, printing of manuals at the school was quickly authorized. During the remainder of the war practically all CWS pamphlets published for the War Department were reproduced at the school plant. Final drafts of manuscripts were produced by electromatic typing and, upon approval, were thus ready for immediate offset reproduction. The proximity of the publications agency, within a few hundred yards of the reproduction plant, was a favor-

---

[18] ASF Administrative Memo S–98, 23 Nov 43, sub: Development and Promulgation of Doctrine, Tactics, Techniques, and Procedure, filed in AGO publications, Air Force and Modern Army Br, War Records Div.

able circumstance. The average time of printing a pamphlet was thus reduced to about two weeks.

The deadline set by the ASF for the completion of official publications ceased to apply to technical manuals after November 1943 since the preparation of these publications was now left entirely to the technical services. A very effective deadline nevertheless remained in the War Department requirement that initial shipment of new munitions to overseas theaters be accompanied by appropriate technical instructions.[19] There is no record that any new chemical equipment was actually held up in shipment because of delays in providing technical literature, although occasionally frantic efforts had to be made to prevent such a contingency. Manufacturers were asked to prepare, in the format of technical manuals, instructions in the operation, care, and maintenance of equipment they were supplying. This was expected to insure the readiness of printed directions in time to accompany new equipment overseas. Chemical Warfare Service experience revealed that this procedure did not always result in producing a satisfactory substitute for a technical manual prepared by the Tactical Doctrine Branch. For example, the producer of the mechanical smoke generator, M–2, was asked in December 1943 to prepare an instructional pamphlet covering this new equipment for which he had been awarded a contract. The pamphlet was ready in April 1944 but it did not satisfy War Department standards. The manufacturer's publication was permitted to accompany the first shipments of these new smoke generators; but the CWS undertook to rewrite, reillustrate, and reprint the pamphlet, which was distributed two months later as TM 3–381.

The measures taken to expedite the preparation of publications during the later stages of the war resulted in reducing by at least 50 percent the time requirements for CWS technical publications. In 1945 these were being produced within approximately three months. In view of all the factors involved, this meant that the program was moving at good speed. Yet study of the official publications issued prior to the end of hostilities show that many of them were distributed too late to have had much effect on military operations. This was true, for example, of the excellent TM's covering mechanized flame throwers; manuals could not be written until weapons were standardized, which in this instance was late in the war.

Although the prewar list of publications was small, it was possible for the individual officer to be acquainted with all manuals relating to chemical

---

[19] AGO Memos No. S310–1–43, 13 Jan 43, and No. S310–4–43, 19 Feb 43, sub: Technical Manuals to Accompany Equipment. Both in AG 353(1–4–4)3.

warfare. The mass of material that had been published by the end of the war precluded this—none but the specialist could become familiar with it all. When the war ended it was not easy—nor was it desirable—to cut off the publications program in mid-air. Many manuals were left only partially written; these in most cases were completed, under the theory that it always is much quicker to revise an existing publication than to bring out a first edition. The publications program, in short, had built up a momentum that inevitably carried it to a point well beyond the end of hostilities. How far it was carried by the enthusiasm of the publications specialist beyond the point of cogent need was a question that only the future can determine.

CHAPTER XII

Replacement Training

While most other elements of the armed forces had made substantial progress in activating and training troops during the early months of partial mobilization, the operations of the Chemical Warfare Service along these lines remained almost at a standstill until the second half of 1941. Even so at the end of December 1941, CWS personnel represented only four-tenths of one percent of the U.S. Army. This ratio was to more than double within the next two years, CWS strength increasing at twice the rate of the entire Army. From 14 chemical units on 7 December 1941, the total rose to 289 on 30 June 1943. (*Table* 9) From 6,269 officers and enlisted men as of 31 December 1941 the service grew to a peak of 69,791 on 30 June 1943. The accelerated expansion represented by the peak figures did not actually get under way until some months after the Pearl Harbor attack.[1]

On 7 December 1941, the existing CWS RTC was quite inadequate. The Chemical Warfare School lacked accommodations for enlisted students, although construction nearing completion would eventually enable it to handle up to two hundred officer students. The branch had no officer candidate school and no unit training facilities. Of even more concern to the CWS was the fact that these deficiencies in its training establishment were indicative of the lack of a suitable chemical troop basis. Although this situation was soon to be improved by a renewed concern in the Army over the probability of gas warfare, this development was by no means foreseeable at the end of 1941.[2]

Soon after the declaration of war the General Staff questioned whether the technical branches were making adequate provision for service units under the augmented protective mobilization plan for 1942. In response to an inquiry on this point, the Chief, CWS, reported that insufficient chemical

---

[1](1) Kent Roberts Greenfield, Robert R. Palmer, and Bell I. Wiley, *The Organization of Ground Combat Troops* (Washington: Government Printing Office, 1947), p. 203, Table 3. (2) App A.

[2] See above, Chapter III.

Table 9—Chemical Warfare Service Units Active During World War II[a]
(As of dates indicated)

Units	31 Dec 41[b]	30 Jun 42	31 Dec 42	30 Jun 43	31 Dec 43	30 Jun 44	31 Dec 44	30 Jun 45	15 Aug 45 (V-J Day)	2 Sep 45[c]
Total	14	98	197	289	264	263	269	283	294	298
Chemical Mortar Battalions	2	6	6	10	11	21	25	25	32	32
Chemical Mortar Companies	3	3	3	2	2	2	3	3	7	11
Chemical Smoke Generator Battalions	0	0	0	0	0	4	6	5	5	5
Chemical Smoke Generator Companies	0	11	28	40	40	33	25	24	22	22
Chemical Companies Air Operations	0	45	66	99	57	47	49	50	50	50
Chemical Depot Companies (Aviation)	0	7	12	14	20	20	20	20	20	20
Chemical Maintenance Companies (Aviation)	0	0	12	14	6	6	3	3	3	3
Chemical Depot Companies	2	5	8	16	25	23	17	18	18	18
Chemical Base Depot Companies	0	0	0	0	0	9	10	11	11	11
Chemical Maintenance Companies	2	5	9	14	15	16	17	18	18	18
Chemical Decontamination Companies	2	7	19	26	29	17	13	12	12	12
Chemical Processing Companies	1	4	22	36	36	36	39	36	36	36
Chemical Service Battalions	0	0	0	0	0	0	0	3	3	3
Chemical Composite Service and General Service Companies	0	2	6	10	16	15	19	20	20	20
Chemical Composite Service Platoons and Detachments	0	0	0	0	0	5	14	27	29	29
Chemical Laboratory Companies	2	3	6	8	7	7	7	8	8	8
Chemical Composite Battalions	0	0	0	0	0	2	2	0	0	0

[a] Data on individual units may be found in Appendix H.
[b] All units shown in this column activated prior to 7 December 1941.
[c] Japanese signed surrender terms.
Source Historical Data Cards, AGO.

units were authorized for ground forces and recommended a ratio of seven chemical service companies per field army.[3] Arrangements then projected for constituting air chemical service units under the current 84-group AAF program were considered satisfactory.

On the combat side the picture was gloomy. Only two chemical mortar battalions had been authorized—and they were a considerable distance from activation. Yet it was clear that if an adequate complement of service troops was needed in connection with defense against enemy gas attack, weapons troops in substantial numbers were just as necessary for retaliation. The two went hand in hand in any balanced gas warfare program.

[3] Memo, C CWS for ACofS G-4, 13 Dec 41, sub: Adequacies of Service Troops. CWS 381/258 (12-13-41).

In comparison to most other arms and services, as already noted, CWS mobilization at the beginning of 1942 was definitely retarded. This situation had been chronic throughout the period of limited emergency. But, with the development of a full and in fact desperate emergency, the War Department began to view more gravely the manifest shortcomings in the chemical troop program. From January 1942 the military strength of the CWS was to follow a rapidly ascending curve. Yet the handicap of a late start upon an eventually ambitious training program was never entirely overcome.

The strength of the CWS at the end of April 1942 was 1,832 officers and 12,068 enlisted men. Four chemical mortar battalions were in training and by the end of June two more were to be mobilized. The air and ground chemical troop basis as of 25 May 1942 called for 4,970 officers and 47,192 enlisted men. It contemplated the mobilization of 105 ground service units and 105 air chemical units. The Army Supply Program called for the activation of twenty-two more chemical mortar battalions in 1943 and 1944.[4] The sharp increases necessitated an immediate step-up of training activities.

The policy on chemical mortar battalions as worked out in the spring of 1942 made Army Ground Forces responsible for the activation and unit training of these organizations; the officers, unit cadres, and filler and loss replacements were to be trained and supplied by the CWS. Officer requirements for these battalions and for the chemical units in prospect for ground and air forces necessitated immediate enlargement of the modest CWS Officer Candidate School that began operations in January 1942. Troop requirements for nearly thirty-five thousand filler and loss replacements during the remainder of the calendar year forced radical changes in the approach to both individual and unit training. A new and vitalized chemical training program for the Army at large coupled with War Department insistence on more realistic chemical situations in ground force maneuvers combined to give the CWS greatly enlarged training responsibilities.

The Upswing in RTC Requirements

Entry of the United States into World War II as an active belligerent presented an immediate challenge to the system of prewar replacement training. If the preparatory training of all individual soldiers under the training center system were to be continued, considerable increase in the number of centers would be necessary. After careful study, the War Department re-

[4] See above, Chapter III.

jected this solution as impractical and instead directed such expansion of existing RTC facilities as was feasible.[5] This decision meant in effect that the Army was falling back in considerable measure to the prewar arrangement of basic training of ground force inductees within units.

One way to stretch existing RTC facilities in meeting the new sharply accelerated load of wartime training was to cut down the training cycle. In December 1941 the War Department, as a temporary measure, directed reduction of RTC training programs from thirteen to eight weeks.[6] An effort was made to meet the cutback in time without disrupting the essential training pattern that had been developed during 1941. Cuts were made in hours allotted to subjects rather than in the subjects themselves with elimination, where necessary, of advanced phases of technical work which bordered upon unit training.

The curtailment of the basic training course by five weeks, while it speeded up the output of the Edgewood Arsenal center, came far short of solving the serious training problem which the CWS was then facing. The steady increase in the RTC load is indicated by the following tabulation of trainees:[7]

Month	Number in Training
December 1941	1,100
January 1942	1,210
February 1942	1,555
March 1942	2,340
April 1942	2,595

To provide for the increasing number of trainees being shipped to Edgewood Arsenal, the training organization of the RTC was progressively expanded. A second training battalion was activated in February 1942 and a third battalion was partially organized a month later. Each battalion consisted of a headquarters and headquarters detachment and four lettered companies. Each company had an authorized cadre of 6 officers and 27 enlisted men and 213 trainees.[8]

Integrated instruction within companies was followed while the RTC remained at Edgewood Arsenal, one lieutenant-instructor teaching nearly all

[5] (1) Palmer, Wiley, and Keast, *Procurement and Training of Ground Combat Troops*, p. 172. (2) Memo, Brig Gen H. R. Bull for G–3, 3 Jan 42, no sub. AGO 381 (12–27–41) (2) (S).

[6] Ltr, TAG to C CWS, 19 Dec 41, sub: Reduction in Length of Tng Program at RTCs. AG 320 2 (12–17–41) MT–C.

[7] CWS Hist of Tng, Pt. IV, Tng of Replacements, Fillers and Cadres, p. 22.

[8] History of Edgewood Arsenal, Vol. I, Ch. 24, App. L. MS.

of the subjects to the men of his platoon. Progress of training was tested by company commanders or, in the case of specialist schools, by the officer in charge. The center commander instituted an individual proficiency chart which was kept for each trainee and forwarded with his service record when he was shipped out. This chart showed at a glance subjects studied, the hours devoted to each, and the instructor's rating of the student. By crossing off each hour of instruction as it was completed, the school readily noted absences which had to be made up by special instruction.

During 1941 and 1942 over 66 percent of the 7,270 trainees who passed through the Edgewood Arsenal RTC were sent to fill chemical units in the zone of interior. (*Table 10*) The RTC also supplied cadres to thirty-nine

TABLE 10—SHIPMENT OF RTC TRAINEES, EDGEWOOD ARSENAL, MARYLAND

Quarter	To Z of I units	To overseas units	Shipped as cadres
Total	ᵃ4,887	1,491	892
1941–2nd	648	0	0
3rd	652	0	0
4th	447	0	0
1942–1st	846	430	0
2nd	1,613	741	832
3rd	681	320	60

ᵃ 57 of these went to OCS.
Source Special orders issued by Hq, Edgewood Arsenal, Md.

newly mobilized chemical companies during the same period, fillers for these organizations being furnished directly from reception centers.

In expanding the Edgewood Arsenal RTC from an initial capacity of 1,000 in the spring of 1941 to 2,500 a year later, it became necessary to house a large portion of the trainees in a tent camp area previously used by the Civilian Military Training Corps. Although this imposed little hardship on the troops, training suffered because of lack of areas and other facilities to accommodate ten companies of over 200 men each.

While the first class of inductees was being processed at Edgewood Arsenal in 1941, the replacement center commander prepared a sketch of what he considered a layout requisite for an RTC capable of handling 1,000 men.[9] The plan provided for the use of an area approximately three miles

[9] Memo, RTC EA for C CWS, 3 Apr 41, sub: RTC. CWS 381.39.

square, with suitable ranges and instructional and exercise areas. The creation of such an installation on the Edgewood Arsenal reservation was not practicable at the beginning of 1941; by the end of the year there was much less chance of adequately accommodating the training load that had developed.

The replacement center was only one of several training activities that burgeoned at Edgewood Arsenal after war was declared. Officer candidate training was soon demanding space. Advanced and specialized courses at the Chemical Warfare School called for greater utilization of ranges. Training activities had pyramided to such size that they required direction by a senior officer who could integrate all of them, consolidate requirements insofar as possible, and see that minimum needs were satisfied. To this task was assigned Brig. Gen. Haig Shekerjian, who became chief of the Troops and Training Division at Edgewood Arsenal on 11 February 1942. For the next three years General Shekerjian was to be intimately concerned with the replacement training program.

In estimating requirements for replacement training during 1942, the CWS in February assumed that it would have to train 14,384 men.[10] Allowing for possible additional activations not yet authorized, the CWS foresaw immediate need for a replacement center having a capacity for 5,000 trainees, which, under a thirteen-week training cycle, would provide 20,000 replacements per year.[11] This figure was so far beyond the capabilities of Edgewood Arsenal that the only possible solution was to look elsewhere for a sizable training area. Construction of new RTC installations in 1942 was contrary to War Department policy. But because of the critical plight of the Chemical Warfare Service at this time, with its urgent need to meet the enlarged requirements for chemical troops which the staff was then formulating, an exception had to be made in the case of the chemical training center. The recommendation of the Chief, CWS, that an adequate RTC facility be provided was accordingly approved. A site near Gadsden, Alabama, was selected in March 1942, and work was begun on the new installation, Camp Sibert, several months later.[12]

Once the decision was taken to develop a new RTC in the south, further improvement of the Edgewood Arsenal installation ceased. Despite the fact that the new facilities were not scheduled for completion before the follow-

---

[10] IOM, 1st Lt F. R. Williams to Ex O, Plans and Training Division, 18 Feb 42, sub: Estimate of facilities for proposed RTC. CWS 314.7 Training File.

[11] The temporary reduction of the RTC course to eight weeks continued only until the spring of 1942, when the thirteen-week course was restored.

[12] For details on the origins of Camp Sibert see above, Chapter VI.

ing December, the Chemical Warfare Service decided to begin occupancy even before the government formally acquired title to the Alabama reservation. What the Edgewood RTC lacked and so desperately wanted at this time was space. And there was space at the new location.

On 3 June a temporary camp area was selected by an advanced detail from Edgewood Arsenal.[13] This section of the reservation soon took the name Tent City. Here shacks were demolished, ground cleared and leveled, and lines of company tents established by the pioneer group so that the temporary camp was habitable by 23 June 1942 when the permanent cadres of Companies E and F, 2d Training Battalion, arrived from Edgewood Arsenal to form the first RTC training units at the new station. On 8 July, 425 inductees arrived for assignment to these two companies. Thereafter no more men were shipped from reception centers to the Edgewood facility; as successive companies completed their training, the cadres moved to Alabama and there prepared to receive fresh trainees. The last RTC elements cleared Edgewood Arsenal on 6 September.

During the remainder of 1942 two projects were going forward simultaneously in different parts of the big reservation—expansion and development of the temporary camp, and construction of the barracks and other facilities for the permanent installation. Work in the Tent City area was done largely with troop labor, assisted by such civilian labor as could be found for the purpose. New troops were now moving in steadily so that by mid-July more than one thousand were present for duty. In order to accommodate them, it became necessary to arrange the training schedule so as to employ trainees on Wednesday afternoons, and even on Sundays, on the improvement and upkeep of the temporary camp and its facilities. On arrival, the recruits "were made aware of the job in front of them by being given a spade, a shovel, and a short pep talk almost before they had officially reported to their company officers." [14] The contribution of trainees to the early development of Camp Sibert was large indeed. Throughout the summer and fall there were endless drainage ditches to be dug, more company streets to be laid out, new areas to be cleared. This work was undertaken cheerfully enough by men who had recently given up civilian life to become soldiers,

[13] Movement of RTC from Edgewood Arsenal was directed by Ltr, AGO to CG 3d Corps Area (CA), 6 Jun 42, sub: Movement of CWS RTC. SPX 370.5 (6–8–42) MS–SP–M.

[14] The Story of Camp Sibert: Training Center of the Chemical Warfare Service (to 31 March 1944). (Hereafter cited as The Story of Camp Sibert), p. 17. Prepared by Historical Branch OC CWS.

though many of them must have questioned the lack of planning which necessitated their employment for such tasks.

During the latter half of 1942, meanwhile, construction proceeded under contracts let by the Corps of Engineers for barracks and other facilities necessary for the permanent housing of five thousand RTC trainees. Unusually heavy rains which began in December and continued until April hampered the work and increased its cost. The rains not only delayed construction—they very seriously interfered with training. The winter of 1942–1943 was one of the worst on record. When the Coosa River overflowed its banks in December, great areas of the main camp were flooded and made unusable for training—a situation very different from the "suitability for year-round training" that had been anticipated.

The completion date for the installation, originally set at December 1942, was not met. In fact, on 3 February 1943 the job was no more than 81 percent complete.[15] Although the first contingent of RTC trainees began moving from tents into their new barracks on 15 November 1942, all construction work was not finished until well into the following spring.

Camp Sibert proved large enough to afford adequate space for all the varied types of training which the CWS undertook at this location. The reservation was fourteen miles long and over five miles wide at its broadest point. Its terrain included open fields, rolling uplands, and well wooded areas. By the summer of 1943 the new RTC was part of a complete and self-sufficient training installation which included 1,500 buildings and 41 miles of roadway. On the large parade ground, twenty battalions could pass in review. There was a 1,000-bed hospital, bakery, laundry, 9 chapels, 3 libraries, 3 service clubs, 5 theaters, and eventually an airport with 2 runways each a mile long. The entire cost of constructing the camp was $17,662,125.[16]

Camp Sibert was built for one purpose only: to facilitate the training of chemical troops. Gradually the ranges, exercise areas, and maneuver fields needed to attain this end were developed, although the training phase of the Army's mobilization had passed its peak before all of them were in use. After the activation of the CWS Unit Training Center at Camp Sibert in

---

[15] Memo, Div Engr, South Atlantic Div, for C Engrs, 5 Feb 43, no sub. CWS 314.7 Facilities File.

[16] Corps of Engineers, Quarterly Inventory of WD Owned, Sponsored, and Leased Facilities, 31 Dec 45. For data on all CW facilities, see Appendix B in Brophy, Miles, and Cochrane, From Laboratory to Field.

CHEMICAL WARFARE TROOPS UNDERGOING TRAINING *on infiltration course,* Camp Sibert, Alabama.

October 1942, many of these training facilities were shared by RTC and UTC.

For basic military training, the normal obstacle and infiltration courses, rifle ranges, and exercise areas were provided. For technical training, some novel facilities were developed. For example, a toxic gas maneuver area of some six square miles was set up in an uninhabited section of the reservation, the first area of this kind ever available to U.S. troops. Another important training adjunct was the decontamination area, where the recruit learned how to reopen terrain contaminated with gas. Here rough ground, covered with underbrush and threaded with trails, was alternately gassed and decontaminated. A range where 4.2-inch chemical mortars could be fired practically at will without conflicting with other range requirements filled a long-felt need. Never in its history had CWS been provided with such a good setup for instruction in the tactics and techniques of chemical warfare. There was elbow room at Camp Sibert. As soon as conditions permitted, the RTC began to use it.

RTC Curriculum

In an introduction to a wartime account of training activities at Camp Sibert, the commanding general (Shekerjian) wrote:

Many trainees who came to Camp Sibert held degrees in science and the arts; but they were considered prospective soldiers rather than specialists. The first duty of the camp was to make soldiers out of them. They had to be made physically hard, receptive to discipline, mentally alert, cooperative and thoroughly versed in the fundamentals of soldiering. Once the men had shed their civilian habits and became coordinated into a military unit, they were far more capable of learning and applying the special chemical warfare techniques covered in the later portion of their Camp Sibert training. The instructors primarily aimed at conditioning the men for war. Having achieved this, they taught them the technical aspects of their military duties.[17]

The issue of military versus technical training was only one of several that had to be settled in connection with the progressive development of the curriculum for RTC training. Other problems were: the amount of time to allow for replacement training; the degree of functional specialization to be aimed at in technical training; and the differing requirements for domestic and overseas replacements. Some of these issues finally had to be decided by higher authority in accord with considerations affecting the Army at large, although in most instances CWS training needs were influential factors. Solutions to these problems were never definitive. They had to be worked out in the light of experience to meet the exigencies of constantly shifting military situations, so that the answers developed in the latter stages of the war would not necessarily have served at the beginning.

The preoccupation of technical branches with their own specialties was reflected in the inadequate provisions that were made for basic military training under the early mobilization training programs. Soon after the Army reorganization of March 1942, the Army Service Forces undertook to correct existing disparities and to insure uniformity in basic military training at all replacement training centers under its control. The concept of RTC's for service troops was new. The Military Training Division, ASF, from the start held the view that the technical soldier should receive the same rigorous basic training as the combatant soldier. The first fruit of this policy was the promulgation in August 1942 of a basic military training program for all replacement (and unit) training centers.[18] Thereafter all inductees assigned

---

[17] The Story of Camp Sibert, pp. 2-3.
[18] Memo, Dir Mil Tng SOS for C CWS, 27 Aug 42, sub: Basic Tng Program. SOS SPTRR 353.01 (8-27-42).

to any branch of the Army Service Forces received identical and generally adequate instruction in the fundamentals of soldiering.

This uniformity of programing was extended to cover specialist training that was common to all branches. The early specialist schools conducted while the RTC was located at Edgewood Arsenal had trained truck drivers, motor mechanics, clerks, and cooks. These students were designated "administrative specialists" in contrast to "technical specialists" such as toxic gas handlers whose training in specialist schools qualified them primarily for duty with the Chemical Warfare Service. The "21-series" of mobilization training programs drawn up by the Army Service Forces provided for unified training of all administrative specialists, leaving the training of technical specialists in the hands of the technical branches.

This same principle was observed throughout the war. For training that was basic or common to all technical branches, programs were prepared by the Military Training Division, ASF; for strictly technical instruction, programs were prepared by the training division of the technical branch concerned. For example, the "3-series" of chemical warfare MTP's followed at Camp Sibert were modified from time to time to conform to the "21-series" of basic programs promulgated by the Army Service Forces.

The question of how much time should be allowed for the replacement center training of newly inducted soldiers was frequently reviewed as the war progressed. The insufficiency of the eight-week program has been noted. The thirteen-week program in effect at the outset of war had to be dropped back to eight weeks during the first three months of 1942, for reasons which were pressing at the time. The thirteen-week schedule was resumed in March and continued to serve reasonably well until that stage of the war when the need for combat loss replacements became of paramount importance.

As a result of his observations in North Africa, General Marshall stated (at a conference on 10 June 1943) that RTC training should be revised to afford better preparation for active combat in overseas theaters.[19] This pronouncement marked a turning point in RTC training. In the course of two years, the centers had come to rely on having their graduates received into units where their military education could be rounded out and any defects in individual training corrected. With most of the thirteen-week trainees this procedure was possible, even where replacement center graduates were sent to units overseas. But once conflict was fully joined, as it was in 1943, organizations in combat zones wanted replacements who were ready for

[19] Notes on Conference, Tng Div ASF, 22 Jul 43. CWS 314.7 Tng File.

battle. To provide them, the War Department had to assign more time for basic training, and in August 1943 the replacement training cycle was increased to provide seventeen weeks of training time.[20]

Under ideal conditions, the most desirable over-all arrangement might have been to allow a total of six months for preparing a civilian to become an effective member of a small-unit military team, with three months devoted to individual and three months to unit training. Such an orderly approach to mobilization has seldom been possible within the vagaries of American military policy. The seventeen-week replacement training cycle represented a satisfactory if not perfect solution to the problem of individual training during the latter stages of the war. It was based, however, on two assumptions which were subject to some question:

a. That individual training for all technical services required identical time.

b. That all technical soldiers (except medical) needed the same basic military training.

The trend of ASF training policy was toward the development of a basic individual soldier who could wear equally well the insignia of any technical service. There was noticeable resistance on the part of the services to the sacrifice of individual service identification implied by this policy. This again is a question which must be considered in relation to progressive stages of mobilization. To have applied the concept of composite training of the individual soldier at the start of the war may well have given validity to objections of the technical services. Later, after the peak of mobilization had been passed, advantages of composite training became evident. Units by that time had assumed a definite mold and were able more easily to assimilate nondescript newcomers without risk of sacrifice to tradition and esprit.

Among matters of technical training initially left to the discretion of the CWS was the question whether a soldier should be trained for duty in a specific type of chemical unit or for general assignment in any type of unit. This problem was complicated by the varied nature of CWS units. Replacements had to be trained for duty in mortar battalions and in smoke generator companies, for processing companies, and for air chemical companies. As long as there was assurance that men trained for specific types of chemical organizations would be assigned to those units, specialized training in the RTC course was advantageous. Such specialization was the rule at the outset

---

[20] WD, MTP 21–2, 1 Aug 43.

of the war. Of the five RTC lettered companies to which trainees were being assigned in December 1941, two were designated as weapons companies, two as chemical service (aviation) companies, and one as a decontamination company.[21]

In practice, it was found that the number of RTC trainees who actually reached the types of units for which they had been specifically trained was small. This was especially true as increasing numbers of RTC graduates began to move directly overseas. It was the uncertainties of the replacement depot system that forced a change from specialized to more general technical training.

This fact is to be noted in comparing the original MTP 3–3 issued in November 1941 with the revision of this MTP dated May 1943. Technical training under the first program was on a functional basis and was intended to prepare replacements for assignment to one of seven specific combat or service type chemical units. Technical training under the 1943 program was aimed primarily at developing a basic chemical soldier. Specialization was here limited to a few individuals who in the tenth, eleventh, and twelfth weeks of training received special instructions as decontamination equipment operators, maintenance repairmen, toxic gas handlers, or as members of communication or mortar squads of chemical weapons companies. The number of replacements currently needed in these particular categories was indicated to RTC headquarters by the OC CWS, according to existing troop requirements. In this way clearly foreseeable (and usually limited) needs for technical specialists were met under a program definitely oriented to the development of the type of replacement principally called for during the latter stages of the war—that is, a basically trained chemical soldier.

The pattern of RTC training in the spring of 1943 was at once simple, flexible, and effective. All men assigned to a training company for the thirteen-week course received the same basic military training during the first four weeks; then, at the beginning of the technical training phase, a few men were usually selected for eight weeks of specialized schooling as cooks, clerks, motor vehicle operators, or automotive maintenance men. The remainder of the company at this point began instruction in the technique of chemical warfare, which was given for the next five weeks. Selected men were then screened out for the three weeks of specialized technical training referred to in the preceding paragraph, while all other trainees completed basic technical training. In the last week of the course the entire company

---

[21] Ltr, C CWS to TAG, 15 Dec 41, sub: T/O for CWS RTC. CWS 400/169 (12–8–41).

was brought together again in unit exercises in which the specialists as well as the basic trainees learned to function as a team.

Eighty percent or more of RTC graduates were listed as basic chemical soldiers. Early in the war they were assigned specification serial number (SSN) 521, a general classification which was not in fact indicative of the training they had received. A more descriptive designation was authorized by Technical Manual 12–427, 12 July 1944, which set up the classification "chemical warfare man, general (979)." This manual had the effect of sanctioning the training procedure already instituted, a chemical warfare basic soldier being described as one who had received technical training in the functioning of the 4.2-inch chemical mortar and also in the duties of chemical service units. In April 1945, the description of a chemical warfare basic soldier, SSN 979, was modified to exclude mortar training.[22] This change again regularized the training practice that evolved toward the end of the war, under which the AGF assumed responsibility for training replacements for chemical combat units, while the CWS trained replacements for chemical service units.

Although the number of men processed through the specialists schools conducted in conjunction with regular RTC training was relatively small, such instruction represented an important feature of the replacement training program. The demand for administrative specialists—cooks, clerks, and automotive men who attended specialist schools during the entire eight-week period of technical training—was fairly constant. The requirement for chemical technicians who attended specialist schools during the last three weeks of the technical training phase of instruction began to fall off in the latter stage of replacement training; by this time units had learned to develop their own specialists and preferred to receive basically trained rather than specialist trained replacements.

The lengthening of the training cycle to seventeen weeks in August 1943 involved no essential change in technical training, which continued as before to extend over eight weeks of the RTC course. The two additional weeks allowed at the beginning of the course for basic military training were intended to better preparation of the individual soldier for life in the combat zone. The two additional weeks provided for basic team or unit training was in substitution for the rounding out that earlier RTC graduates received after joining their organizations, but which under operational conditions after 1943 could no longer be assured to replacements. The final end product

_____

[22] TM 12–427, C 1, 12 Apr 45.

of RTC training was thus a more rounded soldier than his predecessor. If he was not always exactly tailored to meet an overseas requirement, this circumstance must be attributed at least in part to the widely varying demands of global war.

Training Procedures

After the transfer of RTC activities from Maryland to Alabama, the training load followed an ascending curve until May 1943, when a total of 5,850 replacement trainees were being accommodated. The plan of organization had to be flexible enough to permit both expansion and contraction. A second training regiment was organized in the spring of 1943. The following winter the second regiment was disbanded; six months later it had to be reconstituted.

From the training viewpoint the important units were the platoon and the company. As already indicated, the company normally included 213 trainees, but frequently it was necessary to assign as many as 300 trainees to one company. In such cases training suffered. The battalion had four training companies, or 852 men. Thus the CWS RTC, with two regiments of three battalions each, could handle 5,112 trainees.

The system of integrated instruction at Edgewood, where the lieutenant commanding a training platoon taught his men nearly all the subjects in the MTP, had some obvious advantages. But as training programs were successively lengthened and developed, increasing specialization of instruction became necessary, so that a combination of both integrated and departmentalized instruction was eventually evolved. Under the thirteen- and seventeen-week programs at Camp Sibert, the platoon leader instructed in all (or most) of the *basic military* subjects, while training in technical subjects was generally departmentalized.

The decision of the War Department to mobilize a substantial number of chemical organizations during 1942 presented the immediate problem of providing suitable cadres around which these new units could be built. The limited number of existing chemical companies excluded the possibility of obtaining the necessary cadres from parent organizations. It therefore became necessary to fill cadre positions with replacement trainees.

A special cadre training company was established at the Edgewood Arsenal RTC in June 1942.[23] Since some eight hundred cadremen had already

[23] Ltr, C CWS to Dir of Tng, SOS, 10 Apr 42, sub: Cadre Tng Company at CWS RTC. CWS 320.2/780 (4–10–42).

been shipped out from the RTC, the establishment of a cadre training company at this time can be taken to mean that the system of simply selecting as cadre the more alert men who completed the regular RTC course was not satisfactory and that some specialized training for this type of duty was required. Yet cadres for forty-eight chemical units were furnished from Edgewood Arsenal between 1940 and 1943, most of these men being specially selected rather than specially trained.

The cadre training company at Edgewood Arsenal followed the general pattern of the RTC specialist schools; at the end of the period of basic military training, selected men were transferred to the cadre company where for the remainder of the RTC course they received specialized instruction according to the needs of organizations requiring cadre complements. This procedure was amplified after transfer of the RTC to Camp Sibert, where only men who had completed the entire course of replacement training were selected for additional instruction as cadremen. Selection was made by a board of three officers and was based on demonstrated qualities of leadership, excellent character rating, and an Army General Classification Test rating of ninety or over. Throughout 1943, when the group of cadre trainees was usually in excess of one hundred this training was accomplished in four weeks of additional instruction.

An important use of cadremen was in connection with the activation of the chemical mortar battalions authorized under the 1942 Troop Basis. Although responsibility for unit training of these battalions was delegated by the War Department to the Army Ground Forces, the Chemical Warfare Service was deeply interested in the training of weapons units and accordingly co-ordinated the early cadre training program quite closely with the AGF schedule for the activation of chemical battalions.[24] The needs of the mortar battalions received careful consideration, both in the selection of cadremen and in the attention given to their training. When these cadres left Camp Sibert, they carried with them charts and other training aids to assist in the work of instructing the newly activated weapons units.

As the need for cadre development by the CWS RTC gradually fell off, an increasing number of chemical units completed their mobilization training and were thus expected under existing War Department policy to provide cadres for new units.[25] Yet by 1944 this procedure for developing selected

[24] Memo, C CWS for CO CWS RTC, 22 Mar 42, sub: Cadre for Chemical Battalions. CWS 320.2/762 (3–30–42).
[25] Memo, G–3 for CG AGF, 1 Oct 43, sub: Tng of Replacements for CW Combat & Serv Units. WDGCT 353 (28 Sep 43).

RTC trainees for positions of leadership was producing such good results that in March the period of instruction was extended to nine weeks and established as a "leadership training course." When circumstances permitted, men who completed this training were frequently detailed to attend NCO courses at the Chemical Warfare School.

A variation of the standard RTC course to meet Army Air Force requirements for chemical warfare replacements was undertaken in December 1942. Under a procedure developed at that time, sixty-five AAF trainees were shipped to the CWS RTC every two weeks, after completion of four weeks of basic Air Force training.[26] Upon arrival, they entered the fifth week of instruction under MTP 3–3 at Camp Sibert, completing the course nine weeks later. They were then given four weeks of specialized instruction in the functions of either a chemical noncommissioned officer (SSN 870), a decontaminating equipment operator (SSN 809), or a toxic gas handler (SSN 786). This program was continued throughout 1943. When terminated on 31 January 1944, it had produced 1,450 enlisted men technically trained for duty with various chemical activities of the AAF.

A weakness of the RTC training organization was the inexperience of the instructors upon whom fell the principal burden of training. The NCO instructors of 1943 were often soldiers with less than six months of service. The platoon commanders in the training companies were in many cases OCS graduates who themselves were recent products of RTC training. Those in closest contact with the trainees, those whom the trainees were expected to emulate, were almost always individuals with meager military backgrounds. This was a situation that could only be improved by two courses of action: first, by continuous instruction of trainer personnel; and second, by close supervision of training.

The facilities of the Chemical Warfare School at Edgewood Arsenal were never adequately used in the development of commissioned and enlisted instructors for RTC duty. Had the school been located at the training center during 1943, undoubtedly it would have played a more important role in this connection. As it was, the RTC had to depend upon its own resources for fitting its instructional staff to the specific work at hand.

Such preassignment training was accomplished by means of courses of instruction for both officers and enlisted men which were conducted, after the spring of 1943, in conjunction with the system of specialist schools. These courses included intensive study of the important subjects covered in

<hr>

[26] Ltr, Tng Div OC CWS to Dir Mil Tng SOS, 14 Nov 42, sub: Tech Tng of Enlisted Pers and Services with AAF. CWS 353 Camp Sibert, 1943.

MTP training as well as of approved instructional procedures. After assignment, instructors continued their training in troop schools held twice weekly under the provisions of MTP 3–3. Another measure to strengthen training procedure was the institution of nightly cadre meetings at which the officer and NCO staff of each training company met to review and plan instruction scheduled for the following day. Instructors also were frequently detached to attend courses at other service schools. By these means the capability of instructors was gradually improved. It was not until late in the war that veterans with combat zone experience became available for training center duty.

Officer Pools

The officer pool was a necessary device for adjusting variations between the supply of and the demand for commissioned officers. Its most important function was to serve as a reservoir for the temporary storage of excess officers until they could be absorbed into the military system. As long as the overproduction of officers was not great, pools presented no serious administrative problems. But when as was the case by midsummer of 1943, one out of every four CWS officers was being carried in a pool, the requirements for accommodating and training so many individuals became unduly heavy. The evils of officer pools were an inevitable consequence of large officer surpluses, which in turn came about as an incidental result of the unevenness of military mobilization. The War Department undertook to keep officer production in line with military needs, particularly by regulating the output of officer candidate schools. Where early forecasts of requirements erred, mistakes were in the direction of too many rather than too few. While the situation of the Chemical Warfare Service in this respect was somewhat aggravated by uncertainties as to gas warfare as well as by delays in the mobilization of chemical troop units, the upswing from a paucity to an overproduction of officers, which became evident after two years of war, was reflected in the make-up of all technical services.

Late in 1941, when commissioned officers were in short supply, pools were sponsored by the War Department, especially in order to insure availability of filler and loss replacements as needed. The pools at first were therefore associated with replacement centers and were in fact designated as replacement pools. The CWS was initially authorized a pool strength of 150 officers.[27] This quota thus became included in officer procurement ob-

---

[27] Ltr, AGO to Chiefs, Arms and Services, 19 Dec 41. Sub: Officer Filler and Loss Replacements. AG 320.2 (12–15–41) OP–A–M.

jectives. Once the Officer Candidate School began to produce more graduates than could immediately be absorbed, this authorized strength was disregarded and the pool became a means by which unneeded officers could mark time until their services were finally required. This situation extended over a period of many months.

The first CWS officer pool was established at Edgewood Arsenal, where before long it began to impinge upon the already complicated activities of that post. As soon as conditions permitted, a second pool was established at Camp Sibert. By the end of 1942, CWS officer pools had also been set up at other arsenals and in procurement district headquarters. At the latter stations, officers in pools were given on-the-job training in manufacturing, procurement, and supply operations. They were rotated occasionally in types of activity other than their specialty.[28] At both Edgewood and Sibert pool, officers were organized into self-commanded provisional units which followed successive training courses extending to eight weeks. At the height of the pool load in the spring of 1943 the numbers of CWS officers carried in pools totaled 2,005, distributed as follows:[29]

Camp Sibert	686
Chemical Warfare Center	742
Arsenals	152
Procurement districts	376
Other stations	49

The administration of CWS officer pools was complicated by the fact that the excessively populated pools were located in fifteen different places in the zone of interior. The maintenance of a centralized and uniform control of these groups presented serious difficulties which never were fully resolved. At Camp Sibert the operation of the local pool became a responsibility of the Unit Training Center.[30] Some effort was made to centralize the administration of all pools from Sibert, although this scheme was later dropped and the co-ordination of pool activities was resumed by the office of the Chief, CWS. In these matters, both Personnel and Training Divisions were concerned. The responsibility of each organization was clear-cut; Per-

[28] (1) Ltr, C Tng Div OC CWS to CG ASF, 20 Jul 43, sub: Tng of Officers Assigned to CWS Officer Replacement Pool. (2) Ltr, C CWS to CG ASF, 25 Jan 44, sub: Officer Replacement Pools. Both in CWS 353.

[29] Ltr, C CWS to ASF, 15 Jun 43, sub: Tng Programs for Officers Assigned to Army Serv Forces Officers Replacement Pools. CWS 353.11.

[30] Memo, CG ASF to CG Fourth Serv Comd, 22 Jun 43, sub: CWS UTC at Camp Sibert, Ala. CWS 314.7 Tng File.

sonnel Division shifted individuals from pools into appropriate jobs as soon as these became open, while the Training Division undertook to see that pool officers were profitably engaged without burdening the installations where they were assigned. The fact that the CWS never appeared able or willing to assign qualified and experienced officers to the tasks of devising really satisfactory solutions to the troublesome pool problems was probably due to the optimistic hope that in time the pools would empty themselves. Toward the end of hostilities this situation did ease in considerable measure, although by then the usefulness of many emergency officers had been impaired by periods of stagnation in zone of interior pools as well as in overseas theaters.

Supervisory Control

Although the CWS Replacement Training Center eventually attained high standards of training efficiency, these were reached only after the lapse of considerable time and while a suitable organization was being forged at both operating and supervisory levels. It was the immediate responsibility of Training Division, OC CWS, to direct and control the activities of the replacement training center—first, under the general authority of the War Department General Staff, G–3; and, after March 1942, as supervised by the Military Training Division, ASF.

In March 1942, four agencies were involved in the direction of RTC training. These were: *War Department General Staff, G–3,* which remained the ultimate authority on matters of training doctrine and policy, but whose functions after 1942 were usually limited to co-ordination among the AGF, the AAF, and the ASF; the *Director, Military Personnel Division, ASF,* who controlled the flow of trainees into and out of the centers;[31] *The Director of Military Training, ASF,* who prepared the military training program and established instructional standards for all centers; and the *Chief of the Technical Service,* whose training staff prepared the program for technical training, arranged for provision of training facilities (including personnel), established quotas for specialist training, and conducted inspections to insure compliance with standard directives. This division of operating responsibility was clear-cut, logical, and satisfactory. The injection of the service command into this picture in 1943 came too late to affect the bulk of CWS training.

Before the 1942 reorganization, while training centers were under the

---

[31] Millett, *Army Service Forces,* pp. 158–59.

direct control of the War Department General Staff, considerable latitude had been allowed the technical branches in conducting replacement and other training. The primary concern of G–3 was the training of combat units; and the prewar staff was never adequate to handle this all-important function. In assuming responsibility for control of all supply services training, Brig. Gen. Clarence R. Huebner, ASF Director of Military Training, soon made his influence felt, first in stimulating the strictly military phase of the training program, and eventually in improving the quality as well as increasing the scope of training activities in general.

The Training Division, OC CWS, therefore found strong support from above for its replacement training program. Yet the center itself, as it approached the peak of its activities at the beginning of 1943, was suffering from severe growing pains. As long as the camp was still under construction, while barracks and ranges were still unavailable, and while Camp Sibert lay under a flood of unusual winter rains, shortcomings in training did not always show up distinctly. An inspecting officer then commented: "In spite of most severe handicaps a very creditable showing is being made at this center." [32]

Yet a comprehensive inspection of the CWS RTC by the executive officer of the Training Division, OC CWS, in January 1943 indicated that, as the "severe handicaps" of 1942 were eliminated, commensurate improvement of training performance did not result. At the time of this inspection the replacement trainee load was 5,300. There were also fifty-eight chemical units in training or being activated for training at Camp Sibert. The operational distinction between RTC and UTC was not recognized to the extent that a separate command organization was provided for each—a fault of OC CWS which was soon corrected. The increase in the training load had not been accompanied by a corresponding increase in instructor personnel; the RTC staff was understrength, due especially to a dearth of qualified officers. Supervisory control of training by RTC headquarters was inadequate. Period outlines for guidance of instructors were not being used so that teaching methods varied and the use of training aids was ineffectual. Units went through the motions of complying with instructions from higher authority but without sparking their work with energy and imagination. Poor preparation, hesitancy, and indecision on the part of company officers were noticeable. Supervision by field grade officers of the tactical work of units left

---

[32] Memo, Lt Col C. D. Hill for Dir of Tng SOS, 17 Oct 42, sub: Inspection of CWS RTC. SOS SPTRR 333.1 (Camp Sibert) (10–17–42).

much to be desired.[33] These findings were confirmed by an ASF inspection conducted 26–29 January 1943.[34]

In a visit to Camp Sibert late in January 1943, General Porter reviewed the training situation and determined what assistance could be given the undermanned training organization. He then took steps which resulted in marked improvement of RTC training during and after the spring of 1943. Orders were issued 14 February designating separate commanders for RTC and UTC. Experienced Regular Army colonels were assigned to command the two RTC regiments. The officer complement of the center was increased from 152 to 196.[35] An effective control section was established for continuous inspection of training and improvement of training methods and training aids. General tightening of supervision brought about more effective compliance with the training precepts found in Field Manual 21–5, with the consequent production of consistently better trained replacements.

The centralized control of training aids was a definite improvement which could profitably have been instituted earlier. Many training tools were continually in short supply; for example, the center never had on hand more than one hundred compasses or approximately four hundred sets of intrenching tools. It was thus necessary to spread the use of limited matériel as well as to produce effective visual aids to training. Under arrangements eventually adopted, companies upon arrival at designated areas for scheduled instruction found a truck loaded with the necessary instructional materials. Development, procurement, and distribution of training aids were all controlled by the RTC directors of training and supply.

Unquestionably, the morale of both trainees and instructor staff at the CWS RTC began to improve with the completion of permanent barracks and, with the use of the splendid training facilities, the center eventually obtained. Better housing and better training combined, after the spring of 1943, to raise the CWS RTC to the level of an almost model installation. This improvement is reflected in the report of an inspection made a year later which gives an objective picture of a fully integrated training center whose growing pains were well behind it.[36]

---

[33] Memo, Maj F. R. Williams, CWS, for C CWS, 14 Jan 43, sub: Reporting Inspection of CWS RTC, 4–7 Jan 43. CWS 314.7 Tng File.

[34] Memo, Lt Col W. C. Fisher for Dir of Tng ASF, 4 Feb 43, sub: Inspection of CWS RTC. ASF SPTRR 333.1 (Camp Sibert) (2–4–43).

[35] The CWS RTC was authorized a commissioned strength of 250 officers. 2d Ind, ASF to C CWS, 31 Mar 43, sub: Allotment of Officers, CWS RTC. ASF SPGAO 320.2 CWS (3–5–43).

[36] Memo, Lt Col James D. Strong and Capt Douglas A. Craig for Dir Mil Tng ASF, 5 Apr 44, sub: Inspection of CWS RTC. ASF ASPTT 333.1 (CWS) (5 Apr 44).

By this time (1944) the center was organized into two training regiments; one regiment conducted general basic military training, and the other CWS replacement training. In commenting on the latter, the inspectors reported:

In technical training this center has developed a number of ingenious and excellent training devices whereby such subjects as toxic gas handling, impregnation procedure, depot operations, and decontamination operations are taught effectively. In some cases exceedingly clever yet practical training has resulted where there may be a lack of technical training doctrine. It is believed that this is one of the functions in which a replacement training center can lend much to the established doctrine.[37]

After Camp Sibert had been designated as a Class I activity of the Fourth Service Command in May 1943, CWS activities at the camp were limited to the promulgation of training doctrine, the establishment of student quotas, and the preparation of training programs. While this system was workable, it appears likely that had gas warfare materialized CWS control of the installation would have become necessary.

Movement of Trainees

Under the operating procedure prior to 1942, the training center commander reported to The Adjutant General every ten days the number of inductees he could accommodate within the RTC capacity set by the War Department. On the basis of these reports, the AGO directed reception centers to send to each replacement center enough selectees to keep the center operating at full capacity.

At the beginning of RTC operations at Edgewood Arsenal, when capacity was rated at eight hundred white and two hundred Negro trainees, The Adjutant General found that the most convenient procedure was to fill the camp to capacity and then ship no more trainees until after the camp was emptied at the end of the training cycle. This procedure was followed for the first two groups of trainees while the eight-week MTP was in effect. Beginning with the first thirteen-week cycle in September 1941 The Adjutant General began the practice of moving troops in and out at weekly (or biweekly) intervals, thus maintaining a steady flow of men through the center.

The 1941 procedures were elaborated somewhat to meet the pressure of

[37] *Ibid.*

wartime operations. In 1942 The Adjutant General began to issue early each month a tabulated schedule indicating proposed movement of inductees from reception centers to fill RTC's for the month following. For example, Camp Sibert was informed by mid-June 1943 that a total of 1,675 trainees would be received during July.[38]

Weekly reports submitted by the replacement training centers advised TAG of enlisted men who would complete the training course one month later.[39] For example, the report from Camp Sibert on 29 June 1943 advised that during the week of July 26–31 following, there would be available for shipment 401 graduates with qualifications as indicated:[40]

Classification	SSN	Trainees Available
Truck drivers, light	345	41
Automobile mechanics	014	7
Toxic gas handlers	786	5
Decontamination equipment operators	809	4
Clerk-typists	405	4
Cooks	060	11
Nonspecialists	521	329

Appropriate orders were issued in due course by The Adjutant General according to the priority of requisitions for replacements then on hand. First consideration was given to calls for loss replacements for overseas units. Next, requisitions were filled from units preparing for overseas movement. Remaining RTC graduates were supplied as cadres or, finally, as fillers for other zone of interior units.

Procedure for intake of personnel was modified after the peak of training activities had been passed, when TAG began the practice of informing training centers of the total number of trainees they could expect during specific four-week periods. This number was set for the Camp Sibert RTC as 276 white trainees for the four weeks beginning 30 January 1944, a figure which was changed from time to time as circumstances necessitated.[41]

---

[38] Ltr, TAG to All RTCs, *et al.,* 7 Jun 43, sub: Schedule of Allotments and Movements of Enlisted Men to RTCs for July 1943. AG 220.3 (6–7–43) OC–S–M.

[39] These reports were submitted in compliance with AGO Memorandum No. W615–58–42, 23 Nov 42.

[40] CWS 314 7 RTC File.

[41] Ltr, TAG to C CWS, 4 Jan 44, sub: Intake of Pers RTCs. CWS 320.2 ASF Tng Centers 1944.

Curtailment of the Program

Even before the RTC installation at Camp Sibert was fully completed, it became apparent that its capacity would soon be in excess of foreseeable chemical warfare requirements. The job of individual training, which had loomed so large in the spring of 1942, was about to shrink to a replacement-attrition basis. A splendid training facility, urgently needed at the beginning of the war and finally built at heavy expense, came too late to serve adequately the purpose for which it was originally intended. By the middle of 1943 ASF planners, appreciating this situation, were beginning to seek other uses for this plant.

Reduction of capacity of the CWS RTC from 5,000 to 1,500 ASF trainees was announced in August 1943 in a blanket action which affected all ASF training centers. Within this limit, the monthly reception rate of the Camp Sibert center was established at 300 white and no Negro trainees.[42] This figure was computed to provide replacements for estimated normal attrition and battle losses, without distinction between combat and service chemical units.[43] It proved somewhat low in view of the increased requirements for replacements which developed in early 1944 as a result of the Italian campaign. In March 1944 the ASF raised the CWS RTC capacity to 2,750 trainees with a monthly input of 500.[44]

Nevertheless, after the midsummer of 1943 the peak of technical RTC training at Camp Sibert had been passed. The distinctive character of the center as a chemical warfare training facility began to change as it was increasingly utilized for more general training activities. The CWS was anxious that the good instructional organization and facility that had been developed should be maintained against the continuing possibility of gas warfare, and for this reason opportunities for undertaking other training missions were welcomed. One of these came with the establishment of the Fourth Service Command Basic Training Center at Camp Sibert on 24 December 1943. After this date, all service command personnel lacking basic military training received this instruction in conjunction with chemical troops. Beginning in January 1944, the same six-week course of basic train-

[42] Ltr, CG ASF to C CWS, *et al.*, 28 Aug 43, sub: ASF RTCs. AG 354.1 (20 Aug 43) OC–E–SPTRR–M. Beginning with the September 1943 increments, no more Negro troops were sent to the RTC at Sibert. The last Negro troops left the RTC in November 1943.

[43] See Note 25, above.

[44] ASF Cir 66, 6 Mar 44.

ing was also given to all Special Service enlisted men.[45] Finally, in April 1944, the ASF announced the plan of redesignating as "Army Service Forces Training Centers" the existing training installations which had originally served the technical branches as replacement and unit training centers.[46] This move permitted a pooling of ASF training facilities which was necessitated by critical manpower shortages then existing; it was at the same time a tacit recognition of the fact that the major portion of the job of specialized technical training of inductees had been completed.

Certainly by the summer of 1944 chemical warfare technical training at Camp Sibert was shrinking fast. Unit training of chemical organizations was by that time virtually completed. Responsibility for training of loss replacements for chemical battalions had been transferred from the Chemical Warfare Service to the Army Ground Forces. Requirements for loss replacements for chemical service units had diminished with the stabilization of these organizations. Despite the fact that additional general basic training was being undertaken at Camp Sibert, the total training load was still less than the minimum considered by the staff as justifying retention of a training center installation.

In addition to the normal tendency of any government agency to continue under the momentum it has developed long after the initial impetus has ceased, another consideration influenced the reluctance of the CWS to see this center abandoned. Camp Sibert was the only training center where toxic chemicals could be used freely in tactical exercises; if combat employment of gas should be undertaken, this installation would be urgently needed. In an effort to avert the closing of the center, the Chemical Warfare Service made several proposals:

a. That the Army Ground Forces send chemical battalions to Camp Sibert for advanced training in the firing of toxic gas before being committed for overseas movement.

b. That the AGF utilize the facilities available at Camp Sibert for training of replacements for chemical combat units.

c. That the CWS officer candidate school be transferred from Edgewood Arsenal to Camp Sibert.[47]

[45] These were entertainers who were members of the Special Services, ASF. See Millett, *Army Service Forces,* p 348.

[46] ASF Cir 104, Sec. III, 15 Apr 44.

[47] Ltr, AC CWS to Dir Mil Tng ASF, 14 Aug 44, sub: Utilization of Camp Sibert, Alabama. CWS 314.7 Tng File.

Although these proposals did not materialize, final action on the discontinuance of Camp Sibert was deferred until 1945; this along with four other ASF training centers was closed in April of that year.[48]

Subsequent replacement training was conducted under a plan by which inductees designated for duty with chemical units received basic military training at the ASF training center at Camp Lee, Va., after which they were sent to Edgewood Arsenal on detached service for the technical training called for by current MTP's.[49] This plan was one of the most promising of several that had been tried in connection with replacement training between 1941 and 1945. It appeared to satisfy ASF insistence upon interchangeability of trainees, since after completion of the course at the ASF training center the soldier could be sent to any one of several technical training centers for the remainder of his replacement instruction. It made and held the technical training center responsible *only for technical training,* thus bringing to an end the long and sometimes futile attempt to make the technical branch trainer an expert in general combat. It gave the CWS absolute control of training at the place where this control was most needed, that is, in connection with the technical aspects of chemical warfare.

This arrangement did not undergo an exhaustive test since, in the closing phase of the war, CWS replacement training diminished almost to the vanishing point. During July 1944, trainees were being received at Camp Sibert at the rate of 550 every four weeks. Thereafter incoming shipments declined steadily. In June 1945, replacements were being received for technical training at Edgewood Arsenal at the rate of only thirty-two every four weeks.[50]

Development of the CWS replacement training program was retarded substantially by the transfer of the RTC from Edgewood Arsenal to Camp Sibert during the summer of 1942. A year later a quite satisfactory level of training operation had been attained, but the fact remains that men who passed through the RTC during the last half of 1942, when the need for well-trained replacements was most urgent, were not able to obtain the quality of training to which they were entitled. This was not necessarily a fault of those conducting or supervising CWS training. The difficulty was implicit in circumstances affecting the entire CWS program.

[48] Ltr, ASF to CG Fourth SC, *et al.,* 8 Feb 45, sub: Discontinuance of ASF TCs. AG SPX 354.1 (5 Feb 45) OB–I–SPMDC.

[49] Ltr, CG ASF to CG Third SC, *et al.,* 4 Apr 45, sub: Movement of CWS Pers and Equipment, ASFTC, Camp Sibert, Ala. AG SPX 370.5 (3 Apr 45) OB–S–SPMOT–M.

[50] *Rpt of CWS, 1945,* p. 86.

The CWS RTC operated within a rigidly prescribed orbit. Within this orbit it had some leeway, principally in the matter of technical training. Yet the time-bounds of instruction, both technical and military, were set by the ASF. As regards military training, there was never occasion for the Chemical Warfare Service to question directives which constantly emphasized the need for developing combat effectiveness in the technical soldier; reports from theater chemical officers invariably placed more stress on military than on technical proficiency. The training standards set by the ASF were high; if operating agencies were sometimes left breathless in pursuing them, they always recognized that the raising of training sights resulted in a superior RTC output. As difficulties and handicaps, both operational and instructional, were successively overcome the CWS replacement trainee finally began to emerge with the regularity of a production-line item. However, the question arose whether the rigidity of the process did not at times work against the flexibility of the product.

Actually the output of replacement (or individual) training centers needed to be shaped into four distinct patterns. The outlines of these distinctive products were not foreseen with clarity when the centers were projected in 1935. In the afterlight of war experience they stand out as: Replacements for zone of interior units; fillers for zone of interior units; cadres for new organizations; and replacements for theater of operation units.

Replacement of administrative losses in military organizations that still were training in the United States was the requirement easiest to fill. Once the soldier had received a modicum of basic training, it was not too difficult for him to swing into step with an outfit that was still some distance short of readiness for combat and to complete his more advanced training with comrades with whom he expected to share campaign experiences. If replacement training was to be shortened anywhere, it was at this point that curtailment could best be afforded.

Fillers for newly constituted units that were starting out, with no more than cadres, on the long road to military proficiency, should have been well-trained RTC products. When they were, development of the unit was relatively rapid. Unfortunately neither the ASF nor the AGF replacement centers were large enough to satisfy this need for fillers, so that all too often it was necessary to shunt recruits directly from reception centers to field units.

The cadreman was the most important single product of replacement training—not numerically, but with regard to his influence in the shaping of new and unparented organizations. The CWS RTC had been operating more than a year before a clear-cut solution to the cadre training problem was devised. Meanwhile the thin line of early chemical units was depleted by constant calls for cadres. The need for cadres was urgent only during the early stages of mobilization; thereafter this need was negligible. As was true with many aspects of training, by the time an ideal solution to the problem had been devised, it was found that the problem no longer existed.

Both fillers and loss replacements for zone of interior units were individually trained soldiers who were expected to receive final team training with the units they joined. This was all that was expected of replacement training and all actually that was needed. Before proceeding to a theater of operations, the unit still had time to accommodate newcomers. But once the unit was overseas, this situation changed radically. There was no opportunity during combat to devote much attention to incoming replacements. The new arrivals had to be tailored to fit; they needed team training as well as individual training before assignment; and all together they were, or should have been, quite finished RTC products. By the time demands for replacements for the theaters became insistant, requirements for domestic units had slackened appreciably. And with the Chemical Warfare Service, calls for overseas loss replacements were less than had been anticipated. The one uncorrectible failure of the replacement center system as a whole was its inability to supply fillers for all new units that had to be manned during 1942 and 1943. This and other inadequacies of the replacement centers may possibly be traced to the fact that in early planning the *replacement* function was unduly emphasized. In the CWS it appears that adequate provision for training of fillers for chemical units was not made, although this proved to be numerically the most important aspect of individual training of enlisted personnel.

While there were differences in types of RTC trainees, the underlying requirement for the newly inducted soldier was recruit training. Confusion would have been avoided and better training provided if the replacement installations from the start had been designed and designated as basic training centers.

CHAPTER XIII

Training of Chemical Units

Of the 298 chemical units in existence at the cessation of hostilities (2 September 1945), all but 14 were mobilized after the Pearl Harbor attack. (*See Table 9.*) Taking into account organizations reconstituted and disbanded, a total of 383 chemical units and 31 platoons and detachments were activated while the war was in progress.[1] This unparalleled expansion, unexpected and not provided for in prewar planning, gave rise to a number of problems in connection with unit training.

The Building of Military Organizations

The creation of a new military organization involved much more than mobilizing the personnel and matériel called for by tables of organization and equipment. The assembly of the officers, cadre, and fillers at a given time and place was akin to the act of conception. The period of unit training which followed was in reality a period of gestation, the requirements of which had to be fully satisfied before the organization could emerge to a status of functional unity. The mobilization training program was merely a systematic working pattern under which this objective could be accomplished within a given time—eight weeks, thirteen weeks, seventeen weeks —the period of gestation varying as the war progressed.

From the start the unit contained an embryo, the cadre. This included noncommissioned officers and a handful of key enlisted specialists, all having needed know-how. The cadre was presumably trained and competent. During the period of unit training, the cadre's knowledge and experience was expected to extend throughout the organization until finally the entire company could attain the cadre's level of competence.

Individual Training by Units

In order to insure uniformly successful unit training it was important that properly prepared components be provided for assembly into a com-

---

[1] App. H. In addition to the units listed in this appendix, 142 CWS units were activated at various AAF fields on a provisional basis between August 1940 and September 1942.

pleted end product. The officers had to have preliminary training in order
to insure that they would be able to train the men of their unit and eventually
lead them into action. The cadre had to be selected carefully either from
the ranks of veteran units or from likely RTC graduates. Basically trained
personnel ready to learn the business of military teamwork were needed to
fill the organization to authorized strength. During 1942 and 1943 all of
these desiderata could seldom be satisfied. In the matter of fillers, for
example, new units constantly had to be assigned awkward inductees, a
development which necessitated some compromise between replacement
training and unit training.

To observe the technical distinction that exists between these two types
of training was often impossible. Unit training as such could not be attempted until the individual training of the soldier was at least well advanced. Yet as a matter of general policy the War Department decided
early in 1942 that individual training would have to be undertaken to a
large extent within units. This decision meant in reality that when untrained
fillers were received by a newly activated unit (as was normally the case),
they had to be given basic military training by the officers and cadre of the
organization before actual unit training could be undertaken. Thus much
that went by the name of unit training was actually preunit training conducted by the organization.

A more orderly arrangement would have been completion of individual
training at the replacement training center, with the unit training center
left free to concentrate on its proper function.[2] Where, as at Camp Sibert,
unit and replacement training organizations conducted recruit instruction
simultaneously, it was not always easily justified. Yet there was at least one
advantage to the latter arrangement, which of necessity was so often followed. Officers who accompanied the men of their unit through the individual as well as the teamwork stage of military education came to know and
understand them intimately.

Which of these two systems was preferable? Is it more advantageous to
train the inductee in the elements of soldiering at the replacement center
and limit UTC instruction to the development of military teamwork? Or
should newly activated units develop their own fillers and rely on the RTC
for loss replacement only? Although the second scheme worked satisfactorily
in the training of chemical units during World War II, it does not necessarily follow that it is the better arrangement. Certainly it was adopted

[2] This arrangement eventually became possible, but not until the summer of 1944 when the
chemical unit training program was almost completed. See below, page 324.

through necessity rather than by choice. The problem must also be considered in relation to the evolution of chemical warfare training during the war. A significant training development was the shift, already mentioned in connection with replacement training, from the specialized individual training of 1941 to the generalized individual training of 1944. If the chemical soldier of the future is to be developed in basic training as an all-round rather than a specialized individual, he should receive his elementary military training before he joins his unit.

Purposes of Unit Training

The basic military training of inductees, whether conducted in a unit or a replacement training center, was essentially the same. What unit training undertook was to advance the organization from that state of functional ineptitude characteristic of the newly activated company to a plateau of capability where the unit, with all of its members working in unison, could competently perform the specialized military function for which it was created.

Chemical unit training, like individual training, had its nontechnical phase and its technical phase. It comprised military subjects that could be taught by any fairly competent military instructor, and it comprised technical subjects which only specialists in chemical warfare could teach. In unit as in replacement training, there were tendencies to overemphasize the technical aspects of training in certain instances and to depreciate them in other instances.

Before they could be committed to a theater of operations, units had to know how to live in the field as well as how to perform their technical functions in the field. They had to be able to pack and transport their equipment—whether a chemical laboratory or a smoke generator—and to set up and begin operations where needed in the combat zone. And if they hoped to operate very long in World War II, they had to become skillful in withstanding enemy attack. This meant they had to be proficient in camouflage; resolute under aerial bombing; prepared to defend their positions against paratroopers or infiltrators; in short to be wise in all the methods of modern warfare. Military training requirements included camouflage technique as well as collective protection against gas attack, defense tactics as well as the art of living comfortably in bivouac. These things had to be taught to units while they were mastering their technical functions and before they could be passed out of the stage of unit training.

CWS Participation in Unit Training

The development of chemical units was complicated by the varying sources of authority for their initial training, a situation that in turn was an incidental result of the ground-air-service setup under which the Army operated during the World War II. Since this logical pattern of organization had not been considered in mobilization planning, all of its implications were not appreciated in advance. The virtual autonomy of the Army Air Forces had been anticipated, and the role of the Chemical Warfare Service in training chemical personnel for service with the Air Forces had been reduced to an acceptable procedure. But the relationship between the CWS and an independent ground force command produced unforeseen problems.

Unit Training Responsibility

In July 1941, G–3 delegated to the newly established Army Air Forces authority to activate all units, including service, for duty with air—yet retained within the General Staff control of activation of all other units. This arrangement continued until March 1942, when the reorganization of the War Department made possible and even necessitated decentralizing the work of activating and training other-than-air units, specifically, ground combat and service organizations. The reorganization directive indicated that the AGF would train ground force units; that the ASF would train units under its jurisdiction; and that the AAF would train tactical air units.[3] This simple division of unit training responsibility proved unsatisfactory to the ground and air commands. New War Department instructions issued in May established the more acceptable policy that the prospective zone of employment would determine the command that should train the unit.[4]

Under the revised policy, training responsibilities of Army Service Forces extended only to those service units that were organized to operate ASF-type installations and activities, including overseas service or communication zone operations. Ground and air forces became responsible for training both tactical and noncombat units organized for operation within their respective commands.[5] Flexibility under this policy was provided by authoriz-

[3] WD Cir 59, 2 Mar 42.

[4] Memo, ACofS G–3 for CGs AGF, AAF, SOS, 30 May 42, sub: Responsibility for Training. WDGCT 353 (5–30–42). See Palmer, Wiley, and Keast, *Procurement and Training of Ground Combat Units*, pp. 504–05.

[5] Similar responsibility was given the defense commands, which already were involved in activation of chemical smoke units.

ing the shifting of unit training responsibility by mutual agreement among the AGF, the AAF, and the ASF in order to make better use of existing facilities and to avoid duplication of effort. The CWS thus trained a number of chemical service units at the request of the senior combat commands.

Mortar Battalions

The combat traditions of chemical troops were inherited from World War I, when these troops first appeared as the offspring of combat engineers. The early chemical troops had one mission only—to attack the enemy with chemical weapons. The use of chemical warfare units for such work as impregnating clothing against vesicant fumes and destroying persistent enemy agents developed much later. These service functions of the CWS increased in importance during the peacetime years when CWS combatant functions were being minimized.[6] But this trend was neither understood nor fully accepted by the majority of CWS officers, who assumed that once the use of gas began their branch would be in the front line of offensive action. Duty with chemical mortar battalions was therefore eagerly sought by combat-minded officers.

Throughout the entire period of the war there was never any question as to where these battalions belonged. They were mobilized by the Army Ground Forces, and the Army Ground Forces zealously retained responsibility for their unit training. The Chemical Warfare Service was at no time fully reconciled to the latter arrangement and sought to take an active part in at least the technical training of chemical mortar battalions.

The attitude of General McNair's staff on this point was that the Ordnance Department supplied high explosive shells but did not dictate their tactical employment by the Field Artillery; that by the same token, the CWS should provide the chemical agents and leave to the field forces the task of employing them. This appeared to be sound reasoning. The question the CWS raised was whether these units could be properly trained for effective employment under a command that lacked sympathy with their tactical mission.

The two battalions which the Chief of Staff first authorized for activation in September 1941 were not actually mobilized until January 1942. By that time the activation of four more battalions had been authorized. Two of the additional battalions were mobilized in April and two in June 1942. These

---

[6] See above, Chapter II.

six battalions were created for the primary purpose of providing the U.S. Army with means of retaliating with gas in ground operations. Since they represented an important feature of the War Department's program for improving readiness for gas warfare, the CWS felt considerable responsibility for their technical competence. The battalions fired smoke, yet this mission alone could not justify their existence. Their employment in firing high explosive shell had been proposed by the CWS but was not at this time (spring of 1942) authorized by the General Staff. The original proposal of General Porter that chemical battalions be activated at the rate of one per infantry division was rejected in favor of the plan for mobilizing units on the basis of "special projects." This was taken to mean, in effect, that when gas warfare began or appeared to be imminent, additional battalions provided for under the 1942 Troop Basis would be activated.

The battalions activated or expanded in the winter and early spring of 1942 received their initial cadres from existing chemical units. On 1 January, Company C of the 2d Chemical Regiment at Fort Benning, Ga., was inactivated and its personnel were transferred to the newly activated 3d Separate Chemical Battalion (Motorized). Two weeks later Headquarters Company and Company A of the 2d Battalion moved from their station at Edgewood to Fort Bragg, North Carolina, but the 2d Battalion did not reach full strength until Companies B, C, and D were activated in April.[7] Additional personnel for these battalions came from the Infantry, the Coast Artillery, the Medical Department, and the CWS Replacement Training Center. Officers and enlisted men in both battalions were of high caliber and, spurred on by the memory of the recent Pearl Harbor attack, they were anxious to do a particularly good job. Each battalion had some officers who understood infantry tactics, a requirement in the training of the units for infantry support.[8]

As provided in the mobilization regulations,[9] the battalions carried out

[7](1) Ltr, TAG to CGs Third Army and IV Corps Area, 13 Dec 41, sub: Organization of 3d Separate Chemical Battalion and Inactivation of Company C, 2d Chemical Regiment. AG 320.2 (12-2-41) MR–M–C. (2) Ltr, TAG to CG III Corps Area, 5 Jan 42, sub: Transfer of 2d Separate Chemical Battalion. AG 370.5-2d Cml Bn. (3) Ltr, TAG to CG I Corps Area *et al.*, 3 Mar 42, sub: Constitution and Activation of Units for Ground Forces. AG 320.2 (1-28-42) MR–M–C. (4) The chemical mortar battalions were variously known during World War II as "separate chemical battalions," "chemical battalions (separate)," "chemical battalions (motorized)," and "chemical mortar battalions."

[8] Intervs, CmlHO with the following former officers of the 2d and 3d Battalions: Col Robert W. Breaks, 14 November 1955; Lt Col Floyd B. Mitman, 8 December 1955; and Lt Col Harrison S. Markham, 8 December 1955.

[9] WD MR 3–1, 23 Nov 40.

basic and unit training concurrently. The health and endurance of the individual soldier were emphasized; he was taught to use his weapons and to care for himself in the field. Stress was placed on duty, honorable conduct, and uncomplaining obedience. These remained the essentials of mobilization training during the war.

The tactical training of the early battalions was handicapped by a shortage of mortars and ammunition, a deficiency that was not overcome until 1943. Although the principal mission of the battalions was the firing of toxics and smoke, the 2d also fired some five hundred rounds of high explosives before going overseas.[10] Another handicap in the initial period of training was the lack of a specific training program for chemical battalions. This situation was rectified somewhat in May 1942 with the publication of a program for the mobilization training of the battalions, but it was not until January 1944 that the War Department published a Unit Training Program for chemical battalions.[11]

In July 1942 both the 2d and 3d Battalions, having been trained up to company level, were directed to participate in Army maneuvers. The 2d was ordered to the Carolina maneuver area and the 3d, which had been transferred from Fort Benning to Fort Bliss, Tex., in April, was ordered to the Louisiana maneuver area. From November 1942 to March 1943, companies of the 2d and 3d Battalions were rotated for amphibious training at Camp Gordon Johnston, Florida, under the Chemical Warfare Amphibious Project, the object of which was the training of the companies in the use of smoke in landing operations, a technique which these units never used in combat.[12] Before being sent overseas the 2d Battalion was attached to the 45th Infantry Division for training at Camp Pickett, Va.[13] This was one of the

[10] Interv, CmlHO with Col George R. Oglesby, 20 Mar 56. Colonel Oglesby was acting Ground Chemical Officer in March and April 1943 when he was authorized supply of the 500 rounds. After April 1943 allowances were more liberal.

[11] (1) MTP 3–1, 19 May 42. (2) MTP 3–7, 15 Jan 44.

[12] (1) Marshall O. Becker, The Amphibious Training Center, Hist Sec, AGF, 1946, pp. 67–69. (2) Interv CmlHO with Col Lloyd E. Fellenz, 6 Dec 55. Colonel Fellenz was in charge of the CW Amphibious Project at Camp Gordon Johnston. (3) Ltr, Lt Col Alfred C. Day, Commanding CW Amphibious Project, U.S. Atlantic Fleet, Amphibious Project, NOB, Norfolk, Va., to C CWS, 31 Jan 43, sub: Progress Report, Studies of Smoke Screens. CWS 319.1. (4) Ltr, Col Alfred C. Day to CWS, 30 Apr 43, sub: Progress Report, Studies of Smoke Screens. CWS 319.1. (5) Although there were no amphibious chemical mortar operations in the MTO or ETO, a 1944 amphibious training program in the Pacific led to the successful employment of chemical mortars in assault landings. See Paul W. Pritchard, Brooks E. Kleber, and Dale Birdsell, Chemicals in Combat, a volume in preparation for the series UNITED STATES ARMY IN WORLD WAR II (hereafter cited as Pritchard, Kleber, and Birdsell, Chemicals in Combat).

[13] Journal of 2d Cml Bn (Mtz) in World War II. The Chemical Corps Historical Office has a file on each battalion containing varying amounts of information.

very few instances in World War II where a chemical mortar battalion actually went through a period of training in the zone of interior with a division.

Cadres from the 2d and 3d Battalions, together with some 800 men from the RTC at Edgewood who had been given special mortar training over a period of four to six weeks, were detailed as cadres for the 81st, 83d, and 84th Battalions when they were activated in the spring of 1942. The 81st and 82d were both activated on 25 April 1942 at Forts D. A. Russell and Bliss, Tex., respectively. The 83d was activated 19 June 1942 at Camp Gordon, Ga., and the 84th on 5 June at Camp Rucker, Ala. These battalions, like the 2d and 3d before them, were handicapped by a short-

ARMY MANEUVERS, LOUISIANA, 1942. *Infantryman advancing under cover of smoke screen.*

age of mortars, ammunition, training literature, and training aids.[14] Until mortars were received at the beginning of 1943 emphasis was placed on physical conditioning of the men, identification of chemical agents, and small arms training. In March 1943 the 82d was ordered to the Louisiana maneuver area, and in the following month the 81st was directed to participate in the same maneuvers. This was the last occasion during the war when chemical mortar battalions took part in Army maneuvers, so important for the training of combat units.

Despite the handicaps which the 81st, 82d, 83d, and 84th Battalions

---

[14] (1) Memo, Maj Howard P. McCormick, Planning and Equipment Br for C Planning and Equipment Br, OC CWS, 22 Oct 42, sub: Unit Supply and Matériel Inspection of the 81st and 82d Chemical Battalions. CWS 314.7 Training File. (2) Ltr, Asst IG Third Army to CG Third Army, 31 Oct 42, sub: Lack of Weapons as noted in the Annual General Inspection of the 81st Chemical Battalion. Ret Third Army File 33.1. (3) Intervs CmlHO with the following former officers of the battalions: Lt Cols James A. Richardson, Harrison S. Markham, and George Young, and Maj Charles Brightwell. All interviews, 8 Dec 55.

faced, their training seems to have been quite satisfactory so far as it went. Raw recruits were trained to be good soldiers through long and tedious hours of work and instruction. Ambitious enlisted men were offered opportunities for promotion or for attendance at OCS. The men in the ranks, if the words of one of them can be taken at face value, were motivated by a genuine pride in their accomplishment. "Here we are today," wrote a corporal of the 82d Battalion in his seventh month at Fort Bliss, "products of the military training, better Americans and more interested citizens. We have made new friends and acquaintances. We have learned the ways of the outdoors and of nature, of living together and sharing with our fellow soldier. We have learned to listen and obey and follow for a common cause and for the good and welfare of all." [15]

The Army inspectors were likewise impressed with the results of the training, sometimes to an extraordinary degree. To quote from the critique of a Second Army inspector of the 84th Separate Chemical Battalion, "I was amazed to see the same men who were at the train three months ago, raw recruits, now men who put on such a good showing. I find the 84th Chemical Battalion gave a very enviable account of themselves." [16]

While the principal mission of the mortar battalions was the dispersion of toxic agents and smoke, the CWS was of the opinion that the battalions could be profitably used to fire high explosives in support of the infantry. Before any such assignment was possible two preliminary steps were necessary. First, the War Department would have to approve a military requirement for a high explosive (HE) shell for the 4.2-inch mortar, and secondly, the Army Ground Forces would have to be convinced that the 4.2-inch mortar could be used to advantage in supplementing the 105-mm. howitzer in close support of the Infantry.

The CWS had little difficulty in securing approval for establishing a military requirement for the 4.2-inch high explosive shell; on 10 April 1942 the Chief, CWS, submitted a request to the commanding general, ASF, which was approved on 26 April 1942.[17] Convincing the Army Ground Forces of the potentialities of the mortar for firing HE was a much more

---

[15] Cpl Samuel Gluck, "Recapitulation," *The Retort*, 1 Jan 43, a publication of the 82d Chemical Bn, Fort Bliss, Tex.

[16] Remarks of Col March Houser quoted by Lt Col H. S. Markham, CO, 84th Chem Bn, in *Toxic Times*, 31 Jan 43, publication of the 84th Chemical Bn.

[17] Ltr, C CWS to CG SOS, 10 Apr 42, sub: High Explosive Shell for the 4.2-inch Chemical Mortar, and 3d Ind., 26 Apr 42. By a 2d Indorsement AGF gave approval to the CWS recommendation. CWS 320.2/1–23.

prolonged task. In order to accomplish the latter objective, the CWS had to wage a campaign of persuasion on two fronts; in the North African Theater of Operations and in Washington.

Within a month after U.S. troops had landed in North Africa on 8 November 1942, the chemical officer of the Western Task Force, Col. Maurice E. Barker, called the attention of his commander, Maj. Gen. George S. Patton, to the advantages that might be gained by employing 4.2-inch mortars for firing HE. The less mountainous portions of the North African country side were mostly open except for stone farm houses and country villas, which amounted to small natural forts against which it would be highly profitable to employ the 4.2-inch mortar. In the mountainous regions the mortar could be used to put its shells into gullies and behind steep hills where artillery fire could not reach. In December 1942 General Patton requested that the War Department make available a brigade of chemical troops armed with the latest weapons for firing HE and white phosphorus (WP).[18]

At the same time, the Chief, CWS, was attempting to impress upon the War Department the benefits of utilizing a chemical mortar battalion for firing HE. General Porter had a two-fold objective in mind: first, to guarantee that a sufficient number of battalions would be sent to the theaters to operate in a situation of gas warfare, and secondly, to insure that those battalions would be used as effectively as possible should gas warfare not materialize. Reports coming into the Chief's Office in early 1943 to the effect that the British were using their 4.2-inch mortars to fire HE served to stimulate and challenge the CWS. As the Chief of the Field Requirements Branch, OC CWS, remarked, "The British are far ahead. Their CWS is in their Army." [19]

In February 1943 the Chief, CWS, arranged for a conference among representatives of the Army Service Forces, the Army Ground Forces, and the Chemical Warfare Service, to discuss the feasibility of having a War Department directive issued authorizing chemical troops to fire high explosives. Suggestions emanating from this meeting led to War Department action on 26 April 1943 authorizing the firing of high explosives by chemical troops.[20]

---

[18] Operational History of Chemical Battalions and the 4.2-inch Mortar in World War II, Pt. I, pp. 23–24 (hereafter cited as Operational History of Chem Bn). This is a 154-page monograph prepared by Historical Branch, OC CWS, in World War II.

[19] *Ibid.*, p. 29.

[20] FM 100–5, C 3, 26 Apr 43.

The official change in mission to include the firing of high explosive shells had a marked effect on the training of mortar battalions. From the spring of 1943 on, training was concentrated more on that aspect of the mission than on the dispersion of toxics and smoke. From May 1943 till 1945, twenty-two additional chemical battalions were activated by the AGF and trained in various camps throughout the United States.[21] Of these twenty-two, the first four, the 85th, 86th, 87th, and 88th, all activated in May and June 1943, drained the entire Regular establishment of available battalion commanders. Thereafter battalion commanders came primarily from the ranks of Reserve officers called to active duty.

Although the chemical mortar battalions were activated by the Army Ground Forces and remained under AGF jurisdiction, the Chemical Warfare Service, as indicated above, retained a considerable interest in them. The CWS supplied most of their officers and cadres, procured their mortars and ammunition, and was responsible for the technical aspects of their training. The chemical mortar battalions were accepted in the theaters as stemming from the CWS, even though their early growth was nurtured by the AGF.

The CWS, moreover, had a considerable role in the writing of the tables of organization and mobilization training programs for the mortar battalions. In carrying out these activities the Training Division, OC CWS, worked closely with the Office of the Ground Chemical Officer in Washington. The Ground Chemical Officer was a CWS officer, with the rank of colonel, assigned to the AGF headquarters where he had AGF staff responsibilities for all aspects of chemical warfare training. Since he normally had only two officers and several enlisted men to assist him, the writing of mobilization training programs and tables of organization largely devolved on the Office of the Chief, CWS.[22] Final approval of these rested with the Commanding General, AGF.

With the appearance of the mobilization training program for the unit training of chemical battalions in January 1944, the platoon, company, and

---

[21] Seven of these twenty-two battalions were activated in July 1945 and inactivated in September 1945. For details on the four additional battalions activated overseas during the war see Pritchard, Kleber, and Birdsell, Chemicals in Combat.

[22] Intervs CmlHO with the following: Col James E. McHugh, 17 Nov 55. (Colonel McHugh was on duty in Training Division, OC CWS, from April 1943 until after the close of the war.) Col Thomas J. Ford, 11 Jan 56. (Colonel Ford was Ground Chemical Officer from January 1942 to February 1943). Col. George R. Oglesby, 20 Mar 56. (Colonel Oglesby served in the Office of the Ground Chemical Officer from June 1942 until June 1943.) M/Sgt Ludwig Pross, 29 Nov 55. (Sergeant Pross was on duty in the Office of the Ground Chemical Officer from 1 May 1942 until after the close of the war.)

battalion phases of training were spelled out much more precisely than heretofore.[23] During the platoon and company phases of training, which were to run for five and four weeks respectively, each unit was to be developed into a fighting team capable of operating with other units in various types of battle missions. In these phases, troops were to be psychologically prepared for the shock of battle by being subjected to overhead fire, fire past their flanks, tank attacks against entrenchments of their own construction, and realistic, simulated attacks from the air. During the battalion phase of training, which was scheduled for three weeks, each unit was to be taught to perform its tactical and technical functions in the battalion through movements, maneuvers, and exercises in simulated combat situations. All three training phases called for additional instruction in basic and general subjects, such as military intelligence, security, and physical and mental conditioning.

The commanding officers of the battalions received the mobilization training programs and other official publications from the Army chemical officers, who had responsibility for supervising the technical aspects of the training of the battalions and who conducted occasional inspections. The Training Division, OC CWS, and the Ground Chemical Officer or his representative also inspected the units, as did the AGF inspector general. Actually there was not a great deal of outside supervision or inspection of any kind and the battalion commanders were largely on their own. For administrative and housekeeping purposes the commanding officers reported to the AGF staff officer at their camps who was responsible for the so-called Spare Parts units—those units not organically a part of a division.

The mobilization training program, the official War Department directive for training the battalions, guided the battalion commanders in the compilation of their individual training schedules. These schedules were not simple elaborations of the training programs, but included, in addition to the requirements of the War Department, certain aspects of training which the commanding officers felt should be stressed. In a way these schedules and the training carried out under them reflected the personalities of the individual battalion commanders. If the commander was gifted with imagination, training would tend to be realistic and consideration would be given in such activities as firing the mortar and marches to actual tactical situations. The military background of the commanding officer also tended to influence

---

[23] MTP 3–7, 15 Jan 44.

training. If, as sometimes happened, the commanding officer had an artillery background, the firing of the mortar would be approached from the artillery point of view.

The experience gained by battalions which had been in combat was not overlooked in the training of the later battalions. The commanders overseas would send back comments to the Office of the Chief which would be passed on to the commanding officers of the battalions in the United States. One such letter in September 1943, which summarized the reactions of the commanding officers of the 2d, 3d, and 83d Battalions, had this to say about training:

Experience has shown that the soldier well grounded in the fundamentals of scouting and patrolling, use of camouflage, cover and concealment, and taught to move fast, will individually live to fight many battles. Next to that comes team work, an item particularly important to our mortars. . . . Failures in mission will be the result of poor team work. Failures in battle are inexcusable when such failures are a result of poor training.[24]

The demand for company officers for chemical mortar battalions had the effect of pointing up the whole CWS officer procurement program.[25] More junior officers were needed for chemical service units than for chemical combat units; yet the ideal toward which the officer candidate aimed was the platoon leader of a chemical mortar company. If he could measure up to this job, he was assumed to be capable of filling any CWS assignment in the grade of second lieutenant.

OCS students acquired some basic understanding of the employment of war gases in ground combat. This knowledge was augmented by the theory for the offensive employment of gas in courses which some of them later attended at the Chemical Warfare School. But training of officers in the conduct of HE fire could not be undertaken until the high explosive shell was authorized for chemical battalions, so that this type of instruction was not begun at the Chemical Warfare School until the fall of 1942. The training of CWS officers for duty with chemical battalions was, on the whole, never as well integrated as, for example, the preactivation training of artillery officers scheduled for assignment to field artillery battalions.

This same lack of integration is evident in connection with the unit

---

[24] Ltr, Lt Col Kenneth A. Cunin, CO, 83d Cml Bn to Brig Gen Alden H. Waitt, 12 Sep 43.
[25] The influence of this demand on the organization and operation of the Officer Candidate School is discussed below in Chapter XV.

training of chemical battalions. The AGF did not have available firing areas where toxic agents could be released, and arrangements were never worked out for the battalions to fire gas munitions at CWS proving grounds; the training of these units in gas warfare was therefore theoretical at best. At the same time their training in close support of the infantry with HE was never altogether satisfactory because their mobilization training was entirely unrelated to that of the organizations they eventually supported in battle. When the activation of the initial series of six chemical battalions was begun in 1942, a third of the Army's wartime divisions already were mobilized; and the division mobilization program was virtually completed by the time activation of chemical battalions was resumed in 1943.[26] Most of the battalions thus missed out on the splendid teamwork development of non-divisional units which climaxed AGF training in the United States. In many, if not a majority of cases, the battalions first encountered the units they were to support only after their arrival in the theaters of operation, so that lessons that should have been learned in maneuvers had to be mastered in combat.

Smoke Units

From an operational standpoint, the smoke generator companies were somewhere between combat and service units. When attached to combat echelons in screening military operations from either air or ground attack, they were regarded as combat elements. When they were utilized in the static defense of fixed installations they generally came under communication zone control and were classed as ASF troops. In either case their employment was directly against enemy action, in contrast to the noncombatant work of such purely service units as depot and processing companies. Since the operation of smoke generators was somewhat technical and, at least initially, experimental in nature, the development and training of smoke units was handled by the CWS. Thus administratively, if not operationally, they were classed as CWS service troops.

The earliest smoke generator companies were hastily organized in 1942 specifically for screening the Bremerton (Wash.) Navy Yard, west coast aircraft plants, and the Sault Ste. Marie locks in Michigan against air attack. Formal unit training of these organizations had to be curtailed because of the immediate need for their services in the protection of these sensitive zone

---

[26] See Palmer, Wiley and Keast, *Procurement and Training of Ground Combat Troops,* pp. 489–492, for dates of the activation of U.S. Army divisions.

of interior installations. These companies each manned long lines of stationary oil generators, an adaptation of the California orange grove smudge pot. On-the-job training in the operation of these early smoke devices was undertaken as a special CWS project in conjunction with chemical staff personnel of the defense commands involved. In the spring and summer of 1942, the Chief's Office sent Lt. Col. James N. Hinyard to the west coast and to Sault Ste. Marie to demonstrate the use of M1 mechanical smoke generators recently procured by the Chemical Warfare Service.[27]

It was not until the development of the mechanical smoke generator, M1, that the organization of mobile smoke generator units became feasible. Companies activated independently after the mechanical generator was included in a revised T/O&E (as contrasted with those new companies formed amoeba-like from existing units undergoing reorganization) received all or part of their training at the CWS Unit Training Center. In all, forty smoke generator companies were activated during World War II.[28]

Experimental Company, Jungle Warfare

In September 1943 the Chief, CWS, directed that a special company be organized at Camp Sibert to conduct experiments on methods of reducing Japanese-type pill boxes. This company, consisting of 17 officers and 277 enlisted men, was under rigid training from October 1943 until January 1944. It made use of a number of weapons in its experiments, including the 4.2-inch mortar, portable flame throwers, Thompson submachine guns, carbines, pistols, grenades, and Browning automatic rifles. Early in 1944 the company was deactivated by order of the War Department and its personnel used to furnish cadres to chemical mortar battalions about to be activated.[29]

Ground Service Units

Chemical ground service units were those intended to perform technical or service functions of noncombatant nature with the field forces, under either theater, army, or communications zone control. They included chem-

---

[27] Interv, CmlHO with Lt Col James N. Hinyard, 20 Jun 55.

[28] For employment of smoke units in the zone of interior and overseas see Pritchard, Kleber, and Birdsell, Chemicals in Combat.

[29] Ltr, CG Camp Sibert to C CWS, 22 Jan 44, sub: Final Report on the Operations of the Experimental Company, Jungle Warfare. ASF SPTR 370.2 (22 Jan 44).

FLAME THROWER DEMONSTRATION, *Camp Sibert, Alabama, 1944.*

ical laboratory, maintenance, depot, decontamination, processing, and composite companies.[30] With the single exception of the 412th Chemical Depot Company they were altogether new organizations with no background of technical experience or military tradition. A considerable number of service type units were Negro units.[31]

Unit training of these organizations was in the main handled by the Chemical Warfare Service. This training was facilitated by the fact that activation of the principal block of units, begun in March 1942, was spread evenly over the next twelve months, during which period eighty-nine service companies were mobilized.

The timing of the mobilization of these chemical service companies viewed against the full background of the war was excellent. Their primary mission was to limit the effectiveness of hostile gas attack; such secondary functions as they undertook were quite incidental to this principal purpose. By the time the War Department General Staff activated them, it had be-

[30] Eleven chemical battalion staffs were organized during the war, seven for smoke generator and four for chemical service battalions. These organizations were not involved in chemical unit training, which was essentially company training.

[31] App. H lists Negro and white units.

come clear that if gas were used against the Allies it would be in the final phases of the war. Earlier the employment of toxic chemicals in curtain raising air attacks had been regarded seriously by CWS tacticians, but the Japanese at Pearl Harbor proved beyond doubt that other munitions were more than adequate for such operations. This in fact no more than confirmed experience in the initial stages of the war in Europe. At the same time reported enemy activities in the field of gas warfare strongly suggested that the gas weapon might eventually be brought into play. And from the strategical viewpoint it was fairly obvious that this development would come only after the Axis powers were thrown on the defensive. In short, the strong likelihood was that the employment of gas would not take place until more than a year after the activation of gas defense units was begun, an interval that would allow ample time for their training and disposition.

Since training of the bulk of these service units was not seriously undertaken until the fall of 1942, this activity came under the supervisory control of Army Service Forces. The ASF in time delegated the responsibility to the service commands, except for exempted installations where immediate control of training was exercised by branch chiefs.[32] This meant that unit training conducted at Camp Sibert was theoretically under the jurisdiction of the commanding general, Fourth Service Command, while that conducted at Edgewood Arsenal was directly controlled by the Chief, CWS. In practice the Training Division, OC CWS, retained substantial control of this training at both stations.

Air Service Units

The prewar scheme for organization of chemical units with the Army Air Corps was geared to a defensive rather than to a positive and global strategy. Under the 1939 plan, the principal air chemical service units were assigned to airdromes. Under the 1942 plan, they were assigned to bomber formations.

The air expansion program of 1940 necessitated a substantial increase in the Air Corps complement of chemical troops. This in turn made possible the gradual development of the organizational pattern demanded in World War II. Initially one chemical company was set up in each air district.[33] This

---

[32] ASF policies regarding unit training which applied throughout the war were announced in ltr, Dir of Tng SOS to Chiefs of Supply Service, *et al.,* 28 Jul 42, sub: Unit Training Within the Services of Supply. SOS SPTRU 353 (7–28–42).

[33] The four air districts corresponded to but did not coincide with the four defense commands within the continental United States.

company had platoons located at various bases throughout the district. Under this setup the "company" was merely the holding corporation for a large group of service platoons. These were designated as airdromes, service center, and supply base platoons, 134 of them being activated in the zone of interior. With the unit training of these platoons the CWS served only in a monitoring capacity. Enlisted men were supplied principally from the Edge-wood Arsenal Replacement Training Center, while local training of the platoons was accomplished under the supervision of chemical staff personnel assigned to the several air districts. These early air chemical platoons, although later reorganized, were largely represented in the tactical service units which eventually operated with the AAF during the war.

Three principal types of air chemical service organizations were determined upon in 1942 as necessary to support chemical operations of the Army Air Forces. These were chemical companies, air operations; depot companies, aviation; and maintenance companies, aviation. The air operations company was the principal air chemical service unit. Its function was to handle, under operational and combat conditions, liquid toxic or smoke agents used by the type of bombardment aviation which it served.[34] The company included 4 officers and 130 enlisted men.[35] It consisted of a distributing point section and four operating platoons, the latter capable of operating independently on the basis of one platoon per squadron. The companies were distinctively designated to indicate the type of air unit that served: (M & H) for medium or heavy bombardment, (L) for light bombardment, and (D) for dive bombardment. The air operations company was not trained to handle arsenal-filled gas bombs or incendiaries.[36]

The majority of the air operations companies activated in 1942 were organized from air chemical platoons activated and trained earlier. Twenty-eight of the companies were given unit training by the CWS. Of these 6 were eventually sent overseas, 19 remained at Camp Sibert for periods of from 6 to 8 months, and 14 were disbanded in December 1943. Many of their officers and men were sent overseas as casual replacements.

The aviation maintenance company had the job of higher echelon maintenance, repair, and salvage of all chemical warfare equipment used by the Army Air Forces. The aviation depot company handled and stored all bulk chemical ammunition and spray tanks as well as incendiary munitions. Five

[34] AAF Tng Standard 40–4–1, 20 Jan 43, sub: CWS Tactical Service Units.
[35] T/O 3–457, 1 Jul 42.
[36] Actually the air operations companies were often employed in the theaters to handle all types of chemical bombs.

aviation depot and three aviation maintenance companies were trained by the CWS.

Unit Training at Camp Sibert

Chemical Warfare units were well represented in each component of the Army, yet less than half of these organizations received their unit training directly under CWS auspices. The chemical mortar battalions, as indicated, were all trained by the AGF. Two-thirds of the 1942–1943 AAF units were made up from chemical platoons that had been unit-trained at air installations. CWS unit training was thus narrowed to those technical service organizations which were trained at Edgewood Arsenal and Camp Sibert. (*Table 11*)

TABLE 11—WARTIME TRAINING OF CWS SERVICE UNITS

Type of unit	Trained at Edgewood [a]	Trained at Camp Sibert	Trained elsewhere	Trained units activated
Total	30	163	164	337
Smoke generator	8	34	5	40
Air operations	0	28	72	100
Depot, aviation	1	4	15	20
Maintenance, aviation	0	3	11	14
Depot	2	26	10	37
Maintenance	1	5	14	20
Decontamination	2	10	18	30
Processing	12	36	2	39
Composite-service	1	13	15	28
Laboratory	3	4	2	9

[a] Seven smoke generator, 1 depot, 11 processing, and 1 composite-service companies were trained at Camp Sibert and Edgewood and are included in both columns.

Source App. H.

Although replacement training began at Camp Sibert in July 1942, it was not until August that the CWS formally recommended establishment of its Unit Training Center at that station. By the time the center was officially activated on 5 October 1942, the program for mobilization of chemical service units already was well under way; many of the ground service companies and the majority of the air service companies had been mobilized. Many of the organizations mobilized before October 1942 could not be sent to the new UTC to complete their training, but after 1942 chemical service units activated in the zone of interior normally trained at Camp Sibert. By January 1943, UTC trainees numbered 9,067 as against 5,300 men receiving replacement training. The rapid growth of unit training is indicated in the following figures:

Month	Number of Units
October 1942	4
November 1942	13
December 1942	38
January 1943	54
February 1943	68

Internal organization of the UTC differed from that of the RTC in that the replacement training unit was an artificial structure provided merely to facilitate the training of individuals, while the UTC training unit was a tactical organization as prescribed by an official T/O. The training cadre of the RTC unit remained at the center to train succeeding groups of replacements; but the cadre of the UTC organization was "organic"; it was the heart of the unit.

Although unit training was essentially self-training, that is, training of the company by the company, the instruction of the unit by its officers and noncommissioned officers was furthered in many ways by facilities available at the center. It was possible for an organization to work out its own salvation in the matter of unit training; in fact most of the chemical units mobilized before the UTC was activated were obliged to do so. This was a painful process even when, as at Edgewood Arsenal, it was accomplished in a climate of experience and under the shadow of veteran organizations. For a rapid, production-line operation of unit building such as that which confronted the CWS in 1943 there was no substitute for the training center, even though the true role of the center was merely to assist the unit in its effort to train itself.

In devising the organization of a Unit Training Center there were at the start no more than three tangibles from which to work. The approximate number of new units to begin training at stated intervals was known. The mission of each type of organization was understood. And a governing mobilization training program was available. The aggregate number of units to be trained dictated the battalion-regimental echelonment which provided eventually for four regimental groups. It was therefore necessary to develop a type of training center organization which would permit the commanding general to exercise leadership through this command structure so as to insure rapid development of the units in accordance with the standardized training program.

After an experimental period of growth and development, the organizational pattern of UTC headquarters became fairly well stabilized in March 1943. Three principal offices were included: one to handle military administration; one for all supply matters; and one for operations and training. The latter was the largest and most important office of the center command. Its organization was reflected in a corresponding staff section at each regimental headquarters.

The technical training section of the operations and training office supervised each company in the technical phase of mobilization training. It set the technical standards, and it was largely instrumental in seeing that these standards were met.

The composition of the section was an index to the technical specialization involved in chemical warfare operations. The availability at UTC headquarters of groups specializing as experts in each of the fields for which chemical service units were being trained provided a partial solution to the recurrent problem of general versus specialized training of the individual.

A high degree of technical specialization was never a target in the wartime schooling of company grade officers. A captain or lieutenant when assigned, for example, to a smoke generator company ordinarily knew very little about the technique of smoke production. However, before technical training under the mobilization training program was started, the company officers were required to attend a special course on the operation, maintenance, and tactical employment of smoke generators, conducted by the smoke generator group of the technical training section.

This evening instruction, given while basic unit training was in progress, continued until the officers were judged competent to undertake the technical training of the company. Once this was begun the technical group maintained close contact with the unit, observing its progress in field operations and evaluating its training accomplishments. By the time the company had completed its technical training, its officers were themselves specialists in this field.

This general procedure was followed with each type of unit activated at the Unit Training Center. The principal effort in both replacement and unit training as already mentioned, was toward the development of general military effectiveness rather than the creation of a broad base of technical proficiency. It was the important function of the technical training section to insure that the technical training phase of mobilization training was adequately handled. In addition to the primary mission of aiding in the technical training of units, each group of specialists was employed in developing specialized training programs and in preparing technical manuals and directives.

The functions of the supervisory section of the operations and training office complemented the training supervision conducted by the regiments and battalions. Supervision from training center headquarters emphasized especially the technique of training, while supervision from regimental and battalion headquarters gave more attention to the orderly expediting of training programs.

The supervisory section included specialists in training methods who were required repeatedly to visit units in training, to evaluate training procedures with relation to Army standards set by FM 21–5, and to report their findings by standardized form to the several interested agencies. These reports were designed to help the unit, and they proved most useful in maintaining satisfactory training standards. The supervisory section was also responsible for conducting classes of instruction in teaching methods which all UTC instructors were required to attend.

The schedules section undertook at the beginning of UTC operations to write the weekly training schedules to be followed by each organization in accordance with the general provisions of the mobilization training program. This soon proved to be impracticable; it was in fact undesirable, since it infringed upon the training responsibility of the unit. Although schedule writing was soon delegated to the companies, there remained several important functions to be performed by the schedules section of UTC headquarters. The weekly schedules had to be co-ordinated to avoid conflict in the use of firing ranges, training areas, and other facilities. For this reason it was necessary to have copies of all training schedules transmitted to the schedules section well before their effective dates. This section thus became a steering organization for all training operations at the center. At the same time the data it accumulated provided the basis for procurement of munitions and other matériel required in training operations. The schedules section prepared lesson plans which outlined the instructional approach to be followed in each training period and initiated recommendations for changes in current mobilization training programs.

The schools section was another busy office of UTC headquarters. It was charged with the conduct of the specialist school which trained administrative specialists and chemical technicians. The section also made arrangements for the attendance of selected trainees as students at specialized courses conducted by other Army or civilian schools. In short, all training of unit personnel undertaken away from the unit was channelized through the schools section.

Activities of the remaining sections of the operations and training office were indicated by their titles. The training aids section procured or built the training aids needed by the entire command, stored them, and made them available when and where needed by the companies. The weapons and marksmanship section established standard operating procedure for the firing ranges belonging to the Unit Training Center, supervised their use, and initiated arrangements for the employment of outside ranges when needed. The statistics section centralized in one office the preparation of numerous reports required by higher authority on the progress of unit training. These statistics, necessary in connection with the general personnel administration of the Army, also proved to be of considerable value to the center command. Two additional sections appeared somewhat later to meet special requirements. The POM section (preparation for overseas movement) eventually checked all details incident to the complicated administrative procedure involved in the preparation of units for overseas movement. The camouflage school section operated a special training course for instruction in the techniques of camouflage as they applied to the protection of chemical warfare field establishments.

Although the activities of the operations and training office of necessity were definitely compartmentalized, it did not prevent close co-operation between the sections. The preparation of lesson plans by the schedules section and the examination of teaching methods by the supervisory section covered much common ground. While units were firing on ranges, supervision of their instruction was largely taken over by the weapons and marksmanship section. The technical training section worked closely with the schools section in the operation of the specialist schools.

Organization of Units

Organization of the several companies into provisional training battalions and regiments was dictated by the number of units present for training. By February 1943 the formation of ten battalions of white and three battalions of Negro troops was necessary. The First and Second Regiments each included three battalions, and the Third Regiment four battalions of white troops. The Fourth Regiment comprised three battalions of Negro troops.

This basic organization continued until Camp Sibert was converted into an ASF training center in April 1944. (*Table 12*)

TABLE 12—PROVISIONAL ORGANIZATION, CWS UTC, FEBRUARY 1943

Regiment	Battalion	Companies
1st	1st	5 (processing)
	2d	5 (processing)
	3d	5 (processing)
		1 (laboratory)
2d	4th	3 (smoke generator)
		2 (processing)
	5th	1 (decontamination)
		1 (maintenance)
		3 (composite)
	6th	3 (composite)
3d	7th	1 (maintenance)
		4 (depot)
	8th	7 (air operations)
	9th	1 (maintenance)
		5 (processing)
	10th	3 (processing)
4th	11th	10 (smoke generator)
	12th	1 (decontamination)
		1 (processing)
		4 (smoke generator)
	14th	1 (maintenance) (aviation)
		1 (depot) (aviation)

Source CWS UTC, SO 42, 11 Feb 43.

The battalions and regiments were provisional organizations responsible for the military control of the companies and for certain features of their training operations. The number and type of companies assigned to battalions were determined by administrative convenience. Five or six companies usually constituted one battalion. One type of company predominated in each battalion.

Four command levels were active within the Unit Training Center: UTC headquarters, the regiment, the battalion, and the company. Although each had definitely prescribed responsibilities in the scheme of unit training, the first three existed solely for the purpose of furthering the efforts of the company in preparing itself for field operations.

To the regiment, the center command delegated primary responsibility for the training management of the companies. Some of these duties were performed by the regiment. Others were carried out for the regiment by the battalion, since it was impracticable for the regiment itself to provide the intimate leadership needed in directing the operation of fifteen to twenty companies in various stages of mobilization training. For example, the conduct of troop schools was a responsibility of the regiment.[37] In practice the regiment conducted troop schools for all officers under its command, while the battalion conducted troop schools for noncommissioned officers assigned to its companies. Development of proficiency in military administration within the units was a function of the regiment; supply administration was checked by the regimental staff, while maintenance of training records was scrutinized by battalion commanders. The regimental commander had five principal staff officers: an executive, an adjutant, a supply officer, a motor transport officer, and a training officer.

The important functions of the battalion in unit training were to insure, by immediate personal contact with the training companies, that their training needs were met and that their training progress was steady. The battalion commander observed and weighed the capabilities of the company organization and judged the military effectiveness of the company commander. The battalion staff included, besides the major commanding, a captain as executive and one lieutenant as training officer. Aside from the conduct of NCO troop schools, the staff was essentially a supervisory-management agency; it directed the translation of training directives into training accomplishments.

The company was the pivot for all activities at the Unit Training Center. From the moment of activation, the company commander was charged with full exercise of the command of his organization, which included the conduct of all instruction and drills. He usually had an authorized complement of lieutenants and an experienced cadre of enlisted personnel to assist him in company training, yet the responsibility was his.

The company headquarters prepared the weekly training schedule which transformed the generalities of the mobilization training program into a specific timetable of training activity. The company maintained the training progress chart, and recorded deviations from scheduled training that had to be made either individually or by the unit. The company also initiated the

---

[37] Troop schools are not to be confused with specialists schools, which were conducted by UTC headquarters staff.

bimonthly training status report which indicated the progress made by the unit toward completion of its mobilization training. These basic training records were indispensable to training management, and as such they were carefully scrutinized by higher echelons of the training command.

Unit Training Facilities

The movement of replacement trainees from their original "tent city" camp into newly completed barracks, which began late in 1942, opened the way for the accommodation of unit training at Camp Sibert. Shortly this bivouac area, which had been developed by the Replacement Training Center, became available for the housing of units. But it could shelter no more than five thousand, and in immediate prospect was the unit training of a much larger body of troops.

Putting the UTC in tents would have been a solution to its housing problems. But this was not feasible because the units in training were being filled almost entirely with raw reception center inductees who under existing War Department policy were entitled to solid shelter while undergoing basic training. The Chemical Warfare Service therefore proposed, and the War Department shortly approved, the construction of necessary wooden barracks to accommodate a maximum of ten thousand white and three thousand Negro troops, together with appropriate administrative and recreational structures. Until these buildings were erected, the original RTC area was occupied by the Unit Training Center.

This situation lasted but a few weeks. The UTC construction was pushed to completion much more rapidly than expected, thanks to the ready availability of labor and materials in the Gadsden area. Competent contractors were available to handle architectural and engineering details, building construction, roads, and utilities. Though construction was of the short-life type, the buildings long survived the purpose they were intended to serve. Weather was the principal impediment. Despite exceptionally heavy rainfall, the new UTC headquarters was ready for occupancy in December 1942, and most of the units moved to the new area during the following month. Eighty percent of the training center construction was completed by February 1943, the military following close on the heels of the civilian contractors, and occupying buildings as soon as they were inspected and found acceptable.

The UTC housing scheme was developed on a pattern of regimental areas, with provision for six regiments. Within these areas, groups of five-company battalions were laid out. Seven or eight 34-man barracks were allocated to each company, the company group including also mess hall, orderly and day rooms, and lavatory. Counting chapels, libraries, instructional and administrative buildings, in all 822 structures were authorized for UTC occupancy, well over half the total number at Camp Sibert.[38]

Despite the haste in which the Unit Training Center was laid out and built, it proved to be on the whole an efficient installation. Making the streets wider than originally planned and strict care in the preservation of standing trees, both favorite projects of the camp commander, were measures which added to the pleasant atmosphere of the station. Experience indicated some features of the UTC layout which needed improvement. The training areas were too far from the housing area, so that too much time was wasted in going back and forth. The arrangement of four organizational groups in each battalion area, a practice which was followed in the Replacement Training Center, permitted a more convenient arrangement of barracks, mess halls, and orderly and supply rooms, than was possible under the five-unit group adopted by the Unit Training Center. Particularly regretted was the lack of a swimming pool, a much needed recreational facility.

In addition to barracks and administration buildings, the unit training program called for extensive new instructional facilities to provide for a training load well over twice that of the RTC. With the appearance of the new fields, some built by contract and some by training center personnel, Camp Sibert took on the atmosphere of an efficient instructional institution. Many of the basic ideas employed were derived from other training agencies. In this respect the CWS UTC had an advantage by appearing late in the training picture; it could profit from the mistakes of other centers, reject the unsuccessful and ineffective, and limit its training facilities to those of proven worth. A list of these facilities is therefore more than an indication of the scope of training conducted at the UTC—it is also a record of the instructional aids which experience proved was most valuable for that training.

These facilities included four known-distance ranges and three antiaircraft ranges for the .30-caliber rifle, two 1,000-inch ranges for the .22-caliber rifle and the .30-caliber machine gun, a sub-machine gun range, and an anti-tank weapon range. There was an obstacle-infiltration course which featured machine guns firing live ammunition. More advanced facilities were a "jungle" course with unexpected and unusual targets, an assault range to

---

[38] (1) CWS History of Tng, Pt. V, Training of Units, p. 42 and App. D therein. (2) Story of Camp Sibert, p. 25.

teach street fighting, and a combat range for training in the tactics of small unit operations.

A field fortification area and sanitation, rigging, and camouflage areas were developed in connection with basic military training. Two regimental obstacle courses and one "cross-country" course were designed and built by the Unit Training Center and were extensively used for physical training. A single large gas chamber was sufficient for the phase of instruction which covered defense against chemical attack. While the use of ranges and training areas was controlled by UTC headquarters, it was generally the unit commander who led his organization through these training exercises.

More unusual were those facilities developed for special use in the technical phases of unit training. These included areas devoted to each of the specialties represented by the seven technical sections of the operations and training division of the center. Technical instruction was first undertaken in these areas, followed later by the application of principles in field operations.

Preliminary training of processing companies took place in buildings which housed impregnating machinery in a semipermanent type of installation; after learning the technique of treating clothing with gas-resistant chemicals, units continued their training with their own equipment under field conditions. The depot area contained a typical field depot installation which illustrated principles of perimeter defense and camouflage protection. The toxic filling area included storage facilities and equipment for handling all types of liquid chemicals. In the decontamination area, toxic vesicant agents were neutralized according to approved methods. The laboratory setup provided a standard M1 chemical field laboratory for analysis of chemical agents. Air operations classrooms and training areas contained full-scale models of bomb bays and wing sections of different aircraft so that chemical air operations companies could be trained in the installation of incendiary bombs and in the filling and installation of spray tanks. In the maintenance training shop were gathered all types of machinery used in the maintenance and repair of CWS material. Technical instruction of smoke generator units was begun in a special classroom provided with sectionalized models and other training aids relating to smoke production.[39]

Although on the whole the various physical adjuncts to training that were developed and employed at the Unit Training Center were adequate, the assembly of the necessary matériel and the actual construction of facilities while training was in progress presented many difficulties. The preparation

[39] CWS History of Tng, Pt. V, Training of Units, pp. 156–60.

UNIT TRAINING AT CAMP SIBERT. *Members of a processing company in field training remove clothing from predryer unit. This is the first stage in the processing of clothing for impregnation. Pipes at lower right carry gas-resistant solution to impregnator unit.*

of a table of basic allowances of training equipment for the center followed rather than preceded the procurement of the necessary matériel. The task of procuring what was needed was accomplished only as the result of a great deal of enterprise on the part of UTC personnel. The various training facilities were not substantially complete until after the peak of unit training had passed. Their development was not in all cases foreseen or planned for in advance. Some, such as the sanitation area and the rigging area, were initiated by individual units and later adopted for general use. Others, like the jungle course, owed their existence to the perseverance of individual officers who originated an idea or, having seen it applied elsewhere, insisted that it be utilized at Camp Sibert. An effective diorama illustrating correct and incorrect examples of camouflage was devised by the commanding general of the UTC.

Mobilization Training Programs

The conduct of unit training, like the conduct of replacement training, hinged upon the mobilization training program. The programs for the guidance of unit training underwent constant revision during the war. These revisions were in part a reflection of developing experience gained in training management. They were in part attempts to correct defects which showed up in operational experience. And they were in part the results of changes in departmental organization. Some revisions were based on recommendations made by the training center. Others were initiated by the Military Training Division, ASF, either directly or as a result of War Department General Staff action.

The earlier chemical unit programs, in both their military and technical phases, were unilateral productions of the Chemical Warfare Service. After 1943 the CWS prepared only the technical training features, the strictly military sections being written by the Army Service Forces.[40] Thus the later programs of each technical branch called for identical basic military training despite wide variations in the types of technical training.

In all, ten mobilization training programs, formally published by the War Department, were in effect during the war for the direction of chemical unit training, in addition to a number of tentative or ad interim directives. These were known as the "dash–two" series of programs.[41] Their evolution may be divided into five stages: programs of eight, thirteen, twenty-six, seventeen, and six weeks.

The original eight-week program was followed in the training of chemical service units activated at Edgewood Arsenal and elsewhere during the early stages of hostilities.[42]

The thirteen-week program, which was in effect when the CWS UTC was officially established in October 1942, provided a very necessary extension of training time. It included programs to cover the highly specialized technical instruction of CWS ground and air service units and of smoke generator units.[43]

The twenty-six-week program, unlike the earlier programs which assumed

---

[40] Actually ASF provided a uniform basic training policy in November 1942. 1st Ind, ltr, CG SOS to C CWS, 18 Nov 42, sub: Uses of Revised MTP 3–2. CWS SPCV 300.7.

[41] The "dash–three" and later the "dash–one" series, under the final scheme of nomenclature, covered replacement training.

[42] MTP 3–2, 19 Sep 40.

[43] MTP 3–2, 8 Jun 42.

that units would be filled by replacement center graduates, recognized that recruit training of the individual soldier would have to be accomplished within the scope of unit training. The program provided for an initial thirteen-week period of individual training followed by an additional thirteen weeks devoted to actual unit training.[44]

The seventeen-week individual training program [45] lengthened by four weeks the initial thirteen-week cycle of the twenty-six-week program. In so doing, it allowed more time for basic training of the individual soldier and, in addition, permitted some expansion of technical training.

Originally the technical instruction of the several types of service companies had tended toward rigid specialization along functional lines, whereas the need for greater versatility on the part of these troops had become increasingly evident. The seventeen-week program recognized this fact and made provisions for three stages of technical training: two weeks of elementary technical instruction applicable to all units; six weeks of specialized technical training in the functions of the particular unit; and, finally, three weeks of field or applied training. By this arrangement all organizations were able to acquire some basic knowledge of the functions of all chemical service units as well as competency in their own specialized functions.

The six-week program was instituted in the summer of 1944, by which time the activation of new units had slowed to the point that required fillers could be provided from replacement center trainees.[46] It represented another major change in unit training policy. Given individual soldiers thoroughly schooled under the exacting replacement training program of 1943, it became feasible to curtail the period of strictly unit training.

The numerous revisions of training programs made by the War Department considerably complicated the work of training management at Camp Sibert. Much of the time one group of units would be training under one program while subsequently activated units would be following a revised program. The lack of stabilized programing interfered with the systematic scheduling of unit training as well as with the orderly military administration of the training center. Although there were often sound reasons for revising programs, the burden of the resulting changes in operating procedures fell heavily on the training center.

---

[44] MTP 3–2, 15 Mar 43, outlined the individual training program and MTP 3–4, 21 May 43 prescribed the additional thirteen weeks.

[45] MTP 3–102, n.d. This MTP was in effect for CWS units activated after 25 September 1943.

[46] MTP 3–2, 1 Jul 44.

The revisions were never as radical as mere phraseology of the published programs would suggest. Changes were introduced gradually and often were in effect for some time before issuance of the revised program. Under normal procedure a proposed change would be adopted upon tentative approval, after which a mimeograph issue of a revised program was gotten out for limited distribution some months before the printed version appeared. As in the case of many such formal documents, publication of the official program merely sanctioned a practice already being followed.

It was customary and in fact quite necessary to supplement the formal mobilization training programs with two types of instructional guides which became standardized as the subject schedule and the lesson plan. The subject schedule was a mimeographed sheet, listing the several periods to be devoted to a single subject under an appropriate program, the subject representing one "subcourse" of the whole training course. It announced the instructional objective to be aimed at in this series of periods, and it included general training notes and a brief description of each training period. The lesson plan supplemented the subject schedule by providing precise instructions for the conduct of each scheduled period. It set forth the specific instructional directive, the text references, training equipment needed, and the training technique to be followed.

A number of manuals were prepared by the Unit Training Center to supplement instructional directives and official training literature. These normally were produced in mimeograph form and sometimes reached considerable proportions. For example, the CWS Soldiers Guide, compiled by the operations and training office of UTC headquarters and issued to each trainee as his own copy, was a 260-page pamphlet summarizing both military and technical instruction.[47] Elaborate company guides, comprising one hundred to two hundred mimeographed pages, were also issued to soldiers assigned to each type of chemical unit. The need for these unofficial publications lessened as the coverage of official training literature became more nearly complete.

The Conduct of Instruction

The impressive manner in which units were activated at Camp Sibert provided the clue to much of the success of later training. The activation ceremony was staged formally as soon as 90 percent of the organization's

[47] Issue of 10 Oct 43.

fillers had reached the training center. The exercises were conducted by the commander of the regiment to which the new company was assigned, in a park reserved for that purpose. After an invocation by the chaplain, the activation order was read by the appropriate battalion commander. Then the colonel of the regiment called up each soldier and presented to him individually the rifle which symbolized his new status as a member of the armed forces. This was followed by a brief talk by the commanding general or, in his absence, by a senior officer designated by him. During the ceremony suitable music was played by the training center band. After the benediction, the new unit was marched away to the post theater where its indoctrination was begun.

A principle impressed upon all new soldiers, even before formal training began, was that they were primarily fighting men—whether assigned to service or combat units. This was done in an effort to counteract the natural tendency of the skilled specialist to assume that his technical ability was more important to the Army than his combat effectiveness. An illustration frequently used in this indoctrination was that of the early American who, when he hoed his corn, had a musket conveniently within reach to repel attack by hostile Indians; had he not been a competent rifleman, his skill as a husbandman would have been of little value to him or anyone else. This theme, the instilling of a fighting spirit in both officers and enlisted men, was constantly stressed during the entire period of unit training.

The essential tasks of the Unit Training Center were to see that instruction was scheduled in agreement with official training programs and that it was conducted according to instructional procedures set by the War Department. The center was provided with blueprints to be followed; while these might be changed from time to time for good and sufficient reasons, they delineated the bounds of instruction. The management of training operations was in the hands of the center command and the way this function was discharged determined, finally, the effectiveness with which units prepared themselves for active field service.

The officer complement of the CWS Unit Training Center was set at 115; 101 of these were CWS officers and the rest were branch immaterial officers.[48] Assignments to administration and supply duties were limited to approximately 35 officers; the remaining 80 were employed primarily on

---

[48](1) Ltr, AGO to CG, Fourth SC, 18 Nov 42, sub: T/O for CWS UTC. AG SPX 320.2 (10–31–42) PO–M–SPGAO. (2) Branch immaterial officers were officers not assigned to a particular arm or service.

training work. Of these, 28 provided the headquarters training staff and 52 were assigned to the provisional regiments and battalions.

A formal inspection of the center in February 1943 disclosed a number of difficulties interfering with effective progress in unit training.[49] Besides inclement weather, some uncompleted barracks, and many unfinished ranges, it was evident that training was being undertaken in too many instances by inexperienced company officers and that the direction of this training was in the hands of training center personnel who too often were immature and uncertain of their duties. Although the full quota of 115 officers was then available at Camp Sibert, the great majority of these officers were second lieutenants, mostly recent OCS graduates. The original scheme and functional design of the center were good, but the shortage of experienced officers was seriously hindering efficient training operations. The dearth of properly qualified CWS officers in comparison to mounting demands in the training field showed up more strikingly then than at any other time during the war. While the assignment of inexperienced company grade officers to newly activated units was understandable, it was imperative that the center be provided with mature officers who were capable of assisting and directing the training work of the companies. This matter was given careful study by General Porter, who saw to it that a number of additional field grade officers were shortly assigned to the Unit Training Center. The influence of better supervisory control was quickly evident. A formal inspection of the center made in April 1943 showed marked improvement in the conduct of training and elicited personal commendation from the Director of Military Training, ASF.[50]

The rapid and effective handling of the volume of training undertaken at the CWS Unit Training Center in 1943 required, in addition to competent directors, a large number of younger officers who were skilled in training techniques. But the company officers had to know the subject they were to teach as well as how to teach. Officers with these special qualifications were extremely scarce. To a considerable degree they had to be developed at the training center; the device employed was the troop school.

The troop school differed from the service school in that it was an extra duty project, classes normally being conducted in the evenings. It had the advantage of imparting instruction that applied to work immediately at

[49] Memo, Col H. M. Woodward, Jr., for Dir of Tng SOS, n.d., sub: Inspection of CWS UTC. SOS SPTRU 333.1 (CWS). The name indicates the inspection was made 17–19 February 1943.

[50] 1st Ind, Memo, Tng Div ASF for C CWS, 24 Apr 43, sub: Inspection of CWS UTC. ASF SPTRU 333.1 (CWS).

hand, in contrast to the service school whose instruction was necessarily more academic. Nevertheless, the troop school system, especially as it had to be employed at Camp Sibert, exacted a great deal from physically tired officers whose days were crowded with strenuous duties.

The UTC troop schools were attended by both unit and headquarters staff officers. They taught what to teach and how to teach. They were conducted principally at the regimental level with classes scheduled five evenings per week. The subject of instructor training, including the use of training aids, was studied by company officers insofar as possible before beginning mobilization training of the unit. A general refresher program covering the subjects of basic military training included in the unit training schedules was then begun, this instruction being pushed to completion in advance of the unit training to which it pertained. Specialized technical training of company officers, already discussed, was undertaken while basic military training of the unit was in progress.

The practice of holding nightly cadre meetings began in August 1943. These were conducted by the unit commander and attended by company officers and noncommissioned officers. The meeting began with a critique of the day's training operations, followed by a discussion of plans and procedures for the next day's work. While this arrangement was found to be a necessary and important feature of training management, it involved an excessive amount of overtime duty on the part of trainer personnel.

The Unit Training Center made considerable use of other service schools for the supplementary instruction of officers and in some cases of enlisted personnel. Students were sent in increasing numbers to attend courses at AGF schools as well as the service schools of the several technical branches. Graduates of such courses were generally employed on staff training duties at the center.

One phase of training marked by considerable difficulty in the early stages of unit training at Camp Sibert was getting a suitable proportion of trainees to qualify in rifle marksmanship. This matter was brought directly to the attention of the OC CWS by the Army Service Forces when an analysis of training status reports indicated that as of 1 April 1943 the percentage of soldiers qualifying as rifle marksmen ranged between a low of 16 and a high of only 44 percent.[51]

Weapons training was seriously hampered during 1942 and well into 1943 by uncompleted range construction and by a critical shortage of rifles.

[51] Memo, ASF for C CWS, 19 Apr 43, sub: Rifle Marksmanship Qualification. ASF SPTRU 353.02.

Until 17 December 1942, when the first UTC rifle range was officially opened, the UTC had to utilize the range facilities of Fort McClellan, thirty miles away, for this instruction. Gradually the supply of rifles and ammunition improved, although at one time there was no more than forty M1 rifles available for unit training purposes.

Training in small arms fire as well as all basic military training was stimulated by the attachment of fifty infantry officers to the CWS Unit Training Center in March 1943. These young Ft. Benning OCS graduates soon proved themselves an invaluable addition to the Camp Sibert training staff. Initially attached for a period of six months, many of them remained for nine months, during which time UTC standards in rifle and allied military training steadily improved. By June 1943 the minimum standard of 80 percent qualification of all men firing the rifle was being consistently exceeded.

Specialist Training

A principle of unit training recognized in the earliest mobilization training programs was the division of trainees into two categories, basics and specialists, the latter to be detached during part of the unit training period for specialized instruction. All units, combat as well as service, placed considerable emphasis on the technical knowledge of the group of specialists upon whose capability the functioning of the organization as a whole so largely depended. This development was in fact a concomitant to the growing complexity of modern warfare. Specialists requirements of the several arms and services were compiled by The Adjutant General from current tables of organization and were published from time to time as Requirement and Replacement Rates, Military Specialists. Following is a summary of the distribution per thousand as it stood during 1943:[52]

	CWS	Entire Army
Total	1,000	1,000
Military jobs without civilian counterparts	293	464
Jobs paralleling civilian occupations	409	387
Laborers (SSN 590)	182	37
Basic Soldiers (SSN 521)	116	112

[52] Palmer, Wiley, and Keast, *Procurement and Training of Ground Combat Troops*, Table 1, p. 8.

Specialist training was limited to the first two categories. The first category of jobs required training for duties which had no equivalents in American industry, and the second the adaptation training of men who entered the Army with occupational experience paralleling jobs listed in CWS tables of organization. The first of these requirements was the most exacting, although the number of such jobs in CWS was well below the average for the Army at large. The second requirement, which involved training for military assignment of cooks, clerks, truck drivers, laboratory technicians, and so forth, was slightly above the general Army experience.

In the mobilization training of units it was essential that the initial requirements of the organization for enlisted specialists be fully satisfied, although once the unit had passed to operational status it could be expected to develop many of its own specialist replacements by on-the-job training. For this reason UTC training of specialists was much heavier in volume than was specialist training at the Replacement Training Center. The extent of CWS requirements for specialist training is indicated in Table 13.

Two-thirds of the strength of most chemical service units included men requiring types of training that were beyond the resources of the newly organized company. In many cases the soldier brought with him enough civilian experience to qualify him occupationally under a given specification serial number, the only training required being in the adaption of his trade specialty to military duty. It was the partially qualified or the unqualified, yet likely, trainee who presented the most serious problems to the specialist schooling system.

Specialist training was concentrated in the weeks devoted to technical training and was normally completed in time to permit graduates to participate in their units' final training phase of field operations. Some of this training occupied eight weeks, specifically, the training of clerks, cooks, and automotive specialists.[53] Programs for these courses were prescribed by the ASF and were uniform for all technical branches.

Specialist training of chemical technicians was left to the discretion of the CWS and followed programs prepared by the Training Division, OC CWS. These latter courses of shorter duration were attended during the final weeks of technical training of the unit. (*Table 14*) The aim in specialist training of chemical technicians was primarily to teach the soldier the military application of skills which he already possessed. In most cases it

---

[53] The automobile mechanic course of six weeks was normally accompanied by the chauffeur course of two weeks.

TABLE 13—ENLISTED SPECIALISTS IN EACH CHEMICAL SERVICE TYPE COMPANY, WORLD WAR II

Trade Specialty	SSN	Maintenance	Depot	Processing	Laboratory	Decontamination	Smoke Generator	Composite	Air operations	Total for 8 type companies
Total specialists		61	100	99	30	126	65	77	114	672
Total enlisted strength		(90)	(150)	(141)	(50)	(165)	(131)	(210)	(130)	(1067)
Ammunition handler	901	0	18	0	0	0	0	24	0	42
Carpenter	050	1	5	0	0	0	0	1	0	7
Chemist	292	0	0	0	12	0	0	0	0	12
Chemical laboratory assistant	411	0	0	8	5	0	0	7	0	20
Chauffeur, truck driver	345	4	10	3	1	16	28	12	15	89
Clerks	405	4	19	12	3	2	1	9	1	51
Cooks	060	2	3	4	2	3	2	5	3	24
Decontamination equipment operator	809	0	0	0	0	88	0	2	0	90
Electrician	078	1	0	2	0	0	0	1	0	4
Engineman, stationary steam	082	0	0	6	0	0	0	0	0	6
Gas mask repairing	609	24	0	0	0	0	0	0	0	24
Machinist	114	6	0	0	0	0	0	0	0	6
Mechanic, automobile	014	2	3	0	0	3	2	1	1	12
Mechanic, general	164	0	0	2	0	0	1	3	0	6
Munitions worker (handlers)	505	0	0	0	3	0	0	2	0	5
Operator, smoke generator	731	0	0	0	0	0	24	0	0	24
Pipefitter	162	2	0	2	0	0	0	1	0	5
Pumpman	220	0	0	0	0	14	0	0	0	14
Radio Operator	767	0	0	0	0	0	4	0	0	4
Sewing machine operator	200	8	0	0	0	0	0	2	0	10
Technician physical laboratory	160	0	0	0	1	0	0	1	0	2
Toxic gas handler	786	0	24	0	2	0	0	6	85	117
Tumblerman	103	0	0	60	0	0	0	0	0	60
Utility repairman	121	5	0	0	1	0	3	0	9	18
Warehouseman	188	0	18	0	0	0	0	0	0	18
Welder, acetylene	257	2	0	0	0	0	0	0	0	2

Source· Tables of Organization, World War II.

was neither possible nor necessary to teach a student a new trade.

In conducting enlisted specialist training, little use was made of the Chemical Warfare School. Two reasons for this may be adduced. One was the distance separating Edgewood Arsenal and Camp Sibert. Another and more compelling reason was the fact that when the Unit Training Center needed such help most, the Chemical Warfare School had little assistance

TABLE 14—ENLISTED SPECIALIST SCHOOLING UTILIZED IN CWS UNIT TRAINING[a]

Course	Duration in weeks	Conducted by
Acetylene welder	4	Unit Training Center
Automobile mechanic	6	Unit Training Center
Camouflage technician	1	Unit Training Center
Carpentry	3	Unit Training Center
Chauffeur	2	Regiment
Clerk	8	Replacement Training Center
Cooks and bakers	8	Post Bakery
Decontamination apparatus	1½	Unit Training Center
Depot operations	1	Huntsville Arsenal, Ala.
Electricians	3	Alabama School of Trades, E. Gadsen, Ala.
Engineman	1	Unit Training Center
Flame thrower repair	1	Unit Training Center
Gas mask repair	2	CW School, Edgewood Arsenal, Md.
Pipefitters	2	Gadsen, Ala., High School
Radio operator	4	Unit Training Center
Sewing machine	1	Unit Training Center
Sheet metal worker	2	Unit Training Center
Small arms repair	1	Post Ordnance Office
Toxic gas handler	1	Unit Training Center

[a] This list includes only specialist training that was directly relevant to unit training and omits longer courses at Ordnance and Signal schools to which students were occasionally sent.

Source Pt. V, Training of Units (Through 30 June 1944), CWS History of Training, App. D.

to offer. The center was therefore obliged to develop its own specialist school system.

As long as MTP 3–2 provided for eight weeks of unit technical training, the scheme of accommodating specialist training within this period was followed. But a gradual slowing down of activations after 1943 permitted a better solution to the problem, heretofore compromised, of preactivation training. An outline of the procedure eventually adopted was published in May 1944.[54] The procedure provided for the forecasting of unit activations well in advance and for the preparing of trained specialists to meet such anticipated needs. As part of this procedure the Chief, CWS, was directed to issue regularly to the Unit Training Center, specialist school quotas based upon predicted activations. Informed as to the number of trainees to attend designated courses at specified dates, the commanding general of the center then had the responsibility of selecting suitable specialist trainees to attend

[54] ASF Cir 134, 10 May 44.

the schools, and finally of assigning the graduates to appropriate units as they were activated.

Within a month after the ASF inaugurated the new procedure, the Chief, CWS, was directed to revise his unit mobilization program (MTP 3–2) so that the cycle would be accomplished in six rather than eight weeks.[55] The reduction in time was made possible, the ASF apparently believed, because of the adoption of the new system of building up groups of specialists in anticipation of unit needs. In November 1944 a further refinement of the system was effected when the War Department indicated that specialist courses would be taken during the last two weeks of basic technical training of the individual soldier under the replacement training program.[56] This was a final and satisfactory answer to the problem of specialist training, but it was only put into effect after CWS unit training was substantially completed.

Advanced Training of Units

The CWS UTC was more than a training center—to some extent it was also a depot at which chemical service companies were held until such time as operational need for them arose. In normal UTC practice, organizations were given a standard training course after completion of which they moved out promptly for assignment to senior tactical organizations. But at Camp Sibert units were often held for extended periods after completing their normal unit training schedule—once, in the case of a number of air operations companies, until it was determined that anticipated need for them would not materialize. During 1943 it was not uncommon for units to spend more time at Camp Sibert after completing unit training then they had spent on the unit training cycle. This anomalous situation, brought on largely by uncertainty over the employment of gas warfare, had evidently not been foreseen in mobilization planning.

In order to separate regular and advanced unit training, a provisional advanced training battalion was organized at Camp Sibert in August 1943. Into this command was transferred companies that had satisfactorily completed prescribed unit training and whose field assignments were deferred. A special program for the continued training of these organizations was drawn up in May 1943.[57] What the units needed at this particular stage of

---

[55] Memo, Dir of Mil Tng ASF for C CWS, 3 Jun 44, sub: Revision of Mob Tng Program for Unit Tng. ASF SPTRR 300.8 (3 Jun 44).

[56] MTP 3–1, 1 Nov 44.

[57] MTP 3–4, 21 May 43, which was revised as MTP 3–10, 1 Oct 44.

their development was field maneuvering with large commands, yet the time for such exercises in the zone of interior had largely passed. The advanced training program was an attempt to fill this need. It included a series of field problems, any one of which could be terminated when necessary to permit the units to prepare for overseas duty.

In addition to training at Camp Sibert, a number of organizations were sent to other stations for practical work while awaiting overseas commitment. The amphibious training of smoke generator companies at Camp Gordon Johnston, Fla., has already been mentioned; other units were sent for temporary duty to CWS installations, particularly Edgewood Arsenal, Md., and Dugway Proving Ground, Utah.

The units benefited from experience gained at stations where technical work was being conducted. Three types of chemical units were sent from Camp Sibert to Dugway Proving Ground for what could be called development of operational experience prior to movement overseas. These were processing, decontamination, and air operations companies. At Dugway there was considerable work to be done in the field of each, work directly applicable to the kind of technical training they had recently completed. The clothing impregnation plant, used for treating clothing worn in connection with vesicant gas shoots, was operated by a processing company when one was available. There was always work to be done relating to decontamination at the proving ground—not only the clearing of areas gassed in testing operations, but also the measurement of gas concentrations remaining at various postattack stages. Air operations companies found a great deal of practical work in connection with the servicing of aircraft which were being used constantly in staging experimental chemical attacks. There was also a variety of general work in which all units could participate—spotting for incendiary bombing, firing of chemical mortars and rockets, the servicing of all types of chemical material. The atmosphere of Dugway was charged with realism. Chemical troops spending a brief period there after completion of unit training gained respect for their missions that was often lacking in other organizations.

Supervision of Training

All levels of command, from the company to ASF headquarters, were involved in the supervision of unit training. Formal control measures, designed to evaluate training and to correct deficiences, were instituted by UTC headquarters, by the service command, by the OC CWS, and by the

Military Training Division of Army Service Forces. These all were geared to the attainment of a status of readiness for overseas service that would satisfy representatives of The Inspector General of the Army who had final responsibility for determing the adequacy of training.

Reports made by officers assigned to UTC headquarters represented spot checks of specific periods of instruction. Although these frequent checks were useful in training management, they were more concerned with technique than with over-all progress of training. For control of the latter there were involved training tests, training reports, and training inspections. The training test was a device employed by UTC headquarters to check the training progress of units at three specific stages: upon completion of basic military training; upon completion of basic technical training; and finally upon completion of the entire mobilization training program. Tests were conducted by teams designated by UTC or post headquarters. Phases of training found to be unsatisfactory by these inspection teams had to be repeated.

Another management control of considerable importance was the training status report. This report was devised by the ASF primarily to provide data through which to determine the readiness of the unit for overseas service or for functional employment in the zone of interior.[58] As eventually developed, the report on each unit was prepared twice monthly and finally upon movement to a staging area. It contained considerable data, including strength, status of training, and efficiency rating.

By the end of 1942 it became apparent that the training status report, while a valuable device, could not be depended upon in Washington for final decision as to a unit's training readiness for overseas movement. In a directive dated 5 January 1943, the War Department delegated to The Inspector General responsibility for determining, among other things, the state of technical training of organizations alerted for overseas duty.[59] This procedure was followed during the remainder of the war. It insured that all units moving to theaters of operation were suitably trained and equipped; at the same time the final IG test provided a concrete objective on which training controls could be focused.

The final formal inspection of unit training activities was a means by which training progress was directly measured and difficulties brought to

[58] Ltr, Dir of Mil Tng SOS to Chiefs of Supply Services, *et al.*, 28 Jul 42, sub: Unit Training With the SOS. CWS 353 (7–28–42).

[59] The reasons dictating this policy are discussed in Palmer, Wiley, and Keast, *Procurement and Training of Ground Combat Troops,* p. 584.

light. Policy as to formal inspections was determined by the Army Service Forces. Inspection missions were kept to a reasonable minimum, the service command inspecting military training, the OC CWS inspecting technical features, and the Military Training Division, ASF, periodically sending representatives to Camp Sibert to check training operations in general.

Chemical Service Unit Training in Retrospect

No justification is needed for the staff policy of initiating the chemical service units program in 1942. To have delayed further the activation of chemical troops would have been dangerous in that it could easily have encouraged the Axis powers, especially Germany, to initiate gas warfare. The only postwar question that might be raised is whether there was actual need of so many units.[60]

Between 1940 and 1944 chemical service unit training passed through a complete cycle. It began with a mobilization training program that called for eight weeks of essentially organizational training. This was steadily extended until, by mid-1943, two successive thirteen-week programs were being followed, the first for individual and the second for organizational training. Finally in 1944 unit training was cut back to a single six-week program from which everything but strictly organizational or group training was eliminated. Although circumstances did not permit the exhaustive testing of this curtailed procedure, available evidence indicates that six weeks scarcely allowed sufficient time to permit the rounded development of chemical service units to a state of readiness for active field service. The employment of an eight-week unit training cycle would probably have been advisable—the cycle, in short, which was provided for in the prewar unit training program.

Although it is thus evident that unit training returned in 1944 to approximately the program that was in effect in 1940, it does not follow that the various changes made in the program were inappropriate or ill-advised. It would, in theory, have been preferable to limit unit training exclusively to the molding of military organizations out of duly prepared components and eliminated from the procedure all excursions into the field of individual training. Yet the particular circumstances surrounding the mobilization of chemical troops, together with factors relating to military unpreparedness in

---

[60] For a discussion of German preparations for chemical warfare see Ochsner, History of German Chemical Warfare in World War II.

general, combined to force adoption of the procedure that was actually followed. And on the whole there were certain advantages to that procedure. The combining of basic military with unit training provided in fact a good working solution to the problem of developing chemical service organizations for World War II. Even though the companies were mobilized at relatively late dates, there was still ample time to complete both types of training at the Unit Training Center and to do so before their presence in theaters of operation became really important.

There was no opportunity for the CWS to test the scheme in vogue at the end of the war, under which chemical units were to receive all basic military training at an ASF training center before being sent to Edgewood Arsenal for technical training. To have put the plan into effect at the height of mobilization would have been unfortunate; when it came into force, CWS training activities in the zone of interior had almost ceased.

The training of chemical units, though adequate in many phases, had several weak spots. One practice that caused difficulty at the CWS Unit Training Center was the activating of units before their components were adequately prepared. It is impossible for an organization to begin its growth until its cadre, its specialists, and its fillers have all had requisite training. Much is lost under a system that requires cadre personnel to learn the subjects in which the organization is being trained while unit training is actually in progress. That the activation of units was often too precipitate is borne out by the fact that not infrequently new organizations were obliged to wait for long periods before full quotas of fillers were received. This resulted in repeated starts being made on training programs with consequent lost motion and dulling of zest. The activation of new units by the War Department was an exacting and complicated procedure which generally ran smoothly, yet there were occasions when time could actually have been gained by deferring mobilization until preactivation preparations were further advanced.

The operational requirements for greater functional versatility on the part of chemical service troops brought about eventual changes in training programs which in the light of full experience might well have been introduced from the first. Unit training was initially too specialized, so that organizations even came to resent being called upon to perform functions that normally pertained to another type of organization. For example, a processing company might be directed to take over and operate a depot; reluctance to do so was likely to stem from concepts implanted in early unit training. Later training, in addition to providing some knowledge of the functions of other units, sought to inspire willingness to undertake any type of chemical service operations.

The amount of administrative or nontraining time needed by a unit was not always considered by planning agencies. After an organization completed its training program and was ordered out, a lapse of four weeks was required before another unit could begin training in its place. Not less than two weeks had to be reserved to insure that all men could take advantage of furlough policies—the five days of furlough granted had to be supplemented by five days or more of travel time. After the company was again assembled, one week was spent in final processing by supply, personnel, and inspection teams to comply with POM instructions. Once the unit cleared the post, probably three weeks after finishing its training, its place could be taken by an untrained company. But a full week was required for receiving and organizing the new company—time which, if not allowed for, had to be stolen from training schedules.

The cost of the unit training installation at Camp Sibert was heavy. Only eighteen months elapsed between the completion of the center in October 1943 and its closing in April 1945. Some conception of the cost factors in volved in military training may be gained by prorating the cost of the center against the number of chemical companies that trained them. However, there was never serious criticism of the zone of interior training of chemical service companies. This training, although costly, served its purpose.

CHAPTER XIV

The Chemical Warfare School

The role of the Chemical Warfare School, like that of all service schools, was to present essential instruction which could not be given advantageously within units or in local schools. The World War II military directive governing the school divided such instruction into two clearly defined categories: (1) the training of CWS personnel for branch duties, and (2) the instruction of "officers of other arms and services of Army, Navy, Marine Corps, and Coast Guard in tactics and technique of chemical warfare and in protection against chemical attack.[1]

The importance of the Chemical Warfare School training of branch personnel was emphasized by the fact that chemical officers and enlisted men were, with few exceptions, widely scattered in such small elements as to preclude effective general training at local levels. Excellent schools were conducted at Camp Sibert and at the several CWS arsenals, yet this instruction was for the most part directly related to tasks immediately at hand. It remained for the Edgewood school to attend to the broader aspects of the individual's military education.

Before the war the Chemical Warfare School had not been actively engaged in the training of CWS personnel as such. As a result, when full mobilization began, the school had not developed and tested a series of courses for this purpose. More than two years elapsed after the declaration of war before a clear-cut solution to the problem of school training of CWS officers was reached. Meanwhile, many courses were instituted, employed for a time, and then discontinued. In this respect the experience of the Chemical Warfare School paralleled that of the newly established ground forces schools which, in contrast to the older schools of the statutory branches, offered a diversity of special courses.

Administration

After the Army reorganization of March 1942, administrative control

[1] AR 350–1300, 14 Jul 42.

of technical branch schools passed from the General Staff to the Army Service Forces. Under long-standing procedure, direct operational control of these schools was in the hands of the chiefs of branches. This arrangement continued under the provisions of a regulation which exempted the Chemical Warfare School, among others, from corps area supervision and control.[2] When the service command organization was instituted in July 1942, the ASF adopted the policy of decentralizing all training, including school training, to those commands, and accordingly directed that the CW School be conducted under the immediate supervision of the Commanding General, Third Service Command.[3] Because of the technical nature of the instruction, the CWS contended that this procedure was not feasible. The matter eventually was clarified in May 1943, when the Chemical Warfare School was designated a Class IV installation.[4] For the remainder of the war period the school was operated by the Chief, CWS, for the Commanding General, ASF.

For a few months early in 1942 the school fell under local jurisdiction of the Troops and Training Department of the Chemical Warfare Center.[5] Also included in this department were the Replacement Training Center, Officers Replacement Pool, and the growing number of chemical troop units stationed at the center. This organizational device permitted all military administration and training to be centralized under the command of a single officer (brigadier general).

At this time, as for years past, the Edgewood Arsenal commander was *ex officio* commandant of the Chemical Warfare School. It was, accordingly, customary for the assistant commandant to command the school directly and to delegate to the school executive the academic functions which would normally be performed by the assistant commandant. This awkward procedure was relieved in September 1942 when the functions of the school commandant were in effect separated from those of the arsenal commander.[6] In October Brig. Gen. Alexander Wilson became the school commandant, occupying that position until April 1944. The following month, Col. Maurice E. Barker was returned from combat duty in Italy for assignment to the school where he served as commandant until after the end of the war.

---

[2] AR 350–105, 18 Jun 42.
[3] WD GO 35, 22 Jul 42.
[4] ASF Cir 28, 12 May 43.
[5] The Chemical Warfare Center was officially activated in May 1942 to facilitate management of the diversity of wartime activities centering at Edgewood Arsenal. See above, Chapter VI.
[6] AR 350–110, 1 Sep 42.

The main building of the Chemical Warfare School, reconstruction of which was completed early in 1942, housed the offices of the commandant and his staff as well as the Commissioned Officer Division of the school. Officer candidate instruction centered at first in temporary buildings located near the school proper. This arrangement served for the first six classes; but rapid expansion thereafter necessitated transfer to the troop area, by the summer of 1942, of all OCS training activities. A similar sequence occurred in connection with the schooling of enlisted personnel. This training was negligible during 1941, except for seven small classes of Coast Guard ratings whose instruction proceeded without difficulty in the main school area. The increasing number of enlisted classes conducted in 1942 compelled the CW School to transfer this training to the troop area of the arsenal close to where the students were housed. With the transfer of classroom and field training of both officer candidates and enlisted personnel to the troop area (a distance of approximately two miles from the main school building) the commandant reorganized the school into three academic divisions, namely, Officers, Officer Candidate, and Enlisted.

The development of training facilities for the several divisions of the school was always hampered by the space limitations of the Edgewood Arsenal reservation. Lower Gunpowder Neck contained a number of fairly adequate fields, but competition for them was keen, and use by the school was strictly limited. The school was therefore obliged to locate some new training areas, generally in sections not already pre-empted by research and development or proving ground activities. The gas obstacle course was an outstanding example of the type of training facility designed and constructed by the school for its use during the war. Another was the incendiary training area, in the northeast section of the reservation, where were staged realistic night demonstrations of the employment of incendiary munitions. For group instruction, bleachers were provided near field exercise areas. Indoor classrooms for officer training were adequate; eventually these were also provided in sufficient number to meet the needs of officer candidate and enlisted classes. The school operated a well-equipped reproduction plant, insuring an ample supply of instructional materials and training aids. In spite of space limitations, the school's location at the Chemical Warfare Center was never a critical handicap—in fact in some respects the site was ideal. Yet certainly the accomplishment of the school's mission would have been facilitated if the school could have had more complete control of its operational areas.

The authorized capacity of the Officers Division of the school, which originally provided for 50 students, increased first to 200 and then to 500 in 1942 and again to 600 in 1943. A year later, the capacity fell to 500, and on 5 February 1945 this figure dropped to 400. The capacity for enlisted students in 1942 was 200.[7] These maximum capacity quotas were of value in stabilizing staff and faculty levels and school facilities. Because of wide variation in the duration of school courses, capacity maximums bore little relation to the volume of school training. For example, during the fiscal year 1943 the school graduated 6,699 students, excluding officers candidates, although the authorized officers' and enlisted capacity during this period was no more than 800.

Training of CWS Personnel

The two courses unquestionably needed for the general training of CWS officers were the Basic Course and the Advanced Course. The first was an introductory course for junior officers. The second was a refresher course for older officers, partially as qualification for admission to the Command and General Staff School and partially in preparation for assignment to field grade duties in the Chemical Warfare Service. Ideal training management anticipated that all newly commissioned officers would attend the Basic Course and that a proportion of these officers would later return to the school for the Advanced Course. This objective, in time, was partially realized as far as troop officers were concerned. In the case of officers commissioned from civilian life for technical or procurement duty such progressive training was by no means general.

A basic course had been included in the school's curriculum for many years. At the Chemical Warfare School, the term "basic" was traditionally associated with the training of the unit gas officers of the combat arms. It was not until January 1942 that the first class for the basic training of CWS officers was assembled. The course, then of four-week duration, was intended to provide introductory training for officers newly called to active service, something the school had been recommending for more than a year. By then there were many CWS officers on active duty who had not been given basic training. Detaching these officers to attend school at that stage was a difficult problem. In recognition of this fact, a distinction was made in the original Basic Course between general and field training, the latter being concentrated in the separate Troop Officers Course. Officers graduating from

[7] For capacities for officer candidate training, see below, Chapter XV.

the Basic Course who were on technical or procurement duty returned to their stations, while officers slated for tactical assignment remained at the school another four weeks for additional training in chemical tactics and field operations.

Although this integrated scheme of basic and troop training appeared logical and despite the fact that these courses were spirited and well conducted, actually fewer than 300 officers attended the Basic Course during the first half of 1942, while only 183 graduated from the Troop Officers Course. Clearly, little progress was being made toward meeting the mounting accumulation of officer training problems.

In midsummer 1942 the scheme of separate basic and troop courses was dropped, and a Combined Basic and Troop Course instituted. The consolidated course as finally approved provided for six weeks of instruction, a change which meant a lessening by 25 percent of the total length of the two replaced courses. During the first three weeks of the Basic Troop Course all students received identical instruction; for the remainder of the course, the classes were divided into two groups: (1) troop section and (2) nontroop section. Here a clear distinction was made between the tactical and the nontactical functions of the Chemical Warfare Service. The nontroop section was trained during the second half of the course in such subjects as principles of procurement, manufacture of war gases, and field supply of chemical munitions, areas in which precise knowledge on the part of chemical officers was often lacking.[8]

Again, as in the case of the separate basic and troop courses, this apparently logical approach to officer training produced disappointingly meager results. Only 375 officers graduated from the four classes conducted during the late summer and fall of 1942. By the end of October, less than 15 percent of the CWS officers on active duty had received formal basic schooling. Nevertheless, the school dropped the Basic and Troop Course in October 1942, and basic training did not reappear on the school agenda until the spring of 1943. Meanwhile two new courses for training CWS officers were introduced. A series of four short refresher classes provided instruction for officers with some field experience to bring them up to date on current progress in chemical warfare tactics and technique. A three-week Command and Staff Course began at the same time with the object of preparing company grade officers for chemical staff duty with tactical units. While the aim

[8] Class Record, First Chemical Warfare Combined Basic and Troop Officers Course, 3 Jun 42. For each course conducted at the Chemical Warfare School there was a printed class record which contained a class roster and schedule of instruction.

of both courses was the fulfillment of important training requirements, neither course substituted for the Basic and Troop Course which they had replaced on the school program.

The elimination of basic training of chemical officers at the school at this particular time was to some extent a reaction to the increasing output of the CWS Officer Candidate School. The Officer Candidate Course was considered to be in the nature of basic training, so that the Basic Course was, up to this time, intended primarily for non-OCS-graduates. By the spring of 1943 it was becoming evident that the thirteen-week OCS Course was not turning out an adequately rounded officer—nor was it in fact intended to. The function of the Officer Candidate School was to transmute a soldier into a subaltern who, either by experience or further training, would eventually develop the special know-how needed in the work of a commissioned officer. Yet opportunities to learn by experience were relatively few in the case of the CWS subaltern, and OCS graduates were beginning to draw assignments for which they were inadequately prepared. The answer was to be found in additional training for these young officers.

One place where need for such training was apparent was in connection with OCS graduates slated for duty with Army Air Forces. Special instruction to qualify for air duty had been undertaken in a few OCS classes but it was impossible to cover this field adequately during officer candidate training. A better answer was the Air Forces Chemical Course, designed specifically to acquaint CWS officers with the problems they would encounter in service with air commands. This course was approved in February 1943; nineteen classes, graduating 1,022 students, were held during the next two years.

In line with the trend toward further training of OCS graduates, a revised Basic Course was returned to the school program in April 1943.[9] Patterned after the Basic and Troop Course of 1942, it accommodated both OCS graduates and junior officers. By eliminating repetition of work covered in the OCS program, the new Basic Course was held to a four-week cycle. The classes assigned to this course were divided into two sections—service and troop. A common schedule prevailed during the first two weeks, after which each section followed its own schedule. The emphasis throughout was tactical, the troop section specializing in chemical weapons and the service section in field logistics. The theory behind the 1943 Basic Course was sound, but not enough training hours were allotted for the amount of ground to be covered.

[9] Class Record, Second CWS Basic Course, 24 May–19 June 1943.

Resumption of the mobilization of chemical battalions in May 1943 permitted the school to contribute more directly to the training of battalion officers than had been possible when the first series of battalions was organized a year earlier. A four-week Battalion Officers' Course, inaugurated in the summer of 1943, focused instruction on the functions of mortar company officers. The intent was to co-ordinate classes with the activation of specific battalions, with the designated battalion commander acting as class commander and thus acquainting himself in advance with the officers who were to be assigned to his unit.[10] Although it was not possible to follow this plan exactly for all classes, the establishment of the Battalion Officers' Course did provide an excellent solution to the requirement for qualified CWS officers for the new battalions. Between the summer of 1943 and the summer of 1944 eleven classes, totaling 1,229 students, were graduated.

Conclusion of the series of battalion officers classes in the summer of 1944 coincided with the inauguration of a new course designated as the Combat and Service Course.[11] This supplanted the Basic Course referred to above, and also, in time, the Air Chemical Course. The Combat and Service Course represented the accumulated experience, both at the school and in the field, of two and a half years in the basic school training of younger CWS officers. It extended the range of instruction from the four weeks then allotted to the Basic Course, to a new high of ten weeks. It was frankly designed as an extension of the Officer Candidate Course, graduates of which were, if possible, immediately assigned to the Combat and Service Course. Upon completion of the latter, company grade officers were presumably qualified for duty with both combat and service units, with field supply installations, or for assignment to junior staff positions in the Chemical Warfare Service.

Compared to the training of junior officers, the school instruction of field grade officers was relatively stabilized. The Advanced Course was not initiated until April 1943, but thereafter it was conducted continuously and with little change. Duration was four weeks. Probably the most important accomplishment of this course was the preparation of CWS officers to pursue the Command and General Staff School courses at Fort Leavenworth. By midsummer 1945, the Advanced Course had graduated 544 students in 22 classes.

Although the number of chemical officers who received general training

---

[10] Class Record, First Battalion Officers' Course, 30 August–25 September 1943.
[11] Class Record, First Combat and Service Course, 24 July–30 September 1944.

at the Chemical Warfare School was relatively small, the school training of CWS enlisted men was on a still more modest scale. A total of twenty enlisted courses were presented during the war, yet only one was designed for the general training of chemical noncommissioned officers.[12] Early in 1942 a four-week CWS Enlisted Men's Course was approved. This course intended for instruction of senior NCO's who were assigned to staff sections of major tactical units and who needed a broader knowledge of CWS procedures than could be obtained in local training. The course program included chemical matériel, tactics, and technique; training; military administration; and clerical subjects. Seven classes were conducted, each averaging seventy students, the last class terminating 28 November 1942. Since students were drawn from a wide cross section of military organizations, the influence of this training was greater than is suggested by the relatively small numbers involved.

Of the specialist courses for enlisted men, only two were integrated with chemical unit training. The seven-week Laboratory Course was highly technical; officers as well as enlisted men were trained for duty with chemical laboratory companies. The Special Mortar Operations Course trained small groups of enlisted specialists for assignment to the chemical battalions mobilized in 1943 and 1944. The remainder of the enlisted courses conducted at the Chemical Warfare School were primarily for the instruction of those outside the Chemical Warfare Service.

Training of Other Arms and Services

At least one out of every three commissioned officers trained at the Chemical Warfare School came from another arm or service. The number of students from naval components was greater than the total sent by either the Army Ground Forces or the Army Air Forces. In the enlisted classes, outside students definitely outnumbered those from the Chemical Warfare Service.

Training of students from other branches was essentially specialist training—instruction in some technical phase of protection against gas attack, in the handling of chemical agents in bulk, in the operation of flame throwers, or in the duties of unit gas personnel. Some of the specialist training and the training of unit gas officers and noncommissioned officers was, by prewar concepts, a local training responsibility and not one to be

---

[12] Ten of these courses were given to three classes or less.

undertaken at the special service school level. But this training developed during World War II into a major activity of the Chemical Warfare School. School administrators regarded the Chemical Warfare Center as the best place for this training for two reasons. The first was the authoritative instruction available at the Chemical Warfare School. The second was psychological in nature. Since gas had not been used, field interest in gas defense training had declined; nevertheless both the War and Navy Departments, in the light of their information on the possibility of gas warfare, insisted upon maintenance of high standards of gas discipline. Unit gas defense training was therefore given added prestige by the elevation of instructor training to the specialist school level. And the more thorough training available at that level imbued potential unit instructors with an attitude of realism toward poison gas which was favorably reflected in gas discipline.

Despite the advantages which the Chemical Warfare School offered, outside agencies depended less and less on the school as the war period lengthened. Indications of this development are the action of Army Air Forces in setting up an air chemical school at Barksdale Field, La. (later transferred to Buckley Field, Colo.), and the establishment of the naval chemical warfare school at Dugway Proving Ground. These schools were closer to the technical viewpoints of their arms than was the Chemical Warfare School.[13]

The Unit Gas Officers (UGO) Course was the most active wartime officers course at the Chemical Warfare School, both in number of classes and in students graduated. This course had been developed and improved over a long period of time. Originally one class was conducted each year. The biweekly scheduling of the class, which began early in 1941, was the first tangible step taken at the Chemical Warfare School in the transition from peace to war. Thereafter and until the end of hostilities, UGO classes were conducted almost continuously at the school. The course thus provided a direct link between the school's prewar and its wartime training operations. Although it improved with successive presentations, there was little change in the content of the course.

In the fall of 1942, a sixty-hour course of instruction was outlined for training unit gas officers in unit or local schools.[14] This course was generally followed in training at division or corps levels. The 60 hours of instruction

[13] (1) Craven and Cate, *Men and Planes* pp. 650–59. (2) Bernard Baum, Dugway Proving Ground, pp. 100–102. MS.
[14] FM 21–40, Basic Field Manual: Defense Against Chemical Attack, 7 Sep 42.

was in contrast to the 176 hours, or 4 weeks of resident instruction, in the Chemical Warfare School course. The following tabulation of training hours allotted to the several subjects indicates the differences between the two courses:

	Local UGO Course	CW School Course
Total hours	60	176
Agents	9	15
Matériel	6	23
Operations	8	34
Protection	22	64
Training	8	16
Weather	3	10
General subjects	4	14

In all, the Chemical Warfare School conducted 45 Unit Gas Officers classes between February 1941 and August 1945 from which 3,025 students were graduated. The school organized separate classes for air and ground force trainees whenever the student load justified it. Because of the comprehensive degree of instruction presented at Edgewood Arsenal, the graduate of the Chemical Warfare School course, besides emerging as an exceptionally well-trained unit gas officer, was also qualified to conduct varied chemical warfare training in regiments and battalions.

Paralleling the UGO Course was one for the training of enlisted personnel in specialized duties relating to gas defense in regiments and subordinate units. This training began at the Chemical Warfare School with the institution of the Noncommissioned Officers Staff Course in November 1942. The staff course supplanted the Enlisted Men's Course for CWS personnel already mentioned; it actually was aimed at two separate instructional targets—training of CWS enlisted staff personnel and training of gas NCO's. The NCO Staff Course was never altogether satisfactory and was soon replaced by the Gas Noncommissioned Officers Course, the first class of the latter series commencing 13 April 1943. No attempt was made to train CWS personnel as such in the latter four-week course, although where classes included sizable numbers of chemical enlisted men, these students were occasionally kept at the school for a fifth week to receive special branch instruction. Navy, Marine, and Coast Guard enlisted men came to Edgewood in considerable numbers to attend the Gas NCO Course and in some cases they were grouped into special classes which emphasized naval aspects of gas protection. The school continued gas NCO classes without interruption until after the cessation of hostilities. These represented the most important training activity of the Enlisted Division of the Chemical Warfare School. By the end of the war 50 classes were held, and 4,086 students graduated from the Gas NCO Course.

Allied to the unit gas course, but much more technical in nature, was the Medical Officers Course. Military physicians had studied the medical aspects of chemical warfare exhaustively through the 1920's and 1930's. When war began the Medical Department was, from the standpoint of scientific data, well prepared to cope with the special problems of gas warfare. But professional knowledge on this subject was by no means general, since medical practice provided little experience to guide physicians in the diagnosis and prognosis of gas casualties. Yet, an understanding of the proper treatment of such cases promised unusually good dividends in terms of lessened fatalities and early recoveries.

The Surgeon General of the Army requested, during the summer of 1942, that a course be conducted at the Chemical Warfare School for the instruction of medical officers in the therapy of gassed casualties. The War Department quickly approved the proposal and the first class began 7 September 1942. Originally a four-week course, the time was cut to two weeks after seven classes graduated. This reduction was found to be too drastic, so that the course was finally stabilized at three weeks, a period which proved to be a satisfactory compromise between the amount of material to be taught and the time which the officer students could be spared from field assignments.

The Medical Officers Course was a joint CWS-Medical Corps project. Staff instructors taught such subjects as chemical agents, operations, matériel, and protection, where these involved medical aspects. Experienced physicians presented from the school platform all professional medical subject dealing with gas casualties, e.g., physiopathology, symptoms, treatment, and medical service. The splendid facilities of the medical research laboratory at the Chemical Warfare Center were an important factor in this instructional program. Twenty-seven medical officers' classes were held and 1,973 trainees graduated. These scientifically trained physicians, who eventually became scattered through all elements of the armed forces, represented an important feature of the over-all scheme for defense against enemy gas attack.

The Navy steadily used the Chemical Warfare School facilities throughout the entire war period. Notable in this connection was a consistent trend to widen the scope of instruction and to increase the number of naval students. The naval detachment at Edgewood Arsenal was greatly expanded during the war years, partially in order to facilitate this training. The naval detachment was headed by Captain Michael A. Leahy, USN, Retired, an officer of broad experience whose knowledge of naval procedures and personalities was invaluable to the school.

There were three all-Navy courses of instruction at the Chemical Warfare School when the war ended.[15] The most important of these was the four-week Navy and Coast Guard Officers Course. This was an outgrowth of the semiannual Navy Course which had been a regular feature of the curriculum for many years prior to the war. It stressed defense of Navy and Coast Guard units and shore stations against chemical attack, the offensive use of chemical weapons by naval forces, and the training of instructors in this field. As finally developed, this course consolidated separate courses which had previously been presented to Navy, Marine Corps, and Coast Guard officers.

The Navy Gas Officers and the Navy Gas Enlisted Courses, each of six days' duration, were not comprehensive. These short courses were limited to technical training in protection against war gases, with particular attention to naval protective matériel and protective measures and decontamination procedures afloat. Where more extended instruction of this type was desirable for Navy, Marine Corps, and Coast Guard enlisted personnel, the students were assigned to the NCO Course after April 1943 instead of the special four-week classes.

Other Navy instruction included a series of eleven classes conducted in 1942 for training of petty officers in gas mask repair and a Navy Toxic Gas Handlers Course instituted early in 1943 to permit the practical training of both officers and enlisted men in handling bulk chemicals. The latter was eventually consolidated with the Toxic Gas Handlers Course which provided three weeks of training in this special technique for both Army and Navy students. In all of this work at the Chemical Warfare School, the object of naval instruction was to complement and further the Navy's own extensive training program in the field of chemical warfare.

Like the training of Navy personnel, the instruction at the Chemical Warfare School for the Army Air Forces had roots extending into the prewar era. The training of unit gas officers for duty with AAF commands was accomplished principally through the fifteen special UGO (Aviation) classes conducted between January 1941 and February 1943. Through this program, the AAF was able to implement its widespread scheme of training

[15] ASF Manual M3, 18 Nov 44 and C1, 14 Apr 45.

in defense against enemy gas attack. After the conclusion of this series, the diminishing number of AAF students were included in the regular UGO classes. The instruction of air enlisted personnel was limited to the training of gas NCO's.

Academic Procedures

Variations in the size of classes at the Chemical Warfare School presented a continuing problem in training management. Difficulties arose especially from fluctuations in student enrollments for succeeding classes of the same course. The range of these fluctuations in some cases was great, as is indicated by the following figures:

Course	High	Low
Unit Gas Officers	171	21
Unit Gas Officers (Aviation)	275	38
Unit Gas NCO	105	27
Combined Basic and Troop Officer	140	65
Air Forces Chemical	111	18

One reason for such variations in the size of classes stemmed from the general policy of leaving service school training optional with units. Where schooling was undertaken at the specific request of an agency competent to select and order students to Edgewood, classes were generally uniform in size. This was true, for example, of the Medical Officers Course and of the Navy and Coast Guard Course. On the other hand, when school quotas were distributed subject to acceptance by local commanders, fluctuations were inevitable. Certainly, where the training of unit gas personnel was concerned, only the unit commander could decide whether attendance at a special service school was necessary, a situation which of course made almost impossible an even flow of students.

Prewar academic procedures at the Chemical Warfare School had been adjusted to classes of approximately fifty students. For most indoor instruction, groups much in excess of this number presented a problem because of classroom limitations. Consequently it was often necessary to divide large classes into two or even three sections for classroom work, with the sections uniting for outdoor exercise.

Teaching procedures followed the War Department policy and the school developed a library of lesson plans to implement that policy.[16] These

[16] WD policy was defined in FM 21–5, Basic Field Manual, Military Training, 16 Jul 41, and TM 21–50, Army Instruction, 19 Apr 43.

plans as well as the actual methods of instruction were constantly subject
to review and appraisal by the various Army inspectors. The library of
lesson plans developed by the school faculty to supply this policy was a
major factor in enabling the school to expand its training operations rapidly
after the declaration of war.

A criticism repeatedly directed at the school by officers conducting formal
inspections of training was against excessive use of the lecture method in
the explanation phase of instruction. This practice was gradually discontinued until instructors, probably to too great an extent, were avoiding the
use of this useful teaching method. The officially approved conference
method of explanation, involving active student participation, was difficult
to apply in large classes and was scarcely effective for some types of school
instruction. The trend of training procedure was definitely away from the
academic and toward more out-of-door work involving demonstrations and
group performance of practical problems, even though individual preparation for such exercises was not always perfect. Toward the end of the war
an average of 60 percent of a normal fifty-hour training week consisted of
outdoor instruction.

Inspectors noted a lack of uniform supervisory control in all academic
divisions during the period of transition of the school into a three dimen-
sional institution. This situation was probably a consequence of the fact that
the rapid expansion of school capacity, though inevitable, was late. In the
rush to develop instructors, the creation of an appropriate supervisory staff
was neglected; yet, such a staff was necessary to insure the extension to
other divisions of the excellent instructional methods which the Officers
Division of the school had developed. The condition improved with time
although the instructional standards of the Enlisted Division never seemed
to equal those of the other two divisions.

The building block of each course of instruction was the lesson. A group
of lessons composed a subcourse. A group of subcourses in turn constituted
a course.

Lesson planning required, first, a decision as to the scope of the single
lesson within the pattern of the subcourse. The next step was to determine
the method best suited to that particular unit of the instructional process—
lecture, conference, demonstration, or field problem. In the lesson plan such
miscellaneous notes as text references, location of exercise, training aids required, and other data useful to succeeding instructors could then be
included.

Course planning involved a synthesis of subcourses, each modified to conform to the objective and scope of the particular course. The subcourses included in the curriculum of the Chemical Warfare School were essentially seven: Agents, Protection, Matériel, Field Operations, Training, Weather, and General Subjects. These subcourses had been taught at the school for many years. Occasionally it was necessary to stretch the meaning of words to accommodate all wartime schooling within this pattern of subcourses although on the whole it served well enough.

The examination step of the instructional procedure was informal when applied to the separate lesson but formal when applied to the subcourse. The questioning of individual students from the platform was principally an interest-sustaining device. Informal quizzes were useful in evaluating instructional procedures as well as the student's progress. Graded problems were also considered in rating the individual. The formal written examination was generally used to determine how well the student had assimilated the instruction pertaining to each subcourse—it was the criterion for graduation.

The Faculty Board met before the graduation of each class to consider the work of individual students. The board included the commandant or assistant commandant, director of the appropriate academic division, the course director, the instructors principally concerned, and the school secretary. Frequently the board was expected to assay the qualifications of CWS officers for particular types of duty or for more extended military training, in addition to determining their elegibility for graduation. When records indicated an average of seventy or above on written work, if the student was otherwise qualified, he was voted a certificate of satisfactory completion of the course. If work in any one subcourse fell below the required standard and the work could not be made up, this subcourse was red-lined from the certificate. When there was a failure in more than one subcourse, the Faculty Board determined whether under Army Regulations the student should be graduated or not.[17] This procedure applied both to the Officers Division, where failures were 3.5 percent of all enrollees, and to the Enlisted Division, where failures averaged 3 percent.[18]

Western Chemical Warfare School

The West Coast Chemical Warfare School, as indicated, was established at Camp Beale, Calif., in December 1943 and was transferred to Rocky

[17] AR 350 110, 1 Sep 42.
[18] The procedure followed in the Officer Candidate Division for determining eligibility for graduation is described below, Chapter XV.

Mountain Arsenal in May 1944.[19] Before the school opened, instructors were chosen from among former members of the faculty of the Chemical Warfare School at Edgewood and the recently deactivated War Department Civilian Protection Schools at Seattle, Palo Alto, and Los Angeles.[20] It was fortunate that the CWS had access to competent instructors, for the press of administrative duties accompanying the opening of the new school left little time for close supervision of teachers.[21] The authorized courses were:

Unit Gas Officers (4 weeks): Identical with the course standardized at Edgewood Arsenal.

Gas Noncommissioned Officers (4 weeks): Same course as given at Edgewood Arsenal.

Navy Gas Course (Officers) (6 days): Defense of naval forces and shore stations against gas attack; offensive use of chemicals by naval forces.

Navy Gas Course (Enlisted) (3 days): Special duties involved in protection of naval units and stations against gas attack.[22]

CWS Refresher (10 days): To provide a knowledge of recent developments in chemical warfare and to review the principles of defense against gas attack; intended primarily for instruction of CW-trained company grade officers.

CWS Familiarization (10 days): To demonstrate to field and general officers other than CWS the potentialities of chemical warfare in the Pacific Ocean areas.

Air Raid Protection (6 days): Air raid protection measures applicable to military installations and co-ordinated with civilian protection agencies.[23]

The last three courses were obviously of a precautionary nature to be given only under circumstances which fortunately failed to materialize. The remaining courses, two for Army and two for Navy personnel, represented the real working activities of the school. The orientation of this instruction was definitely toward the war against Japan.

Academic procedures at the western school were identical with those developed and practiced at the Chemical Warfare School. The original corps of instructors were all products of the older school, and relieving officers

---

[19] See above, Chapter VI

[20] See above, Chapter X.

[21] Memo, C Fld Tng Br OC CWS for CG ASF, 11 Feb 44, sub: Inspection of West Coast Chemical School, Camp Beale, Calif. CWS 333.

[22] The length of this course was later extended to six days.

[23] (1) ASF Cir 138, 2 Dec 43. (2) Courses at Rocky Mountain Arsenal were a continuation of those given at Camp Beale.

were generally veterans of the Pacific theaters. Eventually, much of the training was in the hands of instructors with combat experience. The total number of graduates at Camp Beale and Rocky Mountain was as follows: [24]

	Officers	Enlisted students
Total	1,101	1,571
Army	375	854
Navy, Marine, and Coast Guard	725	712
WAC	1	5

Careful plans were made at the Western Chemical Warfare School in connection with the redeployment training projected for the final struggle with Japan. Fortunately, it was possible to discard these plans when the enemy capitulated in August 1945, and the school was inactivated in September 1945.[25]

The Western Chemical Warfare School was an experiment in preparedness which would have paid appreciable dividends had operations in the final stages of World War II taken a different turn. As it was, experience in the conduct of this school demonstrated that, given a nice combination of facilities, training know-how, and proper direction, a gratifying satisfactory end product of instruction will result. The school was small and its immediate training objectives were modest; yet the success with which it accomplished its mission indicated that, if necessary, it could easily have undertaken a more ambitious program.

Other Schools

As the war progressed, the CWS gained fresh knowledge on the performance of gas agents under a variety of climatic conditions and means of dispersion, based on scientific data accumulated in tests at chemical warfare experiment stations in Florida, Panama, and Utah. This development and testing work necessitated some review of logistical data and, equally important, some retraining of personnel. The empirical nature of some of the data was such that the CWS cautiously considered the radical revision of its whole training position in the field of offensive gas warfare. Nevertheless, the War Department was convinced that the new information must be passed on to officers assigned to drawing up gas warfare plans.

In September 1943, a group of four Navy officers was sent to Dugway

[24] Tabulation of Graduates, Western CW School, 31 Aug 45.
[25] ASF Cir 331, 1 Sep 45.

Proving Ground (Tooele, Utah) to study field trials in progress at that station in order to work up instructional material on offensive gas warfare for use within the Navy. Its work gradually expanded until, in November 1943, the group was officially designated as the "U.S. Navy Chemical Warfare Training Unit," with responsibility to the Navy for research and training in offensive chemical warfare. This unit had two principal functions: (1) preparation of training literature, including films, and (2) conduct of a school for the training of Navy aerologists. By agreement with the War Department, the Navy conducted this training at Dugway Proving Ground.

The emphasis in this training was originally on micrometeorology—that is, weather conditions at or within a few feet of the earth's surface, the area in which the antipersonnel effectiveness of gas warfare is ultimately measured. The excellence of Navy instruction in this field soon attracted the attention of the Army Air Forces, the military agency primarily concerned with meteorology. At War Department request, the Navy gladly accepted air officers as students in these classes.

The Navy Chemical Warfare Training Unit was soon pioneering in a hitherto somewhat neglected field of scientific study, the behavior of chemical agents in the "micromet" zone. It was also utilizing quite advanced CWS test data, some of which were still experimental, in its teaching. After observing the progress of this instruction, the Chief, CWS, requested and the Navy agreed to institute a micrometeorology course for CWS Officers. Seven such classes were conducted at irregular periods between October 1944 and September 1945, each running for two weeks. The objective of the course was officially stated as being to train chemical officers in the planning of gas offensive operations, with full cognizance of micrometeorological conditions. A total of 186 officers received this training. The instructional material developed in this course was, after the cessation of hostilities, transferred to the curriculum of the Chemical Warfare School.

Because of apprehension during the latter stages of the war over the possibility of enemy employment of biological agents, the War Department decided in 1944 to improve its defensive position in this field. One measure was the inauguration of a two-week course of instruction in technical measures of defense against biological attack. This training was computed by the CWS at Camp Detrick, Md. Five classes were held between February and July 1944, the attendance being limited to senior and specially qualified chemical and medical officers and their naval counterparts. The assignment of graduates to theaters of operation was a means of insuring that chemical and medical officers could be properly coached in anti-BW procedures should a need to apply them arise. A total of 217 officers was graduated from this course.[26]

Accomplishment of School Training

The training accomplishments of the Chemical Warfare schools can be summarized in the record of 21,673 graduations from the Chemical Warfare School at Edgewood during the emergency and war periods (*Table 15*),

TABLE 15—GRADUATES OF THE CHEMICAL WARFARE SCHOOL, EDGEWOOD ARSENAL, MARYLAND[a]

Date	Army (CWS and service)		Army (ground combat)		Army (Air)		Navy		Marine		Coast Guard		WAC		All warrant officers
	Off	Enl	Off	Enl	Off	Enl	Off	Enl	Off	Enl	Off	Enl	Off	Enl	
Total_____	8,806	3,622	1,953	1,450	1,001	507	1,572	596	378	711	134	779	41	51	72
Jul–Dec 1939____	35	0	57	0	0	0	29	0	0	0	0	0	0	0	0
Jan–Jun 1940____	40	0	0	0	0	0	52	0	1	0	0	0	0	0	1
Jul–Dec 1940____	13	120	56	0	0	0	53	27	2	0	24	2	0	0	0
Jan–Jun 1941____	146	58	232	0	105	0	48	0	4	0	2	91	0	0	5
Jul–Dec 1941____	218	25	373	0	69	0	49	10	4	0	0	52	0	0	2
Jan–Jun 1942____	437	72	121	0	98	0	68	83	6	0	1	150	0	0	4
Jul–Dec 1942____	1,494	410	139	12	196	4	177	24	13	115	25	111	0	0	2
Jan–Jun 1943____	1,706	830	130	232	361	119	150	55	61	155	52	106	6	6	8
Jul–Dec 1943____	1,759	822	249	226	56	87	265	67	131	214	30	266	28	25	26
Jan–Jun 1944____	1,475	527	214	245	51	200	280	194	84	195	0	0	1	7	9
Jul–Dec 1944____	934	460	241	428	45	88	275	103	49	0	0	0	6	6	7
Jan–Jun 1945____	549	298	141	307	20	9	126	33	23	32	0	1	0	7	8

[a] Exclusive of OCS Graduates
Source Chemical Corps School records.

2,672 graduations from the Western Chemical Warfare School, 388 from the course at Dugway Proving Ground, and 217 from the course at Camp Detrick.

Besides the graduation of students, the development of courses represented a major school accomplishment. Forty-six titles designated the various courses presented at the Edgewood and Dugway schools between 1941 and 1945. Some of these courses met only a short-term training requirement. Others were eventually modified or merged under new titles. There

[26] Cochrane, Biological Warfare Research in the United States, Vol. II, p. 46.

still remained during the last months of the war the following approved courses:[27]

Chemical Warfare Combat and Service (10 weeks): For basic training of junior CWS officers.

Advanced (5 weeks): For training captains and field grade officers in chemical operations, staff procedures, and supply functions.

Air Forces Chemical (4 weeks): To qualify CWS officers to perform the duties of chemical officers with the AAF.

ASF Depot, Phase II (4 weeks): For training CWS officers in supply, depot, and toxic gas yard operations supplementing the ASF Depot Course (Phase I), conducted at the Quartermaster School.

CWS Laboratory (7 weeks): To train CWS officers and enlisted men to carry out technical functions of field laboratory companies.

Toxic Gas Handlers (Officers) (3 weeks): To train officers in all phases of handling offensive chemical warfare munitions, naval matériel, and bulk agents.

Medical Department Officers (3 weeks): To train medical officers in the identification of chemical warfare agents, decontamination, and the prevention and care of chemical warfare casualties.

Unit Gas Officers (4 weeks): To train AGF, AAF, and ASF officers other than CWS in the duties of unit gas officers.

Flame Thrower (2 weeks): To qualify officers and enlisted men to instruct in and supervise the operation and maintenance of flame throwers.

Navy and Coast Guard (4 weeks): To give Naval and Coast Guard officers practical and theoretical training in chemical warfare.

Navy Gas (Officer) (6 days): To train Naval officers in methods and recent developments in protection against chemical agents.

CWS Refresher (10 days): A stand-by course for quick retraining of CWS officers upon commencement of gas warfare.

CWS Familiarization (10 days): To demonstrate to ranking officers the potentialities of offensive chemical warfare; a stand-by course to be given in the event of gas warfare.

CWS Officer Candidate (17 weeks): To qualify candidates for commission as second lieutenants, AUS, for duty in the CWS.

Gas Noncommissioned Officers (4 weeks): To qualify members of AGF, AAF, ASF, and of Navy, Marine Corps, Coast Guard, and WAC, to fulfill duties of gas NCO's in their units.

---

[27] ASF Manual M3, 18 Nov 44 and C1, 16 Apr 45.

Navy Gas (EM) (6 days): To train Navy enlisted personnel in duties relative to defense of naval units and shore stations against chemical attack.

Toxic Gas Handlers (2 weeks): To train military and naval service enlisted personnel in the efficient and safe handling of toxic chemicals.

In view of the fact that MTP specialist schooling was offered elsewhere, the number of Chemical Warfare School courses conducted during the war was large, if not excessive, for a school of this size. The diversity of background represented by the students was greater than that found in any other special service school. Since the training facilities of the school were placed so generally at the disposal of agencies outside Army Service Forces control, little was done to regulate the flow of students; consequently, the training load could seldom be anticipated precisely. These factors all combined to make operation of the Chemical Warfare School a challenging and rewarding undertaking.

Although most CWS officers who filled tactical assignments during the war received some training at the Chemical Warfare School, those officers whose principal wartime duties were performed at CWS installations were in many cases not so fortunate. At best, the school training of CWS personnel was spotty.

The primary reason why training of CWS officers was not begun earlier and why it was not given to more individuals was the lack of understanding, both on the part of the school and the Training Division in the Chief's Office, of the true training mission of the CWS. The early school administration lacked a comprehensive view of the over-all functions of the Chemical Warfare Service. Because of the school's preoccupation with the tactics and technique of chemical warfare and with gas defense instruction, it was inclined to overlook the fact that the CWS was primarily a technical and supply branch. It therefore failed to move aggressively in extending school training into the fields of procurement, supply, and related activities; and its faculty was always short of instructors well grounded in such subjects.

The Chief's Office to a considerable extent shared the school's predilection for tactical rather than logistical instruction. At least, it was slow in correcting or compensating for this obvious tendency on the part of the school. It was tardy in presenting to other agencies of the Chemical Warfare Service the importance of school training in facilitating the nontactical functions of the branch. Because of the late date at which the training of CWS personnel was actively undertaken at the school, it was difficult if not impossible to recover the ground that had been lost during the period of partial mobilization. Responsibility for this situation rested more with the

OC CWS than with the school. The essential job of the school was to teach the students who were sent to it, according to programs of instruction approved by higher authority; it had no responsibility for the selection of students and it was only partially involved in the initiation of new courses.

A greater degree of prescience in the period when war was foreshadowed undoubtedly would have simplified the wartime operations of the Chemical Warfare School and provided for increased effectiveness. These operations proved to be much more extensive than had been considered likely for a major war in which toxic chemical agents were not employed. At the same time the development of the school was not in fullest measure in the direction of meeting the immediate training requirements of the Chemical Warfare Service. What was lacking at the outset was a clear picture of the school as an integral part of the larger undertaking of CWS wartime training, a picture which in fact only developed in complete outline as the war progressed. Consequently, false starts were sometimes made and opportunities were lost which could not be retrieved. The whole record of the school's wartime accomplishments, however, is impressive, particularly in the field of protection against chemical attack. Here the impetus of its work extended to all elements and echelons of the armed forces.

CHAPTER XV

Officer Candidates

OCS Role in Officer Procurement

During World War I the Chemical Warfare Service obtained its officers either by transfer from other branches or by the direct commissioning of specially qualified civilians. Prior to World War II a substantial body of Reserve and National Guard officers had been developed, a group which, it was recognized, would have to be reinforced in time of emergency by the temporary commissioning of some technical specialists. While the need for officer candidate training was appreciated, there was no expectation that this training would contribute materially to the officer procurement program in a major war. Actually the CWS Officer Candidate School in World War II provided a total of 6,413 second lieutenants, many of whom rose to field grade before the end of hostilities.[1]

When war was declared, nearly one thousand CWS officers were on active duty, 90 percent of whom were nonregulars. After Pearl Harbor the officer procurement curve began to rise more sharply. The officer strength of the CWS stood at approximately 1,800 when the first OCS class of 20 second lieutenants was commissioned at Edgewood on 4 April 1942. Most of the officers then on duty were Reservists or men having other military background. It became clear by this time that other sources would have to be tapped to provide the large increase of officers required by the expanding CWS program.

Compared to the number of officers procured from other sources, the OCS contribution was negligible even in the late summer of 1942, when CWS officer strength of three thousand included only two hundred OCS graduates (*Chart 11*). The rapid rise in OCS output, which began in the fall of 1942, brought the two lines into approximate balance so that for the next nine months the increase in officer strength had an almost direct

---

[1] CWS OCS class records.

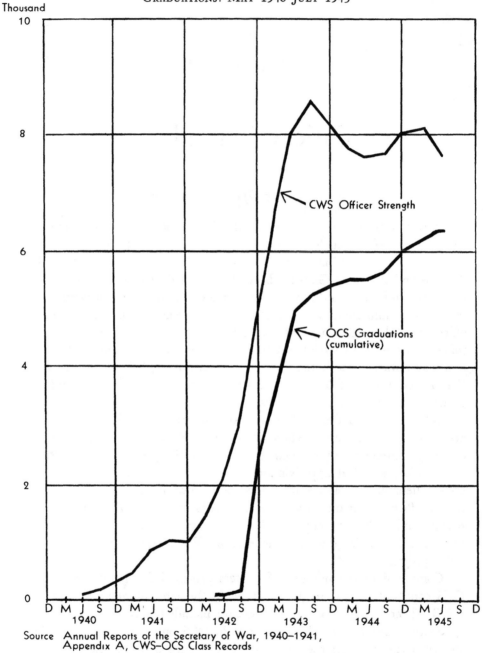

CHART 11—CHEMICAL WARFARE SERVICE OFFICER STRENGTH AND OCS
GRADUATIONS: MAY 1940–JULY 1945

Thousand

CWS Officer Strength

OCS Graduations
(cumulative)

D M J S D M J S D M J S D M J S D M J S D M J S D
1940   1941   1942   1943   1944   1945

Source Annual Reports of the Secretary of War, 1940–1941,
        Appendix A, CWS–OCS Class Records

relation to OCS graduations; in other words, during this period the Officer Candidate School was almost the only source from which the Chemical Warfare Service derived its new officers. When both lines began to level off toward the end of 1943, total officer strength still exceeded OCS graduations by approximately three thousand; yet two out of every three CWS officers had received their commissions at the Officer Candidate School.[2]

Capacity Targets

The Army's officer candidate program of World War II got under way in July 1941 with the opening of ten schools.[3] Each was under direct control of the chief of an arm or service. No school was authorized for the training of CWS officer candidates at this time although provision was made for CWS soldiers selected as officer candidates to be trained and commissioned in other branches.[4] In August the Chief, CWS, was advised by the War Department to be prepared to open a small chemical warfare OCS in January 1942. The War Department confirmed this decision in November 1941, when it increased the number of officer candidate schools from ten to thirteen and established a total capacity for 3,595 students, of which the CWS school was allowed a quota of twenty.[5]

It soon became standard procedure for the War Department to set quarterly the capacity of each officer candidate school. Using this figure as a basis, the branch concerned drew up an allocation of vacancies to senior commands such as armies, corps areas, and replacement training centers. This allocation was reported to The Adjutant General, who then handled the distribution of quotas, including those to overseas commands.[6] The War Department thus retained control over the size of the schools. Such centralized control appeared necessary since capacities of the schools were dictated by requirements for officers which in turn were computed from a frequently changing troop basis.

This arrangement held until March 1943, when control over officer candidate enrollment was delegated to the three major commands of the

[2] Although records as to total CWS officers and of OCS graduates are exact, only a rough estimate is available of the number of OCS graduates transferred to other branches during the war.

[3] The location and type of these schools are indicated in Biennial *Rpt of the Chief of Staff, 1939–41*. Chart 8.

[4] Ltr, AGO to CofS GHQ *et al.*, 30 Aug 41, sub: Officer Candidate Schools. AG 352 (8–23–41) MT–C–M.

[5] WD Cir 245, 26 Nov 41.

[6] WD Cir 126, 28 Apr 42.

War Department. After a year of operation under this arrangement the War Department in March 1944 resumed control over OCS enrollments, returning to a procedure essentially similar to that which had been in force initially.[7]

The Chief, CWS, was advised informally from time to time by the General Staff as to major changes in OCS capacity foreseen by variations in the chemical troop basis. The first of several such notifications came shortly after the declaration of war when the CWS was directed to plan for the expansion of its officer candidate school to a capacity of 100 "at the earliest practicable date," with the understanding that further slight increases might be necessary.[8]

The latter proved to be an understatement. Four months later, the Chemical Warfare Service was instructed to expand its officer candidate school to accommodate a total of 1,150 enrollees, this goal to be reached by 1 September 1942.[9] Within a few weeks, and while plans were being made to accomplish this increase, the CWS studied the current troop basis as then listed for 1942 and computed the CWS officer requirements for 31 December 1942 to be:[10]

Total_____5,091

CWS officers with AAF_____ 800
AGS and ASF units_____1,186
Branch duty_____ _____3,105

On the basis of these figures, the Chief, CWS, recommended to the War Department that capacity of its officer candidate school be increased from the then authorized figure of 1,150 to a new level of 3,068. This recommendation was formally approved in June 1942.[11] By this time the OCS had produced, in two classes, a total of 46 second lieutenants.

Although this ambitious new objective, equaling a thousand graduates a month, was officially adopted, it was never attained. The peak of OCS production came in December, when 895 graduates received commissions.

---

[7] The variations in operating procedure may be traced in the several revisions of AR 625–5 issued during the war.

[8] Memo, ACofS G–3 for C CWS, 16 Jan 42, sub: Increase in CWS OCS. G–3/43276.

[9] Ltr, Dir of Tng SOS to C CWS, 16 May 42, sub: OCS. SOS SPTRS 352.

[10] Memo, C CWS for ACofS G–3, 2 Jun 42, sub: Expansion of Chemical Warfare Officer Candidate School. CWS 353/342. For actual strength figures as of December 1942, see Appendix A.

[11] Memo, Deputy Dir of Tng, SOS for C CWS, 9 Jun 42, sub: Expansion of CW OCS. SOS SPTRS 352 CWS OCS.

But already the trend of enrollments had begun to decline. The situation had been correctly appreciated two months earlier by the Training Division, OC CWS, when an analysis was made of the officer candidate procurement program. This predicted the following officer requirements as of 1 July 1943:[12]

Total	7,740
Plus 5% attrition	387
Grand total	8,127
CWS officers with AAF	1,500
AGF (including CW units)	2,595
Service commands	650
CWS installations	2,995

The CWS therefore had to plan in October 1942 to more than double its commissioned officer strength during the next nine months. It expected to obtain 1,400 officers by direct appointment to the then authorized Army Specialist Corps. A mere handful of ROTC graduates could be counted on. The remainder of the new officers needed would have to come from the Officer Candidate School. The Training Division estimated that classes then in session or scheduled would meet most of this requirement and that after 1 January 1943 the OCS production rate would be greater than needed. The Chief of the Training Division, therefore, recommended that the school capacity be reduced to 1,440 students.[13] As it turned out, this was still somewhat beyond CWS requirements. Decreasing demand for officers was strikingly reflected by the cutback in authorized capacity to 100 as of 1 July 1943.[14]

In March 1944 the Chief, CWS, was advised by The Adjutant General that because of declining requirements the CWS Officer Candidate School would be closed with graduation of the 28th Class on 8 July 1944. This action was viewed with misgivings by the CWS. General Porter immediately submitted a formal recommendation that the school not be closed; that instead it continue to operate on a stand-by status to accommodate three

---

[12](1) Memo, C CWS for Dir of Tng, SOS, 28 Oct 42, sub: Capacity of Chemical Warfare Officer Candidate School. CWS SPCW 352/1. (2) CWS officer strength of 1 July 1943 was 8,177 thus making this an uncannily accurate forecast.

[13] Memo, Col E. F. Bullene for C CWS, 9 Oct 42, no sub. CWS 352/1-370.2.

[14] Memo, AGO for C CWS, 8 Jun 43, sub: Capacity for Chemical Warfare Service Officer Candidate School. AG (5 Jun 43) OB–D–SPGAO.

classes per year of fifty students each.[15] Although the CWS was at this time somewhat overstrength in officers, two good reasons supported this proposal. The requirement for platoon leaders with chemical mortar battalions was continuous. And immediate need for additional officers was forecast should gas warfare materialize—a consideration that always influenced CWS planning. But in spite of these strong arguments against entirely disbanding the efficient OCS organization that had been developed during the preceding two years, the War Department decided otherwise and directed that the school be suspended on 8 July.[16]

This dictum remained in effect for over two months, during which time only one class (the 28th) was in session at the school. Shortly before the graduation of this class the War Department changed its mind and revoked the suspension order.[17] The 29th class was accordingly convened on 17 July 1944, and by October four classes were being accommodated with a total enrollment exceeding 700 students. No further major changes of capacity were directed until after the cessation of hostilities.

The wide fluctuations which thus characterized top level direction of CWS officer candidate training had the inevitable effect of confusing the administrative operation of the school.

Facilities

The first OCS classes conducted at Edgewood Arsenal were housed in newly built structures provided in connection with the Chemical Warfare School enlargement program of 1941. This arrangement was satisfactory as long as the OCS enrollment was small. In order to accommodate the greatly increased student body projected for the summer of 1942, it became necessary to provide much more extensive facilities than could be made available in the immediate vicinity of the Chemical Warfare School. The pending transfer of the Replacement Training Center to Alabama provided an answer to the problems of increased OCS facilities—in fact, the requirement for OCS training at Edgewood Arsenal was one of the reasons influencing the War Department decision to relocate the Chemical Warfare Service RTC.

The inadequacies that hampered the training of replacements at Edgewood Arsenal also hindered the training of officer candidates, once the vacated RTC area was occupied by the Officer Candidate School in the

---

[15] Ltr, C CWS to CG ASF, 6 Apr 44, sub: CW Officer Candidate School. CWS 353 ASF.
[16] WD Cir 150, 15 Apr 44.
[17] WD Cir 261, 26 Jun 44.

summer of 1942. Lack of sufficient barracks was temporarily met by housing several hundred officer candidates in tents; yet need for other facilities was imperative. New temporary construction, authorized by the War Department to meet OCS requirements, and substantially completed by December 1942, included: 8 school buildings, 2 mess halls, 1 administration building, 1 post exchange, 1 supply building, and 17 barracks.[18]

Although academic and administration buildings for the accommodation of officer candidates were eventually provided in adequate measure, field training facilities at the Chemical Warfare Center were never entirely suitable. This was particularly true of ranges for firing of chemical mortars and for the reconnaissance and occupation of mortar positions. Because competition between the Chemical Warfare Center and Aberdeen Proving Ground for the use of the limited range areas on Gunpowder Neck was keen, it was necessary to reschedule a great deal of officer candidate training.

The final location of the Officer Candidate Division at a distance of some two miles from the Chemical Warfare School proper had the inescapable effect of lessening intimate supervisory control of officer candidate training by the school authorities. This minor difficulty might have been avoided had more integrated planning of OCS facilities been feasible.

Selection of Candidates

One out of every five candidates who entered the CWS Officer Candidate School failed to complete the course. Important among the several reasons which explain this waste of training effort were defects in the system of officer candidate selection.

Until the closing months of the war, final selection of students to attend the course was made by senior field commanders to whom quota allotments were made by the OC CWS. Criteria for selection were announced by the War Department. A direct relationship was evident between the caliber of selectees and the size of quotas. As long as enrollment was limited, there was little difficulty in obtaining qualified men to meet the quotas. After the demand for officers rose rapidly in 1942, a less impressive type of officer candidate began to appear at the school. This was a consequence of War Department policy probably as much as it was a result of mistakes by selection boards at Army installations.

Initially, students were required to attend schools of their own arms and

---

[18] CWS History of Training, Pt. I, Training of Officer Candidates, p. 9.

services unless they were found particularly qualified for service in another branch.[19] The acute shortage of officers which developed immediately after the declaration of war necessitated a reversal of this policy. In February 1942, the War Department announced that "it is essential that all schools be filled to capacity for each course with the most highly qualified applicants, irrespective of the arm or service of applicants." [20] The enlisted strength of the Chemical Warfare Service was inadequate to provide enough candidates to fill the quotas that were being set up in the spring of 1942. The classes, therefore, became crowded with airmen, infantrymen, and soldiers from other services, mostly men who for one reason or another were unsuccessful in obtaining admission to officer candidate schools of their own branches. The emphasis placed by the CWS officer candidate course on chemical mortar operations proved extremely difficult for men who lacked basic training with chemical organizations, and this accounted for many turnbacks and eventual separations.

Another factor which in the view of the school authorities interfered with the selection of more suitable candidates was lack of appreciation by selecting officers of the necessary qualifications of an officer candidate. Organization commanders were under constant pressure to fill OCS quotas. That many men were sent to the Edgewood Arsenal school who were ineligible for other courses appeared evident to the instructional staff.

Action was finally taken by the War Department toward remedying what had been a source of irritation for two years—the sending of improperly selected trainees to officer candidate schools. In September 1944 certain technical branches, including the CWS, were authorized to make final selection of candidates provisionally selected by local commanders.[21] The controlling factor in this action on the part of branch chiefs was the academic qualification of the applicant, other qualifications having presumably been passed by field commanders. This promising departure in selection procedure was carefully observed by the Chemical Warfare Service. A board of three officers was appointed to study the individual records of applicants as they came in. Only four classes (Nos. 33–36) were enrolled under the new procedure, so that experience with it was limited. Data relating to these four classes are of some significance.[22]

[19] WD Cir 245, 26 Nov 41.

[20] WD Cir 48. 19 Feb 42.

[21] AR 625–5, 12 Sep 44.

[22] Memo, Lt Col Earl A. Shrader for C CWS, 21 Jun 45, sub: Central Selection of Candidates for CWS OCS. CWS 314.7 Training File. About one third of the candidates were not chosen under the central selection system, but came from overseas.

The CWS selection board rejected approximately two out of every three applications presented to it. The result was to limit enrollment in the four final classes to a total of 253 candidates (not counting turnbacks); these classes were the smallest that the school had accommodated since the summer of 1942. This almost drastic action did have the result of cutting losses, under the system of central selection, to the comparatively favorable figure of 15.9 percent. Reduction of losses due to academic failure was particularly notable. Leadership losses, however, now stood in the order of four to one over academic failures—a proportion much higher than encountered earlier.[23] This merely emphasized a fact already recognized—that it is easier to eliminate potential failures on the academic level than in the field of leadership.

A small percentage of the officer candidates were Negroes. The records of these men were in no way distinguishable from those of white students. The Chemical Warfare Center made no distinction between candidates on the basis of race with no segregation whatever in the dormitories or the mess halls. White and Negro students, of course, sat in the same classes.[24]

Staff and Faculty

Before 1942 the academic organization of the Chemical Warfare School was based on the type of subject taught rather than on the type of student. This division of the faculty into groups of technical specialists was logical since up to that time commissioned officers were almost the only students attending the school. The introduction of the officer candidate course into the school curriculum brought about for the first time the development of a faculty group for a special category of students.

The first class of twenty officer candidates was taught by instructors assigned to the various technical divisions of the school, and most of whose specialties were involved to some extent in the OCS course. From the graduates of the first class, four second lieutenants were selected for detail as OCS instructors. Subsequent classes provided many more instructors and tactical officers to meet the rapidly increasing requirements of late 1942. At the same time older and more experienced instructors were drawn in lesser numbers from other departments of the school.

The CWS Officer Candidate School was headed by a field officer, usually

---

[23] *Ibid.*

[24] These statements are based on interviews with a number of former OCS candidates.

a lieutenant colonel, who was officially styled Director of the Officer Candidate Division of the Chemical Warfare School.

Training operations were divided among three sections—academic, field service, and troop command. The academic section handled all technical instruction. Tactics and basic military instruction were responsibilities of the field service section. Infantry drill, physical training, mass athletics, and guard duty were all conducted by the candidates themselves under supervision of tactical officers who were members of the troop command section. The latter section was also responsible for the military administration of the corps of candidates.

The three operating sections accounted for all the scheduled and non-scheduled activities of officer candidate training on a simple, well-defined basis. The activities of the three sections were in turn co-ordinated by an assistant director in charge of instruction. This officer also was responsible for the provision of training aids, the preparation of schedules, and the maintenance of students' grades and ratings. In 1944, the office of the assistant director in charge of instruction was reorganized as the plans section of the school on a level with the three operating sections without, however, changing these designated functions.

Since the officer candidate course aimed at two distinct objectives—the development of military leadership and training in military techniques—two somewhat distinct types of faculty members were required: the tactical officer and the technical instructor. Tactical officers were assigned to the platoons, companies, and battalions into which the corps of candidates was organized. It was their special function to observe and report on the manner in which the candidates carried out the various staff assignments incident to the command of these units. An important duty of the tactical officer was to detect those disqualifying defects in bearing and personality which, as "leadership deficiency," accounted for the relief of at least one out of every five who failed the course. It was the tactical officer more than anyone else who was responsible for developing the potential leader into a dependable platoon commander. Thus in a broad sense the tactical officer was an instructor, although he taught less by precept than by example and suggestion. Tactical officers were usually recruited from promising graduates of recent OCS classes, the number assigned being directly proportional to the size of the student body. The able manner in which these newly commissioned second lieutenants assumed the role of tactical officer appeared to minimize need for more formal preparation for this important work.

The academic instruction of candidates was in the hands of officers who for the most part were somewhat older, more experienced as teachers, or who were otherwise qualified in specialized subjects. Building up this part of the faculty on the whole presented more of a problem than did selection of the tactical officers and supervision of their work. Well-qualified teachers were difficult to obtain and many of the new instructors did not prove adequate. In an effort to improve the situation the school instituted a teacher training course in November 1942. This course, which was conducted by two officers experienced in teacher training, was ten hours in length and was given over a five-day period. It resulted in considerable improvement in the instruction at the OCS.[25]

Although the job of forging a competent OCS faculty proceeded at a fairly rapid pace, progress along these lines could scarcely keep up with the accelerated growth of the school during the first year of its existence. The factor of instructor competence was directly related to the curve of instructor strength. Between June and October 1942 the strength of the staff and faculty soared from 31 to 215. This rate of expansion definitely exceeded the rate at which new instructors could be assimilated into the school staff. It was not until after the peak had been reached and instructor strength began to recede in the spring of 1943 that the highest standards of training effectiveness were reached.

A fair picture of the school at the end of December 1942 is afforded by the report of a training inspection conducted by an infantry officer, Col. C. L. Irwin.[26] At this time, 1,880 officer candidates were in training, the ratio of instructors to students being 1 to 15.8. Instructors were reported as being well qualified in their subjects. However, their presentations were not being adequately supervised, nor was the instructor training program sufficiently advanced. These were criticisms aimed more particularly at the Chemical Warfare School than at the Officer Candidate Division of the school. For some time the OCS had been separated physically from the administrative headquarters of the Chemical Warfare School and was naturally inclined to seek emancipation from the academic control of the commandant's staff.

An improved situation was reported following a training inspection of the Officer Candidate School in June 1943.[27] At that time the student body was down to 470 officer candidates. Ratio of instructors to students was 1

[25] CWS History of Training, Pt. I, Training of Officer Candidates, p 43.

[26] Memo, C Schools Br for Dir of Tng SOS, 30 Dec 42, sub: Tng Inspection, CWS OCS SOS SPTRS 333 1

[27] Memo, Lt John O Richardson for C CWS, 21 Jun 43, sub: Inspection of CWS OCS. CWS SPCVK 331

to 3.3, a fact which indicated that faculty reductions had not kept pace with the shrinking instructional load of the school. However, the instructor-student relationship was reported as being very satisfactory, largely because sufficient instructors were available to permit organizing small classes of from thirty to thirty-five students. Instructors were found to be well qualified. Instruction was adequately supervised under the general direction of the assistant commandant, Chemical Warfare School. Training of the faculty in instructional procedures was well advanced. The pattern of teaching methods followed in the course indicated real progress in emphasizing applicatory work, as indicated by the following figures:[28]

Teaching method	Percentage of course
Outdoor exercise	52
Conference	26
Classroom exercise	10
Film	5
Map problem	4
Lecture	3

Training Program

The officer candidate course emphasized general military rather than specialist training. It was by no means a satisfactory substitute for a basic course of instruction in the duties of a technical branch such as the CWS. But in 1942 the demand for young officers was urgent and immediate. The time allotted for OCS training was little more than enough to qualify candidates to meet the responsibilities of platoon commanders in modern warfare. Since there was no assurance that once an OCS graduate left the Chemical Warfare Center he could ever return for more schooling, the program for officer candidate training had to be drawn up with this in mind. About two-thirds of the instruction was directed to the duties of junior combat commanders, which by and large were well covered. The remaining third of the program was in the nature of basic training in CWS subjects, the coverage of which was necessarily sketchy.

The primary objective of CWS officer candidate training was, from the start, the production of combat rather than staff officers. A steady demand for lieutenants to serve with chemical mortar battalions quickly absorbed many graduates of the Second to the Eleventh Classes. Once the first phase of battalion mobilization was completed, increasing numbers of graduates

[28] *Ibid.*

went to chemical service-type companies. The stress on qualifications for combat leadership persisted into 1943 when the mobilization of additional chemical mortar battalions was begun. The requirements of the Army Air Forces for junior CWS officers were running so heavy in the last half of 1942 that special emphasis was placed on training in aviation subjects for the Sixth to the Thirteenth Classes. However, the long-range mission of the OCS course was "to train officer candidates in the basic military subjects which will qualify them as combat platoon officers." [29]

Focusing of OCS training upon the needs of mortar battalions had both advantages and disadvantages. Although these units were clearly outside of the operational control of the Chemical Warfare Service, the provision of officers to command them was a CWS responsibility which the branch regarded as of primary importance. If the officer candidate could qualify for mortar company duty, he was presumed to be potentially capable of succeeding in other assignments. The result of this policy was that the CWS officer candidate who survived to graduation emerged as primarily a combat leader even though the proportion of CWS officers who attained combat duty was relatively small. The concentration of OCS training upon a target which varied from the norm for CWS officers may have been objectionable in theory, yet in practice it proved successful.

The prewar plan of the Chemical Warfare Service for officer candidate training had been written in general terms. If an officer candidate school were to be operated under the Protective Mobilization Plan, it would be "established and conducted" by the Chemical Warfare School. Classes of three-month duration would begin at M–30, M–60, and monthly thereafter. Each class would have about 150 candidates. [30]

The length of course as here indicated merely conformed to provisions of Mobilization Regulations 3–1. The schedule for the first course was thus developed by the Chemical Warfare School to cover thirteen weeks of instruction. This period of training continued in effect until May 1943, when the War Department extended the length of all OCS courses to seventeen weeks. [31]

The lengthening of the officer candidate course paralleled the extension of replacement training from thirteen to seventeen weeks, a move also directed by the War Department during the summer of 1943. The selection

[29] Officer Candidate Div, CW School, Instruction Cir 3, 9 Sep 44.
[30] 1940 CWS PMP, Annex 8, 10 Sep 40. AG 381, Mob Plan 1940.
[31] WD Memo S350-29-43, 25 May 43, sub: Extension of Courses at OCS

of identical time-cycles for both enlisted and officer candidate training was somewhat coincidental. The proposal to add four weeks to the OCS course was initiated by Army Service Forces some time before extension of replacement training was taken under consideration.[32] The idea of lengthening the course, although opposed by Army Ground Forces, was approved by the War Department for two special reasons. As was true of replacement training, there was clear need for more emphasis on the strictly military training of officer candidates. Another weighty consideration at the time was the question of failures and turnbacks at all officer candidate schools, a matter which had assumed such proportions by the end of 1942 as to require special study by The Inspector General. A longer training period, it was argued, would result in fewer rejects and more graduates.

The seventeen-week program went into effect at Edgewood Arsenal with the Twenty-sixth Class beginning 5 July 1943. Failures were less in this and succeeding classes than they had been under the thirteen-week program. This was due in part to the fact that training quotas by then had dropped and made possible such a high margin of supply over demand that a more satisfactory type of candidate was being enrolled. The longer course did permit a desirable elaboration of general military training which was principally represented by applicatory field exercises. (*Table 16*)

The Problem of Failures

The officer candidate course differed from all other service school courses in that the OCS student was constantly subjected to searching personal scrutiny. The candidate had to satisfy the staff and faculty as to his aptitude for eventual commissioned rank. At best, the initial selection of candidates had been provisional; it was the responsibility of the school to determine finally, as a result of close observation over an extended period of time, those who actually were qualified, both mentally and physically, to assume the responsibilities of military leadership. In OCS training the function of separating the fit from the unfit ranked barely second in importance to the function of pedagogy.

Under War Department policy, no candidate was relieved from an officer candidate school before completion of one third of the course, except for disciplinary action or at his own request.[33] During the last two thirds of each

---

[32] Memo, CG ASF for ACofS G–3, 23 Apr 43, sub: Increase in Length of OC Courses. ASF SPTRS 352 11
[33] WD Cir 48, 19 Feb 42.

TABLE 16—HOURS OF SCHEDULED INSTRUCTIONS, CWS OCS

SUBJECTS	13–Week Program (to July 1943)	17–Week Program (after July 1943)
General Subjects		
Total	427	562
Assault course	0	8
Bayonet technique	0	8
Booby traps	0	8
Camouflage	5	13
Combat organization tactics	39	0
Combat orientation	0	13
Company administration	26	36
Dismounted drill	19	37
Field fortifications	2	8
General tactics	45	82
Infantry weapons	17	43
Inspections	11	13
Interior guard duty	3	3
Map and aerial photo reading	32	37
Marches and bivouacs	3	3
Mass athletics	18	18
Mess management	7	7
Meteorology	9	9
Methods of instruction	10	10
Military discipline and customs	4	3
Military law	13	10
Miscellaneous subjects	4	19
Motor transport	18	18
Physical training	38	39
Sanitation and first aid	8	13
Scouting and patrolling	19	36
Signal communications	8	8
Student presentations	20	20
Supervised study	12	12
Tactical march	9	0
Training management	28	28
CWS Technical Subjects		
Total	211	296
Antigas protection	54	63
Chemical agents	26	26
Chemical mortar technique	56	70
Chemical tactics	0	59
CWS aviation	30	40
CWS matériel	17	17
Chemical warfare developments	0	3
Gunners' examination	28	18

Source CWS OCS Records.

course, however, there was a constant weeding out of candidates for failure to meet the exacting standards of the schools. This process at the CWS school was fair, it was fully understood by the candidates, and it was impartially administered. The school authorities from the start adopted a firm stand in resisting pressures from any direction that involved discrimination for or against any candidate. The success of the school in withstanding such pressures did much to ease the troublesome question of separations. Candidates who successfully completed the course were convinced, upon graduation, that they had won commissions through their own efforts.

For purposes of supervisory control, the course of instruction was divided into two-week "blocks," with each block given a distinctive initial. The candidate's work was measured in each of these periods, the yardstick of measurement differing for academic and for nonacademic progress. Often the two types of instruction merged to such an extent that it was impossible to draw a clear line between them. In either case, action leading to dismissal usually grew out of formal reports on the student's work. The report on graded papers was a reasonably precise, objective evaluation of academic progress while the report on nonacademic activity often had to be based upon the observer's opinion.

Failure in academic subjects was relatively easy to determine. The school devised a scheme of graduated markings under which a discredit point value was established for all rated papers falling beneath the passing grade of seventy. This table was published in mimeograph form and a copy furnished to each candidate upon enrollment. Whenever accumulated discredit points in any two-week block exceeded designated limits, the student was called before the school executive and warned that he was being placed on a probationary status as to academic deficiency. In many cases this action was sufficient to spur the candidate to better grades. Where deficiency continued, the candidate was eventually directed to appear before a board of officers who considered his case personally. When the established limit for relief had not been exceeded by more than two discredit points and where the candidate was outstanding in leadership or possessed desirable military experience, the board frequently acted to turn him back to a subsequent class or even, in exceptional cases, to permit him to continue into the next block on a probationary status. But, in most instances, separation from the school by reason of academic failure was automatic when the scale of discredit points for relief was exceeded.

Among failures attributable to leadership deficiency, the largest number were rooted in lack of force, aggressiveness, or an unimpressive military bearing. Physical defects, which showed up more sharply in OCS than in basic training, were also the direct cause of many failures.

Each time a candidate was observed in a supervisory or command capacity, such as marching a section to class, or commanding a platoon at infantry drill or calisthenics, he was graded by his commissioned superiors. At biweekly intervals these and other ratings based upon military deportment were tabulated. Twice during the course, each candidate was required to grade every other member of his platoon in military leadership so that the students' own ratings combined with the ratings of the platoon, company, and battalion commanders provided an index to the relative standing of each trainee.[34] This system of marking while not perfect did afford a useful guide in indicating which candidates might be below average in qualities essential to military command.

Demerits assessed for conduct delinquencies were also taken into consideration in determining a candidate's ability to accommodate himself to the disciplinary requirements of the course. Delinquencies were grouped into four classes, each carrying appropriate demerit values. These were published for the information of candidates in an OCS instruction circular.[35] Serious offenses were in most cases brought before an Honor Committee of the student body which recommended to the director of the Officer Candidate School whether the offense merited dismissal. Misconduct, however, accounted for only a small number of separations; on the whole the behavior of officer candidates was exemplary.

When the cumulative class record of the candidate, either academic or nonacademic, definitely fell below the standard set by the school, appearance before the Status Board was mandatory. This board consisted of three officers, at least one being of field grade. The board interviewed the individual, considered the records, and, where deficiency in leadership was involved, discussed the matter with his platoon commander. The personal impression made by the candidate upon the board obviously carried considerable weight in the determination of each case. After the hearing, the Status Board recommended to the commandant, Chemical Warfare School, that the candidate either be relieved from the course, be turned back to a succeeding class, or in exceptional cases be continued on probationary status. The action of the commandant on these recommendations was final.

[34] 2d Ind, Dir CWS OCS, 15 Jan 43, to CG CW Center, to ltr C Tng Div OC CWS to Comdt CW School, 5 Jan 43, sub: Dismissal of Officer Candidates. CWS SPCVK 351.242 CW School 1-5-43.

[35] Officer Candidate Div, CW School. Instruction Cir 3, 4 Sep 44.

There was a relationship, as has been indicated, between the type of selectee sent to the Officer Candidate School and the size of the student quotas. In the first six CWS classes, enrolling an average of thirty-six students, losses from all causes were negligible. The problem of failures began with the Seventh Class, which had 226 students. It became acute late in 1942 under the simultaneous impact of two adverse factors—an accentuated demand for officer candidates and an overrapid development of the instructional staff.

The whole problem of failures was closely studied by the school authorities, especially when (with the Fifteenth Class) losses climbed to the high figure of 33.4 per cent.[36] A survey of failures completed by the school on 4 August 1943, disclosed a number of interesting facts. Of 5,388 enrollees who had entered the school up to and including the Twenty-second Class, only 1,420 candidates had a background of CWS experience; and failures ran consistently higher for men whose basic training had been in other branches.[37] It was notable that the number of Medical Department soldiers sent to the school was disproportionately high, almost equaling the number of candidates selected from CWS units. From the case histories studied at this time it was apparent that:

a) Many candidates came to the school under the misapprehension that the course was primarily scientific rather than tactical in nature.

b) Many listed the CWS school on their applications as a secondary choice without having serious interest in chemical warfare.

c) Others filed applications largely because their organization commanders were required to fill OCS quotas.

The high rate of failures experienced late in 1942 and early in 1943 began to fall off in the latter year, after which a generally downward trend was followed until the end of the war. In the thirty-six OCS classes conducted at the Chemical Warfare Center prior to the cessation of hostilities, a total of 8,068 candidates were enrolled. Of these, 1,660 were relieved from the school before graduation.[38] Academic failures accounted for 696 dismissals. Resignations, unclassified as to cause, totaled 415. Leadership deficiencies were directly responsible for 352 separations. Other causes were: miscellaneous (including physical defects), 144; conduct, 53. Of all OCS

---

[36] CWS OCS class records.

[37] Ibid.

[38] This figure does not include turnbacks, who were either graduated or dropped in later classes

students, 8.6 percent failed for academic reasons, 4.3 percent for leadership deficiencies, and .7 percent for bad conduct. These percentages were somewhat higher than those in AGF officer candidate schools.[39]

Although the full implications of the recorded causes of failure of CWS officer candidates may be subject to some question because of uncertainty as to the real reasons behind separations by resignation, the figures are clear enough to indicate a definite preponderance of losses due to academic deficiency and lack of leadership.[40] Another serious cause of failure was the inability of many candidates to master military tactics and techniques, particularly those relating to chemical warfare.

Losses among trainees returned from overseas garrisons to attend OCS courses ran higher than among other categories of trainees. This was partly the result of selecting overseas veterans on the basis of their combat records rather than their intellectual or educational background. The temptation was also strong for some enlisted men to utilize an OCS assignment as a pretext to return to the continental United States without serious intention of completing the course. Although precautionary instructions in this matter were issued by the War Department in 1943, the high rate of failures among overseas candidates at the CWS Officer Candidate School continued until the end of the war.[41] It is doubtful if, on the whole, full use was made by overseas commands of OCS facilities within the United States, or if, in fact, such use was feasible. Organizations had been carefully combed for CWS candidates before they moved overseas. Battlefield promotions were frequent; in the Mediterranean area where casualties among chemical mortar units were high, this means was frankly adopted in preference to officer candidate training. In the Southwest Pacific an Officer Candidate School was operated for the benefit of deserving enlisted men of most arms and services, including the Chemical Warfare Service. The War Department, seemingly as a matter of equity to forces overseas, regularly allotted OCS quotas to theater commanders; yet in the experience of the CWS Officer Candidate School the training of overseas veterans was scarcely rewarding.

In the record of the Officer Candidate School one sees repeated the pattern so characteristic of other phases of chemical warfare training. The

[39] (1) CWS OCS class records (2) Training of Officer Candidates in AGF Special Training Schools, Historical Section, AGF, Study 31, 1946

[40] Palmer, Wiley, and Keast, Procurement and Training of Ground Combat Troops, p 344

[41] Ltr, TAG to CGs, Overseas Theater & Bases, et al., 31 Mar 43, sub. Trainees Relieved at Own Request AG 220 63 (3–18–42) PE–A

distinct stages of this pattern are: first, the handicap of a deliberately delayed start; second, the sudden imposition of a heavy and actually excessive training load; third, limited progress while the load is heaviest toward achieving satisfactory training standards; and fourth, attainment of a highly satisfactory status of training after the critical stage of mobilization has passed.

A criticism raised by officers intimately concerned with operation of the CWS Officer Candidate School was the lack of planning as a result of which unexpectedly heavy loads were suddenly thrust upon the school. This situation was unquestionably disconcerting to those responsible for OCS operation. Such radical capacity changes as have been recorded were easy to decide upon at high levels of authority, yet they were extremely difficult to carry out at the operating level. It was not feasible for the CWS to plan in detail very much in advance because of unpredictable variations in War Department policy regarding chemical warfare, variations which were so painfully reflected in the efforts of the Officer Candidate School to keep abreast of the increasing demands placed upon it during 1942. At the same time it is clear that in some respects CWS planning for the training of officer candidates was inadequate. For example, in the four months which followed the War Department's warning order of August 1941 that the CWS would inaugurate an officer candidate school, it does not appear that active steps were taken to provide even the modest facilities which the project then entailed.

Experience of the Chemical Warfare Service OCS indicates that where officer candidate training is undertaken as branch schooling rather than as branch immaterial schooling, it is necessary to observe some relationship between the size of the branch and the output of the school. At the time the CWS Officer Candidate School was operating at maximum capacity the branch was able to provide no more than a quarter of the candidates who were being enrolled. It was, therefore, not accidental that in this period the peak of student failures was reached.

The effectiveness of OCS training was influenced by another situation over which the school had no control. There developed in 1943 a sizable overproduction of CWS officers. Despite careful estimates of officer requirements, second lieutenants began coming off the OCS production line much faster than they could be absorbed. The expedient adopted was to put the surplus OCS graduate in an officers' pool until he was needed for an active assignment. But to do this—which usually meant spending several months marking time—had a corroding effect; it dulled the keen edge of zest and enthusiasm which had been built up by OCS training. Some men, after they finally drew manning table jobs, were able to recover from the frustrations of pool assignment. Others were not.

One of the problems never entirely solved in World War II was how to handle the CWS officer candidate who possessed desirable technical qualifications but who nevertheless lacked aptitude for military leadership in the degree demanded by OCS standards. Such men, through no fault of their own, measurably swelled the ranks of rejectees. Many of them compared favorably with officers who entered the CWS directly from civil life, yet neither they nor the Army profited from their unfortunate tussle with the Officer Candidate School. This fact was recognized late in the war, when the practice was begun of rating OCS graduates according to demonstrated capacity for either combat or service assignment.

381-812 O - 70 - 26

CHAPTER XVI

Chemical Warfare Training of the Army

The training of the U.S. Army in chemical warfare involved more then purely defensive training to withstand enemy gas attack. It included, as well, training in the offensive employment of chemical weapons. Under prevailing political policy, the United States was to use toxic chemical agents (war gases) only in retaliation, although once gas warfare was begun by the enemy, U.S. retaliation was to be energetic. As to the other two types of chemical munitions—smokes and incendiaries—no such limitation was ever placed upon their use. The Chemical Warfare Service was intimately concerned with instructing in the defensive and offensive techniques relating to all three groups of chemical weapons.[1]

Antigas Training of Air and Ground Units

The training of the U.S. Army to defend itself against an enemy gas attack was certainly not overlooked before the war. Yet, for reasons described in preceding chapters, the level of this training in December 1941 could not be rated as uniformly high.

The status of gas defense training in air and ground force commands at the outset of hostilities affords an interesting contrast. The training in air units was reasonably good. In ground units it was poor. In each instance, the status of training reflected the predilection of the high command.

Air policy on chemical warfare training at the time of the Pearl Harbor attack called for the training of all individuals and all units of the Army Air Forces in defense against chemical attack, as well as for the tactical readiness of combat units for offensive action.[2] The instructions were comprehensive

---

[1] Defensive procedures were outlined in FM 21-40, the tactics and technique of offensive employment in FM 3-5.

[2] This policy was outlined in Air Force Combat Command Memo 50-7 (27 Nov 41), which was superseded by AAF Regulation 135-11 (27 Jul 42), which was in turn superseded by AAF Regulation 50-25 (31 Aug 44). Chemical warfare training overseas was prescribed in Chapter 14, Booklet IV, The Air Force In Theaters of Operation, prepared by Management Control, Hqs AAF, May 1943.

and exacting and, appearing over General Arnold's name, they were accepted by all AAF elements at face value. The training directives, in short, were offshoots of a long established air policy of realism toward chemical warfare; and while it obviously would have been impossible for the several tactical air forces to carry out the directives in every detail, they did comply substantially with the spirit of these instructions. The program itself was adopted and carried forward by AAF headquarters without special prompting by the War Department. The functions of the Chemical Warfare Service under this program were to train CWS officers for duty with air units and to provide special schooling for AAF unit gas personnel.

Elements of the Eighth Air Force arriving in England in the summer of 1942 quickly recognized the grim seriousness with which the Royal Air Force approached the problems of protecting air establishments from gas attack. AAF defensive preparations were soon permeated by the same sense of realism, one which continued to influence AAF attitudes during the course of hostilities. The air command assumed that in the event of gas warfare, probably as much as 80 percent of the toxic agents employed in retaliation would be released from aerial bombs; and it seemed logical to suppose that the brunt of enemy attack would be against air force bases. Doctrine covering chemical defense of air establishments was set forth in considerable detail by the War Department in May 1942. The AAF followed this doctrine in developing protective procedures for the bases it occupied in England and Northern Ireland and, later, for bases in other theaters.[3] Despite the magnitude of the training problems confronting the Army Air Forces, both G–3 and CWS were satisfied that preparations for gas defense of air bases overseas were reasonably adequate.

The situation as to training of ground force units was, as just mentioned, quite different. Here the high command took but a cursory interest in the subject, an attitude that was quickly reflected at many subordinate command posts. The standards announced in official Army publications had little meaning unless they were sympathetically approached at unit levels. And of the factors affecting gas defense training, the attitude of the commanding officer was the most influential. If the division commander was interested in this training, it was encouraged in the regiments and battalions; if not, then little was accomplished. Next to the unit commander, the chemical officer was in a position to contribute most to the success of the gas defense program.[4] The combination of an interested commanding general and a

[3] WD Tng Cir 31, 16 May 42.
[4] Chemical officers were assigned to armies, corps, and divisions.

competent and energetic division chemical officer meant a satisfactory standard of training and consequently, a good state of gas discipline; but ground force units for the most part lacked such a combination.

Another factor that had a direct effect on the gas defense training picture was the over-all status of training of the organization. Until a unit had acquired some proficiency in the use of its own weapons, there was little time for such specialties as chemical warfare. Only after a commanding general had been satisfied that his organizations could acquit themselves well in their primary missions was he inclined to devote attention to antigas training.

Changes in War Department Policy

The cue as to emphasis to be placed on protection against chemical attack in the troop training program came ultimately from the War Department General Staff. For the first time in many years, the War Department annual training directive in force in 1941 omitted reference to gas defense training. This omission was no doubt a result of General Marshall's insistence that this particular directive be streamlined and condensed; when it was written, other features of military training were more retarded and needed more emphasis than the chemical warfare training program. The reasons for this change were not made known to Chief, CWS, who was merely advised that chemical warfare training had been carefully considered and "purposely omitted." [5] This move, together with the fact that gas warfare situations were deliberately ruled out of early ground force maneuvers, was taken to indicate a general lack of interest by higher authorities in this type of training. As a result, the gas defense training situation for ground units, which had been fairly good in 1939, had deteriorated by the early months of 1942 to an all-time low. The Chemical Warfare Service had become most anxious about this matter during the summer of 1941 and was hopeful that with the perfection of their primary training, the divisions, corps, and armies would soon be able to give more attention to operations in situations of gas warfare. But the stepped-up mobilization that followed the Japanese attack seemed to preclude this possibility.

Although the War Department General Staff declined to interpose in the issue of gas warfare situations in the 1941 army maneuvers, staff policy began to change immediately after Pearl Harbor. As a result of the January 1942 War Plans Division study of the use of toxic gases, the AGF agreed to a more realistic approach to antigas training as well as to the use of smokes

---

[5] Memo, ACofS G–3 for TAG, 16 Mar 40, sub: WD Tng Directive, 1940–1941. G–3/30000.

and nontoxic chemicals in future maneuvers. These measures were incorporated in a letter-directive, sent out from General McNair's headquarters in April 1942, which contained the admission that "recent observation of ground force units indicates the need of added emphasis on the training of troops in defense against gas attacks." [6]

The training situation as it existed at the beginning of 1942 required an explicit War Department statement of policy. The Chemical Warfare Service proposed the issuance of such a statement as one of a number of recommendations made with a view to rectifying the entire chemical warfare position of the U.S. Army.[7] On 15 June 1942, the War Department did publish a definite directive on gas warfare training.[8] This directive was broad enough, yet explicit enough, to serve throughout the remainder of the war as a top-level statement of objectives. It called for a degree of perfection in unit as well as individual training that had not been attempted since the period before mobilization of the wartime Army. It required the introduction of gas situations in field exercises and directed that increased attention be given in all service schools to training in principles and methods of gas defense. If the directive could be substantially fulfilled, the Chemical Warfare Service felt, the Army need have no undue fear of gas warfare. It became one of the training responsibilities of the Chemical Warfare Service to see that War Department policy as thus expressed was carried out in zone of interior training.

Revival of Antigas Training

The turning point in gas defense training in World War II may be dated by the issue of the June 1942 War Department directive for chemical warfare training. Before then some soldiers had been taught, in basic training, how to wear a gas mask. A few had learned the specialized duties of unit gas personnel. Yet individual training had not been continuous, the numbers who had been so trained were insignificant, and the training that was given had atrophied through disuse. Units had not learned to live and fight in gassed areas and they had not been taught the offensive employment of chemical weapons. Almost half of the U.S. Army divisions had been mobilized and trained before the revised War Department policy calling for balanced chemical warfare instruction began to take effect. The question

[6] Ltr, AGF to CG Second Army *et al.,* 16 Apr 42, sub: Gas Defense Training. AGF 353/979-GNTRG.

[7] See above, Chapter III.

[8] Ltr, AGO to CGs AGF *et al.,* 15 Jun 42, sub: CW Tng Directive. AG 353 (6-8-42) MS–C–M. See Appendix I.

now to be answered was, could an established training trend be arrested in mid-channel and its direction reversed?

Actually this was feasible to but a limited degree. Units that had completed mobilization training without consideration of the problems of gas warfare could only with great difficulty retrace their steps for this purpose. Divisions moving into theaters of operation unprepared for gas warfare were obliged to attempt such preparation in conjunction with theater orientation training; this was repeatedly undertaken in Hawaii and in England by units temporarily in those areas. But for divisions mobilized late in 1942 and in 1943, the General Staff insisted that protection against gas attack be woven into their unit training from the start.

In 1943 all divisions were devoting many more hours to chemical warfare training than they had in early 1942.[9] Each division ran a chemical warfare school where instruction was given to selected commissioned and noncommissioned officers over a period of three to five days. The subjects covered included agents, munitions, decontamination, and first aid. The officers who completed this course of instruction were appointed regimental and battalion gas officers, and the noncommissioned officers were appointed gas NCO's. In that capacity they trained their respective units in gas defense. The chemical officer retained responsibility for seeing that such training was up to the standards set by the War Department. A feature of gas defense training throughout the ground forces was the requirement that every man in every unit pass through the gas chamber. This exercise was always closely supervised by the division chemical officer and his staff.

By mid-1943 the War Department was attacking the problem of gas warfare on a global basis. For the theaters, it was setting up standards of readiness; for the zone of interior, it was insisting that troops preparing for overseas movement should be trained in defense against gas attack, at least to a point where no more than maintenance training in this specialty would be required after they arrived overseas. War Department policy was spelled out in a radio message from the Chief of Staff to theater commanders on 31 July 1943. This message reiterated the President's announcement on this subject, made 8 June 1943, and stated that, assuming "our enemies may take the initiative in the use of gas, it is essential that gas training, discipline, and equipment in your theater be such that in the event of surprise use of gas by the enemy, casualties may be reduced and initial retaliation will be

[9] This information is based on interviews and communications between the Historical Office and some twenty-five former chemical officers. Corps and division retired files for the World War II period as well as AGF and Chief of Staff files were searched, but little information on chemical warfare training appeared

WOMEN LEAVING CWS GAS CHAMBER *after instruction in use of gas mask Part of lesson is to remove mask before leaving chamber and thereby experi ence effects of tear gas.*

heavy and prompt." [10] Reports were required from all theaters on readiness for chemical warfare as of 1 January 1944, and periodically thereafter.

The key to the readiness of overseas units to engage in gas warfare was the state of their gas discipline. The radio directive of July 1943 necessarily implied that some retraining in the theaters would have to be done before the degree of readiness called for could be attained. Yet obviously the level of this training would quickly be reduced by the continued shipment from the zone of interior of troops inadequately trained for chemical warfare. This matter was brought directly to the attention of AGF by G-3 in a memorandum which stated: "It is therefore necessary that the training of individuals and units being sent to theaters must comply strictly with established standards." [11] The War Department General Staff was determined to exact more complete compliance with the requirements of the 1942 training directive, not only by direct contact with AGF headquarters but also through employment of the Chemical Warfare Service to inspect the progress of gas defense training.

Service-Wide Inspections

During 1943 and 1944, the activities of the Chemical Warfare Service in the field of antigas training were aimed at helping the ACofS G-3 in his effort to develop a better state of preparedness for chemical warfare on the part of ground units still training in the zone of interior. An important means to this end was the procedure set up on September 1943 which provided for the technical inspection of troops and installations by representatives of technical services in order to determine the suitability of equipment and technical training.[12]

The chiefs of the technical services had two distinct fields of responsibility. Each administered an important procurement and supply agency, supervision of which was delegated by the War Department to Headquarters, Army Service Forces. At the same time each branch chief was a technical adviser to the Chief of Staff and/or the Secretary of War in his special field, the Surgeon General in the field of medicine, the Chemical Officer in the field of chemical warfare, and so forth. In this latter capacity, the relationship of the technical branch to the War Department was naturally direct rather than through the commanding general, ASF. It was the practice of the Chief of Staff, when circumstances demanded, to curtail

[10] CM–OUT 1553 through 1560, 5 Aug 43.
[11] Memo, AofS G–3 for CG AGF, 4 Oct 43, sub: CW Training. WDGCT 353.
[12] WD Memo W265–1–43, 22 Sep 43, sub: Tech Inspection of Troops and Installations by Representatives of the Chief of Tech Services of the ASF. AG 333, 27 Aug 43, Case 1.

formality by dealing directly with the technical branches on important technical matters; this procedure was continually employed for determining the status of antigas training during the latter period of the war.

A system of inspection visits was worked out by the Chemical Warfare Service which brought about an improvement, probably as great as possible under the circumstances, in the gas defense training situation. Inspecting officers were sent out from the Field Training Branch of the Training Division, OC CWS, which was located in Baltimore. In a period of fifteen months, these inspectors visited approximately one hundred training and administrative installations of Air, Ground, and Service Forces, including unit and replacement training centers, air bases, ports of embarkation, and training and maneuver areas of field forces. Reports of each inspection were transmitted quickly to G–3, War Department General Staff, affording that office a timely picture of the state of gas defense training of units remaining in the United States. This inspection procedure did more than inform the staff; it enabled the Chemical Warfare Service to get a clear picture of the strengths and weaknesses of the chemical defense training program of the Army, for which it was technically responsible. Before inauguration of the technical inspections procedure, the rigidity of the three-command organization of the War Department precluded technical branches from gaining intimate knowledge of the status of their specialties within ground and air establishments; after 1943, this situation was greatly improved. The fact that AAF, AGF, or ASF headquarters notified the unit or installation that the CWS inspection team was acting for the War Department was itself a spur to better training and accounted for much of the improvement that was later evident.[13]

The technical inspections resulted in improved administration of chemical warfare training throughout the Army. Chemical officers were assigned to AGF replacement training centers to insure more effective individual training of replacements in protection against chemical attack. The Army Ground Forces made greater use of the Chemical Warfare School to train combat personnel as instructors in chemical warfare. The Chemical Warfare Service sent a dozen junior officers on temporary detail to special troop sections of corps and armies in an effort to correct chronic weakness in antigas training of nondivisional units. Responsibility of post chemical officers in the training of nondivisional units was clarified in 1944.[14]

[13] Reports of inspections by CWS and AGF officers on all aspects of training including chemical warfare are in AGF Cml Sec file, 353.02, Rpt of Visits.
[14] WD Cir 237, 12 Jun 44

Although these measures were helpful, gas defense training remained inadequate. In a report to the Deputy Chief of Staff as late as March 1944, ACofS G-3 (Maj. Gen. Ray E. Porter) stated:

As a result of several reports from overseas theaters indicating a deficiency in chemical warfare training, the Army Ground Forces were directed to include chemical phases in all maneuvers of divisions and larger units. . . . It is the opinion of this division that chemical warfare training in the Army has not yet reached a satisfactory standard. . . . The division will continue to pay particular attention to the progress of chemical warfare training.[15]

This judgment was made at a time when full-dress rehearsals were being staged for the invasion of Europe and when American offensives already were beginning to roll in the Central and Southwest Pacific. A year later the situation had scarcely improved. A survey of units formally inspected by The Inspector General during the second quarter of 1945 showed 30 percent to be deficient in defense against chemical warfare and 35 percent unqualified in decontamination procedures.[16] This was a discouraging picture, coming at the end of two years of intensive effort to improve the readiness of the U.S. Army for gas warfare. Despite explicit directives which eventually were supported by all the pressure that G-3 could bring to bear, the fact remained that gas defense training during World War II did not attain a standard satisfactory to the General Staff. The reasons for this situation are worth considering, since they bear on future training of this type.

Shortcomings in Antigas Training

The apathy with which gas defense training was so often regarded by the ground forces may have been rooted in a basic conviction that gas, like the incendiary, had become primarily an air weapon and that its future employment would be principally strategic rather than tactical. Such views were frankly held by air units and accounted for much of the vitality that marked AAF training in chemical warfare throughout the war. Perhaps the principal reason why AGF preparations for chemical warfare did not more nearly approach the objectives set by the Staff is the fact that many commanders never did take seriously the prospect of gas attack in ground combat.

This attitude, prevalent in GHQ in the early days, became even more

---

[15] Memo, ACofS G-3 for DCofS, 6 Mar 44, sub: Chemical Warfare Training. WDGGT 353.
[16] Rpt, Tng Div OC CWS, 19 May 45, sub: Rpt of Inspections and Findings of the Field Br. CWS 314 7 Tng File. This report contains a detailed analysis of CWS training inspections made under reference cited in Note 12. above.

pronounced as the war drew on toward its end. Among the field forces there continued to persist a widespread belief that such comprehensive training as the General Staff demanded was not required. According to the nature and habit of soldiers, this negative attitude, while never openly expressed, still effectively prevented the breath of life from fully entering the antigas training program.

Actually the gas defense program as set down on paper proved to be more comprehensive than circumstances demanded. It undertook to cover more ground than was feasible in view of the psychological factors involved. Until poison gas was really in the air, it was clear that troops would go so far and no farther in energizing protective measures. This fact emerges from an analysis of reports of inspections of gas defense training made by the Chemical Warfare Service during the latter stages of the war.

Notable was a general lack of carefully prepared standard operating procedures for defense against chemical attack.[17] There was little or no inclination on the part of units to require the occasional wearing of gas masks at work, in firing weapons, or in tactical exercises. Frequent deficiences were reported in methods of decontaminating food, water, and equipment. In the field of collective protection, defects in training showed up most clearly, and it was here that the unit commander's attitude was most influential. If unconvinced of the need for chemical warfare training he assigned chemical officers and unit gas officers to other duties which precluded their attention to gas defense. In half of the units surveyed, gas officers and NCO's were not well trained so that instruction was poor. In many instances there were insufficient local schools for training of instructors; where there were schools, however, the training was either excellent or superior. Finally, the failure of army and corps chemical officers to make regular inspections of gas defense training in subordinate units, the inspection reports stated, appeared to be a contributing reason for many unsatisfactory ratings since 27 percent of the units inspected reported never having been visited by CWS staff officers.[18]

Other weaknesses were disclosed by these reports which pointed to defects in the program itself. For example, the basic War Department training guide (FM 21–40) had certain objectionable features. This 271-page manual was too technical for general training use, and failed to differentiate between what should be taught the instructor and what the average trainee

---

[17] This standing operating procedure was prescribed in Appendix III, FM 21–40.
[18] See Note 16. above.

needed to know about chemical warfare.[19] The designation of unit gas officers and noncommissioned officers by regimental, battalion, and company commanders was called for in the manual but was not prescribed in appropriate tables of organization. Failure of the War Department to provide more authentic authorization for unit gas personnel led to endless difficulties.

While some failures in antigas training were thus attributable to indifference on the part of local commanders, some were due to improper supervision, and others grew out of defects in the gas defense program. All of these defects would probably have been corrected quickly enough in the event of gas warfare. The antigas training program of World War II should be judged in the light of what it actually was—a preparatory rather than a final defensive scheme. As such, it might be rated as satisfactory. Much of the time employed in this training was at the expense of other types of military instruction. If at times the degree of preparedness achieved appeared excessive to local commanders, it was on the other hand a source of assurance to high echelons—which were much more sensitive to threats of hostile gas attack.

Three trends in gas defense training of the U.S. Army during the course of the war were definite enough to deserve notice. These were:

Simplicity: Elimination of technical and nonessential detail from instructional material employed in basic training.

Concentration: Need for more intensive training of selected specialists, and less chemical warfare training for the Army as a whole.

Differentiation: Frank recognition of the essential distinction between training needed before the employment of toxic chemicals and that needed after a gas warfare phase begins.

In the matter of simplifying instruction, a great deal had been accomplished by the end of hostilities. A move toward simplification of gas defense training was made possible by the introduction of gas detector kits and other devices for indicating the presence of toxic chemicals.[20] These lessened the importance that had always been placed on nasal identification of war gases by the individual soldier, a knack which was particularly difficult to teach. Another perennial obstacle in training was the old terminology of toxic agents. This terminology was eventually simplified in line with British practice of grouping casualty agents into three easy

---

[19] Some of the objections to the wartime edition of FM 21–40 were eliminated in the postwar issue of this manual (September 1946).

[20] TM 3–290, 27 Mar 44.

classifications: blister gases, choking gases, and nerve poisons.[21] The trend toward more simplified antigas training is tangibly indicated by the publication of a graphic training aid which reduced to postcard size a summary of protective measures.[22]

While the trend during the latter stages of the war was toward curtailing and streamlining basic instruction in chemical warfare, this tendency was accompanied by a rising emphasis on the specialized training of both officers and enlisted men designated as unit gas personnel. The introduction late in the war of a gas officer at the company level indicated at once the continued concern of the War Department in the scheme of gas protection and the need for concentrating instruction in this field.[23] Less reliance upon local schools and greater utilization of service schools for training of antigas specialists was evident as the war ended.

M9 CHEMICAL DETECTOR KIT. *Developed at Edgewood Arsenal in 1944, the M9 kit was one of several devices used to determine presence and type of toxic chemicals.*

Flame, Smoke, and Incendiaries

The need for training troops in the employment of flame weapons arose largely, although not entirely, from the fact that new flame techniques were introduced in World War II. The flame thrower of World War I had serious limitations which restricted its use to very special situations. For this reason the weapon was not regarded seriously by the CWS and its use was seldom taught at service schools. But the development of thickened fuel from 1940 on, together with mechanical improvements, markedly increased the military

[21] FM 21–40, C 4, 15 Sep 44.
[22] Graphic Training Aid 3–2.
[23] FM 21–40, C 5, 1 May 45.

potential of flame projection and did so at a time when tactical operations in the Pacific demanded a weapon of this type.

Fuel thickened by napalm and other materials was even more widely used by tactical air than it was by ground forces, once its value as a filler for fire bombs had been determined. Training in flame warfare was essentially technical training in the Army Air Forces; yet with ground forces it had to be both technical and tactical.

Little flame-thrower training of any kind was undertaken in the Army until mid-1943 when flame throwers began to be manufactured and distributed on an appreciable scale.[24] While responsible only for the supervision of training in the maintenance and operation of the weapon, the Chemical Warfare Service also became involved in instruction with respect to its tactical use. In 1943 a ten-hour course was introduced at Camp Sibert and given to all replacements. This course covered not only maintenance and operation but also tactical employment of the flame thrower. Many of the replacements who took the course were later assigned to infantry units responsible for the employment of the flame thrower in combat.[25]

Both the Corps of Engineers and Infantry had a responsibility for the employment of the flame thrower. Engineer responsibility stemmed from its mission of demobilizing enemy fortifications, a type of operation in which flame throwers could play an important role. Instruction on the tactical use of the flame thrower was included in a three-week course, "Attack on Fortified Areas," given to field grade officers at the Engineer School, Fort Belvoir.[26]

Instruction in maintenance and operation of the flame thrower was offered in infantry and armored divisions where the commanding generals showed an interest. In these divisions the chemical officers inaugurated courses of instruction for gas officers or a limited number of enlisted men from each company. Generally, the division chemical officer carried on this instruction on his own initiative, but in certain divisions the commanding officer of the engineer battalion co-operated closely with the chemical officer.[27]

All infantry and armored divisions devoted some time to smoke training

[24] CWS Rpt of Production, 1 Jan through 31 Dec 45, p. 13.

[25] Interv, CmlHO with Maj Clifton O. Duty, 11 May 56. Major Duty was in charge of flame thrower instruction at Camp Sibert from 1943 to 1945.

[26] (1) Course on Attack of Fortified Areas (TES Z–9). Archives Section, Engineer School, Fort Belvoir. (2) Interv, CmlHO with Col Ellis O. Davis, 11 Apr 56. Colonel Davis was chemical officer of 6th Armored and 42d Infantry Divisions in World War II.

[27] Ltr, Col Raymond J. Anderson to CmlHO, 10 May 56. Colonel Anderson was chemical officer of the 75th Infantry Division in World War II.

MEDIUM TANK EQUIPPED WITH FLAME THROWER *firing on entrance to enemy cave. Picture taken on Okinawa, 1945.*

although the amount of time varied greatly as between divisions. In the early period of the war the shortage of smoke pots and grenades was a factor in the lack of emphasis placed on smoke training. But the chief factor, as in other phases of chemical warfare training, continued to be the attitude of the individual commander. In some divisions little attention was paid to smoke training at any time during the war, while in others approximately as much time was given to this type training after mid-1942 as to gas defense training.

Training of infantry and armored units in smoke operations emphasized, first of all, the defensive aspects. The chemical officer, in units where smoke training was stressed, had each company march through a smoke screen in order that the men might learn the difficulty of keeping direction. Secondly, the offensive use of smoke was treated. The chemical officer and his staff instructed units in the use of smoke pots, grenades, and colored smokes for marking and signaling. Smoke was employed in battalion exercises and in army maneuvers.

Because of the shortages in the supply of incendiary bombs, particularly in the early period of the war, little stress was laid on training in defense against this type munition. Most divisions limited their activity to mass demonstrations. In the few divisions where the supply situation was satisfactory, much more time was devoted to defense against incendiaries. In the 80th Infantry Division, for example, the chemical officer set up a procedure whereby a number of 4-pound thermite bombs were dropped from trees so that members of his staff could conduct practical training in putting out fires and otherwise neutralizing the effects of the bombs.[28] In at least one division, the 75th Infantry Division, each man in each company was trained in the use of incendiary grenades.[29]

Corps chemical officers were responsible for evaluating the results of chemical warfare training in the divisions of their respective corps. In addition, they conducted such training for nondivisional troops throughout the corps. Generally the corps chemical officer conducted this training in the same manner in which the division chemical officer trained prospective gas officers.[30] A unique practice was introduced by the chemical officer of IV Corps, Col. Hugh M. Milton II. In March and April 1942, Colonel Milton established a traveling school which visited training installations throughout the corps. Courses of instruction were drawn up with the assistance of division chemical officers; a number of whom acted as instructors. First to take the courses was the staff of the corps. This was followed by instruction of division personnel, which took ten days. The purpose behind this type of school—it was generally referred to as the "circus"—was to impress the students right at the start of their divisional training with the importance of chemical warfare.[31]

Supervision of training in defense against gas warfare remained the principal mission of the Chemical Warfare Service so far as training the Army in chemical warfare was concerned. Next came the supervision of training in the use of smoke. This was followed, in order of priority, by training in the use of the flame thrower and defense against the employment of incendiaries.

In summary the effectiveness of training against gas warfare is somewhat difficult to assay, because this type of warfare was not resorted to during the war. That this training, as late as March 1944, was not satisfactory, was

[28] Interv, CmlHO with Col John N. Miles, 12 Apr 56. Colonel Miles was formerly chemical officer of the 80th Infantry Division, where he put this procedure into effect.

[29] See Note 27, above.

[30] Interv, CmlHO with Col Timothy Murphy, former chemical officer XI Corps, 23 May 56.

[31] Interv, CmlHO with Hon Hugh M. Milton II, Asst Secy of Army (Manpower and Reserve Forces), 26 Jun 56. Mr. Milton was chemical officer IV Corps in 1942.

the conviction of the Assistant Chief of Staff, G–3. That his judgment appears to have been correct is borne out by the reports of CWS inspectors as late as 1945. One of the chief reasons behind this lack of preparation was the attitude of certain ground force commanders who were convinced that gas warfare was not imminent and who therefore failed to emphasize this type of training. In all instances commanding generals of divisions assigned additional duties to chemical officers.

While the attitude of those commanders with regard to gas warfare is understandable, it is more difficult to understand their attitude toward other types of chemical warfare—smoke, flame, and incendiaries. There certainly was no question about the probability of the use of those munitions on the battlefield. Yet throughout the various ground force divisions there was anything but uniformity in the amount of time and effort devoted to this type of training. But perhaps it is possible to censure ground force commanders too severely. Under pressure to conduct training programs of all kinds the commanding generals naturally had to rely upon the advice of their chemical officers. And in some instances the chemical officers were not active enough in "selling" chemical warfare to their commanders.

The training of the Army for gas warfare, conceived of as the primary training mission of the CWS in the prewar years, unexpectedly became a secondary mission in World War II. What had loomed in peacetime as a more or less secondary mission—the training of service type units and re placements—actually became the chief training responsibility during the war. Of great importance too was the training of chemical mortar battalions which were organized in numbers not contemplated in the peacetime period. Although the ground forces had jurisdiction over these battalions, the CWS had a very active interest in their training. Thus did the exigencies of war and changes in War Department organization and policies make unforeseen requirements in Chemical Warfare training.

Nor was the distinction between plan and reality confined to the training activities of the Chemical Warfare Service. After responsibility for the development, procurement, and storage of incendiary bombs was transferred from the Ordnance Department in the fall of 1941, the CWS undertook a program for which no peacetime plans had been drawn, a program that developed into one of the most important wartime efforts. The assignment of the biological warfare mission to the CWS shortly before the outbreak of war led to large-scale research and development in this new field of endeavor.

Appendix A

TOTAL CHEMICAL WARFARE SERVICE MILITARY PERSONNEL STRENGTH:[a] 31 DECEMBER 1941 TO 31 DECEMBER 1945

End of Month	Total world-wide[b]		Continental United States												Total overseas	
	Officer	Enlisted	Total Off	Total EM	AGF[c] Off	AGF[c] EM	AAF[c] Off	AAF[c] EM	ASF[c] Off	ASF[c] EM	Def Cmd Off	Def Cmd EM	War Dept[d] Off	War Dept[d] EM	Off	EM
1941																
Dec	993	5,591	953	4,614	(e)	(e)	(e)	(e)	(e)	(e)	(e)	(e)	(e)	(e)	40	977
1942																
Jan	1,091	6,412	1,034	5,359	(e)	(e)	(e)	(e)	(e)	(e)	(e)	(e)	(e)	(e)	57	1,053
Feb	1,265	7,065	1,199	5,906	(e)	(e)	(e)	(e)	(e)	(e)	(e)	(e)	(e)	(e)	66	1,159
Mar	1,599	9,420	1,488	8,137	(e)	(e)	(e)	(e)	(e)	(e)	(e)	(e)	(e)	(e)	111	1,283
Apr	1,832	12,068	1,728	10,553	(e)	(e)	(e)	(e)	(e)	(e)	(e)	(e)	(e)	(e)	104	1,515
May	2,094	14,353	1,950	12,296	(e)	(e)	(e)	(e)	(e)	(e)	(e)	(e)	(e)	(e)	144	2,057
Jun	2,287	17,938	2,099	15,040	(e)	(e)	(e)	(e)	(e)	(e)	(e)	(e)	(e)	(e)	188	2,898
Jul	2,634	20,221	2,389	17,078	(e)	(e)	(e)	(e)	(e)	(e)	(e)	(e)	(e)	(e)	245	3,143
Aug	2,855	23,860	2,517	19,971	(e)	(e)	(e)	(e)	(e)	(e)	(e)	(e)	(e)	(e)	338	3,889
Sep	3,019	27,603	2,650	23,311	323	5,779	144	5,401	2,056	9,358	105	2,769	22	4	369	4,292
Oct	3,547	34,423	3,126	30,126	369	9,032	238	7,270	2,352	11,239	112	2,559	55	26	421	4,297
Nov	4,280	36,878	3,801	32,281	458	10,253	284	7,628	2,907	11,817	132	2,576	20	7	479	4,597
Dec	5,192	40,990	4,702	35,856	483	9,776	631	8,723	3,415	14,208	142	3,143	31	6	490	5,134
1943																
Jan	6,018	47,526	5,479	41,806	518	9,938	790	10,678	3,963	17,979	190	3,210	18	1	539	5,720
Feb	6,218	54,009	5,686	48,075	595	10,835	904	13,704	4,016	21,283	151	2,253	20	0	532	5,934
Mar	6,849	55,596	6,223	49,480	685	11,759	1,006	14,727	4,340	20,771	154	2,223	38	0	626	6,116
Apr	7,698	58,108	6,883	48,668	573	8,494	1,143	17,284	4,978	20,538	152	2,352	37	0	815	9,440
May	8,124	57,856	7,178	46,228	520	8,251	992	15,037	5,459	20,644	173	2,296	35	0	946	11,628
Jun	8,103	61,688	6,921	46,166	523	6,288	1,092	16,919	5,087	20,531	193	2,428	26	0	1,182	15,522
Jul	8,177	56,098	6,891	40,273	556	6,599	1,096	12,037	5,140	19,956	71	1,681	28	0	1,286	15,825
Aug	7,984	57,960	6,530	40,859	553	8,374	1,036	11,128	4,683	19,152	232	2,205	33	0	1,447	17,101
Sep	8,584	58,054	7,034	39,456	549	8,812	1,125	10,382	5,255	18,670	70	1,592	35	0	1,550	18,598
Oct	8,551	56,717	6,768	34,165	535	7,901	1,072	8,286	5,105	17,728	16	250	40	0	1,783	22,552
Nov	8,435	57,870	6,632	33,892	573	7,296	1,006	7,406	4,983	18,944	17	243	53	3	1,803	23,978
Dec	8,125	58,485	6,082	32,546	565	7,065	968	6,330	4,446	18,942	16	207	87	2	2,043	25,939
1944																
Jan	7,891	57,394	5,757	29,503	555	6,750	928	4,030	4,176	18,541	17	178	81	4	2,134	27,891
Feb	7,836	56,288	5,579	26,319	632	7,734	911	3,667	3,940	14,908	6	10	90	0	2,257	29,969
Mar	7,881	57,946	5,388	25,624	622	7,557	883	3,392	3,792	14,666	5	9	89	0	2,344	32,322
Apr	7,729	59,875	5,141	24,642	586	6,657	853	3,176	3,622	14,803	4	6	78	0	2,506	35,233
May	7,760	60,296	4,955	23,723	610	6,583	846	3,066	3,424	14,067	3	7	72	0	2,805	36,573

End of Month															
Jun	7,679	59,244	4,855	22,528	566	6,194	799	2,987	13,340	3	7	78	0	2,824	36,716
Jul	7,768	61,256	4,837	21,524	567	5,995	807	2,924	12,598	3	7	82	0	2,931	39,732
Aug	7,811	59,201	4,784	19,284	547	5,493	787	2,846	10,940	3	5	89	0	3,027	39,917
Sep	7,711	58,459	4,641	17,682	526	5,869	737	2,595	9,213	3	5	88	0	3,070	40,777
Oct	7,698	57,188	4,497	16,097	449	4,660	721	2,726	8,707	2	4	63	0	3,201	41,091
Nov	7,727	57,870	4,507	15,795	378	3,922	709	2,758	9,111	2	4	45	0	3,220	42,075
Dec	8,117	56,446	4,793	15,402	290	4,241	689	2,296	8,861	2	4	104	0	3,324	41,044
1945															
Jan	8,027	56,806	4,538	12,134	193	1,453	675	2,149	8,528	2	4	60	0	3,489	44,672
Feb	8,207	55,940	4,419	10,188	184	1,454	666	2,064	6,666	2	4	61	0	3,788	45,752
Mar	8,169	53,289	4,421	8,116	144	1,367	664	2,009	4,733	2	4	70	3	3,748	45,173
Apr	8,155	51,774	4,314	6,486	147	1,505	613	459	4,518	2	3	64	0	3,841	45,288
May	8,038	52,433	4,205	7,496	152	1,523	536	382	5,588	1	3	67	0	3,833	44,937
Jun	7,686	53,228	3,922	6,947	218	889	326	389	5,666	1	3	58	0	3,764	46,281
Jul	7,630	57,338	4,186	17,223	650	10,559	227	620	6,041	1	3	51	0	3,444	40,115
Aug	7,501	53,062	4,291	16,847	747	9,216	263	1,201	6,427	1	3	47	0	3,210	36,215
Sep	7,112	48,119	4,107	15,173	584	7,853	302	2,061	5,257	1	2	42	0	3,005	32,946
Oct	7,087	36,210	4,505	8,330	420	4,193	209	46	4,089	1	2	37	0	2,582	27,880
Nov	6,843	27,055	4,742	6,054	326	2,171	195	0	3,881	0	2	32	0	2,101	21,001
Dec	6,263	19,919	4,649	5,491	308	1,593	115	0	3,896	0	2	30	0	1,614	14,428

a Army Reports of branch strength were compiled on the basis of branch designation of personnel with each command, and not on the basis of duty assignment. Some of the listed personnel may not, therefore, have been on chemical duty and personnel of other branches or personnel without branch designation may have been assigned chemical duty. Only a portion of the strength shown was under the direct jurisdiction of the Chief, CWS. See footnote c.

b The following breakdown by component was available only for these months:

1942 End of Month	Officers				Enlisted Men				
	RA	NG	ORC	AUS	RA	NG	ERC	AUS	SS
Apr	103	24	1,580	125	2,588	39	135	1,380	7,926
May	109	26	1,741	218	2,619	54	119	1,429	10,132
Jun	109	29	1,872	277	2,536	58	117	1,903	13,324
Aug	119	33	2,049	654	2,933	272	157	2,249	18,249
Sep	122	44	1,971	882	3,109	340	156	2,306	21,692
Oct	126	39	2,067	1,315	3,364	285	401	2,429	27,884
Nov	119	46	2,052	2,063					
Dec	119	41	2,070	2,962					

c Includes both staff and unit personnel. Unit personnel include those chemical units assigned to the command for training or for Z of I operations. Personnel under direct jurisdiction of the Chief, CWS are included under Army Service Forces.

d Includes all personnel detailed to duty with departmental complement of the WD whether for special missions or regular duty.

e Not reported.

Source: Extracts from STM-30, Strength of the Army Report, prepared by Machine Records Branch, TAG, monthly.

Appendix B

CHEMICAL WARFARE SERVICE PERSONNEL STRENGTH, OVERSEAS:[a] 30 APRIL 1942 TO 31 DECEMBER 1945

End of month	Total overseas Officer	Total overseas Enlisted	American Theaters [b] Officer	American Theaters [b] Enlisted	North African, Mediterranean Theaters [c] Officer	North African, Mediterranean Theaters [c] Enlisted	European Theater [d] Officer	European Theater [d] Enlisted	South Pacific Theater [e] Officer	South Pacific Theater [e] Enlisted	Central Pacific Theater [g] Officer	Central Pacific Theater [g] Enlisted	Southwest Pacific Theater [h] Officer	Southwest Pacific Theater [h] Enlisted	Asiatic, China, Burma, India Theaters [i] Officer	Asiatic, China, Burma, India Theaters [i] Enlisted	Middle Eastern Theater [j] Officer	Middle Eastern Theater [j] Enlisted	Mil. Attachés, and WD Groups and Missions [k] Officer	Mil. Attachés, and WD Groups and Missions [k] Enlisted	Enroute U.S. to Theaters Officer	Enroute U.S. to Theaters Enlisted
1942																						
April	104	1,515	31	410	0	0	2	19	1	2	28	365	35	581	2	33	0	0	0	0	5	105
May	144	2,057	34	421	0	0	4	99	2	10	35	494	38	563	8	97	0	0	0	0	23	373
June	188	2,898	38	589	0	0	28	288	6	120	38	725	39	615	8	37	0	0	0	0	31	524
July	245	3,143	51	634	0	0	66	604	5	120	57	759	41	734	8	50	0	0	2	0	15	242
August	338	3,889	55	825	0	0	120	1,080	7	120	66	970	52	773	13	57	1	9	2	0	22	55
September	369	4,292	70	1,305	0	0	142	1,113	9	125	66	906	52	695	13	57	1	9	2	0	14	82
October	421	4,297	89	1,369	0	0	166	1,117	10	126	71	900	61	677	13	57	8	22	2	0	1	29
November	479	4,597	91	1,360	(ᶠ)	(ᶠ)	185	1,236	40	196	72	956	57	775	11	52	9	19	2	0	12	3
December	490	5,134	99	1,417	76	575	129	913	23	200	64	998	64	888	11	52	18	45	2	0	4	46
1943																						
January	539	5,720	112	1,474	98	948	136	981	24	200	67	1,057	65	892	9	69	21	52	2	0	5	47
February	532	5,934	107	1,444	101	1,158	132	854	24	236	62	1,036	65	892	11	64	23	66	1	0	6	184
March	626	6,116	104	1,356	148	1,438	144	1,004	26	221	58	988	79	938	13	64	25	78	1	0	28	29
April	815	9,440	100	1,127	164	1,503	151	1,052	29	191	72	981	111	860	21	74	29	89	1	0	137	3,489
May	946	11,628	99	825	342	5,922	175	1,240	33	223	68	962	98	939	21	80	30	92	2	0	78	1,326
June	1,182	15,522	111	867	457	7,260	274	3,203	38	330	64	953	131	1,391	23	78	29	84	2	0	53	1,347
July	1,286	15,825	111	870	477	7,354	303	3,414	76	1,534	73	932	138	1,433	37	75	27	79	3	0	41	113
August	1,447	17,101	120	867	536	7,211	358	3,924	78	1,644	69	924	142	1,450	85	166	26	47	3	0	30	860
September	1,550	18,598	119	894	553	7,775	436	5,131	80	1,653	69	934	151	1,508	86	168	27	50	3	0	26	495
October	1,783	22,552	115	941	556	7,841	535	7,074	82	1,664	69	961	160	1,713	128	311	24	37	4	0	110	2,037
November	1,803	23,978	112	1,095	529	7,949	707	9,975	81	1,644	78	961	167	1,922	88	267	17	24	3	0	21	241
December	2,043	25,939	111	1,059	571	8,106	816	10,358	92	1,696	87	1,170	180	2,125	101	489	15	19	3	0	67	917
1944																						
January	2,134	27,891	115	1,059	535	7,825	913	12,522	99	1,777	96	1,298	199	2,169	86	479	12	21	4	0	75	741
February	2,257	29,969	111	1,029	492	7,500	991	13,277	117	2,045	99	1,403	207	2,311	108	542	16	11	4	0	96	1,851
March	2,344	30,164	118	1,160	509	7,580	1,087	13,756	155	3,230	109	1,405	214	2,409	137	615	12	9	3	0	149	2,158
April	2,506	34,065	119	1,108	490	7,844	1,184	16,475	166	3,236	115	1,501	262	3,164	152	729	16	8	2	0	82	1,168
May	2,805	36,573	101	1,086	532	7,811	1,281	17,137	173	3,328	150	2,065	289	3,393	156	869	12	10	40	56	71	818
June	2,824	36,716	95	1,078	508	7,727	1,340	17,020	98	1,848	154	2,093	388	5,459	151	901	12	11	48	81	30	498

July	2,931	39,732	95	1,120	535	7,118	1,396	17,711	91	1,816	159	2,040	369	6,200	158	2,896	12	11	49	123	67	697
August	3,027	39,917	92	1,082	514	9,037	1,452	17,769	(e)	(e)	255	3,882	467	6,734	146	1,109	14	5	54	92	28	207
September	3,070	40,777	94	1,118	487	8,738	1,503	18,453	-----	-----	271	4,001	480	7,138	149	1,078	14	4	50	85	22	162
October	3,201	41,091	81	830	511	7,960	1,550	18,989	-----	-----	284	4,024	486	7,353	146	1,050	14	5	53	86	76	794
November	3,220	42,075	77	703	295	3,635	1,765	24,476	-----	-----	295	3,990	505	7,047	149	1,052	13	5	66	292	55	875
December	3,324	41,044	69	530	291	3,821	1,913	23,945	-----	-----	285	3,808	508	7,253	153	1,045	14	10	73	331	18	301
1945																						
January	3,489	44,672	58	562	317	3,856	1,981	26,316	-----	-----	280	3,795	514	7,343	156	1,048	12	9	101	935	70	808
February	3,788	45,752	60	527	313	3,755	2,075	26,685	-----	-----	271	3,460	622	7,771	162	1,083	14	9	204	1,643	67	819
March	3,748	45,173	59	471	315	3,627	2,072	26,909	-----	-----	279	3,543	595	7,709	173	1,060	10	22	215	1,644	30	188
April	3,841	45,288	59	474	316	3,545	2,097	26,506	-----	-----	301	4,100	641	7,686	176	1,207	10	23	222	1,601	19	146
May	3,833	44,937	61	474	289	3,382	2,025	26,247	-----	-----	305	4,083	679	7,698	166	1,179	9	16	264	1,792	35	66
June	3,764	46,281	57	446	271	3,971	1,930	26,151	-----	-----	346	4,578	673	7,929	176	1,195	9	16	277	1,785	25	210
July	3,444	40,115	50	417	246	3,562	1,530	19,643	-----	-----	(e)	(e)	1,088	12,750	159	1,235	9	16	268	1,775	94	717
August	3,210	36,215	45	372	187	2,390	1,274	15,355	-----	-----	-----	-----	1,190	14,507	160	1,221	10	16	286	2,256	58	98
September	3,005	32,946	41	365	162	1,650	1,057	12,149	-----	-----	-----	-----	1,282	15,041	154	1,313	10	17	262	2,317	37	94
October	2,582	27,880	33	354	94	708	835	9,175	-----	-----	-----	-----	1,232	14,965	123	1,024	10	16	235	1,626	20	12
November	2,101	21,001	32	194	53	243	654	5,711	-----	-----	-----	-----	1,013	12,822	115	477	10	2	198	1,530	26	22
December	1,614	14,428	29	160	33	102	500	4,691	-----	-----	-----	-----	833	8,581	69	300	5	1	140	582	5	11

a Army reports of branch strength were compiled on the basis of branch designation of personnel with each command, and not on the basis of duty assignment. Some of the listed personnel may not, therefore, have been on chemical duty and personnel of other branches or personnel without branch designation may have been assigned chemical duty.

b Includes:

May, June 1942–Personnel listed by location in the Americas.

July 1942 to February 1944–Personnel listed under "North American Theater" and "Latin American Theater."

March, April 1944–Personnel listed under "American Theater."

May 1944 to November 1945–Personnel listed under headings:

(1) Alaskan Department.

(2) U.S. Armed Forces in Eastern Canada (combined with (3) below in August 1944; dropped in September 1945).

(3) U.S. Army Forces in Central Canada.

(4) Eastern Defense Command (outside U.S.).

(5) Greenland Base Command (dropped in August 1944).

(6) Caribbean Defense Command.

(7) U.S. Army Forces in South Atlantic (dropped in September 1945).

(8) Northwest Service Command (September 1944 to July 1945).

c North African Theater established 4 February 1943. Prior the March personnel reported in European Theater totals, but identified as in North Africa. Redesignated Mediterranean Theater 1 November 1944.

d Theater established 8 June 1942. Prior reports for command, U.S. Army Forces in the British Isles.

e South Pacific Area forces absorbed by Central Pacific forces 1 August 1944.

f Not reported.

g Central Pacific Area activated 14 August 1943. Prior reports for Hawaiian Department. Central Pacific forces absorbed by U.S. Army Forces, Pacific Ocean Areas on 1 August 1944. Redesignated U.S. Army Forces, Middle Pacific, 1 July 1945. Strength reported under U.S. Army Forces in the Pacific from 1 July 1945.

h Southwest Pacific Area established 18 April 1942. Strength merged under U.S. Army Forces in the Pacific from 1 July 1945.

i Asiatic Theater became U.S. Army Forces, China-Burma-India Theater on 4 March 1942. China Theater and India-Burma Theater established 24 October 1944, but strength reports consolidated for entire period.

j Includes:

August 1942 through September 1943–Persian Gulf Service Command, U.S. Army Forces in Central Africa, U.S. Army Forces in Liberia, Middle Eastern Theater.

September 1943 to March 1945–U.S. Army Forces in the Middle East, Persian Gulf Command (redesignated from Persian Gulf Service Command, 10 December 1943).

March 1945 to 30 November 1945–African Middle East Theater, Persian Gulf Command (absorbed by theater on 1 October 1945).

k Includes:

Military Attachés and all War Department Missions and Groups on duty outside continental United States, May 1944 to November 1945 also includes all missions and groups under the jurisdiction of the Commanding Generals, Army Ground Forces, Army Air Forces, or Army Service Forces.

Source: Extracts from STM-30, Strength of the Army Report, prepared by Machine Records Branch, TAG, Monthly.

Appendix C

Chemical Warfare Service Negro Personnel Strength, World-wide:[a] 30 April 1942 to 31 December 1945

End of month	Continental United States		Overseas	
	Officer	Enlisted	Officer	Enlisted
1942				
April	[b]	1,064	[b]	296
May	[b]	1,527	[b]	215
June	[b]	2,081	[b]	414
July	[b]	2,654	[b]	432
August	[b]	3,066	[b]	412
September	8	3,099	[b]	419
October	4	4,450	[b]	407
November	2	5,608	[b]	391
December	7	6,134	[b]	389
1943				
January	12	7,156	[b]	381
February	13	7,964	[b]	379
March	18	8,257	[b]	381
April	41	9,051	[b]	384
May	51	8,315	[b]	1,468
June	52	8,744	[b]	1,194
July	116	8,402	[b]	1,261
August	77	7,984	[b]	1,660
September	[b]	[b]	[b]	1,836
October	107	8,514	5	1,943
November	107	7,707	5	2,122
December	108	8,148	7	2,369
1944				
January	101	7,412	16	2,879
February	91	6,167	24	3,418
March	50	5,304	39	3,388
April	55	5,429	40	4,053
May	45	3,244	32	4,339
June	42	2,629	38	3,857
July	40	1,978	39	3,699
August	39	1,784	42	3,637
September	23	957	54	4,222
October	25	790	56	4,594
November	27	697	56	4,499
December	31	625	47	4,389

Appendix C—*Continued*

End of month	Continental United States		Overseas	
	Officer	Enlisted	Officer	Enlisted
1945				
January	34	608	49	3,910
February	30	568	60	4,304
March	25	544	60	4,204
April	15	322	59	4,179
May	17	541	55	3,717
June	16	514	65	4,145
July	20	603	54	4,014
August	10	876	61	3,606
September	13	986	48	3,506
October	13	516	35	2,252
November	9	496	27	1,519
December	11	379	20	617

ᵃ Army reports of branch strength were compiled on the basis of branch designation of personnel with each command, and not on the basis of duty assignment. Some of the listed personnel may not, therefore, have been on chemical duty and personnel of other branches or personnel without branch designation may have been assigned chemical duty. This personnel is included in strengths as shown in Appendixes A and B.

ᵇ Not reported.

Source: Extracts from STM—30, Strength of the Army Report, prepared by Machine Records Branch, TAG, Monthly.

Appendix D

OFFICE OF THE CHIEF, CWS, OFFICER PERSONNEL STRENGTH
AUGUST 1939 TO DECEMBER 1945

End of month	Total	Regular Army	Other [a]	End of month	Total	Regular Army	Other [a]
1939				*1942—Continued*			
August	12	12	0	March	164	19	145
September	11	11	0	April	190	21	169
October	11	11	0	May	188	20	168
November	11	11	0	June	177	18	159
December	11	11	0	July	213	19	194
				August	212	17	195
1940				September	217	16	201
January	12	12	0	October	206	18	188
February	11	11	0	November	217	15	202
March	14	11	3	December	232	15	217
April	16	11	5				
May	16	11	5	*1943*			
June	20	12	8	January	221	12	209
July	22	13	9	February	229	12	217
August	24	13	11	March	238	[b] 15	[b]223
September	28	14	14	April	233		233
October	30	15	15	May	242		242
November	31	15	16	June	257		257
December	34	15	19	July	243		243
				August	220		220
1941				September	230		230
January	37	15	22	October	234		234
February	40	16	24	November	234		234
March	41	17	24	December	231		231
April	42	16	26				
May	45	17	28	*1944*			
June	49	18	31	January	230		230
July	52	19	33	February	234		234
August	63	22	41	March	237		237
September	76	22	54	April	236		236
October	92	22	70	May	236		236
November	99	22	77	June	244		244
December	109	22	87	July	245		245
				August	257		257
1942				September	260		260
				October	260		260
January	124	22	102	November	257		257
February	141	21	120	December	254		254

Appendix D—*Continued*

End of month	Total	Regular Army	Other [a]	End of month	Total	Regular Army	Other [a]
1945				*1945—Continued*			
January ----------------	253		253	July-------------------	262		262
February ---------------	258		258	August----------------	259		259
March -----------------	260		260	September-------------	231		231
April ------------------	258		258	October--------------	213		213
May -------------------	252		252	November-------------	208		208
June -------------------	231		231	December-------------	174		174

[a] Includes National Guard, Officer Reserve Corps, and Army of United States officers.

[b] Breakdown by component not made after 20 March 1943.

Source Office of the Comptroller, Department of the Army, Statistics Branch (Squier/Pentagon 2B673) from· (1) Monthly Report of Personnel Activities, WDAGO 73, (2) Monthly Report of Authorizations and Strength for Personnel Operating the Z of I Establishment, WDGS Control Symbol SM–P2–39, (3) Monthly Report of Personnel Authorizations and Strengths for Establishments in Area of District of Columbia and Arlington County, Va., WDMB Form 114, WDGS SM–P2–40, (4) Photostats of Monthly Strength Reports in Statistical Branch, PRAD. OCA.

Appendix E

KEY PERSONNEL, OFFICE OF CHIEF, CHEMICAL WARFARE SERVICE

As of 6 July 1940

Chief, CWS	Maj. Gen. Walter C. Baker
Executive Officer	Lt. Col. Paul X. English
Chief, Personnel Division	Lt. Col. Geoffrey Marshall
Chief, Information Division	Lt. Col. John C. MacArthur
Chief, Training Division	Lt. Col. Edward C. Wallington
Chief, Supply Division	Maj. Norman D. Gillet
Chief, Procurement Division	Lt. Col. George F. Unmacht
Chief, Fiscal Division	Col. Arthur M. Heritage
Chief, Technical Division	Lt. Col. Maurice E. Barker

As of 20 August 1941

Chief, CWS	Maj. Gen. William N. Porter
Executive Officer	Lt. Col. Charles E. Loucks
Chief, Industrial Service	Col. Paul X. English
Chief, Field Service	Col. Edward Montgomery
Chief, Technical Service	Lt. Col. Maurice E. Barker
Chief, Personnel Division	Lt. Col. Geoffrey Marshall
Chief, Intelligence Division	Capt. Thomas E. Rodgers
Chief, Fiscal Division	Col. Arthur M. Heritage
Chief, Supply Division	Maj. Norman D. Gillet
Chief, Plans Training Division	Lt. Col. Crawford M. Kellogg
Chief, Troops Division	Lt. Col. Charles S. Shadle
Chief, Incendiaries Branch	Col. J. Enrique Zanetti

As of 1 May 1942

Chief, CWS	Maj. Gen. William N. Porter
Executive Officer	Col. Charles E. Loucks
Chief, Industrial Service	Brig. Gen. Paul X. English
Chief, Field Service	Brig. Gen. Alexander Wilson
Chief, Technical Service	Col. Edward Montgomery
Chief, Control Division	Col. Lowell A. Elliott
Chief, Civilian Protection Division	Col. George J. B. Fisher
Chief, Personnel Division	Col. Geoffrey Marshall
Chief, Intelligence Division	Col. John C. MacArthur
Chief, Legal Division	Col. John A. Smith

As of 1 May 1942

Chief, Fiscal and Planning Division	Col. Arthur M. Heritage
Chief, Public Relations Division	Maj. William O. Brooks
Chief, Manufacturing Division	Col. Patrick F. Powers
Chief, Procurement Planning Division	Col. Hugh W. Rowan
Chief, Inspection Division	Maj. Elwood H. Snider
Chief, Construction Division	Lt. Col. Lester W. Hurd
Chief, Supply Division	Col. Norman D. Gillet
Chief, Plans Training Division	Col. Ralph G. Benner

As of 26 August 1943

Chief, CWS	Maj. Gen. William N. Porter
Executive Officer	Col. Lowell A. Elliott
Assistant Chief, CWS, for Matériel	Brig. Gen. Rollo C. Ditto
Assistant Chief, CWS, for Field Operations	Brig. Gen. Alden H. Waitt
Chief, Control Division	Col. Harry A. Kuhn
Chief, Personnel Division	Col. Herrold E. Brooks
Chief, Fiscal Division	Col. Arthur M. Heritage
Chief, Medical Division	Col. Cornelius P. Rhoads
Chief, Industrial Division	Brig. Gen. Paul X. English
Chief, Inspection Division	Col. William M. Creasy
Chief, Supply Division	Col. Norman D. Gillet
Chief, Technical Division	Brig. Gen. William C. Kabrich
Chief, Field Requirements Division	Col. George W. Perkins
Chief, Training Division	Col. George J. B. Fisher
Chief, War Plans and Theaters Division	Col. Herbert K. Bear

As of 11 December 1944

Chief, CWS	Maj. Gen. William N. Porter
Deputy Chief, CWS	Col. Lowell A. Elliott
Executive Officer	Col. Eric Lee
Assistant Chief, CWS, for Matériel	Brig. Gen. Rollo C. Ditto
Assistant Chief, CWS, for Field Operations	Brig. Gen. Alden H. Waitt
Chief, Control Division	Col. Harry A. Kuhn
Chief, Personnel Division	Col. Herrold E. Brooks
Chief, Fiscal Division	Lt. Col. Joseph F. Escude
Chief, San José Projects Division	Brig. Gen. Egbert F. Bullene
Chief, Medical Division	Col. Cornelius P. Rhoads
Chief, Industrial Division	Brig. Gen. Charles E. Loucks
Chief, Inspection Division	Col. William M. Creasy
Chief, Technical Division	Brig. Gen. William C. Kabrich
Chief, Supply Division	Col. Norman D. Gillet
Chief, Field Requirements Division	Col. Delancey R. King
Chief, Training Division	Lt. Col. Franklin R. Williams
Chief, War Plans and Theaters Division	Col. Herbert R. Bear

As of 30 June 1945

Chief, CWS	Maj. Gen. William N. Porter
Deputy Chief, CWS	Col. Lowell A. Elliott
Executive Officer	Col. Eric Lee
Assistant Chief, CWS, for Matériel	Brig. Gen. Rollo C. Ditto
Assistant Chief, CWS, for Field Operations	Brig. Gen. Alden H. Waitt
Chief, Control Division	Col. Harry A. Kuhn
Chief, Personnel Division	Col. Herrold E. Brooks
Chief, Fiscal Division	Lt. Col. Joseph F. Escude
Chief, San José Projects Division	Brig. Gen. Egbert F. Bullene
Chief, Medical Division	Col. John R. Wood
Chief, Industrial Division	Brig. Gen. Charles E. Loucks
Chief, Inspection Division	Col. John R. Sharp
Chief, Technical Division	Brig. Gen. William C. Kabrich
Chief, Supply Division	Col. Norman D. Gillet
Chief, Field Requirements Division	Col. Delancey R. King
Chief, Training Division	Lt. Col. Franklin R. Williams
Chief, War Plans and Theaters Division	Col. John C. MacArthur
Chief, Chemical Commodities Division	Col. Samuel N. Cummings

Appendix F

CHEMICAL WARFARE SCHOOL

EDGEWOOD ARSENAL, MARYLAND

DETAILED PROGRAM

(Par. 3c(1), AR 350–110)

REPLACEMENT CENTER OFFICERS' COURSE

December 15, 1940 to February 15, 1941

December 10, 1940

I. SCOPE

To instruct Chemical Warfare Reserve officers in Replacement Center Training and to prepare them for assignment to Replacement Center duty.

II. DURATION OF COURSE

December 15, 1940 to February 15, 1941.

III. PROGRAM

Approximate Hours

1. DEPARTMENT OF TECHNIQUE

    a. *Chemical Warfare Agents.*
       Properties and characteristics; identification. 15

    b. *Protection.*
       Individual; collective; tactical; gas mask drill; inspection and repair of masks; first aid. 47

    c. *Chemical Warfare Weapons.*
       Chemical Warfare Service matériel; chemical weapons of other arms; technique of releasing agents. 12

    d. *Meteorology.*
       Weather elements; instruments; effect on chemical agents; forecasting. 6

2. DEPARTMENT OF MILITARY ART

    a. *Tactics.*
       Organization and tactical employment of chemical troops; chemical troop leading; employment of chemicals by other arms; supply and logistics; combat orders and solutions of problems; operations of combined arms. 48

    b. *Training.*
       Instruction methods; publications; visual aids; programs and schedules; applicatory exercises; conduct of gunners' examinations; chemical staff officers. 79

3. MISCELLANEOUS DEPARTMENT

    a. Administration.

        Army regulations; military law; unit administration; procurement and supply.   28

    b. General Subjects.

        Physical training; map reading; customs of the service; mobilization regulations; interior guard duty; pistol marksmanship; dismounted drill.   129

Total   364

SUMMARY

	Hours
Chemical Warfare Agents	15
Protection	47
Chemical Warfare Weapons	12
Meteorology	6
Tactics	48
Training	79
Administration	28
General Subjects	129
Total	364

Appendix G

HEADQUARTERS SIXTH CORPS AREA

U.S. Post Office Building
Chicago, Illinois

TRAINING MEMORANDUM⎱   December 4, 1940
NO. 13   ⎰

CHEMICAL WARFARE TRAINING

Training Memorandum No. 8, this headquarters, December 28, 1938, is rescinded and this training memorandum substituted therefor.

This training memorandum applies only to troops under the jurisdiction of the corps area commander and does not apply to units assigned or attached to any of the four armies.

SECTION I–TRAINING

1. *GENERAL.—a.* The objective, scope, methods of instruction and standards of proficiency for basic chemical warfare training are prescribed in Basic Field Manual 21–40, Defense Against Chemical Attack.

   b. Recruit training will be conducted as prescribed in paragraph 59, B.F.M. 21–40, and relevant sections of War Department Mobilization Training Programs for the appropriate arm and service.

   c. General information and details on this subject are covered in the appropriate references listed in Section VII of this memorandum.

2. *TRAINING REQUIREMENTS.—a. Regular Army.* The annual training of units of the Regular Army under the jurisdiction of the commanding general, Sixth Corps Area, will include the following:

(1) *Individual and unit training* to meet the requirements set forth in B.F.M. 21–40.

(2) *The training of unit gas officers* in the division chemical warfare school (see par. 4*b*).

(3) *The operation of troop schools* for the qualification of unit gas noncommissioned officers and their replacements.

(4) *Special operations:* Particular stress will be placed on the use of chemicals in special operations under the provisions of W.D. B.F.M., Vol. VII, Military Law, Part Three.

(5) *Training of units in the mechanics of defense against chemical attack.* In order to attain the required standards of proficiency in defense against chemical attack, training of tactical units will include the following: (See paragraphs 60 and 66, B.F.M. 21–40).

(*a*) Gas mask drill, paragraphs 28 and 79, B.F.M. 21–40.

(*b*) Fitting, care and minor repair of gas masks, including the gas chamber exercise, shown in paragraphs 32, 33, 34, B.F.M. 21–40, and Sec. XI, B.F.M. 21–40.

(*c*) Accustoming men to march, maneuver and carry out their normal duties with gas masks adjusted.

(*d*) Characteristics and identification of standard chemical agents.

(*e*) Physiological effects of chemical warfare agents and first aid treatment of gas casualties.

(*f*) Protection of food and water and degassing of areas and equipment.

(*g*) Methods of projecting chemical agents both from the organic weapons of the unit and from the air.

(*h*) Technique in the use of chemical training ammunition.

(*i*) Effect of weather and terrain on chemical attack.

(*j*) Construction and maintenance of gasproof shelters.

(*k*) Alarm devices, procedure to meet a gas attack and procedure during and after such an attack.

(6) *Execution of tactical exercises and combat firing* by small units, with all personnel wearing gas masks. During this phase of chemical warfare training, instruction will be given as prescribed in paragraph 60c, B.F.M. 21–40, and will include the following:

(*a*) Habituating all personnel to marching, patrolling and operating communications and weapons in an atmosphere of nontoxic gas and smoke. To accomplish this mission, the following minimum requirements will govern in the operation of weapons and in the use of matériel.

1. Infantry and Cavalry. Twenty percent of the annual ammunition allowances for combat firing (par. 41*b*, AR 775–10) will be fired, with gas masks adjusted, by all troops participating in combat firing exercises. In addition, infantry troops will be habituated to using the bayonet with gas masks adjusted, and will include at least two practice runs per man through the bayonet qualification course each training year.

2. Field Artillery and Coast Artillery. Twenty percent of the annual allowance of subcalibre ammunition will be fired under conditions involving the wearing of the gas mask by all men employed in the battery, except these detachments which would normally operate in gasproof shelters. (F.M. 21–40, 21–45, 100–5, TM 3–205.)

3. Air Corps. All ground troops will be trained to carry on normal ground activities with masks adjusted, including the preparation of airplanes for takeoff. Stress will be given to decontamination training, not only of ground installations, but also of airplanes. (See W.D. letter, May 9, 1940, Subject: Air Corps Training, 1940–1941, A.G. 353 (3–4–39) Misc.), and paragraphs 11, 25, 26 and 27, B.F.M. 21–40.

4. Staff Troops. Detachments of Signal Corps, Ordnance Department, Quartermaster Corps, Finance Department, Medical Corps and Veterinary Corps, on duty at stations of combat troops, will be trained in the use of gas masks and in gas discipline. Gas masks on hand at stations will be made available for the training of these detachments. Medical Corps units and detachments will, in addition, be given thorough practical training in the administration of first aid to simulated gas cases.

(*b*) Combat units will be well grounded in the tactical use of smoke, and be thoroughly informed concerning its powers and limitations. Stress will be placed on the effect of smoke on aimed fire and on fire control, both in theoretical instruction and by practical demonstration, so far as allowances of chemical munitions will permit. To this end, tactical situations involving the use of smoke and nontoxic agents and intensive measures to assure adequate protection against all types of chemical agents and methods of projection will be included in appropriate problems and terrain exercises. Tactical maneuvers will include operations involving the use of smoke and simulated toxic gas. (See TM 3–305, Use of Smokes and Lachrymators in Training.)

b. National Guard. (1) The chemical warfare training of the National Guard, *prior to induction into Federal Service,* will conform to the instructions issued by the National Guard Bureau and will, insofar as practicable, parallel that of the Regular Army, as herein prescribed. (See paragraphs, 1, 2*a*, 3 and 4*a*).

(2) *Reserve Militia.* Training of Reserve Militia units (State Troops, as authorized, Public Resolutions 874–76, 76th Congress, approved October 21, 1940), if and when authorized by the States concerned, will be as per Chapter 3, Volume VII, B.F.M. Military Law, Part Three.

c. Organized Reserves. Inactive status training schedules will include a minimum of two hours instruction in chemical warfare, in preparation for the active duty period.

d. R.O.T.C. The chemical warfare training for the R.O.T.C. units at colleges will conform to the War Department directive for these units. Camp schedules will include three hours instruction in chemical warfare, as outlined in paragraph 65, B.F.M. 21–40.

e. Enlisted Replacement Centers. (1) Training at Enlisted Replacement Center (Medical Corps), at Camp Grant, Illinois, will be conducted as prescribed in Section II, War Department MTP 8–1, September 9, 1940, and B.F.M. 21–40.

(2) A chemical warfare school will be conducted at Camp Grant for the purpose of training officers and noncommissioned officers as instructors at the Enlisted Replacement Center, Medical Corps.

SECTION II–GAS OFFICERS AND NONCOMMISSIONED OFFICERS

	Paragraphs
Unit Gas officers and noncommissioned officers	3
Qualification of unit gas officers	4
Qualification of unit gas noncommissioned officers	5

3. UNIT GAS OFFICERS AND NONCOMMISSIONED OFFICERS. *a.* As provided in paragraphs 41, 44 and 45, B.F.M. 21–40, each unit under the jurisdiction of the commanding general, Sixth Corps Area, will have detailed at all times the prescribed number of *qualified* gas officers and noncommissioned officers who will function in accordance with the duties therein assigned to them.

b. In order that as many officers and noncommissioned officers as practicable may become familiar with this phase of training, and to provide within each unit a pool of competent instructors in chemical warfare, commanders concerned will rotate officers and noncommissioned officers in assignment to these duties.

c. Post gas officers. In addition to the unit gas officers prescribed above, a line officer of rank commensurate with the duties involved, will be detailed, in addition to his other duties, as post gas officer at each post under the jurisdiction of the commanding general, Sixth Corps Area, and will perform the duties prescribed in paragraph 46, B.F.M. 21–40. Each post gas officer will also function as post property officer for Chemical Warfare Service property at his post.

d. Report of changes. Changes in post and unit gas officers under the jurisdiction of the commanding general, Sixth Corps Area, will be promptly reported to this headquarters.

4. QUALIFICATION OF UNIT GAS OFFICERS.–*a.* Officers will be qualified for appointment as unit gas officers by one of following means:

(1) Satisfactory completion of an appropriate training course at the Chemical Warfare School, Edgewood Arsenal, Maryland.

(2) Graduation from the 5th Division Chemical Warfare School, Fort Custer, Michigan. (See sub-par. *b,* below.)

(3) Satisfactory completion of the Army Extension Course, Common Subcourse 10–3, Defense Against Chemical Warfare; the Chemical Warfare Service Extension Course 40–5; Part II, The Employment of Chemical Agents in Troop Training, and Special Extension Course, entitled, The Unit Gas Officer, supplemented by ten hours practical instruction for Regular Army personnel and by six hours practical instruction for National Guard or Reserve personnel, in the subjects outlined in paragraph 65, B.F.M. 21–40. (Note: Applications for enrollment in Subcourse 10–4 will be submitted through the usual channels. Applications for enrollment in Extension Course 40–5, Part II, and Special Extension Course The Unit Gas Officer will be submitted through channels to the corps area chemical officer, who will conduct this course.)

b. 5th Division Chemical Warfare School. Subject to approval of commanding general, Second Army, unit gas officers will, unless otherwise qualified under the provisions of subparagraphs 4 (1), (2) and (3) above, be trained at the Chemical Warfare School, Fort Custer, Michigan, at a period to be announced later. When this time is announced, unit and post commanders will designate personnel from units under the jurisdiction of the commanding general, Sixth Corps Area, to receive necessary training, as prescribed by paragraphs 43 and 44, B.F.M. 21–40.

5. QUALIFICATION OF UNIT GAS NONCOMMISSIONED OFFICERS.–*a.* At each post under the jurisdiction of the commanding general, Sixth Corps Area, a troop school in chemical warfare will be conducted annually for the training of noncommissioned officers as unit gas noncommissioned officers.

b. The schedule of training for this school will include appropriate portions (approximately 20 hours) of the applicable subjects outlined in paragraph 65, B.F.M. 21–40.

c. Instructors for this school will be carefully selected from among officers who possess the qualifications stated in paragraph 4*a* above. Full use will be made of all officers who are graduates of the Chemical Warfare School, Edgewood Arsenal, Maryland.

d. Noncommissioned officers will be required to attend the school in such numbers as necessary to complete the unit complement of unit gas noncommissioned officers, together with one substitute for each. In addition thereto, all unqualified company, battery and troop commanders will be encouraged to attend this school as observers. (Paragraph 44, B.F.M. 21–40.)

SECTION III–ORGANIZATION

Paragraph

Organization   6

6. ORGANIZATION–*a.* All unit commanders (Regular Army, National Guard and Organized Reserves), under the jurisdiction of the commanding general, Sixth Corps Area, will appoint the appropriate number of gas officers and gas noncommissioned officers, as prescribed in paragraphs 41, 43, 44 and 45, B.F.M. 21–40.

b. Reserve officers who have been qualified and appointed as unit gas officers will conduct the chemical warfare instruction of the Organized Reserve units, where practicable.

c. Post and camp commanders under the jurisdiction of the commanding general, Sixth Corps Area, are responsible that all chemical warfare training under their jurisdiction is conducted by qualified gas officers. They will detail Regular Army officers for the training of the R.O.T.C., and, where necessary, to conduct the training of the Organized Reserves.

SECTION IV–SUPPLY

	Paragraphs
Gas masks	7
Chemical Warfare Service training matériel	8
Requisitions	9

7. GAS MASKS.–*a*. The training allowances of gas masks are governed by Tables of Basic Allowances, 1939, or later revisions.

b. All service type training gas masks, used in normal peacetime training, will be equipped with the MII–R canister (O.D. body, with two horizontal blue stripes), which gives protection against DM (irritant smoke).

c. Present plans contemplate the issuing of the MI training mask as soon as available after January 1, 1941. When issued, paragraphs 77, 78, 79, 80, 81, FM 21–40, will apply as to drill and inspection: paragraphs 34 and 82, FM 21–40, as to storage; and TR 1120–35 (to be published as TM 3–205), as to repair procedure.

d. The size of the gas mask, fitted and tested in tear gas, worn by each soldier will be entered on his service record.

e. Until training masks are issued to each individual, they will be pooled and issued to units, in turn.

f. Inspection, storage and repair of gas masks is set forth in Circular 39, W.D., 1935, and in paragraph 34, B.F.M. 21–40. See also TR 1120–35 The Gas Mask (to be published as TM 3–205).

8. CHEMICAL WARFARE SERVICE TRAINING MATERIEL.–The authorized instructional gas identification sets, and other Chemical Warfare Service training matériel and ammunition, will be requisitioned and used in the training of all components of the Army of the United States. See AR 775–10 and Tables of Allowances, Camps, Posts and Stations (1938), or later revision.

9. REQUISITIONS.–Requisitions for Chemical Warfare Service supplies and ammunition will be addressed to the Chief, Chemical Warfare Service, War Department Annex #1, 401–23rd Street, N.W., Washington, D. C. They will be prepared on W.D.Q.M.C. Form No. 400, and submitted, in quadruplicate, through the commanding general, Sixth Corps Area.

The nomenclature must conform to that shown in the latest annual issue of War Department Standard Nomenclature and Price List of Chemical Warfare Matériel.

CHEMICAL WARFARE SERVICE EXTENSION COURSES FOR SCHOOL YEAR 1940–41

Courses used in 1939–40

CWS Nos.	Titles	Lessons	Hours
10–1	Organization of the Army	4–R	7
10–2	Organization of the Chemical Warfare Service	3–R	9
10–3	Administration	4	8
10–4	Military Law–Law of Military Offenses	7–R	15
10–5	Military Discipline, Court'y. & Cust. of the Serv.	3	6
10–6	Interior Guard Duty	3–R	8
10–7	Map & Aerial Photograph Reading	10–2R	25
10–8	Military Sanitation and First Aid	4–R	10
20–1	Chemical Warfare Agents I	12–R	27
20–2			
20–3	Chemical Warfare Agents II	6–R	15
20–4	Supply and Mess Management	7–2R	18

CWS Nos.	Titles	Lessons	Hours
20–5	Chemical Warfare Agents III	10–R	30
20–6	Property, Emergency Procurement and Funds	5–R	12
20–7	Defense Against Chemical Warfare	8–R	19
20–8	Chemical Warfare Weapons	7–R	21
20–9			
20–10	Military Law-Courts Martial	7–R	18
20–11	Care and Operation of Motor Vehicles	12–R	28
20–12	Chemical Warfare Agents IV–Manufacture	7–R	25
30–1	Storing & Shipping of C.W. Munitions	4–R	13
30–2	Sig. Com. for all Arms and Services	7–R	11
30–3	Chemical Warfare Troops	7–R	19
30–4	Mobilization	5–R	14
30–5	Organization of the Infantry Division	3	6
30–6	Combat Orders and Solution of Problems	3–R	12
30–7	Training Management (Part I)	6–2R	21
30–8	Tactical Employment of Chem. Agents (In Part)	11–2R	43
30–9	Tech. Divisions, Organization & Operation	5–R	16
30–10	Prod. Divisions, its Organization & Operation	4–R	11
30–11	Development Procedure	4–R	15
30–12	Chemical Warfare Service Units of Field Army	4–R	10
40–1	Combat Orders & Solution of Problems	3	24
40–2	Duties of Chem. Off. of Div. & Higher Units	4–R	11
40–3	Tactics & Tech. of Sep. Arms (Parts II & III)	21–3R	83
40–4	Staff & Log. for the Division (In Part)	8	34
40–5	Chem. War. Sup. System; Dep. Org. & Adm.	4–R	10
40–6	Industrial Mobilization	17–2R	51
40–7	Commercial Law–Contracts	0–R	22
40–8	Chemical Warfare Procurement	6–R	14
50–1	Tactics & Tech. of Separate Arms	12–R	106
50–2	Tactical Principles and Decisions	8–R	82
50–3	Troop Lead.; Com. Staff & Log.	5–R	56
50–4	Tactical Principles and Decisions	8–R	78
50–5	Mil. Org., Com. Orders & Est. of Situation	4–R	38
50–6	Troop Lead. & Com., Staff & Log.	5–R	78
50–7	Com. Staff & Log.; Terr. Org.; Mob. Troop. Move.	4–R	56
60–1	Tactical Principles and Decisions	5–R	46
60–2	Special Subjects	6–R	66

LEGEND AND NOTES:

1. R – Examination or review lesson or lessons.
2. X – Required for ——————.
3. 20–3 (1940–41) equivalent to 20–4, Pt. II (1939–40).
4. 40–1 (1940–41) equivalent to 40–3, Pt. I (1939–40).
5. 40–3 (1940–41) partly covered in 30–8 (1939–40).
6. 40–5 (1940–41) equivalent to 30–7, Pt. I (1939–40).
7. 50–5, Pts. II & III (1940–41) equivalent to 40–3. Pts. II & III (1939–40). Part IV is new.
8. When space under Lessons and Examinations is blank, the course will not be given in 1940–41.

CHEMICAL WARFARE SERVICE EXTENSION COURSES FOR SCHOOL YEAR 1940–41

Current Courses

CWS Nos.	Titles	Lessons	Hours	Service with Troops	Special Service
10–1	Organization of the Army	4–R	7	X	X
10–2	Organization of the Chemical Warfare Service	3–R	9	X	X
10–3	Defense Against Chemical Warfare	9–R	20	X	X
10–4	Military Law–Law of Military Offenses	7–R	16	X	X
10–5	Military Discipline, Court'y. & Cust. of the Serv.	3	6	X	X
10–6	Interior Guard Duty	3–R	8	X	X
10–7	Map & Aerial Photography	10–2R	25	X	X
10–8	Military Sanitation and First Aid	4–R	10	X	X
10–9	Chemical Warfare Agents I	12–R	27	X	X
20–1	Use of Smokes and Lacrimators in Train.	3–R	12	X	X
20–2	Scouting and Patrolling	5–R	17	X	
20–3	Mess Management	4–R	10	X	X
20–4	Chemical Warfare Agents II	6–R	15	X	X
20–5	Organization Function & Equip. of Chemical Troops	6–R	21	X	X
20–6	Care and Operation of Motor Vehicles–General	12–R	27	X	
20–7	Chemical Warfare Agents III	10–R	30	X	X
20–8	Chemical Warfare Weapons	7–R	21	X	X
20–9	Military Law–Courts Martial	7–R	18	X	X
20–10	Conduct of Elementary Training	3–R	12	X	
30–1	Tactical Protection and Chemical Reconnaissance	—	—	X	—
30–2	Marches and Shelter	—	—	X	—
30–3	Sig. Com. for all Arms and Services	7–R	11	X	—
30–4	Chemical Warfare Troops	7–R	19	X	—
30–5	Administration	10–R	35	X	—
30–6	Com. Orders & Solution of Problems, C.W.S.	3–R	12	X	—
30–7	Meteorology for Chemical Operations	—	—	X	—
30–8	Advanced Map & Aerial Photograph Reading	7–R	24	X	—
30–9	Combat Principles, Chemical Platoon	—	—	X	—
30–10	Tech. Divisions, Organization & Operation	5–R	16		X
	As prescribed by Chief, C.W.S.	—	—		X
40–1	Tactics & Tech. of Separate Arms–I, Inf.	10–R	33	X	—
40–2	Combat Orders and Solution of Map Problems	7–R	24	X	—
40–3	Combat Principles of the Chemical Company	—	—	X	—
40–4	Mobilization	5–R	14	X	—
40–5	Training Management	6–2R	21	X	—
40–6	Chemical Warfare Service Units of the Field Army	4–R	10	X	—
40–7	Hasty Field Fortifications	—	—	X	—
40–8	Chem. War. Sup. System; Dep. Org. & Adm.	4–R	10	X	—
40–9	Storing & Shipping of C.W. Munitions	4–R	13	X	—
40–10	Prod. Division, its Organization & Operation	4–R	11	—	X
40–11	Chemical Warfare Agents IV	7–R	25	—	X
40–12	Development Procedure	4–R	15	—	X

Current Courses (cont'd)

CWS Nos.	Titles	Lessons	Hours	Service with Troops	Special Service
40–13	Commercial Law–Contracts	9–R	22	–	X
40–14	Chemical Warfare Procurement	6–R	14	–	X
	As prescribed by Chief, C.W.S.			–	X
50–1	Estimation and Use of Terrain	—	—	X	—
50–2	Organization of the Inf. Div. (Triangular)	3–R	9	X	—
50–3	Com., Staff & Log. for the Division	13–2R	45	X	—
50–4	Duties of Chem. Off. of Div. & Higher Units	4–R	11	X	—
50–5	Tac. & Tech. of Sep. Arms, Pts. II, III, IV	19–3R	66	X	—
50–6	Combat Principles of Chemical Battalion	—	—	X	—
50–7	Advanced Military Chemistry I	—	—	—	X
50–8	War Dept. Procurement Planning	—	—	—	X
	As prescribed by Chief, C.W.S.				
60–1	Combat Principles of the C.W.S.	—	—	X	—
60–2	Advance Military Chemistry II	—	—	—	X
60–3	Mob. of Ind. & Control of Econ. Resources	—	—	—	X
	As prescribed by Chief, C.W.S.	—	—	—	X

Compiled 11 December 1940, by Extension Department,
Chemical Warfare School

SECTION V–INSPECTION

10. INSPECTIONS.–Frequent inspections of the methods used and the results obtained in chemical warfare training will be made by post and unit commanders who are under the jurisdiction of the commanding general Sixth Corps Area. Quarterly inspections of chemical warfare matériel will be made by such post and unit commanders or their commanders or their representatives (gas officers). The corps area chemical officer will make an annual technical inspection of chemical warfare matériel, and of the proficiency of unit gas officers and noncommissioned officers. When practicable, training and tactical inspections will include the use of smoke and nontoxic gas.

SECTION VI–REPORTS

11. MONTHLY ACTIVITY REPORTS.–Each camp, post and station commander will submit at the end of each month an Activity Report on chemical warfare training of units under the jurisdiction of the commanding general, Sixth Corps Area. This report will include the following:

a. Number trained.

b. Synopsis of training given.

c. Amount of time devoted to chemical warfare training.

d. List of munitions or other matériel used.

e. Name and grade of officer who conducted the training.

f. Other pertinent comments not covered above.

This report will reach this headquarters *not later than the 5th of the month following.* The corps area chemical officer will incorporate the chemical warfare activities in the monthly report to the Chief of the Chemical Warfare Service, required by paragraph 6, AR 50-5.

12. AMMUNITION EXPENDITURE CERTIFICATES.–Consolidated Chemical Warfare Service ammunition certificates will be submitted semiannually as of June 30th and December 31st, on forms furnished by Headquarters Sixth Corps Area. These certificates will be prepared as per instructions contained in paragraph 2*b*, AR 35-6620: will show the expenditures made by each component of the Army of the United States, and will be mailed to arrive at this headquarters on or before the 15th of the month following the date of the certificate.

13. INVENTORIES.–An inventory of all Chemical Warfare Service property and ammunition on hand as of December 31st each year will be submitted annually to reach this headquarters not later than January 15th, following the date of the inventory. Forms will be furnished by this headquarters.

14. SERVICE CHARGES.–Reference is made to the current War Department letter of June 7, 1939, A.G. 400.23 (6-7-39) Misc. M, C.M.T.C. and Organized Reserves, for use of supplies, equipment and matériel at training camps, to commanding generals of all corps areas, etc. Not later than fifteen (15) days after the close of R.O.T.C. training camps, camp commanders will forward, in quadruplicate, separate Service Charge Reports covering the use of gas masks by each component trained, to the Chief, Chemical Warfare Service, through the corps area commander.

SECTION VII–REFERENCES

Paragraph

References   15

15. REFERENCES.–Appropriate portions of subjects contained in the references listed below should be studied by each unit gas officer in order that he may have a thorough understanding of the whole subject of chemical warfare as pertains to his arm or service. The application of certain portions of these publications to all types of training should not be overlooked.

a. Army Regulations.

    AR 50-5 —Chemical Warfare Service, General Provisions

    AR 750-10—Range Regulations for Firing Ammunition in Time of Peace

    AR 775-10—Ammunition Allowances (As amended)

b. Training Regulations.

    TR 10-5 —Military Training, (paragraphs 9*b* (7) and 26*b*)

    TR 1370-a—Ammunition, General

c. Technical Manuals.

    TM 3-305 —Use of Smokes and Lachrymators in Training

    TM 3-205 —(To be published to supersede TR 1120-35)

d. Field Manuals.

    BFM, Vol. I, Chapter 2—Personal Hygiene and First Aid (paragraph 17)

    BFM, Vol. III, Part One, Chapter 3—Automatic Rifle Marksmanship (paragraph 35)

    BFM, Vol. III, Part Three—Machine Gun Company (paragraph 35)

BFM, Vol. III, Part Four—Howitzer Company (paragraphs 8*b* and 20*d* (2))
BFM, Vol. VII, Part Six, Chapter 1—Antiaircraft Marksmanship (paragraph 4*c*(4))

BFM, Vol. VII, Part Two—Rules of Land Warfare (paragraph 29)
BFM, Vol. VII, Military Law, Part Three
FM 21–40—Defense Against Chemical Attack
FM 23–30—Hand Grenades
FM 30–5 —Combat Intelligence (paragraphs 13b(2), (c)5)
FM 30–35—Military Intelligence (paragraph 10)
FM   3–10—Examination for Gunners
FM 100–5 —Field Service Regulations (paragraphs 88, 89, 263, 268, 443, 514, 617)

FM 101–5 —Staff Officers' Field Manual–The Staff and Combat Orders (paragraph 25)

Cavalry Field Manual, Vol. II, (paragraphs 42, 46 and 114–122)
Cavalry Field Manual, Vol. III, (paragraphs 139, 217 and 247)
CWS Field Manual, Vol. 1—Tactics and Technique
Coast Artillery Field Manual, Vol. I, Part One (paragraphs 180 and 181)
Coast Artillery Field Manual, Vol. II, Antiaircraft Artillery, Part One, Tactics (paragraph 163)

Engineer Field Manual, Vol. II, Part Two, (paragraph 129)
Field Artillery Field Manual, Vol. II (paragraphs 48, 159 and 200*b*)
Infantry Field Manual, Vol. II (paragraphs 328, 333*f* and 395)
Staff Officers' Field Manual, Part One (pages 7, 8, 20, 87, 89, 110, 129, 139, 144)
Staff Officers' Field Manual, Part Two (pages 31–36, 67 and 74)
Staff Officers' Field Manual, Part Three (pages 16 and 57–59)

f. [sic.] *Miscellaneous.*
General Order 67, War Department, 1920, Extermination of Rodent-Vermin (also see War Department Circular 1, 1924, as amended by Circular 33, War Department, 1926).
War Department Letter, May 9, 1940, Subject: Air Corps Training, 1940–1941, A.G. 353 (3–4–39) M–M–C
War Department Mobilization Training Program, W.D., 1940, (Appropriate Arm or Service)
War Department Training Directive, 1940–1941, letter A.G. 353 (12–17–38) Misc. M–C, dated March 2, 1940
Chemical Warfare School Textbooks, 1 to 6, inclusive
Chemical Warfare School Pamphlet No. 2, 1938. (Training Guide–Chemical Warfare)
C.W.S. Pamphlet No. 4, 1936 (Instructions for Using Gas Identification Sets)
C.W.S. Pamphlet No. 5, 1939, (Meteorology)
Standard Nomenclature and Price List
Chemical Warfare Matériel (1940)
C.W.S. Supply Catalog, 1937
Reference Data, Chemical Warfare School (Restricted) (1938)
Circular 15, War Department, 1940—War Department Training Films
TM No. 6, Hq. Sixth Corps Area, October 1, 1938, (Corps Area Training Directive) (As amended)
Tables of Basic Allowances
Circular 39, War Department, 1935, Local Responsibility for Inspection, Storage and Repair of Gas Masks

Circular 28, War Department, 1936, Section II, Gas Masks (Acted on by Inspectors and Surveying Officers, Disposition of)

Circular 49, War Department, 1938, Size of Gas Mask–Entry on Service Record

Circulars 73 and 75, War Department, 1938, Handling Smoke-producing Matériel

By Command of Brigadier General BONESTEEL:

WILLIAM H. WILBUR,
Colonel, General Staff Corps,
Chief of Staff.

OFFICIAL:

EDWARD ROTH, JR.,
Colonel, Adjutant General's Department,
Adjutant General.

Appendix H

CHEMICAL WARFARE SERVICE, UNIT

DATA, WORLD WAR II

This appendix is composed of sixteen tables which list pertinent data on chemical warfare units in World War II. These units correspond to those listed in Table 9 of the text.

There is a table for each type of unit in Table 9 except for chemical depot companies and chemical base depot companies which are combined in one table.

Key to Table Format

Column 1.   "N" indicates Negro unit.

Column 2.   "C" (conversion) or "R" (redesignation) before activation date denotes unit previously existing in another type or service. Activation information appears in Columns 11 and 12.

Column 5.   All zone of interior stations, except ports of embarkation, are listed as training stations.

Columns 6 & 7. In some cases where conversion and/or redesignations occurred overseas, the over-all overseas service dates are given regardless of changes in unit status since information on specific overseas locations is not available.

Column 8.   a. In some cases, the place of inactivation or disbandment, Column 10, is not located in the theater given in Column 8. In this situation, the given theater is that in which a unit either performed the major portion of its active service or where unit activity in a subsequent theater, except for date and place of inactivation or disbandment, is not clearly documented.

        b. Abbreviations:

AD	Alaskan Department
CDC	Caribbean Defense Command
CZ	Canal Zone
ETO	European Theater
HD	Hawaiian Department
I-B	India-Burma Theater
MIDPAC	Mid-Pacific Area
MTO	Mediterranean Theater
NATO	North African Theater
PR	Puerto Rico
SWPA	Southwest Pacific Area

Columns 9&10. Unless otherwise noted all units were inactivated. "D" indicates disbandment. If a unit were converted or redesignated no information is given in either column. For units existing in 1946, precise dates of inactivation or disbandment are not given: "existing in 1946" is entered in Column 9, and last known location is given in Column 10

Column 11.   a. "C" or "R" before date indicates unit conversion or redesignation to another type or service. See Column 2 for original activation.

b. Absence of a symbol ("C" or "R") indicates a date of original activation in another type or service. In this case, conversion or redesignation information is entered in Column 1. See explanatory note on Columns 1 and 2.

Column 12.   a. When a date appears in Column 11 without any information in Column 12, see footnotes.

b. Abbreviations:

AAA	Anti Aircraft Artillery	Maint	Maintenance
Am	Ammunition	Mbl	Mobile
Avn	Aviation	Mort	Mortar
AW	Automatic Weapons	.Mtz	Motorized
Bn	Battalion	Opns	Operations
CA	Coast Artillery	Ord	Ordnance
Cml	Chemical	Plat	Platoon
Co	Company	POA	Pacific Ocean Areas
Comp	Composite	Proc	Processing
Decon	Decontamination	QM	Quartermaster
Det	Detachment	Regt	Regiment
Engr	Engineer	Sep	Separate
FA	Field Artillery	SG	Smoke Generator
Gen	General	Sup	Supply
Hq	Headquarters	Svc	Service
Lab	Laboratory	TD	Tank Destroyer

APPENDIX H-1—CHEMICAL MORTAR BATTALIONS

Unit designation (1)	Date activated (2)	TRAINING			OVERSEAS SERVICE			INACTIVATION OR DISBANDMENT		CONVERSION OR REDESIGNATION	
		From (3)	To (4)	Place (5)	From (6)	To (7)	Theater (8)	Date (9)	Place (10)	Date (11)	Comments (12)
1, Co A^a	C30 Apr 31	30 Apr 31	12 Mar 42	Schofield Barracks, Hawaii	30 Apr 31	12 Mar 42	HD			24 Feb 20 C12 Mar 42	Activated as 2d Sep Cml Co 91 Cml Co (Mtz)
2, Co A^b	16 Apr 35	16 Apr 35 17 Jan 42 10 Jul 42 21 Feb 43	16 Jan 42 9 Jul 42 21 Feb 43 24 May 43	Edgewood Arsenal, Md. Ft. Bragg, N. C. Carolina Maneuver Area Cp. Pickett, Va.	8 Jun 43 10 Jul 43 15 Aug 44	5 Jul 43 14 Aug 44 26 Jul 46	NATO MTO ETO	26 Jul 46	Germany	24 Nov 43 31 Dec 44	Only Hq & Hq Co & Co A were activated in 1935. The remaining units of the bn were activated 1 Jan 42.
3	1 Jan 42	1 Jan 42 7 Apr 42 30 Jul 42 27 Oct 42	3 Apr 42 28 Jul 42 25 Oct 42 16 Apr 43	Ft. Benning, Ga. Ft. Bliss, Tex. Louisiana Maneuver Area Ft. Bliss, Tex.	28 Apr 43 10 Jul 43 15 Aug 44	10 Jul 43 15 Aug 44 2 Jan 46	NATO MTO ETO	2 Jan 46	Cp. Patrick Henry, Va.	24 Nov 43 11 Mar 45	
71	C21 Nov 44	21 Nov 44 25 Nov 44	24 Nov 44 7 Jul 45	Cp. Stewart, Ga. Cp. Shelby, Miss.	12 Jul 45	17 Jan 46	SWPA	18 Jan 46	Seattle, Wash.	20 Nov 42 30 Apr 43	Activated as 479 CA Bn (Sep) Redesignated as 479 AAA AW Bn
72	C 7 Dec 44	7 Dec 44 2 Dec 44	1 Dec 44 1 Jun 45	Ft. Leonard Wood, Mo. Cp. Shelby, Miss.	6 Jun 45	18 Apr 46	MIDPAC	18 Apr 46	Oahu, Hawaii	10 Apr 43 1 Apr 44	Activated as 560 CA Bn (Sep) Redesignated as 560 AAA AW Bn
80^c	30 Jun 44	30 Jun 44	15 Jan 45	Cp. Swift, Tex.	27 Jan 45	30 Jan 46	SWPA	1 Feb 46	Cp. Stoneman, Calif.	4 Mar 45	
81	25 Apr 42	25 Apr 42 4 Apr 43 7 May 43 12 Jun 43 31 Jul 43 9 Aug 43	2 Apr 43 4 May 43 10 Jun 43 31 Jul 43 9 Aug 43 14 Oct 43	Ft. D. A. Russell, Tex. Louisiana Maneuver Area Cp. Gordon Johnston, Fla. Cp. Pickett, Va. Cp. Bradford, Va. Cp. Pickett, Va.	22 Oct 43	2 Sep 45	ETO	7 Nov 45	Ft. Leonard Wood, Mo.	22 Feb 45	

No.	From	To	Station	Overseas — From	Overseas — To	Theater	Inactivated / Status	Location	Date
82	25 Apr 42 10 Mar 43 26 Apr 43	8 Mar 43 25 Apr 43 12 Jun 43	Ft. Bliss, Tex. Louisiana Maneuver Area Cp. Swift, Tex.	28 Jun 43		SWPA	Existing in 1946	In Japan	16 Mar 45
83	10 Jun 42	19 Apr 43	Cp. Gordon, Ga.	28 Apr 43 10 Jul 43 15 Aug 44	5 Jul 43 12 Aug 44 25 Nov 45	NATO MTO ETO	26 Nov 45	Boston, Mass.	31 Dec 44
84	5 Jun 42	18 Apr 43	Cp. Rucker, Ala.	28 Apr 43 8 Jan 44	ca. Jan 44 25 Sep 45	NATO MTO	25 Sep 45	Italy	8 Nov 44
85	5 Jun 43 2 Dec 43	2 Dec 43 1 Jul 44	Ft. D. A. Russell, Tex. Cp. Swift, Tex.	28 Jul 43	31 May 46	SWPA	31 May 46	Philippines	17 Dec 44
86	17 May 43	11 Apr 44	Cp. Swift, Tex.	14 Apr 44	10 Jul 45	ETO	Existing in 1946	At Cp. Campbell, Ky.	15 Feb 45
87	22 May 43 3 Feb 44	31 Jan 44 24 Mar 44	Cp. Rucker, Ala. Tennessee Maneuver Area	31 Mar 44	2 Aug 45	ETO	6 Nov 45	Ft. Benning, Ga.	26 Apr 45
88	29 May 43 2 Feb 44 26 Feb 44	1 Feb 44 25 Feb 44 16 Apr 44	Cp. Rucker, Ala. Tennessee Maneuver Area Cp. Rucker, Ala.	30 Apr 44	28 Dec 45	SWPA	29 Dec 45	Cp. Anza, Calif.	15 Feb 45
89	15 Nov 43 8 Apr 44 20 Sep 44	5 Apr 44 18 Sep 44 16 Nov 44	Cp. Roberts, Calif. Cp. Carson, Colo. Cp. Gruber, Okla.	2 Dec 44	5 Jul 45	ETO	29 Oct 45	Ft. Jackson, S. C.	17 Dec 44
90	10 Feb 44 16 Oct 44	15 Oct 44 22 Oct 44	Ft. Bragg, N. C. Cp. Kilmer, N. J.	22 Oct 44	6 Jul 45	ETO	20 Feb 46	Ft. Jackson, S. C.	3 Dec 44
91	15 Feb 44 4 Apr 44	3 Apr 44 2 Oct 44	Cp. Robinson, Ark. Cp. Swift, Tex.	11 Oct 44	10 Jul 45	ETO	Existing in 1946	At Ft. Lewis, Wash.	22 Feb 45
92	9 Feb 44	17 Jun 44	England	9 Feb 44	3 Aug 45	ETO	27 Oct 45	Cp. S. L. Obispo, Calif.	15 Dec 44
93	24 Mar 44 19 Aug 44 25 Aug 44 4 Oct 44 17 Oct 44	24 Mar 44 19 Aug 44 3 Oct 44 16 Oct 44 9 Jan 45	Cp. Rucker, Ala. Ft. Benning, Ga. Cp. Rucker, Ala. Cp. Sibert, Ala. Cp. Shelby, Miss.	18 Jan 45	4 Jul 45	ETO	20 Oct 45	Ft. Bragg, N. C.	18 Nov 44

APPENDIX H-1—CHEMICAL MORTAR BATTALIONS—Continued

Unit desig-nation (1)	Date activated (2)	TRAINING			OVERSEAS SERVICE			INACTIVATION OR DISBANDMENT		CONVERSION OR REDESIGNATION	
		From (3)	To (4)	Place (5)	From (6)	To (7)	Theater (8)	Date (9)	Place (10)	Date (11)	Comments (12)
94	24 Mar 44	24 Mar 44 11 Apr 44 12 Aug 44 18 Aug 44 30 Sep 44 20 Oct 44 11 Nov 44	10 Apr 44 12 Aug 44 18 Aug 44 29 Sep 44 19 Oct 44 10 Nov 44 22 Dec 44	Ft. Jackson, S. C. Cp. Rucker, Ala. Ft. Benning, Ga. Cp. Rucker, Ala. Cp. Shelby, Miss. Cp. Sibert, Ala. Cp. Shelby, Miss.	21 Jan 45	13 Jul 45	ETO	5 Nov 45	Cp. Shelby, Miss.	11 Jan 45	
95	1 Apr 44	1 Apr 44 20 Oct 44 7 Nov 44	19 Oct 44 6 Nov 44 10 Jan 45	Cp. Polk, La. Cp. Chaffee, Ark. Cp. Polk, La.	18 Jan 45	6 Jul 45	ETO	19 Dec 45	Cp. Shelby, Miss.	14 Nov 44	
96	1 Apr 44	1 Apr 44 10 Nov 44	8 Nov 44 22 Dec 44	Cp. Livingston, La. Cp. Swift, Tex.	11 Feb 45	13 Feb 46	ETO	14 Feb 46	Cp. Kilmer, N. J.	11 Jan 45	
97	5 May 44	5 May 44 9 Dec 44	5 Dec 44 17 Jan 45	Ft. Leonard Wood, Mo. Cp. Gruber, Okla.	3 Feb 45	6 Jul 45	ETO	23 Nov 45	Cp. Polk, La.	16 Feb 45	
98	C 24 Jun 44	24 Jun 44	24 Dec 45	Buna, New Guinea	24 Jun 44	24 Dec 45	SWPA	26 Dec 45	Cp. Anza, Calif.	18 Dec 41 20 Mar 45	641 TD Bn Redesignated as 98 Cml Mort Bn
99	28 Aug 44	28 Aug 44	20 Nov 44	Italy	28 Aug 44 24 Nov 44	20 Nov 44 6 Jul 45	MTO ETO	18 Oct 45	Cp. Chaffee, Ark.	31 Dec 44	
100	30 Aug 44	30 Aug 44	2 Nov 44	Italy	30 Aug 44	12 Oct 45	MTO	13 Oct 45	Cp. M. Standish, Mass.	15 Nov 44	
443	C 1 Jul 45	1 Jul 45	22 Sep 45	Cp. Hood, Tex.				22 Sep 45	Cp. Hood, Tex.	25 Sep 44	Activated as 443 FA Bn (Mtz)
483	C 1 Jul 45	1 Jul 45	22 Sep 45	Cp. Hood, Tex.				22 Sep 45	Cp. Hood, Tex.	25 Sep 44	Activated as 483 FA Bn (Mtz)

534	C 5 Jul 45	5 Jul 45	8 Sep 45	Cp. Gruber, Okla.	8 Sep 45	Cp. Gruber, Okla.	16 Oct 44 Activated as 534 FA Bn (Mtz)
537	C 5 Jul 45	5 Jul 45	8 Sep 45	Cp. Gruber, Okla.	8 Sep 45	Cp. Gruber, Okla.	16 Oct 44 Activated as 537 FA Bn (Mtz)
560	C 9 Jul 45	9 Jul 45	22 Sep 45	Ft. Bragg, N. C.	22 Sep 45	Ft. Bragg, N. C.	25 Sep 44 Activated as 560 FA Bn (Mtz)
781	C 5 Jul 45	5 Jul 45	8 Sep 45	Cp. Bowie, Tex.	8 Sep 45	Cp. Bowie, Tex.	16 Feb 42 Activated as 1st Bn, 30 CA Regt 17 Aug 44 Converted as 781 FA Bn
782	C 5 Jul 45	5 Jul 45	8 Sep 45	Cp. Bowie, Tex.	8 Sep 45	Cp. Bowie, Tex.	16 Sep 40 Activated as 2d Bn 244 CA Regt 5 Jun 44 Converted as 889 CA Bn 17 Aug 44 Converted as 782 FA Bn

a Activated as the 2d Separate Chemical Company, 24 Feb 20. Converted as the 1st Chemical Battalion (Separate) Co A, 30 Apr 31. Again converted as the 91st Chemical Mortar Company, 12 Mar 42. See Columns 11 and 12. This is the only conversion known of a chemical mortar battalion during World War II.

b The 2d and 3d Battalions activated as separate chemical battalions (motorized) (see Column 2). Redesignated chemical battalions (motorized), Column 11. Again redesignated chemical mortar battalions, Column 11, Line 2.

c Units 80 through 97, inclusive, and units 99 and 100 were activated as chemical battalions (motorized) (see Column 2). Redesignated as chemical mortar battalions on dates shown in Column 11.

APPENDIX H-2—CHEMICAL MORTAR COMPANIES

Unit desig-nation (1)	Date activated (2)	TRAINING			OVERSEAS SERVICE			INACTIVATION OR DISBANDMENT		CONVERSION OR REDESIGNATION	
		From (3)	To (4)	Place (5)	From (6)	To (7)	Theater (8)	Date (9)	Place (10)	Date (11)	Comments (12)
1	13 Jul 27	13 Jul 27	1 Feb 29	Corozal, Canal Zone	13 Jul 27	30 Mar 43	CZ	29 May 43	Cp. Sibert, Ala.	1920 / 1 Apr 31 / 24 Mar 42	Activated as Co C, 1st Gas Regt / Converted as 1st Sep Cml Co (Mtz) / Redesig as 1st Sep Cml Co Wpns (Mtz)
4	2 Oct 30	2 Oct 30	15 Mar 33	Ft. Wm. McKinley, P. I.	2 Oct 30	ca. May 42	SWPA	ca. May 42	Philippines		
5a	1 Jan 42	1 Jan 42	6 Jul 45	Edgewood Arsenal, Md.				19 Nov 46	Edgewood Arsenal, Md.	16 Apr 45	
91	C12 Mar 42	12 Mar 42	12 Sep 44	Schofield Barracks, Hawaii	12 Mar 42 / 20 Oct 44	12 Sep 44 / 15 Dec 45	MIDPAC / SWPA	Existing in 1946	In Pacific Area	24 Feb 20 / 30 Apr 31 / 24 Feb 45	Activated 2d Sep Cml Co / Converted as 1st Sep Cml Bn, Co A / Converted as 91 Cml Mort Co
132	21 Jul 45	21 Jul 45	13 Oct 45	France	21 Jul 45	13 Oct 45	ETO	13 Oct 45	Germany		
133	21 Jul 45	21 Jul 45	13 Oct 45	France	21 Jul 45	13 Oct 45	ETO	13 Oct 45	Germany		
134	21 Jul 45	21 Jul 45	13 Oct 45	France	21 Jul 45	13 Oct 45	ETO	13 Oct 45	Germany		
135	21 Jul 45	21 Jul 45	13 Oct 45	France	21 Jul 45	13 Oct 45	ETO	13 Oct 45	Germany		
136	17 Aug 45	17 Aug 45	13 Oct 45	Germany	17 Aug 45	13 Oct 45	ETO	13 Oct 45	Germany		
137	17 Aug 45	17 Aug 45	13 Oct 45	Germany	17 Aug 45	13 Oct 45	ETO	13 Oct 45	Germany		
138	17 Aug 45	17 Aug 45	13 Oct 45	Germany	17 Aug 45	13 Oct 45	ETO	13 Oct 45	Germany		
139	17 Aug 45	17 Aug 45	13 Oct 45	Germany	17 Aug 45	13 Oct 45	ETO	13 Oct 45	Germany		

	189	26 Aug 44	26 Aug 44	18 Aug 45	Hawaii		26 Aug 44	15 Jan 46	MIDPAC	15 Jan 46	Hawaii	8 Nov 44	
Co C, 2d Cml Regt[b]		1 Apr 31	1 Jan 42	Ft. Benning, Ga			1 Jan 42	Ft. Benning, Ga.				1920	Activated as Co C, 1st Cml Regt

[a] The 5th, 91, and 189 units activated as chemical companies (motorized) (see Column 2) Redesignated chemical mortar companies on dates shown in Column 11

[b] Upon inactivation, unit personnel were transferred to the 3d Separate Chemical Battalion, 1 Jan 42.

APPENDIX H-3—CHEMICAL SMOKE GENERATOR BATTALIONS

Unit designation (1)	Date activated (2)	TRAINING			OVERSEAS SERVICE			INACTIVATION OR DISBANDMENT		CONVERSION OR REDESIGNATION	
		From (3)	To (4)	Place (5)	From (6)	To (7)	Theater (8)	Date (9)	Place (10)	Date (11)	Comments (12)
22[a]	5 May 44	5 May 44	31 Aug 44	Italy	5 May 44 / 4 Sep 44	31 Aug 44 / 3 Nov 45	MTO / ETO	3 Nov 45	Germany		
23[b]	27 May 44	27 May 44	14 Sep 44	England, France	27 May 44	12 Nov 45	ETO	12 Nov 45	Germany		
24	1 Jun 44	1 Jun 44	13 Aug 44	England	1 Jun 44	12 Nov 45	ETO	12 Nov 45	Germany		
25[c]	4 Jun 44	4 Jun 44	19 Aug 44	England	4 Jun 44	25 Feb 46	ETO			C30 Jun 45	25 Cml Svc Bn
26	2 Jul 44	2 Jul 44	21 Apr 45	New Guinea	2 Jul 44	25 Jan 46	SWPA	25 Jan 46	Philippines		
27	15 Jul 44	15 Jul 44 / 25 Jul 44	24 Jul 44 / 5 Sep 44	Cp. Sibert, Ala. / Ft. G. Johnston, Fla.	15 Sep 44	12 Nov 45	ETO			C30 Jun 45	27 Cml Svc Bn
28	22 Jan 45	22 Jan 45	ca 15 Apr 45	Cp. Sibert, Ala.	29 Apr 45	15 Apr 46	MIDPAC	15 Apr 46	Okinawa		

[a] All units were hq & hq dets only.

[b] Activation of the 23, 24 and 25 units was concurrent with the disbandment of the 46 Chemical Laboratory Company, 27 May 44.

[c] Overseas service dates for 25 and 27 units include entire period overseas regardless of conversions.

APPENDIX H-4—CHEMICAL SMOKE GENERATOR COMPANIES

Unit desig-nation (1)	Date activated (2)	TRAINING			OVERSEAS SERVICE			INACTIVATION OR DISBANDMENT		CONVERSION OR REDESIGNATION	
		From (3)	To (4)	Place (5)	From (6)	To (7)	Theater (8)	Date (9)	Place (10)	Date (11)	Comments (12)
67	8 Jun 42	8 Jun 42 25 Nov 44	1 Aug 42 3 Apr 45	Cp. Haan, Calif. Cp. Sibert, Ala.	3 Sep 42 12 Apr 45	21 Nov 44 10 Nov 46	CZ SWPA	10 Nov 46	Philippines		
68	1 Jun 42	1 Jun 42 25 Nov 44	31 Jul 42 3 Apr 45	Cp. Haan, Calif. Cp. Sibert, Ala.	3 Sep 42 12 Apr 45	21 Nov 44 25 Jan 46	CZ SWPA	25 Jan 46	Okinawa		
69	20 Jun 42	1 Jul 42 22 Oct 42	18 Oct 42 24 Nov 42	Cp. Haan & Burbank, Calif. Cp. Edwards, Mass.	11 Dec 42 29 Jul 43 9 Sep 44	27 Jul 43 6 Sep 44 26 Nov 45	NATO MTO ETO	26 Nov 45	Cp. Patrick Henry, Va.		
70(N)	25 May 42	25 May 42	1 Sep 43	Sault Ste Marie, Mich.	25 Sep 43	8 Nov 44	SWPA	D 8 Nov 44	New Guinea		
71(N)	25 May 42	25 May 42 24 Dec 44 28 Mar 45	22 Dec 44 28 Mar 45 16 Jun 45	Edgewood Arsenal, Md. Cp. Sibert, Ala. Cp. Gordon Johnston, Fla.	27 Jun 45	25 Jan 46	SWPA	25 Jan 46	Okinawa		
72(N)	25 May 42	25 May 42 26 Oct 43 14 Apr 44 16 Jul 44	20 Oct 43 12 Apr 44 12 Jul 44 25 Jul 44	Ft. Lewis, Seattle, Wash. Cp. Sibert, Ala. Edgewood Arsenal, Md. Ft. Lewis, Wash.						C25 Jul 44	1532 Engr Dump Truck Co
73(N)	1 Jun 42	1 Jun 42 11 Jun 42 8 Oct 42 28 Oct 43 29 Mar 44	11 Jun 42 8 Oct 42 22 Oct 43 28 Mar 44 31 Mar 44	Cp. Haan, Calif. Cp. S. L. Obispo, Calif. Santa Monica, Calif. Cp. Sibert, Ala. Cp. Claiborne, La.						C31 Mar 44	1368 Engr Dump Truck Co
74(N)	20 Jul 42	20 Jul 42 28 Oct 43 20 Apr 44	22 Oct 43 19 Apr 44 15 Sep 44	Cp. S. L. Obispo & Burbank, Calif. Cp Sibert, Ala. Cp. Gordon Johnston, Fla.	15 Sep 44	4 Apr 46	ETO	5 Apr 46	Cp. Kilmer, N. J.		

No.	Activated	Station dates	Stations	Theater	Departed	Overseas	Disposition
75(N)	8 Apr 42	8 Apr 42 / 22 Oct 43; 27 Oct 43 / 29 Mar 44; 31 Mar 44	Cp. Haan & Inglewood, Calif.; Cp. Sibert, Ala.; Cp. Claiborne, La.				C 31 Mar 44, 1369 Engr Dump Truck Co
76(N)	8 Apr 42	8 Apr 42 / 22 Oct 43; 28 Oct 43 / 29 Mar 44; 31 Mar 44	Cp. Haan & Long Beach, Calif.; Cp. Sibert, Ala.; Cp. Claiborne, La.				C 31 Mar 44, 1370 Engr Dump Truck Co
77(N)	8 Apr 42	8 Apr 42 / 11 Aug 42; 20 Oct 43 / 12 Apr 44; 25 Jul 44 / 16 Jul 44	Ft. Rosecrans, Calif.; San Diego, Calif.; Cp. Sibert, Ala.; Edgewood Arsenal, Md.; Ft. Lewis, Wash.				C 25 Jul 44, 1533 Engr Dump Truck Co
78	25 Jun 42	25 Jun 42 / 15 Jul 42; 16 Jul 42 / 20 Oct 42	Edgewood Arsenal, Md.; Cp. Edwards, Mass.	NATO MTO ETO	2 Nov 42 / 18 Jun 43; 23 Jun 43 / 1 Sep 44; 4 Sep 44 / 27 Nov 45	28 Nov 45	Cp. Kilmer, N. J.
79	20 Jul 42	20 Jul 42 / 2 Dec 42; 2 Dec 42 / 12 Mar 43; 13 Mar 43 / 8 Aug 43	Ft. McClellan, Ala.; Cp. Sibert, Ala.; Norfolk Navy Yard, Va.	ETO	20 Aug 43 / 13 Jun 45	D 13 Jun 45	Germany
80	20 Jul 42	20 Jul 42 / 2 Dec 42; 2 Dec 42 / 15 Mar 43; 16 Mar 43 / 20 Aug 43; 20 Aug 43 / 16 Nov 43	Ft. McClellan, Ala.; Cp. Sibert, Ala.; Norfolk Navy Yard, Va.; Cp. Sibert, Ala.	ETO	5 Dec 43 / 5 Jul 45	D 5 Jul 45	Germany
81(N)	10 Aug 42	10 Aug 42 / 4 Dec 42; 6 Dec 42 / 25 Mar 44	Cp. Blanding, Fla.; Cp. Sibert, Ala.	ETO	7 Apr 44 / 28 Jan 46	29 Jan 46	Cp. Kilmer, N. J.
82(N)	10 Aug 42	10 Aug 42 / 4 Dec 42; 6 Dec 42 / 14 Mar 44	Cp. Blanding, Fla.; Cp. Sibert, Ala.	ETO	28 Mar 44 / 6 Oct 45	6 Oct 45	France
83(N)	10 Aug 42	10 Aug 42 / 4 Dec 42; 6 Dec 42 / 17 Jun 43; 20 Jul 43 / 3 Jul 43; 14 Jul 43 / 20 Oct 43; 26 Oct 43 / 19 Apr 44; 20 Apr 44 / 5 Sep 44	Cp. Blanding, Fla.; Cp. Sibert, Ala.; Alamogordo AAB, N. M.; Seattle, Wash.; Cp. Sibert, Ala.; Cp. Gordon Johnston, Fla.	ETO	15 Sep 44 / 5 Jan 46	5 Jan 46	Germany
84(N)	15 Sep 42	15 Sep 42 / 5 Dec 42; 6 Dec 42 / 29 May 43; 31 May 43 / 28 Aug 43; Sep 43 / 3 Feb 44	Cp. Shelby, Miss.; Cp. Sibert, Ala.; Orlando, Fla.; Cp. Sibert, Ala.	ETO	1 Mar 44 / 3 Dec 45	4 Dec 45	Boston, Mass

APPENDIX H-4—CHEMICAL SMOKE GENERATOR COMPANIES—Continued

Unit designation (1)	Date activated (2)	TRAINING			OVERSEAS SERVICE			INACTIVATION OR DISBANDMENT		CONVERSION OR REDESIGNATION	
		From (3)	To (4)	Place (5)	From (6)	To (7)	Theater (8)	Date (9)	Place (10)	Date (11)	Comments (12)
85(N)	15 Sep 42	15 Sep 42 / 6 Dec 42 / 31 May 43 / ca. Sep 43	5 Dec 42 / 29 May 43 / 24 Sep 43 / 14 Jan 44	Cp Shelby, Mss / Cp. Sibert, Ala / Orlando, Fla. / Cp Sibert, Ala.	29 Jan 44	6 Oct 45	ETO	6 Oct 45	France		
86(N)	26 Dec 42	26 Dec 42	14 Jan 44	Cp. Sibert, Ala.	29 Jan 44	6 Oct 45	ETO	6 Oct 45	France		
87(N)	26 Dec 42	26 Dec 42	14 Mar 44	Cp Sibert, Ala.	28 Mar 44	6 Oct 45	ETO	6 Oct 45	France		
161(N)	25 Sep 42	25 Sep 42 / 6 Dec 42	6 Dec 42 / 3 Feb 44	Cp Shelby, Miss. / Cp Sibert, Ala.	11 Feb 44	1 Dec 45	ETO	2 Dec 45	Cp Kilmer, N. J.		
162(N)	15 Jan 43	15 Jan 43 / 20 Apr 44	19 Apr 44 / 5 Sep 44	Cp. Sibert, Ala / Cp Gordon Johnston, Fla	15 Sep 44	1 Apr 46	ETO	2 Apr 46	Cp. Kilmer, N. J.		
163(N)	15 Jan 43	15 Jan 43	9 Aug 43	Cp. Sibert, Ala	21 Aug 43 / 30 Nov 43 / 9 Sep 44	25 Nov 43 / 6 Sep 44 / 23 Oct 45	NATO MTO ETO	23 Oct 45	Cp Patrick Henry, Va		
164(N)	15 Jan 43	15 Jan 43	9 Aug 43	Cp. Sibert, Ala.	21 Aug 43 / 30 Nov 43 / 13 Sep 44	25 Nov 43 / 11 Sep 44 / 30 Oct 45	NATO MTO ETO	31 Oct 45	Cp Shanks, N. Y		
165(N)	1 Feb 43	1 Feb 43	14 Dec 43	Cp. Sibert, Ala	29 Dec 43	3 Dec 45	ETO	4 Dec 45	Cp M. Standish, Mass		
166(N)	1 Feb 43	1 Feb 43 / 20 Apr 44	19 Apr 44 / 20 Aug 44	Cp. Sibert, Ala / Cp. Gordon Johnston, Fla						C20 Aug 44	488 Amphibian Truck Co
167(N)	1 Feb 43	1 Feb 43	1 May 44	Cp Sibert, Ala.	7 May 44	20 Mar 46	ETO	21 Mar 46	Cp Kilmer, N. J.		
168a	13 Oct 42	13 Oct 42 / 3 Jan 43 / 18 Oct 45	1 Jan 43 / 16 Mar 43 / 10 Apr 46	Cp Edwards, Mass / Norfolk Navy Yard, Va. / Edgewood Arsenal, Md	13 Apr 43 / 27 Sep 43 / 29 Sep 44	25 Sep 43 / 27 Sep 44 / 17 Oct 45	NATO MTO ETO	10 Apr 46	Edgewood Arsenal, Md.		

Unit	Activated	Station dates	Station	Date	Theater	Date	Date	Location	Redesignation
169	1 Nov 42	1 Nov 42 / 2 Dec 42 2 Dec 42 / 14 Feb 43 18 Feb 43 / 25 Aug 43 29 Aug 43 / 29 Jan 44 31 Jan 44 / 15 Feb 44 15 Feb 44 / 28 Feb 44 28 Feb 44 / 15 May 44 16 May 44 / 20 Aug 44	Ft McClellan, Ala Cp Sibert, Ala Cp Young, Calif Ft Hancock, N J Cp Sibert, Ala Eglin Field, Fla Cp Sibert, Ala Edgewood Arsenal, Md.						C20 Aug 44 | 185 Cml Proc Co
170(N)	1 Nov 42	1 Nov 42 / 1 Sep 43	Sault Ste Marie, Mich	25 Sep 43	SWPA	8 Nov 44	D 8 Nov 44	New Guinea	
171(N)	10 Nov 42	10 Nov 42 / 10 Jul 43 11 Jul 43 / 14 Dec 43	Edgewood Arsenal, Md Cp Sibert, Ala	29 Dec 43	ETO	6 Oct 45	6 Oct 45	France	
172	26 Oct 42	26 Oct 42 / 1 Jan 43 3 Jan 43 / 16 Mar 43	Cp Edwards, Mass Norfolk Navy Yard, Va	13 Apr 42 / 10 Oct 43	NATO MTO	1 Oct 43 / 3 Aug 45	D 3 Aug 45	Italy	
173(N)	1 Feb 43	1 Feb 43 / 22 Oct 43 28 Oct 43 / 29 Mar 44 29 Mar 44 / 31 Mar 44	Santa Monica, Calif. Cp. Sibert, Ala Cp Claiborne, La.						C31 Mar 44 | 1371 Engr Dump Truck Co
174(N)	1 Jan 43	1 Jan 43 / 22 Oct 43 28 Oct 43 / 12 Apr 44 14 Apr 44 / 12 Jul 44 17 Jul 44 / 25 Jul 44	Burbank, Calif. Cp. Sibert, Ala Edgewood Arsenal, Md Ft Lewis, Wash.						C25 Jul 44 | 1534 Engr Dump Truck Co
175(N)	10 Feb 43	10 Feb 43 / 22 Oct 43 28 Oct 43 / 28 Mar 44 29 Mar 44 / 31 Mar 44	Inglewood, Calif Cp. Sibert, Ala Cp Claiborne, La						C31 Mar 44 | 1372 Engr Dump Truck Co
176(N)	10 Jan 43	10 Jan 43 / 22 Oct 43 27 Oct 43 / 12 Apr 44 15 Apr 44 / 12 Jul 44 17 Jul 44 / 25 Jul 44	Long Beach, Calif. Cp. Sibert, Ala. Edgewood Arsenal, Md Ft Lewis, Wash						C25 Jul 44 | 1535 Engr Dump Truck Co
177(N)	1 Jan 43	1 Jan 43 / 20 Oct 43 25 Oct 43 / 28 Mar 44 29 Mar 44 / 31 Mar 44	San Diego, Calif Cp. Sibert, Ala. Cp Claiborne, La						C31 Mar 44 | 1373 Engr Dump Truck Co
178(N)	1 Jan 43	1 Jan 43 / 20 Oct 43 26 Oct 43 / 28 Mar 44 29 Mar 44 / 31 Mar 44	Ft Lewis, Seattle, Wash. Cp. Sibert, Ala. Cp Claiborne, La						C31 Mar 44 | 1451 Engr Dump Truck Co
179	20 Dec 42	20 Dec 42 / 15 Mar 43 16 Mar 43 / 11 Aug 43	Cp Sibert, Ala Norfolk Navy Yard, Va.	21 Aug 43 / 25 Sep 43 29 Sep 43 / 8 Sep 45	NATO MTO		8 Sep 45	Italy	

a Activation of the 168 through 179 Smoke Generator Companies was concurrent with the respective reorganization of the 78, 79, 70, 71, 69, 73, 74, 75, 76, 77, 72, and 80 Smoke Generator Companies

APPENDIX H-5—CHEMICAL COMPANIES, AIR OPERATIONS

Unit desig-nation (1)	Date activated (2)	TRAINING From (3)	TRAINING To (4)	TRAINING Place (5)	OVERSEAS SERVICE From (6)	OVERSEAS SERVICE To (7)	Theater (8)	INACTIVATION OR DISBANDMENT Date (9)	INACTIVATION OR DISBANDMENT Place (10)	CONVERSION OR REDESIGNATION Date (11)	Comments (12)
801	29 Apr 42	29 Apr 42	2 Oct 42	Will Rogers Fld, Okla.				D 1 May 44	Key Fld, Miss.		
		3 Oct 42	21 May 43	H. Smart Aprt, Ga.							
		22 May 43	15 Jul 43	Harding Fld, La.							
		16 Jul 43	18 Sep 43	H. Smart Aprt, Ga.							
		19 Sep 43	29 Oct 43	Drew Fld, Fla.							
		30 Oct 43	15 Mar 44	H. Smart Aprt, Ga.							
		15 Mar 44	1 May 44	Key Fld, Miss.							
802	29 Apr 42	29 Apr 42	17 May 42	Will Rogers Fld, Okla.	19 Dec 44	19 Dec 45	MIDPAC	19 Dec 45	San Francisco, Calif.		
		19 May 42	8 Oct 42	Blythe, Calif.							
		ca. Oct 42	13 Jan 43	Merced, Calif.							
		30 Jan 43	24 Mar 43	Rice Aprt, Calif.							
		26 Mar 43	7 Jul 43	Reno AAB, Nev.							
		8 Jul 43	17 May 44	Fresno, Calif.							
		20 May 44	15 Jun 44	Barksdale Fld, La.							
		18 Jun 44	21 Sep 44	Dugway P.G., Utah							
		23 Sep 44	7 Dec 44	March Fld, Calif.							
803	29 Apr 42	29 Apr 42	25 Sep 42	Will Rogers Fld, Okla.	18 Jan 44	8 Jul 45	ETO	27 Oct 45	Buckley Fld, Colo.		
		25 Sep 42	4 Feb 43	H. Smart Aprt, Ga.							
		4 Feb 43	22 May 43	Cp. Sibert, Ala.							
		29 May 43	15 Jul 43	Drew Fld, Fla.							
		16 Jul 43	2 Jan 44	H. Smart Aprt, Ga.							
804	29 Apr 42	29 Apr 42	3 Jul 42	Savannah, Ga.				D20 Dec 43	H. Smart Aprt, Ga.		
		4 Jul 42	24 Sep 42	Meridian, Miss.							
		25 Sep 42	15 May 43	Macon, Ga.							
		20 Jun 43	20 Dec 43	H. Smart Aprt, Ga.							
805	29 Apr 42	29 Apr 42	26 Sep 42	Savannah, Ga.	24 Mar 44	29 Jun 45	MTO	26 Dec 45	San Francisco, Calif.		
		26 Sep 42	17 Jul 43	H. Smart Aprt, Ga.	4 Aug 45	24 Dec 45	MIDPAC				
		18 Jul 43	13 Aug 43	Key Fld, Meridian, Miss.							
		19 Sep 43	11 Nov 43	Barksdale Fld, La.							
		13 Nov 43	24 Dec 43	H. Smart Aprt, Ga.							

No.	Activated	Stations (with dates)	Overseas dates	Theater	Status date	Final station
806	29 Apr 42	25 Dec 43 – 24 Jan 44 Ft. Knox, Ky. (Goodman Fld); 25 Jan 44 – 15 Mar 44 H. Smart Aprt, Ga.	5 May 43 – 17 Aug 45	ETO	12 Feb 46	Buckley Fld, Colo.
807	29 Apr 42	29 Apr 42 – 7 Jun 42 Ft. Crockett, Tex.; 7 Jun 42 – 20 Nov 42 Will Rogers Fld, Okla.; 25 Nov 42 – 1 Apr 43 H. Smart Aprt, Ga.; 2 Apr 43 – 20 May 43 Drew Fld, Fla.; 21 May 43 – 9 Sep 43 H. Smart Aprt, Ga.	20 Sep 43 – 1 Jan 46	ETO	1 Jan 46	Hampton Roads, Va.
808	29 Apr 42	29 Apr 42 – 27 Jun 42 Savannah, Ga.; 28 Jun 42 – 25 Sep 42 Meridian, Miss.; 25 Sep 42 – 18 May 43 H. Smart Aprt, Ga.	1 Jun 43 – 1946	ETO	Existing in 1946	In France
809	4 Sep 42	4 Sep 42 – 4 Sep 44 Australia; New Guinea	4 Sep 42 – 20 May 46	SWPA	20 May 46	Philippines
810	26 Jun 42	26 Jun 42 – 3 Oct 42 Barksdale Fld, La.; 4 Oct 42 – 14 Dec 43 H. Smart Aprt, Ga.	29 Dec 43 – 14 Oct 45	ETO	15 Oct 45	Cp. Shanks, N. Y.
811	1 Jul 42	1 Jul 42 – 24 Sep 42 MacDill Fld, Fla.; 24 Sep 42 – 16 Jul 43 H. Smart Aprt, Ga.; 17 Jul 43 – 20 Dec 43 Drew Fld, Fla.			D 20 Dec 43	Drew Fld, Fla.
812	26 Jun 42	26 Jun 42 – 30 Jul 42 Barksdale Fld, La.; 30 Jul 42 – 2 Oct 42 Columbia AAB, S. C.; 2 Oct 42 – 21 May 43 H. Smart Aprt, Ga.; 22 May 43 – 1 Jun 43 Waycross, Ga.; 2 Jun 43 – 10 Aug 43 H. Smart Aprt, Ga.	21 Aug 43 – 23 Jan 44; 29 Jan 44 – 29 Jun 45; 4 Aug 45 – 19 Dec 45	NATO; ETO	19 Dec 45	San Francisco, Calif.
813	17 Jul 42	17 Jul 42 – 12 Mar 43 MacDill Fld, Fla.; 27 Mar 43 – 10 Apr 44 Leesburg, Fla.; 10 Apr 44 – 2 Jun 44 Barksdale Fld, La.; 5 Jun 44 – 22 Aug 44 Glendale, Calif.; 22 Aug 44 – 7 Dec 44 March Fld, Calif.	19 Dec 44 – 24 Dec 45	MIDPAC	26 Dec 45	Los Angeles, Calif.
814	4 Aug 42	4 Aug 42 – 26 Sep 42 Columbia AAB, S. C.; 26 Sep 42 – 4 Feb 43 H. Smart Aprt, Ga.; 4 Feb 43 – 22 May 43 Cp. Sibert, Ala.; 22 May 43 – 27 Jun 43 H. Smart Aprt, Ga.; 28 Jun 43 – 12 Sep 43 Lake Charles, La.; 13 Sep 43 – 21 Nov 43 H. Smart Aprt, Ga.	5 Dec 43 – 25 Aug 45	ETO	3 Jan 46	Buckley Fld, Colo.
815	6 Jul 42	6 Jul 42 – 23 Jul 42 Salt Lake City, Utah; 23 Jul 42 – 12 Oct 42 Alamogordo AAB, N. M.; 14 Oct 42 – 12 Oct 42 Merced, Calif.; 13 Jan 43 – 1 Jul 43 Reno AAB, Nev.; 2 Jul 43 – 5 Jan 44 Fresno, Calif.	19 Jan 44 – 14 Oct 45	ETO	15 Oct 45	Cp. Shanks, N. Y.

APPENDIX H-5—CHEMICAL COMPANIES, AIR OPERATIONS—Continued

Unit desig- nation (1)	Date activated (2)	TRAINING			OVERSEAS SERVICE			INACTIVATION OR DISBANDMENT		CONVERSION OR REDESIGNATION	
		From (3)	To (4)	Place (5)	From (6)	To (7)	Theater (8)	Date (9)	Place (10)	Date (11)	Comments (12)
816	6 Jul 42	6 Jul 42 29 Oct 42 13 Jan 42 2 Jul 43	29 Oct 42 12 Jan 43 1 Jul 42 13 Feb 43	Salt Lake City, Utah Merced, Calif. Reno AAB, Nev. Fresno, Calif.	23 Feb 44	14 Jan 46	I-B	14 Jan 46	India		
817	13 Jul 42	13 Jul 42 12 Sep 42 6 Oct 42 15 Jan 43 2 Jul 43 23 Aug 44 21 Jan 45 1 Apr 45	12 Sep 42 6 Oct 42 14 Jan 43 1 Jul 43 20 Dec 43 19 Jan 45 1 Apr 45 14 May 45	Salt Lake City, Utah Hill Fld, Ogden, Utah Merced, Calif. Reno AAB, Nev. Fresno, Calif. Barksdale Fld, La. Columbia AAB, S. C. Buckley Fld, Colo.	16 May 45	14 May 46	MIDPAC	14 May 46	Okinawa		Unit disbanded 20 Dec 43. Reconstituted as the same numbered unit—23 Aug 44.
818	13 Jul 42	13 Jul 42 25 Sep 42 28 Jul 43 25 Sep 43	25 Sep 42 26 Jul 43 23 Sep 43 20 Dec 43	Conestee Aprt, S C H Smart Aprt, Ga. DeRidder AAB, La. H. Smart Aprt, Ga.				D20 Dec 43	H. Smart Aprt, Ga.		
819	13 Jul 42	13 Jul 42 4 Oct 42 4 Feb 43 25 May 43 30 Jun 43 16 Sep 43	3 Oct 42 4 Feb 43 25 May 43 28 Jun 43 14 Sep 43 21 Nov 43	Barksdale Fld, La. H Smart Aprt, Ga. Cp Sibert, Ala H. Smart Aprt, Ga. Will Rogers Fld, Okla. Macon Aprt, Ga.	5 Dec 43	23 Aug 45	ETO	27 Oct 45	Buckley Fld, Colo.		
820	13 Jul 42	13 Jul 42 24 Sep 42 4 Feb 43 25 May 43 30 Aug 43	24 Sep 42 4 Feb 43 25 May 43 30 Aug 43 20 Dec 43	MacDill Fld, Fla. H Smart Aprt, Ga Cp Sibert, Ala. H Smart Aprt, Ga Cp Sibert, Ala.				D20 Dec 43	Cp. Sibert, Ala.		
821	15 Mar 43	15 Mar 43 25 Mar 43	25 Mar 43 3 Jul 43	Daniel Fld, Ga Cp. Sibert, Ala.				D20 Dec 43	H. Smart Aprt, Ga.		

Unit	Activated	Station dates	Stations	Disposition date	Disposition place	Remarks
822	15 Mar 43	15 Mar 43–25 Mar 43; 25 Mar 43–3 Jul 43; 3 Jul 43–20 Dec 43	Daniel Fld, Ga.; Cp Sibert, Ala; H. Smart Aprt, Ga.	D20 Dec 43	H. Smart Aprt, Ga.	
823	15 Mar 43	15 Mar 43–25 Mar 43; 25 Mar 43–3 Jul 43; 3 Jul 43–20 Dec 43	Daniel Fld, Ga.; Cp. Sibert, Ala.; H. Smart Aprt, Ga.	D20 Dec 43	H. Smart Aprt, Ga.	
824	15 Mar 43	15 Mar 43–25 Mar 43; 25 Mar 43–1 Nov 43; 1 Nov 43–10 Dec 43	Daniel Fld, Ga; Cp. Sibert, Ala.; H. Smart Aprt, Ga.	D20 Dec 43	De Ridder AAB, La	
825(N)	15 Mar 43	15 Mar 43–25 Mar 43; 25 Mar 43–1 Nov 43; 11 Nov 43–20 Dec 43	Daniel Fld, Ga.; Cp. Sibert, Ala; De Ridder AAB, La.	C20 Dec 43		770 Cml Depot Co (Avn)
826	15 Mar 43	15 Mar 43–25 Mar 43; 25 Mar 43–1 Nov 43; 1 Nov 43–18 Nov 43; 20 Nov 43–20 Dec 43	Daniel Fld, Ga.; Cp. Sibert, Ala.; H. Smart Aprt, Ga.; Barksdale Fld, La.	D20 Dec 43	Barksdale Fld, La	
827	15 Mar 43	15 Mar 43–25 Mar 43; 5 Nov 43; 19 Nov 43–22 Dec; 23 Dec 43–27 Jan 44; 23 Aug 44–12 Mar 45; 12 Mar 45–9 Apr 45; 13 Apr 45–17 Aug 45; 25 Aug 45–20 Mar 46; 20 Mar 46	Daniel Fld, Ga.; Cp. Sibert, Ala.; Ft. Knox, Ky. (Goodman Fld); H Smart Aprt, Ga; Barksdale Fld. La.; Columbia AAB, S. C.; Buckley Fld, Colo.; MIDPAC; Hawaii	D20 Dec 43	H. Smart Aprt, Ga.	Unit disbanded 27 Jan 44. Reconstituted as the same numbered unit—23 Aug 44.
828	15 Mar 43	15 Mar 43–10 Apr 43; 11 Apr 43–5 Nov 43; 6 Nov 43–15 Mar 44; 15 Mar 44–1 May 44	Daniel Fld, Ga.; Cp. Sibert, Ala.; H. Smart Aprt, Ga.; Key Fld, Miss	D 1 May 44	Key Field, Miss.	
829	15 Mar 43	15 Mar 43–10 Apr 43; 11 Apr 43–20 Dec 43	Daniel Fld, Ga.; Cp Sibert, Ala.	C20 Dec 43		771 Cml Depot Co (Avn)
830	15 Mar 43	15 Mar 43–10 Apr 43; 11 Apr 43–4 Nov 43; 5 Nov 43–30 Dec 43; 1 Jan 44–27 Jan 44; 23 Aug 44–21 Apr 45; 24 Apr 45–28 Aug 45; 29 Aug 45–22 Oct 45	Daniel Fld, Ga; Cp Sibert, Ala; H Smart Aprt, Ga.; De Ridder AAB, La.; Barksdale Fld, La.; Buckley Fld, Colo; Ft. Lawson, Wash.	22 Oct 45	Ft Lawton, Wash	Unit disbanded 27 Jan 44 Reconstituted as the same numbered unit—23 Aug 44
831	15 Mar 43	15 Mar 43–10 Apr 43; 11 Apr 43–18 Dec 43	Daniel Fld, Ga.; Cp. Sibert, Ala	D27 Jan 44	H Smart Aprt, Ga.	

APPENDIX H-5—CHEMICAL COMPANIES, AIR OPERATIONS—Continued

Unit designation (1)	Date activated (2)	TRAINING			OVERSEAS SERVICE			INACTIVATION OR DISBANDMENT		CONVERSION OR REDESIGNATION	
		From (3)	To (4)	Place (5)	From (6)	To (7)	Theater (8)	Date (9)	Place (10)	Date (11)	Comments (12)
832	15 Mar 43	15 Mar 43 11 Apr 43	10 Apr 43 18 Dec 43	Daniel Fld, Ga Cp. Sibert, Ala.				D20 Dec 43	Macon, Ga		
833	15 Mar 43	15 Mar 43 11 Apr 43 27 Dec 43 1 Feb 44 15 Mar 44	10 Apr 43 26 Dec 43 28 Jan 44 15 Mar 44 1 May 44	Daniel Fld, Ga. Cp Sibert, Ala. Greenville AAB. S. C. H. Smart Aprt, Ga. Dale Marberry Fld, Fla.				D 1 May 44	Barksdale Fld, La.		
834	15 Mar 43	15 Mar 43 11 Apr 43	10 Apr 43 18 Dec 43	Daniel Fld, Ga. Cp. Sibert, Ala.				D20 Dec 43	H. Smart Aprt, Ga.		
835	15 Mar 43	15 Mar 43 16 May 43 18 Jan 44 5 Feb 44 18 Mar 44 1 Apr 44 7 Jun 44 7 Oct 44	15 May 43 18 Jan 44 5 Feb 44 18 Mar 44 31 Mar 44 2 Jun 44 2 Oct 44 14 Oct 44	Daniel Fld, Ga. Cp. Sibert, Ala. H Smart Aprt, Ga. Greenville AAB. S. C. H. Smart Aprt, Ga. Barksdale Fld, La. Portland AAB, Ore. Barksdale Fld, La.				D14 Oct 44	Barksdale Fld, La.		
836	15 Mar 43	15 Mar 43 16 May 43	15 May 43 18 Dec 43	Daniel Fld, Ga. Cp. Sibert, Ala				D20 Dec 43	H. Smart Aprt, Ga.		
837	15 Mar 43	15 Mar 43 16 May 43	15 May 43 18 Dec 43	Daniel Fld, Ga. Cp. Sibert, Ala.				D20 Dec 43	H. Smart Aprt, Ga.		
838	15 Mar 43	15 Mar 43 16 May 43	15 May 43 18 Dec 43	Daniel Fld, Ga. Cp. Sibert, Ala.				D20 Dec 43	H. Smart Aprt, Ga.		
839	15 Mar 43	15 Mar 43 16 May 43	15 May 43 18 Dec 43	Daniel Fld, Ga. Cp. Sibert, Ala.				D20 Dec 43	H. Smart Aprt, Ga.		
840	15 Mar 43	15 Mar 43 16 May 43	15 May 43 18 Dec 43	Daniel Fld, Ga. Cp. Sibert, Ala.				D20 Dec 43	H. Smart Aprt, Ga.		

No.	Activated	Stations (dates)			Theater	Inactivated	Location
841	15 Mar 43	Daniel Fld, Ga. 15 Mar 43 – 13 May 43; Cp Sibert, Ala. 14 May 43 – 18 Dec 43				D20 Dec 43	H. Smart Aprt, Ga.
842	15 Mar 43	Daniel Fld, Ga 15 Mar 43 – 20 Dec 43				D20 Dec 43	Daniel Fld, Ga
843	15 Mar 43	Daniel Fld, Ga. 15 Mar 43 – 20 Dec 43				D20 Dec 43	Daniel Fld, Ga
844	15 Mar 43	Daniel Fld, Ga. 15 Mar 43 – 20 Dec 43				D20 Dec 43	Daniel Fld, Ga
845	15 Mar 43	Daniel Fld, Ga. 15 Mar 43 – 20 Dec 43				D20 Dec 43	Daniel Fld, Ga
846	15 Mar 43	Daniel Fld, Ga 15 Mar 43 – 20 Dec 43				D20 Dec 43	Daniel Fld, Ga.
847	15 Mar 43	Daniel Fld, Ga. 15 Mar 43 – 20 Dec 43				D20 Dec 43	Daniel Fld, Ga.
848	15 Mar 43	Daniel Fld, Ga. 15 Mar 43 – 20 Dec 43				D20 Dec 43	Daniel Fld, Ga
849	15 Mar 43	Daniel Fld, Ga. 15 Mar 43 – 20 Dec 43				D20 Dec 43	Daniel Fld, Ga
850	15 Mar 43	Daniel Fld, Ga. 15 Mar 43 – 20 Dec 43				D20 Dec 43	Daniel Fld, Ga
851	1 May 42	Langley Fld, Va. 1 May 42 – 28 Sep 42; H. Smart Aprt, Ga. 29 Sep 42 – 22 May 43; Key Fld, Miss. 23 May 43 – 16 Jun 43; H. Smart Aprt, Ga. 18 Jun 43 – 23 Aug 43; Norfolk, Va. 24 Aug 43 – 23 Sep 43; H. Smart Aprt, Ga. 24 Sep 43 – 20 Dec 43				D20 Dec 43	H. Smart Aprt, Ga.
852	1 May 42	Manchester, N.H. 1 May 42 – 2 Oct 42; H. Smart Aprt, Ga. 4 Oct 42 – 4 Feb 43; Cp. Sibert, Ala. 4 Feb 43 – 24 May 43; H. Smart Aprt, Ga. 24 May 43 – 3 Jun 43; Waycross, Ga. 3 Jun 43 – 2 Jul 43; H. Smart Aprt, Ga. 2 Jul 43 – 4 Aug 43; Greenville AAB, S.C. 4 Aug 43 – 2 Sep 43; H. Smart Aprt, Ga. 2 Sep 43 – 15 Oct 43	15 Nov 43	10 May 46	SWPA	10 May 46	Japan
853	1 May 42	Westover Fld, Mass. 1 May 42 – 1 Oct 42; H. Smart Aprt, Ga. 3 Oct 42 – 4 Feb 43; Cp. Sibert, Ala. 4 Feb 43 – 26 May 43; Dugway P.G., Utah 29 May 43 – 26 Mar 44; Barksdale Fld, La. 30 Mar 44 – 1 May 44				D 1 May 44	Barksdale Fld, La.
854	1 May 42	Tuscon, Ariz. 1 May 42 – 24 Jul 42; Ft. G. Wright, Wash. 24 Jul 42 – 8 Oct 42; Merced, Calif. 11 Oct 42 – 14 Jan 43; Reno AAB, Nev. 15 Jan 43 – 14 May 43	1 Jun 43	1 Sep 45	ETO	27 Oct 45	Buckley Fld, Colo.

APPENDIX H-5—CHEMICAL COMPANIES, AIR OPERATIONS—Continued

| Unit desig-nation (1) | Date activated (2) | TRAINING | | | OVERSEAS SERVICE | | | INACTIVATION OR DISBANDMENT | | CONVERSION OR REDESIGNATION | |
		From (3)	To (4)	Place (5)	From (6)	To (7)	Theater (8)	Date (9)	Place (10)	Date (11)	Comments (12)
855	15 Nov 42	15 Nov 42 13 Jan 43 2 Jul 43	13 Jan 43 1 Jul 43 20 Dec 43	Merced, Calif. Reno AAB, Nev. Fresno, Calif.				D20 Dec 43	Fresno, Calif.		
856	15 May 42	15 May 42 3 Jul 42 7 Oct 42 13 Jan 43 2 Jul 43 13 Aug 43 24 Aug 43	1 Jul 42 7 Oct 42 13 Jan 43 1 Jul 43 13 Aug 43 24 Aug 43 1 Apr 44	Geiger Fld, Wash. Muroc Lake, Calif. Merced, Calif. Reno AAB, Nev. Fresno, Calif. Salinas, Calif. Fresno, Calif.				7 Apr 44	Barksdale Fld, La.		
857	13 Jun 42	13 Jun 42 17 Oct 42 13 Jan 43 2 Jul 43 15 Aug 43 2 Nov 43	16 Oct 42 13 Jan 43 1 Jul 43 13 Aug 43 31 Oct 43 10 Dec 43	Tuscon, Ariz. Merced, Calif. Reno AAB, Nev. Fresno, Calif. Corvalis, Ore. Fresno, Calif.	29 Dec 43	30 Jun 46	ETO	Existing in 1946	At Eglin Fld, Fla.		
858	15 Jun 42	15 Jun 42 17 Oct 42 13 Jan 43 12 May 43 ca. Aug 43	16 Oct 42 13 Jan 43 10 May 43 ca. Aug 43 ca. Sep 43	Tuscon, Ariz. Merced, Calif. Reno AAB, Nev. Rice AAB, Calif. Fresno, Calif.	20 Sep 43	21 Nov 45	ETO	21 Nov 45	England		
859	10 Jun 42	10 Jun 42 11 Oct 42 13 Jan 43 2 Jul 43	9 Oct 42 12 Jan 43 1 Jul 43 10 Dec 43	McChard Fld, Wash. Merced, Calif. Reno AAB, Nev. Fresno, Calif.	29 Dec 43	13 Oct 45	ETO	25 Oct 45	Cp. Shanks, N. Y.		
860	1 May 42	1 May 42 12 May 42 17 Oct 42 13 Jan 43 2 Jul 43	9 Jun 42 15 Oct 42 13 Jan 43 1 Jul 43 2 Nov 43	Ft. G. Wright, Wash. Tuscon, Ariz. Merced, Calif. Reno AAB, Nev. Fresno, Calif.	17 Nov 43	21 Nov 45	ETO	21 Nov 45	England		

No.	Constituted	From	To	Station	Overseas From	Overseas To	Theater	Status Date	Location
861	1 May 42	1 May 42	8 Oct 42	Ft. G. Wright, Wash.	25 Jun 43	31 Aug 45	ETO	27 Oct 45	Buckley Fld, Colo.
		11 Oct 42	14 Jan 43	Merced, Calif.					
		15 Jan 43	29 May 43	Reno AAB, Nev.					
862	15 May 42	15 May 42	15 May 42	Pendleton Fld, Ore.	20 Sep 43	19 Jul 45	ETO	Existing in 1946	At Buckley Fld, Colo.
		15 May 42	9 Jun 42	Ft. G. Wright, Wash.					
		12 Jun 42	15 Oct 42	Tuscon, Ariz.					
		17 Oct 42	13 Jan 43	Merced, Calif.					
		13 Jan 43	1 Jul 43	Reno AAB, Nev.					
		2 Jul 43	4 Sep 43	Fresno, Calif.					
		24 Jul 45	1 Apr 46	Buckley Fld, Colo.					
863	15 May 42	15 May 42	16 Jun 42	Ft. G. Wright, Wash.	5 Aug 42	17 Jun 46	ETO	17 Jun 46	England
		22 Jun 42	19 Jul 42	Richmond, Va.					
864	15 Nov 42	15 Nov 42	13 Jan 43	Merced, Calif.				D20 Dec 43	Fresno, Calif.
		13 Jan 43	1 Jul 43	Reno AAB, Nev.					
		2 Jul 43	20 Dec 43	Fresno, Calif.					
865	15 Nov 42	15 Nov 42	13 Jan 43	Merced, Calif.				D20 Dec 43	Fresno, Calif.
		13 Jan 43	1 Jul 43	Reno AAB, Nev.					
		2 Jul 43	20 Dec 43	Fresno, Calif.					
866	15 May 42	15 May 42	7 Jun 42	Geiger Fld, Wash.				D20 Dec 43	Fresno, Calif.
		17 Jun 42	9 Oct 42	Ephrada, Wash.					
		11 Oct 42	14 Jan 43	Merced, Calif.					
		15 Jan 43	1 Jul 43	Reno AAB, Nev.					
		2 Jul 43	20 Dec 43	Fresno, Calif.					
867	15 May 42	15 May 42	18 Jun 42	Gowen Fld, Idaho	9 Jan 44	20 Aug 45	ETO	27 Oct 45	Buckley Fld, Colo.
		11 Jun 42	12 Aug 42	Alamogordo, N. M.					
		14 Aug 42	12 Jan 43	Merced, Calif.					
		13 Jan 43	1 Jul 43	Reno AAB, Nev.					
		2 Jul 43	10 Dec 43	Fresno, Calif.					
868	29 Apr 42	29 Apr 42	16 May 42	Sarasota AAB, Fla.	21 Oct 43	1946	ETO	Existing in 1946	In Germany
		16 May 42	19 May 42	MacDill Fld, Fla.					
869	7 May 42	7 May 42	24 Jun 42	MacDill Fld, Fla.	23 May 43	21 Sep 45	ETO	7 Jan 46	Buckley Fld, Colo.
		1 Jul 42	8 Oct 42	Gowen Fld, Idaho					
		11 Oct 42	13 Jan 43	Merced, Calif.					
		15 Jan 43	5 May 43	Reno AAB, Nev.					
870	29 Apr 42	29 Apr 42	1 Oct 42	Esler Fld, La.	1 Oct 44	12 Feb 46	MIDPAC	12 Feb 46	Saipan
		3 Oct 42	16 May 43	H. Smart Aprt, Ga.					
		16 May 43	10 Jun 43	W. Northern AAB, Tenn.					
		10 Jun 43	9 Aug 43	H. Smart Aprt, Ga.					
		10 Aug 43	22 Sep 43	Barksdale Fld, La.					
		23 Sep 43	28 Dec 43	H. Smart Aprt, Ga.					

APPENDIX H-5—CHEMICAL COMPANIES, AIR OPERATIONS—Continued

Unit desig-nation (1)	Date activated (2)	TRAINING From (3)	To (4)	Place (5)	OVERSEAS SERVICE From (6)	To (7)	Theater (8)	INACTIVATION OR DISBANDMENT Date (9)	Place (10)	CONVERSION OR REDESIGNATION Date (11)	Comments (12)
		29 Dec 43	3 Feb 44	Barksdale Fld, La.							
		5 Feb 44	16 May 44	H. Smart Aprt, Ga.							
		17 May 44	19 Sep 44	Barksdale Fld, La.							
871	29 Apr 42	29 Apr 42	24 May 42	Columbia AAB, S. C.	25 Jun 43	31 Dec 45	ETO	31 Dec 45	England		
		25 May 42	25 Jun 42	Key Fld, Miss.							
		27 Jun 42	24 Sep 42	MacDill Fld, Fla.							
		29 Sep 42	10 Jun 43	H. Smart Aprt, Ga.							
872	29 Apr 42	29 Apr 42	1 Sep 42	Ft. Myers, Fla.	5 Dec 43	17 Aug 45	ETO	27 Oct 45	Buckley Fld, Colo.		
		1 Sep 42	24 Sep 42	MacDill Fld, Fla.							
		24 Sep 42	4 May 43	H. Smart Aprt, Ga.							
		6 May 43	21 Jun 43	Will Rogers Fld, Okla.							
		25 Jun 43	21 Nov 43	H. Smart Aprt, Ga.							
873	29 Apr 42	29 Apr 42	16 May 42	MacDill Fld, Fla.	20 Sep 43	8 Oct 45	ETO	10 Oct 45	Cp. Kilmer, N. J.		
		16 May 42	19 Jul 42	Sarasota AAB, Fla.							
		19 Jul 42	24 Sep 42	MacDill Fld, Fla.							
		24 Sep 42	15 May 43	H. Smart Aprt, Ga.							
		15 May 43	7 Jun 43	DeRidder AAB, La.							
		9 Jun 43	9 Sep 43	H. Smart Aprt, Ga.							
874	29 Apr 42	29 Apr 42	3 Oct 42	Barksdale Fld, La.	25 Jun 43	31 Dec 45	ETO	31 Dec 45	England		
		4 Oct 42	9 Mar 43	H. Smart Aprt, Ga.							
		11 Mar 43	9 May 43	Will Rogers Fld, Okla.							
		10 May 43	10 Jun 43	H. Smart Aprt, Ga.							
875	29 Apr 42	29 Apr 42	14 May 42	MacDill Fld, Fla.	7 Feb 43	24 Oct 43	NATO	29 Dec 45	Cp. Anza, Calif.		
		14 May 42	14 Jun 42	Ft. Myers, Fla.	29 Oct 43	29 Jun 45	ETO				
		14 Jun 42	19 Jun 42	Barksdale Fld, La.	4 Aug 45	28 Dec 45	MIDPAC				
		21 Jul 42	25 Sep 42	Greenville AAB, S. C.							
		25 Sep 42	24 Jan 43	H. Smart Aprt, Ga.							
876	29 Apr 42	29 Apr 42	25 Jun 42	MacDill Fld, Fla.	5 Aug 42	8 Dec 45	ETO	8 Dec 45	England		
		29 Jun 42	19 Jul 42	Walla Walla, Wash.							

No.	Constituted	Redesignation / movement dates and stations	Departed US	Theater	Inactivated	Location
877	29 Apr 42	29 Apr 42 / 23 Jun 42 (25 Jun / 3 Jun) — Columbia AAB, S. C.; Barksdale Fld, La.	25 Jun 43 — 21 Nov 45	ETO	21 Nov 45	England
878	29 Apr 42	29 Apr 42 / 26 Jun 42; 30 Jun / 7 Oct 42; 9 Oct / 12 Jan 43; 13 Jan / 17 Apr 43; 19 Apr / 8 May 43; 9 May / 29 May 43 — Barksdale Fld, La.; Pendleton Fld, Ore.; Merced, Calif.; Reno AAB, Nev.; Rice AAB, Calif.; Reno AAB, Nev.	25 Jun 43 — 31 Dec 45	ETO	31 Dec 45	England
879	29 Apr 42	29 Apr 42 / 26 Sep 42; 26 Sep / 9 May 43 — Columbia AAB, S. C.; H. Smart Aprt, Ga.	23 May 43 — 21 Nov 45	ETO	21 Nov 45	England
880	29 Apr 42	29 Apr 42 / 25 Jun 42; 25 Jun / 2 Oct 42; 2 Oct / ca. Jan 43; 13 Jan / 1 Jul 43; 2 Jul / 20 Dec 43 — MacDill Fld, Fla.; Pendleton Fld, Ore.; Merced, Calif.; Reno AAB, Nev.; Fresno, Calif.			D20 Dec 43	Fresno, Calif.
881	29 Apr 42	29 Apr 42 / 26 Sep 42; 26 Sep / 27 Jan 43; 28 Jan / 17 May 43 — Columbia AAB, S. C.; H. Smart Aprt, Ga.; Key Fld, Miss.	24 May 43 — 2 Aug 45	ETO	Esixtng in 1946	At MacDill Fld, Fla.
882	29 Apr 42	29 Apr 42 / 5 Jun 42; 5 Jun / 2 Oct 42; 2 Oct / 19 Jan 43; 22 Feb / 8 May 43; 11 May / 10 Sep 43 — Barksdale Fld, La.; Ft. Myers, Fla.; H. Smart Aprt, Ga.; DeRidder AAB, La.; H. Smart Aprt, Ga.	20 Sep 43 — 19 Jul 45	ETO	3 Jan 46	Buckley Fld, Colo.
883	5 May 42	5 May 42 / 26 Jun 42; 26 Jun / 31 Dec 42; 1 Jan / 14 Jan 43; 15 Jan / 1 Jul 43; 2 Jul / 20 Dec 43 — Barksdale Fld, La.; Pendleton Fld, Ore.; Merced, Calif.; Reno AAB, Nev.; Fresno, Calif.			D20 Dec 43	Fresno, Calif.
884	6 May 42	6 May 42 / 7 Oct 42; 7 Oct / 13 Jan 43; 13 Jan / 1 Jul 43; 2 Jul / 20 Dec 43 — March Fld, Calif.; Merced, Calif.; Reno AAB, Nev.; Fresno, Calif.			D31 Jan 44	Fresno, Calif.
885	30 Apr 42	30 Apr 42 / 6 Oct 42; 7 Oct / 12 Jan 43; 13 Jan / 18 Mar 43; 20 Mar / 20 Apr 43; 22 Apr / 14 May 43 — Fresno, Calif.; Merced, Calif.; Reno AAB, Nev.; Rice AAB, Calif.; Reno AAB, Nev.	1 Jan 43 — 31 Aug 45	ETO	27 Oct 45	Buckley Fld, Colo.
886	8 Jun 42	8 Jun 42 / ca. Jul 43 — Hickham Fld, Hawaii	8 Jun 42 — ca. Jul 43; 6 Jul 43 — 15 Mar 46	MIDPAC SWPA	15 Mar 46	Philippines
887	8 Jun 42	8 Jun 42 / 29 Jan 45 — Wheeler Fld, Hawaii	8 Jun 42 — 29 Jan 45; 16 Feb 45 — 1 May 46	MIDPAC SWPA	1 May 46	Philippines

APPENDIX H-5—CHEMICAL COMPANIES, AIR OPERATIONS—Continued

Unit desig- nation (1)	Date activated (2)	TRAINING			OVERSEAS SERVICE			INACTIVATION OR DISBANDMENT		CONVERSION OR REDESIGNATION	
		From (3)	To (4)	Place (5)	From (6)	To (7)	Theater (8)	Date (9)	Place (10)	Date (11)	Comments (12)
888	1 Jul 42	1 Jul 42 12 Apr 43	31 Mar 43 20 Dec 43	Howard Fld, Canal Zone Daniel Fld, Ga.	1 Jul 42	31 Mar 43	CZ	D20 Dec 43	Daniel Fld, Ga.		
889	1 Jul 42	1 Jul 42 15 May 43 ca. Jul 43 2 Sep 43 1 Nov 43	15 May 43 ca Jul 43 1 Sep 43 1 Nov 43 27 Jan 44	British Guinea, Trinidad Daniel Fld, Ga. H. Smart Aprt, Ga. Freenville AAB, S. C. Macon, Ga.	1 Jul 42	15 May 43	CDC	D27 Jan 44	H. Smart Aprt, Ga		
890	1 Jun 42	1 Jun 42 19 Oct 44	8 Oct 44 18 Apr 45	Ft. Richardson, Alaska Barksdale Fld, La.	5 May 45	20 May 46	MIDPAC	20 May 46	Guam		
891	15 Aug 42	15 Aug 42 26 Sep 42 4 Feb 43 22 May 43 5 Jun 43 4 Aug 43 8 Sep 43 15 Oct 43	26 Sep 42 4 Feb 43 22 May 43 5 Jun 43 2 Aug 43 7 Sep 43 14 Oct 43 8 Jan 44	Columbia AAB, S. C H. Smart Aprt, Ga. Cp. Sibert, Ala. H. Smart Aprt, Ga. DeRidder AAB, La. H. Smart Aprt, Ga. MacDill Fld, Fla. H. Smart Aprt, Ga.	21 Jan 44	15 May 46	MIDPAC	15 May 46	Tinian		
892	4 Sep 42	4 Sep 42	14 Mar 43	Australia	4 Sep 42	1 Feb 46	SWPA	1 Feb 46	Korea		
893	1 Jul 42	1 Jul 42 25 May 43	13 May 43 20 Dec 43	Berinquen Fld, P. R. Daniel Fld, Ga	1 Jul 42	13 May 43	CDC	D20 Dec 43	Daniel Fld, Ga.		
894	4 Sep 42	4 Sep 42	20 Dec 43	Australia	4 Sep 42 13 Aug 45	1 Aug 45 20 Feb 46	SWPA MIDPAC	20 Feb 46	Japan		
895	4 Sep 42	4 Sep 42	23 Jun 44	Australia	4 Sep 42 11 Aug 45	6 Aug 45 15 Jan 46	SWPA MIDPAC	15 Jan 46	Ryukyus		
896	1 Jul 42	1 Jul 42 1 Nov 42 25 May 43	1 Nov 42 13 May 43 20 Dec 43	Losey Fld, P. R. Berinquen Fld, P. R. Daniel Fld, Ga.	1 Jul 42	13 May 43	CDC	D20 Dec 43	Daniel Fld, Ga.		

897	15 Mar 43	15 Mar 43	20 Dec 43	Daniel Fld, Ga				D20 Dec 43	Daniel Fld, Ga.
898	15 Mar 43	15 Mar 43	20 Dec 43	Daniel Fld, Ga.				D20 Dec 43	Daniel Fld, Ga.
899	15 Mar 43	15 Mar 43	20 Dec 43	Daniel Fld, Ga.				D20 Dec 43	Daniel Fld, Ga.
900	10 May 45	10 May 45	3 Nov 45	India	10 May 45	3 Nov 45	1-B	5 Nov 45	Cp Kilmer, N. J.

APPENDIX H-6—CHEMICAL DEPOT COMPANIES (AVIATION)

Unit desig-nation (1)	Date activated (2)	TRAINING			OVERSEAS SERVICE			INACTIVATION OR DISBANDMENT		CONVERSION OR REDESIGNATION	
		From (3)	To (4)	Place (5)	From (6)	To (7)	Theater (8)	Date (9)	Place (10)	Date (11)	Comments (12)
751	1 May 42	1 May 42	21 Jul 42	Mitchel Fld, N. Y.	5 Aug 42 14 Dec 42 20 Dec 43	14 Dec 42 10 Dec 43 13 Nov 45	ETO NATO MTO	13 Nov 45	Italy		
752	15 May 42	15 May 42 10 Oct 42 15 Jan 43 13 Mar 43 4 Oct 44	8 Oct 42 14 Jan 43 8 Mar 43 4 Oct 44 8 Dec 44	Ft. G. Wright, Wash. Merced, Calif. Reno AAB, Nev. Orlando, Fla. Barksdale Fld, La.	19 Dec 44	20 May 46	MIDPAC	20 May 46	Guam		
753	7 May 42	7 May 42	20 Jan 43	MacDill Fld, Fla.	7 Feb 43 29 Jan 44	23 Jan 44 2 Nov 45	NATO MTO	2 Nov 45	Italy		
754	30 Apr 42	30 Apr 42 11 Nov 42	10 Nov 42 25 Nov 42	March Fld, Calif Merced, Calif.	6 Jan 43	29 Nov 45	ETO	1 Dec 45	New York, N. Y.		
755(N)	3 Sep 42	3 Sep 42 12 Nov 42	11 Nov 42 10 Jun 43	MacDill Fld, Fla. Columbia AAB, S. C.	24 Jun 43	31 Dec 45	ETO	31 Dec 45	Germany		
756	1 Jul 42	1 Jul 42 11 Apr 43 20 May 43 14 Oct 43	30 Mar 43 20 May 43 13 Oct 43 14 Dec 43	France Fld, Canal Zone Daniel Fld, Ga. Cp. Sibert, Ala. H. Smart Aprt, Ga.	1 Jul 42 29 Dec 43	30 Mar 43 16 Aug 45	CZ ETO	27 Oct 45	Buckley Fld, Colo.		
757	8 Jun 42	8 Jun 42	5 Feb 46	Hawaii	8 Jun 42	5 Feb 46	MIDPAC	5 Feb 46	Hawaii		
758	29 Apr 42	29 Apr 42	10 Dec 42	Savannah, Ga.	10 Dec 42 27 Mar 43 8 Jan 44	27 Mar 43 1 Jan 44 1 Feb 46	ETO NATO MTO	1 Feb 46	Italy		
759(N)	3 Sep 42	3 Sep 42 14 Nov 42 4 Feb 43	14 Nov 42 2 Feb 43 15 May 43	Savannah, Ga. Columbia AAB, S. C. Cp. Sibert, Ala.	9 Jul 43	31 Dec 45	ETO	31 Dec 45	Germany		

No.	Activated	Arrived	Departed	Station	Departed US	Returned	Theater	Inactivated	Inactivation Station	Remarks
760	29 Apr 42	29 Apr 42 2 Dec 42	1 Dec 42 15 May 43	Patterson Fld, Ohio Edgewood CW Depot, Md.	24 May 43	25 Mar 46	SWPA	25 Mar 46	Philippines	
761(N)	3 Sep 42	3 Sep 42 16 Oct 42 13 Jan 43 27 Mar 43	16 Oct 42 12 Jan 43 26 Mar 43 4 Sep 43	Muroc Lake, Calif. Merced, Calif. Reno AAB, Nev. Merced, Calif.	1 Oct 43	22 Aug 45	ETO	27 Oct 45	Buckley Fld, Colo	
762(N)	3 Sep 42	3 Sep 42 29 Oct 42 15 Jan 43 27 Mar 43	29 Oct 42 28 Dec 42 26 Mar 43 1 Aug 43	McChord Fld, Wash. Merced, Calif. Reno AAB, Nev. Merced, Calif.	20 Aug 43	15 Sep 45	ETO	10 Nov 45	Buckley Fld, Colo.	
763	15 Apr 43	15 Apr 43	19 Jul 45	England	15 Apr 43	19 Jul 45	ETO	27 Oct 45	Buckley Fld, Colo.	
764(N)	20 May 43	20 May 43 28 May 43 4 Feb 44	28 May 43 4 Feb 44 10 Apr 44	Merced, Calif. Cp. Sibert, Ala. H. Smart Aprt, Ga.	14 Apr 44	26 Dec 45	SWPA	31 Dec 45	Cp. Stoneman, Calif.	
765	1 Nov 43	1 Nov 43	20 Dec 45	England	1 Nov 43	20 Dec 45	ETO	21 Dec 45	Cp. Kilmer, N. J.	
766	28 Oct 43	28 Oct 43	5 Aug 44	England	28 Oct 43	28 Jul 45	ETO	27 Oct 45	Buckley Fld, Colo.	
767	5 Dec 43	5 Dec 43	15 Oct 44	England	5 Dec 43	8 Oct 45	ETO	10 Oct 45	Cp. Kilmer, N. J.	
769(N)	C20 Dec 43	20 Dec 43 5 Apr 44	3 Apr 44 4 Oct 44	Columbia AAB, S. C. Barksdale Fld, La.	22 Oct 44 2 Sep 45	6 Aug 45 15 Apr 46	I-B MIDPAC	15 Apr 46	Okinawa	Activated as 706 Cml Maint Co (Avn) 3 Sep 42
770(N)	C20 Dec 43	20 Dec 43 1 Apr 44	1 Apr 44 1 Jul 44	DeRidder AAB, La. Barksdale Fld, La.	21 Jul 45	15 Apr 46	MIDPAC	15 Apr 46	Okinawa	Activated as 825 Cml Co, Air Opns 15 Mar 43
771	C20 Dec 43	20 Dec 43 10 Feb 44	9 Feb 44 14 Mar 44	Cp. Sibert, Ala. H. Smart Aprt, Ga.	13 Apr 44 1 Jun 44	15 May 44 10 Jan 46	NATO I-B	10 Jan 46	India	Activated as 829 Cml Co, Air Opns 15 Mar 43

Appendix H-7—Chemical Maintenance Companies (Aviation)

Unit desig- nation (1)	Date activated (2)	TRAINING			OVERSEAS SERVICE			INACTIVATION OR DISBANDMENT		CONVERSION OR REDESIGNATION	
		From (3)	To (4)	Place (5)	From (6)	To (7)	Theater (8)	Date (9)	Place (10)	Date (11)	Comments (12)
701(N)	17 Jul 42	17 Jul 42 ca. Nov 42	ca. Nov 42 14 Aug 43	MacDill Fld, Fla. Columbia AAB, S. C.	21 Aug 43 19 Dec 43	10 Dec 43 19 Aug 45	NATO ETO	27 Oct 45	Buckley Fld, Colo.		
702(N)	3 Sep 42	3 Sep 42 ca. Nov 42	ca. Nov 42 4 Feb 44	MacDill Fld, Ala. Columbia AAB, S. C.	15 Feb 44	5 Feb 46	MIDPAC	5 Feb 46	Hawaii		
703(N)	3 Sep 42	3 Sep 42 12 Nov 43 5 Apr 44	11 Nov 43 3 Apr 44 14 Oct 44	MacDill Fld, Fla. Columbia AAB, S. C. Barksdale Fld, La.				D14 Oct 44	Barksdale Fld, La.		
704(N)	3 Sep 42	3 Sep 42 ca. Nov 42	ca. Nov 42 11 Jan 44	MacDill Fld, Fla. Columbia AAB, S. C.	7 Feb 44 3 Aug 45	21 Jul 45 1 Feb 46	SWPA MIDPAC	1 Feb 46	Japan		
705(N)	3 Sep 42	3 Sep 42 14 Nov 42 13 May 43 23 Jun 43 10 Apr 44	14 Nov 42 13 May 43 22 Jun 43 10 Apr 44 14 Oct 44	Savannah, Ga. (Hunter Fld) Columbia AAB, S. C. Daniel Fld, Ga. Orlando, Fla. Barksdale Fld, La.				D14 Oct 44	Barksdale Fld, La.		
706(N)	3 Sep 42	3 Sep 42 14 Nov 42 2 Feb 43 21 Jul 43	14 Nov 42 2 Feb 43 20 Jul 43 20 Dec 43	Savannah, Ga. (Hunter Fld) Columbia AAB, S. C. Cp. Sibert, Ala. Columbia AAB, S. C.						C20 Dec 43	769 Cml Depot Co (Avn)
707(N)	3 Sep 42	3 Sep 42 16 Oct 42 15 Jan 43 27 Mar 43 8 Sep 43	16 Oct 42 14 Jan 43 26 Mar 43 8 Sep 43 20 Dec 43	Muroc Lake, Calif. Merced, Calif. Reno AAB, Nev. Merced, Calif. Fresno, Calif.				D20 Dec 43	Fresno, Calif.		
708(N)	3 Sep 42	3 Sep 42 16 Oct 42	16 Oct 42 11 Jan 43	Muroc Lake, Calif. Merced, Calif.				D20 Dec 43	Fresno, Calif.		

Unit	Activated	From	To	Location				Disposition	Location	Conversion	Converted to
709(N)	3 Sep 42	11 Jan 43	26 Mar 43	Reno AAB, Nev.				D 20 Dec 43	Fresno, Calif.	C 1 Dec 44	211 Cml Maint Co
		27 Mar 43	8 Sep 43	Merced, Calif.							
		8 Sep 43	20 Dec 43	Fresno, Calif.							
710(N)	3 Sep 42	3 Sep 42	ca. Nov 42	McChord Fld, Wash.				D 20 Dec 43	Fresno, Calif.		
		ca. Nov 42	8 Sep 43	Merced, Calif.							
		8 Sep 43	20 Dec 43	Fresno, Calif.							
711•	3 Sep 42	3 Sep 42	3 Aug 43	Langley Fld, Va.	10 Aug 43	16 Nov 45	ETO				
712	3 Sep 42	3 Sep 42	8 Oct 42	Ft. G. Wright, Wash.				D 20 Dec 43	Fresno, Calif.		
		10 Oct 42	14 Jan 43	Merced, Calif.							
		15 Jan 43	1 Jul 43	Reno AAB, Nev.							
		2 Jul 43	20 Dec 43	Fresno, Calif.							
713(N)	20 May 43	20 May 43	ca. Jun 43	Merced, Calif.				D 20 Dec 43	W. Robbins Fld, Ga.		
		ca. Jun 43	ca. Dec 43	Cp. Sibert, Ala.							
		ca. Dec 43	20 Dec 43	W. Robbins Fld, Ga.							
714(N)	20 May 43	20 May 43	ca. Jun 43	Merced, Calif.				D 20 Dec 43	W. Robbins Fld, Ga.		
		ca. Jun 43	ca. Dec 43	Cp. Sibert, Ala.							
		ca. Dec 43	20 Dec 43	W. Robbins Fld, Ga.							

• Overseas service dates for unit include entire period overseas regardless of conversion.

APPENDIX H-8—CHEMICAL DEPOT COMPANIES AND CHEMICAL BASE DEPOT COMPANIES

Unit desig-nation (1)	Date activated (2)	TRAINING From (3)	To (4)	Place (5)	OVERSEAS SERVICE From (6)	To (7)	Theater (8)	INACTIVATION OR DISBANDMENT Date (9)	Place (10)	CONVERSION OR REDESIGNATION Date (11)	Comments (12)
3	1 Jun 41	1 Jun 41 25 Dec 41	21 Dec 41 7 Mar 42	Ft. Sam Houston, Tex. Ft. Lewis, Wash.						R 7 Mar 42	63 Cml Depot Co
6	25 Mar 42	25 Mar 42	20 Jun 42	Ft. Sam Houston, Tex.	30 Jun 42 4 Dec 42 6 Oct 43 30 Aug 44	24 Nov 42 28 Sep 45 27 Aug 44 17 Nov 45	ETO NATO MTO ETO	19 Nov 45	Cp. Kilmer, N. J.		
7	30 Apr 42	30 Apr 42 20 Jul 42 8 Nov 42	18 Jul 42 7 Nov 42 27 Nov 42	Cp. Bowie, Tex. Louisiana Maneuver Area Cp. Bowie, Tex.	7 Dec 42	19 Dec 45	ETO	20 Dec 45	Cp. Kilmer, N. J.		
8	13 Mar 42	13 Mar 42	1946	Ft. Shafter, Hawaii	13 Mar 42	1946	MIDPAC	Existing in 1946	In Hawaii		
9	1 Jul 42	1 Jul 42 27 Aug 42 9 Nov 42	27 Aug 42 8 Nov 42 18 Sep 43	Cp. Rucker, Ala. Nashville, Tenn. Cp. Rucker, Ala.	8 Oct 43	5 Jan 46	ETO	6 Jan 46	Cp. Kilmer, N. J.		
36	20 Dec 44	20 Dec 44	28 Jul 45	France	20 Dec 44 2 Sep 45	28 Jul 45 10 Apr 46	ETO SWPA	10 Apr 46	Philippines		
37	C15 Apr 44	15 Apr 44 15 Jun 44 26 Jul 44 28 Aug 44	15 Jun 44 25 Jul 44 28 Aug 44 12 Sep 44	Cp. Sibert, Ala. Cp. Rucker, Ala. Huntsville, Ala. Cp. Rucker, Ala.				12 Sep 44	Cp. Rucker, Ala.	29 Dec 42	Activated as 37 Cml Decon Co
60	15 Aug 42	15 Aug 42 1 Feb 43	31 Jan 43 2 Jun 43	Cp. Shelby, Miss. Cp. Polk, La.	1 Jul 43	16 Dec 45	ETO	17 Dec 45	Cp. Shanks, N. Y.		
61	15 Jan 43	15 Jan 43 21 Mar 43 16 Aug 43	16 Mar 43 12 Aug 43 13 Oct 43	Cp. Sibert, Ala. San Bernadino, Calif. Cp. Sibert, Ala.	21 Oct 43	29 Dec 45	ETO	31 Dec 45	New York, N. Y.		

No.	Activated	Station dates	Station	Overseas dates	Theater	Inactivated / Final date	Final location	Remarks
62•	R 12 Mar 42	12 Mar 42	Australia	12 Mar 42	SWPA	1946		16 Apr 35 / C 1 Nov 44 — Activated as 412 Cml Depot Co; 62 Cml Gen Svc Co
63	R 7 Mar 42	7 Mar 42 / 4 May 42 4 May 42 / 19 Jul 42 23 Jul 42 / 21 Sep 42 21 Sep 42 / 23 Feb 43	Pacos, Wash. Ft. Lewis, Wash. Cp. Kilmer, N. J. Cp. Pickett, Va.	1 Mar 43 / 28 Jul 43 30 Jul 43 / 11 Sep 44 14 Sep 44 / 12 Oct 45	NATO MTO ETO	13 Oct 45	Boston, Mass.	1 Jun 41 — 3d Cml Depot Co
64	15 Jan 43	15 Jan 43 / 21 Oct 43	Cp. Sibert, Ala.	3 Nov 43 / 28 May 46	ETO	28 May 46	France	
65	1 Feb 43	1 Feb 43 / 10 Sep 43	Cp. Sibert, Ala.	20 Sep 43 / 22 Nov 45	ETO	23 Nov 45	Boston, Mass	
66ᵇ	6 Jul 42	6 Jul 42 / 31 Mar 44	Iceland	6 Jul 42 / 23 Nov 45	ETO	23 Nov 45	Boston, Mass.	12 Apr 44
190	1 Feb 43	1 Feb 43 / 1 Mar 44 3 Mar 44 / 23 May 44 24 May 44 / 13 Jun 44 14 Jun 44 / 30 Jun 44	Cp. Sibert, Ala. Edgewood Arsenal, Md. Ft. Niagara, N. Y. Edgewood Arsenal, Md.			D 30 Jun 44	Edgewood Arsenal, Md.	Two platoons were in SWPA from Feb 1943 until Jun 1944.
191	4 Mar 43	4 Mar 43 / 15 Jul 43 17 Jul 43 / 18 Aug 43 20 Aug 43 / 28 Feb 44 3 Mar 44 / 2 Aug 44	Cp. Sibert, Ala. Ft. Sam Houston, Tex. Desert Training Ctr, Ariz. Cp. Shelby, Miss.	11 Aug 44 / 15 Dec 45	ETO	15 Dec 45	England	
192	9 Apr 43	9 Apr 43 / 1 Oct 43 2 Oct 43 / 6 Nov 43 8 Nov 43 / 29 Feb 44 29 Feb 44 / 1 Apr 44	Cp. Sibert, Ala. Cp. Rucker, Ala. Tennessee Maneuver Area Cp. Forrest, Tenn.	7 Apr 44 / 18 May 46	ETO	18 May 46	Germany	
193	5 May 43	5 May 43 / 15 Sep 43 16 Sep 43 / 25 Nov 43 26 Nov 43 / 26 Mar 44	Cp. Sibert, Ala. Cp. Polk, La. Ft. Sam Houston, Tex.	20 Apr 44 / 1946	ETO	Existing in 1946	In Austria	
194	15 Jun 43	15 Jun 43 / 26 Nov 43 29 Nov 43 / 24 Apr 44 29 Apr 44 / 21 Aug 44	Cp. Sibert, Ala. Calif.-Ariz. Maneuver Area Ft. Dix, N. J.	7 Sep 44 / 29 Jul 45 23 Sep 45 / 31 May 46	ETO SWPA	31 May 46	Philippines	
195	15 Jul 43	15 Jul 43 / 4 May 44 5 May 44 / 5 Aug 44	Cp. Sibert, Ala. Ft. Dix, N. J.	11 Aug 44 / 28 May 46	ETO	28 May 46	England	
198	1 Feb 44	1 Feb 44 / 21 May 44 21 May 44 / 10 Jun 44 10 Jun 44 / 15 Jul 44 16 Jul 44 / 22 Aug 44 24 Aug 44 / 6 Oct 44 7 Oct 44 / 9 Jan 45	Cp. Sibert, Ala. Huntsville, Ala. Cp. Sibert, Ala. Cp. Campbell, Ky. Louisiana Maneuver Area Cp. Swift, Tex.	17 Jun 45 / 21 Jul 45 12 Aug 45 / 11 Feb 46	ETO MIDPAC	11 Feb 46	Saipan	
199	21 Feb 44	21 Feb 44 / 13 Nov 44	Cp. Sibert, Ala.	25 Nov 44 / 20 Dec 44	ETO	D 20 Dec 44	France	1 Jul 44

APPENDIX H-8—CHEMICAL DEPOT COMPANIES AND CHEMICAL BASE DEPOT COMPANIES—Continued

Unit designation (1)	Date activated (2)	TRAINING			OVERSEAS SERVICE			INACTIVATION OR DISBANDMENT		CONVERSION OR REDESIGNATION	
		From (3)	To (4)	Place (5)	From (6)	To (7)	Theater (8)	Date (9)	Place (10)	Date (11)	Comments (12)
200	21 Mar 44	21 Mar 44	13 Nov 44	Cp. Sibert, Ala.	25 Nov 44	20 Dec 44	ETO	D20 Dec 44	France	1 Jul 44	
222	14 Aug 43	14 Aug 43	3 Feb 44	Cp. Sibert, Ala.	11 Feb 44	31 Aug 45	ETO	5 Nov 46	Huntsville, Ala.		
223	14 Aug 43	14 Aug 43	29 Mar 44	Cp. Sibert, Ala.	7 Apr 44	14 Dec 45	ETO	15 Dec 45	New York, N. Y.	24 Feb 44	
224	14 Aug 43	14 Aug 43	29 Mar 44	Cp. Sibert, Ala.	13 Apr 44	3 Jan 46	ETO	4 Jan 46	New York, N. Y.	24 Feb 44	
225	14 Aug 43	14 Aug 43	29 Mar 44	Cp. Sibert, Ala.	13 Apr 44	30 Nov 46	ETO	30 Nov 46	France	24 Feb 44	
226	27 Sep 43	27 Sep 43	29 Mar 44	Cp. Sibert, Ala.	13 Apr 44	22 Apr 46	ETO	22 Apr 46	France	24 Feb 44	
227	27 Sep 43	27 Sep 43	29 Mar 44	Cp. Sibert, Ala.	13 Apr 44	1946	ETO	Existing in 1946	In Germany	24 Feb 44	
228	15 Oct 43	15 Oct 43	29 Mar 44	Cp. Sibert, Ala.	13 Apr 44	29 Dec 45	ETO	29 Dec 45	Hampton Roads, Va.	24 Feb 44	
229	15 Oct 43	15 Oct 43	31 Mar 44	Cp. Sibert, Ala.	6 Apr 44	22 Nov 45	ETO	22 Nov 45	Boston, Mass.	24 Feb 44	
230	1 Feb 44	1 Feb 44	22 Aug 44	Cp. Sibert, Ala.	30 Aug 44 / 4 Sep 45	29 Jul 45 / 5 Apr 46	ETO / SWPA	5 Apr 46	Philippines		Co was constituted on inactive list of cml depot cos.
231	5 Feb 45	5 Feb 45 / 2 Apr 45	1 Apr 45 / 10 Jul 45	Cp. Sibert, Ala. / Cp. Shelby, Miss.	23 Jul 45	15 Apr 46	MIDPAC	15 Apr 46	Okinawa		
236	21 Mar 44	21 Mar 44	19 Nov 44	Cp. Sibert, Ala.	25 Nov 44	20 Dec 44	ETO	D20 Dec 44	France	1 Jul 44	
237	14 Apr 44	14 Apr 44 / 14 Nov 44	10 Nov 44 / 15 Dec 44	Cp. Sibert, Ala. / Dugway P. G., Utah				D15 Dec 44	Dugway P. G., Utah	1 Jul 44	
238	14 Apr 44	14 Apr 44 / 14 Nov 44	12 Nov 44 / 15 Dec 44	Cp. Sibert, Ala. / Dugway P. G., Utah				D15 Dec 44	Dugway P. G., Utah	1 Jul 44	

239	1 Aug 44	1 Aug 44	12 Apr 45	England	1 Aug 44 29 Aug 45	25 Jul 45 5 Apr 46	ETO SWPA	5 Apr 46	Philippines		
247	25 Jan 45	25 Jan 45	7 Apr 45	New Guinea	25 Jan 45 25 Jan 46	5 Apr 46 25 Jan 46	SWPA	25 Jan 46	Philippines		
412	16 Apr 35 23 Feb 42	16 Apr 35 12 Mar 42	23 Feb 42 12 Mar 42	Edgewood Arsenal, Md. Ft. Dix, N. J.						R12 Mar 42	62 Cml Depot Co

a Overseas service dates for unit include entire overseas regardless of conversion.

b Companies 66, 199, 200, 236, 237, 238 and 223 through 230 were redesignated, without change in number, as chemical base depot companies on dates shown in Column 11. Companies 239 and 247 were the only units activated as chemical base depot companies.

APPENDIX H-9—CHEMICAL MAINTENANCE COMPANIES

Unit designation (1)	Date activated (2)	TRAINING			OVERSEAS SERVICE			INACTIVATION OR DISBANDMENT		CONVERSION OR REDESIGNATION	
		From (3)	To (4)	Place (5)	From (6)	To (7)	Theater (8)	Date (9)	Place (10)	Date (11)	Comments (12)
2	4 Dec 44	4 Dec 44	ca. Apr 45	Italy	4 Dec 44 4 Aug 45	29 Jun 45 15 Feb 46	MTO MIDPAC	15 Feb 46	Okinawa		
3	15 May 41	15 May 41 2 Jan 42	25 Dec 41 12 Mar 42	Ft. Sam Houston, Tex. Cp. Haan, Calif.						R12 Mar 42	15 Cml Maint Co
10ª	1 Jul 40	1 Jul 40	1 Mar 42	Edgewood Arsenal, Md.	4 Mar 42	1946	SWPA			C 1 Nov 44	10 Gen Svc Co
11	25 Mar 42	25 Mar 42	26 Dec 42	Ft. Sam Houston, Tex.	14 Jan 43 10 May 44 1 Nov 44	10 May 44 1 Nov 44 28 Sep 45	NATO MTO ETO	28 Sep 45	Germany		
12	1 May 42	1 May 42 5 Sep 42	3 Sep 42 20 Feb 43	Ft. Custer, Mich. Cp. Sutton, N. C.	5 Mar 43 10 Jul 43 11 Sep 44	7 Jul 43 11 Sep 44 27 Mar 46	NATO MTO ETO	27 Mar 46	New York, N. Y.		
13	1 Jun 42	1 Jun 42 10 Feb 43	5 Feb 43 25 Oct 43	Cp. Rucker, Ala. Cp. Young, Calif.	28 Oct 42	1946	ETO	Existing in 1946	In Germany		
14	1 Aug 42	1 Aug 42 9 Apr 43 18 Jun 43 25 Jun 43 2 Jul 43 9 Jul 43 16 Jul 43	8 Apr 43 18 Jun 43 25 Jun 43 2 Jul 43 9 Jul 43 16 Jul 43 26 Nov 43	Cp. Rucker, Ala. Tennessee Maneuver Area Ft. Oglethorpe, Ga. Ft. McClellan, Ala. Ft. Benning, Ga. Cp. Wheeler, Ga. Cp. Gordon, Ga.	2 Dec 43	7 Jul 45	ETO	20 Oct 45	Cp. Polk, La.		
15	R12 Mar 42	12 Mar 42 24 Apr 42 5 Aug 42 31 Aug 42 29 Dec 42	24 Apr 42 5 Aug 42 28 Aug 42 29 Dec 43 24 Jan 43	Cp. Haan, Calif. Cucamonga, Calif. Desert Training Ctr., Calif. Ft. Ord, Calif. Cp. Stoneman, Calif.	24 Jan 43	26 Nov 45	SWPA	26 Nov 45	Philippines	15 May 41	Activated as 3d Cml Maint Co

No.	Activated	Stations (arrived – departed)	Departed U.S.	Returned U.S.	Theater	Inactivated	Location	Remarks
16	3 Aug 42	Cp. Bowie, Tex. (3 Aug 42 – 3 Apr 43); Louisiana Maneuver Area (4 Apr 43 – 13 Jun 43); Cp. Bowie, Tex. (14 Jun 43 – 15 Dec 43)	29 Dec 43	20 Jul 45	ETO	9 Nov 45	Cp. Shelby, Miss.	
17	25 Sep 42	Cp. Maxey, Tex. (25 Sep 42 – 9 Jun 43); Cp. Polk, La. (10 Jun 43 – 6 Aug 43); Cp. Maxey, Tex. (7 Aug 43 – 7 Sep 43); Cp. Shanks, N.Y. (17 Sep 43 – 1 Oct 43); Ft. Dix, N.J. (4 Oct 43 – 17 Nov 43)	5 Dec 43	15 Dec 45	ETO	15 Dec 45	France	
18	12 Dec 42	Cp. Campbell, Ky. (2 Dec 42 – 11 Jun 43); Tennessee Maneuver Area (11 Jun 43 – 29 Aug 43); Cp. Campbell, Ky. (29 Aug 43 – 21 Oct 43)	5 Nov 43	20 Feb 47	ETO	Existing in 1946	In Germany	
19	15 Jan 43	Cp. Sibert, Ala. (15 Jan 43 – 28 May 43); Cp. Blanding, Fla. (29 May 43 – 15 Jul 43); Perryville, Mo. (17 Jul 43 – 20 Aug 43); Tullahoma, Tenn. (22 Aug 43 – 8 Nov 43); Ft. Jackson, S.C. (9 Nov 43 – 18 Nov 43); Cp. Sutton, N.C. (18 Nov 43 – 26 Nov 43); Cp. Butner, N.C. (26 Nov 43 – 6 Dec 43); Ft. Bragg, N.C. (6 Dec 43 – 4 Feb 44)	1 Mar 44	23 Dec 45	ETO	24 Dec 45	Cp. M. Standish, Mass.	
20	15 Jan 43	Cp. Sibert, Ala. (15 Jan 43 – 6 Jun 43); Ft. Sam Houston, Tex. (8 Jun 43 – 17 Mar 44)	11 Apr 44	11 May 46	MIDPAC	11 May 46	Hawaii	
38	20 Dec 44	France (20 Dec 44 – ca. Apr 45)	20 Dec 44 / 28 Aug 45	22 Jul 45 / 31 Dec 45	ETO / SWPA	31 Dec 45	Japan	
56	15 Jan 43	Cp. Sibert, Ala. (15 Jan 43 – 28 May 43); Cp. Maxey, Tex. (29 May 43 – 16 Sep 43); Louisiana Maneuver Area (16 Sep 43 – 20 Nov 43); Cp. Maxey, Tex. (20 Nov 43 – 29 Mar 44)	29 Mar 44	20 Dec 45	ETO	21 Dec 45	Cp. Kilmer, N.J.	
57	1 Feb 43	Cp. Sibert, Ala. (1 Feb 43 – 28 May 43); Cp. Blanding, Fla. (29 May 43 – 15 Jul 43); Perryville, Mo. (17 Jul 43 – 20 Aug 43); Tennessee Maneuver Area (22 Aug 43 – 8 Nov 43); Cp. Campbell, Ky. (8 Nov 43 – 16 Nov 43); Ft. Knox, Ky. (16 Nov 43 – 23 Nov 43); Cp. Atterbury, Ind. (23 Nov 43 – 2 Dec 43); Cp. Grant, Ill. (2 Dec 43 – 11 Dec 43); Cp. McCoy, Wis. (11 Dec 43 – 4 Jan 44); Tennessee Maneuver Area (6 Jan 44 – 15 Feb 44); Cp. Tyson, Tenn. (15 Feb 44 – 27 Mar 44)	10 Apr 44	19 Sep 45	ETO	30 Nov 45	Cp. Campbell, Ky.	
58	15 Feb 43	Cp. Sibert, Ala. (15 Feb 43 – 6 Jun 43); Ft. Sam Houston, Tex. (8 Jun 43 – 18 Aug 43); Desert Training Ctr, Calif. (20 Aug 43 – 4 Apr 44)	30 Apr 44	31 Mar 46	SWPA			C 1 Nov 44 58 Gen Svc Co

Appendix H-9—Chemical Maintenance Companies—Continued

Unit desig- nation (1)	Date activated (2)	TRAINING			OVERSEAS SERVICE			INACTIVATION OR DISBANDMENT		CONVERSION OR REDESIGNATION	
		From (3)	To (4)	Place (5)	From (6)	To (7)	Theater (8)	Date (9)	Place (10)	Date (11)	Comments (12)
59	15 Aug 43	15 Aug 43 17 Jan 44 24 Mar 44	17 Jan 44 24 Mar 44 3 Mar 44	Cp. Campbell, Ky. Tennessee Maneuver Area Cp. Campbell, Ky.	13 May 44	3 Sep 45	ETO	Existing in 1946	At Ft. Lewis, Wash.		
211	a 1 Dec 44	1 Dec 44	2 Apr 45	Holland	10 Aug 43	16 Nov 45	ETO	18 Nov 45	New York, N. Y.	3 Sep 42	Activated as 711 Cml Maint Co (Avn)
220	21 Mar 44	21 Mar 44	15 Dec 44	Cp. Maxey, Tex.	3 Jan 45	2 Feb 46	ETO	4 Feb 46	Cp. Kilmer, N. J.		
221	13 Feb 45	13 Feb 45	29 Jul 45	France	13 Feb 45 4 Sep 45	29 Jul 45 5 Apr 46	ETO SWPA	5 Apr 46	Philippines		

a Overseas service dates for the 10, 58 and 211 units include entire period overseas regardless of conversions.

APPENDIX H-10—CHEMICAL DECONTAMINATION COMPANIES

Unit desig-nation (1)	Date activated (2)	TRAINING From (3)	To (4)	Place (5)	OVERSEAS SERVICE From (6)	To (7)	Theater (8)	INACTIVATION OR DISBANDMENT Date (9)	Place (10)	CONVERSION OR REDESIGNATION Date (11)	Comments (12)
1	1 Aug 40	1 Aug 40 17 Mar 41 23 Dec 41	16 Mar 41 23 Dec 41 1 Mar 42	Ft. Eustis, Va. Edgewood Arsenal, Md. Ft Dupont, Del.						R12 Mar 42	28 Cml Decon Co
2	3 Jun 41	3 Jun 41 1 Oct 41 8 Dec 41 28 Dec 41	25 Sep 41 6 Dec 41 23 Dec 41 12 Mar 42	Edgewood Arsenal, Md. Ft. Bragg, N. C. Edgewood Arsenal, Md. Ft. Ord, Calif.						R12 Mar 42	29 Cml Decon Co
21	30 Mar 42	30 Mar 42	18 Apr 43	Cp. Bowie, Tex.	13 May 43 26 Jul 43 13 Aug 44	2 Jul 43 13 Aug 44 22 Apr 46	NATO MTO ETO	22 Apr 46	France		
22(N)	1 May 42	1 May 42 18 Feb 44 12 Mar 44	17 Feb 44 11 Mar 44 10 May 44	Cp. Gordon, Ga. Tennessee Maneuver Area Cp. Gordon, Ga.						C10 May 44	208 Ord Am Co
23	1 Jul 42	1 Jul 42 9 Apr 43 18 Jun 43 26 Aug 43	8 Apr 43 17 Jun 43 21 Aug 43 27 Feb 44	Cp Rucker, Ala. Tennessee Maneuver Area Cp. Rucker, Ala. Desert Training Ctr, Calif.	5 Mar 44	25 Jan 46	SWPA	25 Jan 46	Philippines		
24(N)	31 Aug 42	31 Aug 42	2 May 43	Cp Butner, N. C.	10 May 43 11 Sep 43	1 Sep 43 26 Oct 45	NATO MTO	27 Oct 45	New York, N. Y.		
25(N)	25 Mar 42	25 Mar 42	1 May 43	Cp. Blanding, Fla.	10 May 43 10 Oct 43 14 Sep 44	7 Oct 43 12 Sep 44 22 Apr 46	NATO MTO ETO	22 Apr 46	Germany		
26	15 Aug 42	15 Aug 42	2 May 43	Cp. Carson, Colo.	10 May 43 25 Feb 45	22 Feb 45 25 Oct 45	NATO MTO			C15 May 45	26 Cml Svc Co
27	9 Feb 42	9 Feb 42 5 Jun 43	4 Jun 43 23 Feb 44	Ft. Buchanan, P. R. Cp. Sibert, Ala.	9 Feb 43 24 Feb 44	4 Jun 43 25 Nov 44	CDC CZ	D25 Nov 44	Panama		

Unit	Activated	Stations in U.S. (arrived – departed)	Departed U.S.	Theater	Returned U.S.	Inactivated	Station at inactivation	Date / Remarks
28(N)	R12 Mar 42	Australia (12 Mar 42)	12 Mar 42	SWPA		30 Nov 45	Philippines	1 Aug 40 — Activated as 1st Cml Decon Co
29(N)	R12 Mar 42	Ft. Ord, Calif. (12 Mar 42 – 16 Jun 42)	16 Jun 42 / 8 Nov 44	MIDPAC SWPA	24 Oct 44	25 Jan 46	Philippines	3 Jun 41 — Activated as 2d Cml Decon Co
30	14 Jul 42	Cp. Bowie, Tex. (14 Jul 42 – 15 Mar 43); Cp. Young, Calif. (17 Mar 43 – 14 Aug 43); Cp. Pickett, Va. (20 Aug 43 – 4 Sep 43); Cp. Bradford, Va. (4 Sep 43 – 24 Sep 43); Cp. Pickett, Va. (24 Sep 43 – 11 Oct 43)	21 Oct 43	ETO		27 Dec 45	Germany	
31	14 Jul 42	Cp. Bowie, Tex. (14 Jul 42 – 2 Sep 43); Cp. Pickett, Va. (6 Sep 43 – 15 Dec 43); Cp. Polk, La. (8 Jul 45 – 20 Oct 45)	22 Dec 43	ETO	6 Jul 45	20 Oct 45	Cp. Polk, La.	Co had seven separate detachments
32(N)	11 Aug 42	Cp. Claiborne, La. (11 Aug 42 – 4 Apr 43); Louisiana Maneuver Area (4 Apr 43 – 5 Jul 43); Cp. Claiborne, La. (5 Jul 43 – 19 Oct 43); Ft. Bragg, N.C. (21 Aug 45 – 1 Nov 45)	3 Nov 43	ETO	19 Aug 45	1 Nov 45	Ft. Bragg, N. C.	
33	11 Aug 42	Cp. Blanding, Fla. (11 Aug 42 – 7 Nov 43); Cp. Swift, Tex. (8 Aug 45 – 17 Oct 45)	16 Nov 43	ETO	3 Aug 45	17 Oct 45	Cp. Swift, Tex.	Co had four separate platoons.
34(N)	1 Sep 42	Cp. Claiborne, La. (1 Sep 42 – 5 Apr 43); Louisiana Maneuver Area (5 Apr 43 – 10 Jun 43); Cp. Claiborne, La. (10 Jun 43 – 7 Jan 44); Cp. Shelby, Miss. (5 Jul 45 – 9 Nov 45)	18 Jan 44	ETO	2 Jul 45	9 Nov 45	Cp. Shelby, Miss.	
35	25 Sep 42	Cp. Maxey, Tex. (25 Sep 42 – 22 Jun 43); Louisiana Maneuver Area (22 Jun 43 – 16 Aug 43); Cp. Maxey, Tex. (16 Aug 43 – 17 Nov 43); Ft. Jackson, S.C. (17 Jul 45 – 26 Oct 45)	5 Dec 43	ETO	16 Jul 45	26 Oct 45	Ft. Jackson, S. C.	
36(N)	15 Dec 42	Cp. Sibert, Ala. (15 Dec 42 – 28 May 43); Cp. Pickett, Va. (29 May 43 – 26 Mar 44); Elkins, W. Va. (27 Mar 44 – 24 May 44); Cp. Pickett, Va. (24 May 44 – 15 Jul 44)						C15 Jul 44 — 4296 QM Gasoline Sup Co
37	29 Dec 42	Cp. Sibert, Ala. (29 Dec 42 – 12 Jun 43); Manchester, Tenn. (12 Jun 43 – 1 Sep 43); Cp. Breckinridge, Ky. (2 Sep 43 – 22 Sep 43); Dugway P. G., Utah (25 Sep 43 – 28 Dec 43); Calif.-Ariz. Maneuver Area (29 Dec 43 – 10 Feb 44); Cp. Roberts, Calif. (11 Feb 44 – 1 Apr 44); Cp. Sibert, Ala. (5 Apr 44 – 15 Apr 44)						C15 Apr 44 — 37 Cml Depot Co
38(N)	4 Mar 43	Cp. Sibert, Ala. (4 Mar 43 – 30 Nov 43); Cp. Breckinridge, Ky. (1 Dec 43 – 20 Jan 44); Tennessee Maneuver Area (20 Jan 44 – 21 Feb 44); Cp. Breckinridge, Ky. (21 Feb 44 – 10 May 44)						C10 May 44 — 209 Ord Am Co

APPENDIX H-10—CHEMICAL DECONTAMINATION COMPANIES—Continued

Unit designation (1)	Date activated (2)	TRAINING From (3)	TRAINING To (4)	TRAINING Place (5)	OVERSEAS SERVICE From (6)	OVERSEAS SERVICE To (7)	OVERSEAS SERVICE Theater (8)	INACTIVATION OR DISBANDMENT Date (9)	INACTIVATION OR DISBANDMENT Place (10)	CONVERSION OR REDESIGNATION Date (11)	CONVERSION OR REDESIGNATION Comments (12)
39(N)	9 Apr 43	9 Apr 43	30 Nov 43	Cp. Sibert, Ala.						C30 May 44	241 Ord Am Co
		30 Nov 43	28 Feb 44	Cp. Shelby, Miss.							
		29 Feb 44	4 Apr 44	Lousiana Maneuver Area							
		4 Apr 44	30 May 44	Cp. Van Dorn, Miss.							
141(N)	9 Apr 43	9 Apr 43	13 Feb 44	Cp. Sibert, Ala.						C14 Jul 44	4297 QM Gasoline Sup Co
		14 Feb 44	23 Feb 44	Cp. Shelby, Miss.							
		25 Feb 44	18 Mar 44	Tennessee Maneuver Area							
		20 Mar 44	14 Jul 44	Cp Shelby, Miss.							
142(N)	5 May 43	5 May 43	14 Feb 44	Cp. Sibert, Ala.						C10 May 44	238 Ord Am Co
		15 Feb 44	2 Mar 44	Cp Breckinridge, Ky.							
		3 Mar 44	25 Mar 44	Tennessee Maneuver Area							
		25 Mar 44	10 May 44	Cp. Breckinridge, Ky							
143(N)	10 Aug 42	10 Aug 42	20 Feb 44	Cp Pickett, Va.						C10 May 44	239 Ord Am Co
		22 Feb 44	25 Mar 44	Tennessee Maneuver Area							
		25 Mar 44	10 May 44	Cp. Breckinridge, Ky.							
144(N)	5 May 43	5 May 43	14 Feb 44	Cp. Sibert, Ala						C30 May 44	240 Ord Am Co
		15 Feb 44	30 May 44	Cp McCann, Miss.							
145(N)	15 Jun 43	15 Jun 43	14 Feb 44	Cp. Sibert, Ala.						C15 July 44	4298 QM Gasoline Sup Co
		15 Feb 44	14 Jul 44	Cp. Polk, La.							
146(N)	15 Jun 43	15 Jun 43	14 Feb 44	Cp. Sibert, Ala.						C15 May 44	846 QM Gasoline Sup Co
		15 Feb 44	28 Feb 44	Cp. Shelby, Miss.							
		3 Mar 44	6 Apr 44	Tennessee Maneuver Area							
		7 Apr 44	15 May 44	Cp Shelby, Miss.							
149(N)	15 Aug 43	15 Aug 43	11 Feb 44	Cp Breckinridge, Ky						C15 Jun 44	4295 QM Gasoline Sup Co
		13 Feb 44	4 Mar 44	Tennessee Maneuver Area							
		4 Mar 44	15 Jun 44	Cp. Breckinridge, Ky.							

									Remarks
150(N)	15 Aug 43	15 Aug 43 / 1 Mar 44 / 4 Apr 44	1 Mar 44 / 4 Apr 44 / 15 May 44	Cp McCain, Miss / Louisiana Maneuver Area / Cp. McCain, Miss				C15 May 44	848 QM Gasoline Sup Co
151	20 Jun 42	20 Jun 42 / 9 Jul 42	7 Jul 42 / 21 Jul 42	Cp. Bowie, Tex / Pittsburg, Calif	21 Jul 42	1 Jul 43	SWPA	1 Jul 43 Guadalcanal	Only one section of the company was ever activated
152(N)	15 Aug 43	15 Aug 43	15 May 44	Cp. Livingston, La.				C15 May 44	849 QM Gasoline Sup Co
153(N)	15 Aug 43	15 Aug 43 / 18 Feb 44 / 13 Mar 44	15 Feb 44 / 11 Mar 44 / 15 May 44	Cp. Shelby, Miss. / Tennessee Maneuver Area / Cp. Shelby, Miss.				C15 May 44	847 QM Gasoline Sup Co

APPENDIX H-11—CHEMICAL PROCESSING COMPANIES

Unit desig-nation (1)	Date activated (2)	TRAINING			OVERSEAS SERVICE			INACTIVATION OR DISBANDMENT		CONVERSION OR REDESIGNATION	
		From (3)	To (4)	Place (5)	From (6)	To (7)	Theater (8)	Date (9)	Place (10)	Date (11)	Comments (12)
1	3 Jun 41	3 Jun 41	12 Mar 42	Edgewood Arsenal, Md						R12 Mar 42	51 Cml Proc Co
51	R12 Mar 42	12 Mar 42	22 Jun 42	Edgewood Arsenal, Md.	30 Jun 42	25 Nov 45	ETO	27 Nov 45	New York, N. Y	3 Jun 41	Activated as 1st Cml Proc Co
52	30 Apr 42	30 Apr 42 13 Aug 42 21 Sep	10 Aug 42 21 Sep 42 22 Apr 43	Cp. Bowie, Tex. New York, N. Y. Cp. Pickett, Va.	13 May 43 31 Dec 44 4 Aug 45	31 Dec 44 29 Jun 45 23 May 46	NATO MTO MIDPAC	23 May 46	Korea		
53(N)	10 Apr 42	10 Apr 42 23 Aug 20 Nov 42	22 Aug 42 19 Nov 42 20 Apr 43	Cp. Blanding, Fla Huntsville, Ala. Cp. Sutton, N. C.	13 May 44 21 Sep 44	18 Sep 44 10 Nov 45	NATO MTO			C15 May 45	53 Cml Svc Co
54	1 Jun 42	1 Jun 42 24 Nov 42 2 May 43 3 Sep 43	24 Nov 42 1 May 43 3 Sep 43 29 Oct 43	Cp. Rucker, Ala. Cp. Sibert, Ala. Cp. Pickett, Va. Ft Dix, N. J.	29 Oct 43 29 Aug 45	25 Jul 45 25 Jan 46	ETO SWPA	25 Jan 46	Philippines		
55(N)	21 Aug 42	21 Aug 42 8 Dec	7 Dec 42 27 Jan 44	Edgewood Arsenal, Md. Cp. Sibert, Ala.	9 Mar 44	25 Jan 46	SWPA	25 Jan 46	New Guinea		
101(N)	11 Jul 42	11 Jul 42 21 Mar 43	19 Mar 42 21 Feb 44	Edgewood Arsenal, Md. Cp. Sibert, Ala.	6 Mar 44	30 Nov 45	SWPA	30 Nov 45	Philippines		
102	11 Aug 42	11 Aug 42 8 Dec	7 Dec 42 12 Oct 43	Edgewood Arsenal, Md. Cp. Sibert, Ala.	13 Nov 43 3 Mar 44	3 Feb 44 11 Nov 45	NATO I-B	12 Nov 45	New York, N. Y.		
103	18 Aug 42	18 Aug 42 8 Dec 42 24 Sep 43	7 Dec 42 20 Sep 43 1 Jul 44	Edgewood Arsenal, Md. Cp. Sibert, Ala. Digway P.G., Utah	12 Jul 44	25 Jan 46	SWPA	25 Jan 46	Philippines		
104	18 Aug 42	18 Aug 42 8 Dec	7 Dec 42 4 Jun 42	Edgewood Arsenal, Md. Cp. Sibert, Ala.	24 Jun 43	16 Nov 45	ETO	17 Nov 45	Cp. M. Standish, Mass.		

No.	Activated	Dates	Location	Dates	Theater	Date	Status/Location	Redesignation
105	18 Aug 42	18 Aug 42 / 8 Dec 42 — 7 Dec 42	Edgewood Arsenal, Md. / Cp. Sibert, Ala.	15 May 43 / 30 Nov 45	SWPA	30 Nov 45	Philippines	
106	25 Sep 42	25 Sep 42 / 25 Feb 43 — 24 Feb 43 / 30 Aug 43	Cp. Sibert, Ala / Edgewood Arsenal, Md.	16 Sep 43 / 20 Dec 45	ETO	21 Dec 45	Cp. Kilmer, N J	
107	25 Sep 42	25 Sep 42 — 15 Mar 44	Cp. Sibert, Ala.	31 Mar 44 / 25 Jan 46	SWPA	25 Jan 46	Philippines	
108	25 Sep 42	25 Sep 42 / 19 May 43 — 15 May 43 / 29 Dec 43	Cp. Sibert, Ala. / Dugway P. G., Utah	25 Jan 44 / 10 Dec 45	SWPA	10 Dec 45	Guadalcanal	
109	25 Sep 42	25 Sep 42 — 22 Feb 44	Cp. Sibert, Ala.	9 Mar 44 / 28 Feb 46	SWPA	28 Feb 46	Japan	
110	15 Nov 42	15 Nov 42 / 17 Jul 43 — 16 Jul 43 / 6 Dec 43	Cp. Sibert, Ala. / Edgewood Arsenal, Md.	20 Dec 43 / 30 Jan 46	MIDPAC	30 Jan 46	Hawaii	
111	15 Nov 42	15 Nov 42 — 23 Sep 43	Cp. Sibert, Ala.	11 Oct 43 / 27 Nov 45	ETO	29 Nov 45	Cp. Kilmer, N. J.	
112	15 Dec 42	15 Dec 42 — 1 Oct 43	Cp. Sibert, Ala.	21 Oct 43 / 24 Aug 45	ETO	Existing in 1946	At Edgewood Arsenal, Md.	
113	15 Dec 42	15 Dec 42 — 1 Oct 43	Cp. Sibert, Ala.	21 Oct 43 / 2 Aug 45	ETO	20 Oct 45	Edgewood Arsenal, Md.	
114	15 Dec 42	15 Dec 42 — 1 Oct 43	Cp. Sibert, Ala.	13 Oct 43 / 26 Mar 46	ETO	27 Mar 46	Cp. Kilmer, N. J.	
115	29 Dec 42	29 Dec 42 — 1 Oct 43	Cp. Sibert, Ala.	13 Oct 43 / 12 Oct 45	ETO	13 Oct 45	Boston, Mass.	
116	29 Dec 42	29 Dec 42 — 29 Apr 44	Cp. Sibert, Ala.	16 May 44 / 25 Jan 46	SWPA	25 Jan 46	Philippines	
117	29 Dec 42	29 Dec 42 — 9 Aug 43	Cp. Sibert, Ala.	21 Aug 43 / 4 Jul 44 — 7 Jul 44 / 24 Nov 45	NATO MTO			C15 May 45 — 117 Cml Svc Co
118	15 Jan 43	15 Jan 43 / 25 Apr 44 / 29 Jan 44 — 24 Apr 44 / 28 Jun 44 / 9 Aug 44	Cp. Sibert, Ala. / Bushnell Fld, Fla. / Cp. Sibert, Ala.	4 Sep 44 / 25 Jan 46	SWPA	25 Jan 46	Philippines	
119	15 Jan 43	15 Jan 43 / 13 May 44 — 10 May 44 / 3 Oct 44	Cp. Sibert, Ala. / Dugway P. G., Utah	11 Nov 44 / 25 Jan 46	SWPA	25 Jan 46	Philippines	
120	15 Jan 43	15 Jan 43 — 21 Oct 43	Cp. Sibert, Ala.	3 Nov 43 / 29 Aug 45 — 29 Aug 45 / 25 Jan 46	ETO SWPA	25 Jan 46	Philippines	
121	15 Jan 43	15 Jan 43 / 9 Jun 44 — 5 Jun 44 / ca. Nov 44	Cp. Sibert, Ala. / Dugway P. G., Utah	17 Nov 44 / 28 Feb 46	SWPA	28 Feb 46	Japan	
122	1 Feb 43	1 Feb 43 — 1 Oct 43	Cp. Sibert, Ala.	13 Oct 43 / 14 Aug 45	ETO	30 Oct 45	Edgewood Arsenal, Md.	

APPENDIX H-11—CHEMICAL PROCESSING COMPANIES—Continued

Unit designation (1)	Date activated (2)	TRAINING			OVERSEAS SERVICE			INACTIVATION OR DISBANDMENT		CONVERSION OR REDESIGNATION	
		From (3)	To (4)	Place (5)	From (6)	To (7)	Theater (8)	Date (9)	Place (10)	Date (11)	Comments (12)
123	1 Feb 43	1 Feb 43	22 Jan 44	Cp. Sibert, Ala.	7 Feb 44	20 Jan 46	SWPA	20 Jan 46	Guadalcanal		
124	1 Feb 43	1 Feb 43	22 Jan 44	Cp Sibert, Ala	7 Feb 44	10 Feb 46	SWPA	10 Feb 46	Japan		
125	1 Feb 43	1 Feb 43 / 7 Jun 44 / 26 Sep 44	6 Jun 44 / 25 Sep 44 / ca Nov 44	Cp. Sibert, Ala. / Bushnell Fld, Fla. / Cp. Sibert, Ala.	17 Nov 44	31 May 46	SWPA	31 May 46	Japan		
126	26 Apr 43	26 Apr 43	22 Feb 44	Cp Sibert, Ala.	25 Feb 44	30 Jan 46	SWPA	30 Jan 46	Philippines		
127	25 Mar 43	25 Mar 43 / 2 Nov 43	31 Oct 43 / 26 Jan 44	Cp. Sibert, Ala. / Edgewood Arsenal, Md.	26 Jan 44	30 Jan 46	SWPA	30 Jan 46	Philippines		
128	25 Mar 43	25 Mar 43	22 Jan 44	Cp Sibert, Ala	24 Jan 44	20 Apr 46	SWPA	20 Apr 46	Guadalcanal		
129	25 Mar 43	25 Mar 43	13 Apr 44	Cp Sibert, Ala.	23 Apr 44	11 Nov 45	I-B	12 Nov 45	Cp. Kilmer, N. J.		
130	26 Apr 43	26 Apr 43	16 Apr 44	Cp. Sibert, Ala.	24 Apr 44 / 29 Aug 45	25 Jul 45 / 25 Jan 46	ETO / SWPA	25 Jan 46	Philippines		
131	26 Apr 43	26 Apr 43 / 3 Mar 44	1 Mar 44 / ca. Oct 44	Cp. Sibert, Ala. / Edgewood Arsenal, Md.	21 Oct 44	25 Jan 46	SWPA	25 Jan 46	Philippines		
185	R20 Aug 44	20 Aug 44 / 24 Aug 44	22 Aug 44 / 16 Nov 44	Edgewood Arsenal, Md. / Cp. Sibert, Ala.	29 Nov 44	25 Jan 46	SWPA	25 Jan 46	Philippines	1 Nov 42	Activated as 169 Cml SG Co
249	30 Dec 44	30 Dec 44	ca. Apr 45	Cp Sibert, Ala.	16 Apr 45	19 Apr 46	MIDPAC	19 Apr 46	Saipan		
250	30 Dec 44	30 Dec 44	18 Feb 45	Cp. Sibert, Ala.				D18 Feb 45	Cp. Sibert, Ala.		

APPENDIX H-12—CHEMICAL SERVICE BATTALIONS

Unit desig- nation (1)	Date activated (2)	TRAINING			OVERSEAS SERVICE			INACTIVATION OR DISBANDMENT		CONVERSION OR REDESIGNATION	
		From (3)	To (4)	Place (5)	From (6)	To (7)	Theater (8)	Date (9)	Place (10)	Date (11)	Comments (12)
13a	R 6 Mar 45	6 Mar 45	20 Apr 45	Ft. Richardson, Alaska	15 Mar 44	20 Apr 45	AD	D20 Apr 45	Ft. Richardson, Alaska	15 Mar 44	Activated as 13 Cml Comp Bn
14	R25 Apr 45	25 Apr 45	1946	Hawaii, Midway	19 Aug 44	1946	MIDPAC	Existing in 1946	At Midway	20 May 44	Activated as 14 Cml Comp Bn
25b	C30 Jun 45	30 Jun 45	25 Feb 46	France, Germany	4 Jun 44	25 Feb 46	ETO	25 Feb 46	Germany	4 Jun 44	Activated as 25 Cml SG Bn
27	C30 Jun 45	30 Jun 45	12 Nov 45	France	15 Sep 44	12 Nov 45	ETO	12 Nov 45	France	15 Jul 44	Activated as 27 Cml SG Bn

a All units were hq & hq detachments only.
b Overseas service dates for the 25 and 27 units include entire period overseas regardless of conversions.

APPENDIX H-13—CHEMICAL COMPOSITE SERVICE AND GENERAL SERVICE COMPANIES

Unit designation (1)	Date activated (2)	TRAINING			OVERSEAS SERVICE			INACTIVATION OR DISBANDMENT		CONVERSION OR REDESIGNATION	
		From (3)	To (4)	Place (5)	From (6)	To (7)	Theater (8)	Date (9)	Place (10)	Date (11)	Comments (12)
10a	C 1 Nov 44	1 Nov 44	4 Jul 45	New Guinea	4 Mar 42	1946	SWPA	Existing in 1946	In Japan	1 Jul 40	Activated as 10 Cml Co (Maint)
26(N)	C15 May 45	15 May 45	25 Oct 45	Italy	25 Feb 45	25 Oct 45	MTO	25 Oct 45	Italy	15 Aug 42	Activated as 26 Cml Decon Co
53(N)	C15 May 45	15 May 45	10 Nov 45	Italy	21 Sep 44	10 Nov 45	MTO	10 Nov 45	Italy	10 Apr 42	Activated as 53 Cml Proc Co
58	C 1 Nov 44	1 Nov 44	ca. Jul 45	New Guinea	30 Apr 44	31 Mar 46	SWPA	31 Mar 46	Japan	15 Feb 43	Activated as 58 Cml Maint Co
62	C 1 Nov 44	1 Nov 44	8 Jun 45	Australia	12 Mar 42	1946	SWPA	Existing in 1946	At Okinawa	12 Mar 42	Activated as 62 Cml Depot Co
89a	21 Aug 44	21 Aug 44	17 Nov 44	Cp. Sibert, Ala.	12 Dec 44	31 May 46	SWPA	31 May 46	Philippines		
90	9 Sep 44	9 Sep 44	20 Apr 45	Adak, Alaska	9 Sep 44	20 Apr 45	AD	D20 Apr 45	Alaska		
92	26 Dec 42	26 Dec 42	20 Apr 43	Cp. Sibert, Ala.	28 Apr 43 / 16 Aug 43	15 Aug 43 / 16 Jun 46	NATO / MTO	16 Jun 46	Italy		
93	26 Dec 42	26 Dec 42	27 May 43	Cp. Sibert, Ala.	4 Jun 43	31 Jan 46	SWPA	31 Jan 46	Philippines		
94	26 Dec 42	26 Dec 42	25 Sep 43	Cp. Sibert, Ala.	27 Sep 43	2 Nov 44	SWPA	D 2 Nov 44	Philippines		
95	3 Mar 42	3 Mar 42 / 12 Nov 44	24 Oct 44 / 11 Mar 45	Corozal, Canal Zone / Cp. Sibert, Ala.	3 Mar 42 / 28 Apr 45	24 Oct 44 / 1 Nov 45	CZ / I-B	Existing in 1946	At Edgewood Arsenal, Md.		
96	18 Apr 42	18 Apr 42	9 May 42	Ft. Ord, Calif.	26 May 42	20 Apr 46	SWPA	20 Apr 46	Guadalcanal		
97	18 Jul 42	18 Jul 42 / 25 Jul 42	21 Jul 42 / 12 Aug 42	Ft. Bragg, N. C. / Ft. Murray, Wash.	18 Aug 42	1 Nov 44	AD	D 1 Nov 44	Ft. Richardson, Alaska		

Unit	Organized / activated dates	Station	Overseas dates	Theater	Inactivation / date	Location	Remarks date	Remarks
98	15 Jan 43|15 Jan 43| 3 Jul 43 4 Jul 43|28 Oct 43 30 Oct 43| 5 Mar 44	Cp. Sibert, Ala. Norfolk, Va. Cp. Sibert, Ala.	22 Mar 44|12 Feb 46	SWPA	12 Feb 46	Philippines		
99	15 Jan 43|15 Jan 43|28 May 43	Cp. Sibert, Ala.	14 Jun 43|28 Feb 46 25 Sep 45	SWPA	28 Feb 46	Japan		
100	15 Jan 43|15 Jan 43|26 Jan 44 27 Jan 44|10 Apr 46	Cp. Sibert, Ala. Edgewood Arsenal, Md.			10 Apr 46	Edgewood Arsenal, Md.		
117	C15 May 45|15 May 45|24 Nov 45	Italy	7 Jul 44|24 Nov 45	MTO	24 Nov 45	Italy	29 Dec 42	Activated as 117 Cml Proc Co
147	10 Apr 45|10 Apr 45|11 Jul 45	Ft. Ruger, Hawaii	10 Apr 45| 1946	MIDPAC	Existing in 1946	In Korea		
148	10 Apr 45|10 Apr 45|15 Sep 45	Ft. Ruger, Hawaii	10 Apr 45|15 Sep 45 15 Sep 45|15 Mar 46	MIDPAC SWPA	15 Mar 46	Philippines		
216	14 Aug 43|14 Aug 43|23 Mar 44	Cp. Sibert, Ala.	31 Mar 44|31 May 46	SWPA	31 May 46	Philippines		
217	10 Jul 43|10 Jul 43|29 Apr 44	Cp. Sibert, Ala.	9 May 44|31 Jan 46	SWPA	31 Jan 46	Japan		
218	1 Jul 43|1 Jul 43|14 Jun 44	Guadalcanal	1 Jul 43|14 Jun 44	SWPA	D14 Jun 44	Guadalcanal		Only a depot section activated
219	1 May 43|1 May 43|14 Jun 44	New Caledonia	1 May 43|14 Jun 44	SWPA	D14 Jun 44	New Caledonia		Only a depot section activated
240[a]	14 Aug 43|14 Aug 43|17 May 44	Cp. Sibert, Ala.	26 May 44|31 Aug 46	SWPA			C12 Feb 45	236, 237, 238, & 240 Cml Svc Plat(s)
241	14 Aug 43|14 Aug 43|11 May 44	Cp. Sibert, Ala.	23 May 44|15 Jan 46	I-B	15 Jan 46	Burma		
242	31 Dec 43|31 Dec 43|12 Jan 46	Corozal, Canal Zone	31 Dec 43|12 Jan 46	CZ			C12 Jan 46	242 Cml Sup Det
243	15 Mar 44|15 Mar 44|20 Apr 45	Alaska	15 Mar 44|20 Apr 45	AD	D20 Apr 45	Alaska		
245[d]	15 Nov 44|15 Nov 44|ca. Feb 45	Cp. Sibert, Ala.	23 Feb 45|28 Feb 46	SWPA			C 6 May 45	245, 263, 264, & 265 Cml Svc Plat(s)

ᵃ Overseas service dates for the 10, 58, 62, 240, and 245 units include entire period overseas regardless of conversions.
ᵇ Companies 89, 90, 92, 93, 95, 96, 98, 99, 100, 148, 216, 217, 241, and 243 activated as chemical composite companies; redesignated chemical service companies in period 15 Mar 45 to 15 May 45.
ᶜ Activated as 240 Chemical Warfare Composite Company; converted, 12 Feb 45, as the 236, 237, 238, and 240 Chemical Service Platoons.
ᵈ Activated as 245 Chemical Composite Company; redesignated, 20 Apr 45, as the 245 Chemical Service Company; converted, 6 May 45, as the 245, 263, 264, and 265 Chemical Service Platoons.

APPENDIX H-14—CHEMICAL COMPOSITE AND SERVICE PLATOONS AND DETACHMENTS

Unit desig-nation (1)	Date activated (2)	TRAINING			OVERSEAS SERVICE			INACTIVATION OR DISBANDMENT		CONVERSION OR REDESIGNATION	
		From (3)	To (4)	Place (5)	From (6)	To (7)	Theater (8)	Date (9)	Place (10)	Date (11)	Comments (12)
1a	25 Jun 44	25 Jun 44	26 Aug 44	Schofield Barracks, Hawaii	25 Jun 44	26 Aug 44	MIDPAC	D 26 Aug 44	Hawaii		
1b	20 Jan 45	20 Jan 45	2 Jun 45	Hawaii	20 Jan 45	31 Jan 46	MIDPAC			R 2 Jun 45	411 POA Provisional Cml Det
180c	14 Jun 44	14 Jun 44	25 Sep 44	New Georgia	14 Jun 44	10 Nov 45	SWPA	10 Nov 45	Japan	26 Apr 45	
181	14 Jun 44	14 Jun 44	21 Dec 44	Russell Island	14 Jun 44	11 Mar 46	SWPA	11 Mar 46	Japan	29 Apr 45	
182	14 Jun 44	14 Jun 44	13 Jun 45	Espiritu Santo Island	14 Jun 44	20 Apr 46	SWPA	20 Apr 46	New Caledonia	29 Apr 45	
183	14 Jun 44	14 Jun 44	16 Dec 44	Bougainville	14 Jun 44	10 Nov 46	SWPA	10 Nov 46	Philippines	20 Apr 45	
184	26 Aug 44	26 Aug 44	15 Sep 44	Hawaii	26 Aug 44 / 15 Sep 44	15 Sep 44 / 31 Jan 46	MIDPAC / SWPA	31 Jan 46	Japan	26 Apr 45	
187	5 Sep 44	5 Sep 44	28 Dec 45	India	5 Sep 44	28 Dec 45	I-B	28 Dec 45	India		
236d	C 12 Feb 45	12 Feb 45	5 Nov 45	Philippines	12 Feb 45	5 Nov 45	SWPA	5 Nov 45	Philippines	14 Aug 43	Activated as 240 Cml Warfare Comp Co
237	C 12 Feb 45	12 Feb 45	25 Jan 46	Philippines	12 Feb 45	25 Jan 46	SWPA	25 Jan 46	Philippines	14 Aug 43	Activated as 240 Cml Warfare Comp Co
238	C 12 Feb 45	12 Feb 45	4 Sep 45	Philippines	12 Feb 45	28 Feb 46	SWPA	28 Feb 46	Japan	14 Aug 43	Activated as 240 Cml Warfare Comp Co
240	C 12 Feb 45	12 Feb 45	ca Feb 46	Philippines	26 May 44	31 Aug 46	SWPA	31 Aug 46	Japan	14 Aug 43	Activated as 240 Cml Warfare Comp Co
245e	C 6 May 45	6 May 45	28 Feb 46	Philippines	23 Feb 45	28 Feb 46	SWPA	28 Feb 46	Philippines	15 Nov 44	Activated as 245 Cml Svc Co
246	28 Jul 45	28 Jul 45	ca. Oct 45	Philippines	28 Jul 45	17 Jan 46	SWPA	17 Jan 46	Japan		
247	28 Jul 45	28 Jul 45	ca Oct 45	Philippines	28 Jul 45	17 Jan 46	SWPA	17 Jan 46	Japan		

Unit												Remarks
251[f]	26 Aug 44	26 Aug 44	30 Jan 46	Hawaii	26 Aug 44	30 Jan 46	MIDPAC	30 Jan 46	Hawaii	25 Apr 45	C25 Apr 45	256 Cml Lab Co (Mbl)
256	30 Nov 44	30 Nov 44	25 Apr 45	New Guinea	30 Nov 44	1946	SWPA	5 Nov 45	Saipan	25 Apr 45	25 Apr 45	
261[b]	26 Aug 44	26 Aug 44	5 Nov 45	Saipan	26 Aug 44	5 Nov 45	MIDPAC	5 Nov 45	Saipan	25 Apr 45	25 Apr 45	
263	C 6 May 45	6 May 45	ca. Sep 45	Philippines	6 May 45	31 Aug 46	SWPA	31 Aug 46	Japan	15 Nov 44	15 Nov 44	Activated as 245 Cml Svc Co
264	C 6 May 45	6 May 45	24 Aug 45	Philippines	6 May 45	31 Oct 46	SWPA	31 Oct 46	Japan	15 Nov 44	15 Nov 44	Activated as 245 Cml Svc Co
265	C 6 May 45	6 May 45	25 Jan 46	Philippines	6 May 45	25 Jan 46	SWPA	25 Jan 46	Japan	15 Nov 44	15 Nov 44	Activated as 245 Cml Svc Co
266[h]	20 Apr 45	20 Apr 45	1946	Ft Richardson, Alaska	20 Apr 45	1946	AD	Existing in 1946	In Alaska			
267	20 Apr 45	20 Apr 45	1 Nov 45	Adak, Alaska	20 Apr 45	1 Nov 45	AD	1 Nov 45	Alaska			
268	20 Apr 45	20 Apr 45	1 Nov 45	Cp. Earle, Alaska	20 Apr 45	1 Nov 45	AD	1 Nov 45	Alaska			
269	20 Apr 45	20 Apr 45	27 Nov 45	Shemya, Alaska	20 Apr 45	27 Nov 45	AD	28 Nov 45	Ft. Lewis, Wash.			
270	20 Apr 45	20 Apr 45	1 Nov 45	Amchitka, Alaska	20 Apr 45	1 Nov 45	AD	1 Nov 45	Alaska			
271	8 Dec 44	8 Dec 44	28 Mar 45	Hawaii	8 Dec 44	1946	MIDPAC	Existing in 1946	On Iwo Jima			
272[a]	25 Nov 44	25 Nov 44	15 Dec 45	Philippines	25 Nov 44	15 Dec 45	SWPA	15 Dec 45	Philippines			
273	25 Nov 44	25 Nov 44	2 Feb 45	Hollandia	25 Nov 44	31 Jan 46	SWPA	31 Jan 46	Japan			
274	25 Nov 44	25 Nov 44	26 Dec 44	Toem, New Guinea	25 Nov 44	31 Oct 46	SWPA	31 Oct 46	Japan			
275	25 Nov 44	25 Nov 44	26 Dec 44	Atape, New Guinea	25 Nov 44	28 Feb 46	SWPA	28 Feb 46	Japan			
411[b]	R 2 Jun 45	2 Jun 45	ca. Sep 45	Hawaii	20 Jan 45	31 Jan 46	MIDPAC	D31 Jan 46	Okinawa	20 Jan 45	20 Jan 45	Activated as 1st Provisional Cml Det

a 1st Provisional Chemical Warfare Composite Platoon

b 1st Provisional Chemical Detachment.

c Units 180 through 184 activated as chemical composite platoons, redesignated chemical service platoons, without change in number, on dates shown in Column 11.

d Service Platoons 236, 237, 238, and 240 activated in conjunction with reorganization and conversion of the 240 Chemical Warfare Composite Company, 12 Feb 45

e Service Platoons 245, 263, 264, and 265 activated in conjunction with reorganization and conversion of the 245 Chemical Service Company, 6 May 45.

f Activated as 251 Chemical Composite Detachment (Supply), redesignated 251 Chemical Supply Detachment, on date shown in Column 11.

g Activated as 261 Chemical Composite Section, redesignated 261 Chemical Service Detachment on date shown in Column 11.

h Units 266 through 270 organized in conjunction with the disbanding of the 90 and 243 Chemical Service Companies, 20 Apr 45.

i Units 272 through 275 organized in conjunction with the disbanding of the 94 Chemical Composite Company, 2 Nov 44.

j Overseas service dates for the 1st Provisional Chemical Detachment and units 240, 245, 256, and 411 include the entire period overseas regardless of conversions or redesignation.

APPENDIX H-15—CHEMICAL LABORATORY COMPANIES

Unit desig-nation (1)	Date activated (2)	TRAINING			OVERSEAS SERVICE			INACTIVATION OR DISBANDMENT		CONVERSION OR REDESIGNATION	
		From (3)	To (4)	Place (5)	From (6)	To (7)	Theater (8)	Date (9)	Place (10)	Date (11)	Comments (12)
1	1 Aug 40	1 Aug 40	12 Mar 42	Edgewood Arsenal, Md.						R12 Mar 42	41 Cml Lab Co
3a	15 May 41	15 May 41	13 Nov 41	Edgewood Arsenal, Md.	21 Nov 41 / 7 Jan 46	7 Jan 46 / 23 Sep 46	SWPA / MIDPAC			R12 Mar 42	42 Cml Lab Co
40	3 May 42	3 May 42 / 18 Feb 43 / 13 Oct 43 / 30 Jul 45	18 Feb 43 / 13 Oct 43 / 9 Dec 43 / 4 Nov 46	Cp. S.L. Obispo, Calif. / Sunnyvale, Calif. / Ft. Ord, Calif. / Edgewood Arsenal, Md.	29 Dec 43	30 Jul 45	ETO	4 Nov 46	Edgewood Arsenal, Md.		
41	R12 Mar 42	12 Mar 42	20 Apr 43	Edgewood Arsenal, Md.	28 Apr 43 / 14 Jul 44 / 27 Aug 45	12 Jul 44 / 22 Jul 45 / 30 Nov 45	NATO / MTO / SWPA	30 Nov 45	Philippines	1 Aug 40	Activated as 1st Cml Lab Co
42	R12 Mar 42	12 Mar 42	8 Jun 45	Australia	21 Nov 41 / 7 Jan 46	7 Jan 46 / 23 Sep 46	SWPA / MIDPAC	23 Sep 46	Hawaii	15 May 41	Activated as 3d Cml Fld Lab Co
43	26 Aug 42	26 Aug 42	9 Dec 43	Edgewood Arsenal, Md.	16 Dec 43	15 Mar 46	MIDPAC	15 Mar 46	Hawaii		
44	15 Nov 42	15 Nov 42 / ca. Jun 45	10 Sep 43 / 20 Oct 45	Cp. Sibert, Ala. / Edgewood Arsenal, Md.	20 Sep 43	20 Jun 45	ETO	20 Oct 45	Edgewood Arsenal, Md.		
45	26 Dec 42	26 Dec 42	11 Oct 43	Cp. Sibert, Ala.	23 Oct 43 / 10 Feb 45	15 Nov 44 / 12 Nov 45	NATO / I-B	12 Nov 45	Cp. Kilmer, N. J.		
46	1 Feb 43	1 Feb 43	14 Jan 44	Cp. Sibert, Ala.	22 Jan 44	17 Jan 46	ETO	17 Jun 46	France		
47	25 Jun 43	25 Jun 43	20 Dec 43	Cp. Sibert, Ala.				D20 Dec 43	Cp. Sibert, Ala.		
256	C25 Apr 45	25 Apr 45	6 Jun 45	New Guinea	30 Nov 44	1946	SWPA	Existing in 1946	In the Philippines	30 Nov 44	Activated as 256 Cml Svc Det

• Overseas service dates for the 3d, 42, and 256 units include the entire period overseas regardless of conversions or redesignations.

APPENDIX H-16—CHEMICAL COMPOSITE BATTALIONS

Unit desig- nation (1)	Date activated (2)	TRAINING			OVERSEAS SERVICE			INACTIVATION OR DISBANDMENT		CONVERSION OR REDESIGNATION	
		From (3)	To (4)	Place (5)	From (6)	To (7)	Theater (8)	Date (9)	Place (10)	Date (11)	Comments (12)
13ᵃ	15 Mar 44	15 Mar 44	6 Mar 45	Ft. Richardson, Alaska	15 Mar 44	20 Apr 45	AD			R 6 Mar 45	13 Cml Svc Bn
14ᵇ	20 May 44	20 May 44 9 Aug 44	6 Aug 44 19 Aug 44	Cp. Sibert, Ala. Ft. Lawton, Wash.	19 Aug 44	1946	MIDPAC			R 25 Apr 45	14 Cml Svc Bn

ᵃ Both units were hq and hq detachments only.
ᵇ Overseas service dates for both units include the entire period overseas regardless of redesignations.

Appendix I

WAR DEPARTMENT

The Adjutant General's Office
Washington

RESTRICTED

15 June 1942

AG 353 (6–8–42) MS–C–M

SUBJECT: War Department Chemical Warfare Training Directive.

TO: The Commanding Generals,
                  Army Ground Forces;
                  Army Air Forces;
                  Services of Supply;
                  Defense Commands;
                  All Armies; Departments; Army Corps;
                  Divisions; and Corps Areas;
                  Air Forces, Ports of Embarkation;
             The Commandants,
                  General and Special Service Schools;
             The Superintendent,
                  United States Military Academy;
             The Commanding Officer,
                  Base Commands.

1. *General.*

The probability of the early use of toxic gas by the enemy in the present war requires imparting to our troops a thorough knowledge of how chemical warfare can be waged by an enemy against us and the placing of added emphasis upon training in defense against chemical attack. In short, it is now necessary to review training directives of all commands in the light of the probable use of chemicals in combat.

2. *References.*

a. The principles governing offensive and defensive use of chemicals, together with combined operations and security in connection therewith, are found in FM 100–5, Operation; FM 3–5, Tactics of Chemical Warfare (now published as CWS FM VOL. 1); and TM 3–305, Use of Smoke and Lacrimators in Training.

b. The principles governing defense against chemical attack, together with the object of training and standards of proficiency for individuals and organizations, are covered in FM 21–40, Defense against chemical Attack.

3. *Objective.*

a. Defense Against Chemical Attack. The proficiency of every individual and every unit in security against chemical attack.

b. Employment of Smoke.   The proficiency of all appropriate units in the employment of smoke in various types of combat.

c. Employment of Incendiaries.   The ability of appropriate units efficiently to employ incendiaries in the destruction of hostile matériel and installations.

d. Employment of Toxic Gas.   The training of all appropriate units in the projection of toxic chemicals to the end that in case it becomes necessary to retaliate in the use of such chemicals, they can do so promptly and efficiently.

4. *Gas Defense.*

Proficiency in gas defense requires:

a. The perfection in each unit of gas warning system including gas reconnaissance, and gas intelligence.

b. The training of every individual in the care and use of the protective equipment issued to him.

c. The training of every individual in appropriate first aid measures after gas exposure and of medical personnel in first aid treatment of gas casualties.

d. The ability of each individual to decontaminate the weapon with which armed and the provision in each unit of special decontaminating squads for the decontamination of ground and organizational equipment.

e. The training of all units in the collective measures and tactical procedure necessary to minimize or avoid gas casualties.

f. The introduction of gas situations in various types of field exercises.

5. *Employment of Smoke.*

a. Properly used, smoke greatly reduces the number of casualties in attacking forces and contributes to the success of the mission upon which engaged. Improperly used, smoke may interfere with other operations and aid the enemy rather than our own troops.

b. The proper use of smoke requires the training of the firing units in the technique of firing this agent and the supported units in operations in smoke. Infantry mortar units, chemical warfare units and appropriate field artillery units will be trained in the technique of firing smoke to deny hostile observation and to screen the movements of attacking infantry, cavalry, and armored units. The combined training of these units as essential.

6. *Employment of Incendiaries.*

The employment of incendiaries is primarily a function of the Army Air Forces. However, infantry, cavalry, field artillery, tank destroyer, parachute, engineer, armored, and chemical warfare units also will be trained to use appropriate incendiaries in the destruction of hostile materiel and installations.

7. *The Employment of Toxic Gases.*

The field forces must be prepared to use chemicals promptly, efficiently, and on a large scale if forced to do so by enemy action. Therefore, thorough training is required by appropriate chemical warfare, Army Air Forces, field artillery, and engineer units. This training will be initiated without delay by all commanders concerned.

8. *Training Methods.*

To the maximum extent possible, all instruction will be practical rather than theoretical. Simulated materials available locally will be used to supplement the training munitions and supplies authorized by AR 775–10., Tables of Allowances, and Tables of Basic Allowances.

9. *Instruction at Service Schools.*

It is directed that increased attention be given all service schools to the training of students in the principles and methods of gas defense. Attention will also be directed to the training of appropriate personnel of the infantry, cavalry, armored force, field artillery, engineers, chemical warfare, and air forces in the tactics and technique of the offensive employment of chemical agents.

10. *Responsibility.*

Immediate action will be taken by all commanders to initiate the program of training outlined herein. Special attention will be given to the basic requirements of security against chemical attack to the end that every individual and every unit will be able to take proper protective measures in case of subjection to a surprise gas attack. Both offensive and defensive chemical warfare will be included in training and tactical inspections by appropriate commanders.

By order of the Secretary of War:

J. A. ULIO
Major General,
The Adjutant General

COPIES FURNISHED

Chiefs of Supply Services
The Divisions of the War Department
General Staff

Bibliographical Note

World War I

There are several published volumes which discuss the origin and activities of the Chemical Warfare Service in World War I. These include Benedict Crowell, *America's Munitions, 1917–1918* (Washington: GPO, 1919); Amos A. Fries and Clarence J. West, *Chemical Warfare* (New York: McGraw Hill, 1921); and *Medical Aspects of Gas Warfare,* Volume XIV of the series MEDICAL DEPARTMENT OF THE UNITED STATES IN THE WORLD WAR (Washington: GPO, 1926). Volumes XV and XVI of the series UNITED STATES ARMY IN THE WORLD WAR (Washington: GPO, 1948), prepared by the Historical Division, Special Staff United States Army, contain data on the Chemical Warfare Service, American Expeditionary Forces (AEF). More valuable as a source of information is the official history of the Chemical Warfare Service, American Expeditionary Forces, a copy of which is on file in the Chemical Corps Historical Office. Especially useful in this history are the appendixes which are copies of pertinent directives. On the organizational development of the Chemical Warfare Service in the zone of interior, the most fruitful sources of information are M. T. Bogert's and W. H. Walker's History of the Chemical Service Section, on file at the Technical Library, Army Chemical Center, Maryland, and the annual reports of the CWS for the years 1918, 1919, and 1920. The retired CWS files in the National Archives contain some important documents.

Peacetime

A brief account of the development of the Chemical Warfare Service from World War I up through the end of World War II appears in a volume entitled *The Chemical Warfare Service in World War II: A Report of Accomplishments,* published in 1948. This volume was prepared by the Historical Office for the Chief of the Chemical Corps and was published by the Reinhold Publishing Corporation, New York City, for the Chemical Corps Association. The brief survey of the CWS in the peacetime period which appears in this volume is the only such account in print. The sources for this period include annual reports of the Chemical Warfare Service, the annual reports of the Secretary of War, War Department general orders and other directives dealing with chemical warfare activities, and correspondence and reports in the retired files of the War Department General Staff, The Adjutant General, and the Chemical Warfare Service. Copies of much of the correspondence between the War Department and the Chemical Warfare Service on policy matters were kept on file in the Office of the Chief, CWS, in a loose-leaf notebook, known as the "black book." After World War II, Miss Helen McCormick, secretary to successive chiefs of the CWS, graciously turned over this notebook to the Historical Office. Military and civilian personnel data for the peacetime period and the World War II period were obtained from the files of the Civilian Personnel Division, Office of the Secretary of War, and from working files maintained in the Office of the Comptroller of the Army and in the Office of the Deputy Chief of Staff for Personnel.

The Emergency

On the period from the emergency through World War II, several volumes in the series UNITED STATES ARMY IN WORLD WAR II make reference to CWS administration or training activities. These include *The Organization and Role of the Army Service Forces* by John D. Millett, *The Women's Army Corps* by Mattie E. Treadwell, *The Procurement and Training of Ground Force Troops* by Robert R. Palmer, Bell I. Wiley, and William R. Keast, and *The Organization of Ground Combat Troops* by Kent R. Greenfield, Robert R. Palmer, and Bell I. Wiley.

In June 1943 the Chemical Corps Historical Office was established as part of the War Department historical program. This office prepared a number of monographs on various phases of CWS activities, including administration, military training, research, procurement, and supply. These studies were written on the basis of research in a limited number of sources available in the Office of the Chief, CWS, and at certain CWS installations. In addition to the monographs, the Historical Office initiated and supervised an historical program throughout the Chemical Warfare Service, which resulted in the compilation of historical monographs by the CWS installations. These various monographs proved useful in the compilation of the present volume. Copies of these histories are on file in the Chemical Corps Historical Office and the Office of the Chief of Military History. The Historical Office also collected a number of valuable records.

World War II

With the increase of CWS activities from the period of the national emergency on, came a concomitant expansion of the volume of records, reports, and pieces of correspondence which these activities entailed. The bulk of CWS retired files for the World War II period, now located in the Technical Services Records Section, Military Records Branch, Region 3, General Services Administration (formerly the Departmental Records Branch, The Adjutant General's Office), is many times that of the World War I and peacetime periods combined. The voluminousness of these files is not necessarily an indication of their value to the historian. They contain much material that is not useful for historical purposes, and they lack data on some of the more important developments in the Chemical Warfare Service. To fill in gaps in the history of CWS administration, research was conducted with the following sources: records of the United States Chemical Warfare Committee on file in the Historical Office; the retired files of the Chief of Staff, of the Assistant Chiefs of Staff, G–1, G–2, G–3 and G–4, the War Plans Division (WPD), and its successor the Operations Division (OPD), all sections of the War Department General Staff; the central file maintained by The Adjutant General's Office (AG); and the files of Headquarters, Army Service Forces. All of the foregoing were located in the Departmental Records Branch, The Adjutant General's Office, at the time this volume was compiled. Footnote citations throughout the volume which give file numbers preceded by the abbreviation "CWS" indicate documents currently filed in the Technical Services Records Section. Other records, such as those of the Assistant Chief of Staff, G–1, are indicated by the appropriate organizational abbreviation.

To supplement the data in these files, the author of Part I of this volume corresponded with and interviewed key soldiers of all ranks as well as civilians who participated in the events described. These letters and interviews proved extremely valuable because many times the reasons behind administrative actions were not made a matter of record. At the time of writing, these letters and interviews were on file in the Chemical Corps Historical Office. Copies of these documents will be retired to Technical Service Records Section under file reference 314.7, Interviews and Correspondence.

The sources described above were researched for material for both parts of the volume. In the writing of Part II extensive use was also made of the collection of Chemical Warfare Service records on military training located in the Chemical Corps Historical Office. This collection includes blocks of records pertaining to the following Chemical Warfare Service training areas: unit training, replacement training both at Edgewood Arsenal and Camp

Sibert, the Chemical Warfare Schools (including class records for most courses), Officers Candidate School, War Department Civil Defense Schools (conducted by the CWS), the administration of training, training literature, and the chemical warfare training of other services and arms. Also researched were the training records among the retired CWS files in the Technical Services Records Section, and the historical data cards and orders on chemical units furnished by the Organization and Directory Section, Operations Branch, Administrative Services Division, The Adjutant General's Office.

Glossary

THE CHEMICAL WARFARE SERVICE
GLOSSARY

AAB	Army Air Base
AAF	Army Air Forces
AC	Hydrogen cyanide (war gas); Assistant Chief
ACmlC	Army Chemical Center, Md.
ACofS	Assistant Chief of Staff
Actg	Acting
Adm	Administration; Administrative
Adm O	Administrative Order
AEF	American Expeditionary Forces
AGF	Army Ground Forces
AGO	Adjutant General's Office
ANMB	Army and Navy Munitions Board
APG	Aberdeen Proving Ground, Md.
App.	Appendix
Aprt	Airport
AR	Army Regulation
ARCADIA	U.S.-British conference held in Washington, December 1941 January 1942
ASC	Army Specialist Corps
ASF	Army Service Forces
ASFTC	Army Service Forces Training Center
ASGS	Assistant Secretary, General Staff
ASW	Assistant Secretary of War
AUS	Army of the United States
AV	Antivapor
BCWPD	Boston Chemical Warfare Procurement District
Bd	Board
BFM	Basic Field Manual
Bn	Battalion
Br	Branch
Bull	Bulletin
BW	Biological Warfare

C	Chief
CA	Corps Area
Ca.	About; approximately
CC	Chemical Corps
CC (CK)	Cyanogen chloride
CCS	Combined Chiefs of Staff
CCW	Publications symbol for the British Inter-Service Committee on Chemical Warfare
CCWC	Combined Chemical Warfare Committee
C CWS	Chief, Chemical Warfare Service
CD	Civilian Defense
CDC	Caribbean Defense Command
CG	Commanding General; Phosgene (war gas)
Ch.	Chapter
CinC	Commander-in-Chief
CINCSWPA	Commander-in-Chief, Southwest Pacific Area
Cir	Circular
C Log Gp	Chief Logistics Group
Cml	Chemical
Cml C	Chemical Corps
CmlHO	Chemical Corps Historical Office
Cml O	Chemical Corps Office
CNO	Chief of Naval Operations
CO	Commanding Officer
Co	Company
CofEngrs	Chief of Engineers
CofOrd	Chief of Ordnance
CofS	Chief of Staff
Com	Committee
Comd	Command
Comdr	Commander
Comdt	Commandant
COMINCH	Commander-in-Chief
Comm	Commission
Comp	Composite
Conf	Conference
Cong	Congress
Contl	Control
Co-ord	Co-ordination
Corres	Correspondence
CRL	Chemical Corps Chemical and Radiological Laboratories
Cp.	Camp

CPS	Combined Staff Planners
CsofS	Chiefs of Staff
Ctr	Center
CWP	Chemical Warfare Program
CWPD	Chemical Warfare Procurement District
CWS	Chemical Warfare Service
D	Dive [bombardment company]
DA	Department of the Army
DANC	Decontaminating Agent, Noncorrosive
DC	Deputy Chief
DCofS	Deputy Chief of Staff
DCWPD	Dallas Chemical Warfare Procurement District
Decon	Decontamination
Dep	Depot
Det	Detachment
DF	Disposition form
Dir	Director
Div	Division
DM	Irritant Smoke
DRB	Departmental Records Branch, The Adjutant General's Office
dtd	Dated
EA	Edgewood Arsenal
EM	Enlisted men
Engr	Engineer
ERC	Enlisted Reserve Corps
ETO	European Theater of Operations
ETOUSA	European Theater of Operations, U.S. Army
Ex	Executive
Ex O	Executive Officer
Fld	Field
FM	Field Manual
FS	Solution of sulfur trioxide in chlorosulfonic acid (smoke)
Ft.	Fort
FY	Fiscal year
G–1	Personnel Division, War Department General Staff
G–2	Intelligence Division, War Department General Staff
G–3	Operations & Training Division, War Department General Staff
G–4	Supply Division, War Department General Staff
Gen	General
GHQ	General Headquarters
GO	General Orders
GP	General Purpose

Gp	Group
GPI	Granite Peak Installation
GSC	General Staff Corps (British)
GTA	Graphic Training Aid
HA	Huntsville Arsenal
HE	High explosive
Hist	History
HO	Historical Office
Hon	Honorable
Hq	Headquarters
IGD	Inspector General's Department
Impreg	Impregnation
Incl	Inclosure
Ind	Indorsement; Industrial
Insp	Inspection
Intel	Intelligence
Interv	Interview
IOM	Interoffice memo
IPF	Initial Protective Force
ISCCW	Inter-Service Committee on Chemical Warfare (British)
JB	Joint Board
JCS	Joint Chiefs of Staff
JLC	Joint Logistics Committee [of the Combined Chiefs of Staff]
JLPC	Joint Logistics Plans Committee
JPS	Joint Staff Planners [of the Combined Chiefs of Staff]
Jt	Joint
L	Light [bombardment company]
Lab	Laboratory
Lib	Library
Log	Logistics
M&H	Medium or heavy [bombardment company]
M-Day	Mobilization Day
Maint	Maintenance
Mfg	Manufacturing
Mil	Military
Min	Minutes
MIT	Massachusetts Institute of Technology
Mob	Mobilization
Mob Plan	Mobilization Plan
Mob Reg	Mobilization Regulation
Mort	Mortar
MS	Manuscript

Mtg	Meeting
MTP	Mobilization Training Program
Mtz	Motorized
NA	National Army; National Archives of the United States
NCO	Non-commissioned officer
n.d.	No date
NDD	New Developments Division
NDRC	National Defense Research Committee
NG	National Guard
NOB	Naval Operating Base
NRC	National Research Council
NYCWPD	New York Chemical Warfare Procurement District
OASW	Office of the Assistant Secretary of War
O/C	Officer in Charge
OCA	Office of the Comptroller of the Army
OC CWS	Office of the Chief, Chemical Warfare Service
OCD	Office of Civilian Defense
OCMH	Office, Chief of Military History
OCofS	Office of the Chief of Staff
OCS	Officer Candidate School
Off	Office
Off O	Office Order
OLYMPIC	Plan for March 1946 invasion of Kyushu, Japan
OPD	Operations Division, War Department General Staff
Opns	Operations
ORC	Officers' Reserve Corps
Ord	Ordnance
OSRD	Office of Scientific Research and Development
OSS	Office of Strategic Services
OSW	Office of the Secretary of War
OUSW	Office of the Under Secretary of War
Par	Paragraph
PBA	Pine Bluff Arsenal
Pers	Personnel
P. G.	Proving Ground
Plng	Planning
PMP	Protective Mobilization Plan
POM	Preparation for Overseas Movement [Section]
POW	Prisoner of War
PRAD	Progress Review and Analysis Division
Proc	Procurement; Processing
Prof	Professor

Proj	Project
Pt.	Part
QM	Quartermaster
QMG	Quartermaster General
R.	Republican
RA	Regular Army
Rad	Radio
RAF	Royal Air Force
R&D	Research and Development
Rcd	Record
Reqmts	Requirements
Res	Reserve; resolution
Ret.	Retired
RMA	Rocky Mountain Arsenal
ROTC	Reserve Officers Training Corps
Rpt	Report
RTC	Replacement Training Center
Sec	Section
Secy	Secretary [of State]
Sep	Separate
Serv	Service
SFCWPD	San Francisco Chemical Warfare Procurement District
SGO	Surgeon General's Office
SGS	Secretary, General Staff
SJP	San José Project
Smk Gen	Smoke Generator
SN	Secretary of the Navy
SO	Special Orders
SOS	Services of Supply
S&P	Strategy & Policy
SPD	Special Project Division
SPHINX	An over-all Army project concerned with testing of equipment and tactics for detecting and reducing Japanese field fortifications.
SS	Selective Service
SSN	Specification serial number
SSUSA	Special Staff United States Army
Stat	Statute; Statistics
Sub	Subject
Subcom	Subcommittee
SW	Secretary of War
SWPA	Southwest Pacific Area
TAG	The Adjutant General

TB	Technical Bulletin
T/BA	Table of Basic Allowances
TC	Training Center
Tech	Technical
TIG	The Inspector General
TM	Technical Manual
Tng	Training
T/O	Table of Organization
T/O&E	Table of Organization & Equipment
TQMG	The Quartermaster General
TSG	The Surgeon General
Trans	Translator
TWX	Teletype message
UGO	Unit Gas Officer
UN	United Nations
USA	United States Army
USAFFE	United States Army Forces Far East
USASOS	United States Army Services of Supply
USBWC	United States Biological Warfare Committee
USCWC	United States Chemical Warfare Committee
USES	U.S. Employment Service
USSR	Union of Soviet Socialist Republics
USMC	United States Marine Corps
USN	United States Navy
USW	Under Secretary of War
UTC	Unit Training Center
VCNO	Vice Chief of Naval Operations
WAAC	Women's Army Auxiliary Corps
Waac	A member of the WAAC
WAC	Women's Army Corps
Wac	A member of the WAC
WBC	Reversal of initials for Committee on Biological Warfare
WD	War Department
WDCP	War Department Civilian Protection
WDGS	War Department General Staff
WDMB	War Department Manpower Board
WDSS	War Department Special Staff
WP	White phosphorus
WPD	War Plans Division, War Department General Staff
WRS	War Research Service
Z of I	Zone of Interior

Index

CPSIA information can be obtained
at www.ICGtesting.com
Printed in the USA
LVHW101453171019
634538LV00006B/244/P

9 781410 204875